The question of "life style," or choosing how to live, encounters the regime of the logo and its image.

Disney's planned community of Celebration, Florida

We live in a twenty-four-hour market world where less and less terrain remains unregulated.

AT&T Global Network Operations Center, Bedminster, New Jersey

The new image infrastructure consists of systems, agreements, alliances, and standards.

AOL Chairman and Chief Executive Steve Case, Time Warner Chairman and CEO Gerald Levin, and Turner Broadcasting Chairman Ted Turner (left to right) announce their intent to form a merger of AOL and Time Warner, January 10, 2000.

What is the focus of the new image infrastructure? Attention. It's all designed for capturing, tracking, quantifying, manipulating, holding, buying, selling, and controlling attention.

The enormous Manhattan office of DoubleClick, the Internet advertising services company that has attracted attention and controversy for its Website banner ads and data-mining (or customer "profiling") tools.

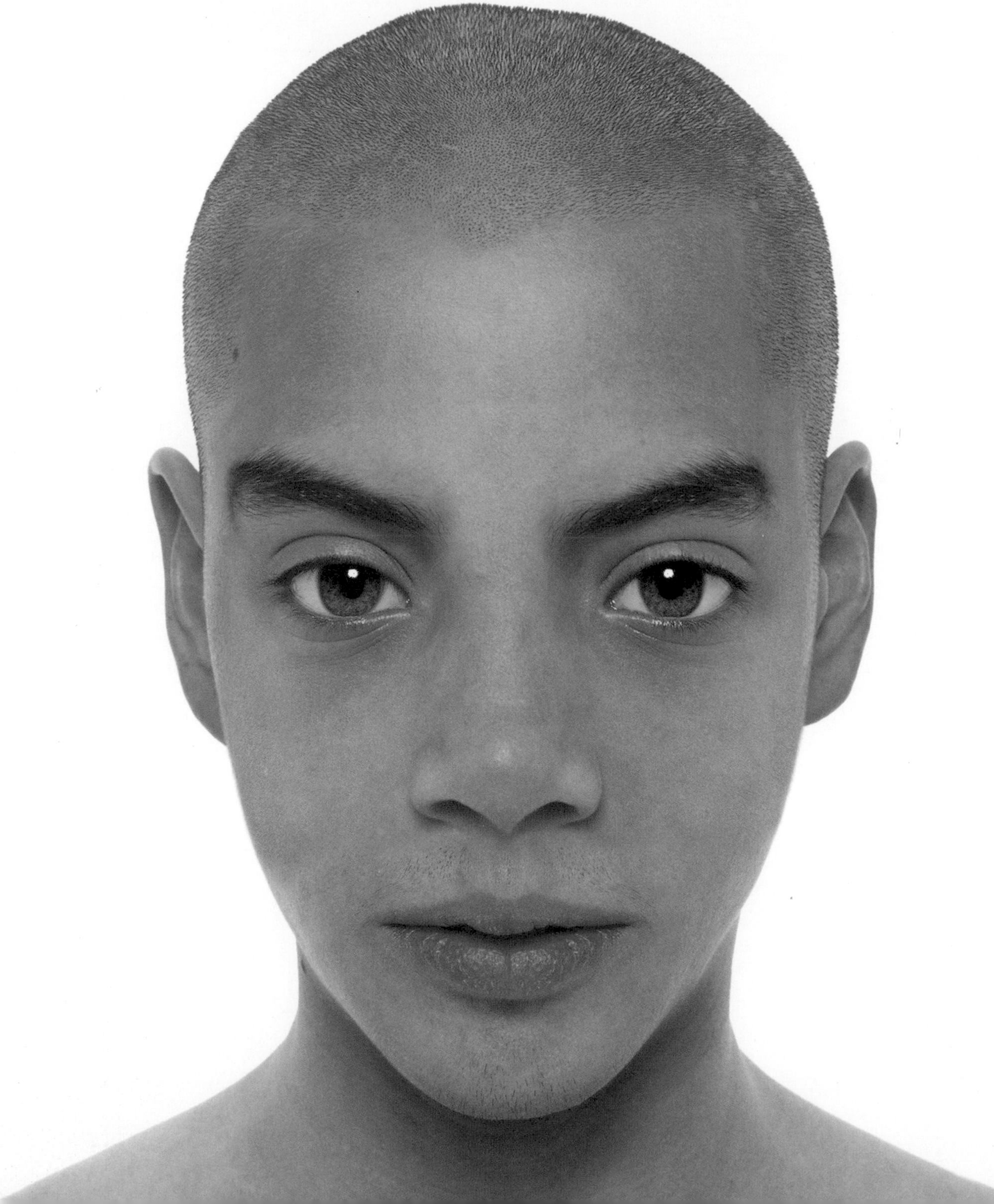

As visual landmarks melt and reform before our eyes, we sense that somehow the world itself dissolves beneath us.

Jurgen Ostarhild's "Humanoid" portraits combine features of different faces, races, and genders.

NETWORK
Casuals
anand
KILLER LOOP
Ray-Ban
MULANI OPTICAL GALARY
ಕರೋನ
Carona
FAVOUR
NEWPORT
Bata
TOYS
3K
CASUAL WEAR

Global markets demand a predatory colonization of open space.

Rush hour on Commercial Street, Bangalore, India, 2000

Destinations themselves are increasingly design-driven.

Ski Dome indoor sports facility, Tokyo, Japan

Unless we can come to terms with the global image economy and the way it permeates the things we make and see, we are doomed to a life of decorating and redecorating.

S,M,L,XL as a life-style pillow from the cover of a Dutch newspaper supplement

Every city is now in the business of not only making itself, but also marketing itself.

The Venetian Resort & Casino, Las Vegas

Franchise supersedes national boundaries. It utterly dissolves local and regional thresholds.

KFC's Colonel Sanders, Tokyo, Japan

Steele's
MOTEL
HEATED POOL
HILTON
THE NATURE COMPANY

The most successful "attractions"... are franchised and reproduced around the world with subtle local inflection, increasing attendance and decreasing travel time.

Universal CityWalk at Universal City, California, designed by the Jon Jerde Partnership International

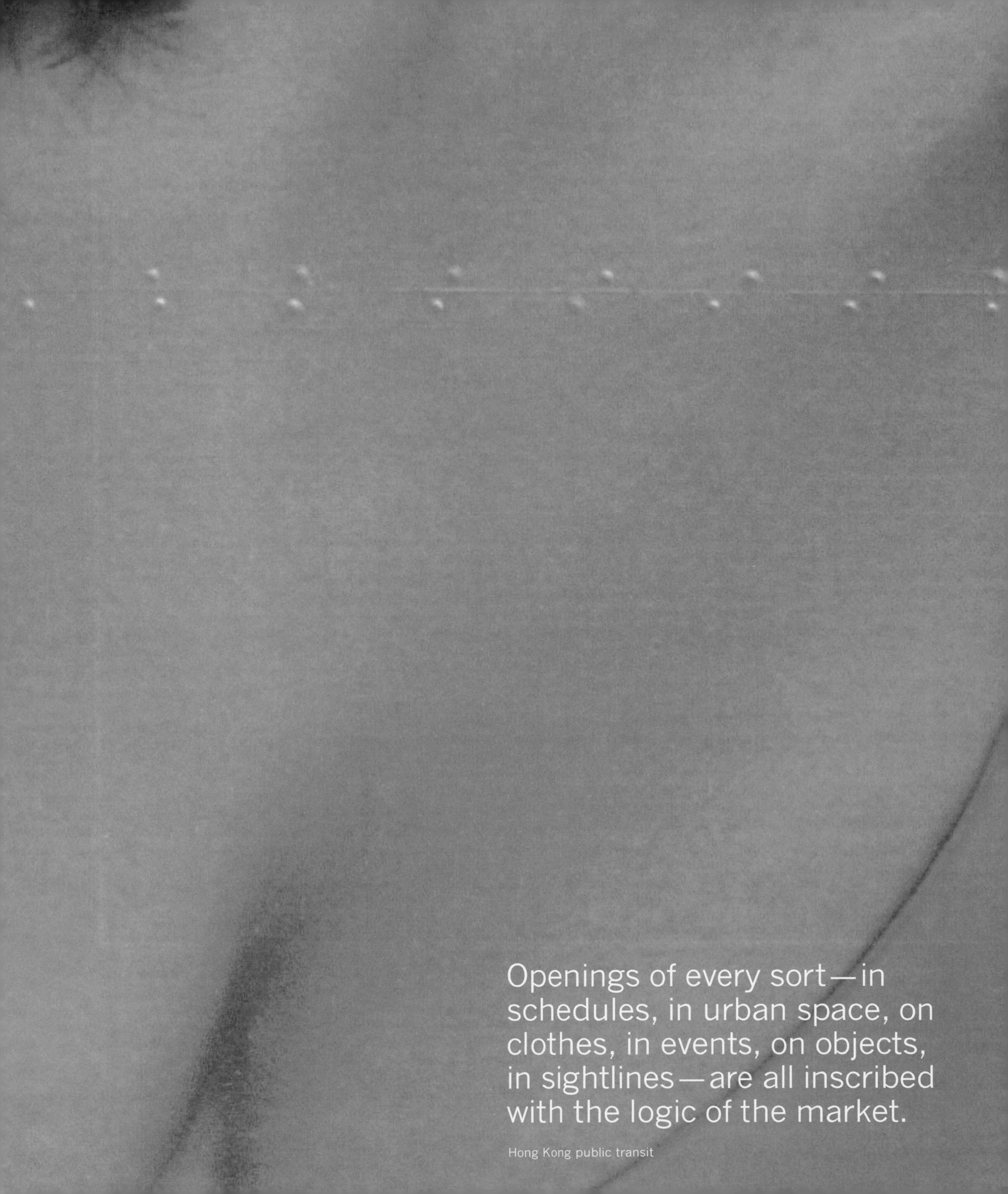

Openings of every sort—in schedules, in urban space, on clothes, in events, on objects, in sightlines—are all inscribed with the logic of the market.

Hong Kong public transit

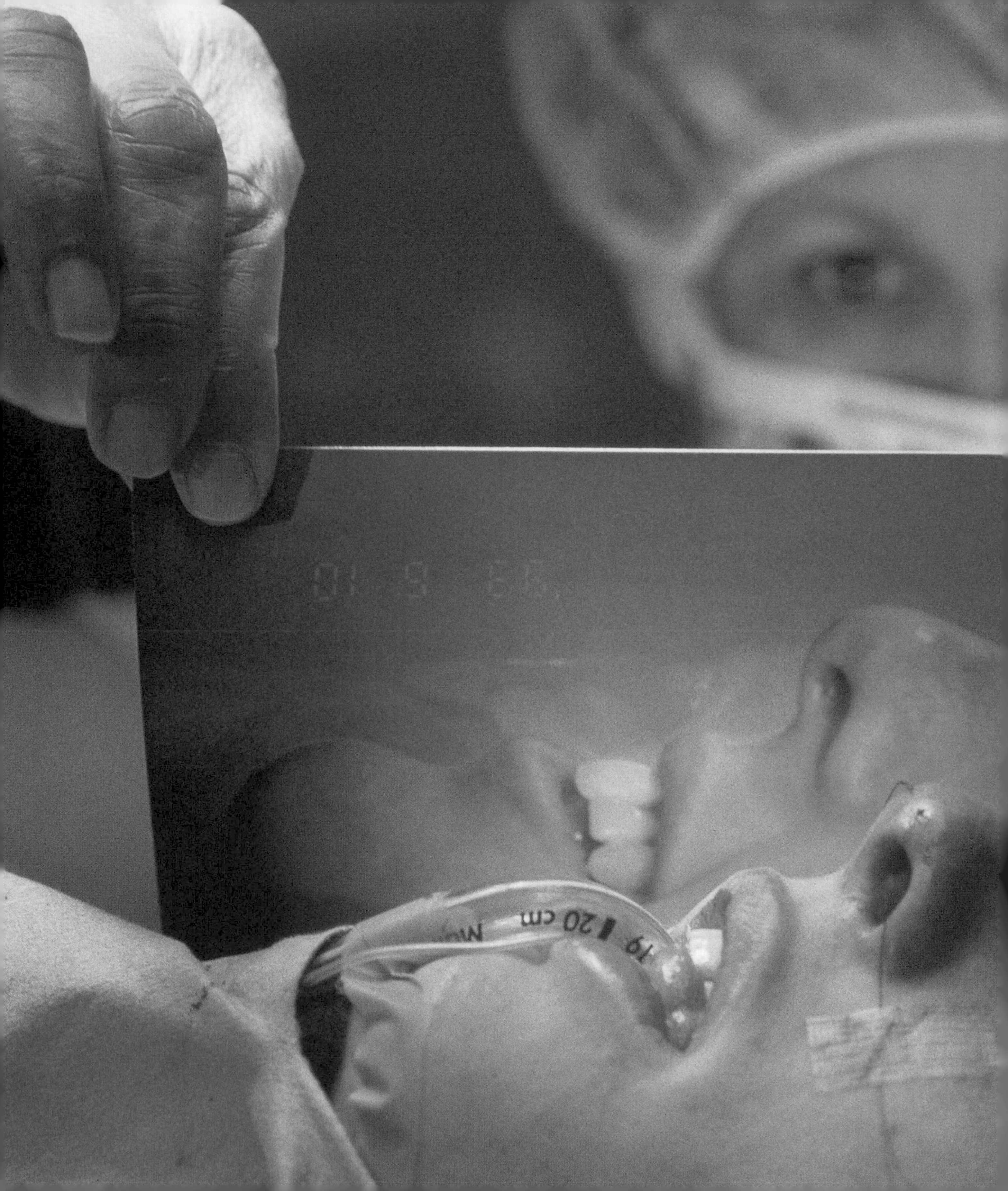
20 cm

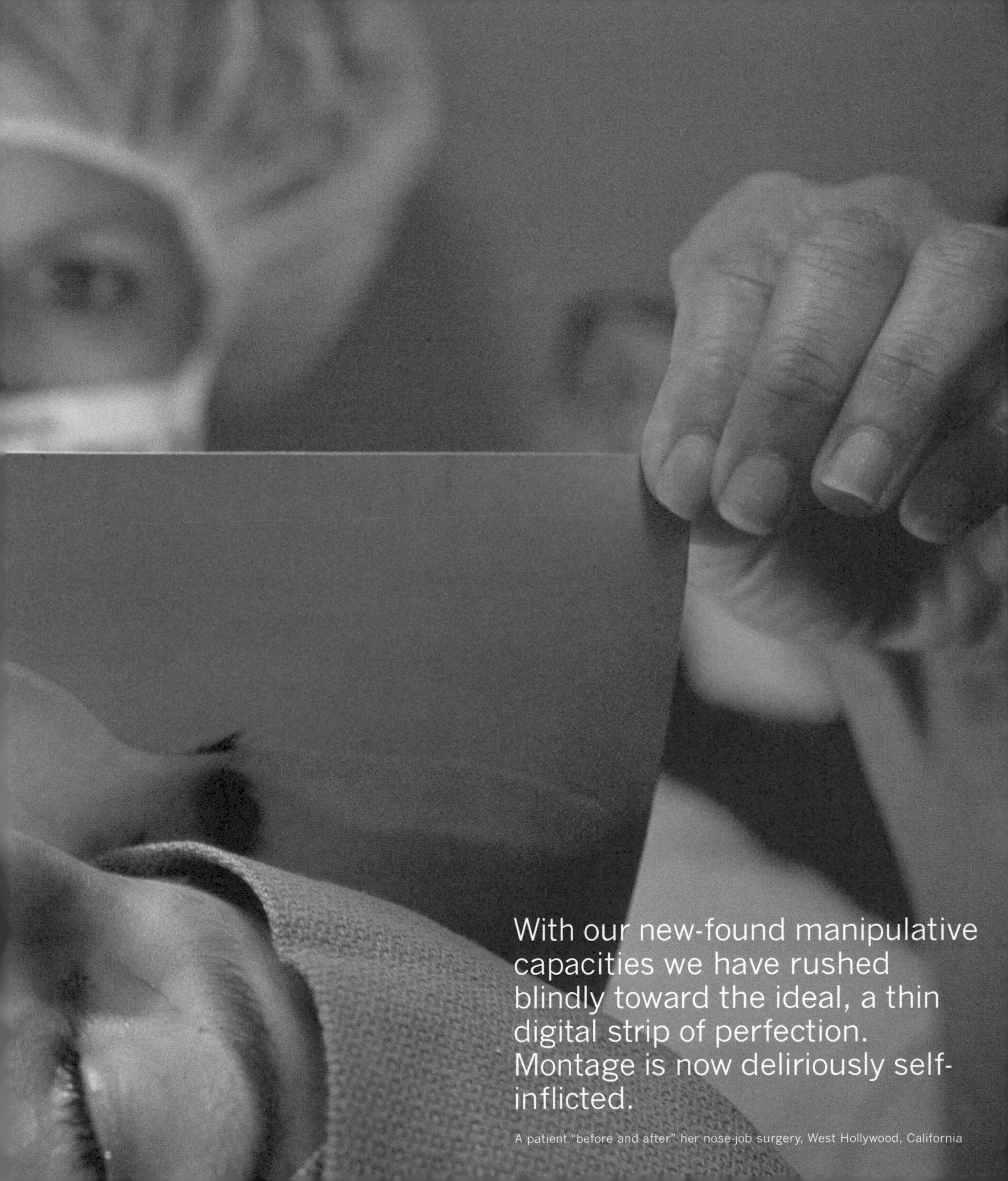

With our new-found manipulative capacities we have rushed blindly toward the ideal, a thin digital strip of perfection. Montage is now deliriously self-inflicted.

A patient "before and after" her nose-job surgery, West Hollywood, California

Styling Life

Life style. There are few terms that have been as savagely commodified and gutted of meaning in recent years. Our first instinct is to leave its empty carcass to the vendors and merchants. But in the spirit of *détournement*, we are wresting it back. We are interested in recuperating and reinvesting the term "life style" so that it speaks of the designer's role in shaping the lives we lead and the world in which we live.

One of the revelations in the studio has been that life doesn't simply happen to us, we produce it. That's what style is. It's producing life. Rather than accepting that life is something that we passively receive, accept, or endure, I believe that life is something we generate. We use our capacities. And that all boils down to style. Style may be presented as theory, serendipity, or happenstance. But fundamentally style is a decision about how we will live. Style is not superficial. It is a philosophical project of the deepest order.

Style is intrinsically rhetorical, the expression of a series of more or less convincing propositions about life and the way it might be ordered. I am a firm believer in what Jean-Luc Godard says: "Style is merely the outside of content, and content the inside of style." This observation engenders the two principal issues that animate our practice: formal innovation and content development. While the former has established the reputation of the practice, the latter is the focus of our work.

This book is conceived and designed as an active field, not a classical object that follows a chronological, linear model. There are developmental lines, moments of attack and decay that evolve in a network relation to every other. We accept the accidents, the encounters, the interruptions, and the failures of design practice along with its successes and elations. It is a documentary portrait of the culture of design seen through the lens of one practice — our own — as we attempt an ongoing, problematic, and evolutionary engagement with the world.

Life

Bruce Mau

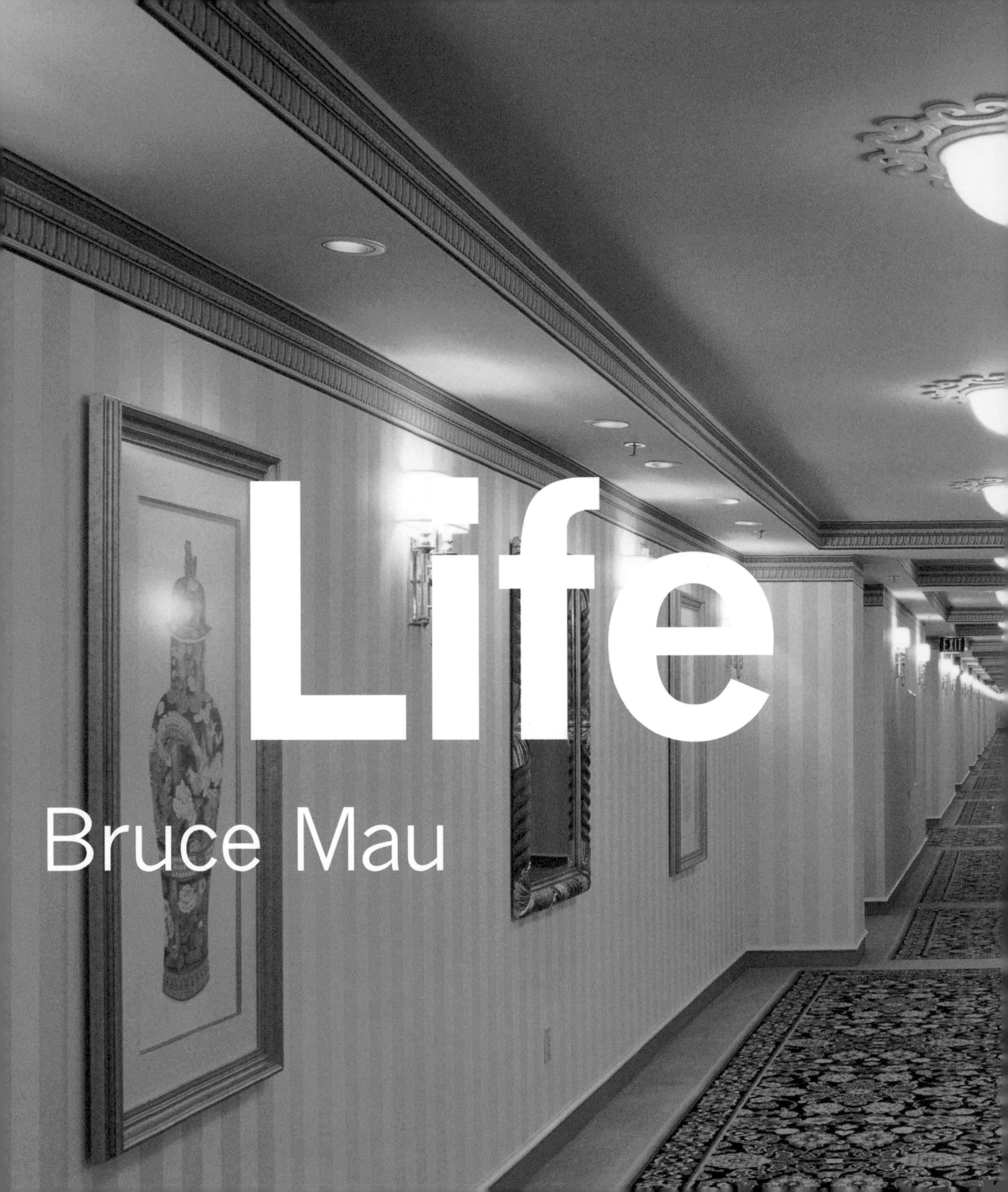

Style

Edited by Kyo Maclear with Bart Testa

Life Theories

Life Projects

Zone

Identity

Life Stories

Acknowledgments

Life Style is a studio project. The book is the culmination of a collective research project undertaken by the people who have worked at and with Bruce Mau Design. It presents projects produced in the studio over a fifteen-year period from 1985 to 2000.

The book would not have been realized without Kyo Maclear, who has steered the project for years researching ideas and images, editing texts, and making possible the impossible.

Bart Testa joined the project at a crucial moment and brought his acute thinking to bear on it.

Chris Rowat led the design of the book as a collaborative process with the design team of Michael Barker, who also played a major role in the project, Henry Hong-Yiu Cheung, David Wilkinson, Reto Geiser who piloted solo for a time, and Nancy Nowacek who flew without instruments. Anita Matusevics and Kevin Sugden who, along with Chris Rowat, are veteran studio members, worked on earlier versions of the project. Jim Shedden acted as its producer.

Amanda Sebris, Kevin Sugden, Jim Shedden, Cathy Jonasson, Norah Farrell, and Bisi Williams offered valuable insight on the texts. Barr Gilmore, Catherine Rix, Maris Mezulis, Simon Chan, Donald Mak, Gary Westwood, Lisa Molnar, Robert Kennedy, Chris Pommer, Tania Boterman, Alan Belcher, Jason Halter, and Jackie Rothstein contributed in important ways to the project.

Sanford Kwinter, who has been a collaborator since the studio's inception (and my closest friend), wrote a generous introduction to the book.

Michel Feher, also a close friend and one of the studio's most nurturing, trusting (and sometimes forgiving) collaborators, wrote an afterword that brilliantly understands the contradictions the studio so enthusiastically embraces.

Branden Hookway collaborated on the first published version of Twelve Strategies. Carol Moukheiber worked with me on several short texts including *A Studio is not a Tree*. Bolaji Williams first commissioned *An Incomplete Manifesto for Growth*.

Armin Linke produced some of the most striking photographs of our studio, our work, and the world around us. See Spot Run made images of the finished work that are unmatched in their subtlety.

Phaidon has shown a remarkable commitment to the adventures of this project. The unerring support and dedication of Richard Schlagman, Karen Stein, and Megan McFarland have been crucial. David McAninch, Paul Hammond, Karl Shanahan, and Julia Joern also offered crucial support in realizing the book.

Over the years, John Macfarlane, Greg Van Alstyne, Lisa Naftolin, Nigel Smith, Alison Hahn, Kathleen Oginski, Robert Soar, Archie Harris, Richard Hunt, Sara Borins, James Lahey, Bosede Williams, Howard Saginur, Rod Fraser, John Scinnocco, and Guy Poulin made significant contributions to the work and intelligence of the studio. Adele Freedman provided valuable critical feedback.

Our partners and clients make possible the privilege of doing the work we do.

Michel Feher, Sanford Kwinter, Jonathan Crary, and Ramona Naddaff from Zone are the reason the studio began. They introduced me to intellectual life and convinced me that I could have one.

Julia Bloomfield of the Getty Research Institute became first a client and then a dear friend, allowing, supporting, and insisting on the best we could do.

Frank Gehry has been a friend, advisor and business mentor and opened doors for our recklessly ambitious redefinition of design.

Rem Koolhaas systematically dismantled the boundaries between our work and his, and continues to test our capacity to keep pace.

Lars Lerup made possible my presence as the Cullinan Professor at Rice University School of Architecture where many of the texts in this volume had their first tentative expression.

Hans Ulrich Obrist introduced our studio to new aesthetic and intellectual orbits.

Hortensia Völckers imagined new vistas into uncharted terrain and invited us to join her on the excursion.

Peter Noever, director of the MAK in Vienna, insisted

that we do something we had never done.
Gianfranco Monacelli held his breath long enough to produce S,M,L,XL. Helena Kontova and Giancarlo Politti were our gracious hosts during its Milanese production.
Andrew Cogan and Chee Pearlman, my colleagues at I.D., allowed me to produce a New York magazine in Toronto.
Heather Reisman, in a leap of faith, showed a commitment to the talent in the studio that took me years to understand and appreciate.
Dufflet Rosenberg was a patron in the early years and saved the studio from certain ruin on more than one occasion.
Tony Scherman, Margaret Priest, Brian Boigon, and Susan Speigel are friends who helped me through a bumpy transition from a hobby to a business.

Kerri Kwinter, Steven Bock, Elisabeth Matheson, Tom Allin, Francesco Bonami, Mark Francis, Lynne Cooke, Christian Hubert, Nadia Tazi, Meighan Gale, Sherri Geldin, Kurt Forster, Tom and Carol Reese, Bob Tannen, Scott Cowen, John Barry, Anthony Mumphrey, Gene D'amour, Lindy Roy, Michael Maltzan, Randy Jefferson, Jim Glymph, Bill and Jan Schmidt, Russell Ferguson, Barbara Vanderlinden, Chris Dercon, Francine Fort, Michel Jacques, Terry Riley, Paola Antonelli, Adam Weinberg, Kathleen Fleming, Sandy and Joe Rotman, Claes Oldenburg and Coosje van Bruggen, Glenn Lowry, Michael Snow, Maurizio Nannucci, Richard Hamilton, Micah Lexier, Steve Pozel, Gordon Monahan, Douglas Gordon, Glen Seator, Chuck Helm, Meg Stuart, Michel Uytterhoeven, André Lepecki, Louise Dennys and Ric Young, Michael Budman and Don Green, Bruce Kuwabara, Stéphane Beel, Larry Tanenbaum, Rachel Gotlieb, John Goodwin, Jane Corkin, Sandy Simpson, Donald Mackay, Detlef Mertins, Larry Richards, John Knechtel, Carol McBride, Frank Comella, Bill Boyle, Matthew Teitelbaum, Ron Dembo, Burton Hamfelt, Steve Snyder, Naomi Klein, Dennis Reid, Ken Dryden, Nicholas Metivier, John Shnier and Marty Kohn, Gerry Sheff, David Sadowski, Philip Monk, François Girard, Petra Blaisse, Jennifer Sigler, Jeffrey Inaba, Joshua Ramus, Dan Wood, Deborah Jacobs, Cynthia Davidson, Annie Philben, Phyllis Lambert, Larry Gagosian, Kay Pallister, Ealan Wingate, Bob Monk, Vanessa Beecroft, Jessie Washburn-Harris, Terry Winters, Judith Brauner, Ben Watson, Federica Zanco, and Rolf Fehlbaum have all supported the work of the studio at critical moments. The studio grows with them because of their vision, and courage.
To all I am deeply grateful.
Bisi Williams, my wife, has shared the stresses and exhilarations of the adventure for more than a decade, and now we have three wonderful passengers, Osunkemi, Omalola, and Adeshola, along for the ride. Hi ho.

The Gay Science (What is Life?)
Sanford Kwinter

> *What one should learn from artists: How to make things beautiful, attractive and desirable for us, when in themselves, they never are.*
>
> —Friedrich Nietzsche, *Die fröhliche Wissenschaft*

Every object around us is a composition of forces, as important for how it is made as for the elements of which it is made up. Design is not about making things beautiful, but simply about making them what they are ... *for us.* If the general public is neither instructed nor accustomed to understanding design in this way, it is hardly a surprise. Most designers are also unaware of the obscure logic of forces that composes our object world, of the cues and compulsions that provoke in us the patterns and routines that animate our nervous and mental life. If this sounds more like engineering than design, well, isn't that, at bottom, what it is?

We are, more than ever today, prisoners of design. Our world is so saturated with design that we can hardly separate ourselves from it. Though much of design is explicit enough to amuse, focus, quicken, or infuriate us, we hardly notice that in so doing, it continually enters and reorganizes us. With art now faded irretrievably into entertainment, we are left to conjecture the ways that design may be taking its place. More radically, is it not possible that design is now taking over the social role that music has served for the last three decades, at least in the Anglo-Saxon world? Design is arguably among the most important, ubiquitous, and least understood shapers of public consciousness today. But to fully appreciate this, one must know where to look for it.

As Nietzsche's statement suggests, no thing is beautiful or compelling in and by itself. All beauty—all power to affect—derives from the way in which things are invested with disposition, how they are made to *appear*. Design, then, has to do with the shape of *appearance* (no small thing!), with the critical proviso that someone or something (some force!) is always responsible for that shape.

Nietzsche called this shape-giving aspect of life (and the things it catches up in its movement), "meaning," largely because he was interested in irritating the blind belief in static things like Truth. In the rare passages where he gave himself over to deep and personal passions, however, he referred to the culminating point of "meaning" as *style*.

Nothing is more important, more necessary, he proposed in a famous passage in *The Gay Science*, "than to *give style* to one's character." And no one was more adept at this, he argued, than the healthy, form-loving Greeks. If philosophy is one day to be reborn as a gay science it would need to be put back in service of Life (not Truth!). And the purpose of life is to bring into the world a system of novel forms that reflect the constraint of a single will or viewpoint. Style.

Style is often dismissed as a mere effect of surface, and this might well be valid if one could understand by surface the most profound of all things. In sports, for example, style means nothing less than *a whole new way of doing things*. Think of Jean-Claude Killy's "*avalement*" skiing style that brought him three Olympic gold medals and a revolution to the sport; think of the two-handed backhand in tennis, the Fosbury Flop, Pele's bicycle kick, Jordan and Gretzky, or in music, of Jimi Hendrix's right thumb. What is so profound about these examples? Simply this: that each innovation is the product of a single and novel way of being in the world, an invention that then redisposes that world according to entirely new rhythmic values. It changes the underlying music of a given world and in so doing changes the very notion of what will become possible in it.

Objects too—books, buildings, clothes, tools—embody and emit styles, establish and constrain possibilities, introduce and limit freedoms. When we "give style" to our character, we do nothing else than to claim and renounce freedoms. We compose an environment of possibility that we enter into and use with either grace or awkwardness. Either way, in the end, the final product is who we are. Life, too, is composition, and style is what our lives are about.

To see the world as style (is it not, after all, the goal

of every ambitious composer to forge a new and personal style, so that even the task of achieving a work "with no style" is an heroic act of style-making?) is to take possession of much more than just a theory of the world. It is to possess a theory of all the activity in it, perhaps an entire science, an ethology that could tell us everything we want to know about human behavior. To live in a technological society is not just to submit to the imperative of style but rather to face the challenge of creating a science of it. This may well imply a new use of the intelligence, but if that is so, then we may be on our way to inventing a new (life) style here as well.

Design invests raw, even base, matter with "performativity"; it endows an inert thing with a capacity for action. One could see this process as the forceful subjection of one thing to the goals and will of another, or one could see it as investing something with "anima" or intelligence (in the purely technological sense, at least). Design is, in fact, a cybernetic process because it takes the functions of communication and control from a human operator and embeds these (as in a microprocessor) into the thing itself. Design makes things move, but that is the least of its power. For the type of movement that design projects into objects has the intention to make other things move. Design modifies objects so that they, in turn, can modify the world.

This certainly sounds like science fiction: design as the invention of formulas, algorithms, chants, matrixes, diagrams, and songs that quicken the world and make it alive. If life is a "pattern in time," and design is the practice of impressing pattern into things, it stands to reason that the highest ambition of design would be to target the forms of life itself. But this would serve no good if it were simply to open the door to new, increasingly sophisticated techniques of human and social engineering. To "give style" to life is, on the contrary, to free life of routine, to place it into syncopation so that it can find new, entirely unexpected patterns of unfolding. All improvisation is life in search of a style.

It took years for the BMD studio to settle comfortably into this project. Each step toward life was experienced first as treason, as an *abandonment* of design (I remember an uprising once to have my own provocations banned from the office). In time, the "design" project itself came to be seen as increasingly suspicious and deficient, an intolerable submission to a client's imagined need to conform to a market. We spoke in those days of "through-designing," a process by which an action or set of forces is transmitted to the *agora*, or social sphere, through the object but in no way limited to it. We spoke of sheepdogs and whistles and landscapes and the way a shepherd moves a troupe through and over a terrain by transmitting tonal signals remotely to a dog, who moves the fluid sheep-mass precisely yet improvisationally and according to his own way. We invented concepts, built models, and ran experiments.

I learned about design in its most dizzying and exhilarating states. In turn, BMD developed a practice that became at once increasingly collaborative and independent of the client. Collaborative because "through-design" meant re-engineering the impetus by first designing (rethinking) the client's task itself; independent, because a fully confident set of social researches was forming within the BMD milieu, a constant interrogation of "what is possible?" and "how can this be put at the service ... of life?"

In the last few years the project of (post-Swiss, bourgeois) design appears to have been abandoned almost wholesale by the office, in favor of a new style of working. Years of reflection on the social aspects of design have transformed the practice from one focusing on graphics to one intimately involved in a struggle with the forces that shape markets and consciousness today: the image. There simply is no greater or more obscure force than pictures compelling action, reflex, behavior, and routine in our society today. No denser or more tacit form of communication, no shaping or organizing force more comprehensive or more insidiously embedded in our lifeworld than images. They make up the true lingua franca of commerce, politics, and psyche; they are the "cloaking devices" par excellence of the human social world. The twentieth century saw to this transformation: it is the first century in a millennium to have left a larger and more constitutive record of itself in images than in words and ledgers.

If working with BMD for the last fifteen years has taught me one thing, it is that design and life can be raised with impunity, each to the power of the other. It does not trivialize life to see its task as the attempt to give birth to a new style (just as an author, over an entire career, creates a "voice"), nor does it elevate design ludicrously to place it at the service of living. The wars to be fought within our own historical period and in the future are increasingly about the shaping of consciousness. In this state of affairs, design could only be demonized unless we were to propose a method of action whereby design becomes a kind of "de-design." Amid the hysterical cacophony of commercial messages and cues, de-design would provide a way to clear a space where the subtle structures of coercion could momentarily be suspended. Nothing would happen in such a space except ... what was completely unforeseen. In other words, the autonomous processes of life itself.

Not all life forms are good (soldier ants, for example), and not all of BMD's designs are uniformly brilliant. But a commitment to the *cultivation of life* is a practice whose value far transcends the pettiness of individual products; it represents a heroic enlargement of work to an ethics, and a commitment to a human social ecology that far exceeds the usual posture of voluntary submission to the law of markets. No one knows where such an experiment will go, and it is one certainly rife with traps and dead ends. What is most beautiful about it, in fact, might well be its potential to magnify risk. To bring design into such close proximity with life is to make laughter a necessary component of work and action. For only laughter makes risk tolerable. To the attentive reader, it will not be surprising as one looks over this book that as the game gets bigger, the mood gets increasingly light. Design, it tells us softly, *can* have pretensions; it can aspire, not only to activism but to science and thought.

I, for one, detect the risk and the laughter everywhere here, as well as a remarkable lack of the cynicism that has invaded so much of design work today. The power of BMD's work is not at all a function of being "critical" in the banal sense in which the word is now used, but rather of being deliberately out of step with the contemporary current, and even dismissive of collective expectation. There is something in the work that is a pure dismantler of design. It establishes a demilitarized zone of sorts, a place whose serene and confident atmosphere places all bets on hold yet at the same time raises the stakes beyond the reach of any player, BMD included. You will recognize it in those quirky silent moments in the work that allow—even provoke—thought to begin.

It is in these moments—rare now anywhere in our culture—that one is tentatively permitted to dream of a day when design might merge with philosophy itself, and even lead the way to a truly gay science.

New York City
May 27, 2000

The Ball Player
EBONY
VANESSA WILLIAMS
MICHAEL JORDAN
EBONY
JANET:
PEBBLES!
SHIRT TALES
HOW TO HANDLE BEAUTIFUL WOMEN
STEPHANIE
What Pleases Men?

Getting Engaged: The Global Image Economy

To say that the twentieth century has been an era of change is to understate the obvious. The last century has seen the world swept by a tide of massive transformations. We have been exposed to moments of invention, discovery, growth, and rupture that have altered our lives in ways that we are only beginning to fully comprehend. To varying extents, the effects of global modernization continue to connect and shape us.

If we are to fully engage our moment in history, we must develop speculative strategies and illuminate the context in which we produce our work. Only through a willingness to tackle the big questions, the tough assignments, the issues we often consider to be beneath us or beyond us, can we hope to reinvigorate the practice of design.

Only through full-fledged, exuberant engagement—not mud-stuck nostalgic resistance, on the one hand, or FastWired boosterism on the other—can we hope to fashion a practice of depth, meaning, and significance. Lamenting brand hegemony and cheerleading the "revolution" are both simplistic, reductionist postures. On the one hand, we pin our hopes on anti-corporate agit-prop—culture jammers and their oppositional energy and gestures. On the other, we are asked to abandon common sense and critical discourse in an orgasmic embrace of every new gadget, every new application of software, no matter how alienating, invasive, or destructive.

This sort of engagement means calculating every move within the volatile milieu that envelops any new object, gesture, or configuration. Engagement means tenacity and entrepreneurship, along with creative, intellectual, and even physical stamina. It means postponing judgment while we search for an exit. It means not knowing the answers but at least asking the questions.

To better understand the work we produce, and the work we ought to produce, I have attempted a preliminary inventory of the background conditions that increasingly constitute the ecology of our work. The inventory touches on a range of phe-

Even at home, we are embedded in the image.
Fred H. Photograph by Adrienne Salinger

Naive prototypes: Times Square, New York, 1904

Times Square, 1910s

Times Square, 1952

nomena currently shaping and constituting what I call the global image economy. It includes:

surfaces of inscription,
the unstable image,
circulation,
surveillance,
new image infrastructure,
camouflage industries,
tourism,
Postscript world,
freeway condition,
franchise,
celebrity,
cinematic migration,
electronic media,
violence,
aura,
and spin.

The overall effect of this inventory pushes us to see that there is no longer a distance between foreground and background. On the contrary, what we consider our work—that is, the objects we produce, whether they are books, cinema, systems, spaces, or language—is, in fact, embedded in the thickness between foreground and background. The objects, in effect, are formed of the world beyond them. And that world has produced a new and volatile set of forces, conditions, and practices.
What becomes apparent in assembling and studying the inventory is that things are now less discrete than ever. We live in a twenty-four-hour market world where less and less terrain remains unregulated. Less terrain falls outside of the regime of the logo and its image. Today, events, styles, cultures, technologies, memes—as well as rumors, scares, and insults—pass through and are incorporated into the global image economy, reverberating with and distorting one another, all with the capacity to produce—and to erase—wealth, value, and meaning. Attempting to declare the discrete boundary of any practice, where one ends and another begins, has become arbitrary and artificial. On the contrary, the

Times Square, 1967

EIGHT O'CLOCK BEAN COFFEE
The Company You Know. The People You Trust.
SONY THEATRES
OUTDOOR SYSTEMS
VIDEO CAMERAS
CD's & TAPES
ONE WAY
THE VIRGIN TRADING COMPANY

overlap is where the greatest innovation is happening. For example, the intersection of cinema and software, or of the analog and the digital, is charged with hybridity. The work emerging from that zone—here one thinks of the bullet-time process developed for Gap ads and the movie *The Matrix*—is neither cinema nor software but a monstrous and beautiful child of the two. The fact that the same technique can be used to sell both khakis and science-fiction violence tells us that the end products have more in common than simply the means of their production. Nietzsche describes the birth of character as the moment when the first soloist stepped forward from the Greek chorus and defined himself as a singular persona against the collective voice of his peers. What we are undergoing in the global image economy is an analogous yet altogether different type of birth. Imagine a chorus composed entirely of soloists, each one singing a different song, each one attempting to step forward at once in order to out-sing the other. Now imagine that the chorus is mobile and disembodied and fractal. And when we take a step back, they take a step forward and press up against us. And if we step to the side, they, too, step to the side. And when we turn to evade them we discover they're also behind us. We are embedded in them, and they in us.

The new image vista: Times Square, New York, 1997

Above, from left: Openings of every sort — Cultural memory (a church in Germany), public transport, urban space, and the human body (Florida Governor Lawton Chiles in a self-promotional T-shirt, 1997)
Below, from left: Sporting events, virtual and real; children's toys, public restrooms

Image of a logo-printed raw egg,
from *The Medium is the Massage*, by
Marshall McLuhan and Quentin Fiore

Surfaces of Inscription

Image technology, global markets, and digital infrastructure all demand a predatory colonization of open space—whatever the physical or virtual, extensive or temporal form that may take. The imperative of inscribed and inscribable surfaces is now an endless need.

Marshall McLuhan and Quentin Fiore opened their 1967 book *The Medium is the Massage* with an image of a logo "printed" on a raw egg. Even then, they saw fit to comment on the colonization of attention through the inscription of surfaces. Their caption reads: "A trademark is printed on a raw egg yolk by a no-contact, no-pressure printing technique. Imagine the possibilities to which this device will give birth!" At the beginning of the twenty-first century, we no longer need to imagine. Today we have ads on bananas.

Openings of every sort—in schedules, in urban space, on clothes, in events, on objects, in sightlines, in democracy, in philanthropy, in cultures, on bodies—are all inscribed with the logic of the market. Spheres once thought free from this logic, and even resistant or opposed to it—the museum, the academy, public democratic space—find it ever more difficult to retain autonomy in the face of corporate culture and its sponsorships, educational initiatives, and so-called civic gestures.

At the same time, smaller and smaller temporal and physical crevices are being packed with the message of the market. Print ads in front of urinals and video ads in elevators occupy moments once assumed free from the engineered capture of attention. Downtime, or time free from economy, is an endangered species.

Entirely new domains are being invented for eventual inscription. The Internet is a surface of limitless dimension in a high-stakes race to capture eyeballs, or page views, as they say. It is the quintessential chorus of soloists, with every site desperate to express "personality," and every innovation set to trigger collective adoption. The chorus takes another step forward.

In this context, nature (what remains of it) is perhaps all we have left that is free from the hostile takeover of space by the logo, by the predatory regime of inscription.

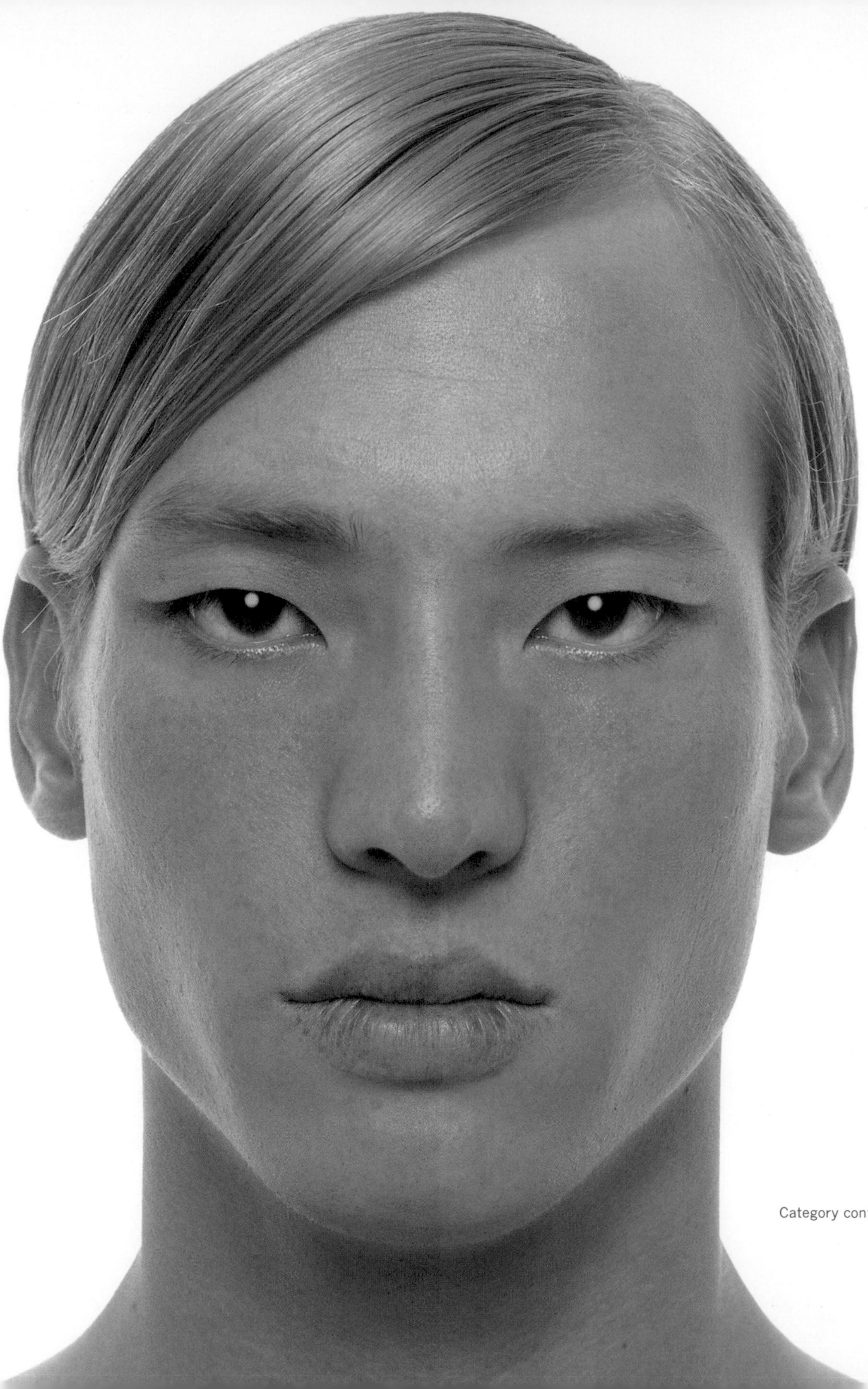

Category confusion

The Unstable Image (or, Photoshop till You Drop)
At work in the field of the image, we are faced with a fundamental paradox: as special effects become more real (that is, more convincing), the original image becomes less real—drained of its connection to an actual moment in time. At its apparent apotheosis, the photographic image arrives with its credibility damaged. Even the straight shot seems suspect, easily accused of having been digitally manipulated. (Deadpan, amateur, snapshot chic is inflated with the potential of providing an "honest" alternative.)
At the other extreme, the morphed image exposes us to deeply disturbing feelings of instability: call it ontological vertigo. As visual landmarks melt and reform before our eyes, we sense that somehow the world will never be the same again. Our only comparable vertiginous experience is the sickening sensation during an earthquake that the very firmness beneath our feet is moving. All our foundations, the stabilities, the fixed entities that we know as singularities, as forms, are in fact only momentarily stable. They are, instead, in perpetual transformation, and all of the in-between forms exist alongside them.

"Manimal"

Photoshop is a two-way street. If the image can be altered and reshaped, so, too, can practice. Are these bodybuilders leading or following Photoshop?

STARDUST
HILTON
BALLY'S
MGM GRAND
MGM

Circulation

What goes around, goes around: circulation is the lingua franca of the global image economy. Every object, even apparently stable and singular ones like buildings and places, now exists everywhere simultaneously. Statues of Liberty (the original appropriately conceived as a love letter from its French creators) now proliferate across the globe.

Within our reprographic culture, value is a function of circulation. Michael Jordan and Dennis Rodman function as currency. Their value, initially pegged to their performance on the court, almost immediately comes to rely on their freedom to circulate fluidly as brand images, in their capacity to compress and package values to suit various communication formats, and in their ability to demand attention.

Clockwise from top: New York-New York Hotel, Las Vegas; replica, Japan; the real statue as seen from New Jersey; more replicas in Japan; aerial view of Las Vegas; replica in Tiananmen Square, Beijing, and surrounded by a student demonstration, 1989 (insets)

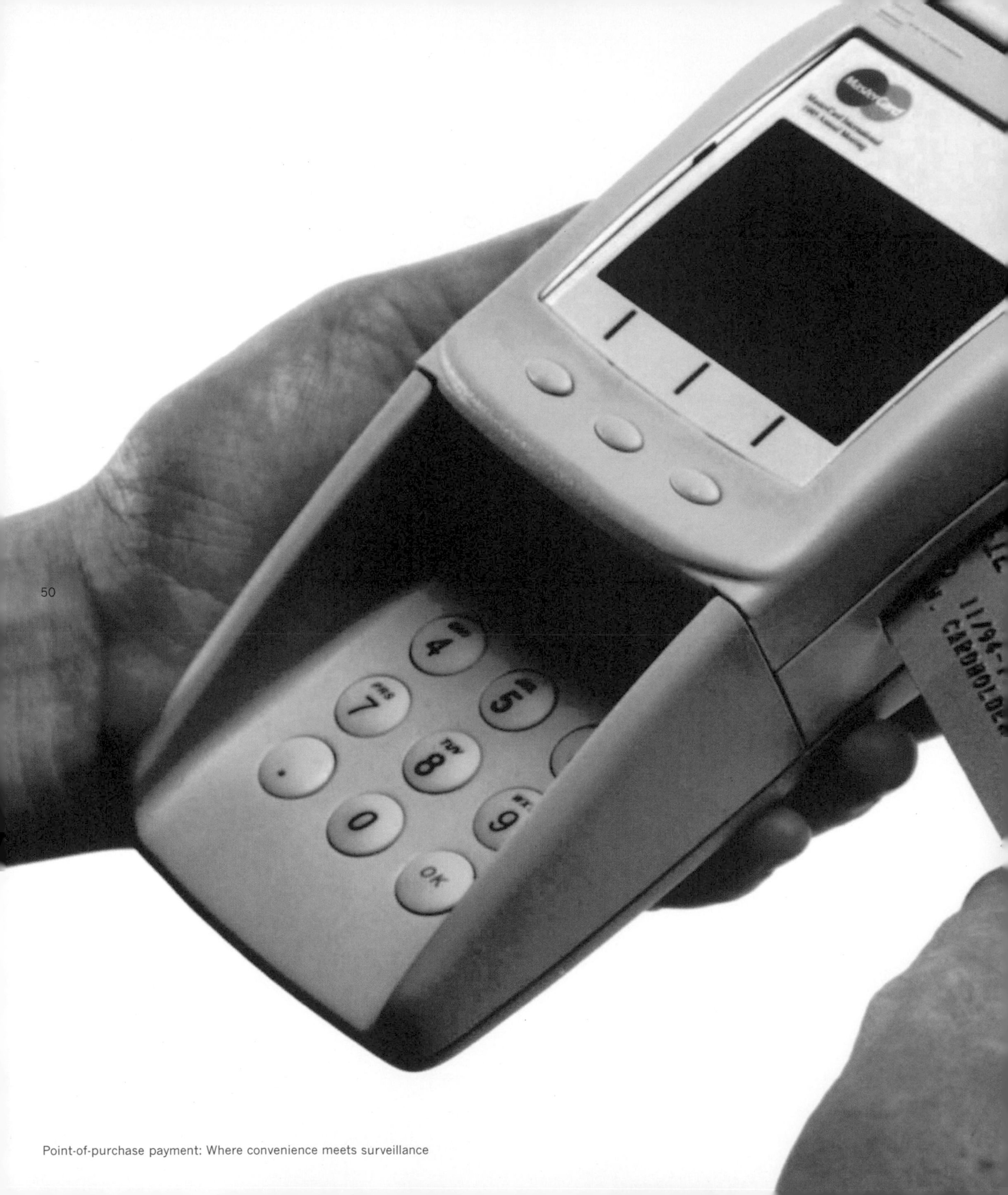

Point-of-purchase payment: Where convenience meets surveillance

Surveillance

Surveillance is the logical, even inevitable, outcome of a system with unlimited capacity to record. Today, credit cards, cash machines, magazine subscriptions, tollbooths, and mail-order catalogs are part of a vast network of data mining. Biometrics, the use of the human body for electronic identification through iris scanning and DNA matching, is a rapidly growing field. On the Internet, cookies and intelligent agenting technology gather massive amounts of data on patterns of attention. ("If you bought this book you probably like that book," etc.) This information, or consumer DNA, is ostensibly captured with the best of intentions—to improve service, to improve a product, to give us more of what we want, to enhance convenience. Yet, as the recording systems become increasingly responsive to our interests, as expressed by our purchasing patterns, we may only encounter things that we are told should interest us. Picture a world that rolls out in front of us like a red carpet of our own design, a projection of our own desires.

Hip e-commerce both records and produces our desires. (On-line businesses come and go, but the data remains.)

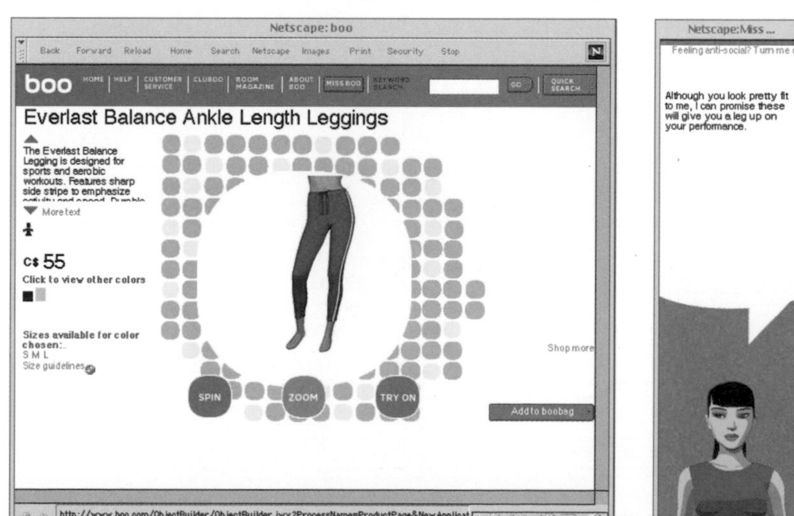

Super-brand systems: Time Warner Inc. agrees to buy Turner Broadcasting System, September 1995. Ted Turner (left) and Gerald Levin announce the deal.

Negative celebrity endorsement: Canadian sprinter Ben Johnson was disqualified for testing positive for steroids after winning the gold medal for the 100-meter sprint at the 1988 Olympics in Seoul.

Credit systems: Retail connections increasingly depend on electronic networks rather than on physical space.

Marketing demographics: The underground vault at Iron Mountain, Pennsylvania, a company that provides data storage and related services for major corporations.

New Image Infrastructure

The old infrastructure we all know about. It involves large-scale, materially concentrated capital projects that are often physically prominent, politically sensitive, and typically the pinnacle of their chief architect's career. These monuments of the past include railway terminals, hydroelectric projects, and museums on hilltops (with railway terminals).

The new infrastructure, by contrast, is dispersed, decentralized, and evolutionary. Built or grown by users, or in response to users, the new image infrastructure consists of systems, agreements, alliances, and standards. Here, we might include:

1. Super-brand systems

Systems designed to capture events and add their energy to the equity of a visual signature (Coca-Cola).

2. Credit systems

A vast e-commerce network where connection is more important to retail practice than is physical real estate.

3. Incentive clubs

In virtually every category, from airlines to coffee shops, frequent-purchase "loyalty" programs exchange benefits for detailed information on consumer preferences.

4. Marketing demographics

By superimposing a matrix of differentiation, meaning, and access, marketing demographics provide a use value to the mountains of data piling up around us.

5. The Olympics

The Olympic Games are the stock exchange of sports-celebrity endorsement, where global brands come to bet on local favorites. (It was an American named Peter Ueberroth who first made the Olympics profitable by selling the 1984 games in Los Angeles to corporate sponsors.) The value of the brand relationship is a function of an athlete's image as a winner or loser; a drug scandal or bribery accusations drive the market down.

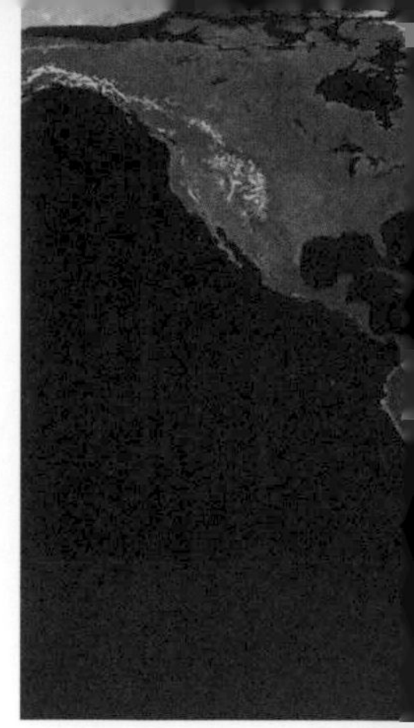

Global airlines

Global currency exchange

The global media business

The global color industry

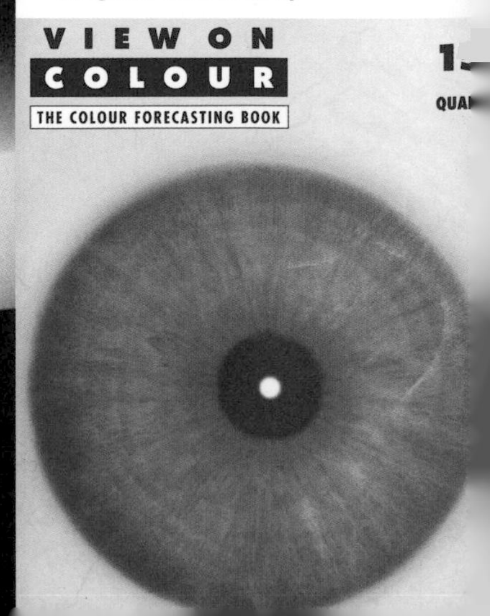

The global photo business

6. Global airlines
The Star Alliance, a sinister name describing the cooperation of eleven national airlines, produces a super-airline with thousands of flights and hundreds of thousands of passengers daily. The effect is that you never travel beyond their realm; they are always there for you, and you for them.

7. Global currency exchange
An ever-expanding system of shifting values. Once a currency is posted, everything within its domain enters the realm of infrastructure, and of surveillance.

8. The global photo business
World standards allow global circulation of visual documents: film purchase in Jakarta, processing in Toronto, projection in Zurich.

9. The global media business
This is the system that promotes the free circulation of items and clips measured in column inches and sound bites. (Paparazzi are the infrastructural parasites.)

10. The global color industry
The International Color Consortium is determined to color our world, systematically exchanging complex color systems for a worldwide standardization of color.

11. The software business
Software is the infrastructure within the new image infrastructure. Software is infrastructure produced line by line by millions of programmers. In the global contest to generate market share and gain control of the infrastructure (what is called "an installed base"), this race is giving software away. The most significant change wrought by software is that it has generated a realm in which every system talks to every other system.

The global software business

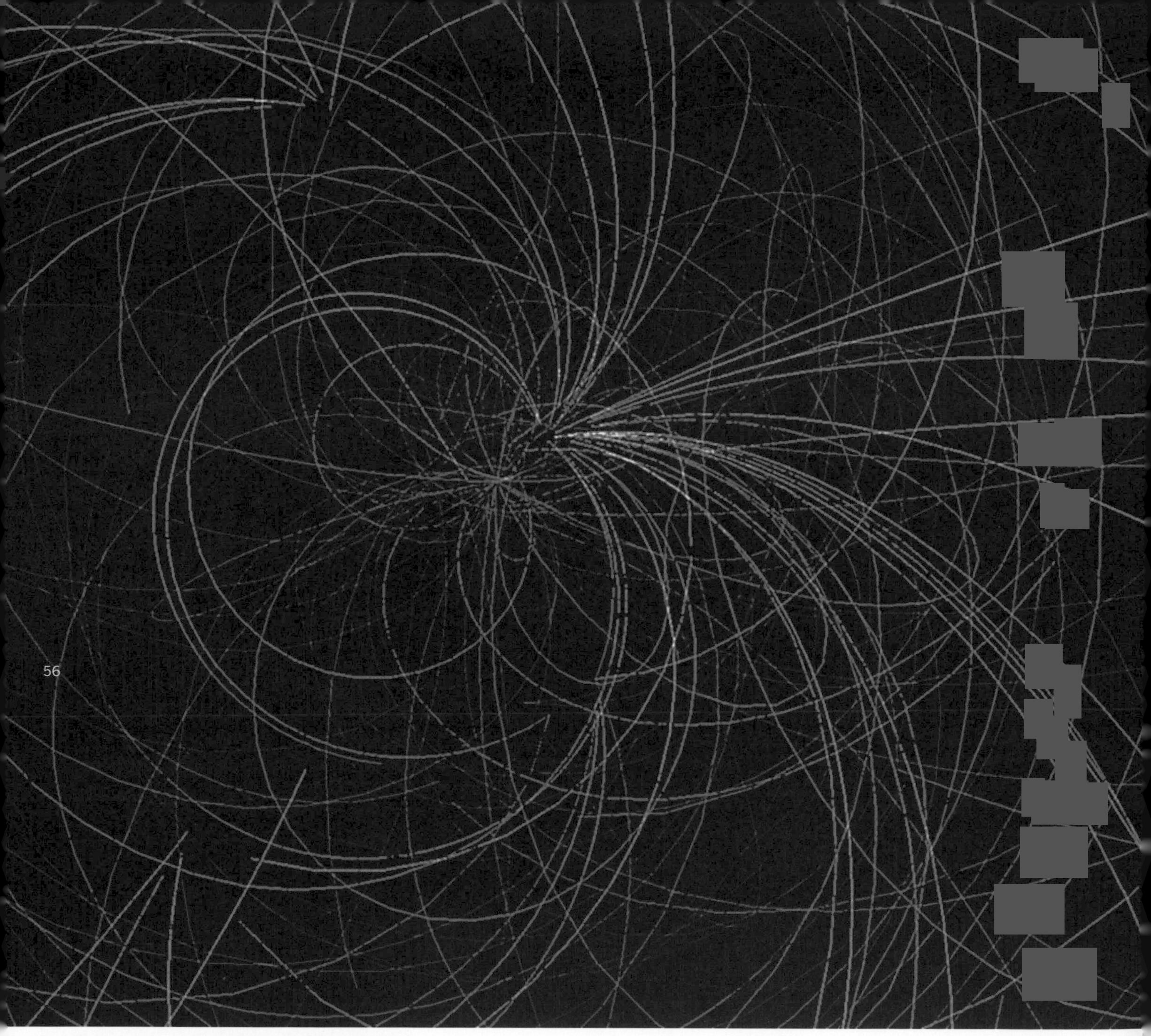

Visualizing internet traffic at the MIT Media Laboratory,
Massachussetts Institute of Technology, Cambridge, Massachussetts

Research from the Aesthetics of Computation Group at MIT

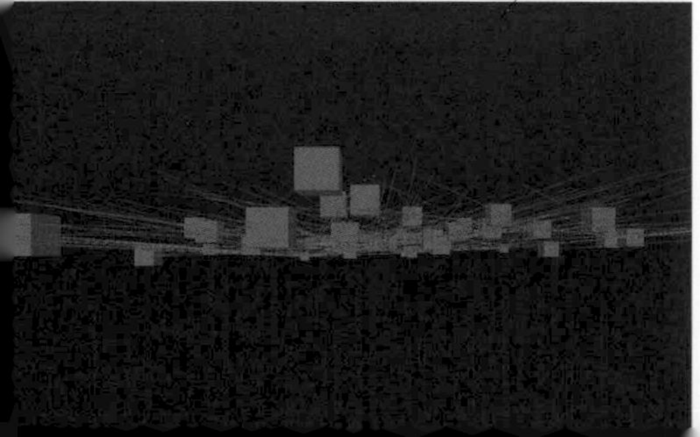

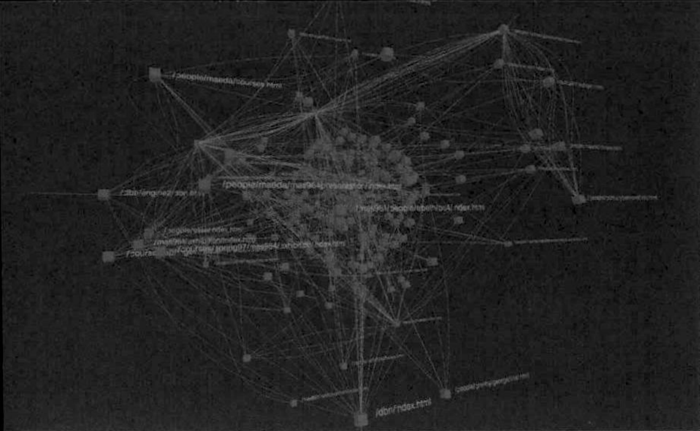

12. The Internet

The greatest distributed evolutionary infrastructure ever conceived is still in its infancy. Developed as a defense apparatus to protect an old military infrastructure, the Internet is still linked to an American system of command and control.

What do the components of the new image infrastructure have in common? Attention. It's all designed for capturing, tracking, quantifying, manipulating, holding, buying, selling, and controlling attention.

If the digital age is a revolution, it is sadly also its opposite — a totalizing, predatory regime, an infrastructure built to channel our own desires and ambitions, to articulate and further extend its own reach. Where do I want to go today? Never mind. It's none of your business.

The old infrastructure can be characterized by one quality that is notably lacking in the new: its civic visibility and presence. It stood as a rendering of a collective project — however politically problematic — and a projection of shared values. The new image infrastructure presents a real challenge to those of us who would imagine a collective project or at least a life made richer by commitment and access to something other than shopping and the market.

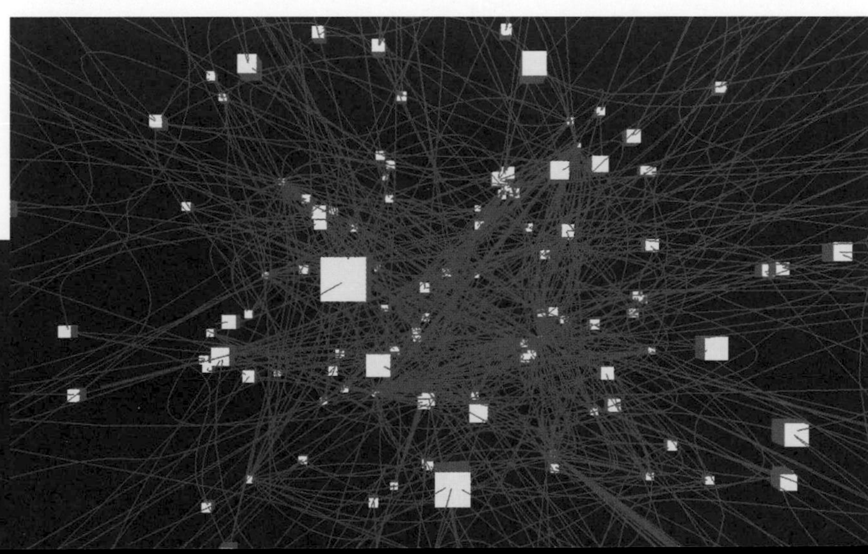

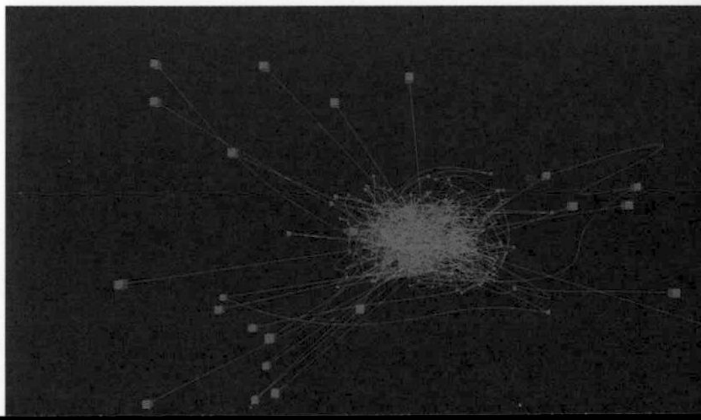

The fateful face-off between presidential candidates
Richard Nixon and John F. Kennedy, October 21, 1960

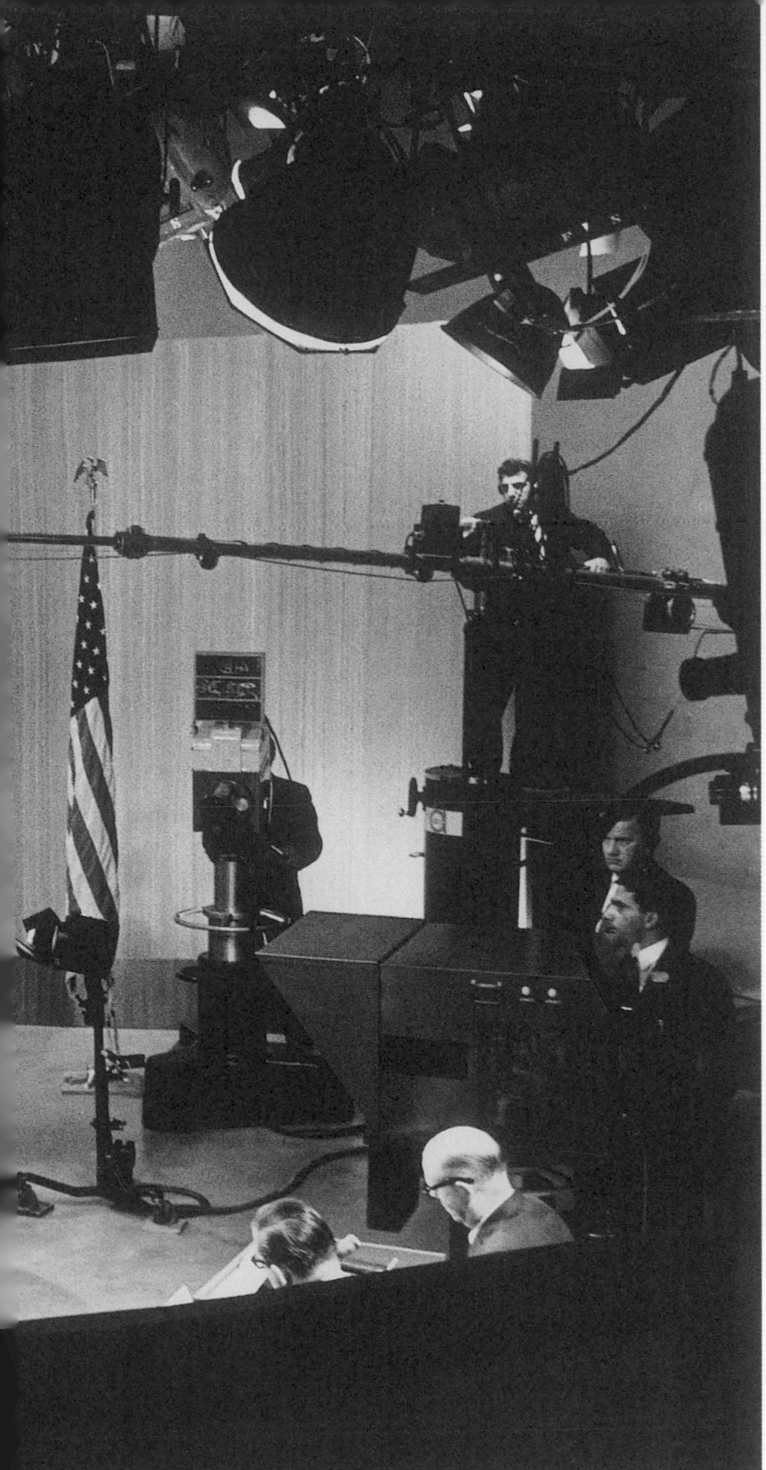

Camouflage Industries

The last half-century has seen the creation of a vast industry devoted to manufacturing appearances that are subtly at odds with reality. As if we couldn't take the collective stress of the real world changes we are undergoing, we have dedicated enormous resources to propping up and confirming our shared state of denial. We deny our newness, our ruthlessness, our violence, our modernity. Instead, we focus on managing our image through public relations.

Consider, for instance, the practice of political debate. In the early days of the American political system, debates would transpire over the course of many hours and even days. Today, the increasingly abbreviated sound bite is the weapon of choice in an effort to control the political brand image in the market.

The media, fully integrated into the camouflage industries, shift the debate from content to form, from what she said to how she said it. The effect of all this, paradoxically, is that reality now seems at odds with appearances. It's not surprising, then, to discover that the Kosovo Liberation Army hired one of New York's top public relations firms, Ruder-Finn, to help them prepare to lobby the U.S. Congress. Such practices reduce the complexities of a civilizational clash to a useful cartoon.

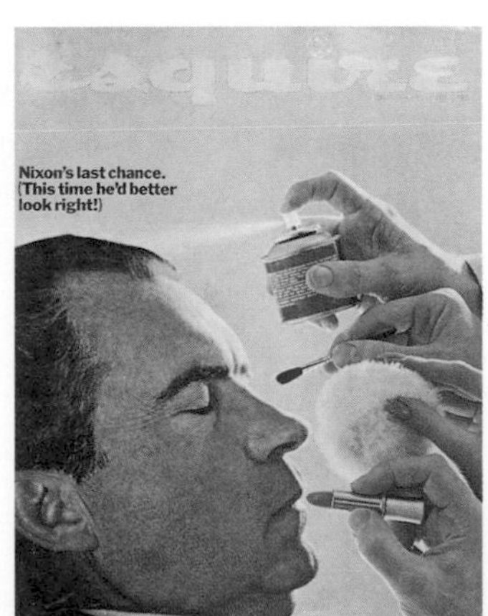

Manufacturing appearance

This synthetic beach sits inside a massive dome in Miyazaki, Japan. Such design-driven destinations short-circuit the desire to experience the full bandwidth of reality—sights, sounds, feelings, tastes, and smells functioning in concert, as opposed to the single-channel world of the plastic image.

Tourism

Every city is now in the business of not only making itself, but also marketing itself. Decisions that affect tourist "optics"—for example, whether a city has a pro sports franchise, or a crime problem, or a police problem—take on unprecedented significance. Thanks to Milton Glaser, who brought us the "I ♥ New York" logo, cities around the globe compete for tourism dollars using their own city logos and slogans. Celebrities, some brought back from the grave, are pressed into promotional service. Destinations themselves are increasingly design-driven: nighttime golf courses carved from the Asian jungle, cinematically engineered theme parks, or the latest massive-scale cruise liners. (Too big to actually dock anywhere, these ships are no longer a form of transportation but have become floating destinations.)

Abetted by transnational designers and architects, the forces of globalism are working their way into every pocket of the world. As a result, the places we arrive at are virtually identical to the places we depart from. The most successful "attractions," like Jon Jerde's CityWalk at Universal Studios in Southern California, are franchised and reproduced around the world with subtle local inflection, increasing attendance and decreasing travel time.

As the global middle class expands exponentially and global infrastructure transports vast bourgeois tourist tribes to distant and exotic destinations, every local difference becomes fodder for touristic exploitation. Then, as franchise operations continue to extend their global presence, they eradicate uniqueness in cuisine, culture, custom, and product. The practices that remain distinctive become increasingly extreme and eccentric—bullfights, sex industries, violence, risk, fundamentalism, primitivism, isolation, disaster, even architecture. In our age of global tourism, the natural environment represents the only significant and unmanufacturable difference between places, but even nature is not holding on very well.

Top: The genteel side of simulated environments: Huis ten Bosch, a life-size replica of a Dutch town built in Kyushu, Japan, is billed as one of Asia's largest theme parks.

Bottom: A destination in itself: when P&O cruises' *Grand Princess* debuted in May 1998, it was the largest and costliest cruise liner ever built.

Toilet peeping at the Treasure House, a drive-in peepshow in Niigata, Japan

One can imagine tomorrow's eccentric niche-market offerings: South Central Los Angeles Survival Adventures, Ethiopian Famine Tours, Antarctic Isolation Treks (you may simply never come back), Disease Excursions (complete with guaranteed cure). Thrill-seeking tourists look farther and farther afield to experience the ideal trip. Panama, for instance, is planning an ecotourism strategy that will attempt to turn the entire country into an eco-corridor. The first bookings for outer-space holidays have probably already been taken.

Macintosh
insanely great!

Postscript World

Until the invention of Postscript, so aptly named by Adobe Systems, the simultaneous production of image and text made for an awkward marriage. There were some attempts at integration, most notably in cinema, where designers like Saul Bass synthesized text and image to powerful effect. But these undertakings were costly, cumbersome, and time-consuming. In print, filmstripping, every bit as cumbersome and costly as in film, remained the technique of marrying text and image. Postscript changed all that. Its principal innovation was the invention of a "page description language" used to describe any point on the surface, whether it was text or image. There is no longer any distinction between text and non-text, image and non-image. The entire surface is now described in one language. Everything is now image. With the elimination of that distinction Adobe ushered in an entirely new aesthetic and a new model of "thinking the page" that will change the way typography itself is conceived.
If we look closely at the history of typography, it's principally a history of evolving typographic production techniques. The forms are in fact inseparable from the ways in which they were produced. The same will apply to Postscript. The consequences remain to be seen.

Above: Text and image become equal partners: Title sequence designed by Saul Bass, from the film *Vertigo*.

Opposite: Steve Jobs (left) and John Scully launch the new Apple Macintosh computer, January 16, 1984.

Under freeway condition only robust entities survive.

Freeway Condition

To drive the Pasadena 110 in Los Angeles — the first so-called freeway in America, famous for the treachery of its twenty-meter-long on-ramps — is to understand the cultural significance of the freeway condition, the profoundly modern idea that we enter a flow, are carried along with it, and exit again effortlessly, unscathed.

As actual places decline in significance and particularity, the space between them increases in prominence and "quality." As Tracy Metz notes in the book *Snelweg: Highways in the Netherlands*: "Roads no longer merely lead to places: they are places."

The metaphor of freeway condition, of constant movement and velocity, has become so ingrained in our collective psyche that it is now applied to politics, to assembly-line, just-in-time manufacturing, and to the information industry. It is even applied to parenting. We are now a culture going with the flow, looking for the best ramps. It is only when we try to decelerate that we perceive a problem. At freeway velocities only robust entities survive. Only brand franchise signals can be apprehended. With culture set at cruise-control, clarity trumps complexity. Known-quantity Toys-R-Us wins out every time over enterprising but ambiguous mom-and-pop stores.

Uniqueness becomes a traffic hazard when you're traveling at breakneck speed. Difference, no matter how subtle, constitutes an unnecessary detour. Both are impossible with life lived on the fly.

Franchise

Franchise is the application of reproduction technologies to intangibles. Franchise is founded on the idea that one can design, produce, circulate, and brand not only products, but also space and time, attitude and atmospheres. Franchise is the packaging of sensibility—smiles, greetings, prompts, and employee behavior.

Franchise supersedes national boundaries. It utterly dissolves local and regional thresholds. Franchise thrives on and sometimes generates a tabula rasa—a flat-nothing-on-the-edge-of-nowhere. For Franchise, no context is the best context.

Franchise is ruthlessly efficient, a form of centralized economy where development costs are endlessly amortized, where worldwide profits go on to support the next phase of planned innovation back at headquarters.

Franchise is the logical outcome of the freeway condition. The known quantity, even if its quality is dubious, wins every time.

Franchise demands clarity. The capsule, the slogan, is the format of choice. For Franchise, we bring good things to life = even finicky eaters love the meaty taste = bye good bye good, bye good bye good.

The perceived limit of temporal, physical, and attention-based real estate that one franchise can occupy now prompts production of false variety. The Gap, Banana Republic, and Old Navy, apparent competitors, are all owned by one company and engineered by one design enterprise.

In a double-twist of irony, ubiquity of Franchise has also provided a common Esperanto of media formulas and clichés for culture jammers. Images now circulate out of the control of central planners. The Swoosh, The Colonel, the Arches, the Bunny: all these become fodder for culture jammers who threaten to blow apart the system of brand value.

Top: A McDonald's franchise in Hazeldonk, The Netherlands

Above: Brand synergy, McDonald's and Beanie Babies team up

Opposite: Culture-jamming, The Colonel circulates out of control

Below: Clear signal, Teletubbies in an official product shot

"We pioneered a new media category which is called lifestyle. Nobody else ever did it before, and we did it, and we intend to really dominate this area for a very long time to come."

Martha Stewart announcing that her empire has gone public, 1999 (Associated Press)

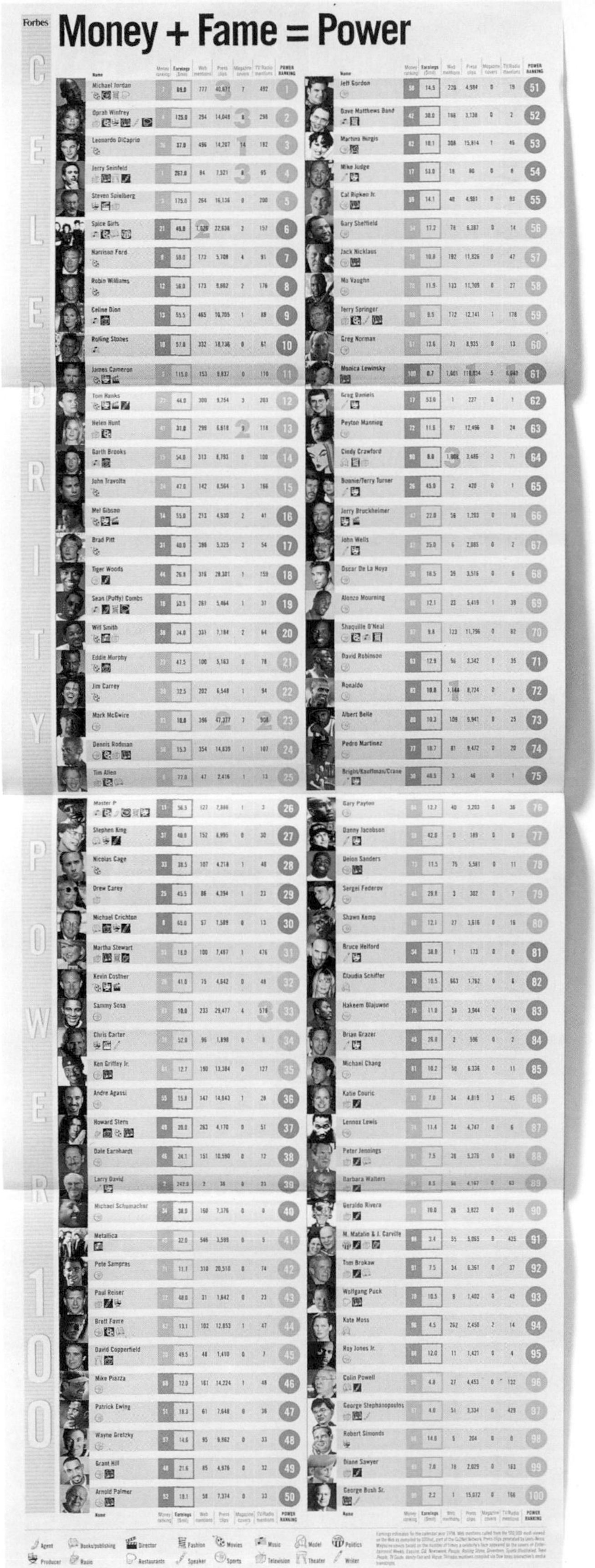

Celebrity (Branded Humans)

Celebrity is a clear human signal in a noisy corporate world.

Celebrity is short-form personality—a way of stuffing complexity into a package that need never be opened.

Celebrity is efficiency applied to qualities.

Celebrity is a brand of DNA—it functions as a reductive index of personality and behavior.

Celebrity is the knife that cuts all of human history into fifteen-minute slices. It is the price you pay for being part of the future.

No longer based on accomplishment, celebrity can be bestowed by virtue of mere proximity (Kato Kaelin), victimization (Nicole Brown Simpson), mistaken identity (the Atlanta bomber), relation (Nicole's parents), evil intent (Mark Fuhrman), incompetence (Mark Fuhrman), or mere happenstance (Marcia Clark).

Celebrity occurs at every scale. Madonna = XXL celebrity, but every small town has one—typically seen hawking cars or carpets on late-night TV.

Money + fame = power
One-hundred celebrity power brands, as identified by *Forbes* magazine, March 1996

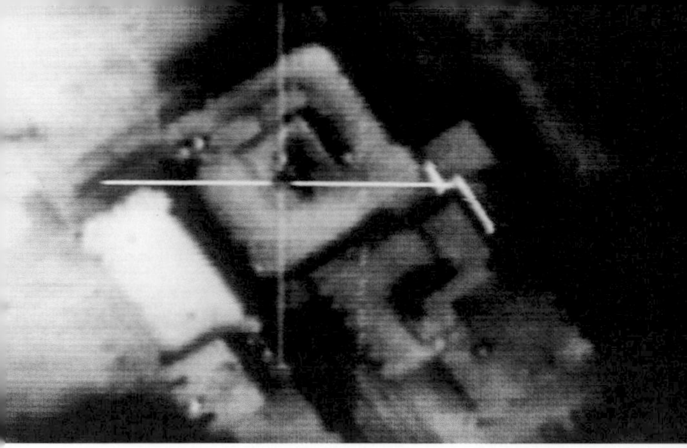

Cinema at war

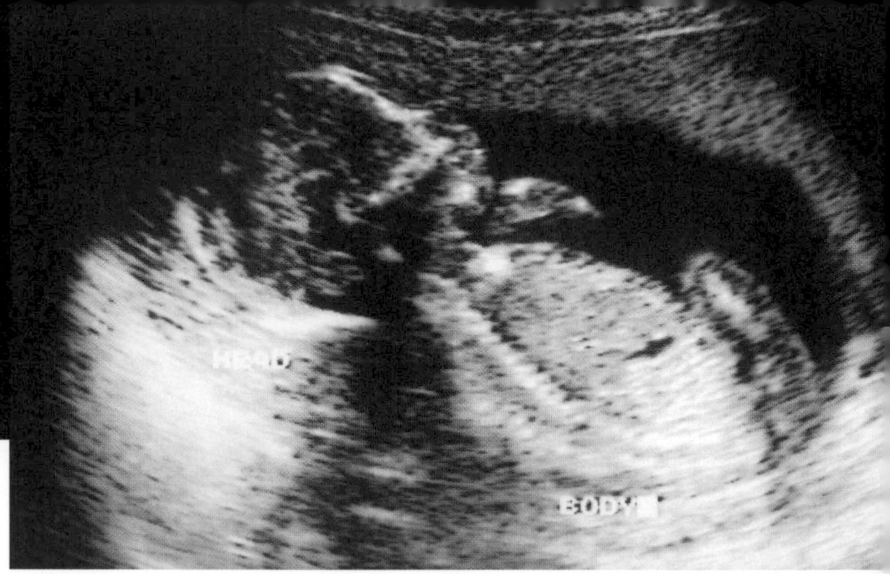

In the womb

At the checkout counter

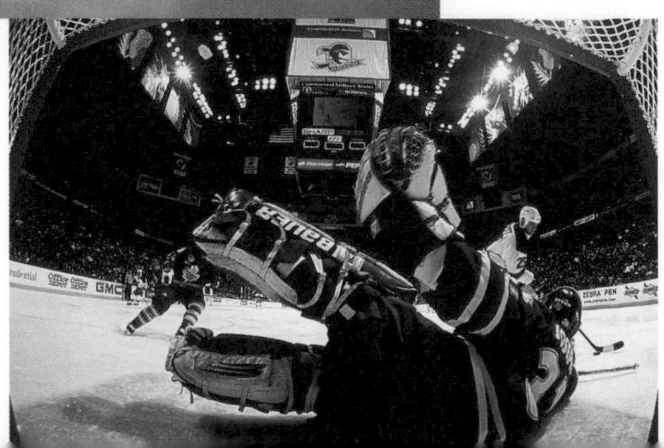

In the net

Cinematic Migration

Cinema will not rest. The moving image is on the move.

While Hollywood cinema becomes paralyzed by the vertiginous numbers of dollars spent and tickets sold and traps itself in epicycles of prequels, sequels, and remakes, the cinematic meme has proven unstoppable, tearing its way into practically every practice and place.

The moving image is now taking us to places we've never been: intimate, first person, mobile, extreme. We are now with the driver inside the cockpit for the Formula One crash. We see what the hockey goalie sees as forwards rush to the net. We witness the shooting in choppy security-camera footage. And we're present for the police chase, the adrenaline rush of the arrest, the melancholic interrogation. Like Slim Pickens in Stanley Kubrick's film *Dr. Strangelove*, we travel on the nose of an American bomb to the moment of impact with its precise target. On the Internet there is simply no intimate act not available to us through the cinematic interface. From bestiality to "college dorm cams" to the most banal and touchingly intimate recordings of boyfriends and girlfriends, Internet access means cinematic intimacy.

In the college dorm

On the slopes

Urban cinema

Cinema in transit

Christoph Kolumbus, an opera with stage design by Peter Greenaway and Saskia Boddeke that incorporates film and video

Video screens in a restaurant

At the same moment, cinema is occupying more and more places—more physical real estate, public and private—and tearing holes in the urban fabric. Ever since the Jumbotron was installed in Tokyo we have seen a proliferation of large-screen urban installations that seem to effortlessly cut apertures in the world. Jumbotrons now dominate even sports stadiums, where the main event is supposedly happening. But the moving image is also using small-screen technologies in its relentless attention grab. In elevators, at the checkout counter, on shopping carts, in cars, in airports, in airplanes—cinema is unstoppable.
On another front, cinema is migrating into other objects: building surfaces, books, paper, Websites, attractions, rides, T-shirts. Cinema is the attention-getter of choice.
And, finally, cinema is evolving a predatory integration with other cultural forms, practices, and techniques. Books, dance, and opera, for instance, have all taken on the mode of cinema as if a form of cultural gene-splicing had occurred.

Prototype of a public video pay phone

Sega's new virtual reality shooting game, with video headsets

Bottom feeding: *The Jerry Springer Show*

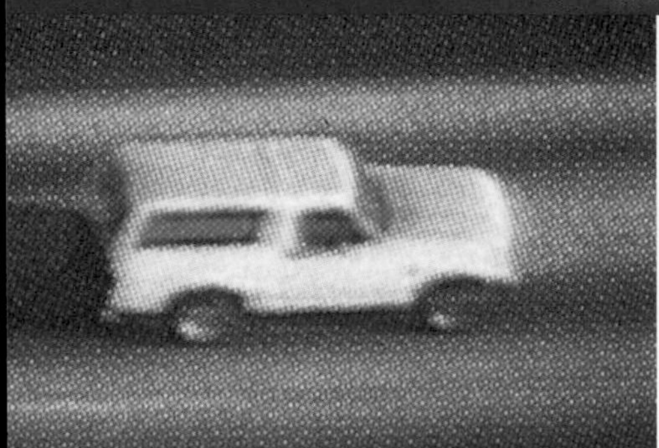

Aerial surveillance: Competing for the live feed

Television verité: In the operating room

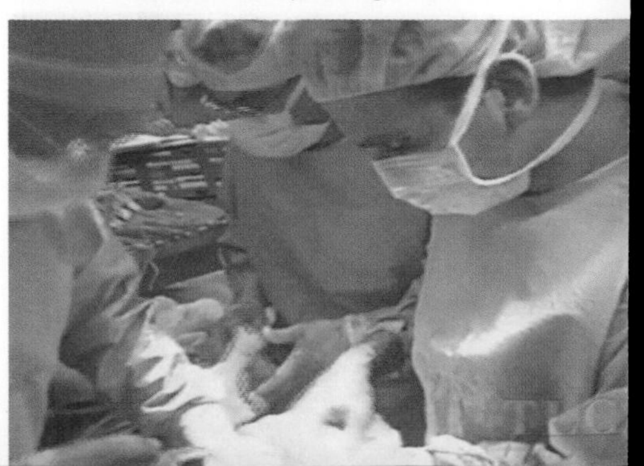

Depth: The Weather Channel broadcasts endless detail.

Officer Charles Huth
Kansas City, Mo. Police Dept.

Television verité: In the patrol car

Mutating Media

With five-hundred channels distributing events twenty-four hours a day, we have created a need for twelve thousand hours of drama every day of the year. Since we can't possibly generate that volume naturally, elaborate and sometimes bizarre strategies have been developed to produce it artificially.

1. Bottom feeding: My ______'s _____ is sleeping with my ______. A dismal format, but one capable of infinite variation.

2. Depth: Never thought possible in this medium, but an imagined demand for more creates mind-numbing mountains of detail.

3. Television verité: The MTV of police work, television verité, or reality-based TV, has all the harshness of its cinematic cousin without the aesthetic ambition.

4. Aerial surveillance: The grafting of the prototypical American military technology—the helicopter—to the news camera means that reporters scour the landscape for a competitive live feed. A recent shotgun suicide on the L.A. freeway was broadcast live in the middle of children's cartoons, prompting bizarre apologies from the networks (as if radical interruption isn't precisely the point).

5. Media daisy chain: The coverage of the coverage of the coverage. A feeding frenzy on major stories results in increasingly abstract and minimalist programming where waiting—for the jury, for a confrontation, for the standoff to end—is the content.

6. Amateur footage: There is a growing market for amateur footage of violence, disaster, and pratfalls. The Rodney King video, one of the most widely broadcast clips in television history, had far-reaching consequences—not least of which were the Los Angeles riots, which, in turn, produced ample opportunity for all of the above media strategies.

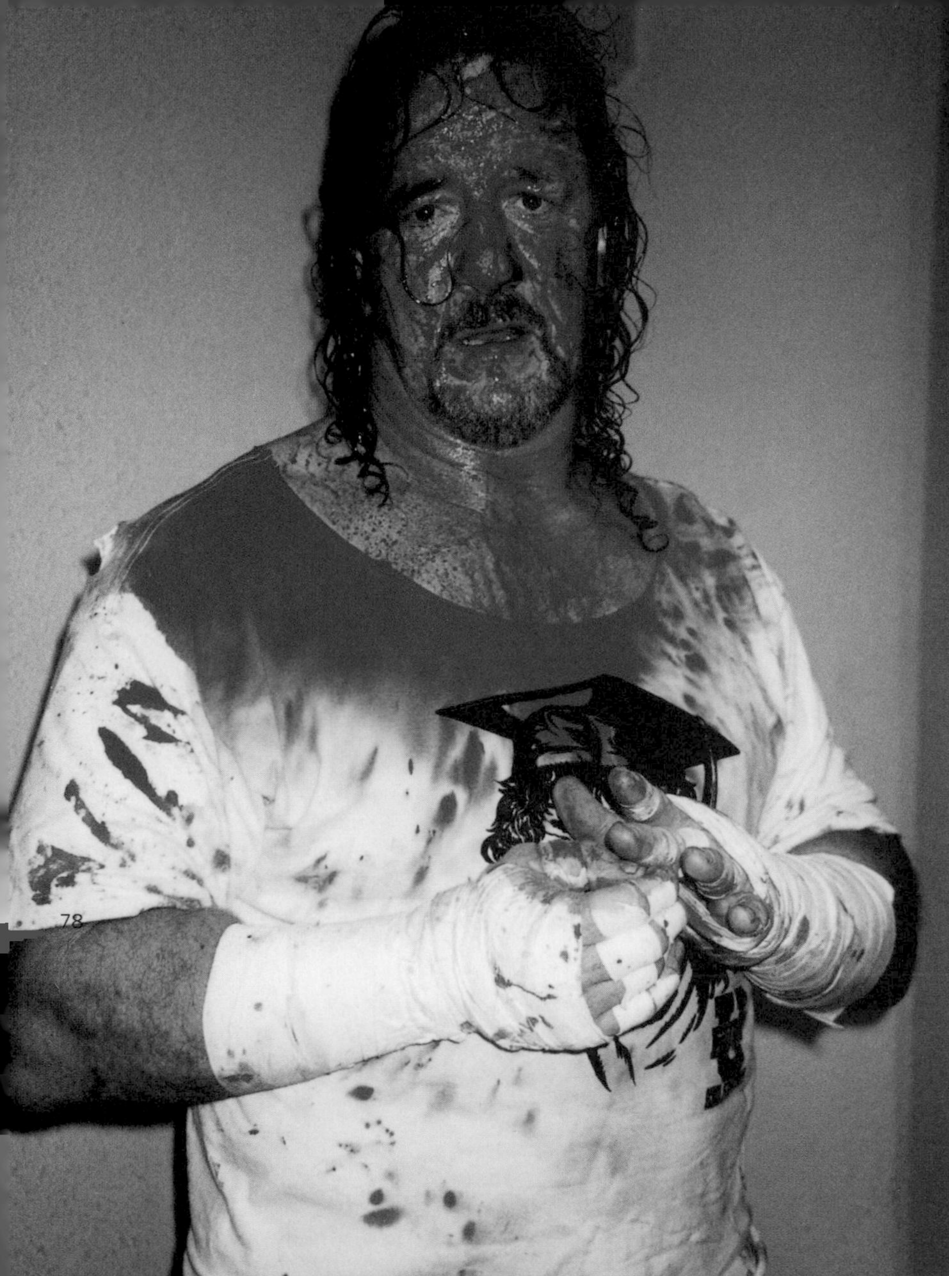

Above: Bar brawls in "Bouncer" video game

Left: Ultimate violence: No-holds-barred wrestling

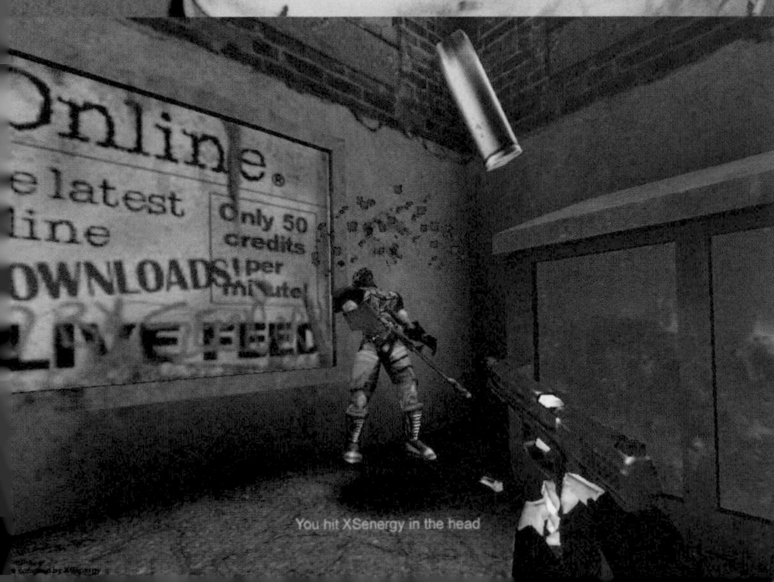

Global kill-fest as seen in "Quake," a multi-player Internet game

Violence

The music industry is in love with love. The image industry is in love with violence.
The image industry splits broadly into two sectors: the utopian (advertising + Hollywood) and the dystopian (media + Hollywood).
Commerce produces utopia. Their line is: There will be a future. It will be good. You will be there.
Violent dystopia is the domain of today's newsmakers. Their line: If there is a future, it will be violent and brutish and you will be there.

Violence caught on a surveillance camera

Moment of truths: Armin Linke photographs a photocopy reproduction of a Thomas Struth photo of a Georges Seurat painting. Who's stealing whose aura?

Aura

Contrary to Walter Benjamin's prediction, made in the 1930s, that mechanical reproduction would drain the work of art of its aura, the circulated image has not stolen the aura from the original; it has borrowed and reinvested it. Today, the works of the greatest value, both in monetary terms and in auratic density, are precisely those images most reproduced.
It seems more and more apparent that the space simulated by virtual reality will never substitute for real space. To the contrary, the virtual now acts as an enormous and unwitting advertisement for the real. Because the reproduction can never hope to generate the dynamic range or bandwidth of the original, the desirability of the original merely grows as the quality of the reproduction improves.

In a "pre-spin" photo

Confronting the media melée

Posing for posterity

Arriving at a post-Oscar awards party, March 1999

With Barbara Walters, March 1999

Spin

It is what it is and it is what it says. Spin is an infinitely flexible yardstick capable of measuring anything. Every gesture, every object, every event has a spin dimension that can be calculated and controlled. But that dimension is not stable.
It changes with perspective, with time, and with market conditions. Those capable of effectively handling the yardstick have an uncanny ability to calibrate these factors.
An example:
1. In a contemporary business context, the old-fashioned device says, "We care about our history," provided the service isn't bad, in which case it says, "We're poorly managed and haven't yet upgraded our equipment," unless the business is convincingly grassroots, in which case it says, "We care about the environment."
No meaning system is sacred. Every market sign is fundamentally unstable.
2. A stylish new haircut says, "I'm hip to the latest trends," unless I'm a White House intern, in which case it says, "I'm being handled by a book agent," unless I'm being attacked by the president's wife, in which case it says, "I'm not trailer-park trash. I'm just a gullible, ambitious girl from the West Coast, being handled by a book agent."
It is what it is and it is what it says.
Bhopal for Union Carbide. Valdez for Exxon. And Nazi gold for Switzerland's banks. These are events with a considerable communications dimension; their meanings are enlarged or reduced by the way in which they are managed.

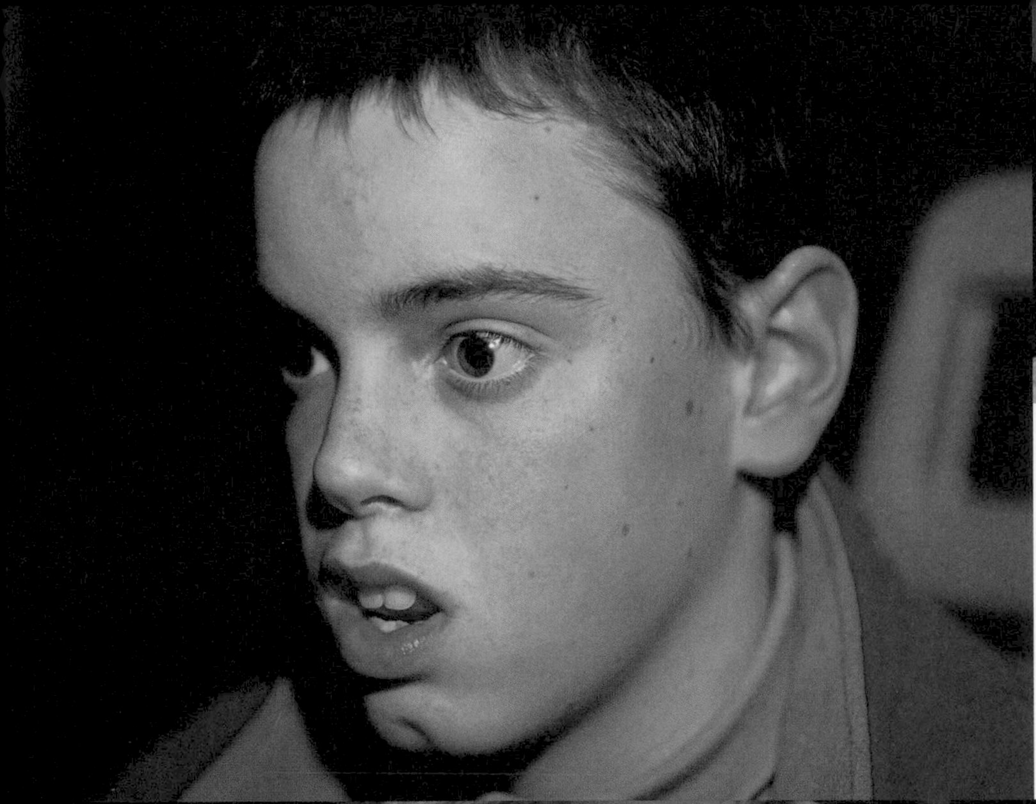

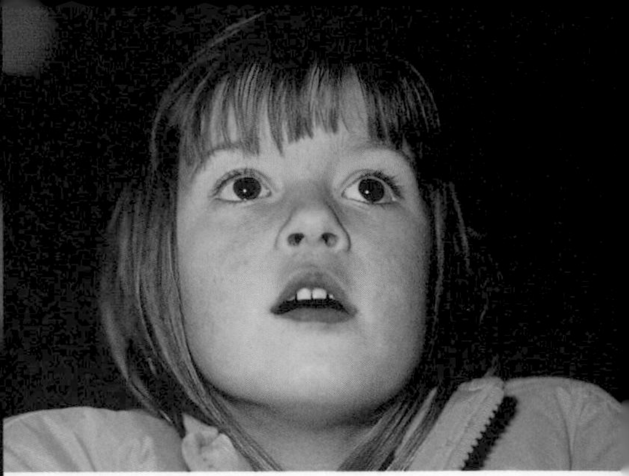

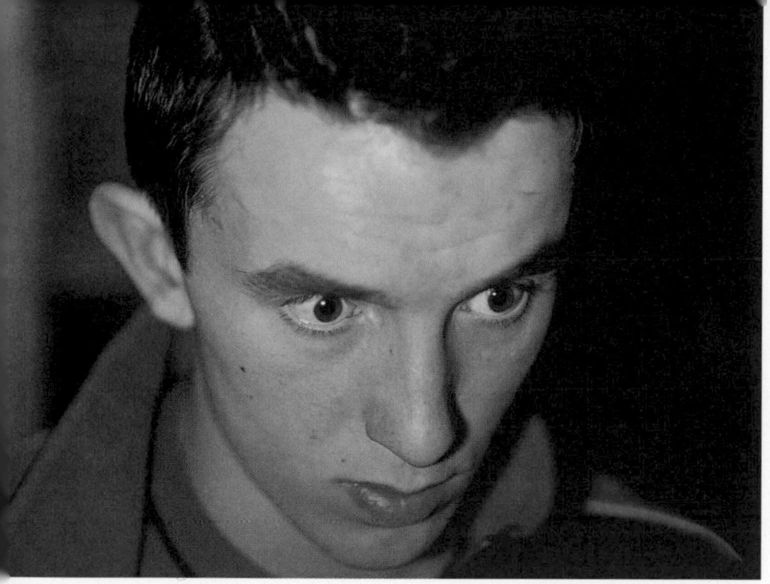

Hitched: A Conclusion

Designers today experience a condition of ambiguity and compromise: building, aiding, and abetting the global image economy seem inevitable consequences of our work. Prospects of that condition changing seem remote. Nonetheless, our obligation to exploit the situation is compelling, provided that we are willing, given our position, to recognize the potential of radical contradiction and to take an eagerly opportunistic posture in looking for the openings that appear before us.

What I am attempting, in response to the torrential acceleration of the global image economy, is engaged design. Engagement means enlisting all the restrictions, conditions, and limitations of the context in which we work. It means taking on the background, like it or not, and bringing it to every foreground. The question we have to ask is: What is our relationship to this beast?

Every set of the developments we have inventoried has a downside and an upside. The downside is obvious and depressingly easy to catalog. The upside is up to us to discover, or more importantly, to invent. We must, then, be super-provisional and hyper-opportunistic. Contrary to the popular maxim, the digital age does not behave like a revolution, but its opposite, an apparently predatory totality surrounding us. And yet, it is transforming human capacities for communication, for environmental reform, for productivity and creativity. Every aspect of the global image economy is darkly problematic, yet every aspect of it also carries a potential for human reinvention.

If the accelerated image-production technologies have saturated society, they have also put image-making capability into the hands of non-professionals. Technology has miniaturized the image-making process. Today, a feature film that once would have required a large technical facility backed by a huge financial apparatus (Paramount Pictures, say) can now be fully realized in a medium-size room rented in a typical provincial town.

Proliferation also means dispersion. Dispersion means new potential strategies constantly appear, if we are

Children photographed while playing video games.
Photographs from the series "Trust,"
by Adam Broomberg and Oliver Chanarin, 2000

"Look Painting," by Canadian professor Steve Mann on "Shoot Back" day. Sporting his "wearable computer" invention, Prof. Mann shoots back at video surveillance technology and unsuspecting security personnel in symbolic protest against the loss of privacy in modern life.

willing to look for the openings. But people tend only to look at the contradiction and then stop, because they cannot resolve it, cannot get the pieces to fit. Having looked and seen, they prefer to look away, to keep their heads down and get on with their work. Unless we keep our heads up and come to terms with the global image economy and the way it permeates the things we make and see, we are doomed to a life's work of decorating and redecorating. And coming to terms means maintaining the dialogue with the context and facing the contradictions it imposes on our work.

But there is another reason to be openly and critically engaged. If freedom can be defined as the ability to apply one's energy to objects of one's own choosing, then our attention, our time, and our energy — our most precious human resources — ought to be guarded jealously. The onus is on us to devise attitudes, postures, flexible and imaginative strategies to exploit the situation.

Every gesture we make now is cinematic because it gets swept up into a swift sequence of gestures that precede and follow it. The condition of montage, as Eisenstein so radically conceived it, has become the condition of our culture. No single gesture can be preserved from that condition, none can be regarded as completed or closed. Every gesture is held to a context in which it is made. And the context is moving and absorbing so fast that new gestures constantly have to be invented. No matter how bleak the situation into which we have been thrown by the global image economy, it offers opportunities — we need only invent them. By understanding our living and working context, we open — even if only temporarily — avenues of liberty not yet charted or even explored.

An Incomplete Manifesto for Growth

1. Allow events to change you. You have to be willing to grow. Growth is different from something that happens to you. You produce it. You live it. The prerequisites for growth: the openness to experience events and the willingness to be changed by them.

2. Forget about good. Good is a known quantity. Good is what we all agree on. Growth is not necessarily good. Growth is an exploration of unlit recesses that may or may not yield to our research. As long as you stick to good you'll never have real growth.

3. Process is more important than outcome. When the outcome drives the process we will only ever go to where we've already been. If process drives outcome we may not know where we're going, but we will know we want to be there.

4. Love your experiments (as you would an ugly child). Joy is the engine of growth. Exploit the liberty in casting your work as beautiful experiments, iterations, attempts, trials, and errors. Take the long view and allow yourself the fun of failure every day.

5. Go deep. The deeper you go the more likely you will discover something of value.

6. Capture accidents. The wrong answer is the right answer in search of a different question. Collect wrong answers as part of the process. Ask different questions.

7. Study. A studio is a place of study. Use the necessity of production as an excuse to study. Everyone will benefit.

8. Drift. Allow yourself to wander aimlessly. Explore adjacencies. Lack judgment. Postpone criticism.

9. Begin anywhere. John Cage tells us that not knowing where to begin is a common form of paralysis. His advice: begin anywhere.

10. Everyone is a leader. Growth happens. Whenever it does, allow it to emerge. Learn to follow when it makes sense. Let anyone lead.

11. Harvest ideas. Edit applications. Ideas need a dynamic, fluid, generous environment to sustain life. Applications, on the other hand, benefit from critical rigor. Produce a high ratio of ideas to applications.

12. Keep moving. The market and its operations have a tendency to reinforce success. Resist it. Allow failure and migration to be part of your practice.

13. Slow down. Desynchronize from standard time frames and surprising opportunities may present themselves.

14. Don't be cool. Cool is conservative fear dressed in black. Free yourself from limits of this sort.

15. Ask stupid questions. Growth is fueled by desire and innocence. Assess the answer, not the question. Imagine learning throughout your life at the rate of an infant.

16. Collaborate. The space between people working together is filled with conflict, friction, strife, exhilaration, delight, and vast creative potential.

17. ________________. Intentionally left blank. Allow space for the ideas you haven't had yet, and for the ideas of others.

18. Stay up late. Strange things happen when you've gone too far, been up too long, worked too hard, and you're separated from the rest of the world.

19. Work the metaphor. Every object has the capacity to stand for something other than what is apparent. Work on what it stands for.

20. Be careful to take risks. Time is genetic. Today is the child of yesterday and the parent of tomorrow. The work you produce today will create your future.

21. Repeat yourself. If you like it, do it again. If you don't like it, do it again.

22. Make your own tools. Hybridize your tools in order to build unique things. Even simple tools that are your own can yield entirely new avenues of exploration. Remember, tools amplify our capacities, so even a small tool can make a big difference.

23. Stand on someone's shoulders. You can travel farther carried on the accomplishments of those who came before you. And the view is so much better.

24. Avoid software. The problem with software is that everyone has it.

25. Don't clean your desk. You might find something in the morning that you can't see tonight.

26. Don't enter awards competitions. Just don't. It's not good for you.

27. Read only left-hand pages. Marshall McLuhan did this. By decreasing the amount of information, we leave room for what he called our "noodle."

28. Make new words. Expand the lexicon. The new conditions demand a new way of thinking. The thinking demands new forms of expression. The expression generates new conditions.

29. Think with your mind. Forget technology. Creativity is not device-dependent.

30. Organization = Liberty. Real innovation in design, or any other field, happens in context. That context is usually some form of cooperatively managed enterprise. Frank Gehry, for instance, is only able to realize Bilbao because his studio can deliver it on budget. The myth of a split between "creatives" and "suits" is what Leonard Cohen calls a "a shining artifact of the past."

31. Don't borrow money. Once again, Frank Gehry's advice. By maintaining financial control, we maintain creative control. It's not exactly rocket science, but it's surprising how hard it is to maintain this discipline, and how many have failed.

32. Listen carefully. Every collaborator who enters our orbit brings with him or her a world more strange and complex than any we could ever hope to imagine. By listening to the details and the subtlety of their needs, desires, or ambitions, we fold their world onto our own. Neither party will ever be the same.

33. Take field trips. The bandwidth of the world is greater than that of your TV set, or the Internet, or even a totally immersive, interactive, dynamically rendered, object-oriented, real-time, computer graphic–simulated environment.

34. Make mistakes faster. This isn't my idea — I borrowed it. I think it belongs to Andy Grove.

35. Imitate. Don't be shy about it. Try to get as close as you can. You'll never get all the way, and the separation might be truly remarkable. We have only to look to Richard Hamilton and his version of Marcel Duchamp's large glass to see how rich, discredited, and underused imitation is as a technique.

36. Scat. When you forget the words, do what Ella did: make up something else... but not words.

37. Break it, stretch it, bend it, crush it, crack it, fold it.

38. Explore the other edge. Great liberty exists when we avoid trying to run with the technological pack. We can't find the leading edge because it's trampled underfoot. Try using old-tech equipment made obsolete by an economic cycle but still rich with potential.

39. Coffee breaks, cab rides, green rooms. Real growth often happens outside of where we intend it to, in the interstitial spaces—what Dr. Seuss calls "the waiting place." Hans Ulrich Obrist once organized a science and art conference with all of the infrastructure of a conference—the parties, chats, lunches, airport arrivals—but with no actual conference. Apparently it was hugely successful and spawned many ongoing collaborations.

40. Avoid fields. Jump fences. Disciplinary boundaries and regulatory regimes are attempts to control the wilding of creative life. They are often understandable efforts to order what are manifold, complex, evolutionary processes. Our job is to jump the fences and cross the fields.

41. Laugh. People visiting the studio often comment on how much we laugh. Since I've become aware of this, I use it as a barometer of how comfortably we are expressing ourselves.

42. Remember. Growth is only possible as a product of history. Without memory, innovation is merely novelty. History gives growth a direction. But a memory is never perfect. Every memory is a degraded or composite image of a previous moment or event. That's what makes us aware of its quality as a past and not a present. It means that every memory is new, a partial construct different from its source, and, as such, a potential for growth itself.

43. Power to the people. Play can only happen when people feel they have control over their lives. We can't be free agents if we're not free.

What is Good?

One of the first things that impressed me as a young designer was the politics of form. The way I saw it, the most important formal developments were intimately linked to social discoveries and political action. People forged new visions of the world and needed to express them. The connection between social and formal innovation could not be ignored.

The first company I started was called Public Good. It was an enterprise very much concerned with the social implications of the work we produced. Previously, I had been in London working with a corporate design agency world-renowned for its "good design." While there, I had lived through the ascent of Thatcherism. I had experienced first-hand the British class system, which to a young Canadian was at once opaque and absurd. I eventually left London and hooked up with two friends in New York, Steven Bock and Elisabeth Matheson, who proposed that we return to Toronto and launch Public Good. Our ambition was to bring meaning to the work we produced. In that context, the notion of "good" was liberated from any visual or aesthetic expression. Some of our work generated no visual evidence. It involved, for instance, analyzing and assisting the organization of a union initiative, or producing an educational program. Our work revolved around social effects and objectives—literacy, education, health, justice, workplace issues—and design was deployed in the service of achieving results. My work could look deadpan but have profound effect. In some way I think this is the genesis of the approach that Bruce Mau Design would take later.

My role at Public Good lasted only a few years. It ended when I became involved with Zone. My two partners did not want to pursue the project but I did. I had no idea at the time that the project would extend into an extraordinary fifteen-year intellectual adventure.

KAGEL
WEEKEND
Featuring German Composer Mauricio Kagel
Friday, April 6
Saturday, April 7
8:00 P.M.
Films/Music by Kagel
at the Funnel
507 King Street East
$3.00/Subscribers Free
Un chien andalou
Buñuel and Dalí
MM51
Collage from
Murnau's "Nosferatu"
Hallelujah
Match
Sunday, April 8
4:00 P.M.
Kagel lectures
at the Music Gallery
30 St. Patrick Street
$3.00/Subscribers Free
Monday, April 9
8:00 P.M.
An All-Kagel Concert
at the Town Hall,
St. Lawrence Centre
$9.00 Adults $6.00 Students
Featuring Boris Carmeli, bass
and the Elmer Iseler Singers
Ten Marches to Miss the Victory
Chorbuch
Mitternachtsstük
Fürst Igor, Strawinsky
Two Machault Ballades
All North American Premieres
Tickets available from
Five Star Tickets
Tickets Available from
New Music Concerts
24 Mercer Street
593-0436
Produced in cooperation
with the Goethe Institute

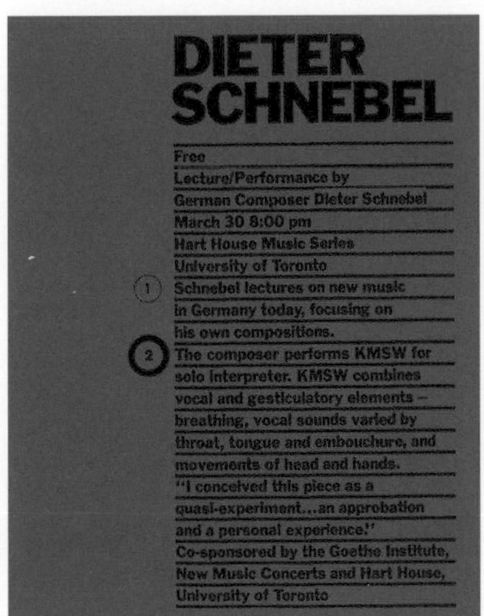

DIETER
SCHNEBEL
Free
Lecture/Performance by
German Composer Dieter Schnebel
March 30 8:00 pm
Hart House Music Series
University of Toronto
1
Schnebel lectures on new music
in Germany today, focusing on
his own compositions.
2
The composer performs KMSW for
solo interpreter. KMSW combines
vocal and gesticulatory elements –
breathing, vocal sounds varied by
throat, tongue and embouchure, and
movements of head and hands.
"I conceived this piece as a
quasi-experiment...an approbation
and a personal experience."
Co-sponsored by the Goethe Institute,
New Music Concerts and Hart House,
University of Toronto

SUNDAY
FEBRUARY
19
Great Hall, Hart House
8:00 P.M. $9.00 adults $6.00 students
THREE PREMIERES
MUSIC IN
SPACE
New Music Concerts
24 Mercer Street
593-0436
STEVE REICH
Vermont Counterpoint flute and 13 pre-recorded flutes
JOHN REA
Treppenmusic 12 musicians and tape
JAN JARVLEPP
Time Zones 17 musicians spatially arranged
PHILLIP WERREN
Hurricaneum 7 musicians and tape

Super low-budget: lettersize photocopy posters designed at Public Good between the years 1983 and 1985

Model City

In 1985 I was approached by Urzone, a new publishing venture based in New York that was about to launch a cultural journal. Its editors, Sanford Kwinter, Jonathan Crary, Michel Feher, and Hal Foster, wanted to structure the first issue around the idea of the contemporary city. It would consist of commissioned art works, essays, and replies to questionnaires sent to a wide range of scholars and practitioners who work with contemporary urbanism.

When *Zone 1/2* came out, public reception was surprisingly strong given the scale of Urzone's operation. A number of factors contributed to this success, but principally, *Zone 1/2*'s power derived from the fact that it performed its subject. It modeled urbanism rather than illustrated it. The book behaved like a city—it even had the abrasive quality that cities have.

Today it is hard to imagine the state of academic and intellectual discourse that existed when *Zone 1/2* emerged. Intellectual publishing as we now know it has been radically transformed. In the mid-1980s, however—when *Zone 1/2* appeared—there simply was nothing like it. The magazine declared itself in an entirely new way. It was a radical object.

Zone 1/2
New York: Urzone, 1985
Zone 1/2 was produced before computers appeared in design studios. It is a kind of pre-digital digital work. The cover looks as though it is computer-rendered, but it is actually composed of multiple photocopies of an image from a popular science magazine that eventually were retouched by hand.

The first mock-up.

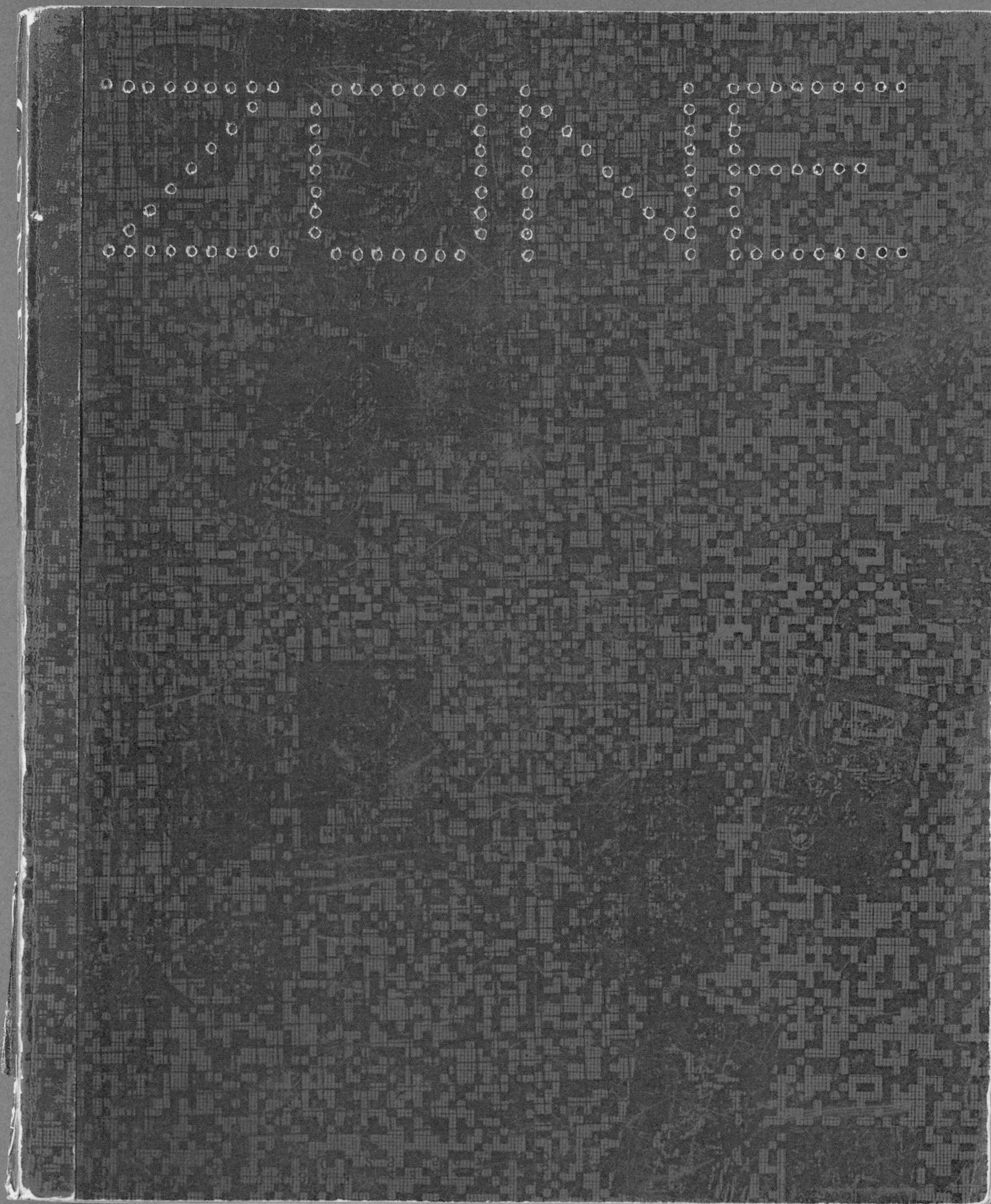
ZONE

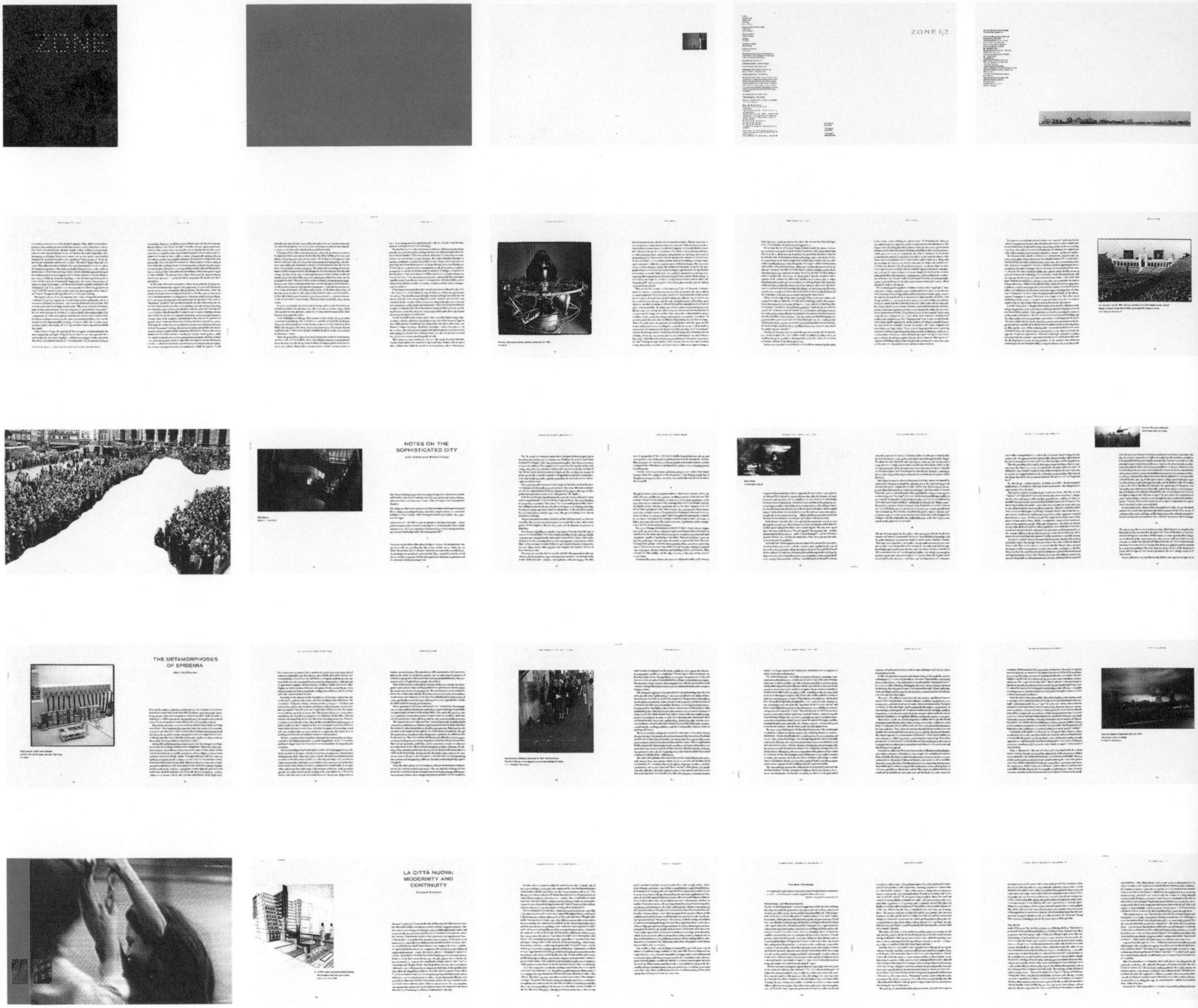

The editors' foreword speaks of how the Chinese master draws a carp. It is not enough to draw the body of the carp — one must somehow render its life passage and draw the traces that the carp leaves behind. We referred to this precept throughout the design process. In this case, we were rendering the jittery, furious passage of urban life.

The following pages reproduce *Zone 1/2* in its entirety.

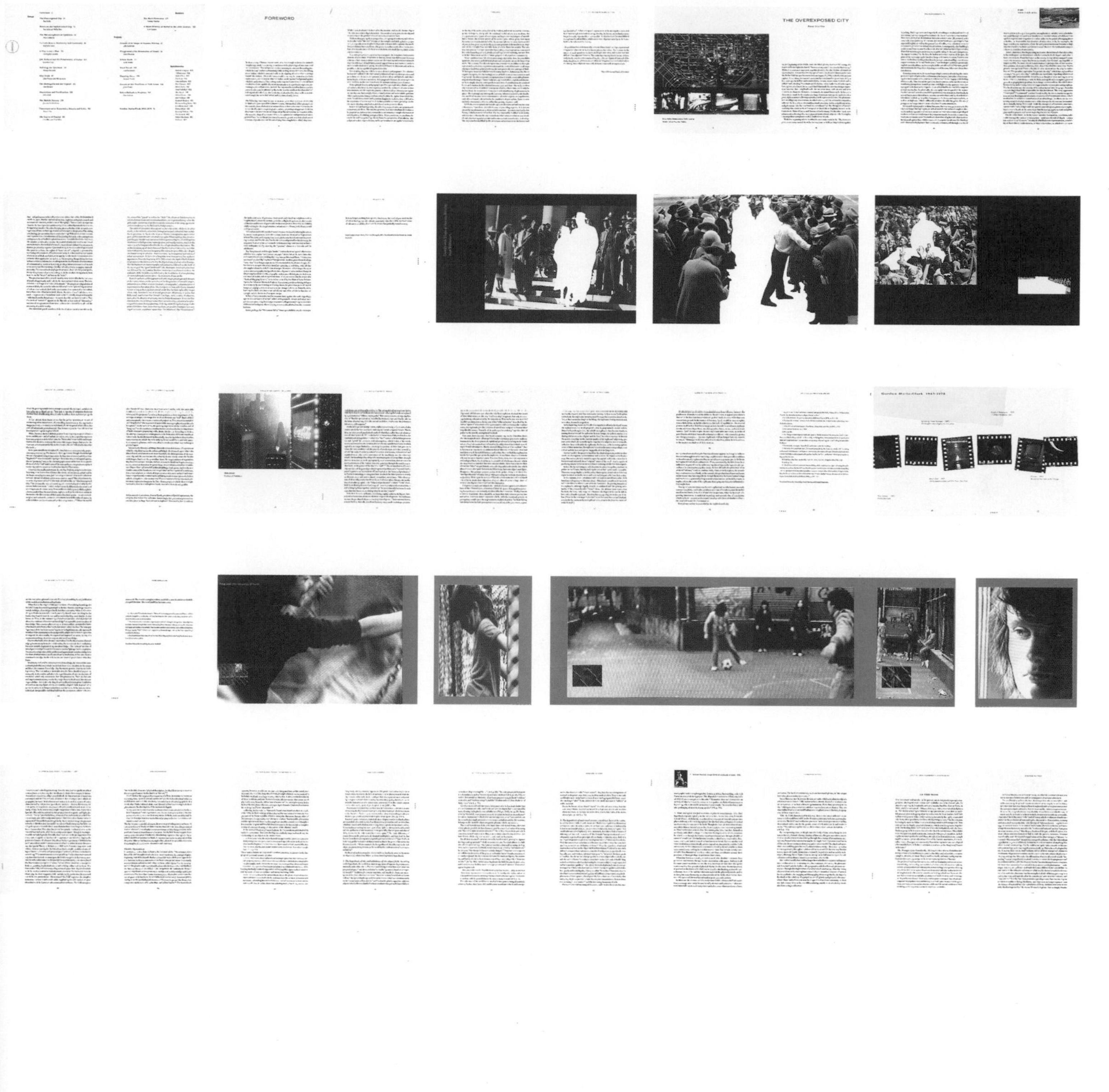
FOREWORD
THE OVEREXPOSED CITY

Urban Feeds
J.G. BALLARD AND THE
PROMISCUITY OF FORMS

A CITY IS NOT A TREE
POLICING THE SPECTRUM
CITY/STATE
POLICE SUR LA VILLE

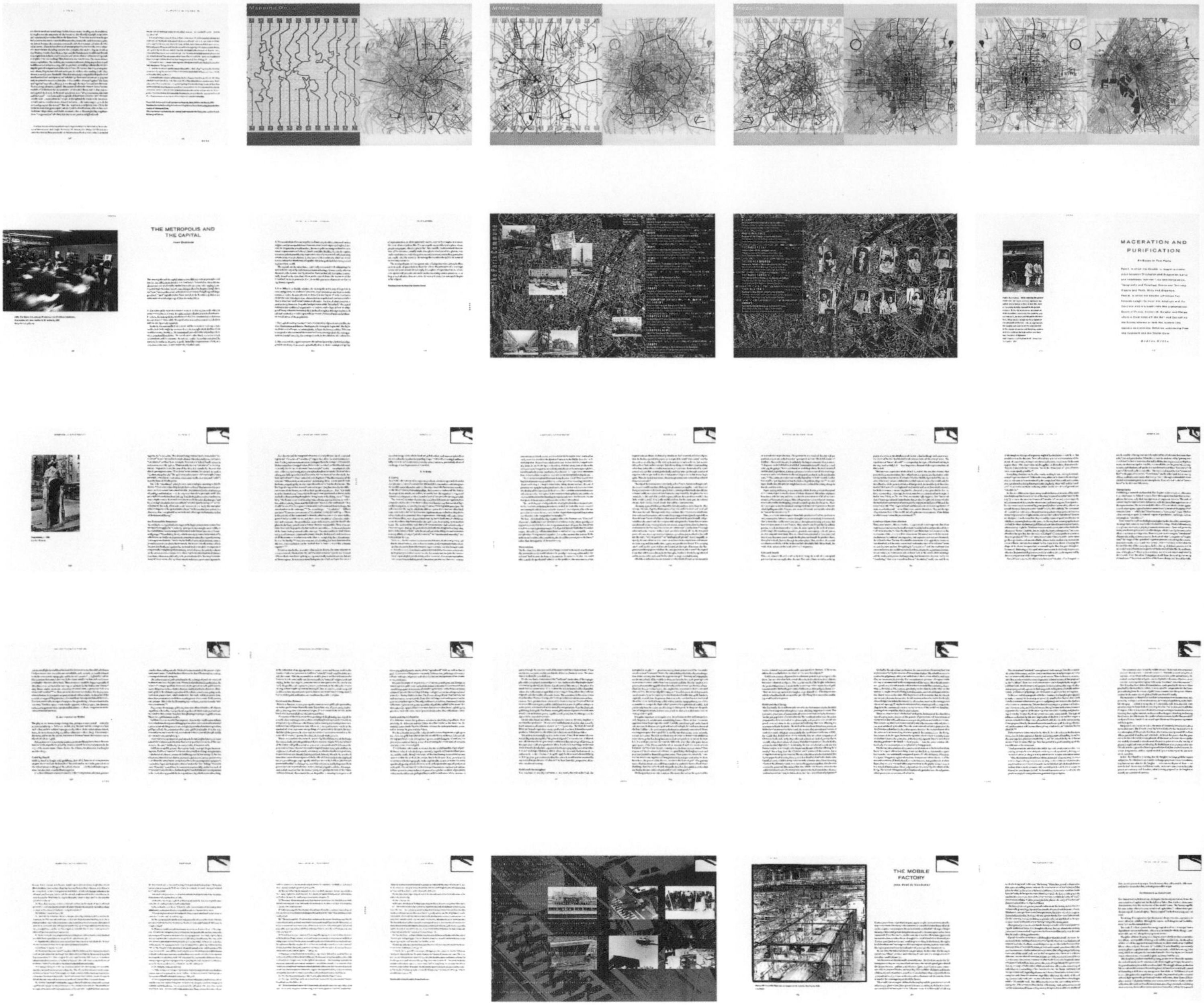
THE METROPOLIS AND THE CAPITAL
MACERATION AND PURIFICATION
THE MOBILE FACTORY

MAPS AND MODELS
CHARACTER STUDIES
CONCLUSIONS
NEOCONSERVATIVE
ECONOMICS, UTOPIA
AND CRISIS

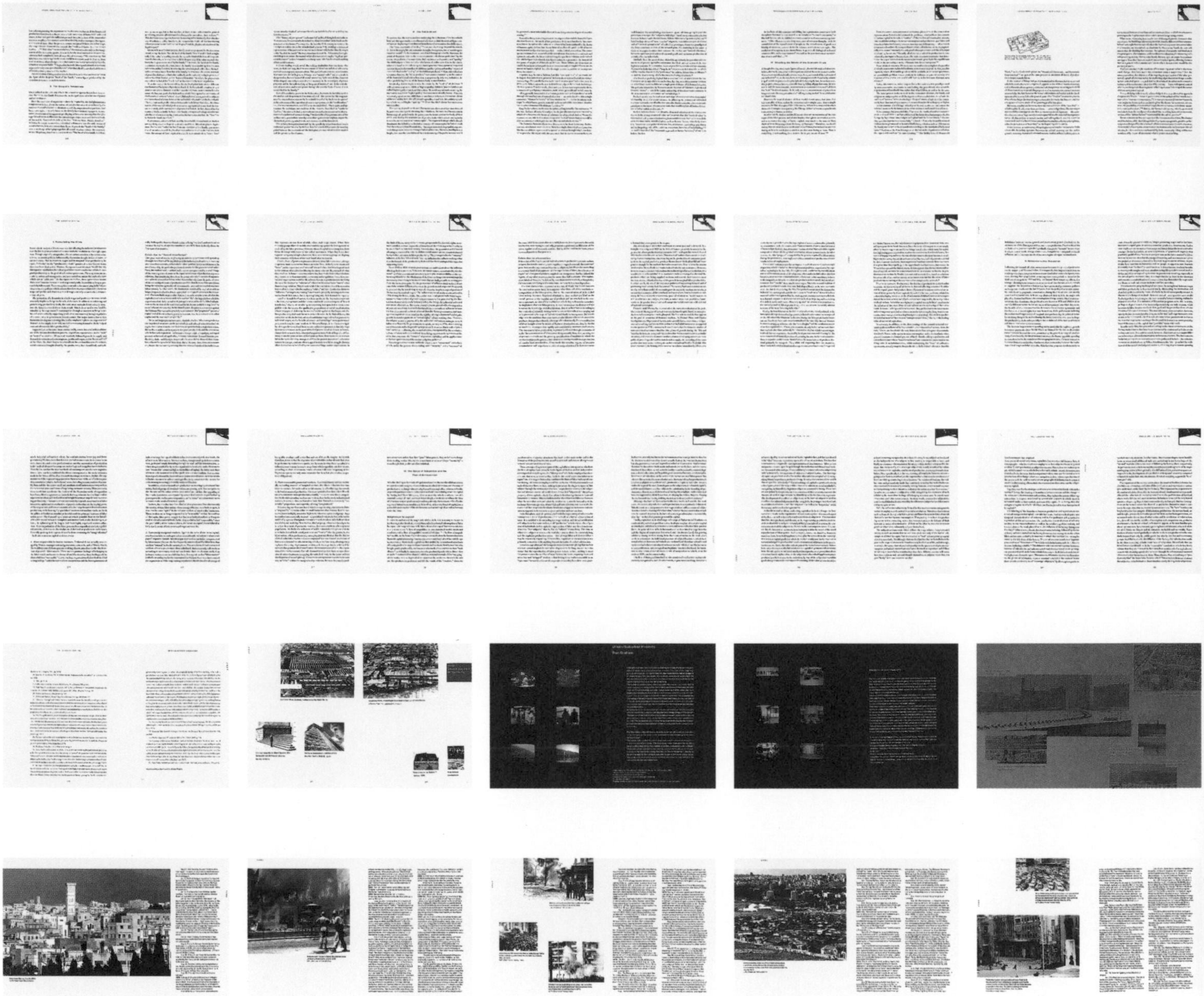

THE LUSTER
OF CAPITAL

The idea of a pantheistic, or living, surface became part of the Zone identity. Pantheism is the notion that God is in everything. This means that the whole field of the object is charged with potential life and energy.

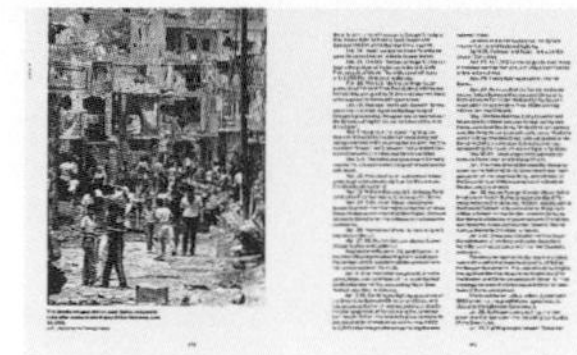
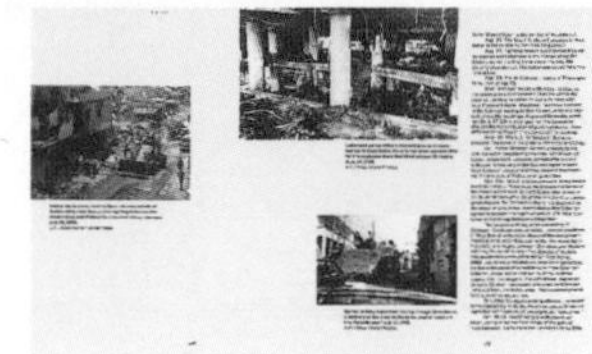
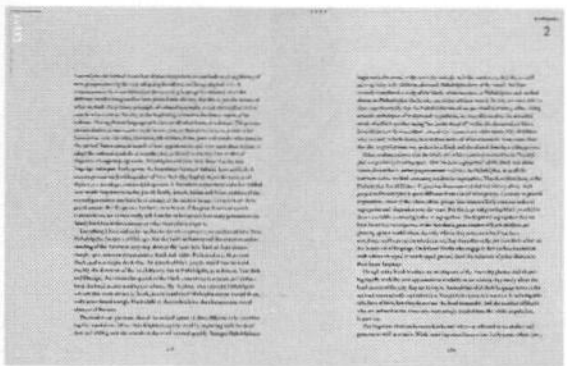
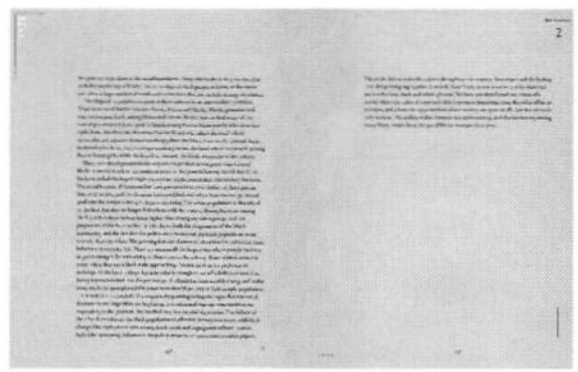
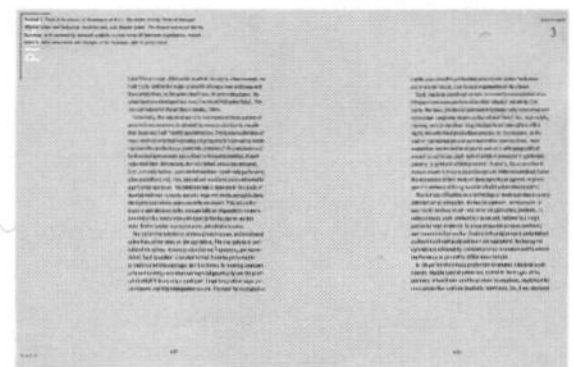
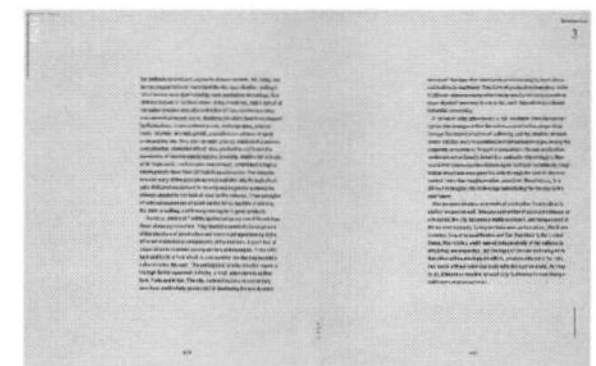
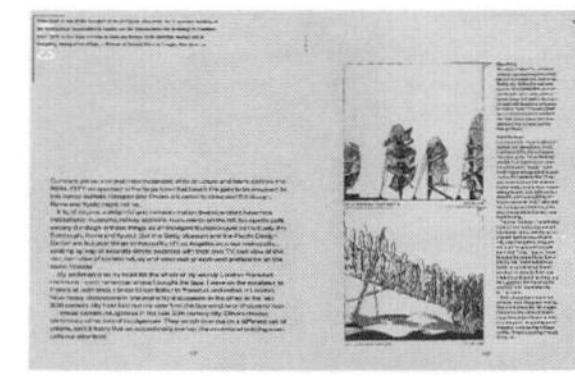
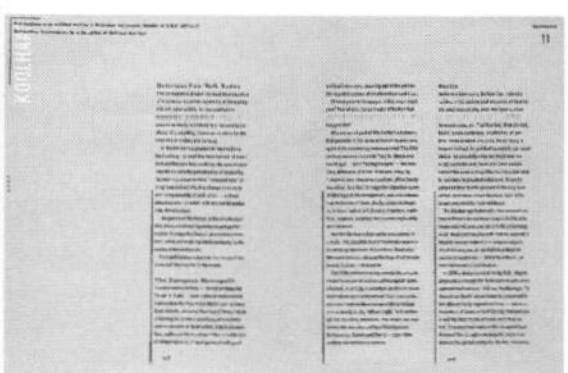
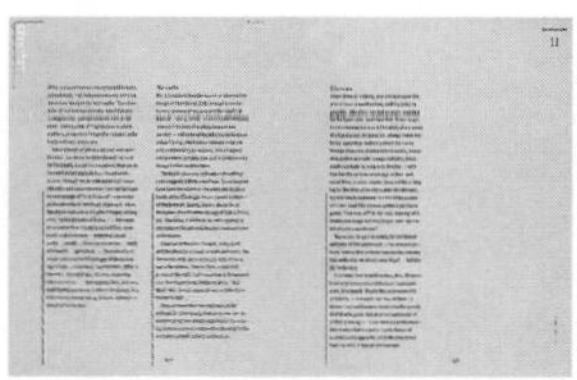
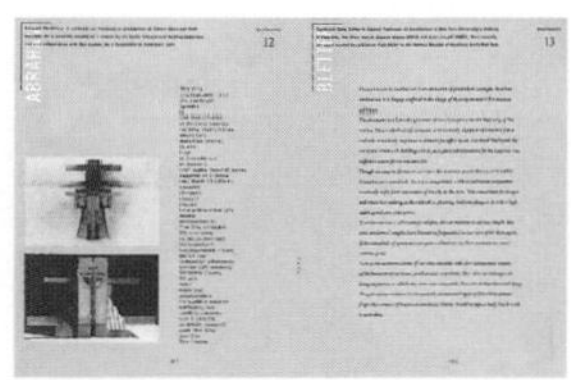
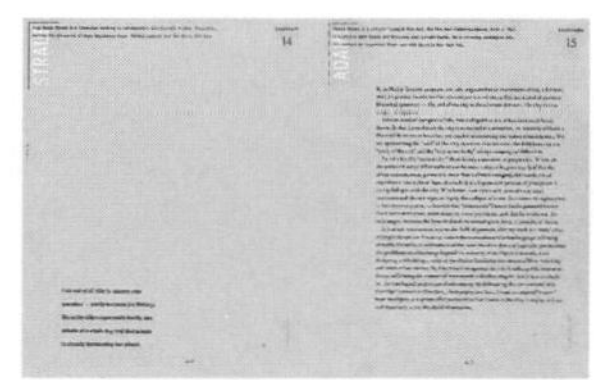

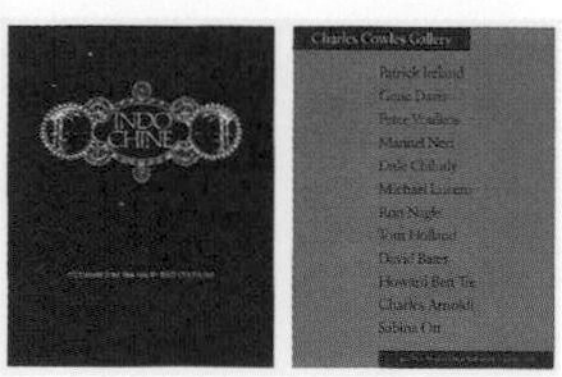
INDO CHINE
Charles Cowles Gallery
Patrick Ireland
Dale Chihuly
Ron Nagle
Tom Holland
David Bates
Howard Ben Tré
Charles Arnoldi
Sabina Ott
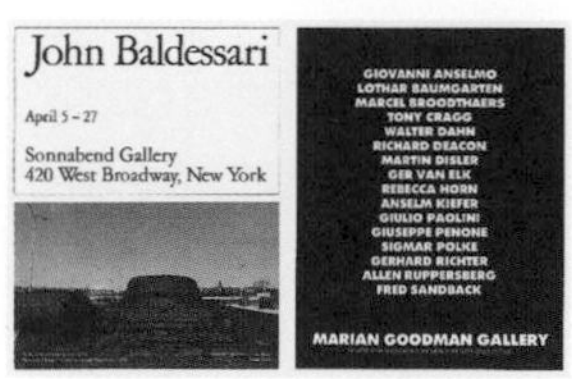
John Baldessari
April 5 – 27
Sonnabend Gallery
420 West Broadway, New York
GIOVANNI ANSELMO
LOTHAR BAUMGARTEN
MARCEL BROODTHAERS
TONY CRAGG
WALTER DAHN
RICHARD DEACON
MARTIN DISLER
GER VAN ELK
REBECCA HORN
ANSELM KIEFER
GIULIO PAOLINI
GIUSEPPE PENONE
SIGMAR POLKE
GERHARD RICHTER
ALLEN RUPPERSBERG
FRED SANDBACK
MARIAN GOODMAN GALLERY

MICHAEL BYRON
PETER CHEVALIER
LYDIA DONA
JON KESSLER
49TH PARALLEL
GERMANS VAN ECK
420 WEST BROADWAY NEW YORK NY
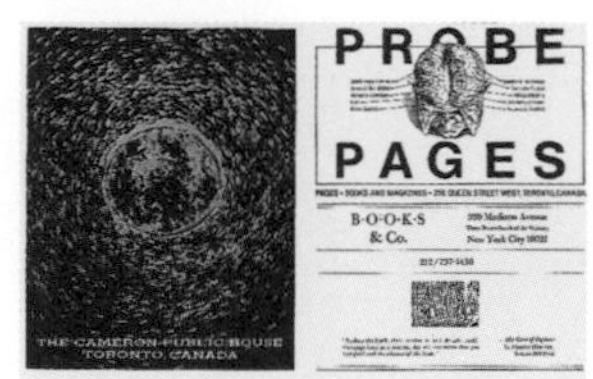
THE CAMERON PUBLIC HOUSE
TORONTO, CANADA
PROBE
PAGES
B·O·O·K·S
& Co.
New York City
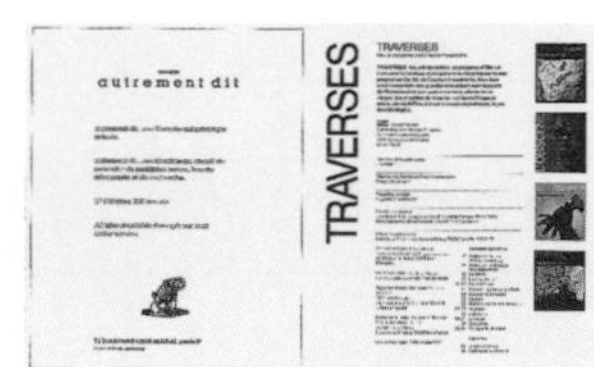
autrement dit
TRAVERSES
TRAVERSES

The Spelling of Mr. Kwinter's Proper Name

During the final preparation of *Zone 1/2*, Mr. Kwinter, one of the editors, until that time in his life known by the diminutive "Sande," decided to declare his nom de plume "Sanford." So it was with extraordinary attention and thoroughness that he checked and rechecked every instance of the appearance of his name in the book. But a change of that sort is sometimes easier done than said. And many of his friends and colleagues continued to hail him in a casual and offhanded manner as "Sande." This struggle caught the attention of his sister, Kerri, and she paid me a visit late one afternoon. We would, she suggested, spell Mr. Kwinter's name incorrectly, only once, somewhere in the book. As a contributor, Mr. Kwinter's name appeared at the top of every left-hand page for a run of fifty pages or so. We chose one, and I meticulously cut into place an extra *d* to spell "Sandford." The book was published, we had a party on a barge in the Hudson River, and we hung out in New York that summer, basking in the pleasure of one another and in the satisfaction of having actually done something. A month or so later, we were sitting at a sunny sidewalk café on West Broadway with a group of "gallerists" visiting from Los Angeles. One gallerist from the Valley was grappling with Mr. Kwinter's spelling problem. "Then . . . why do they call you 'Sandy'? If there's no *d* it should be 'Sanny.' Is it not 'Sandford'?" In frustration, Mr. Kwinter casually paged the copy of *Zone* we took with us everywhere that summer. "No, no, no. You see, it's right here." Somehow, he had turned to page ninety-five.

Shelf Life

I designed my first book, *Zone 1/2,* in 1985. Since then the perils faced by the book have intensified and multiplied to become ever more glaring and obvious. We who believe in the book must come to its defense. We must reiterate its power, capabilities, and bonds to life. Nostalgic laments for a dying form are false and deserve ridicule. We must make new formulations that simply outperform competitors.

Zone Books, New York
1986–present
After the success of *Zone 1/2* in 1985, Urzone launched an ambitious publication program, with a list of important titles on social, philosophical, and cultural issues. BMD designs all aspects of Urzone's publishing—Zone's visual identity, all of the books, the advertising, and the catalogs—and shares editorial and planning responsibilities.
Zone Books, currently fifty-one volumes in five distinct book series, includes titles by European thinkers such as Georges Bataille, Gilles Deleuze, Guy Debord, and Henri Bergson. Subject to the most intense conceptual consideration, each book is designed to perform its subject matter—whether it be the consumer society, Spinoza's philosophy, or contemporary art.

The original Zone Books mock-up: plain white covers, serial uniformity, a minimalist riff on the European design approach

Bergsonism
BY
Gilles Deleuze
Translated by Hugh Tomlinson
and Barbara Habberjam
ZONE BOOKS

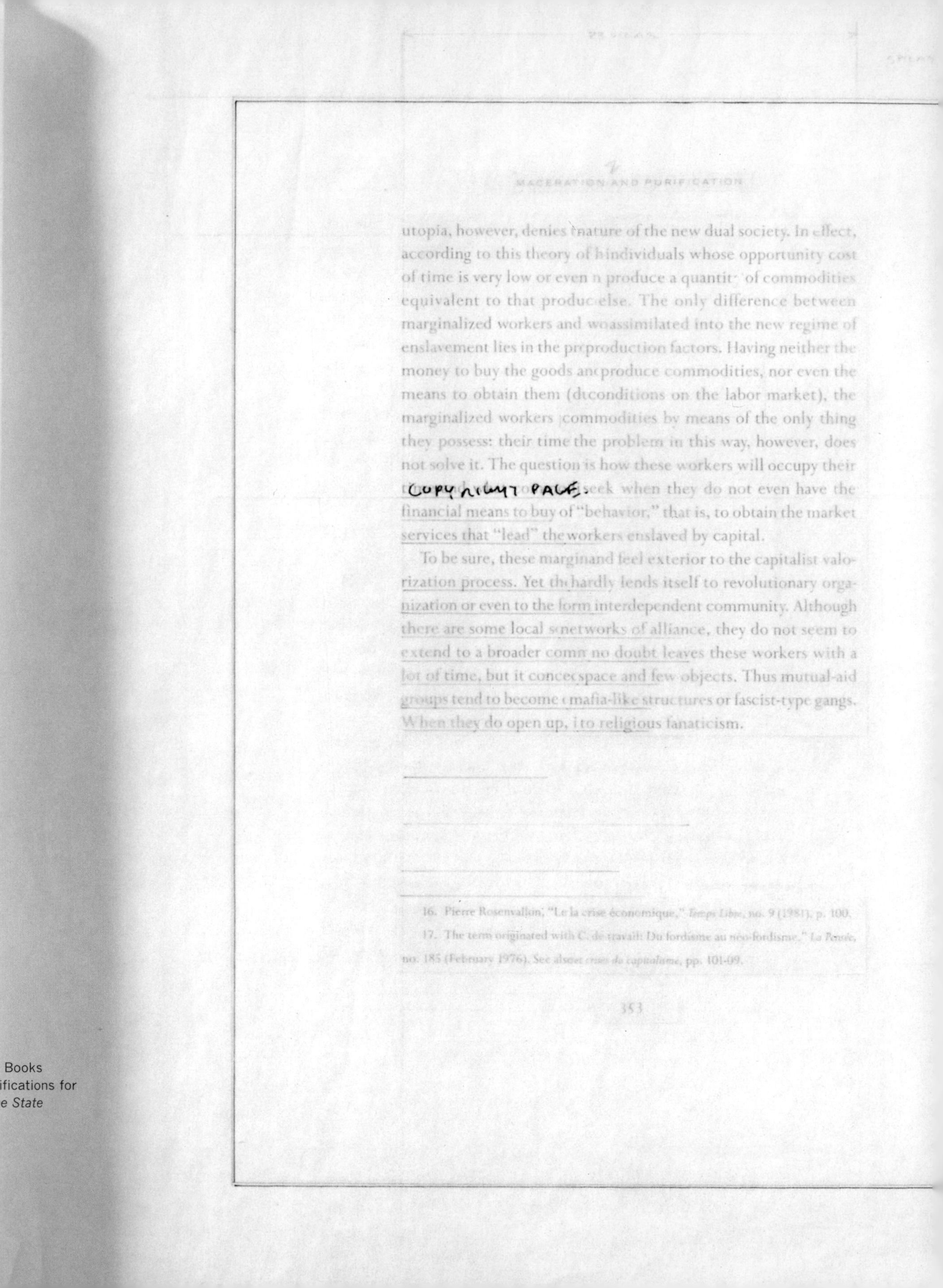
MACERATION AND PURIFICATION

utopia, however, denies t nature of the new dual society. In effect, according to this theory of h individuals whose opportunity cost of time is very low or even n produce a quantit of commodities equivalent to that produc else. The only difference between marginalized workers and wo assimilated into the new regime of enslavement lies in the pr production factors. Having neither the money to buy the goods an produce commodities, nor even the means to obtain them (d conditions on the labor market), the marginalized workers commodities by means of the only thing they possess: their time the problem in this way, however, does not solve it. The question is how these workers will occupy their t seek when they do not even have the financial means to buy of "behavior," that is, to obtain the market services that "lead" the workers enslaved by capital.

To be sure, these margin and feel exterior to the capitalist valorization process. Yet th hardly lends itself to revolutionary organization or even to the form interdependent community. Although there are some local s networks of alliance, they do not seem to extend to a broader comm no doubt leaves these workers with a lot of time, but it conce space and few objects. Thus mutual-aid groups tend to become mafia-like structures or fascist-type gangs. When they do open up, i to religious fanaticism.

16. Pierre Rosenvallon, "Le la crise économique," *Temps Libre*, no. 9 (1981), p. 100.

17. The term originated with C. de travail: Du fordisme au néo-fordisme," *La Pensée*, no. 185 (February 1976). See also *crises du capitalisme*, pp. 101-09.

353

COPYRIGHT PAGE.

The original Zone Books typographic specifications for *Society Against the State*

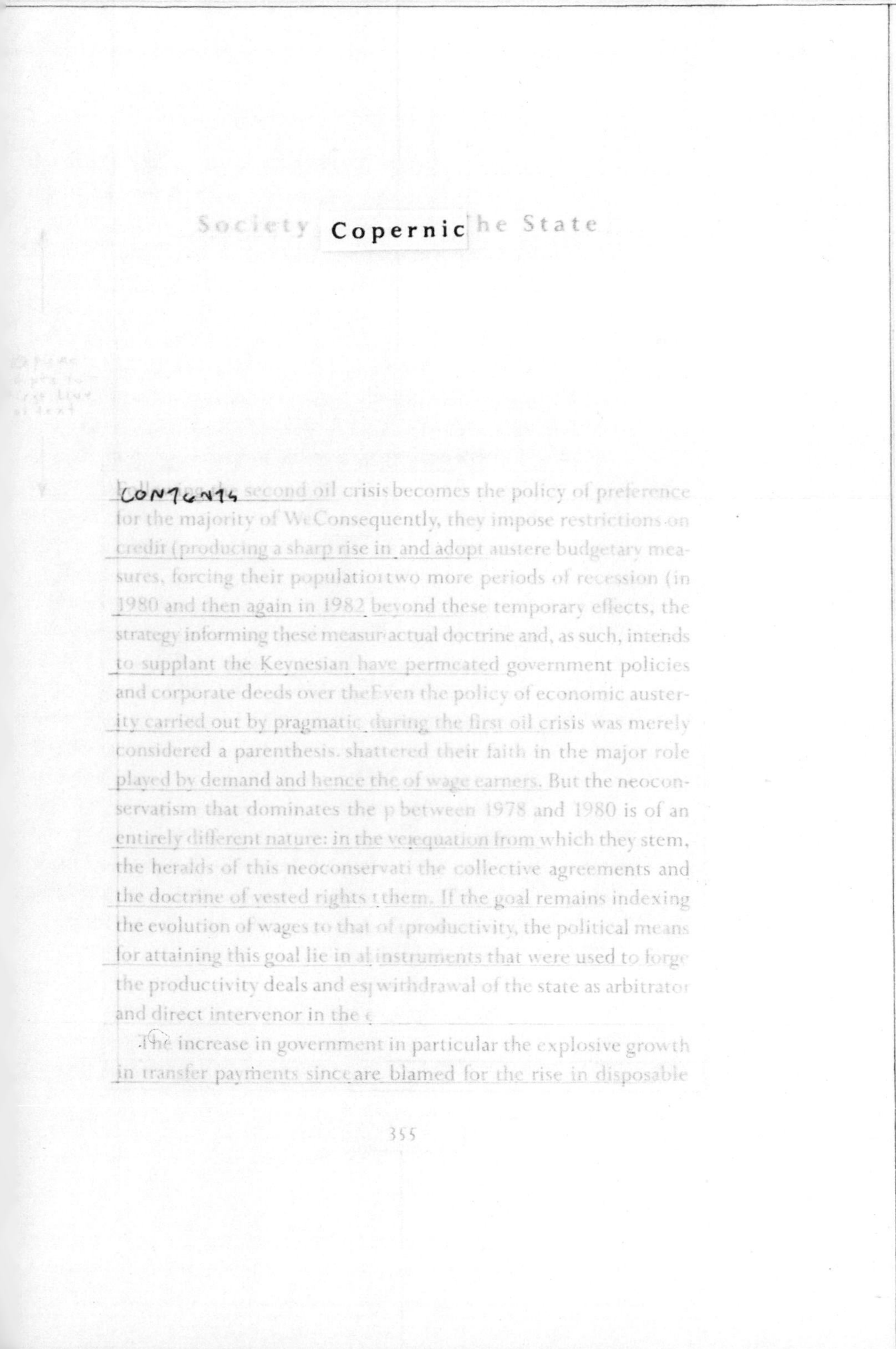
Society Copernic he State

CONTENTS

Following the second oil crisis becomes the policy of preference for the majority of WeConsequently, they impose restrictions on credit (producing a sharp rise in and adopt austere budgetary measures, forcing their populatiortwo more periods of recession (in 1980 and then again in 1982 beyond these temporary effects, the strategy informing these measur actual doctrine and, as such, intends to supplant the Keynesian have permeated government policies and corporate deeds over theEven the policy of economic austerity carried out by pragmatic during the first oil crisis was merely considered a parenthesis. shattered their faith in the major role played by demand and hence the of wage earners. But the neoconservatism that dominates the p between 1978 and 1980 is of an entirely different nature: in the ve equation from which they stem, the heralds of this neoconservati the collective agreements and the doctrine of vested rights t them. If the goal remains indexing the evolution of wages to that of productivity, the political means for attaining this goal lie in al instruments that were used to forge the productivity deals and es withdrawal of the state as arbitrator and direct intervenor in the e

The increase in government in particular the explosive growth in transfer payments since are blamed for the rise in disposable

355

Zone Books Composition Rules
(Based on Jan Tschichold's specifications for Penguin Books)

Omit indent in the first line of the first paragraph of the text and at the beginning of a new section.

If a chapter is divided into several parts without headings, these parts should be divided by a 2-line space. If asterisks are indicated, set 3 "stars" centered in a 2-line space. In both cases the beginning of the text should be flush left. Space above separate line subheads and space-break indicator is not retained at the top of a new page.

The indent of the paragraph should be the same number of points as the leading (i.e. 11/14 = 14 pt indents).

Extracts are indented a regular paragraph indent and are set 1 point size smaller than the main text, but on the same leading. Extracts should be preceded and followed by a full line space.

Instead of em rules, use "in-between dashes" consisting of 2 en-dashes kerned together and set centered on an em-dash space. At end or beginning of the line set flush out.

Running headlines, unless otherwise stated, should consist of the title of the book on the left-hand page and the chapter title on the right. (Max. no. of characters = 45.)

Folios should be set in the same size and face as the text. Use old-style figures from the small-caps font. Maintain this size throughout notes, bibliography, and index.

Running heads and folios maintain constant position. Folios do not move up with short pages.

Pagination should begin with the first leaf in the book with type on it, but folios should not appear before the first page of body text.

Widows should be avoided; however, widows over 3/4 of a line are permitted at the top of the page. Less than this should be corrected. If a separate line subheading falls on the last line of the page, move it over to the next page even if the previous page appears short. Two lines of type below a subhead are essential.

situation of atomized compe result in a logic of universal monopolization, conforming to what and leading inevitably to the seizing of the economy by a cent Secondly, and most importantly, the neoconservative econon an essential viscosity which, in any complex society, hampers the m(and things as well as the flow of information. From this point on, th(of a market economy lies less in its role as a balancer of supply that is, in its homeostatic character, than in its role as accelerat(the circulation of various resources, that is, in its dynamic chara words, the market is no longer merely the anonymous place wh services are exchanged, no longer a static mechanism where the shortag(in the social body are supposed to cancel each other out. It no dynamic instrument for the optimal "mobilization" (in both senses of scarce resources: by taking the form of exchangeable goods, th are both recruited by capital and assigned a coefficient of maximum

Such was the fate of labor in the capitalism: although defined as a production factor, it was under the form of labor power that it could and would be more effecien Today neonconservative spokesmen such as Friedrich Von Haye Stigler intend to inflict the same fate on what they call "informa it has been accepted that (1) the importance of research and has made information a production factor; (2) the dissemination o in the social body (which alone makes it productive) is inevitab and (3) the boom in cybernetics, communications sciences and th application relies on the ability to quantify information (thanks t(in Boole's algebra), it becomes both necessary and possible to tur into a commodity and thereby to insure the optimum mobilization c Even if productivity gains resulting from the introductio technology into the industrial and service sectors can be seen as of this conversion, the latter, above all, indicates an extension sector to new resources in response to the limits reached by exploitation of old resources. But this transformation of inf(merchandise in the name of the optimization of

36 PICAS
2 pts.

23 P 5 P

6"

4 picas 8 pts to baseline of running head

7 picas from top of page to first baseline of text

28 pts

the years 1968-73 (excesses thhowever, in comparison to the social unrest they were trying to ward oa profound modification of the social regulation of economic activ the usual institutions, procedures and practices that govern it.

Crisis due to attenuation

If the crisis of the last 15 years is ind productivity, certain authors propose that it is due not only to the rig downward, the continued growth in transfer payments and the risebut also to the unravelling of a certain kind of arrangement of theof labor, the allocation of capital and the types of products arrangement that has defined the regime of capitalist accumulation fchalf a century. This regime, often labelled "Fordist," is defined by two c which, although they did not come into being at the same time, ar interdependent.

The first characteristic appeared at the eWar I and concerns the production sector itself. It completecalled the machinic recomposition of the labor process concentration of little-skilled labor in large factories. Deprived these workers are blind to the overall process of the manufactureand are attached to the evermore automatic motion of the machithey will soon be secondary. To implement this new labor proce necessary to abstract and systematize the knowledge of skilled lto redistribute it according to the methods of scientific managc worker collectives carrying out only piecework (the stage of Tcfinally to incorporate this knowledge into the machines that comelaborers who run them and the products they produce directly (the sta itself). The intensification of labor brought about by meanatomization and then by Fordist or machinic recompositiorconsiderably increases productivity. This increase in labor piprimarily effected through economies of

28 pts 1 line space between last line of text + footnote.

8. On the development of newly industrialized count "Fordisme, fordisme périphérique et métropolisation." *CEPREMAP*, No. 8514 (1985), pp. 10-23.

28 pts 1 line space between last line of text + folio.

5P 23 P

11.5 P 11.5 P

Folio centred on text column

434

A minimum of 4 lines of text is preferable on the last page of a chapter. Less than this is tolerated, but if it is possible to correct, please do so.

Notes should be set 2 points smaller than the text but set on the same leading. Indent the first line of each note with the same number of points as the paragraph indents in the main text. For the numbering of notes use normal figures followed by a full point and an en-space.

Books should, with certain exceptions, be organized in the following order:

- **I Preliminary pages: 1. half title 2. frontispiece 3. title 4. imprint or date of publication 5. dedication 6. acknowledgments 7. contents 8. list of illustrations 9. list of abbreviations 10. preface 11. introduction 12. errata**
- **II The text of the book**
- **III Backmatter: 1. appendix 2. author's notes 3. glossary 4. bibliography 5. index**

Each of the above elements should begin on a right-hand page, imprint and frontispiece excepted.

9"

The index should be set in two columns and in 9/10 type. The first entry of each letter of the alphabet should be set in cap/small caps. Leave 1 line space before the beginning of each section. Continued-line notices are set at the top of the column when an entry follows from recto to verso. Turnovers indent 10 points. Index is set in two columns of 11 picas each, with a 1-pica gutter. At end of index, allow text to run on so that left column is full measure and right ends when it ends. Forty-five lines on a full column. Space between last line of text and folio is 21 points b/b. (Folio position remains constant throughout book.) First line of index begins on line 16 (counting with index line count).

Turned-page tables and illustrations read correctly when book is turned to right.

Maximum number of consecutive line-end hyphens is 2. Minimum number of characters before and after a hyphen is 3.

When Greek is called for use the Times italic font set to match the x-height of Perpetua.

Society Against the State came shortly after *Zone 1/2*. It is the second book I designed. This was 1987, and the idea was to establish a method to "mass produce" the books. The challenge was to design a system for making high-caliber, text-based books relatively inexpensively. With this purpose in mind, the original design strategy for Zone Books, with their plain white covers and serial uniformity, was a minimalist riff on the European approach. While European books are certainly beautiful, we quickly realized that they would not travel well. They would be unworkable in North American bookstores and invisible in Europe. We had to decide to go either above that European norm or below it. There was insufficient room below to make it work, so we went above. The solution was two-fold. We maintained a minimalist typography, but we slid a cinematic layer behind it. This layer created Zone's distinctive appearance. The beauty of the original template, as we conceived it, was that the typography could be laid down in forty-five minutes. We have never managed to execute that lightning efficiency. On the contrary, every project that we undertake with Zone begins with the idea to make it cheap and fast and easy. Then it ends up becoming super-articulated and hypernuanced.

Society Against the State: Essays in Political Anthropology
by Pierre Clastres
New York: Zone Books, 1987

Society Against The State

BY

Pierre Clastres

hilosophy has made
e 'true' experience
ts itself in the stan-
zed masses. It is
ınder the heading of
this literature is
/latter and Memory."
r Benjamin
ɔsis of a crisis in
reality in the external
ality in conscious-
he Bergsonian dis-
ıore profoundly, of a
ess today that it is
s have been drawn."
Deleuze
minimize the amaz-
iven in Matter and
hus described the
In unveiling it along
iscovers in the heart
ı' sense of the world."
ce Merleau-Ponty
er and Memory
Henri Bergson
ned by Bruce Mau
printed in Canada

Matter and Memory
by Henri Bergson
New York: Zone Books, 1988

Matter and Memory

BY

Henri Bergson

Translated by N.M. Paul and W.S. Palmer

Zone Standards

Creating Specifications

Our design attitude is inspired by the text because the Zone editors put enormous effort into ensuring that every text is absolutely right. Their precision editing is microscopically exact. Beautifully crafted, the texts evidence a level of commitment that sets the standard for the whole project and this commitment emerges in every other aspect of the work. As a result of this intense editorial process, we found ourselves investing great care in each object and in the entire Zone project—the way the books are designed, produced, and presented in the catalogs.

The typographic system was established for the lucid and perfectly structured book by Pierre Clastres, *Society Against the State*, the first in the Zone series, and for which I created a very detailed typographic specification. I went back to Jan Tschichold, author of the twentieth century's two great books on typography. In 1935, Tschichold theorized the asymmetric typography associated with the Bauhaus and threw off the yoke of nineteenth-century conventions. Then, a decade later, as the designer of Penguin Books, Tschichold rejected his previous theories to embrace serif symmetric typography. The design of Zone reconciles Tschichold's apparent contradictions, playing one off the other in a new field of potential. It deploys the grid and then subverts it to its own ends and to new effect.

Tschichold's Penguin specs were published in a book on his work. Using these as a starting point, I updated and revised them to reflect contemporary technology and our own design. I worked with an extraordinary typesetter named Archie (she has a one-word name, like Cher). Together, we evolved a unique and very detailed typographic approach for Zone. Archie had been a croupier in England and had worked the casinos for years; she could type two hundred words a minute flawlessly. This was before visual-display advances in computer typography, so we had to work with a system that required the user to type in codes that would tell the computer what to do with the text. Once the codes were entered, you saw nothing until the type was printed out. Archie was amazing in executing this typographical design.

One of Zone's objectives from the outset was to bring these texts to readers at a relatively low cost. The fact that the design was systematized made that possible because we could do very large projects cheaply. For a long time, we used the back end of the technological cycle. We salvaged discarded typesetting equipment regarded as obsolete and found that it was of higher quality and infinitely cheaper to use than the new machines. People were switching over from old code-based systems to visual-display systems. Companies were throwing out equipment that our typesetter bought for $200. It worked for us at the time. The problem was that this older equipment required a highly skilled operator like Archie, who could look at a page of numbers and codes and know what the page was going to look like. These efficiencies made the Zone project possible.

Reading Zone

There is something else that contributes to the Zone identity, a factor that is at once obvious and indispensable; that is, we actually read the books that we design. Many years ago, I had the experience of working in a large design company where every book designer had to generate five covers a week. At this pace, all the designer could do was read one paragraph describing what the book was about, and then he or she would design the cover. Doing five covers a week in this manner is like applying Henry Ford's production-line methods to literature. There is no real learning from it; you're not changing yourself in any way; it is not a transformative experience.

The conditions at Zone are entirely different. Aspects of the text are allowed to surface gradually. Sometimes the editors have specific images they think might be right, and they bring them to the process. Occasionally, the author proposes an image as well. Often, we do research to help produce ideas. We consider it part of the work. What it means is that you can do things that are very subtle, and so much richer because you have taken time to acquaint yourself with the intricacies of the manuscript.

I have the greatest respect for writers, and I think their work should be treated well and presented to the public intelligently and compellingly. Our task is to build a bridge between a potential reader and the mind and sensibility of the author. It is common sense that such a bridge can be based only on an honest presentation of the work, and that an understanding of the work is a starting point for building the bridge. Sadly, it's so rarely done this way; authors are generally treated poorly in the design process. This is an absolutely astounding aspect of the publishing business. Authors do huge amounts of work in developing their manuscripts, and then have no input into the covers of their books. They suffer a total disconnection from their work.

Writing Zone

Most writers are performing a kind of public service. They are doing their work and contributing it to the culture, and the return on that work, if quantified monetarily, is abysmally poor. The returns are so far out of proportion to their labors that authors must be regarded as doing a form of charity work. In fact, it is work for civilization. There is, therefore, an obligation to treat a text with a sense of that level of contribution and to do everything you can to present it in the right way. When you pick up J. G. Ballard's novels, you recognize not only that these are incredible pieces of literature, but that somebody took a mere fifteen minutes to package them. This is somebody's life work, and the culture is enriched if the contribution is recognized and presented in the right way.

When a designer makes decisions based on a developed affinity with the reader, an altogether different kind of work evolves. In our case, a commitment to actually reading and thinking about the texts has produced two tangible results. The first is that the design resonates more closely with what the text is saying and doing. The second is that we have ended up with one of the most highly educated design studios in the world, because we are reading philosophy, architecture criticism, literary history, and psychology with authors who are leading their fields.

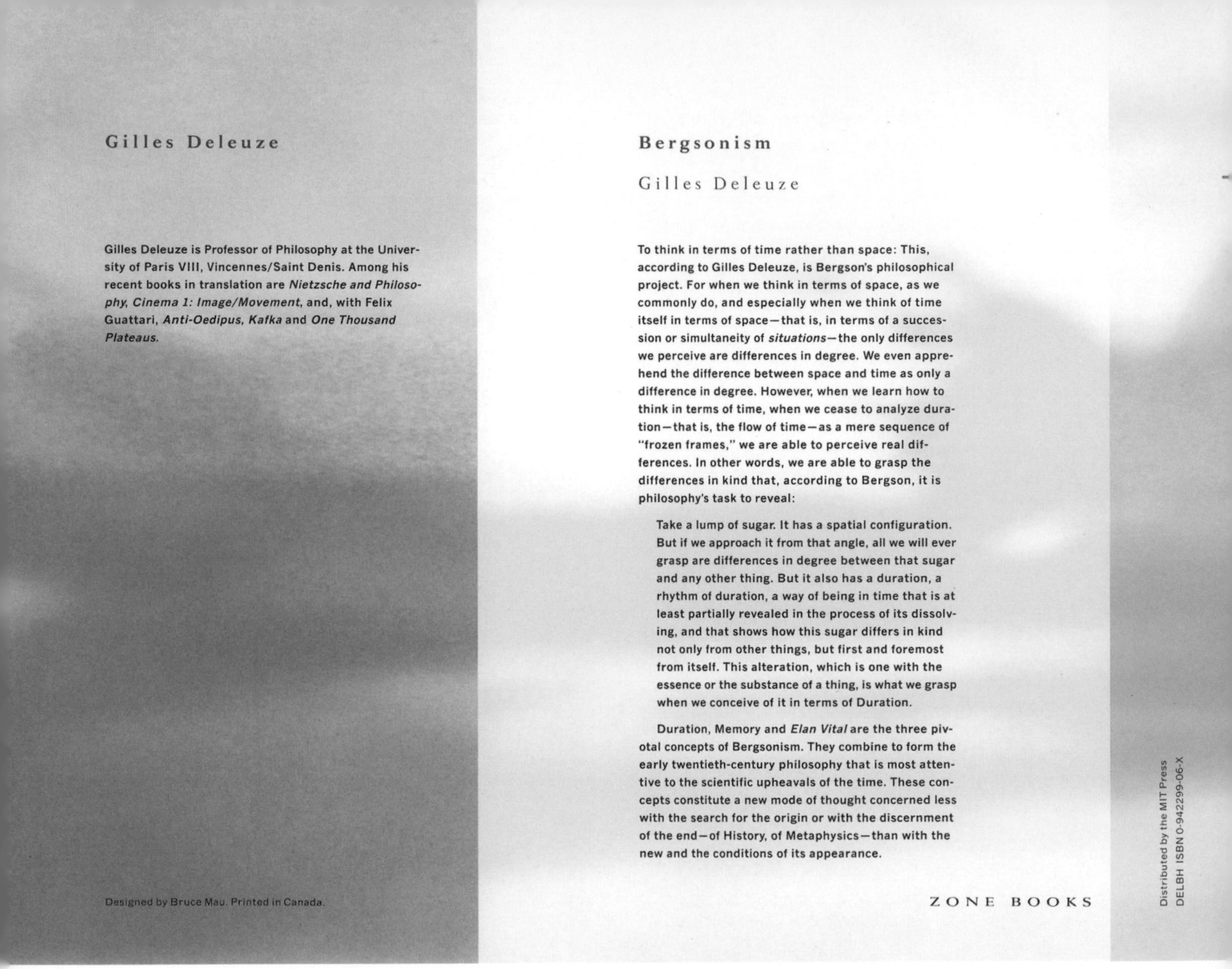

Gilles Deleuze

Gilles Deleuze is Professor of Philosophy at the University of Paris VIII, Vincennes/Saint Denis. Among his recent books in translation are *Nietzsche and Philosophy, Cinema 1: Image/Movement*, and, with Felix Guattari, *Anti-Oedipus, Kafka* and *One Thousand Plateaus.*

Designed by Bruce Mau. Printed in Canada.

Bergsonism

Gilles Deleuze

To think in terms of time rather than space: This, according to Gilles Deleuze, is Bergson's philosophical project. For when we think in terms of space, as we commonly do, and especially when we think of time itself in terms of space—that is, in terms of a succession or simultaneity of *situations*—the only differences we perceive are differences in degree. We even apprehend the difference between space and time as only a difference in degree. However, when we learn how to think in terms of time, when we cease to analyze duration—that is, the flow of time—as a mere sequence of "frozen frames," we are able to perceive real differences. In other words, we are able to grasp the differences in kind that, according to Bergson, it is philosophy's task to reveal:

> Take a lump of sugar. It has a spatial configuration. But if we approach it from that angle, all we will ever grasp are differences in degree between that sugar and any other thing. But it also has a duration, a rhythm of duration, a way of being in time that is at least partially revealed in the process of its dissolving, and that shows how this sugar differs in kind not only from other things, but first and foremost from itself. This alteration, which is one with the essence or the substance of a thing, is what we grasp when we conceive of it in terms of Duration.

Duration, Memory and *Elan Vital* are the three pivotal concepts of Bergsonism. They combine to form the early twentieth-century philosophy that is most attentive to the scientific upheavals of the time. These concepts constitute a new mode of thought concerned less with the search for the origin or with the discernment of the end—of History, of Metaphysics—than with the new and the conditions of its appearance.

ZONE BOOKS

Distributed by the MIT Press
DELBH ISBN 0-942299-06-X

Bergsonism
by Gilles Deleuze
New York: Zone Books, 1988

Bergsonism

BY

Gilles Deleuze

Translated by Hugh Tomlinson and Barbara Habberjam

ZONE BOOKS

ZONE BOOKS

Bergsonism
By Gilles Deleuze

Matter and Memory
By Henri Bergson

Your Money or Your Life
Economy and Religion in the Middle Ages
By Jacques Le Goff

Foucault/Blanchot
Maurice Blanchot: The Thought From Outside
By Michel Foucault
Michel Foucault as I Imagine Him
By Maurice Blanchot

Society Against the State
Essays in Political Anthropology
By Pierre Clastres

e
organism ordi-
cessary for main-
npletely absorbed
gly or not, glori-
es Bataille intro-
are, the surplus
ltural, must ex-
g to Bataille, that
amples include
among the North-
m and Buddhist
aille proposes a
on excess and
ventional eco-
brilliant blend
The Accursed Share Volume I
Georges Bata

124

The Accursed Share: An Essay on General Economy
Volume 1
by Georges Bataille
New York: Zone Books, 1988

The Accursed Sha

Volume I

BY

Georges Bataille

Translated by Robert Hurle

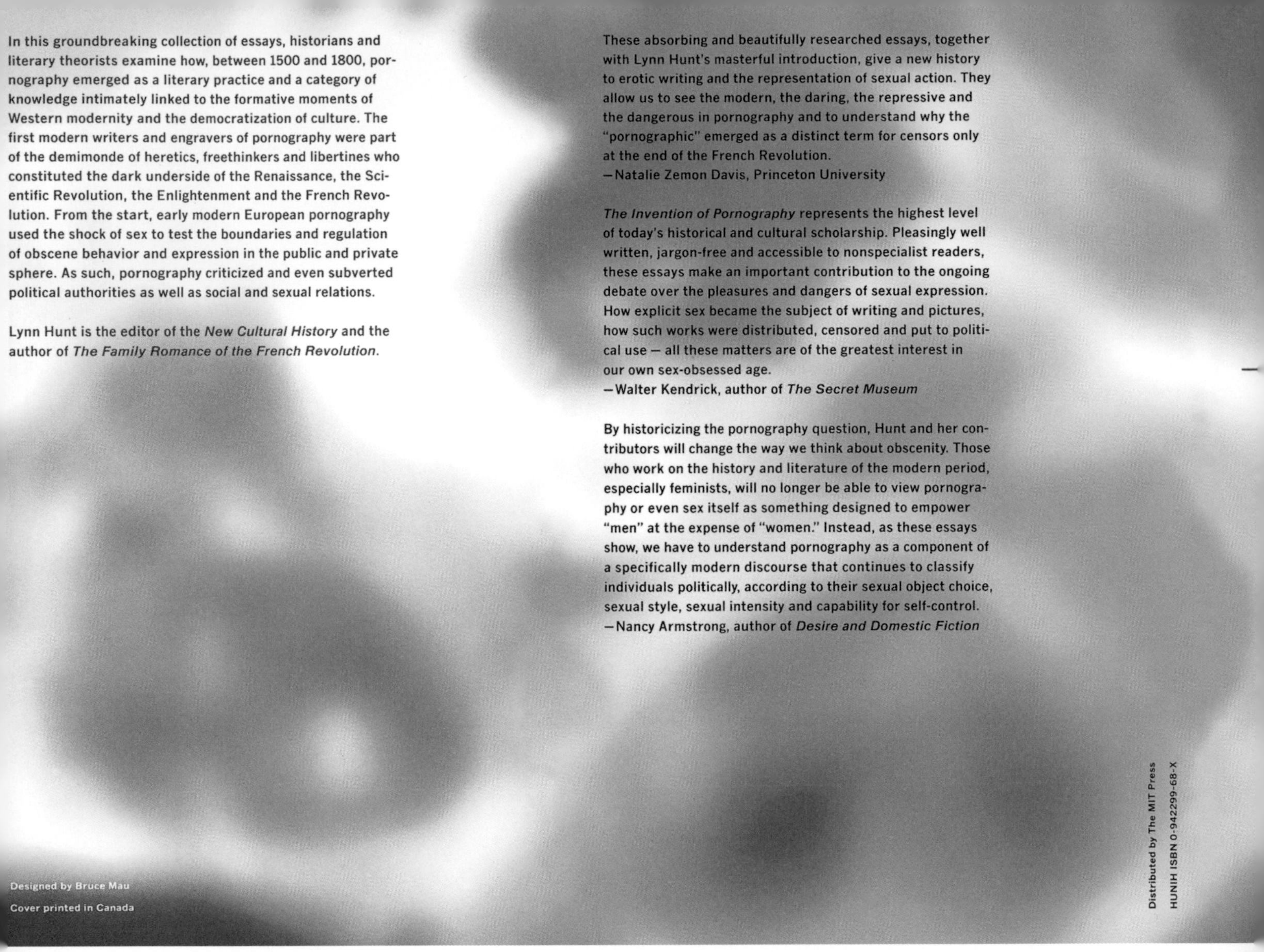
In this groundbreaking collection of essays, historians and literary theorists examine how, between 1500 and 1800, pornography emerged as a literary practice and a category of knowledge intimately linked to the formative moments of Western modernity and the democratization of culture. The first modern writers and engravers of pornography were part of the demimonde of heretics, freethinkers and libertines who constituted the dark underside of the Renaissance, the Scientific Revolution, the Enlightenment and the French Revolution. From the start, early modern European pornography used the shock of sex to test the boundaries and regulation of obscene behavior and expression in the public and private sphere. As such, pornography criticized and even subverted political authorities as well as social and sexual relations.

Lynn Hunt is the editor of the *New Cultural History* and the author of *The Family Romance of the French Revolution*.

These absorbing and beautifully researched essays, together with Lynn Hunt's masterful introduction, give a new history to erotic writing and the representation of sexual action. They allow us to see the modern, the daring, the repressive and the dangerous in pornography and to understand why the "pornographic" emerged as a distinct term for censors only at the end of the French Revolution.
—Natalie Zemon Davis, Princeton University

The Invention of Pornography represents the highest level of today's historical and cultural scholarship. Pleasingly well written, jargon-free and accessible to nonspecialist readers, these essays make an important contribution to the ongoing debate over the pleasures and dangers of sexual expression. How explicit sex became the subject of writing and pictures, how such works were distributed, censored and put to political use — all these matters are of the greatest interest in our own sex-obsessed age.
—Walter Kendrick, author of *The Secret Museum*

By historicizing the pornography question, Hunt and her contributors will change the way we think about obscenity. Those who work on the history and literature of the modern period, especially feminists, will no longer be able to view pornography or even sex itself as something designed to empower "men" at the expense of "women." Instead, as these essays show, we have to understand pornography as a component of a specifically modern discourse that continues to classify individuals politically, according to their sexual object choice, sexual style, sexual intensity and capability for self-control.
—Nancy Armstrong, author of *Desire and Domestic Fiction*

Designed by Bruce Mau
Cover printed in Canada

Distributed by The MIT Press
HUNIH ISBN 0-942299-68-X

The Invention of Pornography: Obscenity and the Origins of Modernity 1500–1800
by Lynn Hunt
New York: Zone Books, 1993
This book is a collection of scholarly essays exploring the largely political arena of pornographic writing over three centuries, comprising what the author identifies as the first era of the genre's formation. The cover image was borrowed from a skin magazine; it was cropped so that genitalia fill the cover and then softened beneath recognition in order to both tap and frustrate the voyeuristic desire to see more. The image becomes "explicit" only when the dust jacket is opened, spread flat, and seen from a distance. In this way it inverts the obsession with close-ups that drives the pornographic gaze in late modernity.

The Invention of Pornography

Obscenity and the Origins of Modernity, 1500–1800

Edited by

Lynn Hunt

ZONE BOOKS

The Invention of Pornography
Obscenity and the Origins of Modernity, 1500–1800
Edited by Lynn Hunt

The Movement of the Free Spirit
By Raoul Vaneigem

Etienne-Jules Marey
A Passion for the Trace
By François Dagognet

La Jetée
Ciné-roman
By Chris Marker

The Accursed Share
Volumes II & III
By Georges Bataille

Perspective as Symbolic Form
By Erwin Panofsky

Fragmentation and Redemption
Essays on Gender and the Human Body in Medieval Religion
By Caroline Walker Bynum

Expressionism in Philosophy: Spinoza
By Gilles Deleuze

The Poetic Structure of the World
Copernicus and Kepler
By Fernand Hallyn

The Life of Forms in Art
By Henri Focillon

The Normal and the Pathological
By Georges Canguilhem

Masochism
Coldness and Cruelty
By Gilles Deleuze
Venus in Furs
By Leopold von Sacher-Masoch

Theory of Religion
By Georges Bataille

Myth and Society in Ancient Greece
By Jean-Pierre Vernant

Myth and Tragedy in Ancient Greece
By Jean-Pierre Vernant and Pierre Vidal-Naquet

Mitra-Varuna
By Georges Dumézil

The Accursed Share
Volume I
By Georges Bataille

Bergsonism
By Gilles Deleuze

Matter and Memory
By Henri Bergson

Your Money or Your Life
Economy and Religion in the Middle Ages
By Jacques Le Goff

Foucault/Blanchot
Maurice Blanchot: The Thought from Outside
By Michel Foucault
Michel Foucault as I Imagine Him
By Maurice Blanchot

Society Against the State
By Pierre Clastres

ZONE BOOKS

Few works of political

have been as enduring

Debord's *The Society*

its publication amid th

the 1960s up to the p

theses of this book ha

debates on the shape

Debord wrote *The Society of the Spectacle* to attack the transformation of all social life into the perpetual staging of consumerist desire. As designers, we are implicated in facilitating this transformation. By creating a seductive, image-bearing object for a marketplace, we help convert discourse into commodity. We confront this paradox again and again in our work, but nowhere is the contradiction so frontal as in *The Society of the Spectacle*. A real dilemma arises with a book that says the seductive techniques that make it desirable are evil, but at the same time that book must enter a commodity universe to have its intended effect.

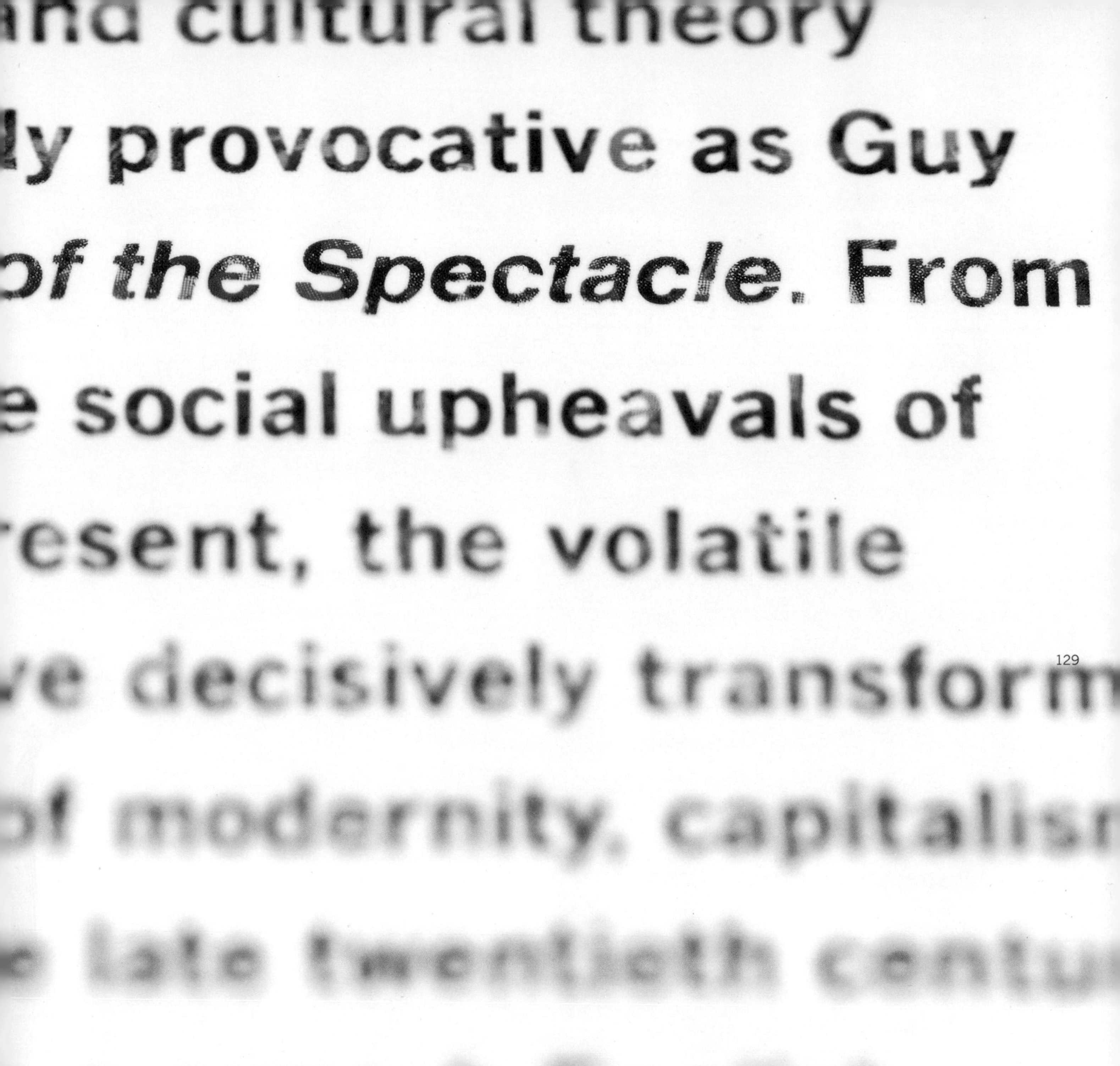
and cultural theory
ly provocative as Guy
of the Spectacle. From
e social upheavals of
resent, the volatile
ve decisively transform
of modernity, capitalis
e late twentieth centu

The Society of the Spectacle
by Guy Debord
New York: Zone Books, 1994
First published in Paris in 1967, *La Société du spectacle* served as a revolutionary user's manual for the events of May '68, and today stands as the classic statement of the Situationist movement. The new English translation was made by Donald Nicholson-Smith, with Guy Debord's approval, for Zone Books. The cover is an inversion of the usual Zone Books strategy. In this case, the typography is filled with image. The empty white field functions as a screen floating between the reader's eye and the spectacle of a massed crowd beyond. What the crowd has gathered to observe remains beyond perception.

The Movement of the Free Spirit

The Movement of the Free Spirit
by Raoul Vaneigem
New York: Zone Books, 1994

La Jetée ciné-roman
by Chris Marker
New York: Zone Books, 1992
This book is a study in translation, not across languages but across media. The challenge was to find a way to use time and memory to interpret in book form Marker's classic 1962 science fiction film *La Jetée*. Given that cinematic time differs fundamentally from book time, graphic techniques were employed to create sympathetic effects. Typography was used to produce the cadence of cinema, and the page turn to create a base rhythm.

La Jetée ciné-roman

Chris Marker

This is the story of a man, marked by an image from his childhood.
The violent scene that upset him,
and whose meaning he was to grasp only years later,
happened on the main jetty at Orly, the Paris airport,
sometime before the outbreak of World War III.

Ceci est l'histoire d'un homme marqué par une image d'enfance.
La scène qui le troubla par sa violence,
et dont il ne devait comprendre que beaucoup plus tard la signification,
eut lieu sur la grande jetée d'Orly,
quelques années avant le début de la troisième guerre mondiale.

Orly, Sunday. Parents used to take their children there to watch the departing planes.

A Orly, le dimanche, les parents mènent leurs enfants voir les avions en partance.

On this particular Sunday, the child whose story we are telling was bound to remember the frozen sun, the setting at the end of the jetty,

De ce dimanche, l'enfant dont nous racontons l'histoire devait revoir longtemps le soleil fixe, le décor planté au bout de la jetée,

Nothing sorts out memories from ordinary moments.
Later on they do claim remembrance when they show their scars.
That face he had seen was to be the only peacetime image
to survive the war. Had he really seen it?
Or had he invented that tender moment to prop up
the madness to come?

Rien ne distingue les souvenirs des autres moments:
ce n'est que plus tard qu'ils se font reconnaître, à leurs cicatrices.
Ce visage qui devait être la seule image du temps de paix à traverser
le temps de guerre, il se demanda longtemps s'il l'avait vraiment vu,
ou s'il avait créé ce moment de douceur pour étayer
le moment de folie qui allait venir,

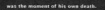

was the moment of his own death.

c'était celui de sa propre mort.

Chris Marker's Favorite Photos

Chris Marker is a difficult artist. Among the most original filmmakers working today, Marker is famous for the last-minute about-face. Known for pulling his works from retrospectives and festivals, he refuses travel, interviews, publicity, and celebrity. For six years we tried to coax Marker to do a book version of his 1962 science fiction film classic, *La Jetée*. At first, he insisted that it wouldn't be of interest. Then he insisted it couldn't be done. We pressed. Years passed.

Finally, he allowed us to try. If we could produce a convincing prototype, he would permit the production. But there was a hitch. Marker would not allow the original photographs to be sent from Paris. We would have to send someone to carry the images back personally. A Zone editor did just that, arriving in Toronto with the precious cargo.

Marker's original film is composed entirely of still images, with the exception of a single sequence. I thus thought that the translation from film to book would be a cinch, merely a matter of placing the images in sequence. I couldn't have been more naive or misguided. Because cinematic time differs fundamentally from book time, graphic techniques must be employed to create film effects. Our work consisted of inverse filmmaking. We watched the film over and over, extracting the film sense and then producing its effect in book form. Day after day we designed sequences; night after night we screened and rescreened. Finally, we had a section ready to show Marker. The result was a subtle marriage of image and text, pause and effect.

We called FedEx and held our breath. A few days later a fax came from Marker.

"Your work on *La Jetée* is astonishingly beautiful. If you keep this pace throughout the entire story, it will be not a film's book, but a book by itself, the real *ciné-roman* announced in the film's credits.... I am totally with you in your approach. Best wishes, Chris Marker, Paris."

We set about producing the complete book but soon hit a roadblock. One segment was missing. We sent a message to Marker: Is it possible images are missing? destroyed? still in Paris?

Several days later I was casually opening my mail while talking on the telephone. A flimsy airmail envelope crossed the desk. Without thinking, I tore it open. To my amazement it contained the precious missing originals, their only protection provided by the back of the envelope, where Marker had written in small script, "photos—please do not bend."

Chronicle of the Guayaki Indians
by Pierre Clastres
New York: Zone Books, 1998
Clastres's account of his 1963–64 encounter with a small Paraguayan Indian tribe is a precise and detailed recording of the history, rituals, myths, and culture of a remarkably unique, and now vanished, people.
The book begins with a rather coy, innocent picture of one of the youngest members of the tribe; it ends with a picture of a dying elder. The story of the tribe's decline and impending extinction unfolds on the pages in between. The cover features an abstracted, close-focus photograph of the Guayaki chief's painted chest.

Pierre Clastres
Chronicle of the Guayaki Indians
Translation & Foreword by
Paul Auster
ZONE BOOKS
ZONE BOOKS

Transformation Loop

When you see a color in a certain light, you're changed forever. When you do a project like *Society Against the State*, you're changed. When you do a project like *Zone*, you can't go back.
The studio is not an isolated, discrete object. It is an organic system with machine parts; it is a space partly fixed, partly fluid, willing to engage fluctuations and disturbances. The studio functions as a transformation loop. Information flows through the studio as liberated particles of matter belonging to various other systems, triggering—in an attempt to resolve conflict—the emergence of new form.
A residual flow is captured, and that captured flow in turn triggers an almost chemical transformation of the studio. (With each event, the studio is changed; try as we might we can no longer return to a previous state.) Like a self-sustaining composition, there are several of these loops running simultaneously. The studio becomes a turbulence amplifier.
What tipped me off to the existence of the transformation loop was an uncanny synchronicity between producing volumes of *Zone* and losing my girlfriend. It seemed that during the course of each big project the script of my life was rewritten and her character was always ruthlessly written out. When I recognized this pattern, I suddenly understood the difference between information, which is passive and external, and transformation, which is active and integral—an event. It's the difference between owning a book and reading a book. Owning a book is easy. It demands a commitment on only the lowest level. Reading a book means integrating the book into one's life. It means incorporating a new flow in the existing flow.

Student protests, Paris, May 1968

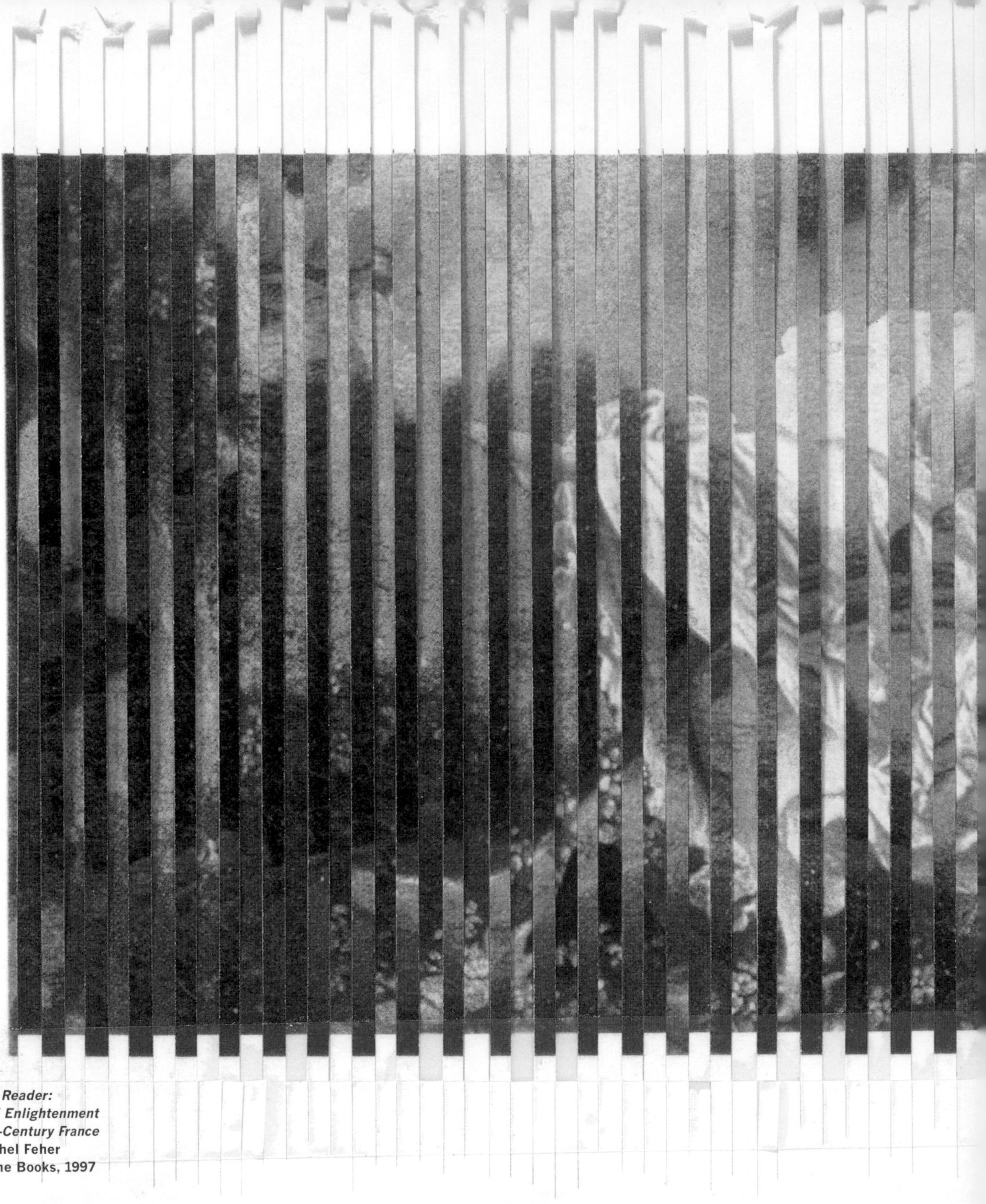

The Libertine Reader: Eroticism and Enlightenment in Eighteenth-Century France
Edited by Michel Feher
New York: Zone Books, 1997

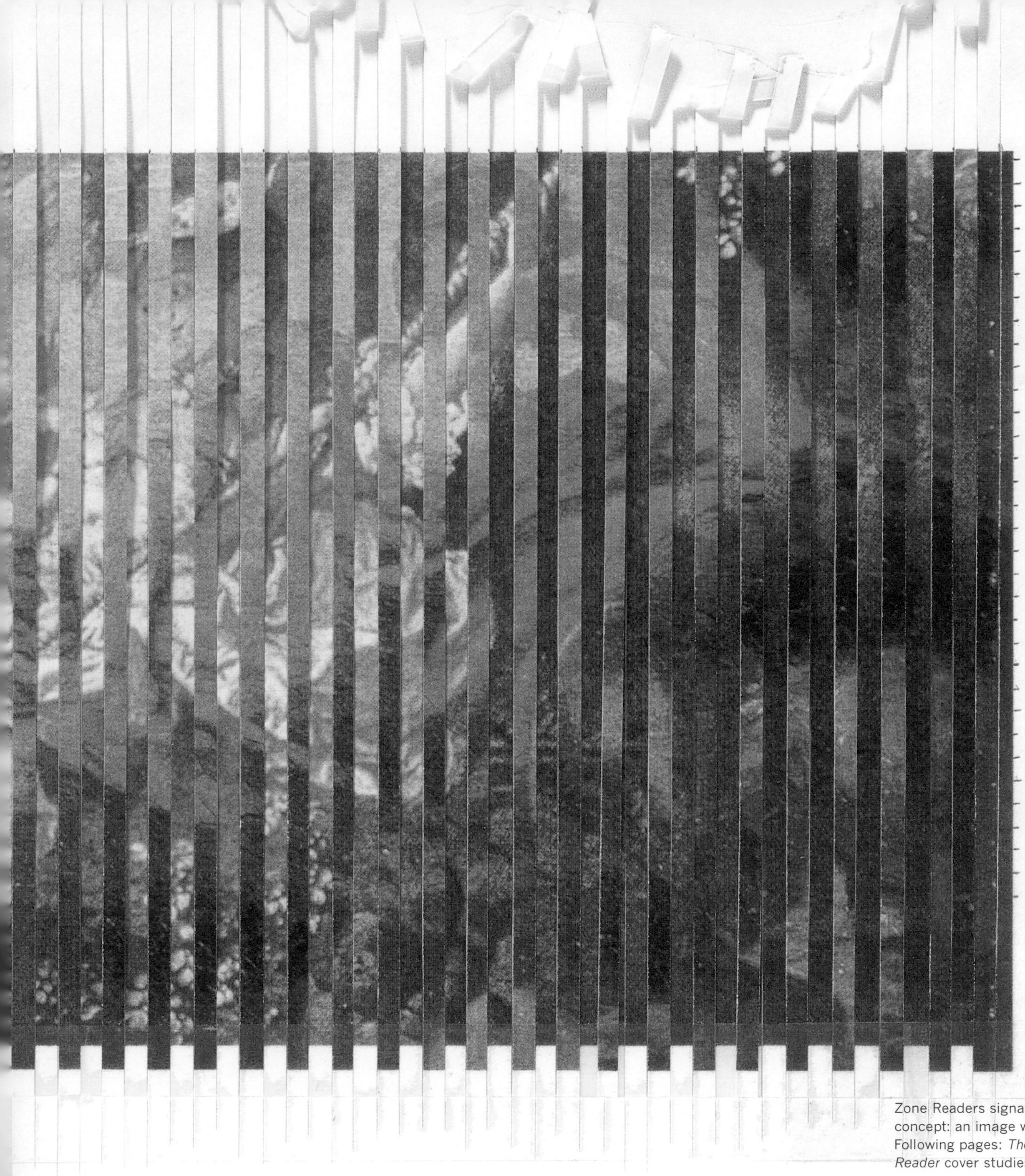

Zone Readers signature image concept: an image weave. Following pages: *The Libertine Reader* cover studies.

148

Michel Feher, the Zone Readers series co-editor, imagined that we were going into the archives, finding dusty volumes, and discovering hidden jewels left buried for centuries. We were lifting them back up to the surface of the culture, weaving them together, and presenting them as a literary genre. Feher's editorial conceit inspired the idea of doing the image weaves for the covers. For each volume we produced an image in which two aspects of the collection could vibrate on the surface. It was a technique that allowed two images to be seen simultaneously, through one another, flickering as our attention attempts to apprehend them.

The Libertine Reader is a compilation of erotic letters, fiction, and other texts from eighteenth-century France, including selected works by authors such as Crébillon fils, Choderlos de Laclos, and the Marquis de Sade. The soft cover is a weave of colorfully manipulated details taken from two works by Fragonard: *The Furtive Kiss* and *The Bolt*. A removable, translucent vellum dust jacket acts as protective lingerie. When the vellum is removed, the cover image beneath it stands alone—naked, harmless, and discreet. *The Libertine Reader* becomes a private book, one that can be read in public on the subway.

The
EROTICISM AND ENLIGHTENMENT
Libertine
IN EIGHTEENTH-CENTURY FRANCE
Reader
EDITED BY MICHEL FEHER
ZONE READERS

The Decadent Reader: Fiction, Fantasy, and Perversion from Fin-de-Siècle France
Edited by Asti Hustvedt
New York: Zone Books, 1998
Given their ambitious assembly of specialized, historical literature, the Zone Readers demanded a format that could contain, at a low cost, as much as possible between the two covers. There were two major issues at stake. One was the interior typography, made complex by the quantity and nature of the content and the economy of scale. The second was the production of the book as an object, which led to the choice of a paper used for bibles that had just the right opacity and weight.

The

FICTION, FANTASY, AND PERVERSION

Decadent

FROM FIN-DE-SIECLE FRANCE

Reader

155

EDITED BY ASTI HUSTVEDT

OKS

ZONE READERS

Zone Readers are edited by
Michel Feher and Ramona Naddaff

The

FICTION, FANTASY, AND PERVERSION

Decadent

FROM FIN-DE-SIÈCLE FRANCE

Reader

EDITED BY ASTI HUSTVEDT

ZONE BOOKS NEW YORK 1998

Contents

THE FUTURE EVE
by Villiers de l'Isle Adam

CONTENTS

THE FUTURE EVE
by Villiers de l'Isle-Adam

Advice to the Reader

IT SEEMS PROPER to forestall a possible confusion regarding the principal hero of this book.

Everyone knows nowadays that a most distinguished American inventor, Mr. Edison, has discovered over the last fifteen years a prodigious number of things, as strange as they are ingenious – among others, the Telephone, the Phonograph, the Microphone, and those admirable electric light bulbs which have now spread across the earth's surface – not to speak of a hundred other marvels.

In American and in Europe a LEGEND has thus sprung up in the popular mind regarding this great citizen of the United States. He has become the recipient of thousands of nicknames, such as "THE MAGICIAN OF THE CENTURY," "THE SORCERER OF MENLO PARK," the "PAPA OF THE PHONOGRAPH," and so forth and so on. A perfectly natural enthusiasm in his own country and elsewhere has conferred upon him a kind of mystique, or something like it, in many minds.

Henceforth, doesn't the PERSONAGE of this legend – even while the man who inspired it is still alive – belong to the world of literature? For example, if Doctor Johann Faust had been living in the age of Goethe and had given rise to his symbolic legend at that time, wouldn't the writing of *Faust*, even then, have been a perfectly legitimate undertaking?

Thus, the EDISON of the present work, his character, his dwelling, his language, and his theories, are and ought to be at least somewhat distinct from anything existing in reality.

Let it be understood, then, that I interpret a modern legend to the best advantage of the work of Art-metaphysics that I have conceived; and that, in a word, the hero of this book is above all "The Sorcerer of Menlo Park," and so forth – and not the engineer, Mr. Edison, our contemporary.

I have no other qualifications to note.

Villiers de l'Isle-Adam

To the Dreamers, To the Deriders

BOOK I

MR. EDISON

CHAPTER I

Menlo Park

The garden like a lady fair was cut,
That lay as if she slumbered in delight
And to the open skies her eyes did shut;
The azure fields of heaven were 'sembled right
In a large round, set with the flowers of light,
The flowers de luce, and the round sparks of dew,
That hung upon their azure leaves did show
Like twinkling stars, that sparkle in the evening blue.
– Giles Fletcher

Twenty-five leagues from New York, at the heart of a network of electric lines, is found a dwelling surrounded by deep and quite deserted gardens. The doorway looks out across a grassy lawn crossed by sanded paths and leading to a kind of large isolated pavilion. To the south and west, two long avenues of ancient trees bend their shadows in the direction of this pavilion. This is Number One Menlo Park; and here dwells Thomas Alva Edison, the man who made a prisoner of the echo.

Edison is forty-two years old. A few years ago his features recalled in a striking manner those of a famous Frenchman, Gustave Doré. It was very nearly the face of an artist *translated* into the features of a scholar. The same natural talents, differently applied – mysterious twins. At what age did they completely resemble one another? Perhaps never. Their two photographs of that earlier time, blended in the stereoscope, would evoke an intellectual impression such as only certain figures of the superior races ever fully realize, and then only in a few occasional images, stamped as on coins and scattered through Humanity.

When one compares the features of Edison with those on ancient

Without question, the Readers represent the most comprehensive, economical typographic system the studio has devised for any project. The literature is, for historical reasons, extremely complicated in its textual arrangement. *The Decadent Reader* is 1088 pages divided into three thematic parts and includes five full novels, a novella, eight lengthy extracts, and a full set of critical introductions. The result is fourteen works of fiction, as well as critical essays, each with its own set of typographic parameters dealing with things like chapter headings and subheads. If we differentiated the volume's numerous parts by bumping up the text by even a single point size, the whole volume would have inflated like a balloon. Instead, the typography is an application of the modernist principle of a single difference: only one variable changed at each step. So if the size is different, it is the only distinction. If it is italic, that is the only distinction.

By keeping the steps to an absolute minimum, clear differentiation is maintained without catastrophic inflation. Within just six lines, a chapter number, a chapter title, and a chapter subtitle could appear, and the text could begin.

The same tactic applies to the critical essays. They occupied exactly the same text area on the page as did the literary pieces and had exactly the same typeface and size; but the scholarly text is set unjustified, following contemporary critical convention, and the literary text margins are justified, following a classic literary convention.

These projects exemplify how we work in the space of the

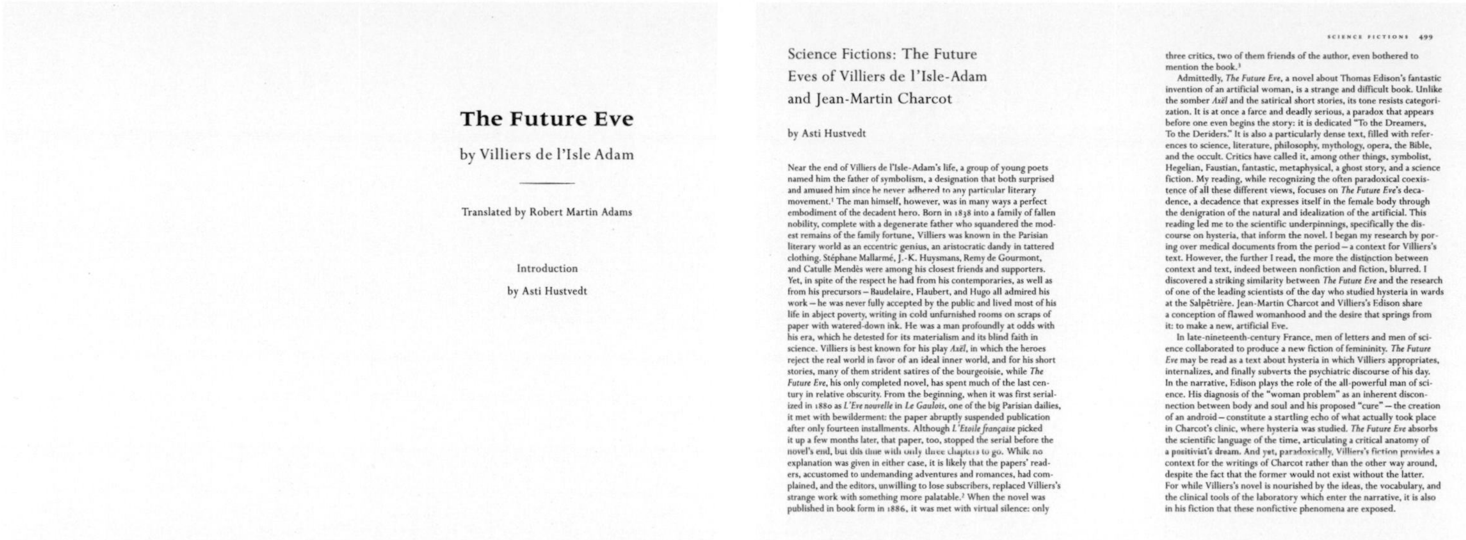

The Future Eve

by Villiers de l'Isle Adam

Translated by Robert Martin Adams

Introduction

by Asti Hustvedt

Science Fictions: The Future Eves of Villiers de l'Isle-Adam and Jean-Martin Charcot

by Asti Hustvedt

Near the end of Villiers de l'Isle-Adam's life, a group of young poets named him the father of symbolism, a designation that both surprised and amused him since he never adhered to any particular literary movement.[1] The man himself, however, was in many ways a perfect embodiment of the decadent hero. Born in 1838 into a family of fallen nobility, complete with a degenerate father who squandered the modest remains of the family fortune, Villiers was known in the Parisian literary world as an eccentric genius, an aristocratic dandy in tattered clothing. Stéphane Mallarmé, J.-K. Huysmans, Remy de Gourmont, and Catulle Mendès were among his closest friends and supporters. Yet, in spite of the respect he had from his contemporaries, as well as from his precursors – Baudelaire, Flaubert, and Hugo all admired his work – he was never fully accepted by the public and lived most of his life in abject poverty, writing in cold unfurnished rooms on scraps of paper with watered-down ink. He was a man profoundly at odds with his era, which he detested for its materialism and its blind faith in science. Villiers is best known for his play *Axël*, in which the heroes reject the real world in favor of an ideal inner world, and for his short stories, many of them strident satires of the bourgeoisie, while *The Future Eve*, his only completed novel, has spent much of the last century in relative obscurity. From the beginning, when it was first serialized in 1880 as *L'Eve nouvelle* in *Le Gaulois*, one of the big Parisian dailies, it met with bewilderment: the paper abruptly suspended publication after only fourteen installments. Although *L'Etoile française* picked it up a few months later, that paper, too, stopped the serial before the novel's end, but this time with only three chapters to go. While no explanation was given in either case, it is likely that the papers' readers, accustomed to undemanding adventures and romances, had complained, and the editors, unwilling to lose subscribers, replaced Villiers's strange work with something more palatable.[2] When the novel was published in book form in 1886, it was met with virtual silence: only

SCIENCE FICTIONS 499

three critics, two of them friends of the author, even bothered to mention the book.[3]

Admittedly, *The Future Eve*, a novel about Thomas Edison's fantastic invention of an artificial woman, is a strange and difficult book. Unlike the somber *Axël* and the satirical short stories, its tone resists categorization. It is at once a farce and deadly serious, a paradox that appears before one even begins the story: it is dedicated "To the Dreamers, To the Deriders." It is also a particularly dense text, filled with references to science, literature, philosophy, mythology, opera, the Bible, and the occult. Critics have called it, among other things, symbolist, Hegelian, Faustian, fantastic, metaphysical, a ghost story, and a science fiction. My reading, while recognizing the often paradoxical coexistence of all these different views, focuses on *The Future Eve*'s decadence, a decadence that expresses itself in the female body through the denigration of the natural and idealization of the artificial. This reading led me to the scientific underpinnings, specifically the discourse on hysteria, that inform the novel. I began my research by poring over medical documents from the period – a context for Villiers's text. However, the further I read, the more the distinction between context and text, indeed between nonfiction and fiction, blurred. I discovered a striking similarity between *The Future Eve* and the research of one of the leading scientists of the day who studied hysteria in wards at the Salpêtrière. Jean-Martin Charcot and Villiers's Edison share a conception of flawed womanhood and the desire that springs from it: to make a new, artificial Eve.

In late-nineteenth-century France, men of letters and men of science collaborated to produce a new fiction of femininity. *The Future Eve* may be read as a text about hysteria in which Villiers appropriates, internalizes, and finally subverts the psychiatric discourse of his day. In the narrative, Edison plays the role of the all-powerful man of science. His diagnosis of the "woman problem" as an inherent disconnection between body and soul and his proposed "cure" – the creation of an android – constitute a startling echo of what actually took place in Charcot's clinic, where hysteria was studied. *The Future Eve* absorbs the scientific language of the time, articulating a critical anatomy of a positivist's dream. And yet, paradoxically, Villiers's fiction provides a context for the writings of Charcot rather than the other way around, despite the fact that the former would not exist without the latter. For while Villiers's novel is nourished by the ideas, the vocabulary, and the clinical tools of the laboratory which enter the narrative, it is also in his fiction that these nonfictive phenomena are exposed.

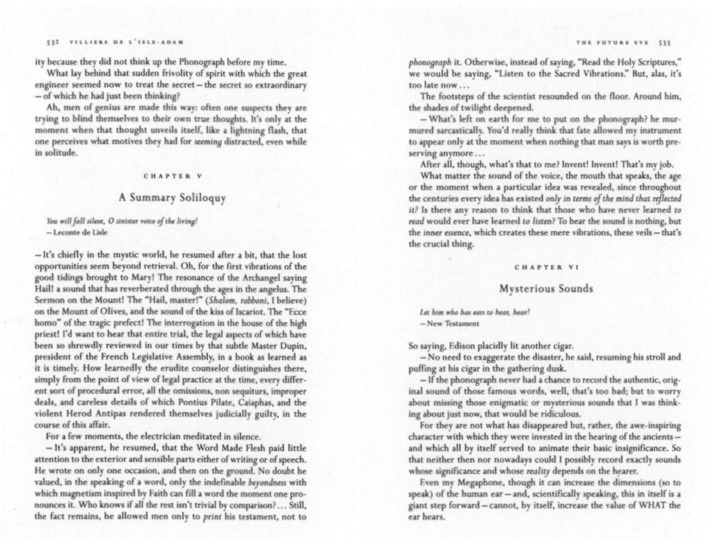

532 VILLIERS DE L'ISLE-ADAM

ity because they did not think up the Phonograph before my time.

What lay behind that sudden frivolity of spirit with which the great engineer seemed now to treat the secret – the secret so extraordinary – of which he had just been thinking?

Ah, men of genius are made this way: often one suspects they are trying to blind themselves to their own true thoughts. It's only at the moment when that thought unveils itself, like a lightning flash, that one perceives what motives they had for *seeming* distracted, even while in solitude.

CHAPTER V

A Summary Soliloquy

You will fall silent, O sinister voice of the living!
– Leconte de Lisle

– It's chiefly in the mystic world, he resumed after a bit, that the lost opportunities seem beyond retrieval. Oh, for the first vibrations of the good tidings brought to Mary! The resonance of the Archangel saying Hail! a sound that has reverberated through the ages in the angelus. The Sermon on the Mount! The "Hail, master!" (*Shalom, rabboni*, I believe) on the Mount of Olives, and the sound of the kiss of Iscariot. The "Ecce homo" of the tragic prefect! The interrogation in the house of the high priest! I'd want to hear that entire trial, the legal aspects of which have been so shrewdly reviewed in our times by that subtle Master Dupin, president of the French Legislative Assembly, in a book as learned as it is timely. How learnedly the erudite counselor distinguishes there, simply from the point of view of legal practice at the time, every different sort of procedural error, all the omissions, non sequiturs, improper deals, and careless details of which Pontius Pilate, Caiaphas, and the violent Herod Antipas rendered themselves judicially guilty, in the course of this affair.

For a few moments, the electrician meditated in silence.

– It's apparent, he resumed, that the Word Made Flesh paid little attention to the exterior and sensible parts either of writing or of speech. He wrote on only one occasion, and then on the ground. No doubt he valued, in the speaking of a word, only the indefinable *beyondness* with which magnetism inspired by Faith can fill a word the moment one pronounces it. Who knows if all the rest isn't trivial by comparison?... Still, the fact remains, he allowed men only to *print* his testament, not to

THE FUTURE EVE 533

phonograph it. Otherwise, instead of saying, "Read the Holy Scriptures," we would be saying, "Listen to the Sacred Vibrations." But, alas, it's too late now...

The footsteps of the scientist resounded on the floor. Around him, the shades of twilight deepened.

– What's left on earth for me to put on the phonograph? he murmured sarcastically. You'd really think that fate allowed my instrument to appear only at the moment when nothing that man says is worth preserving anymore...

After all, though, what's that to me? Invent! Invent! That's my job.

What matter the sound of the voice, the mouth that speaks, the age or the moment when a particular idea was revealed, since throughout the centuries every idea has existed *only in terms of the mind that reflected it?* Is there any reason to think that those who have never learned *to read* would ever have learned *to listen*? To hear the sound is nothing, but the *inner essence*, which creates these mere vibrations, these veils – that's the crucial thing.

CHAPTER VI

Mysterious Sounds

Let him who has ears to hear, hear!
– New Testament

So saying, Edison placidly lit another cigar.

– No need to exaggerate the disaster, he said, resuming his stroll and puffing at his cigar in the gathering dusk.

– If the phonograph never had a chance to record the authentic, original sound of those famous words, well, that's too bad; but to worry about missing those enigmatic or mysterious sounds that I was thinking about just now, that would be ridiculous.

For they are not what has disappeared but, rather, the awe-inspiring character with which they were invested in the hearing of the ancients – and which all by itself served to animate their basic insignificance. So that neither then nor nowadays could I possibly record exactly sounds whose significance and whose *reality* depends on the hearer.

Even my Megaphone, though it can increase the dimensions (so to speak) of the human ear – and, scientifically speaking, this in itself is a giant step forward – cannot, by itself, increase the value of WHAT the ear hears.

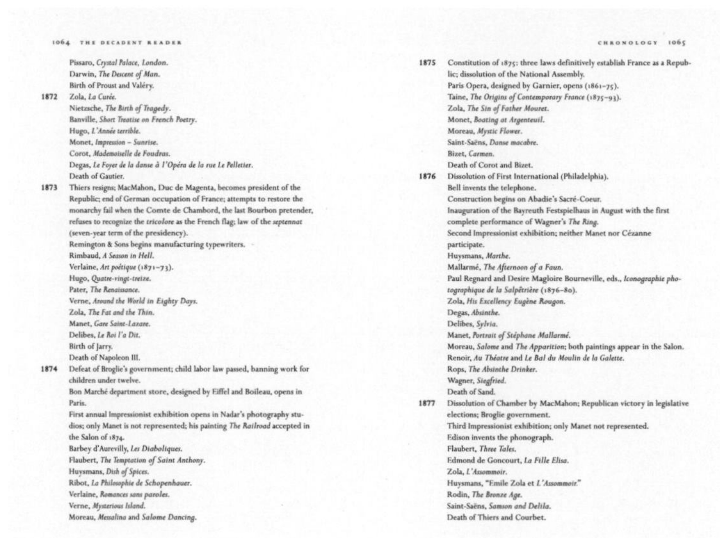

1064 THE DECADENT READER

Pissaro, *Crystal Palace, London.*
Darwin, *The Descent of Man.*
Birth of Proust and Valéry.
1872 Zola, *La Curée.*
Nietzsche, *The Birth of Tragedy.*
Banville, *Short Treatise on French Poetry.*
Hugo, *L'Année terrible.*
Monet, *Impression – Sunrise.*
Corot, *Mademoiselle de Foudras.*
Degas, *Le Foyer de la danse à l'Opéra de la rue Le Pelletier.*
Death of Gautier.
1873 Thiers resigns; MacMahon, Duc de Magenta, becomes president of the Republic; end of German occupation of France; attempts to restore the monarchy fail when the Comte de Chambord, the last Bourbon pretender, refuses to recognize the *tricolore* as the French flag; law of the *septennat* (seven-year term of the presidency).
Remington & Sons begins manufacturing typewriters.
Rimbaud, *A Season in Hell.*
Verlaine, *Art poétique* (1871–73).
Hugo, *Quatre-vingt-treize.*
Pater, *The Renaissance.*
Verne, *Around the World in Eighty Days.*
Zola, *The Fat and the Thin.*
Manet, *Gare Saint-Lazare.*
Delibes, *Le Roi l'a Dit.*
Birth of Jarry.
Death of Napoleon III.
1874 Defeat of Broglie's government; child labor law passed, banning work for children under twelve.
Bon Marché department store, designed by Eiffel and Boileau, opens in Paris.
First annual Impressionist exhibition opens in Nadar's photography studios; only Manet is not represented; his painting *The Railroad* accepted in the Salon of 1874.
Barbey d'Aurevilly, *Les Diaboliques.*
Flaubert, *The Temptation of Saint Anthony.*
Huysmans, *Dish of Spices.*
Ribot, *La Philosophie de Schopenhauer.*
Verlaine, *Romances sans paroles.*
Verne, *Mysterious Island.*
Moreau, *Messalina* and *Salome Dancing.*

CHRONOLOGY 1065

1875 Constitution of 1875: three laws definitively establish France as a Republic; dissolution of the National Assembly.
Paris Opera, designed by Garnier, opens (1861–75).
Taine, *The Origins of Contemporary France* (1875–93).
Zola, *The Sin of Father Mouret.*
Monet, *Boating at Argenteuil.*
Moreau, *Mystic Flower.*
Saint-Saëns, *Danse macabre.*
Bizet, *Carmen.*
Death of Corot and Bizet.
1876 Dissolution of First International (Philadelphia).
Bell invents the telephone.
Construction begins on Abadie's Sacré-Coeur.
Inauguration of the Bayreuth Festspielhaus in August with the first complete performance of Wagner's *The Ring.*
Second Impressionist exhibition; neither Manet nor Cézanne participate.
Huysmans, *Marthe.*
Mallarmé, *The Afternoon of a Faun.*
Paul Regnard and Desire Magloire Bourneville, eds., *Iconographie photographique de la Salpêtrière* (1876–80).
Zola, *His Excellency Eugène Rougon.*
Degas, *Absinthe.*
Delibes, *Sylvia.*
Manet, *Portrait of Stéphane Mallarmé.*
Moreau, *Salome* and *The Apparition*; both paintings appear in the Salon.
Renoir, *Au Théatre* and *Le Bal du Moulin de la Galette.*
Rops, *The Absinthe Drinker.*
Wagner, *Siegfried.*
Death of Sand.
1877 Dissolution of Chamber by MacMahon; Republican victory in legislative elections; Broglie government.
Third Impressionist exhibition; only Manet not represented.
Edison invents the phonograph.
Flaubert, *Three Tales.*
Edmond de Goncourt, *La Fille Elisa.*
Zola, *L'Assommoir.*
Huysmans, "Emile Zola et *L'Assommoir.*"
Rodin, *The Bronze Age.*
Saint-Saëns, *Samson and Delila.*
Death of Thiers and Courbet.

reader and how within that space we are able to generate subtle variances that can structure large, complex books. The Readers are staggeringly large and maddeningly complex. The scale of single differences lets readers know at every point where they are vis-à-vis the overall project. It is a flashlight in the labyrinth.

In "The Tao of D.E.," William Burroughs wrote that certain things in life were meant to be "done easy." Some things just don't require a struggle.

Human Rights in Political Transitions: Gettysburg to Bosnia
Edited by Carla Hesse and Robert Post
New York: Zone Books, 1999
This series is designed to be easy to handle and easy to produce. As political texts, they are meant to be turned around more quickly than Zone's philosophical works, which do not have the pressing urgency of activist writings. To expedite the process, we worked out a very simple text format that is heavily templated. It is not like other Zone projects, where we spend a lot of time creating the image and working out intricate relationships with text. In this case, we even removed the cinematic background from the cover. The whole book was conceived as a single solid object created out of uncoated paper. The edges are the same color as the cover, and we use foil stamping to produce a distinctive kind of tactility. The internal layout is also economical and simple: it fills the page. We finally did something inexpensive as well as easy.

Human Rights
in Political
Transitions:
Gettysburg
to Bosnia
ZONE BOOKS

FORMLESS A User's Guide

Yv

I went with Michel Feher in 1996 to meet Rosalind Krauss in Paris and spent several hours with her in the galleries of the Pompidou Center, where she and Yve-Alain Bois had mounted *L'Informe* (Formless). As often happens with thematic art shows, even with Krauss's supremely articulate commentary, it was a struggle to grasp the exhibition's complex frame. Each room contained a collection of modern masterpieces—Rauschenberg's black paintings, Fontana's extraordinary punctured canvases, Oldenburg's *Green Beans*—and was organized around a theme that no viewer could have teased out of the installation itself. The Pompidou had produced a catalog of the exhibition that only served to demonstrate the degree to which the French are allergic to graphic design. Our work would be to give form to the *Formless*.

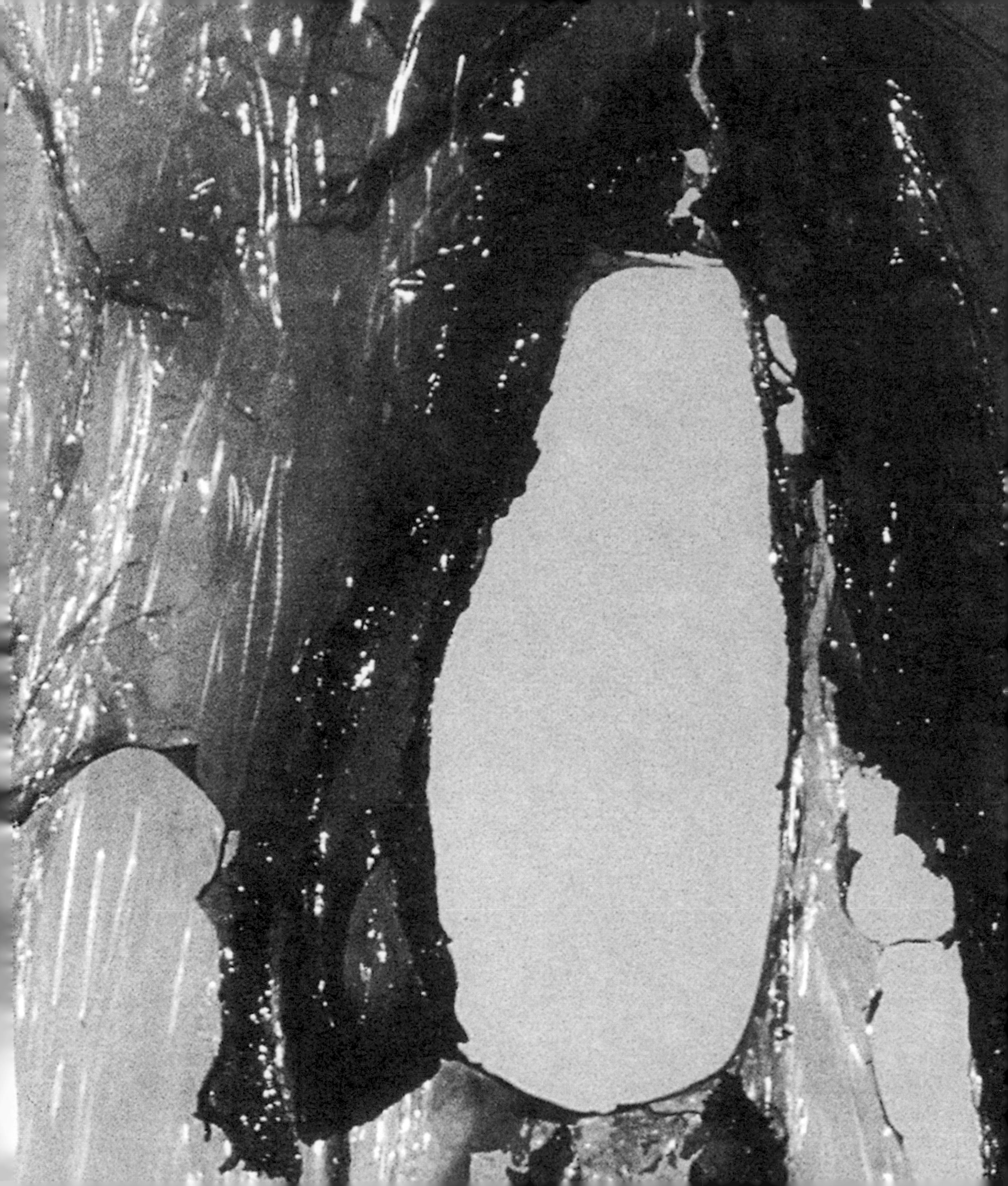

Contents

Formless: A User's Guide
by Yve-Alain Bois and
Rosalind E. Krauss
New York: Zone Books, 1997

Surrealist Georges Bataille invented the term *informe*, or "formless," for a "dictionary" he published serially during the 1930s. Drawing on Bataille's term for inspiration, Yve-Alain Bois and Rosalind Krauss curated an exhibition at the Georges Pompidou Center in Paris in 1996. The book *Formless* represents a reworked English translation of the original French exhibition catalog. Bataille randomized the entries in his "dictionary." BMD followed the lead of curators Bois and Krauss and reversed Bataille's strategy, organizing *Formless* alphabetically, complete with tabs along the right margin to provide reference for the reader.

Figure 14.
Eli Lotar,
Aux abattoirs de la Villette,
1929.
Silver print.
Musée National d'Art
Moderne-CCI, Centre
Georges Pompidou, Paris.

A

Abattoir

Yve-Alain Bois

The three Eli Lotar photographs with which Bataille illustrates his article "Abattoir" (Slaughterhouse) in the *Documents* "critical dictionary" form a kind of climax, within the journal, of the iconography of horror.[1] Cruelty and sacrifice, terror and death are often enough broached in articles there (beginning with Bataille's essay, in the second issue of *Documents*, on the illuminated manuscript of *The Apocalypse of Saint Sever*), but no other image appearing in the journal is as realistically macabre as these photographs taken at La Villette in the company of André Masson – except perhaps, in the penultimate issue, the nearly illegible reproduction (from *X Marks the Spot*) of a crude montage of press photos depicting the brutality of gang warfare in Chicago. "It seems that the desire to see is stronger than horror or disgust," Bataille remarked in relation to this book.[2]

For his own part, however, he refused to cater to this voyeurism in *Documents* (only much latter – in 1961, in *Les Larmes d'Eros* – did he publish the famous photograph of a young Chinese hacked to pieces *alive*, which his psychoanalyst, Dr. Adrien Borel, had given him in 1925).[3] It is possible that self-censorship played a role in this reserve (after all, the editorial life of *Documents* depended on the continuing support of a publisher), but that is somewhat doubtful: Bataille did not even reproduce the shot of the sliced eye from *Un Chien andalou* to which he refers, while other journals did not hold back (for example, *Cahiers d'Art*, the much more conformist magazine, to which he directed readers who wished to see the picture) – and he suppressed the image even though it would have compellingly supported his argument ("How can one not appreciate the extent of horror's fascination, and that it alone is sufficient to shatter everything that stifles us").[4] Even when it is a matter of depicting the shrunken heads of the Javaro Indians, the iconographic violence in *Documents* is mediated, distanced through

and its dogma of pure visuality: it could already seem repulsive there, made to prevent the spectator from entering into an illusory world.[9]

In this reading of it, kitsch does not go with the grain of the culture industry: making us see Monet's *Waterlilies* as so many "Multiple Originals," for example, undermines modernism's certainty by detecting in it the poison that had always been there.

(See "Base Materialism," "No to . . . the *Informel*," and "X Marks the Spot.")

L

Liquid Words

Yve-Alain Bois

The essence of language is to be articulated. Such articulations can be as smooth as one wishes; they are no less divisive for all that. In order for language to function, signs must be isolable one from the other (otherwise they would not be repeatable). At every level (phonetic, semantic, syntactic, and so on) language has its own laws of combination and continuity, but its primary material is constructed of irreducible atoms (phonemes for spoken language, and for written, signs whose nature varies according to the system in question: in alphabetical writing, for example, the distinctive unit is the letter). Whoever says "articulation" always says, in the final instance, "divisibility into minimal units": the *articulus* is the particle. Language is a hierarchical combination of bits.

Liquid, on the contrary (except on the molecular level), is indivisible (of course one can divide up a certain quantity of liquid into different containers, but it remains identical to itself in each of its parts).

Thus, properly speaking, there cannot be liquid words (we only speak of a flow of language and of liquid consonants metaphorically), except in terms of the brief moment at which they have just been penned and the ink is not yet dry. It is just such a moment that Edward Ruscha's series of paintings titled *Liquid Words* (figure 41) makes us think of, except that, in trompe-l'oeil, these paintings represent an imaginary inverse process: not the drying out of

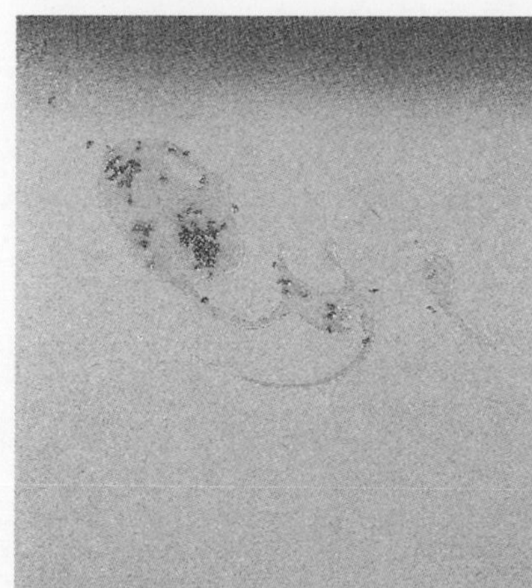

Figure 41.
Edward Ruscha,
Eye, 1969.
Oil on canvas,
60 x 54 inches.
The Oakland Museum of
California, Art Guild
and NEA.

The Panorama
by Stephan Oettermann
New York: Zone Books, 1997

For the original cover concept of *The Panorama*, we took a panoramic image of a mountain range and squeezed it to make the cover look like a Cinemascope film compressed for television broadcast. This cover concept was abandoned in favor of the cover reproduced above.

The French Army Entering Switzerland (Bourbaki Panorama) is a 360-degree panorama painted in 1880–81 by Edouard Clastres, who personally witnessed the event as a Red Cross helper during the Franco-Prussian War of 1870–71. The restored panorama is one of the world's largest, extending to a height of 14 meters and a circumference of 112 meters.

Edited by Michel Feher

with Ramona Naddaff and Nadia Tazi

Corpus

In 1989, the editors of Zone, Michel Feher, Ramona Naddaff, and Nadia Tazi, came to Toronto to work with us on Zone volumes 3, 4, and 5. Our collaboration was incredibly civilized. We began every day with a big breakfast and continued to work all day and into the night. Nadia would sit next to my table and talk to me while I worked. She said to me that *Zone 1/2* was like Jean-Luc Godard. This Zone had to be like Robert Bresson.
It had to be super-tight and resolved in the way Bresson's films are formally measured and internally complete.
When it came time to print, we manufactured our own paper because we couldn't find precisely what we wanted in the marketplace. We mixed our own inks, developing what we now call "Zone Black"— a special, high-density black ink that permits us to print on uncoated paper and get very rich images. For the covers, we developed a new printing technique. Really, it arose out of an effort to resolve a crisis. We had made three covers for the volumes

Zone 3, 4, and 5
Fragments for a History of the Human Body
Part One, Part Two, Part Three
Edited by Michel Feher with Ramona Naddaff and Nadia Tazi
New York: Urzone, 1989

Fragments for a History of the Human Body is a trilogy of essays exploring the cultural history of the human body. Each volume emphasizes a particular axis of investigation: the first, a vertical axis from the divine to the animal; the second, a transversal axis from the inside to the outside; the third, the classical distinction between organ and function.

To convey the idea of the book as a total body, BMD devised gate-folded covers for each volume. Each cover featured a single figure — taken from key moments in European art history — unfolding in a drama of scale and literally incorporating the contents of the book.

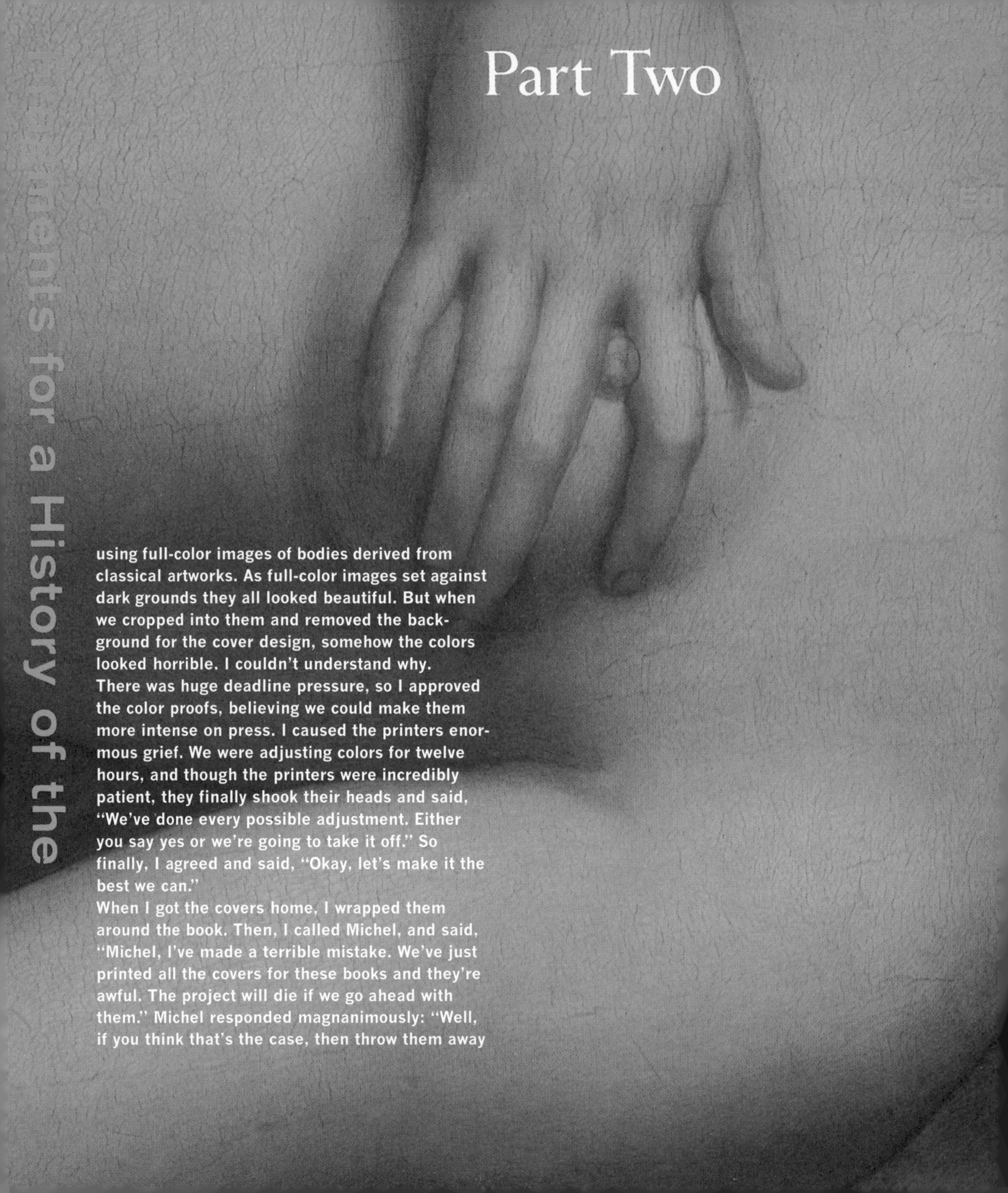

Part Two

using full-color images of bodies derived from classical artworks. As full-color images set against dark grounds they all looked beautiful. But when we cropped into them and removed the background for the cover design, somehow the colors looked horrible. I couldn't understand why.

There was huge deadline pressure, so I approved the color proofs, believing we could make them more intense on press. I caused the printers enormous grief. We were adjusting colors for twelve hours, and though the printers were incredibly patient, they finally shook their heads and said, "We've done every possible adjustment. Either you say yes or we're going to take it off." So finally, I agreed and said, "Okay, let's make it the best we can."

When I got the covers home, I wrapped them around the book. Then, I called Michel, and said, "Michel, I've made a terrible mistake. We've just printed all the covers for these books and they're awful. The project will die if we go ahead with them." Michel responded magnanimously: "Well, if you think that's the case, then throw them away

d by Michel Feher
Ramona Naddaff and Nadia Tazi

Part Three

Edited by M

with Ramon

and start again." His generosity meant an additional $25,000 from Zone's budget. "I must insist on one thing, however," Michel added. "You have to figure out what you're going to do and do it today. If we miss the delivery, it will be a disaster."

I went into my office, locked the door and I stayed in that room until I figured out how to solve the problem.

The originals worked, I knew, because of the contrast between figure and ground. The mistake I had made was to eliminate the ground, bleeding the figures of their richness and contrast. We were left with brown books.

The solution was to use the existing film but reassign the colors. Instead of four standard process colors over a full spectrum, we used four special colors within one narrow spectrum. So, in the case of Part Three, they are all reds, and in the case of Part Two, they are all blues. The result was an intricate and unprecedented range of densities and tonal values.

hel Feher
Naddaff and Nadia Tazi

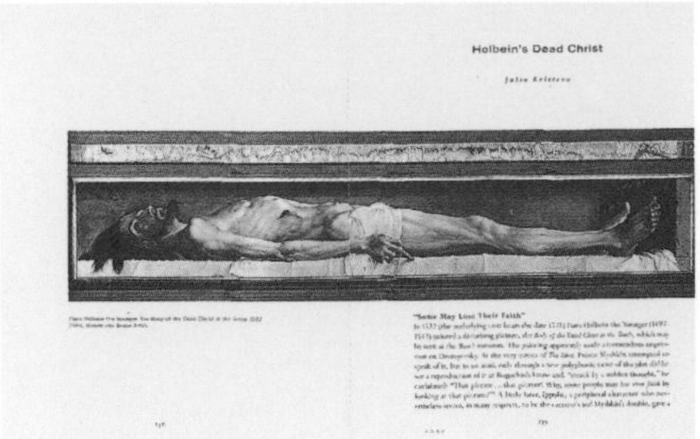

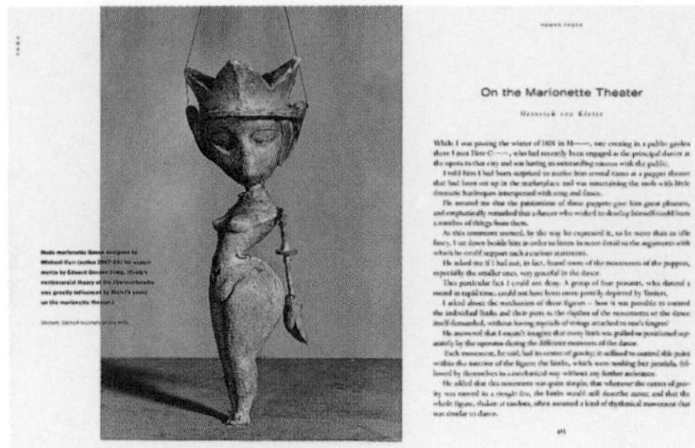

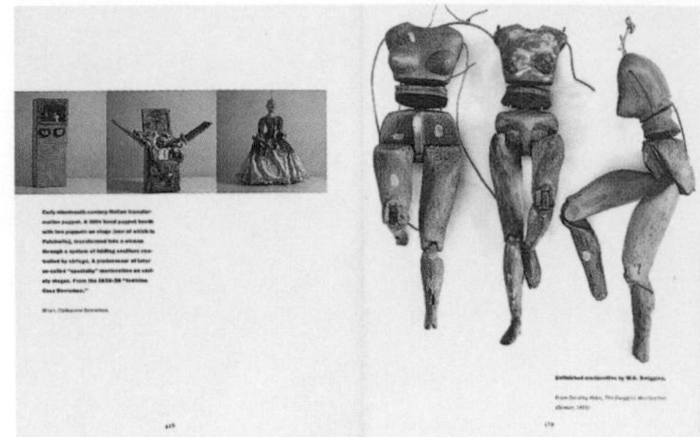

Zone 3. *Fragments for a History of the Human Body*, Part One

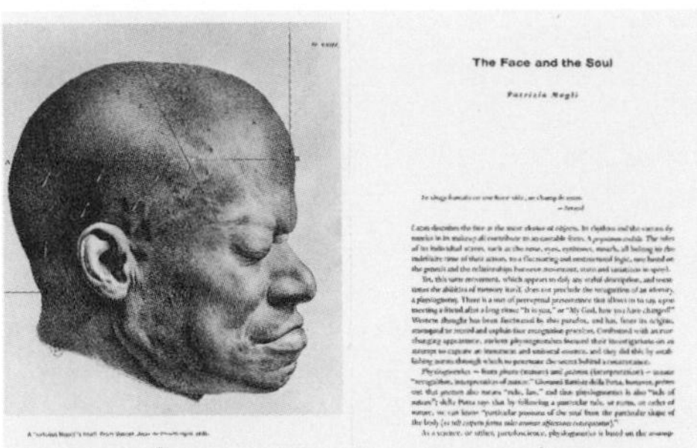

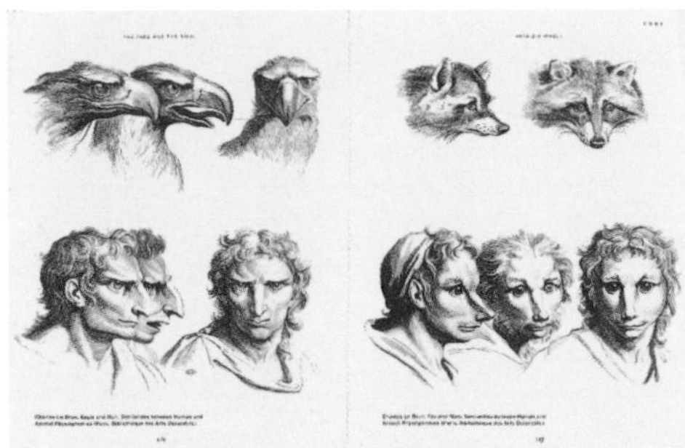

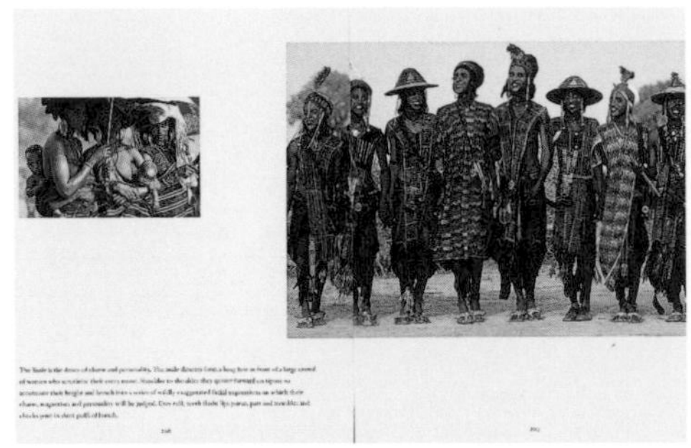

Zone 4. *Fragments for a History of the Human Body*, Part Two

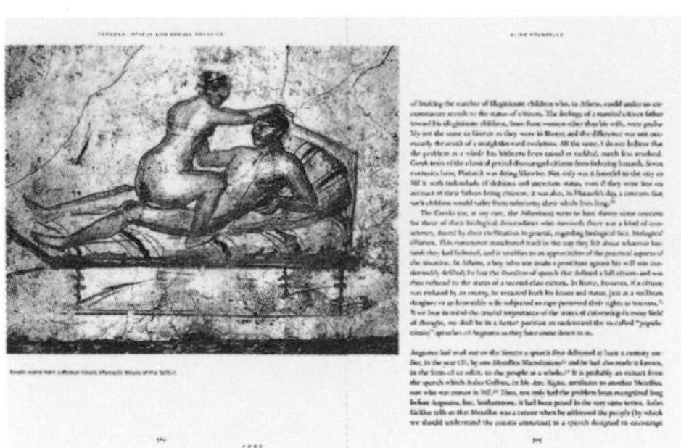

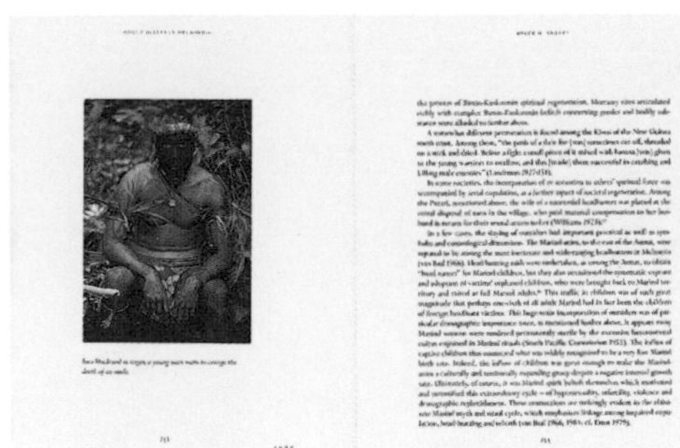

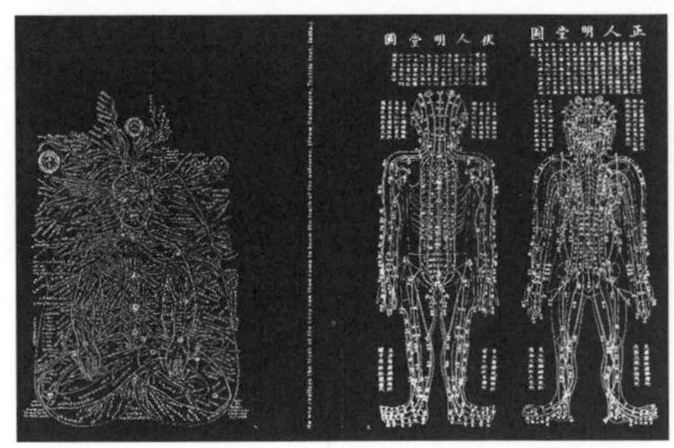

Zone 5. *Fragments for a History of the Human Body*, Part Three

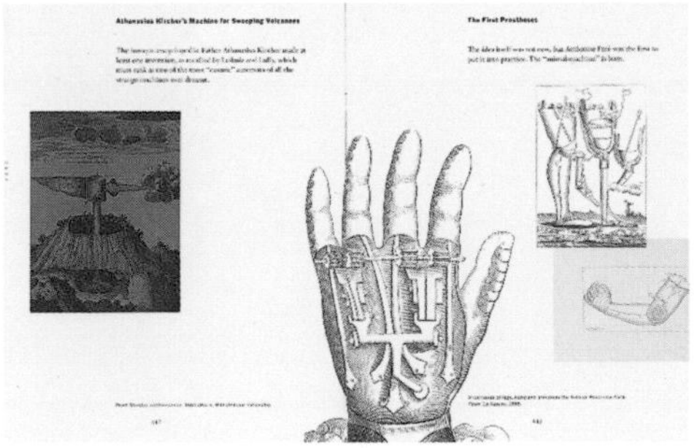
Athanasius Kircher's Machine for Sweeping Volcanoes
The First Prosthesis

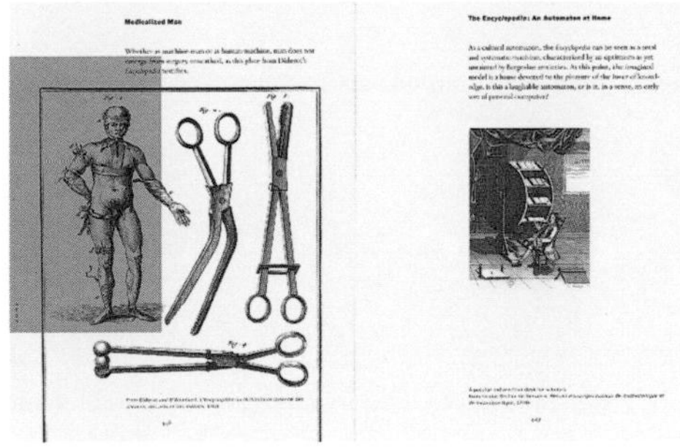
Medicalized Man
The Encyclopedia: An Automaton at Home

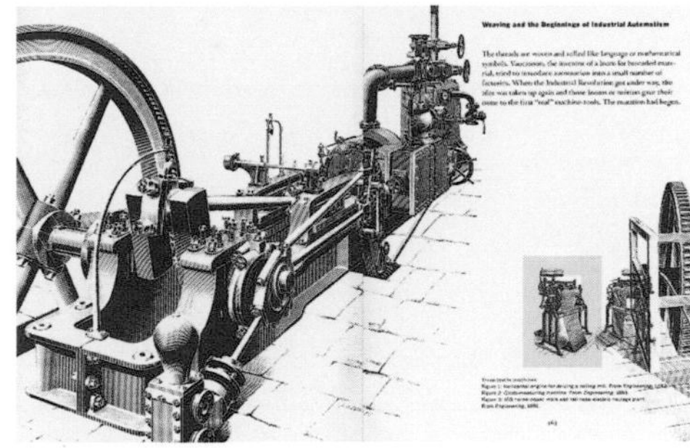
Weaving and the Beginnings of Industrial Automatism

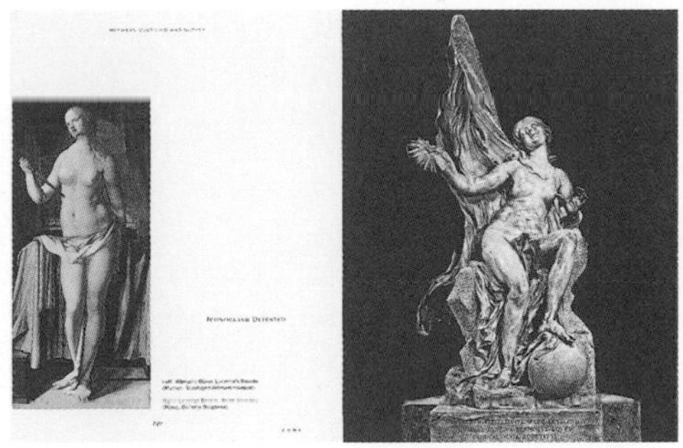

The Natural and Literary
History of Bodily Sensation
Jean Starobinski

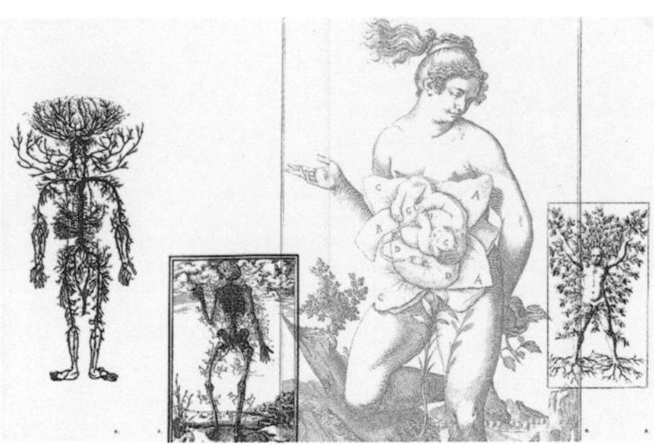

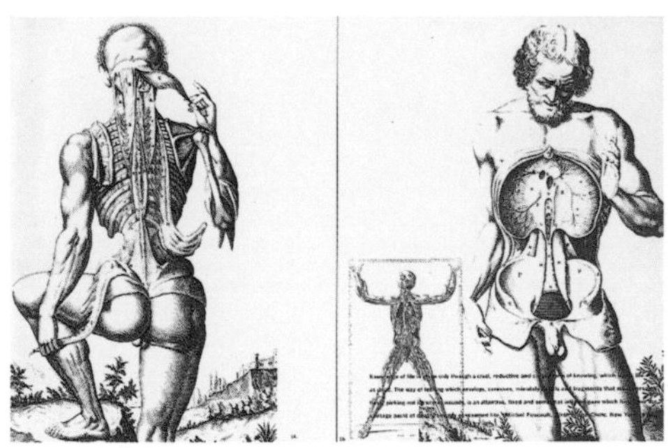

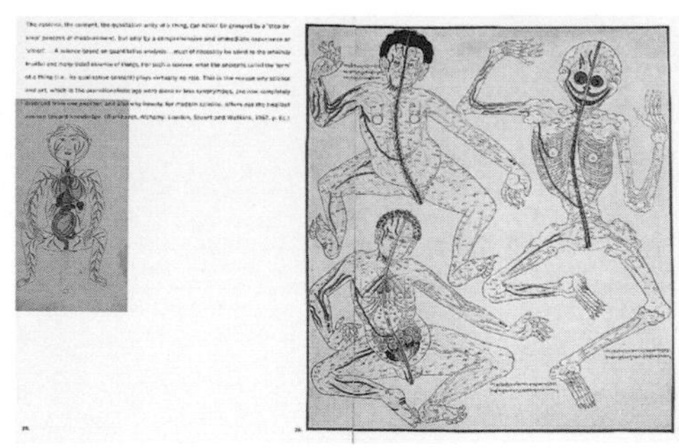

Educating Olivia

Olivia decided to study philosophy in Paris, the world capital of philosophy. On her departure from Boston, her mother had given her one telephone number, that of my friend Michel, a young man who might help her find her way in Paris and who happened also to be a philosopher.

On our way to dinner Michel informed Bisi and me that Olivia would be joining us. We enjoyed a perfectly elegant dinner in a restaurant not far from Beaubourg. During coffee, Michel suggested that we take in a couple of Russ Meyer flicks that were screening nearby. I thought the idea rather odd and said so, my vague impression of Meyer's films being that they were crude and grotesque quasi-pornography. Michel protested and defended Meyer's oeuvre: "*Non, non,* they're blue at most!"

I can remember very little of the film we saw. But as the opening credits rolled, I knew Michel was wrong, and I was right. We sat through most of *Faster Pussycat Kill! Kill!*—trademark Meyer, an endless parade of antigravity bosoms inflated with cinematic pretensions. We emerged, bewildered, into the Paris night.

By then it was nearly 2:00 A.M. Bisi and I were staying with Michel, who lived nearby, but Olivia had an apartment in the sixteenth arrondissement. Michel, somewhat embarrassed, offered to escort her home. "No," she insisted, panic in her voice. She would be fine, it was only a few hundred blocks.

Staying Alive

In the foreword to *Incorporations*, the editors, Jonathan Crary and Sanford Kwinter, write, "Every thing and every individual emerges, evolves and passes away by incorporating, and being incorporated, into other emerging, evolving or disintegrating structures that surround and suffuse it."
In other words, the discrete object is no longer possible or even conceivable. One can no longer design something in the city that exists separate from the city. Every object is incorporated into flows that will pass through it and around it.
The design schema for *Incorporations* was a collaboration with Sanford Kwinter. Our ambition was to make a book that behaved like a living thing. This meant that we had to keep it alive and crackling until the very last instant, when we would perform a final iteration and temporarily "freeze" the process. The book's motion and momentum could resume again in the reader's hands.

Zone 6: *Incorporations*
Edited by Jonathan Crary and Sanford Kwinter
New York: Urzone, 1992
Incorporations is an attempt to model growth and life. Its theme is the fluid relationship between the organic and the mechanical, and the ways in which one incorporates the other. It takes as its premise the unity of all things, beings, and systems, irrespective of size. Our ambition was to allow the book to perform its subject by moving away from a mechanistic design approach toward one based on growth. Yet, as with most life forces and processes, the action often occurs gradually and imperceptibly.

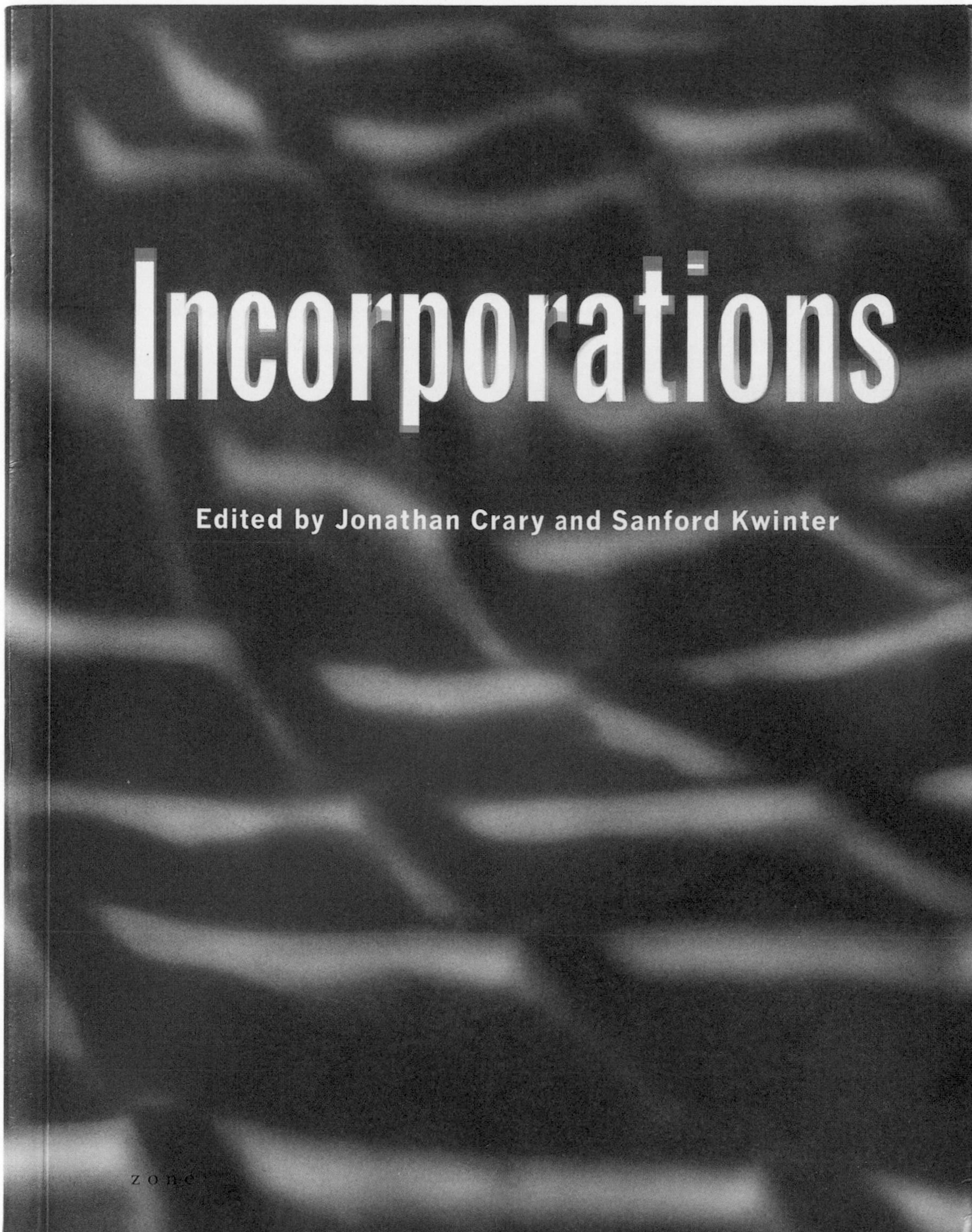
Incorporations
Edited by Jonathan Crary and Sanford Kwinter

1. The Cover Envelope

We conceived the cover as a membrane with a thickness that would penetrate the book and fold in on itself. The cover runs for sixteen pages at the front of the book, and six at the back, and it is epic. It recalls the opening and closing credits of a film. It begins with a transformation of scale that moves gradually from the urban, an image of Kowloon City in Hong Kong; via the body, an impression of a man who has fallen out of a zeppelin (an unfortunate but beautiful event); to the organs, an early minaturized pacemaker; and finally to the molecular level.

The cover envelope: *Incorporations*

This page
Title page: Fallen WWI zeppelin aviator

Following pages
Imprint page: Ovoid operating theater (Paul Nelson);
Early miniaturized pacemaker (1967)
Photo credits page: Anabaena filaments;
FBI fingerprint division (1943);
Mobile home library (Frederick Kiesler)
Contents page: Epigenetic landscape
Contributors page: Chromosome sky

Incorporations

Edited by Jonathan Crary and Sanford Kwinter

ZONE Editors: Jonathan Crary, Michel Feher, Sanford Kwinter, Ramona Naddaff
Editors of this volume: Jonathan Crary and Sanford Kwinter
Managing Editor: Elizabeth Felicella
Design: Bruce Mau
Design Schema: Sanford Kwinter and Bruce Mau
Production: Ed Cleary, Alison Hahn, Vilip Mak, Kathleen Oginski, Nigel Smith, Gregory Van Alstyne.

Image Research Coordinator: Elizabeth Felicella with Naomi Jackson, Suzanne Jackson, Carole Naggar, Keith Seward, Steve Snyder, Kristen Vallow, Timothy Wright
Manuscript Editor: Ted Byfield
Editorial Coordinators: Rennie Childress and Meighan Gale with Suzanne Jackson, Linda Kelly, Rachel Robbins, Keith Seward, Kristen Vallow, Thad Ziolkowski.
Translations: Randall Cherry, Mark Cohen, Robert Hurley, Martin Joughin, Donald Leslie, Brian Massumi, Delphine Bechtel, Ted Byfield.
Fundraising and Advertising: Céline Cazals de Fabel
Initiating Projects Editor: Kerri Kwinter
Special Thanks: Brian Boigon, Lois Burke, Anne Dixon, Ed Epstein, Jason Greenberg, Virginia Heckert, Barbara Hoffman, Christian Hubert, Alex Kessler, Gus Kiley, Andy Levine, Kerry McCarthy at AP/World Wide, Melissa Mathis, Jeffrey Meikle, Erica Meinhardt, Anne Mensior of CLAM, Guillaume Paris, Gilles Peress, Guy Poulin, Jackie Raynal, Wendelin Scott, Carina Snyder, Susan Spiegel, Tim Sternberg, Aiyemobisi Williams, Thomas Jean Yee; Aperture Magazine, Avery Library, CRT Artificio, Museum of Modern Art Photography Department, Photofest, Telescope Magazine, University of California at Riverside Photography Museum.

We gratefully acknowledge the generous support of the National Endowment for the Arts, Tom Cugliani Gallery, Lorence Monk Gallery, Nahan Gallery, Marian Goodman Gallery, Vincent Wapler, John Weber Gallery, Salvatore Ala Gallery, Leo Castelli Gallery, Vrej Baghoomian, Sidney Janis.

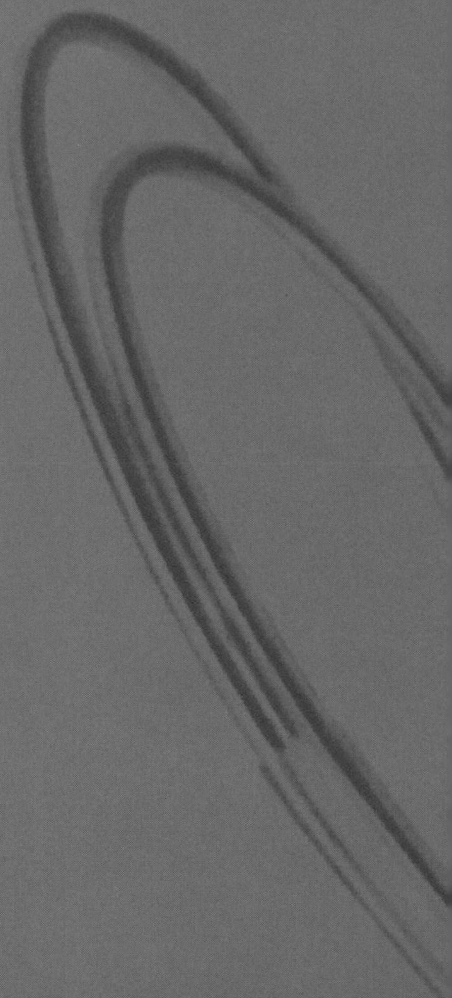

ZONE 611 Broadway Suite 608
New York, NY 10012

Printed in Canada by Bradbury Tamblyn & Boorne Ltd.
Distributed by The MIT Press.
ISBN: 0-942299-29-9 (paper) 0-942299-30-2 (cloth)
Library of Congress Catalog Card Number: 88-051439

ZONE 6

John Cage 1912–1992

Félix Guattari 1930–1992

in memoriam

Photo Credits

Courtesy of John Anthony Gallery, London, 481

AP/Wide World, 104, 270, 274, 477, 646

Art Resource, 186

Courtesy of Ana Barrado, 169–77

Biosphere 2, 499

British Imperial War Museum, 9

Clark University Archive, 202

CRT Artificio, 255

Culver Pictures Inc., 7, 90, 222, 272, 543

Courtesy of Robert Dawson, 235

Courtesy of Orshi Drozdik and Tom Cugliani Gallery, 181

Friends of Jacques-Henri Lartigue, Paris, 70, 274

Buckminster Fuller Institute, 508

J. P. Getty Museum, 608

Courtesy of Jean-Pierre Gorin, 450–53

Courtesy of Jon Kessler and Luhring Augustine Gallery, 427

Magnum Photos, 44, 270, 274, 276, 302, 455

Courtesy of Ryuji Miyamoto, 1, 32

Barbara Morgan and Morgan Press Archive, 489

Museum of Modern Art Film Archive, 28, 435, 588

National Archive, 72, 76

Courtesy of Joseph Nechvatal and Brooke Alexander Gallery, 339

Courtesy of OMA, 373, 377, 381, 384

People for the Ethical Treatment of Animals, 52

Photofest, 257, 276, 447, 585, 588

Collection of Ellen Salween, 516

Courtesy of Elaine Scarry, 340

Scientific American, 266

Courtesy of Toshio Shibata and Koko Yamagishi Gallery, 323, 326

U.S. Holocaust Memorial Museum, 271

Courtesy of Albert Watson, 574–5, 578–9

Contributors: **J. G. Ballard** is a novelist. His works include *The Crystal World*, *Crash*, *High-Rise*, *The Atrocity Exhibition* and *Concrete Island*. **Judith Barry** is an artist and writer who lives in New York City. She is represented by the Nicole Klagsbrun Gallery. **Ana Barrado** is a photographer whose work has been featured in international publications in the U.S. and Japan. A monograph of her work was published by Atelier Peyto! in Tokyo. **Georges Canguilhem**, philosopher of science, is professor emeritus at the Sorbonne and is former director of the Institut d'Histoire des Sciences et des Techniques at the University of Paris. His works include *The Normal and Pathological*, *Connaissance de la vie* and *Ideology and Rationality: The History of the Life Sciences*. **Lisa Cartwright and Brian Goldfarb:** Lisa Cartwright teaches film and media studies at the University of Rochester and writes on cinema, science and technology. She is the author of *Physiological Modernity*. Brian Goldfarb is a computer graphics and video artist. He teaches multimedia art at the University of Rochester. **François Dagognet** is a philosopher and medical doctor who has taught at the universities of Lyon and Paris. He is the author of *La maîtrise du vivant*, *Philosophie de l'image*, and *Etienne-Jules Marey*. **Manuel DeLanda** is a film/video artist and author of *War in the Age of Intelligent Machines*. **Didier Deleule** is a philosopher and the author of *Le Corps productif* (with François Guéry) and *La Psychologie: Mythe scientifique*. **Gilles Deleuze** is a philosopher. Among his works are *Masochism*, *The Logic of Sense* and *Différence et répetition*. He co-authored (with Félix Guattari) *Anti-Oedipus* and *A Thousand Plateaus*. **Diller + Scofidio** is a collaborative team involved in cross-disciplinary work incorporating architecture, performing and visual arts. Elizabeth Diller is an Assistant Professor of Architecture at Princeton University. Ric Scofidio is Professor of Architecture at the Irwin S. Chanin School of Architecture, Cooper Union. **Peter Fend** is cofounder of Ocean Earth Construction and Development Corporation. He is represented by American Fine Arts Company in New York. **Leif Finkel** teaches in both the Department of Bioengineering and the Institute of Neurological Sciences at the University of Pennsylvania. **Susan L. Foster** is a choreographer, dancer, writer and Professor of Dance at the University of California, Riverside. She has published articles on semiotics and dance and is author of *Reading Dancing: Bodies and Subjects in Contemporary American Dance*. **Heidi Gilpin** teaches in the Department of Dance, University of California, Riverside. She is editor of *Parallax* and director of the Institute for New Dramaturgy. **Jean-Pierre Gorin** is a filmmaker, whose works include *Poto and Cabengo* and *Routine Pleasures*. He is co-director, with Jean-Luc Godard, of *Tout Va Bien* and was a member of the Dziga Vertov Group. He is currently teaching at University of California, San Diego. **Félix Guattari** is the author of *La Revolution moleculaire* and *Cartographies schizoanalytiques*. He co-authored (with Gilles Deleuze) *Anti-Oedipus* and *A Thousand Plateaus*. **Donna Haraway** is a professor in the History of Consciousness Board at the University of California, Santa Cruz, where she teaches feminist theory, techno-science studies, and women's studies. She is author of *Simians, Cyborgs, and Women: The Reinvention of Nature* and *Primate Visions: Gender, Race, and Nature in the World of Modern Science*. **Ronald Jones** teaches in the Yale School of Art and Architecture and is represented by Metro Pictures and the Sonnabend Gallery.

Leone & Macdonald is the collaborative team of Hillary Leone and Jennifer Macdonald. They are represented by the Joe Fawbush Gallery and have exhibited throughout the United States and in South America. **Ellen Lupton and J. Abbott Miller** are graphic designers and writers. Ellen Lupton is Curator of Contemporary Design at the Cooper-Hewitt National Museum of Design. J. Abbott Miller is principal of the studio Design Writing Research in New York. Both teach the history and theory of graphic design at Cooper Union. **Bill Krohn** is the Los Angeles correspondent for *Cahiers du Cinema* and a regular contributor to *Traffic* and *Modern Times.* **John O'Neill** is Distinguished Research Professor of Sociology at York University and author of *Plato's Cave: Desire, Power and the Specular Functions of the Media* and *Sociology as a Skin Trade: Essays Towards a Reflexive Sociology.* **Mark Poster** teaches at the University of California, Irvine. His recent books include *The Mode of Information, Critical Theory and Poststructuralism* and *Baudrillard: Selected Writings.* **Anson Rabinbach** teaches European History at Cooper Union. He is coeditor of *New German Critique* and author of *The Human Motor: Energy, Fatigue, and the Origins of Modernity.* **Paul Rabinow** is Professor of Anthropology at the University of California, Berkeley and is author of *French Modern: Norms and Forms of the Social Environment.* **Paul Rogers** is a Senior Lecturer in the Department of Peace Studies at Bradford University. He also writes for *The Guardian* and *The Observer* in London. **Nina Rosenblatt** is an art historian currently completing a study of the technologies and economies of French modernism in the 1920s and 1930s. **Elaine Scarry** teaches English at Harvard University and is the author of *The Body in Pain: The Making and Unmaking of the World* and *Resisting Representation.* **Hillel Schwartz** is a visiting scholar at the University of California at San Diego. He is author of *Century's End: A Cultural History of the Fin de Siècle from the 1890s through the 1990s* and *Never Satisfied: A Cultural History of Diets, Fantasies and Fat.* **Eve Kosofsky Sedgwick** is a Professor of English at Duke University and author of *Between Men: English Literature and Male Homosocial Desire* and *The Epistemology of the Closet.* **Gilbert Simondon** is a philosopher and was a professor at the Sorbonne. He is the author of *Du mode d'existence des objets techniques* and *L'individu et sa genèse physico-biologique.* **Alluquère Roseanne Stone** teaches in the department of Sociology at the University of California, San Diego. She is director of the Group for the Study of Virtual Systems at the Center for Cultural Studies at the University of California, Santa Cruz. **Klaus Theweleit** is a freelance writer working in West Germany. He is the author of *Male Fantasies.* **Frederick Turner** is Founders Professor of Arts and Humanities at the University of Texas, Dallas. He is author of *Beauty: The Value of Values, Rebirth of Value* and *Tempest, Flute and Oz.* **Paul Virilio** has been Director of the Ecole Spéciale d'Architecture and is a founding member of the Center for Interdisciplinary Research in Peace Studies and Military Strategy. His books include *Speed and Politics, La Machine de vision,* and *War and Cinema: The Logistics of Perception.* **Francisco J. Varela** is Director of Research at the Institute of Neurosciences of the CNRS in Paris. His books include *Principles of Biological Autonomy, The Tree of Knowledge: The Biological Roots of Human Understanding* (with Humberto Maturana), and *The Embodied Mind: Cognitive Science and Human Experience.*

2. Trials and Tribulations

We found a signature image for the book in a photograph by the Japanese photographer Toshio Shibata. The image, which we eventually used on the top cover, shows a structural grid applied to the unstructured surface of a hillside. What you have is an incredible condition where the rectilinear deforms and adheres to the organic. We took that as a metaphor for what we were doing.

Our initial idea was to take the Shibata image and run a weather pattern through it, so that each layer of the image would register force.

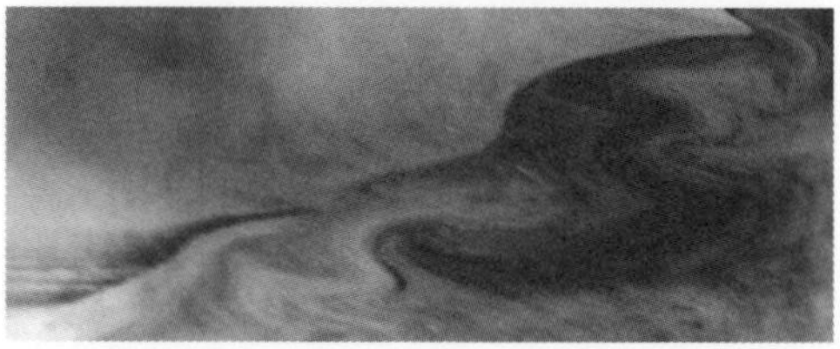

We wanted to go to press and continuously adjust the flow of ink, starting with yellow, moving to green, and so on. Our objective was to produce a beautiful, randomized effect: a mass object of unique specimens. It proved more difficult than it seemed. What happened is that everything turned brown. We'd adjust the color and it would still look brown. So in the end we decided we would do just one version and get it right.

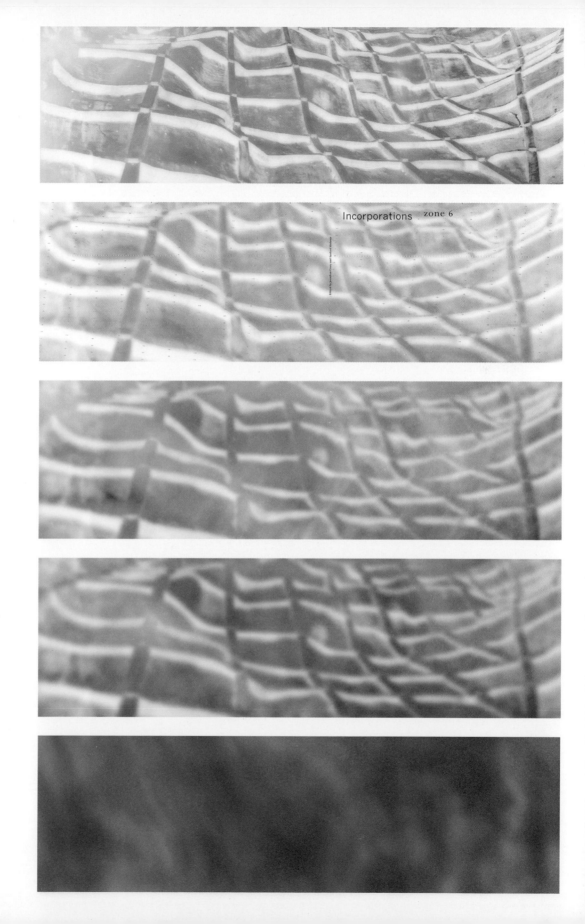

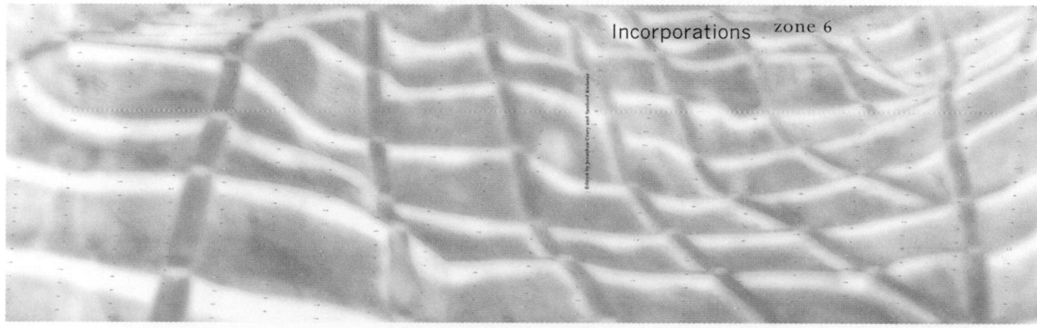
Incorporations zone 6
Edited by Jonathan Crary and Sanford Kwinter

3. Cover Typography
The cover title is an experiment in typographic transition. Each letterform was created through the averaging of four distinct but related fonts. We rendered the effects using strategies of addition, subtraction, and superimposition, exploring the space between existing moments of typographic stability. The results test the definition of form as a fixed entity.

corp

4. The Grid

This is the grid for *Incorporations.*

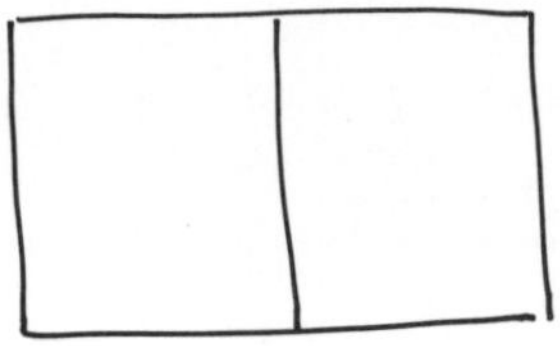

This grid has no privileged points. In a typical grid there are regulating lines. One of the exciting aspects of this work was to develop coherence out of a free movement where every point in the space was charged with an equal potential. At the same time, we remained concerned with legibility. The fact is that readers access information according to a history of access. This history determines how people read books and how, in turn, information will be organized. Our task as designers has involved deciding how to work with or against these inherited conventions.

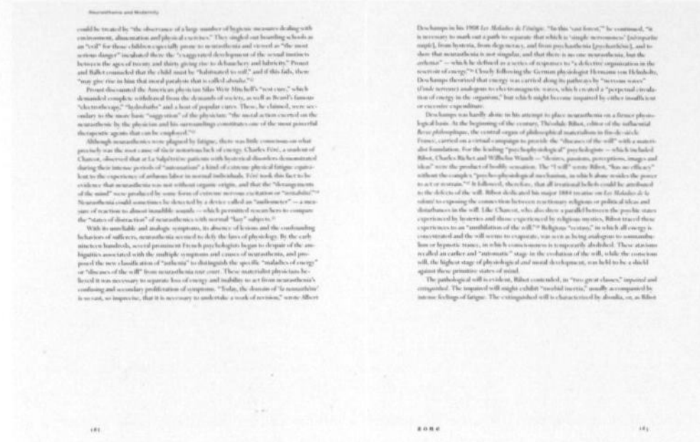

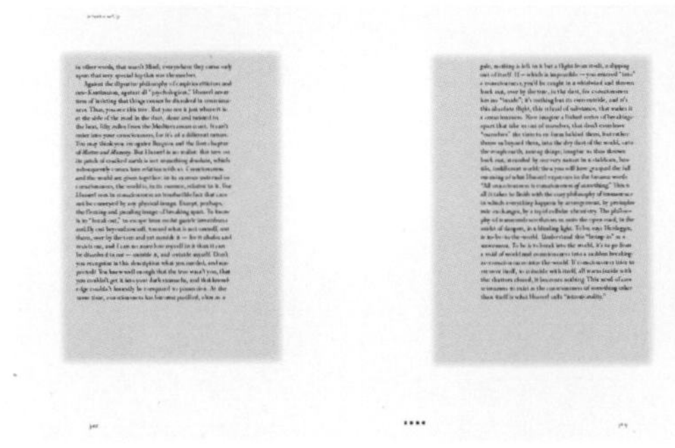

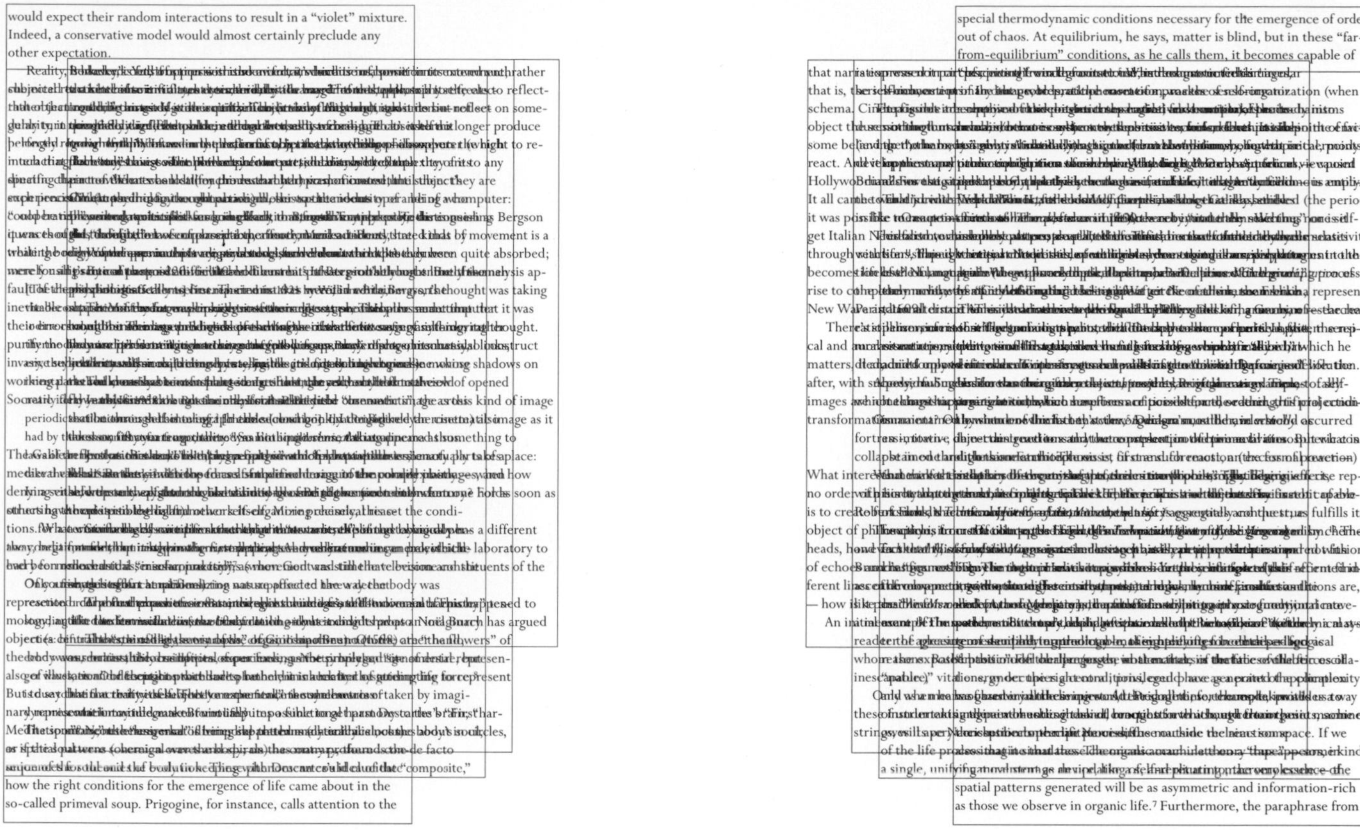

would expect their random interactions to result in a "violet" mixture.
Indeed, a conservative model would almost certainly preclude any
other expectation.
how the right conditions for the emergence of life came about in the
so-called primeval soup. Prigogine, for instance, calls attention to the
special thermodynamic conditions necessary for the emergence of order
out of chaos. At equilibrium, he says, matter is blind, but in these "far-
from-equilibrium" conditions, as he calls them, it becomes capable of
spatial patterns generated will be as asymmetric and information-rich
as those we observe in organic life.7 Furthermore, the paraphrase from

Four superimposed text areas show the consistency of the baseline grid. Unlike *Zone 1/2*, *Zone 6* uses bilateral symmetry.

5. Transformational Solids and the Schmoo

Very early on, we decided that we wanted to introduce a curve into the book. We tackled the problem in a number of ways. First, we developed the idea of "transformational solids," then we built a shape that could generate non-rectilinear text areas, and, finally, we placed pages in an animated sequence. The problem was, it looked like a Schmoo. It looked too silly to use. Despite our valiant efforts, we were stuck between a high concept and a goofy application.

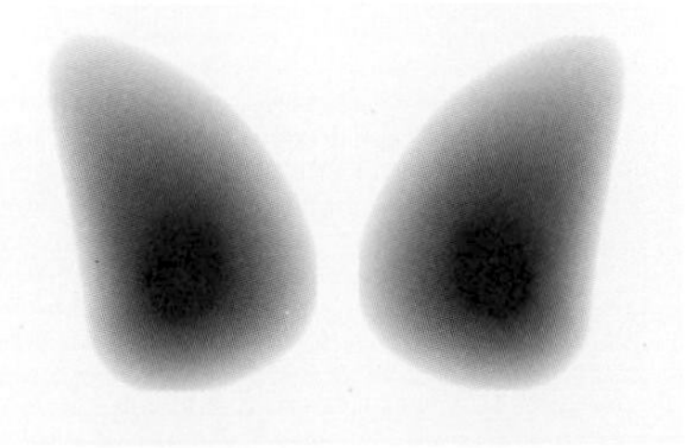

At the depth of our despair, we came up with an alternate idea that involved maintaining the rectilinear within the space of the page. We imagined the page as having depth, and into that space we inserted a series of shapes (or templates) that would evolve in a nonlinear way, changing from one text surface area to another along a curve.

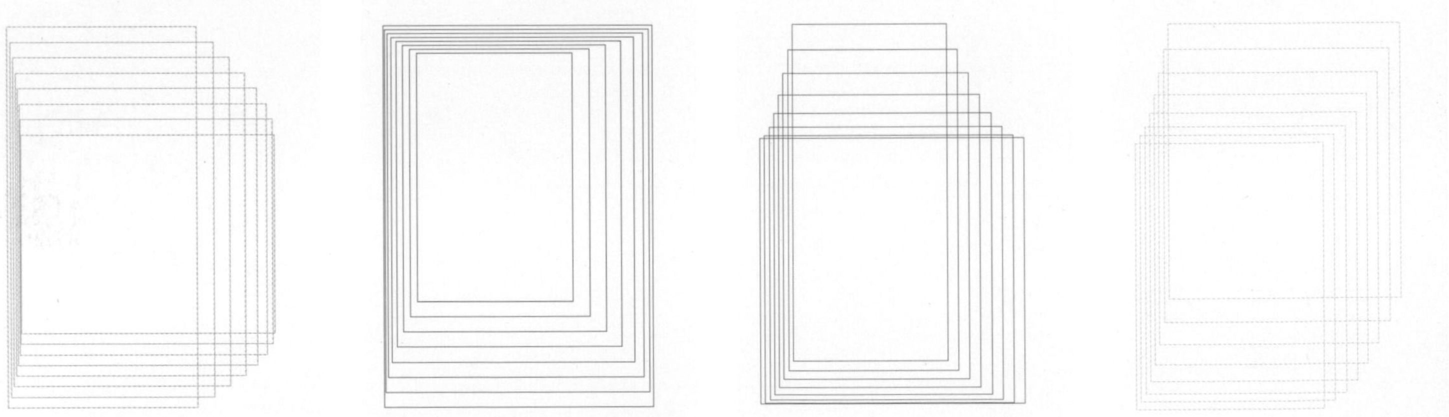

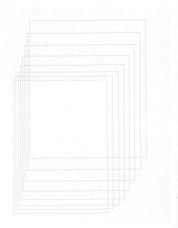

We eventually created four solid objects, which we sliced into thirteen sections. On the surface of any given page, the solid is not readily apparent. Yet, as an intervening force, it produces an effect on a structural level.

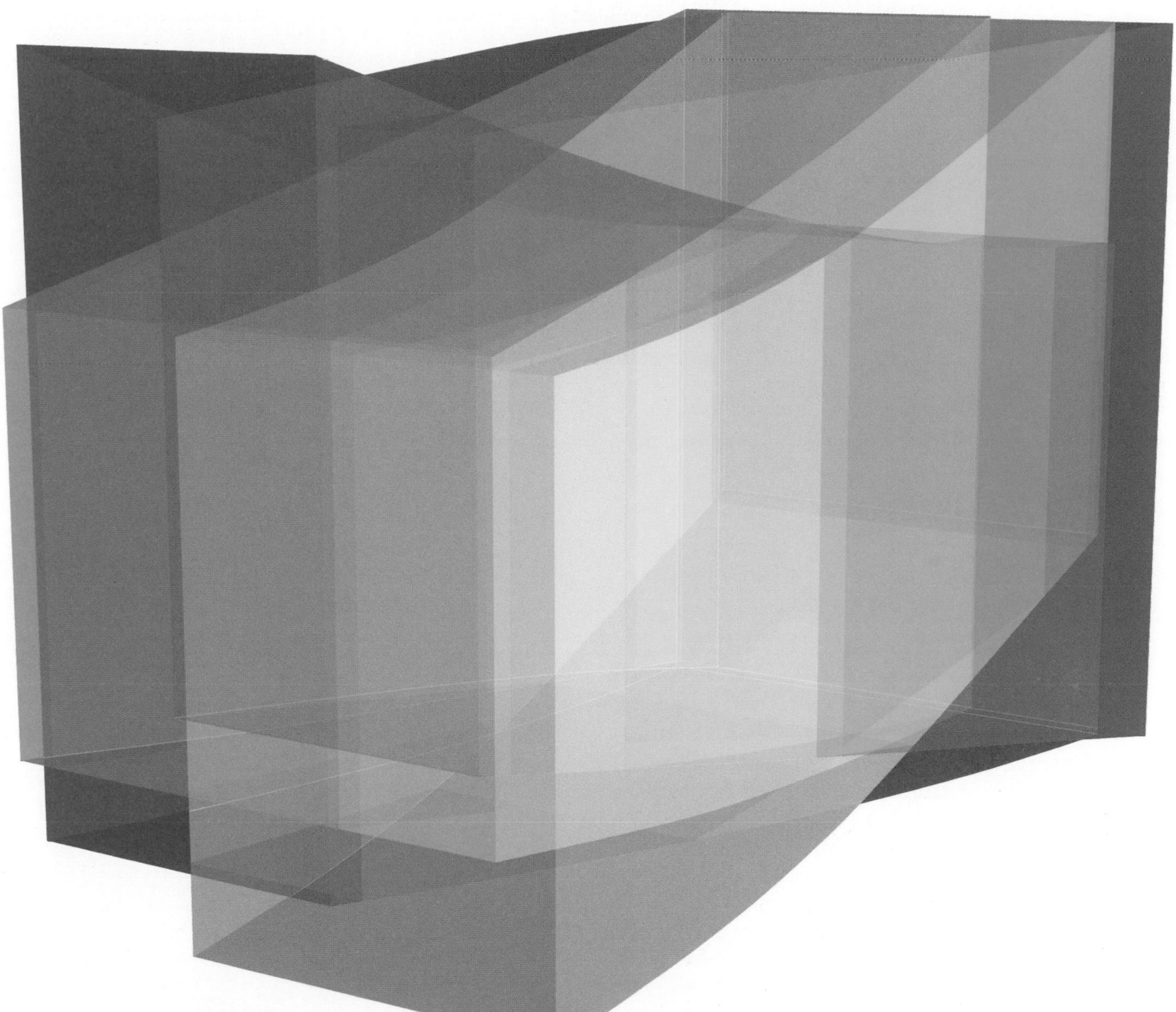

Four transformational solids

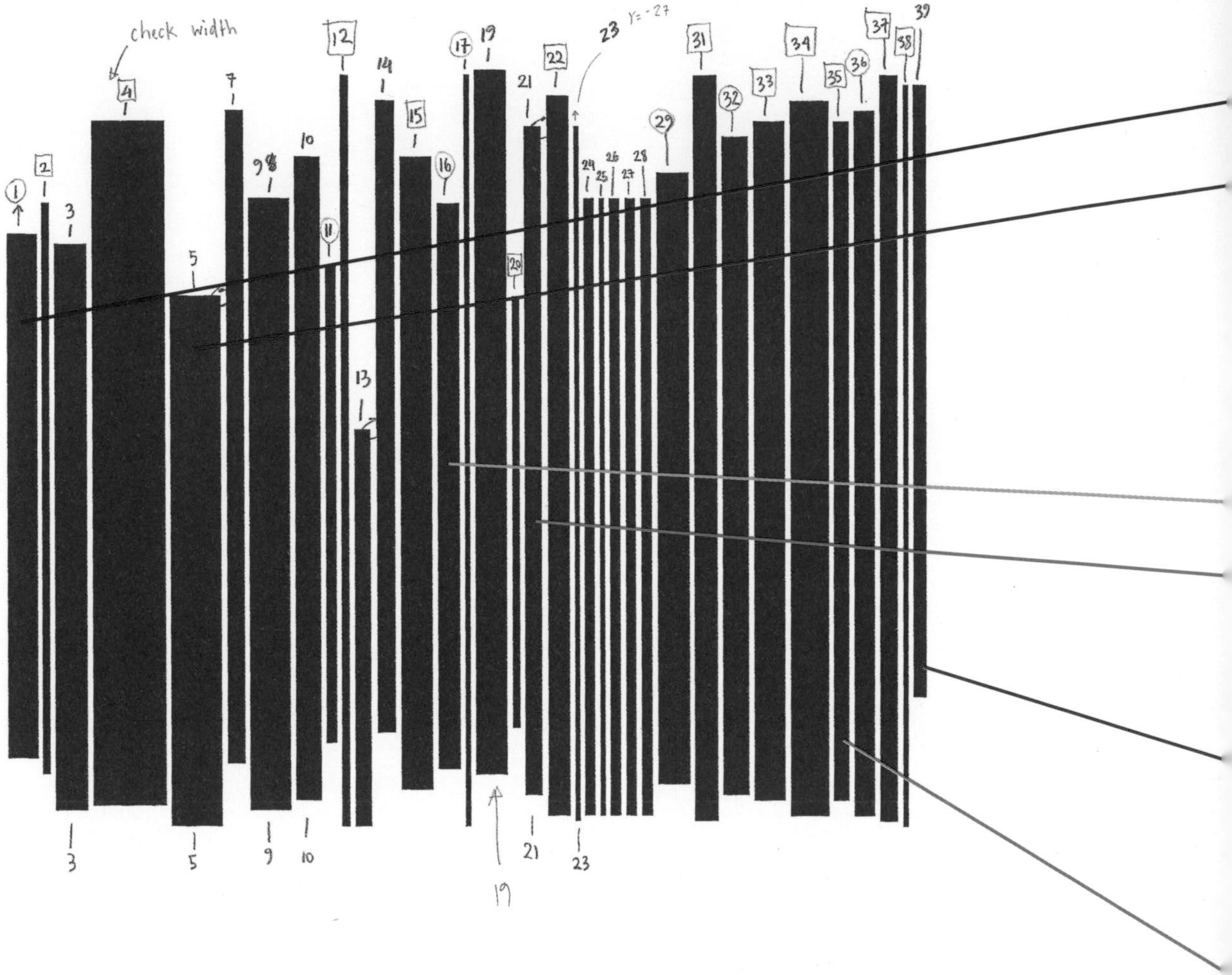

6. Constant Total Length

When it came to the organizing concept for the final object, Sanford and I developed something we called the "constant total length approach." The idea was to imagine that the book was a long piece of string—a constant length with two fixed points and some slack. Instead of designing the book as a sequence of discrete units, we approached everything in the book via its connection to everything else. Information is expected to travel within this formulation. Every time you "pull" one section, it ripples through the book, particularly affecting those elements in close proximity.

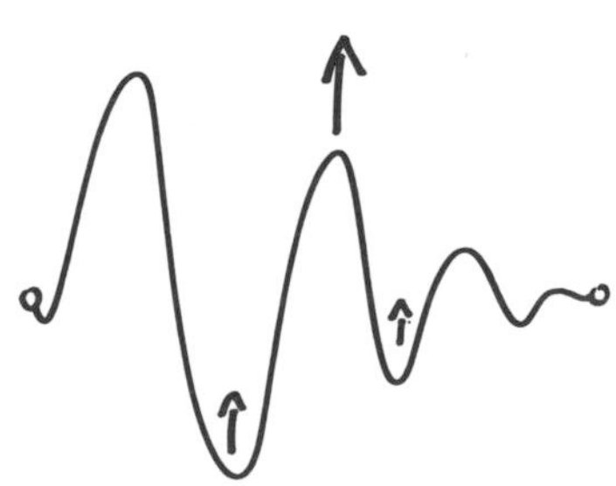

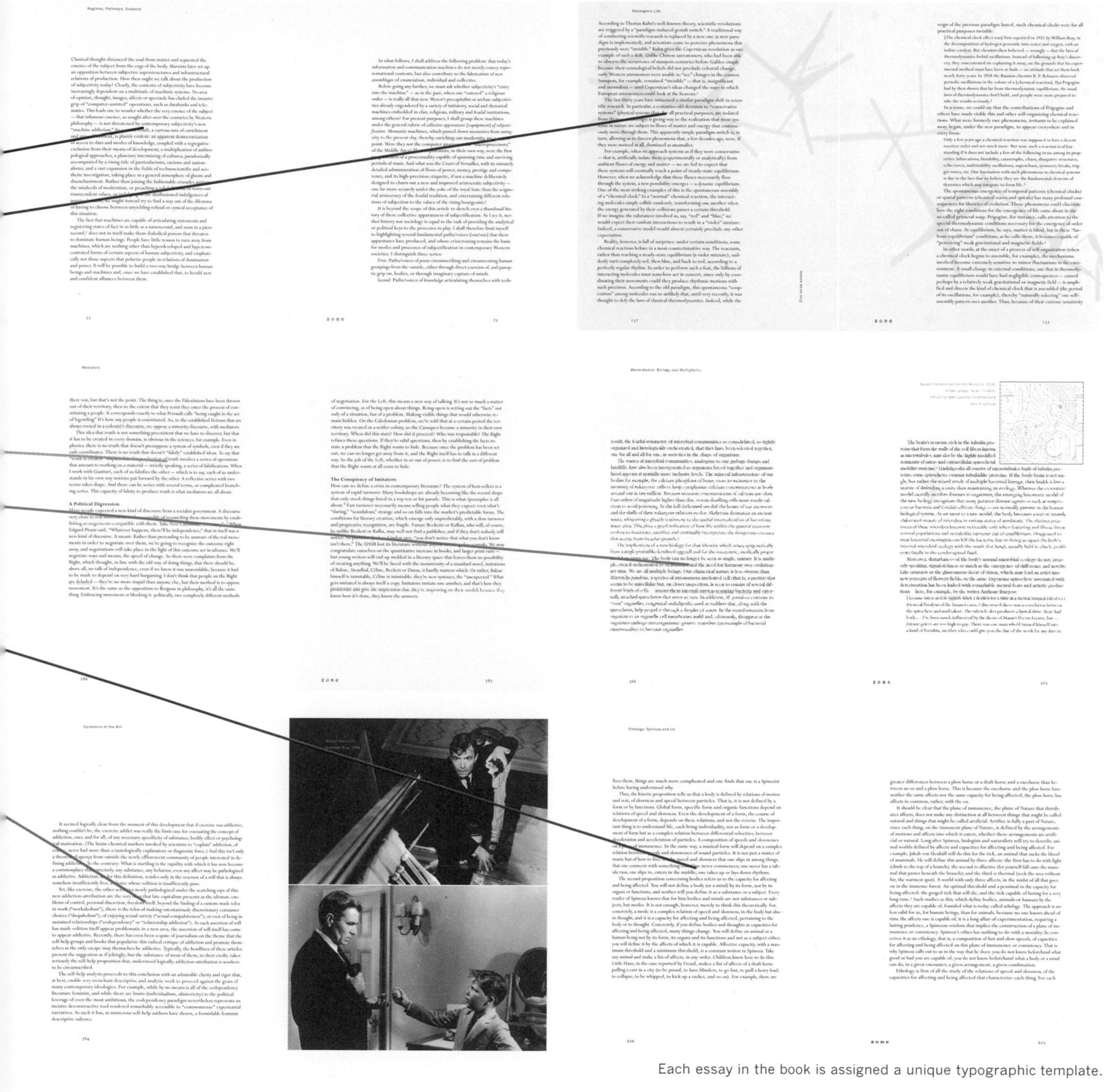

Each essay in the book is assigned a unique typographic template.

7. Triggers and Blooms

While working on *Zone 6*, Sanford Kwinter and I had numerous telephone conversations that were often deliriously exciting. In one, we came up with the idea of triggers and blooms. It describes our interest in catalytic thresholds, those moments when you trip a wire and initiate an effect. (A bloom might denote that moment when a sequence of images comes to the surface.) We imagined a system where information enclosed in blooms could be explosively released by a series of triggers. Each bloom was like a loaded film projector standing in an unlit, stainless-steel room. A gun fires, the bullet ricochets off every surface, finally hitting the trigger on the projector. Then the film plays. Our idea was to embed these triggers and blooms in the work. At some interval the switch will be released. It may take a long time, it may take a few seconds. The point is that you can't calculate when it's going to happen, but you know it will.

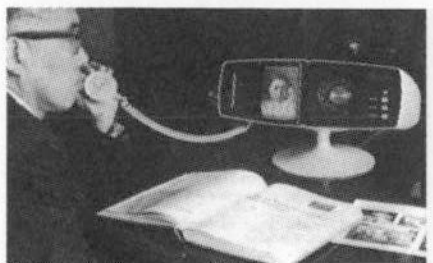

Project for a Glossary of the Twentieth Century

J. G. Ballard

X-ray Does the body still exist at all, in any but the most mundane sense? Its role has been steadily diminished, so that it seems little more than a ghostly shadow seen on the X-ray plate of our moral disapproval. We are now entering a colonialist phase in our attitudes to the body, full of paternalistic notions that conceal a ruthless exploitation carried out for its own good. This brutish creature must be housed, sparingly nourished, restricted to the minimum of sexual activity needed to reproduce itself and submitted to every manner of enlightened and improving patronage. Will the body at last rebel, tip all those vitamins, douches and aerobic schedules into Boston harbor and throw off the colonialist oppressor?

Typewriter It types us, encoding its own linear bias across the free space of the imagination.

Zipper This small but astute machine has found an elegant way of restraining and rediscovering all the lost enchantments of the flesh.

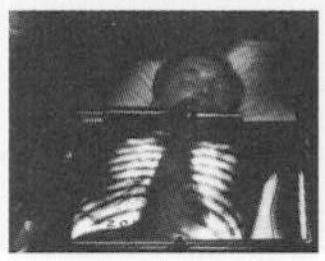

Jazz Music's jettisoned short-term memory, and no less poignant for that.

Telephone A shrine to the desperate hope that one day the world will listen to us.

Chaplin Chaplin's great achievement was to discredit totally the body, and to ridicule every notion of the dignity of gesture. Ponderous men move around him

like lead-booted divers trying to anchor the central nervous system to the seabed of time and space.

Trench warfare The body as sewer, the gutter of its own abattoir, flushing away its fears and aggressions.

The pill Nature's one step back in order to take two steps forward, presumably into the more potent evolutionary possibilities of wholly conceptualized sex.

Aerodynamism Streamlining satisfies the dream of flight without the effort of growing wings. Aerodynamics is the motion sculpture of non-Euclidean space-time.

Pornography The body's chaste and unerotic dream of itself.

Time and motion studies I am both myself and the shape that the universe makes around me. Time and motion studies represent our attempt to occupy the smallest, most modest niche in the surrounding universe.

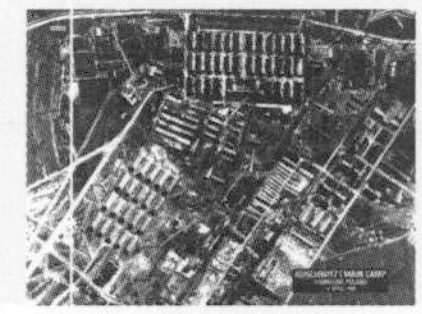

Prosthetics The castration complex raised to the level of an art form.

Biochemical warfare Nerve gases — the patient and long-awaited revenge of the inorganic world against the organic.

Hallucinogenic drugs The kaleidoscope's view of the eye.

The Warren Commission Report The novelization of the Zapruder film.

Genocide The economies of mass production applied to self-disgust.

Phenomenology The central nervous system's brave gamble that it exists.

Crowd theory Claustrophobia masquerading as agoraphobia or even, conceivably, Malthusianism.

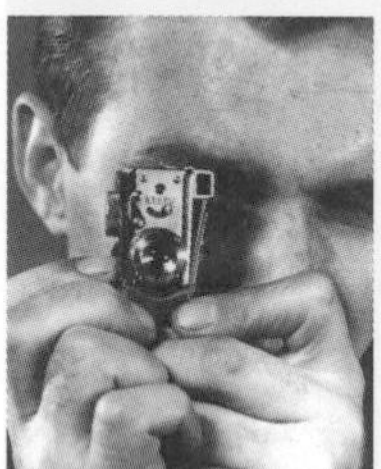

Lysenkoism A forlorn attempt not merely to colonize the botanical kingdom, but to instill a proper sense of the puritan work ethic and the merits of self-improvement.

Robotics The moral degradation of the machine.

Suburbs Do suburbs represent the city's convalescent zone or a genuine step forward into a new psychological realm, at once more passive but of far greater imaginative potential, like that of a sleeper before the onset of REM sleep? Unlike its unruly city counterpart, the suburban body has been wholly domesticated, and one can say that the suburbs constitute a huge petting zoo, with the residents' bodies providing the stock of furry mammals.

Forensics On the autopsy table science and pornography meet and fuse.

Miniaturization Dreams of becoming very small predate Alice, but now the probability grows that all the machines in the world, like the gold in Fort Knox, might be held in one heavily guarded location, protected as much from themselves as from the rest of us. Computers will continue to miniaturize themselves, though, eventually disappearing into a microverse where their ever-vaster calculations and mathematical models will become one with the quarks and the charms.

The Vietnam War Two wholly incompatible martial systems collided, with desperate result. Could the Vietcong, given a little more TV savvy, have triumphed sooner by launching an all-women guerrilla army against the *Playboy*-reading GIs? "First Air Cavalry ground elements in Operation Pegasus killed 350 enemy women in scattered contacts yesterday, while Second Division Marines killed 124 women communists...."

Isadora Duncan The machine had its own fling with her overdisciplined body, the rear wheel of her car dancing its lethal little jig around the end of her scarf.

Furniture and industrial design Our furniture constitutes an external constellation of our skin areas and body postures. It's curious that the least imaginative of all forms of furniture has been the bed.

Schizophrenia To the sane, always the most glamorous of mental diseases, since it seems to represent the insane's idea of the normal. Just as the agnostic world keeps alive its religious festivals in order to satisfy the vacation needs of its workforce, so when medical science has conquered all disease certain mental afflictions, schizophrenia chief among them, will be mimicked for social reasons. By the same token, the great appeal of alcoholism, and the reason why it will never be eliminated, is that it provides an opportunity for honorable and even heroic failure.

Body-building Asexual masturbation, in which the entire musculature simulates a piece of erectile tissue. But orgasm seems indefinitely delayed.

Epidemiology Catastrophe theory in slow motion.

Fashion A recognition that nature has endowed us with one skin too few, and that a fully sentient being should wear its nervous system externally.

Automobile All the millions of cars on this planet are stationary, and their apparent motion constitutes mankind's greatest collective dream.

Skyscraper The eight-hour city, with a tidal population clinging to the foreshore between Earth and the yet to be navigated oceans of space.

Pasolini Sociopath as saint.

Transistor If the wheel is 1 on the binary scale, the transistor is 0 — but what will be 1000001?

Retroviruses Pathogens that might have been invented by science fiction. The greater the advances of modern medicine, the more urgent our need for diseases we cannot understand.

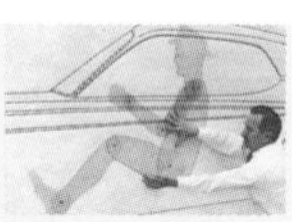

Money The original digital clock.

Abortion Do-it-yourself genocide.

Science fiction The body's dream of becoming a machine.

Answering machines They are patiently training us to think in a language they have yet to invent.

Genetics Nature's linguistic system.

Food Our delight in food is rooted in our immense relish at the thought that, prospectively, we are eating ourselves.

Neurobiology Science's Sistine Chapel.

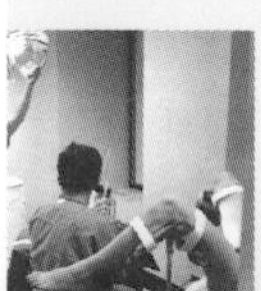

Criminal science The anatomizing of illicit desire, more exciting than desire itself.

Camouflage The camouflaged battleship or bunker must never efface itself completely, but confuse our recognition systems by one moment being itself, and the next not itself. Many impersonators and politicians exploit the same principle.

Cybernetics The totalitarian systems of the future will be docile and subservient, like super-efficient servants, and all the more threatening for that.

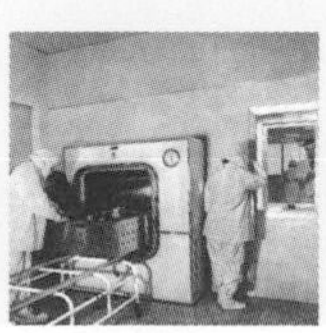

Disease control A proliferation of imaginary diseases may soon be expected, satisfying our need for a corrupt version of ourselves.

Ergonomics The Protestant work ethic disguised as a kinaesthetic language.

Personal computers Perhaps unwisely, the brain is subcontracting many of its core functions, creating a series of branch economies that may one day amalgamate and mount a management buy-out.

War The possibility at last exists that war may be defeated on the linguistic plane. If war is an extreme metaphor, we may defeat it by devising metaphors that are even more extreme.

International Standard Time Is time an obsolete mental structure we have inherited from our distant forebears, who invented serial time as a means of dismantling a simultaneity they were unable to grasp as a single whole? Time should be decartelized, and everyone should set his or her own.

Satellites Ganglions in search of an interplanetary brain.

Modernism The Gothic of the information age.

Apollo mission The first demonstration, arranged for our benefit by the machine, of the dispensability of man.

Note: The glossary headings were among a list supplied by the editors to Mr. Ballard, who provided their substance.

8. The Zone Morph

In an effort to find a solution to the running head, we created the concept of typographic moguls. Imagine that there is a hillside with moguls on it, and the tips of the moguls are typefaces. We began at the top, rolled a marble down the curved slope, and animated a sequence that made each typographic mogul one moment in a continuous transformation. We traced the effects.

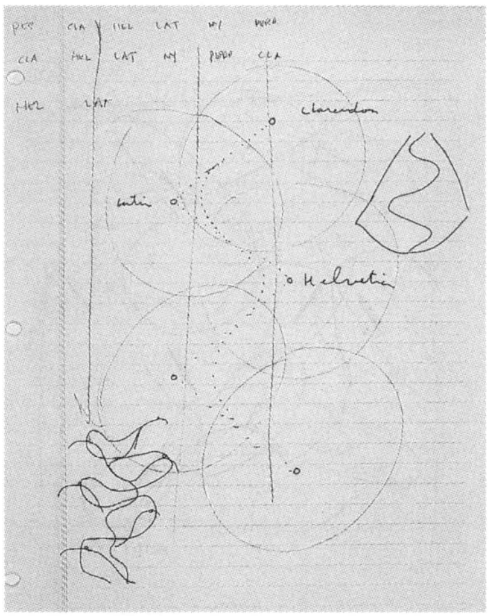

The end result is 380 new fonts; every page has a unique rendering of the word "zone" that is different from that of the page before it. If you glance through the book, it's almost imperceptible, but the type changes continually, from Bodoni to DIN and then to Futura, and so on, each font slipping slowly into the other.

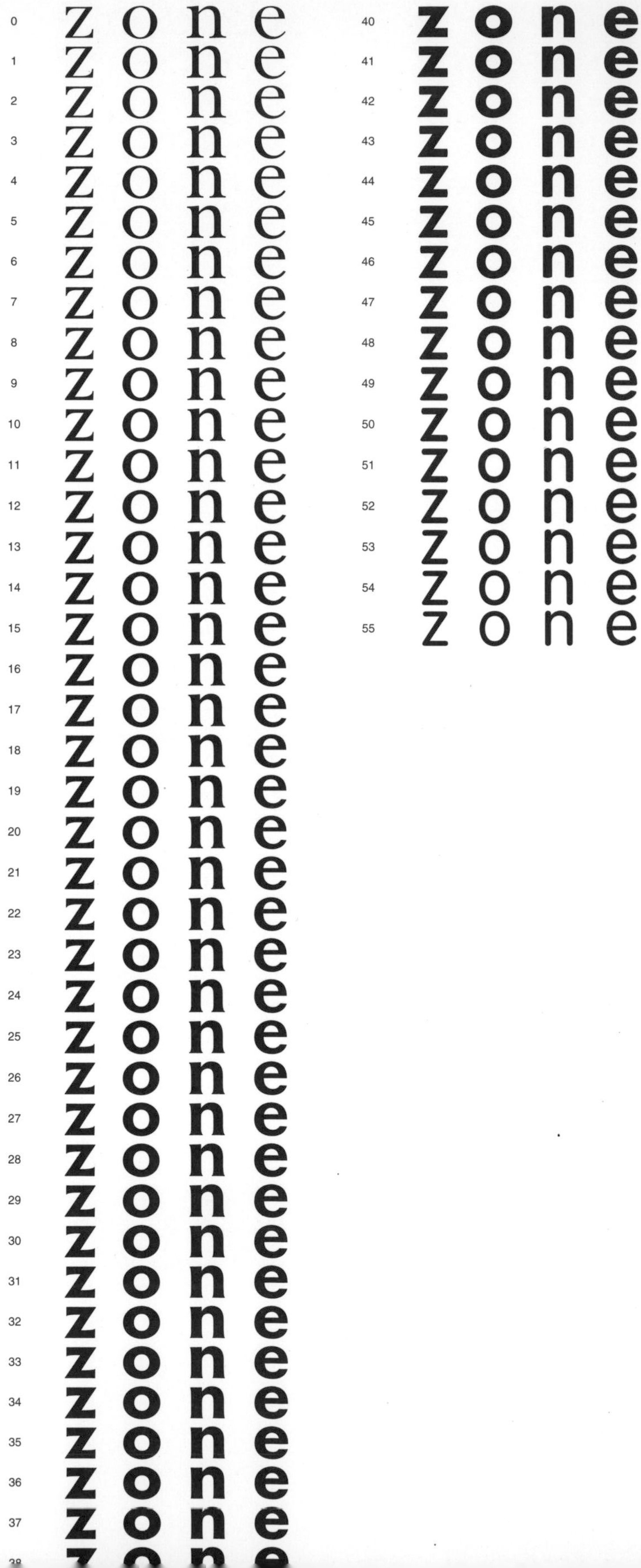

170 z o n e
171 z o n e
172 z o n e
173 z o n e
174 z o n e
175 z o n e
176 z o n e
177 z o n e
178 z o n e
179 z o n e
180 z o n e
181 z o n e
182 z o n e
183 z o n e
184 z o n e
185 z o n e
186 z o n e
187 z o n e
188 z o n e
189 z o n e
190 z o n e
191 z o n e
192 z o n e
193 z o n e
194 z o n e
195 z o n e
196 z o n e
197 z o n e
198 z o n e
199 z o n e
200 z o n e
201 z o n e
202 z o n e
203 z o n e
204 z o n e
205 z o n e

285 z o n e
286 z o n e
287 z o n e
288 z o n e
289 z o n e
290 z o n e
291 z o n e
292 z o n e
293 z o n e
294 z o n e
295 z o n e

295 z o n e
296 z o n e
297 z o n e
298 z o n e
299 z o n e
300 z o n e
301 z o n e
302 z o n e
303 z o n e
304 z o n e
305 z o n e
306 z o n e
307 z o n e
308 z o n e
309 z o n e
310 z o n e
311 z o n e
312 z o n e
313 z o n e
314 z o n e
315 z o n e
316 z o n e
317 z o n e
318 z o n e
319 z o n e
320 z o n e

345 z o n e
346 z o n e
347 z o n e
348 z o n e
349 z o n e
350 z o n e
351 z o n e
352 z o n e
353 z o n e
354 z o n e
355 z o n e
356 z o n e
357 z o n e
358 z o n e
359 z o n e
360 z o n e
361 z o n e
362 z o n e
363 z o n e
364 z o n e
365 z o n e
366 z o n e
367 z o n e
368 z o n e
369 z o n e
370 z o n e
371 z o n e
372 z o n e
373 z o n e
374 z o n e
375 z o n e
376 z o n e
377 z o n e
378 z o n e
379 z o n e
380 z o n e

9. Color

One of the things we were working with in this book is *Klangfarbenmelodiekompozition* (a long way of describing our approach to color composition). In homage to Schoenberg and Stockhausen, we decided to produce one near-constant pitch. Instead of having a composition that is about dramatic pitch change, we maintained the pitch and changed the timbre to produce effects. The timbre is hue, the pitch is tone.

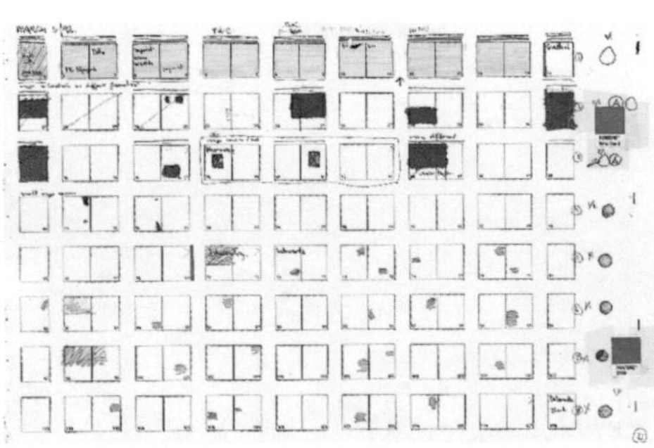

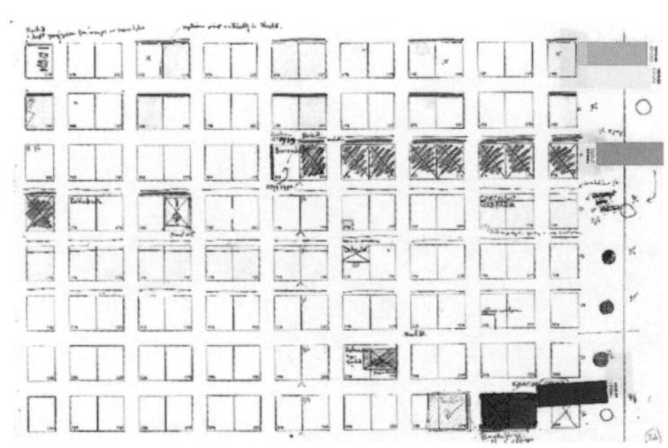

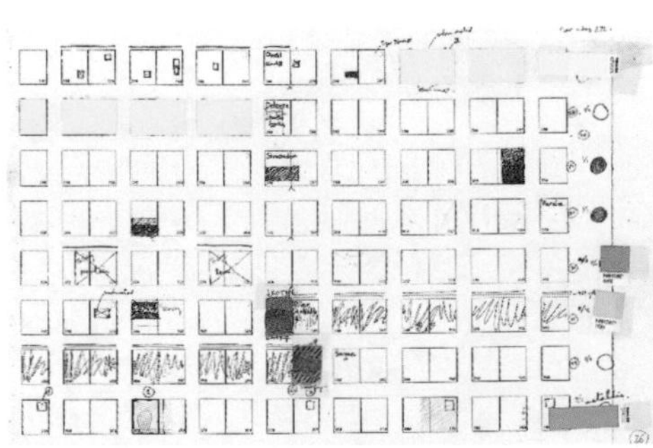

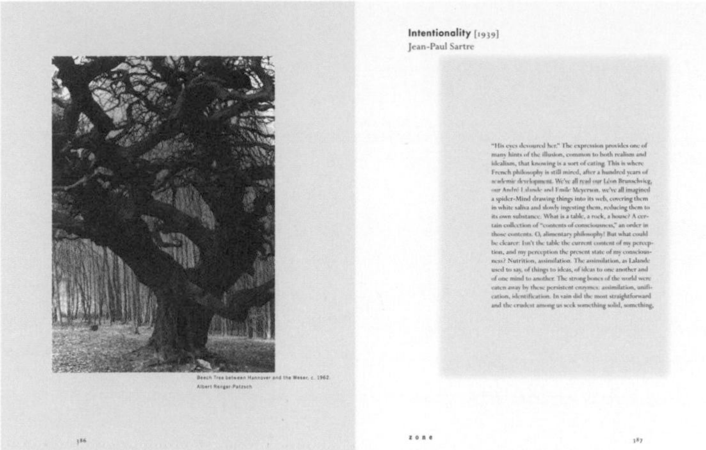

Intentionality [1939]
Jean-Paul Sartre
Beech Tree between Hannover and the Weser, c. 1962.
Albert Renger-Patzsch
386
zone
387

Nonorganic Life
Liquid crystals.
zone

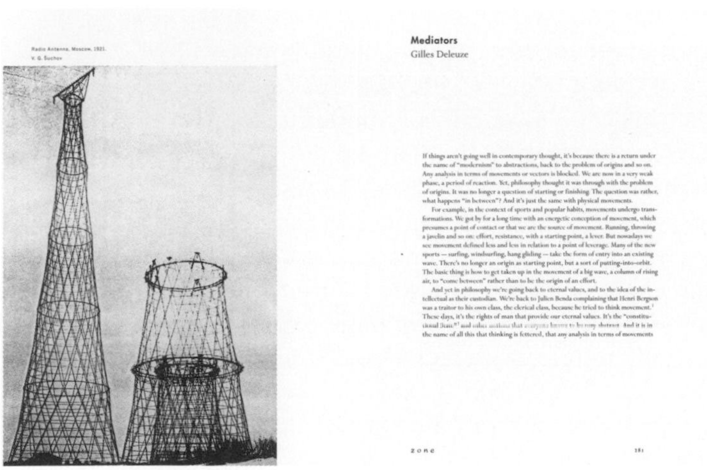

Radio Antenna, Moscow, 1921.
V. G. Suchov
Mediators
Gilles Deleuze
zone

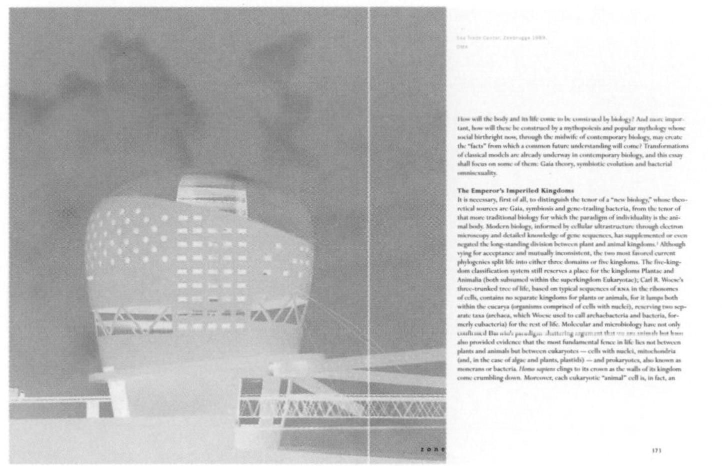

The Emperor's Imperiled Kingdoms
zone

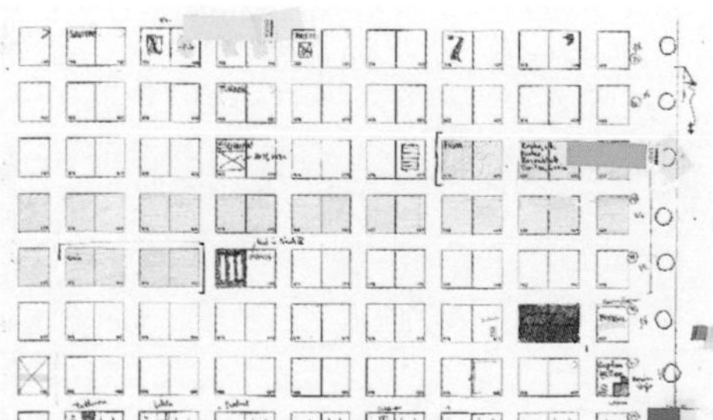

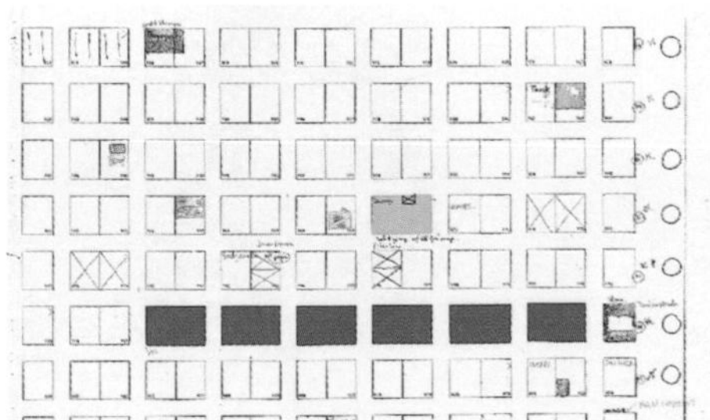

Conclusion

Readers don't immediately register the book's many layers. They may say, "I love the color," or "It feels great"; but it usually takes them longer to get to a place of deeper access. But even when the reader can't articulate his or her response, it doesn't mean the book is not working, or that it's not moving them in a different way. In fact, our argument is that it has more impact because it is happening below the surface.

Contemporary image culture colonizes our attention at a certain level and arrests it there. I like to think that our work unfolds on a subliminal level—that is, it works beneath the threshold of conscious perception. This is where we want the effects to be felt.

A distinction that applies to all the work of the studio can be found between the *image* of complexity and real complexity. Is the work an illustration of a complex thing or is it actually a complex thing? Today, there is huge production of illustrative complexity striving to be convincingly complex.

Imagine a cone of vision. The eyeball is the narrowest point of the cone, which expands to meet the page. What has happened in design is that designers have begun to put filters into the cone by adding layers between the eye and the content. Designers insert substance between the page and the reader, effectively filling up the cone of vision and, in some cases, clogging it. This phenomenon does not pertain only to magazines. Videos, films, billboard treatments, posters, and print advertising are similarly caught up in illustrating complexity, using superimpositions, out-of-register photographs, hypersaturated colors—all the cool stuff of recent vintage. The content may still be there, but it becomes illegible. The problem is that the cone of vision is a limited space and will accommodate only so much before it is oversaturated. Once this occurs, the reader can no longer see through the filters to the content.

Incorporations is our first conscious effort to clear the cone. Instead of working in the cone, we worked in the depth of the page and produced an entirely different kind of work. The beauty of this approach is that there's no limit to what can be done because you always maintain clarity in the cone, and you can, if you need more space, simply excavate more.

The tendency in the world is to label the people who want clarity as conservative, and the people who want "hip" or "funky" as innovative. If you think about it for even a second, you realize that it's a ridiculous division. Taking away clarity of communication: Who wanted that in history? Not the innovators.

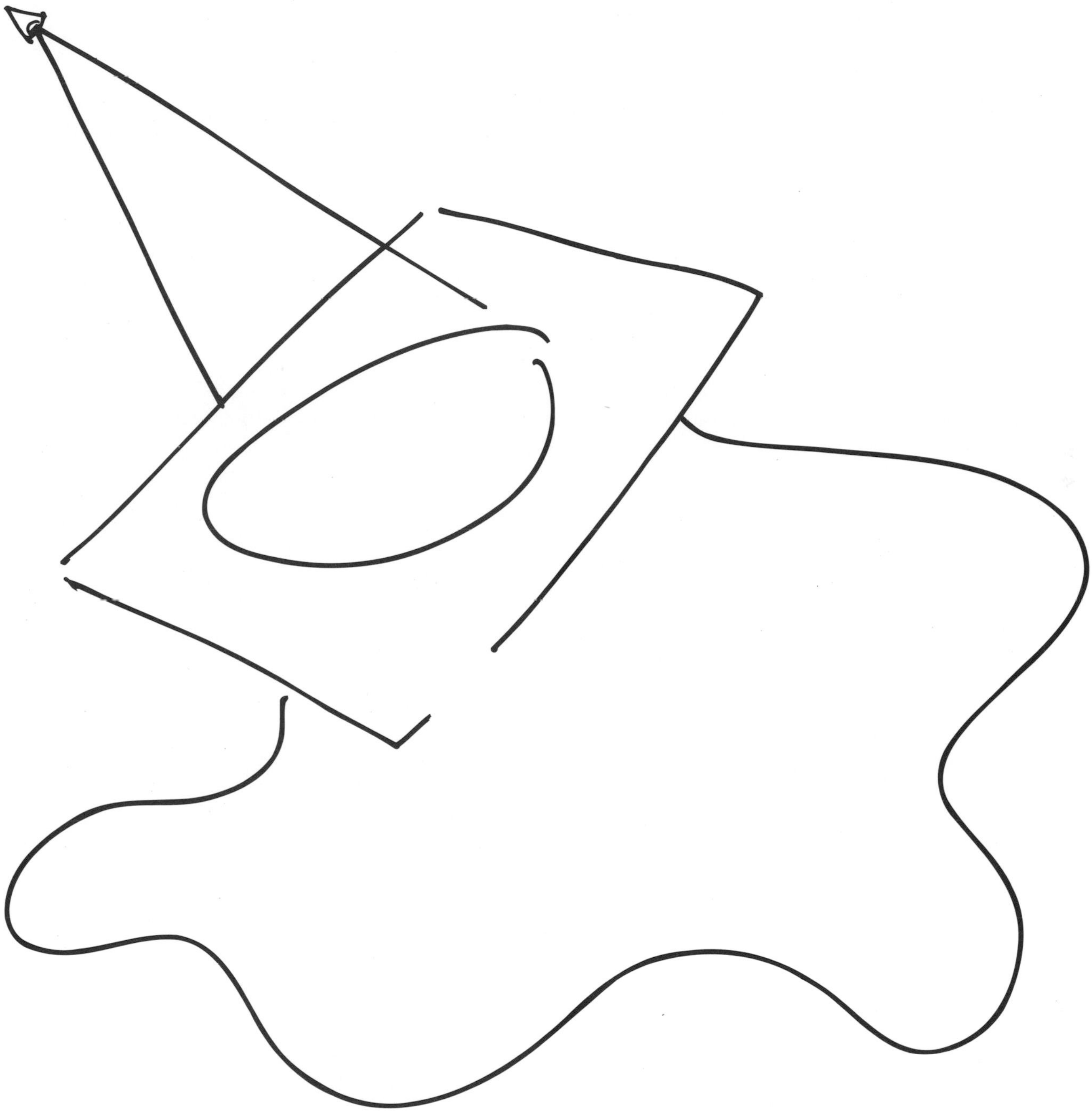

Imprint

Swerve came out of a crisis at Zone. When Zone Books started, the intention was to bring a European intellectual project to an English-speaking audience that had not had access to it previously. Even though the Zone authors—Henri Bergson, Gilles Deleuze, Pierre Clastres—had invented an outsider discourse, they had themselves become giants of Continental thought. To add something less prestigious to the list became increasingly difficult as Zone Books took on a greater aura in the publishing context. The barriers to a book's inclusion kept climbing.

Still, some of us wanted to do things that were more speculative, more grassroots, and which involved work by new, less-established figures. Writers need the process of publishing to become who they will be. It is impossible to know in advance where the next profound work will emerge, so you have to experiment. But it becomes difficult to experiment in a context where every author published is of formidable stature. Herein lay the dilemma. Swerve provided the way out by creating an imprint for which some editors could take exclusive responsibility. That's how Swerve was born.

An abandoned cover study.

Swerve Editions
Edited by Jonathan Crary, Sanford Kwinter, and Bruce Mau
New York: Zone Books, 1991–present

The published cover.

War in the Age of Intelligent Machines
by Manuel De Landa
New York: Zone Books, Swerve Editions, 1991

The paperback cover for *War in the Age of Intelligent Machines* ranks as one of the worst the studio has ever done. Yet, despite this dubious distinction, the book has many redeeming qualities. It helped map the way for subsequent projects. The opening credit sequence, for example, takes the reader directly into the thick of things. The vertical typography on the cover became a template for our work with the Getty Research Institute. Projects like this show that even when things are not perfectly realized initially, their energy remains in the system and may come back to inform other projects.

We did a series of visual spreads that compressed the book's key concepts. The idea was that if you took them out to make a pamphlet, you would have the essence of the book. This produced an agit-prop feel, an aura of authenticity, which was augmented by the project's super-cheap production.

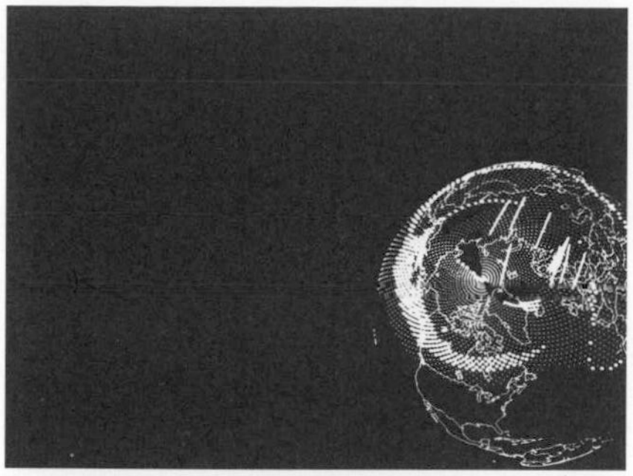

Swerve Editions
Edited by Jonathan Crary, Sanford Kwinter and Bruce Mau

Manuel DeLanda War in the Age of Intelligent Machines

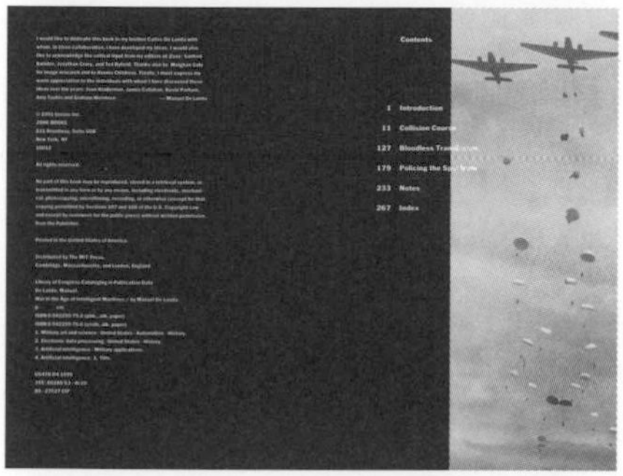
Contents
1 Introduction
11 Collision Course
127 Bloodless Transition
179 Policing the Spectrum
233 Notes
267 Index

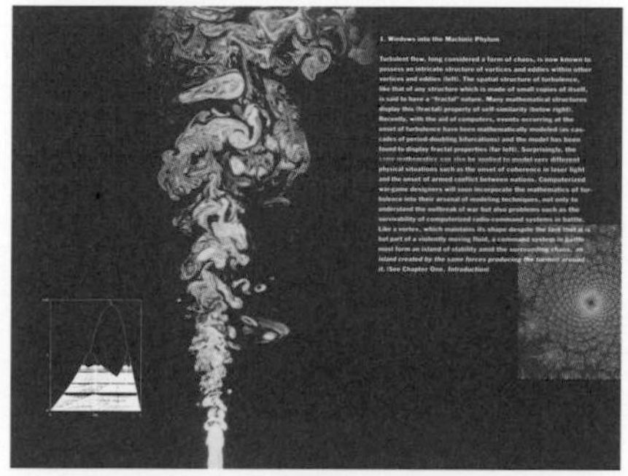
1. Windows into the Machinic Phylum

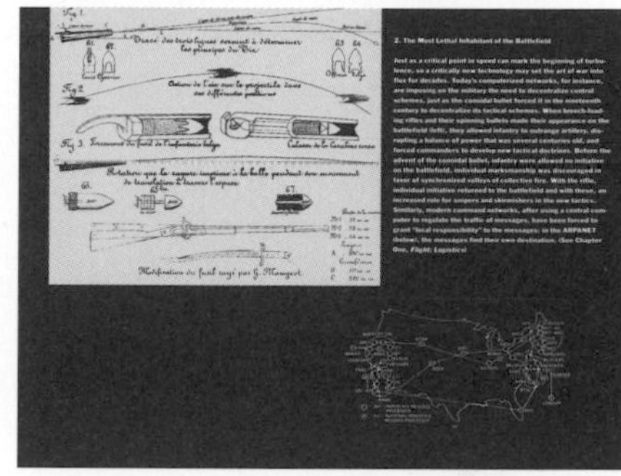
2. The Most Lethal Inhabitant of the Battlefield

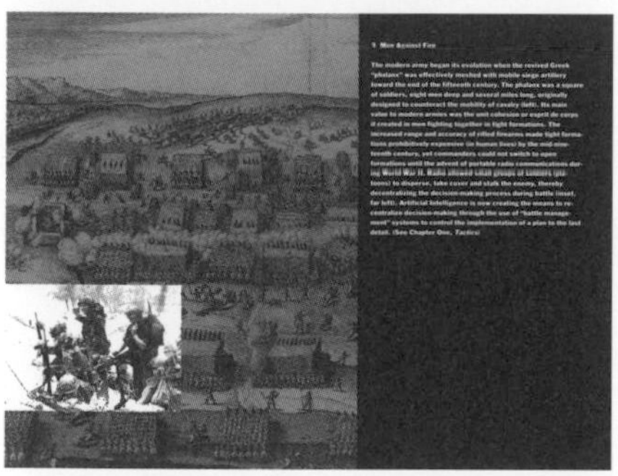
3. Man Against Fire

4. Fortified Walls: Dematerialize To Become Radar Curtains

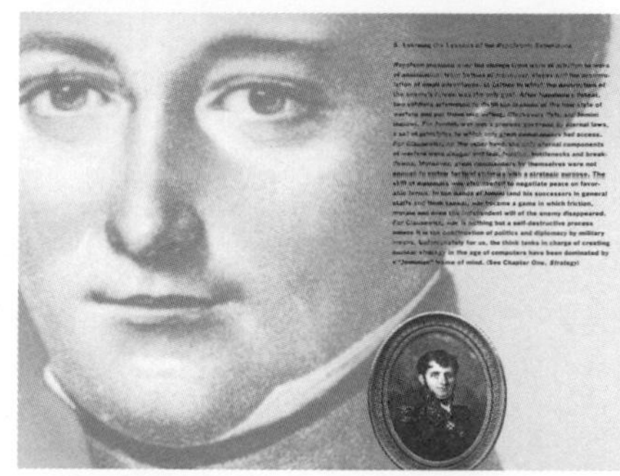

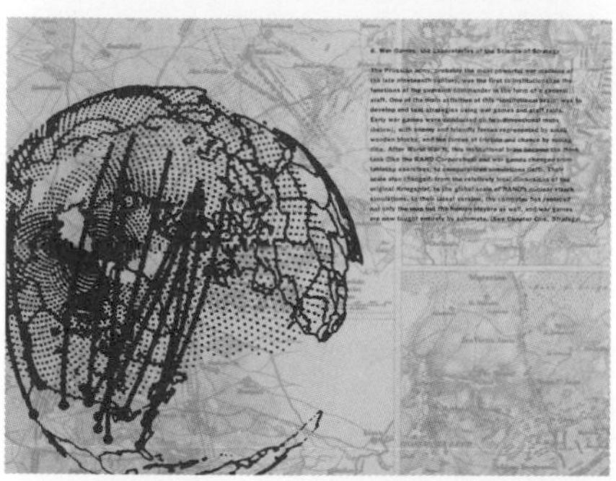

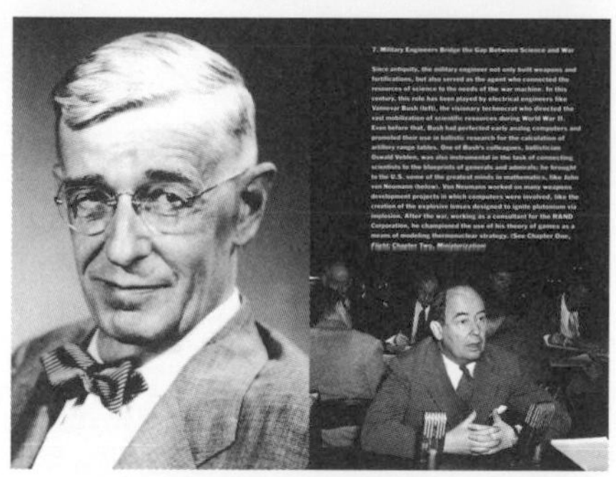
7. Military Engineers Bridge the Gap Between Science and War

9. The Phylogenetic Lineage of Robotic Weapons

10. The Worlds of Visible and Invisible Radiation

Following in the wake of his groundbreaking work, *War in the Age of Intelligent Machines*, Manuel De Landa presents a brilliant, radical synthesis of historical developments during the last one thousand years. *A Thousand Years of Nonlinear History* sketches the outlines of a renewed materialist history in the tradition of Fernand Braudel, Gilles Deleuze, and Félix Guattari, while engaging—in an unprecedented manner—the critical new understanding of material processes derived from the sciences of dynamics. Working against prevailing attitudes that see history merely as the arena of texts, discourses, ideologies, and metaphors, De Landa traces the concrete movements and interplays of matter and energy through human populations in the last millennium. The result is an entirely novel approach to the study of human societies and their always mobile, semi-stable forms, cities, economies, technologies, and languages.

De Landa attacks three domains that have given shape to human societies. In every case—economics, biology, and linguistics—he discloses the self-directed processes of matter and energy interfacing with the whim and will of human history itself to form a panoramic vision of the West, free of rigid teleology and naive notions of progress, and even more important, free of any deterministic source for its urban, institutional, and technological forms. The source of all concrete forms in the West's history rather, are shown to derive from internal morphogenetic capabilities that lie within the flow of matter-energy itself.

Distributed by The MIT Press
DELTH ISBN 0-942299-31-0

A THOUSAND YEARS OF NONLINEAR HISTORY

Manuel De Landa

SWERVE

MANUEL DE LANDA A THOUSAND YEARS OF NONLINEAR HISTORY

ZONE BOOKS

When atoms are travelling straight down through empty space by their own weight, at quite indeterminate times and places, they swerve ever so little from their course, just so much that you would call it a change of direction. If it were not for this swerve, everything would fall downwards through the abyss of space. No collision would take place and no impact of atom on atom would be created. Thus nature would never have created anything.

—Lucretius

Swerve Editions text logo

A Thousand Years of Non-Linear History
by Manuel De Landa
New York: Zone Books, Swerve Editions, 1997

In contrast to *War in the Age of Intelligent Machines*, this is one of the best covers the studio has ever produced. The approach was to slice through a section of an image, like they do in DNA testing. The effect is consistent with the content of the book. It taps into a range of associations: abstraction, speed, layers, sediment, history, digital technology, surface, and depth. It manages to make all those things resonate simultaneously. You have a sense of history and of speed as signs operating at the same time—a sense of strong forward momentum, and of sedimentation, locked into a single image. The design is also completely inclusive, even incorporating the bar code (usually a hideous blot on the design).

On the inside, the text is designed to swell up and meet the reader at every chapter opening. We used blue ink for the text rather than black, and a sans-serif font, which was a real departure from Zone.

This book was also cheaply produced in keeping with the economic mandate of Swerve.

When atoms are travelling straight down through empty space by their own weight, at quite indeterminate times and places, they swerve ever so little from their course, just so much that you would call it a change of direction. If it were not for this swerve, everything would fall downwards through the abyss of space. No collision would take place and no impact of atom on atom would be created. Thus nature would never have created anything.

—Lucretius

Swerve Editions

Edited by Jonathan Crary, Sanford Kwinter, and Bruce Mau

A
THOUSAND
YEARS
OF
NONLINEAR
HISTORY
Manuel De Landa
Swerve Editions New York 1997

Geological History 1000–1700 A.D.

We live in a world populated by structures—a complex mixture of geological, biological, social, and linguistic constructions that are nothing but accumulations of materials shaped and hardened by history. Immersed as we are in this mixture, we cannot help but interact in a variety of ways with the other historical constructions that surround

us, and in these interactions we generate novel combinations, some of which possess emergent properties. In turn, these synergistic combinations, whether of human origin or not, become the raw material for further mixtures. This is how the population of structures inhabiting our planet has acquired its rich variety, as the entry of novel materials into the mix triggers wild proliferations of new forms.

In the organic world, for instance, soft tissue (gels and aerosols, muscle and nerve) reigned supreme until 500 million years ago. At that point, some of the conglomerations of fleshy matter-energy that made up life underwent a sudden *mineralization*, and a new material for constructing living creatures emerged: bone. It is almost as if the mineral world that had served as a substratum for the emergence of biological creatures was reasserting itself, confirming that geology, far from having been left behind as a primitive stage of the earth's evolution, fully coexisted with the soft, gelatinous newcomers. Primitive bone, a stiff, calcified central rod that would later become the vertebral column, made new forms of movement control possible among animals, freeing

them from many constraints and literally setting them into motion to conquer every available niche in the air, in water, and on land. And yet, while bone allowed the complexification of the animal phylum to which we, as vertebrates, belong, it never forgot its mineral origins: it is the living material that most easily petrifies, that most readily crosses the threshold back into the world of rocks. For that reason, much of the geological record is written with fossil bone.

The human endoskeleton was one of the many products of that ancient mineralization. Yet that is not the only geological infiltration that the human species has undergone. About eight thousand years ago, human populations began mineralizing again when they developed an urban *exoskeleton*: bricks of sun-dried clay became the building materials for their homes, which in turn surrounded and were surrounded by stone monuments and defensive walls. This exoskeleton served a purpose similar to its internal counterpart: to control the movement of human flesh in and out of a town's walls. The urban exoskeleton also regulated the motion of many other things: luxury objects, news, and food, for

example. In particular, the weekly markets that have always existed at the heart of most cities and towns constituted veritable motors, periodically concentrating people and goods from near and faraway regions and then setting them into motion again, along a variety of trade circuits.[1]

Thus, the urban infrastructure may be said to perform, for tightly packed populations of humans, the same function of motion control that our bones do in relation to our fleshy parts. And, in both cases, adding minerals to the mix resulted in a fantastic combinatorial explosion, greatly increasing the variety of animal and cultural designs. We must be careful when drawing these analogies, however. In particular, we must avoid the error of comparing cities to organisms, especially when the metaphor is meant to imply (as it has in the past) that both exist in a state of internal equilibrium, or homeostasis. Rather, urban centers and living creatures must be seen as *different* dynamical systems operating far from equilibrium, that is, traversed by more or less intense flows of matter-energy that provoke their unique metamorphoses.[2]

Indeed, urban morphogenesis has depended, from its ancient beginnings in the Fertile Crescent, on intensification of the consumption of nonhuman energy. The anthropologist Richard Newbold Adams, who sees social evolution as just another form that the self-organization of energy may take, has pointed out that the first such intensification was the cultivation of cereals.[3] Since plants, via photosynthesis, simply convert solar energy into sugars, cultivation increased the amount of solar energy that traversed human societies. When food production was further intensified, humanity crossed the bifurcation that gave rise to urban structures. The elites that ruled those early cities in turn made other intensifications possible—by developing large irrigation systems, for example—and urban centers mutated into their imperial form. It is important to emphasize, however, that cereal cultivation was only one of several possible ways of intensifying energy flow. As several anthropologists have pointed out, the emergence of cities may have followed *alternative routes to intensification*, as when the emergence of urban life in Peru fed off a reservoir of fish.[4] What matters is not agriculture per se, but the great increase in the flow of matter-energy through society, as well as the transformations in urban form that this intense flow makes possible.

From this point of view cities arise from the flow of matter-energy, but once a town's mineral infrastructure has emerged, it reacts to those flows, creating a new *set of constraints* that either intensifies or inhibits them. Needless to say, the walls, monumental buildings, streets, and

houses of a town would make a rather weak set of constraints if they operated on their own. Of course, they do not. Our historical exploration of urban dynamics must therefore include an analysis of the *institutions* that inhabit cities, whether the bureaucracies that run them or the markets that animate them. Although these institutions are the product of collective human decision making, once in place they also react back on their human components to limit them and control them, or, on the contrary, to set them in motion or accelerate their mutation. (Hence institutions constitute a set of emergent positive and negative constraints, but on a smaller scale.)

The birth of Europe, around the eleventh century of our era, was made possible by a great agricultural intensification. As Lynn White, Jr., a historian of medieval technology, has shown, in the centuries preceding the second millennium, "a series of innovations occurred which consolidated to form a remarkably efficient new way of exploiting the soil."[5] These innovations (the heavy plow, new ways of harnessing the horse's muscular energy, the open-field system, and triennial field rotation) were mutually enhancing as well as interdependent, so that only when they fully meshed were their intensifying effects felt. The large increase in the flow of energy created by this web of technologies allowed for the reconstitution of the European exoskeleton, the urban framework that had for the most part collapsed with the Roman Empire. Beginning around 1000 A.D., large populations of walled towns and fortified castles appeared in two great zones: in the south, along the Mediterranean coast, and in the north, along the coastlands lying between the trade waters of the North Sea and the Baltic.

As city historians often point out, urbanization has always been a discontinuous phenomenon. Bursts of rapid growth are followed by long periods of stagnation.[6] The wave of accelerated city building that occurred in Europe between the eleventh and thirteenth centuries is no exception. Many of the great towns in the north, such as Brussels and Antwerp, were born in this period, and the far older cities of Italy and the Rhineland experienced enormous growth. This acceleration in urban development, however, would not be matched for another five hundred years, when a new intensification in the flow of energy—this time arising from the exploitation of fossil fuels—propelled another great spurt of city birth and growth in the 1800s. Interestingly, more than the proliferation of factory towns made possible by coal, the "tidal wave of medieval urbanization"[7] laid out the most enduring features of the European urban structure, features that would continue to influence the course of history well into the twentieth century.

Zone Life

Beginnings

The times were extraordinary—the middle 1980s, the height of American yuppie culture gorging itself on wealth. The Macintosh computer had only just been introduced and was making itself felt in the world of typography by virtue of its capacity to distort fonts. It would eventually transform the field of design, disseminating expertise and clustering capacities vertically. Fax and FedEx were making possible a new level of international collaboration that would soon put a Toronto designer at the center of a transatlantic intellectual project. That project was Zone. Today we take all these developments for granted, but they occurred just as we were trying to accomplish something. A new kind of infrastructure was sliding underneath us, making it possible to mount a New York project from Toronto and to work with people in Paris—to go everywhere at any time.

Since 1986, all of Zone's production has taken place in Toronto. When we did big projects, like *Zone 3*, *4*, and *5*, the editors would come and live here for six months. I really spent every day with the editors, and every night with them, too. For the first few years, I experienced total immersion. I did nothing else but Zone. Those were extraordinary times.

Zone Identity

The most unusual aspect of Zone's operation is probably the fact that one design studio has produced all the imprint's output for over fifteen years, allowing it to develop its image and identity over time and to explore certain terrain that would not have been accessible in the higgledy-piggledy production hierarchies of conventional publishing. This relationship has produced two effects. First, it makes design akin to research. We can travel along a trajectory and make mistakes, then do it better, and then do it right. It allows for exploratory latitude, innovation, and growth. When you do one-off designs all the time, as most

The Normal and the Pathological
Georges Canguilhem
ZONE BOOKS
ZONE
Incorporations
Edited by Jonathan Crary and Sanford Kwinter
6

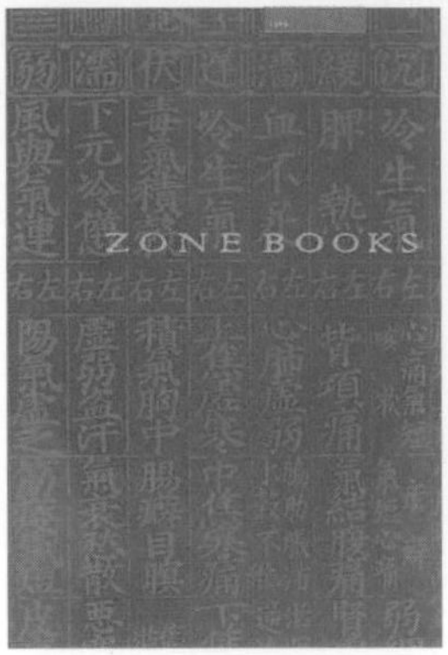

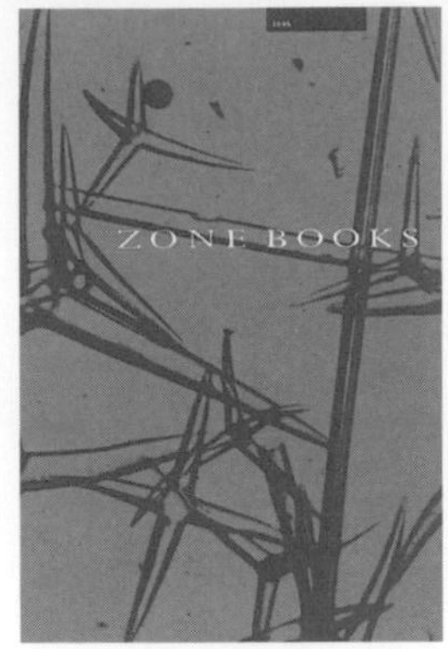

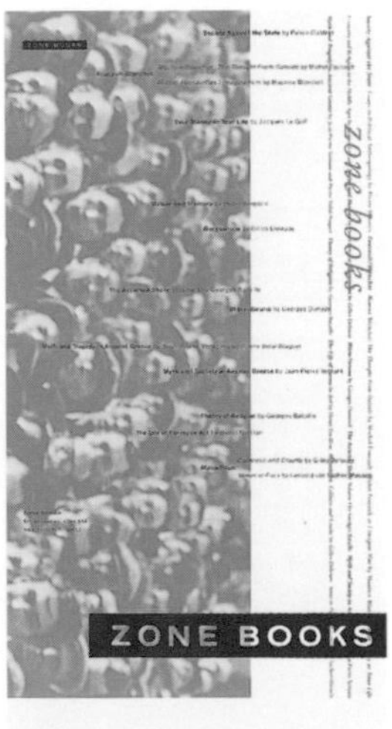

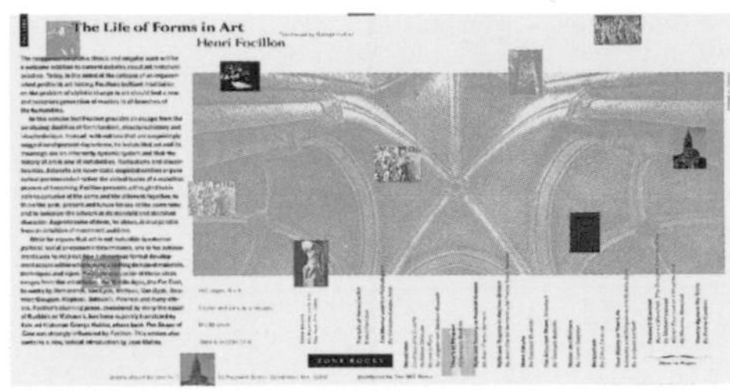

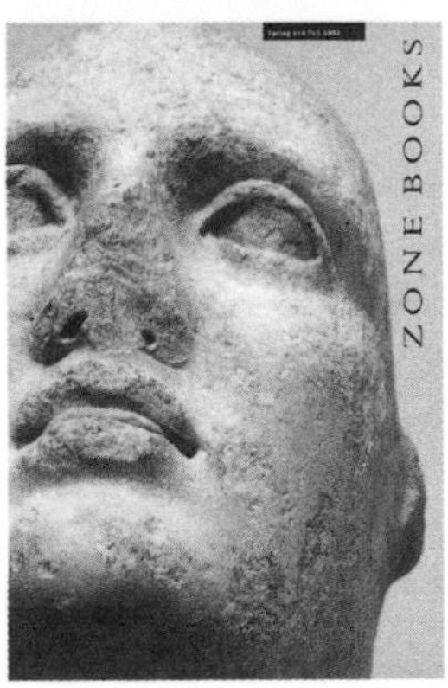

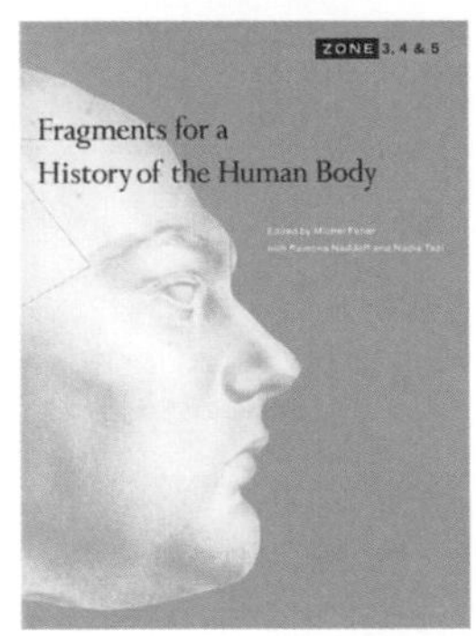

Catalog
Flyer
Catalog

Compliments slip
Flyer
Advertisement

Catalog
Catalog
Flyer

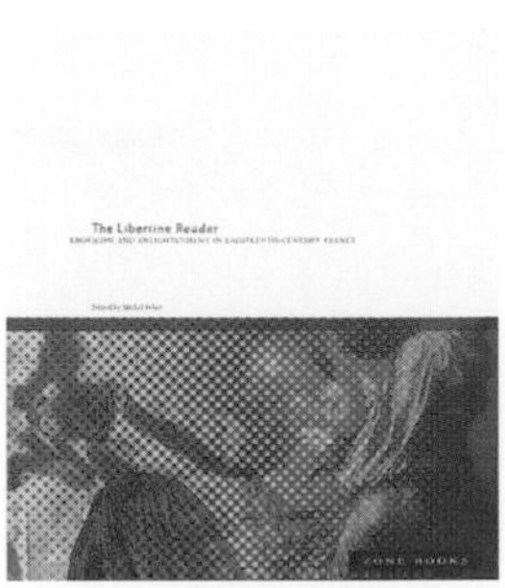

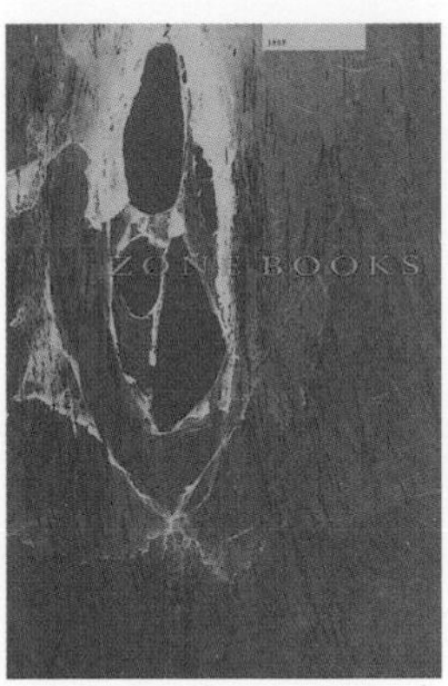

Catalog
Flyer
Catalog

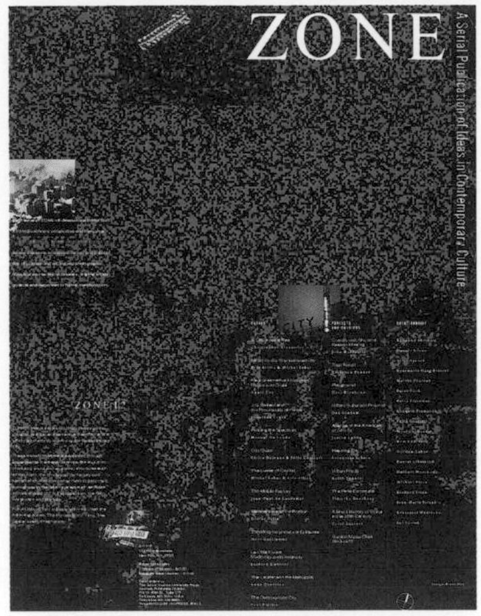

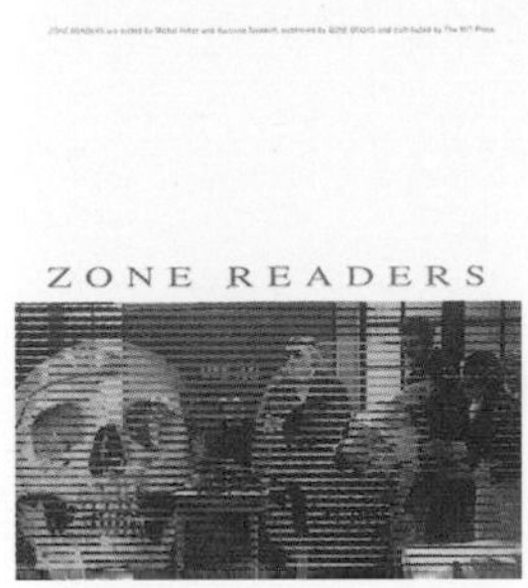

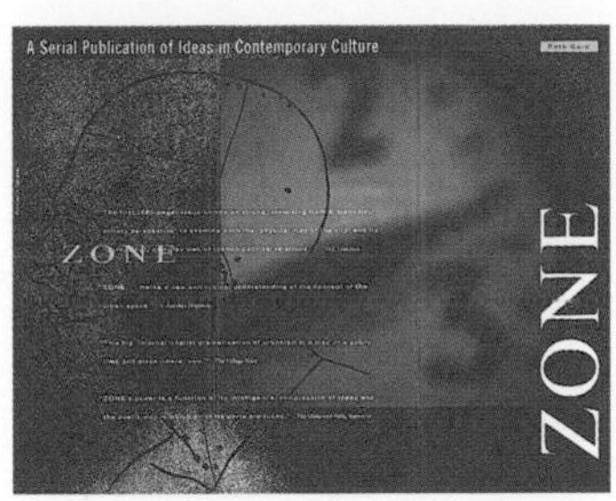

Poster
Flyer
Flyer

Poster (folded)
Catalog
Catalog

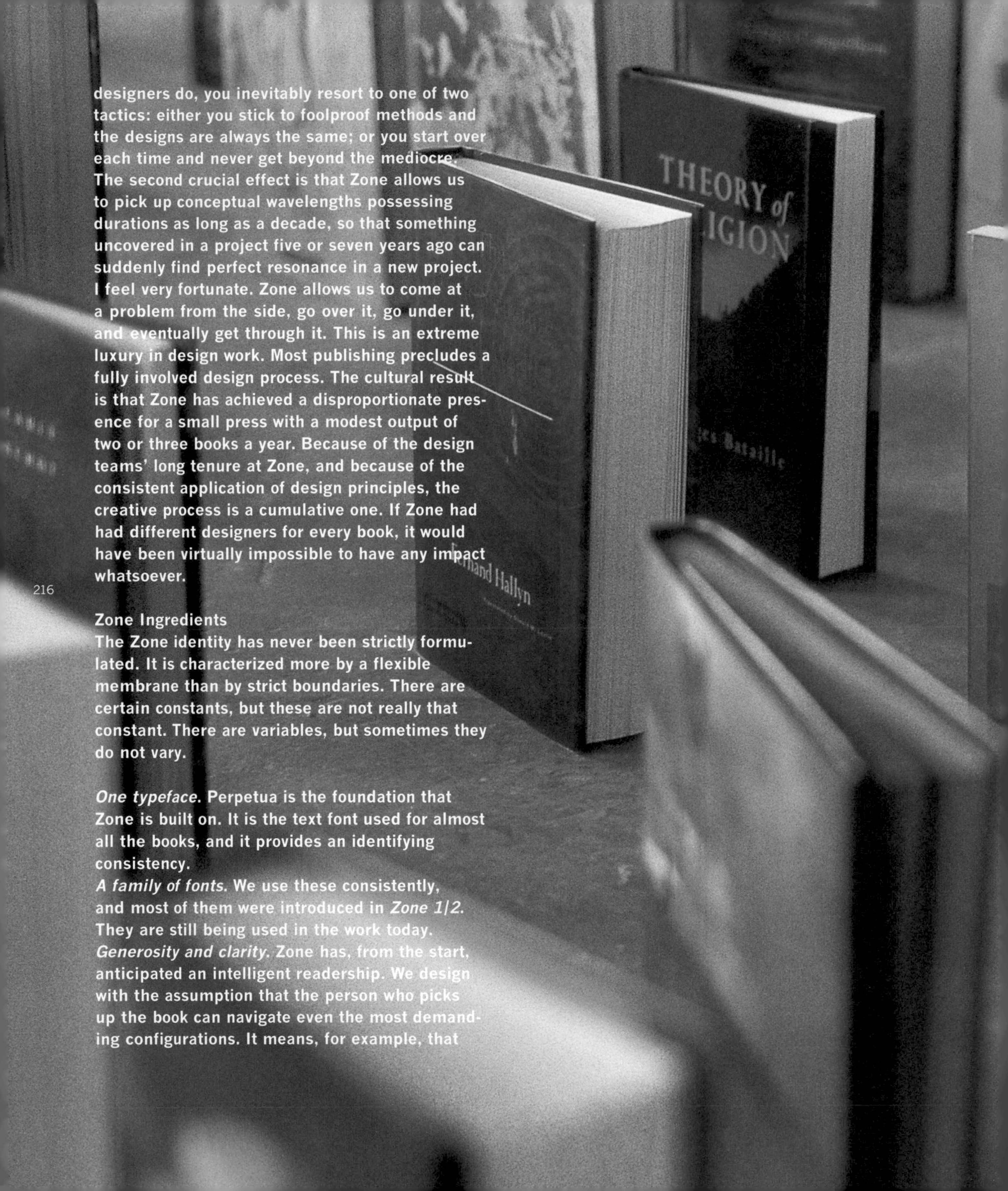

designers do, you inevitably resort to one of two tactics: either you stick to foolproof methods and the designs are always the same; or you start over each time and never get beyond the mediocre.
The second crucial effect is that Zone allows us to pick up conceptual wavelengths possessing durations as long as a decade, so that something uncovered in a project five or seven years ago can suddenly find perfect resonance in a new project. I feel very fortunate. Zone allows us to come at a problem from the side, go over it, go under it, and eventually get through it. This is an extreme luxury in design work. Most publishing precludes a fully involved design process. The cultural result is that Zone has achieved a disproportionate presence for a small press with a modest output of two or three books a year. Because of the design teams' long tenure at Zone, and because of the consistent application of design principles, the creative process is a cumulative one. If Zone had had different designers for every book, it would have been virtually impossible to have any impact whatsoever.

Zone Ingredients

The Zone identity has never been strictly formulated. It is characterized more by a flexible membrane than by strict boundaries. There are certain constants, but these are not really that constant. There are variables, but sometimes they do not vary.

One typeface. Perpetua is the foundation that Zone is built on. It is the text font used for almost all the books, and it provides an identifying consistency.
A family of fonts. We use these consistently, and most of them were introduced in *Zone 1/2*. They are still being used in the work today.
Generosity and clarity. Zone has, from the start, anticipated an intelligent readership. We design with the assumption that the person who picks up the book can navigate even the most demanding configurations. It means, for example, that

in the Age of Intelligent Machines
Manuel De Landa
The Masters of Truth in Archaic Greece

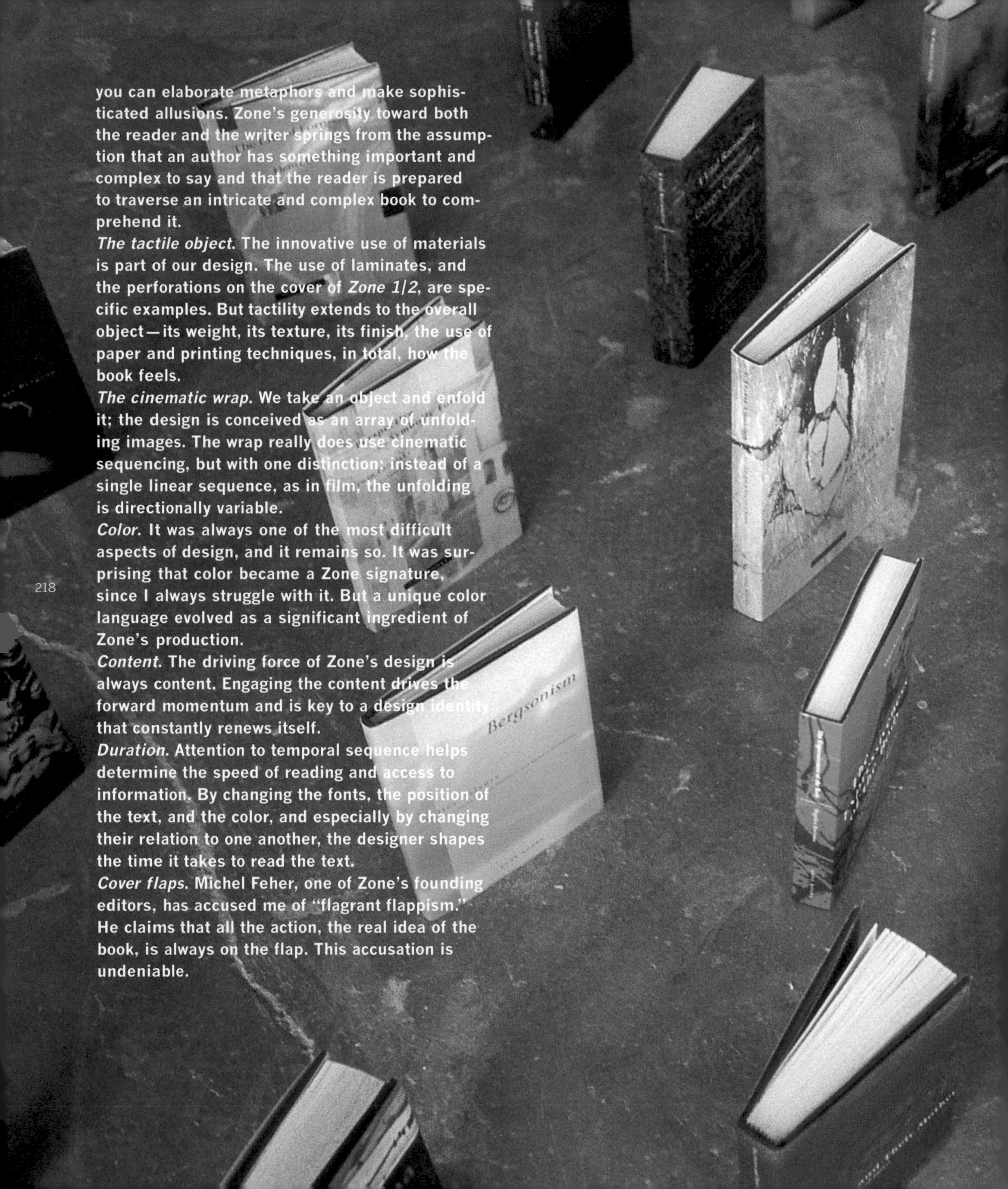

you can elaborate metaphors and make sophisticated allusions. Zone's generosity toward both the reader and the writer springs from the assumption that an author has something important and complex to say and that the reader is prepared to traverse an intricate and complex book to comprehend it.

The tactile object. The innovative use of materials is part of our design. The use of laminates, and the perforations on the cover of *Zone 1/2*, are specific examples. But tactility extends to the overall object—its weight, its texture, its finish, the use of paper and printing techniques, in total, how the book feels.

The cinematic wrap. We take an object and enfold it; the design is conceived as an array of unfolding images. The wrap really does use cinematic sequencing, but with one distinction: instead of a single linear sequence, as in film, the unfolding is directionally variable.

Color. It was always one of the most difficult aspects of design, and it remains so. It was surprising that color became a Zone signature, since I always struggle with it. But a unique color language evolved as a significant ingredient of Zone's production.

Content. The driving force of Zone's design is always content. Engaging the content drives the forward momentum and is key to a design identity that constantly renews itself.

Duration. Attention to temporal sequence helps determine the speed of reading and access to information. By changing the fonts, the position of the text, and the color, and especially by changing their relation to one another, the designer shapes the time it takes to read the text.

Cover flaps. Michel Feher, one of Zone's founding editors, has accused me of "flagrant flappism." He claims that all the action, the real idea of the book, is always on the flap. This accusation is undeniable.

Incorporations

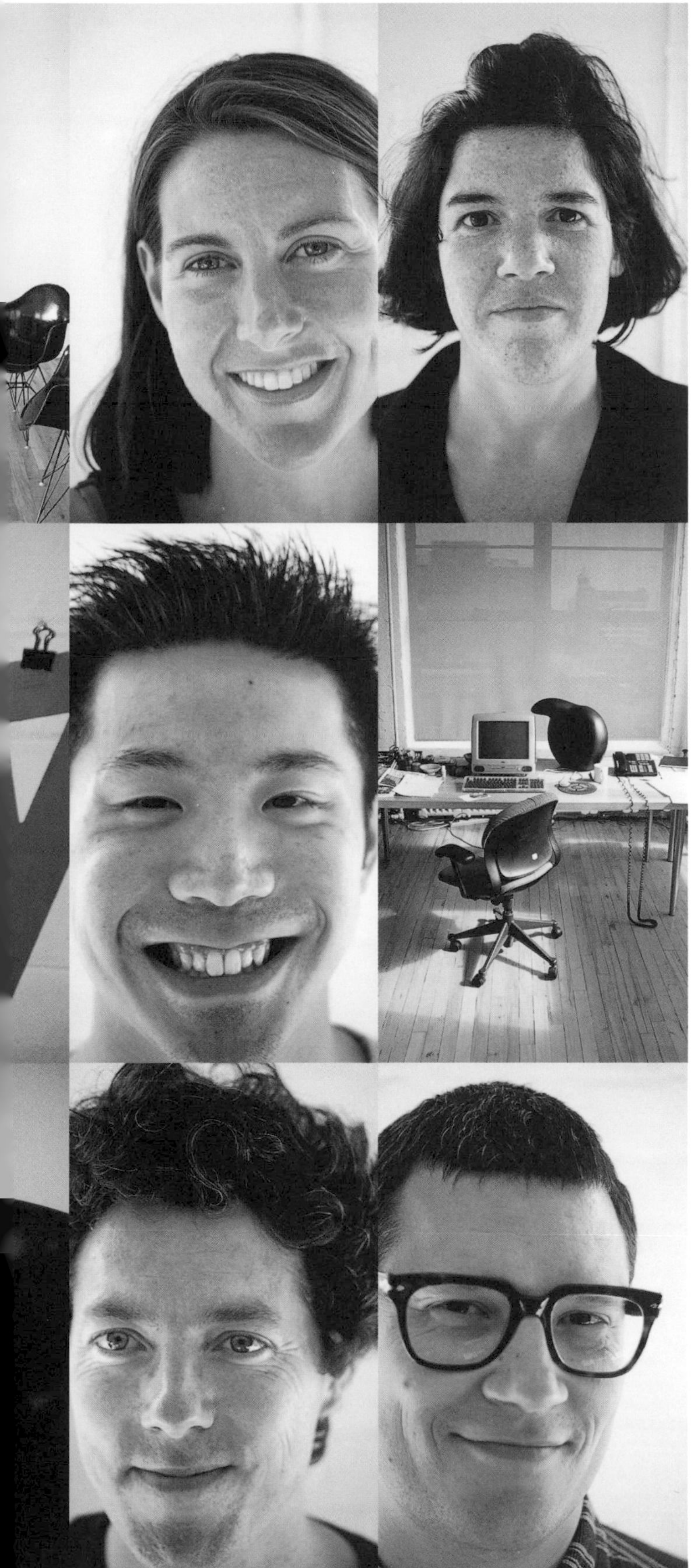

A Studio is Not a Tree

The studio is a kind of self-propelled entity: agile and resilient, drifting in search of events (problems and accidents), selecting and inserting itself as an active force within the realities it chooses to engage in — those that surround it, and those that make it up.
We have withstood the corrosive environment of capital, media, gravity, magnetism, misrepresentation, translation, error, absence, dispersal, malfeasance, and BAD LUCK, by remaining flexible.
Our work exists between the purity of invention and the contamination of compromise. It is a strategy that seems impossible, expressing a maximum innocence on the one hand, and a willingness to accommodate almost any input on the other. But, by activating these contradictory modes, by pushing each to its logical conclusion, we make new work.
We are developing a methodology that is without boundaries. One that implies a continuous variation in activity and defines a movement from work to free action. The practice avoids being consumed or spent in this activity by continually borrowing or siphoning energy from adjacent fields and practices such as cinema, philosophy, and science; and from the works of Chris Marker, Marshall McLuhan, and John Cage, among others. In sum, this is a model not only of survival but of cultivation — the cultivation of pleasure.
Within a conservative definition of design, I would be expected to put on the mask of my client and say what he or she told me to say. In essence, I would live as a ventriloquist's dummy. I cannot imagine ever accepting that as a way of life. By formulating our practice the way we have, we find in our water glass an ocean of possibility.

The edge of the studio is defined by an increasingly permeable membrane, a sort of informational Gore–Tex. In fact, it's harder to find the edge as studio collaborators push out, and as outside collaborators penetrate.
To understand the studio, you must understand the way we have defined collaboration. A collaborator comes to the studio with an undefined relationship to the proposed work. They approach with an understanding that anything is possible. They arrive prepared to ignore limits, engage content, and develop something new. They may have expectations, even quite specific ones, but within those expectations or desires, there is space for invention. We, on the other hand, enter an open space of learning. It is an enviable position. At the best of times we have been students with the world's greatest teachers. We have studied:

architecture with Frank Gehry,
urbanism with Rem Koolhaas,
furniture with Rolf Fehlbaum,
technology with Manuel De Landa,
composition with Gordon Monahan,
art with Michael Snow,
dance with Meg Stuart,
economics with Michel Feher,
Paris with Nadia Tazi,
film with Chris Marker,
Los Angeles with Julia Bloomfield,
modernity with Jonathan Crary,
the future with John Cage,
the past with Lynne Cooke,
and life with Sanford Kwinter.

Our collaborators have helped create a situation in which we have more at the end of our work than we had at the beginning.

ROCK CIRCUS

Identity

Notes

> *Life is a continuum and does not begin or end at some arbitrary point. Despite the belief of some people that life begins at conception, all life, including human life, actually never ends.... [Our] germ plasma (the source of sperm and eggs) is immortal. If it weren't immortal, we would not be here to discuss the matter.*
>
> —Leonard Hayflick, *How and Why We Age*

Consider identity to be a life problem. How does an entity declare itself within an environment? How does it find friends or other entities that can connect to it in a beneficial relationship?

The contours of identity are developed against and within a shifting and mutable environment. As the environment evolves, design strategies must also evolve if they are to function. Design strategies must therefore be living entities themselves—dynamic feedback systems taking information from the background, processing it, and pumping it out in new forms.

One can imagine that every identity program or strategy has a life expectancy that is a function of the volatility of the environment. In the 1950s and 1960s, when the communication environment was evolving rather slowly, design programs could expect to have a ten- or even twenty-year life span, during which time they could sustain their integrity against the background noise. Today, a period in which computing power doubles every nine months, new, complex, evolutionary strategies are possible and, in some sense, necessary.

Is the future of identity design rule-based, performance-driven design programs with consistent conceptual behavior which, like perennials, maintain their basic seed characteristics, but grow and bloom in a new way every season?

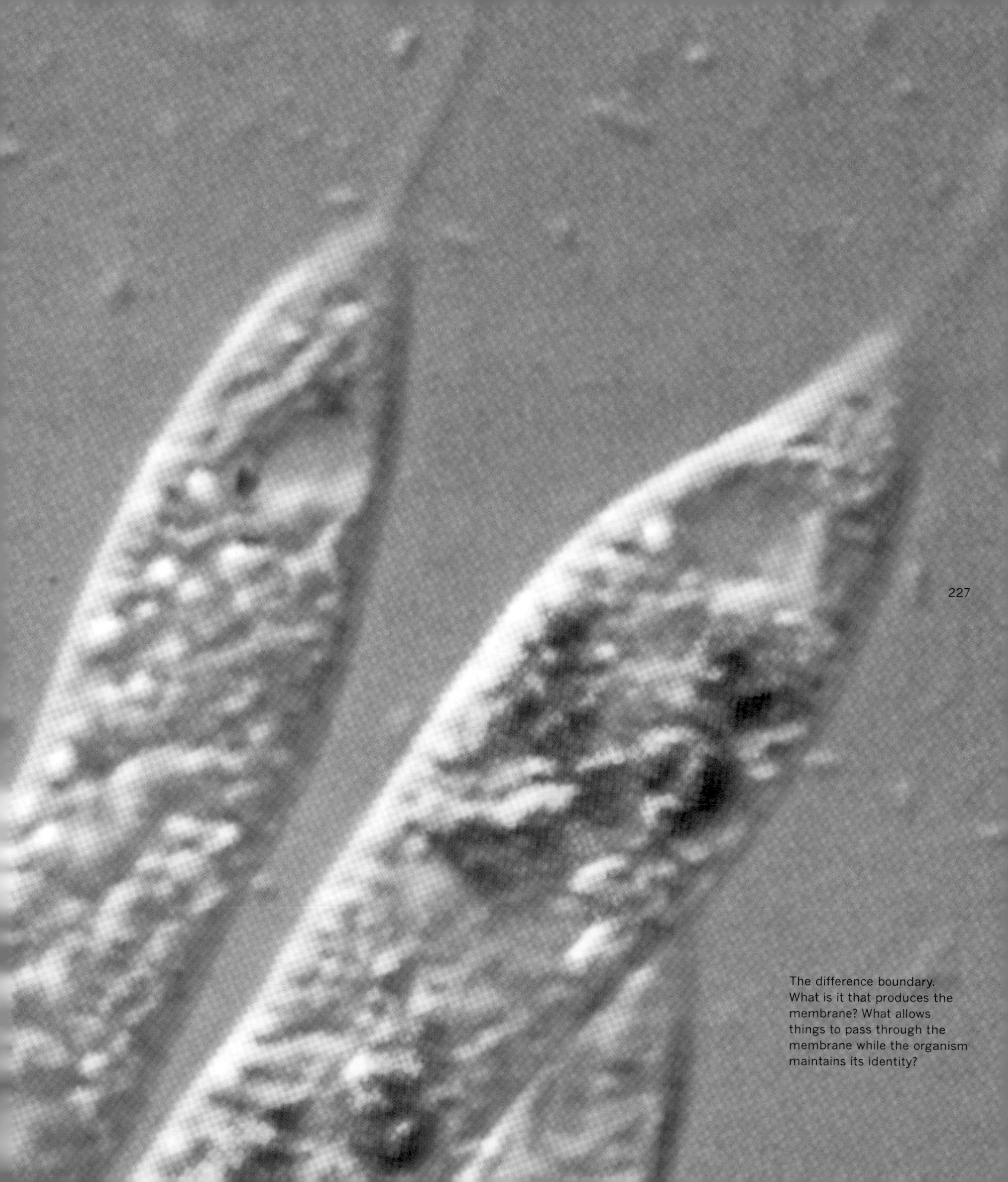

The difference boundary. What is it that produces the membrane? What allows things to pass through the membrane while the organism maintains its identity?

Life Expectancy

Over the last couple of years BMD has become known for producing identity. At first, we were principally known as the Zone designers, then as book designers, and then, slowly, we came to be seen as an enterprise with its own identity. Now that identity is evolving into something else. It is an interesting exercise to play with an identity (once you have one), to work against it in some ways and, in other ways, to make it more complex, to make it harder to fit into clear-cut categories and yet, simultaneously, work to maintain that identity's distinctiveness.

We started doing identity work for friends. First, some people asked me to create an identity for their bookstore. Then Zone needed some business cards. These were small, even incidental tasks, but, over time and incrementally, they built toward further developments. Identity work has since grown into a kind of science for us. As the studio becomes more adept at identity projects, I have come to realize that the potential value of identity is enormous. It has thus become essential to uncover what produces value in the form of identity.

Life Signals

First of all, we want to understand signal. Signal is a key to determine how an identity defines itself as a life-form in a communications environment, how it defines its presence against a background. We want to understand how signal is produced. Signal is noise with a pattern. It is not *materially* different from the background noise against which it appears. Signal and noise are not different substances. Instead, signal is background material that gains form and contour, and this is the way it becomes an identifiable figure against a field of noise.

Imagine that there are one thousand people in a room, all of them speaking and each of them saying something different. The result would be a lot of background noise. Now imagine that you step among them and say, "Just start saying the word 'violin, violin, violin'." And you convince more and more of these people to repeat the word "violin."

Seven sets of twins, Malaysia, 1996

1936

1955

1965

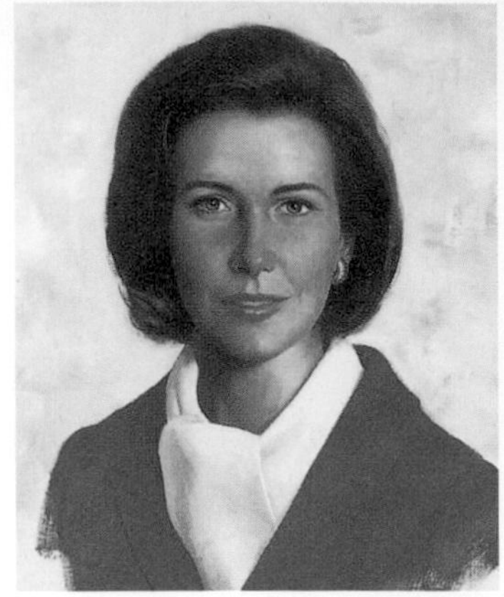

1968

1972

1980

1986

Life Brands

Example 1:
Here is Betty Crocker, circa 1936. Betty Crocker is very interesting because she's a brand based on a life, so there's an interesting swirl of attributes that move around her. What is it about Betty Crocker that remains consistent and integral to her as a branded personality even as her image changes over the years? The red-and-white wardrobe remains constant, the posture and body shape, the way Betty Crocker places herself before us as the image, and the ways she addresses and solicits us. But Betty Crocker is also a barometer of changing gender expectations and opportunities.

1936: Motherly—the slightly stern nurturer, bearer of food.
1955: Softer, smiling version—the icon of the freshly defined, suburban domestic space where pleasure and comfort accompany nurturing.
1965, 1968: The maternal sophisticate—the wider world is carefully incorporated into the domestic space; its pleasures expand. The white in the 1965 edition is carried by an elegant string of pearls.
1972: More businesslike—the pressures of the global economic sphere are met by a crisply confident and efficient family provider.
1980: Soft and casual—the relaxation of the domestic space is gently ruled by maternal ease.
1986: Friendly, confident professional—the stress-free and efficient mother can be everything to her family now.

At some point, a critical mass is achieved—let's say, two hundred people speaking in unison. An aural shape emerges from the background and pulls the contour of "violin" out of the noise of a thousand voices. Shaping that contour is the essence of signal production. The exercise of producing identity is all about giving environmental noise a defined pattern. The question is, how do we produce pattern? How do we go about convincing any two people in the room, much less two hundred, to say the word "violin"?

In a more realistic (or at least typical) scenario than the fiction I have just proposed, quality will produce pattern. The issue is not good quality vs. bad, but quality in the sense of difference. In our fictional theater of the signal, the word "violin" has a differential capacity that permits it to endure repetitions. This quality of difference is one that less idiosyncratic words like "hello" or "excuse me," for example, might not have under these circumstances.

To understand the contemporary problem of identity and the enterprise of producing signal, we have to understand the changing nature of the life-world of identity—the background against which an identity can be made to stand as an entity, or a life-form.

We're living through a period in which the production of background is both expanding and mutating more than at any other moment in history. There are several reasons for this. One is connectiveness. The web of communications media connecting us has drawn tighter than ever before. The density of the communications environment makes it difficult for a single entity to maintain presence and integrity—or to manifest its identity.

1996

Consider a distinction between the sociology of a village and that of a city. In a village, like the one in which I grew up in northern Ontario, anything a bit odd about a man could push him out of the local social background and make him stand out as the village eccentric. In contrast, in New York or any urban context, only extreme peculiarity can push a man out of the social background and cause him to break the surface and be recognized as eccentric —the peculiarity, for example, of someone like Moondog, the tall blind man who every day for years stood at the corner of 53rd Street and Sixth Avenue dressed in the complete regalia of a Viking. Eventually, Moondog became so well known for his eccentricity that he was given the opportunity to record an album of the music he had been composing under his Viking robes all that time. The difference here concerns background. In New York, everybody is louder and bigger. Personalities are outsized. The scale of the place creates a powerful, socially loud background against which an individual striving to establish a presence must make that presence equivalent to a thunderclap.

When it comes to contemporary background noise levels, we are all living in the city. There is no village. Everyone and everything is urban. The proliferation of interconnected communications media means that every signal is in fierce competition with every other signal. Every signal pumps up the volume, and, in response, identity is being pushed toward an extreme condition.

This new condition also raises the value of signal. This is the paradox. With infinitely more competing signals and tighter connections among them, their value should diminish. This is what was supposed to happen with any system of overproduction. The truth, however, is that the more signals there are, the greater the value we place on the clarity and contour produced by any successful signal. Difference is a crucial, and now rare quality that permits an identity to stand out as a figure against the background.

Another change in the background is simultaneously technological and temporal: the background is now rapidly reproducing itself. This presents a radically

1996: For her seventy-fifth anniversary, a nationwide search identified seventy-five women of diverse backgrounds and ages who embody the characteristics and spirit of Betty Crocker. To achieve this, according to General Mills, you must: (1) enjoy cooking and baking; (2) be committed to family and friends; (3) be resourceful and creative in handling everyday tasks; and (4) be involved in the community. The final portrait of Betty Crocker is a computerized composite of the seventy-five women.

Betty Crocker is a classic brand identity, in this case a vivid branded personality, a media life-form, that has passed through a series of rebirths. Her evolution encompasses a rapidly changing series of domestic ideals running from the Great Depression through 1950s suburbanization to 1990s third-wave feminism. Yet Betty Crocker has maintained her identity. She remains a clear signal and a strong configuration because her identity possesses great powers of incorporation—the power to shape and reshape the noise of the communications environment into her distinct signal-form.

1963

1969

1973

Example 2:
1953: British writer Ian Fleming begins the James Bond series with the novel *Casino Royale*. Fleming's Bond is a postwar British bureaucrat. In contrast to the abrupt way he writes action scenes, Fleming devotes endless pages to the obsessive details of Bond's style: the martinis ("shaken, not stirred"), the Bentley, the gunmetal cigarette lighters, the Barretta semiautomatic (followed by the Walther PPK), the dexedrine dosages, the worsted blue suits and knit ties, the women, and the cuisine. Bond is born and bred on the page as a convention of style traits, organizational attitudes, and consumer tastes, and Fleming has synthesized them into a signal called "Bond, James Bond."
1963: Sean Connery in *Dr. No*, initiates the Bond film franchise (he would go on to make five films by 1971 and a sixth in 1983). The bureaucrat gains a cruelly handsome face, a hard body, and a dangerous walk. The high-tech gizmos and growled quips were screenwriting conventions, enlargements of Bond. They mutate Fleming's life-style-detailing into Hugh Hefner–style consumerism. Bond becomes the risk-taking business traveler with NASA-styled toys. The assembly of signals solidifies Bond's cinematic identity.
1969: George Lazenby stars in one Bond film, *On Her Majesty's Secret Service*, demonstrating that anyone can carry the Bond signal.
1973: Roger Moore takes over the role in *Live and Let Die*, and Bond grows softer and middle-aged in six subsequent films. But the Bond identity adjusts seamlessly to

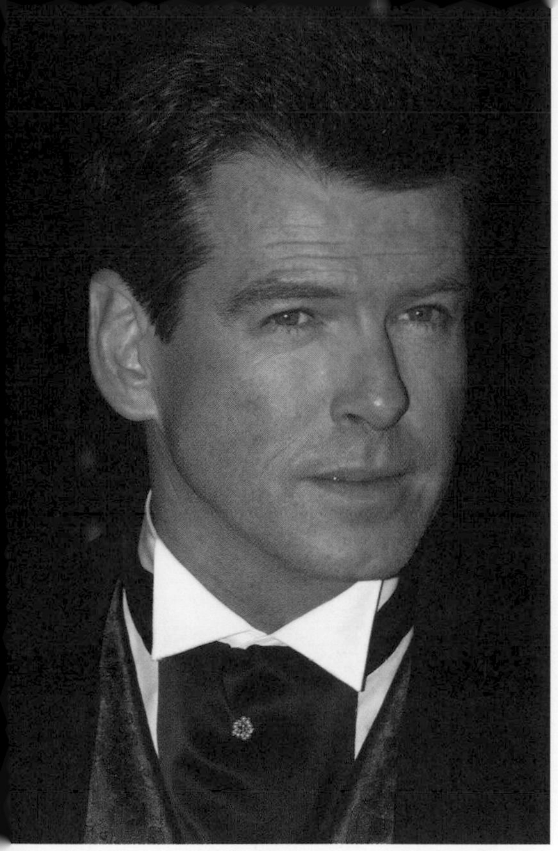

1995

new kind of problem. For some time now, computers have taken over the job of developing and inventing new computers. They have immensely accelerated the pace of innovation and improvements in flexibility and communication capacity. Moore's law, which states that computing power doubles every eighteen months, was recently revised to a time-frame of nine months. And so the background, the environment, becomes volatile in ways that were previously unimaginable. As computers generate new computing power, they also generate more connections and greater bandwidth and produce more background noise. More noise actually—and paradoxically—increases the value of signal.

Life Conventions

If we are to produce signal within that dense and ever-accelerating context, what role does convention play? Technical complexity and speed are increasing but the reservoir of memory remains; all the historic precedents maintain their forms into the present. Convention is generic pattern. It takes the noise of the background and organizes it into a form, but that form does not yet have specificity. Perhaps the most pervasive and deeply held convention underlying today's media culture is the notion of the individual human being as a social, legal construct. The individual is the irreducible unit of measure when it comes to rights, boundaries, and accountability, superseding family, tribe, corporation, or nation.

It is through this conventional notion of the individual that signals are received, differentiated, and interpreted. It is this convention that gives meaning to person-specific signals such as hairstyle, dress, and language. It is this convention that allows us to read these specifics. Convention is a significant piece of the signal puzzle because it allows us to decompress and differentiate signals against the background of their forms, a necessary preliminary to reading them.

Convention, while it seems to operate as both signal and carrier of the signal, is, strictly speaking, neither. One differentiates between signal and carrier in

1970s safari suits and the trappings of exotic tourism. The playboy globetrotter becomes a suburban executive—older, slower, and more indulged and relaxed on the road, but still ruthless.
1987 to the present:
Like Lazenby, Timothy Dalton and Pierce Brosnan inhabit the Bond identity with almost no effect, beyond renovation. Dalton returns some threat and hardness to Bond, and Brosnan revives some fashion-sense. The consumerism is upscale again. Both renovations coincide with ever more brazen luxury product-placement, from BMW motorcycles to Omega watches.

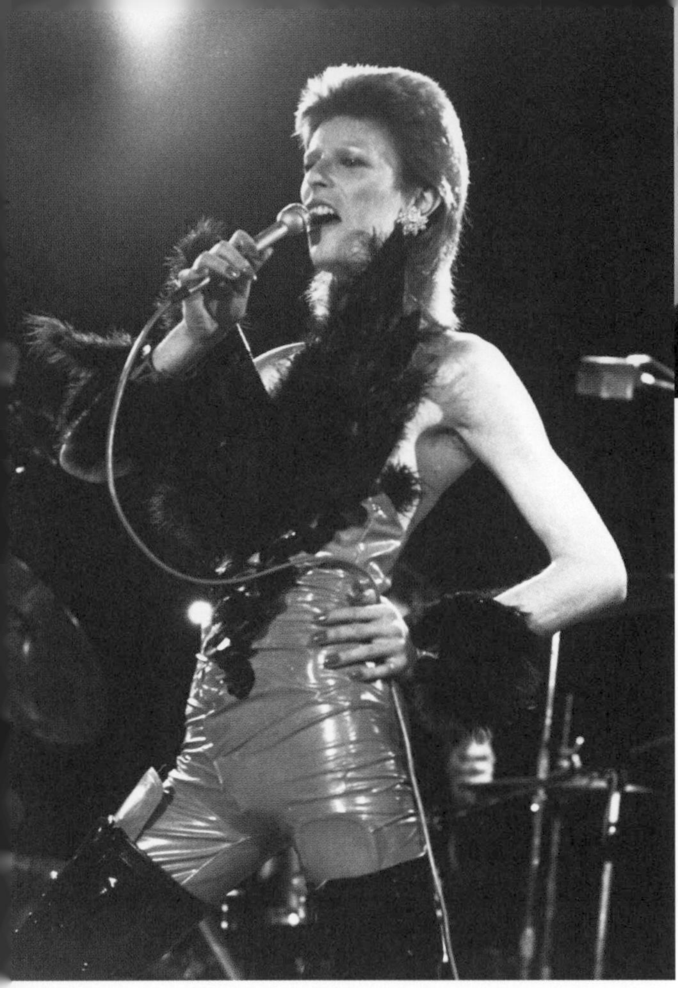

1973

1975

1983

1965

Example 3:
The synthetic identity of the rock star is the quickest to produce because its signal is forced to operate at a speed closest to the rate of the environment's mutation. Elvis Presley experienced this necessity as a series of disasters. David Bowie, by contrast, perfected a serial signal production by creating the ambiguous identity of space alien Ziggy Stardust in 1972 and then, just three years later, creating the Thin White Duke. As his personal and musical styles switched, they nonetheless contributed to the same Bowie identity—the rock star who is always Bowie plus someone else.

1990

1997

terms of where they are situated in the communication matrix. The carrier, as its name implies, is a vehicle and not the producer of the signal. The carrier typically disappears behind (or under) the signal. In a sense, what masks the carrier of a signal is convention; it can make the carrier vanish. The book page, for example, is the carrier of text and illustration, the signals of the book that we read and interpret. The conventions of typography and page design, however, cause the book page effectively to be eclipsed by the arrangement of text and illustration. The conventions of typesetting and design provide the controlling conditions in which the signals borne by the page are received and interpreted by the reader.

Ordinarily, we are not aware of carriers and conventions. For example, we don't regularly experience or think about the fact that we are in a physiological sense biped mammals or members of the species *homo sapiens*. I experience myself as "Bruce Mau." The material carrier of my identity — my biophysical composition — disappears behind the civilizational conventions of personhood, beginning with the very rudiments of consciousness ("I am ...") and self ("... Bruce Mau").

If we consider identity as reaching beyond the scope of a person's intimate experience of subjectivity (but without losing sight of the fact that every identity operates very much like a person does), we begin to discover the real set of operations that produce identity on different scales. Not only do I think to myself, "I am Bruce Mau," but, when I present myself to another person, I voice these words. It is a simple gesture announcing my identity, but it consists of a complex of signals that involve conventions of politeness, language, and even physical posture. I am a social entity subject to all manner of energy flows and conventions that affect me materially, socially, and culturally. Though only I can truly speak the words that announce my identity, that gesture expands enormously beyond me, the person who makes it. If we think about identity as a life problem — how entities define themselves within energy flows then we can use metaphors at different scales to

1985

1986

1988

Example 4:
The reason that we're able to differentiate Madonna from everything else around her is that she produces a peculiar signal that, even more than Bowie's, we attribute to an identity. Bowie staged his identity in exaggerated scale to the point where each new staging ceased to feel new. Madonna, however, continues to pull herself constantly out of the background; indeed, her gestures are so effective that she convinces us that this act of reinvention is what life's all about. From the moll on the run in *Desperately Seeking Susan* to the hard-body diva of the Blonde Ambition tour to the yogic rave-mother of *Ray of Light*, Madonna stages exaggeration, ceaselessly and with great finesse. She is a life-form that shifts its shape, and more important, makes those shifts resonate and matter. Madonna is a signal like all the others but much stronger in shape and force.

1998

discover how an identity signal is produced and how it behaves against its background. At present, identity seems an obscure, even mysterious process for designers struggling in an extremely volatile communications environment. But, if we focus on identity as a life problem, our ease with and understanding of the interaction of identity and that environment become second nature.

47-6738
MEET MISS SUBWAYS
SARALEE SINGER
Senior at Brooklyn College... preparing to teach elementary school. Recently married her childhood sweetheart. Both love sports: skiing in winter and sailing in summer.

Elvis lookalikes at a Manhattan diner, 1994

100 Logos, 1000 Colors

We began with several questions: Is it possible for a visual identity to resist the imposition of a master narrative and opt instead for maximum difference? How elastic can it be? How far can it stretch? What are the boundaries? And what is the thread that sews it all together? The answers mark a departure from modern identity programs and their list of "don't"s. This program, which consists entirely of "do"s, is an embrace of promiscuity.

Netherlands Architecture Institute (NAi)
Rotterdam, 1993

When the Netherlands Architecture Institute (NAi) relocated to its new facility in 1993, Bruce Mau Design was commissioned to develop an identity program. Given the institute's status in the local design community and the high standard of design culture in The Netherlands in general, our objective was to develop an innovative program that would give the local and in-house designers maximum freedom for interpretation and experimentation.

The word-mark images were generated by projecting an "NAi" logotype onto one hundred different surfaces. The resulting projections, with their vague, corroded contours, achieved a sense of movement and transformation and inspired the development of more than one hundred logotypes, which were combined with a palette of more than one thousand colors, which in turn were derived from a 1973 painting by Gerhard Richter.

Identity is an increasingly challenging problem because of the corrosive effect of technological developments and media-saturation on people's attention. Previously stable relationships between foreground and background are collapsing as everything surges toward the foreground. It used to be that a local business, like a pizza shop, only had to push itself to the front of the neighborhood's attention. Now, with global networks like the Internet, that pizza shop has to share the foreground with every other pizza shop in the world. What identity involves is the production and rezoning of attention. In order to generate an identity, things have to be linked together in the foreground so that a gesture made today attaches to a different gesture made tomorrow, so that eventually all these gestures accrete and produce a recognizable unity. Identity, in other words, preserves and channels the energies emanating from various gestures.

In even the recent past, the production of identity could assume a fairly open and unjaded public. When Paul Rand made the original IBM identity, for example, he was able to bring the company to the forefront of people's attention in a novel but straightforward way. The communication ecology has changed since then. Our contemporary environment has become more complicated and volatile. Because the foreground is itself so crowded, the public's reception threshold is correspondingly much higher.

The NAi is a highly respected, well-known Rotterdam institute dealing with design through a wide range of programs that attract a variety of audiences. It offers programs for school children, design practitioners, and scholars, and it has a generally interested public. Taken together, these activities represent a tremendous expenditure of energy, but the problem was enabling people to see these disparate activities collectively as the NAi. What was needed was a mechanism that would channel the energy and the responses so that they could accumulate for the NAi as a whole.

Now, in the quiet recesses of the contemplating mind, such a linking mechanism can be gentle and staid. But in the real-world media environment, the mechanism has to attract attention because people are no longer neophyte receivers, they are increasingly acute critics. To attract attention, the device has to be different and changing and yet maintain consistency. Mere consistency, however, results in a practical invisibility. Mere novelty or variety, on the other hand, dissipates identity. When marketing people speak about branding, they talk about differentiation, meaning that you have to produce a difference from everything in the environment. Because the environment is over-saturated and everything that previously appeared as

background has heaved into the foreground, the situation approaches a state of white noise. Thus, if you produced a steady-state identity, and kept it the same for every application, it would be virtually imperceptible.

The strategy we devised for NAi was to create an identity that exists as a carrier or genetic code, one level removed from specific applications. We made a mark that was a flat, characterless logo inscription. But it was never seen in its first-generation form. Instead, using light, we projected the flat inscription onto one hundred surfaces to produce an array of versions, each of them unique but legible. Then we borrowed one thousand colors from Gerhard Richter. In application, the mark acts as a vector passing through a large set of variations, so that the logo blossoms anew in every instance it is used. The result is a fully kinetic identity program.

The history of identity has been shaped by the idea of subtraction, the process of cutting everything away that does not look like the identity. The NAi project used an additive process, and this resulted in an identity that could be characterized as differences-within-consistency. In this way it responds to the advent of image software that permits each image to be infinitely plastic. For instance, when the publishing arm of the NAi asked for a specific solution dealing with the spines for their books, we suggested that they take the mark, keep its height consistent, and stretch or compress its image to fill the varying widths of their books.

The design we made for NAi may only be practical in a country like the Netherlands, which has a culture extraordinarily rich in skilled practitioners who can interpret a program and perform its applications. A primary reason why identity programs tend to be ruthlessly reductive is that they often must eliminate the need for design talent, an element that our design assumes in its ongoing reinterpretation and application. Fundamental to the idea is that "100 logos, 1000 colors" continues to evolve.

NAi

NAi

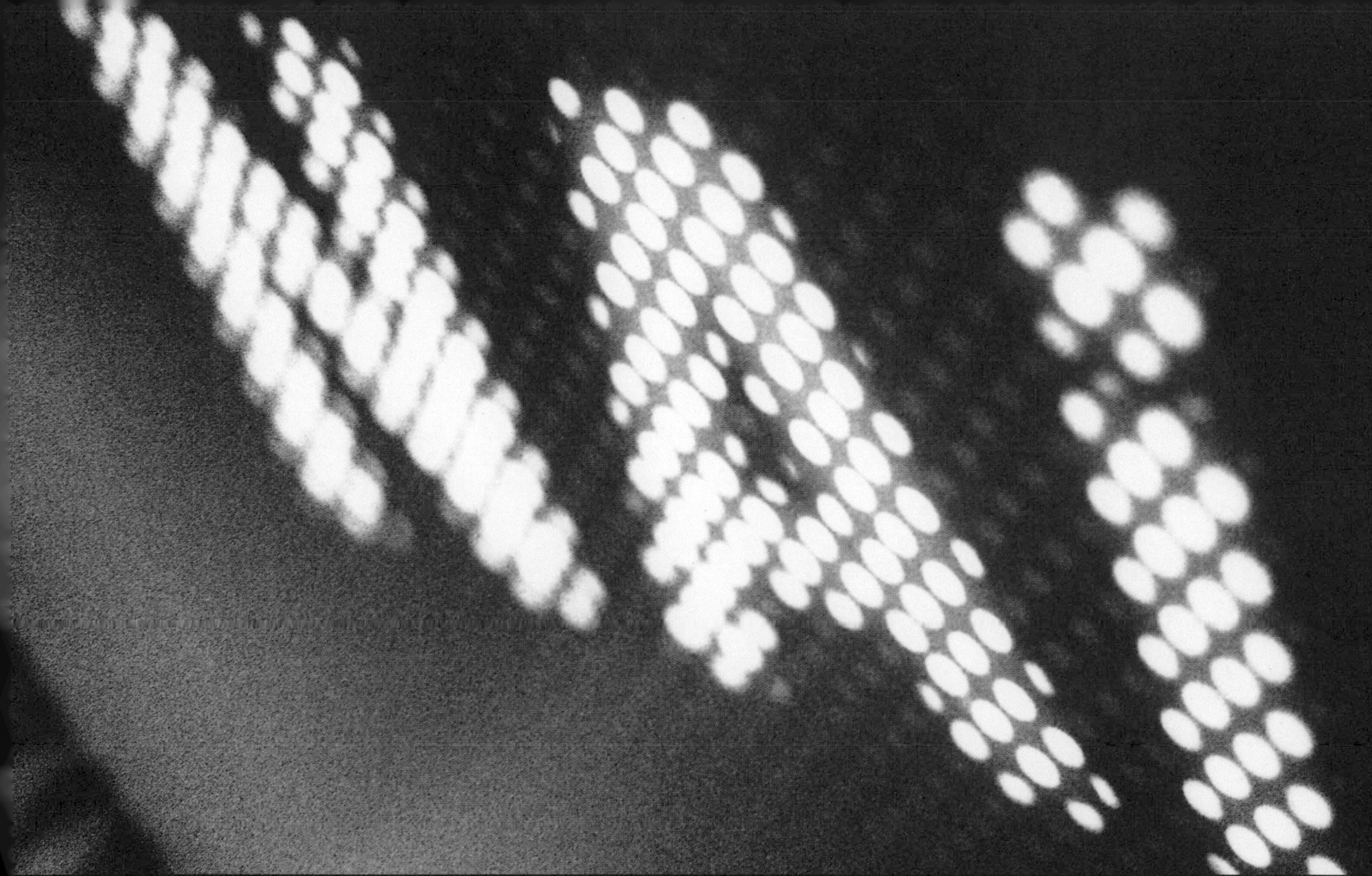
NAi

NAi

NAi
NAi
NAi
NAi
NAi
NAi
NAi
NAi
NAi
NAi
NAi
NAi
NAi
NAi
NAi
NAi
NAi
NAi
NAi
NAi
NAi
NAi
NAi
NAi
NAi
NAi
NAi
NAi

NAi

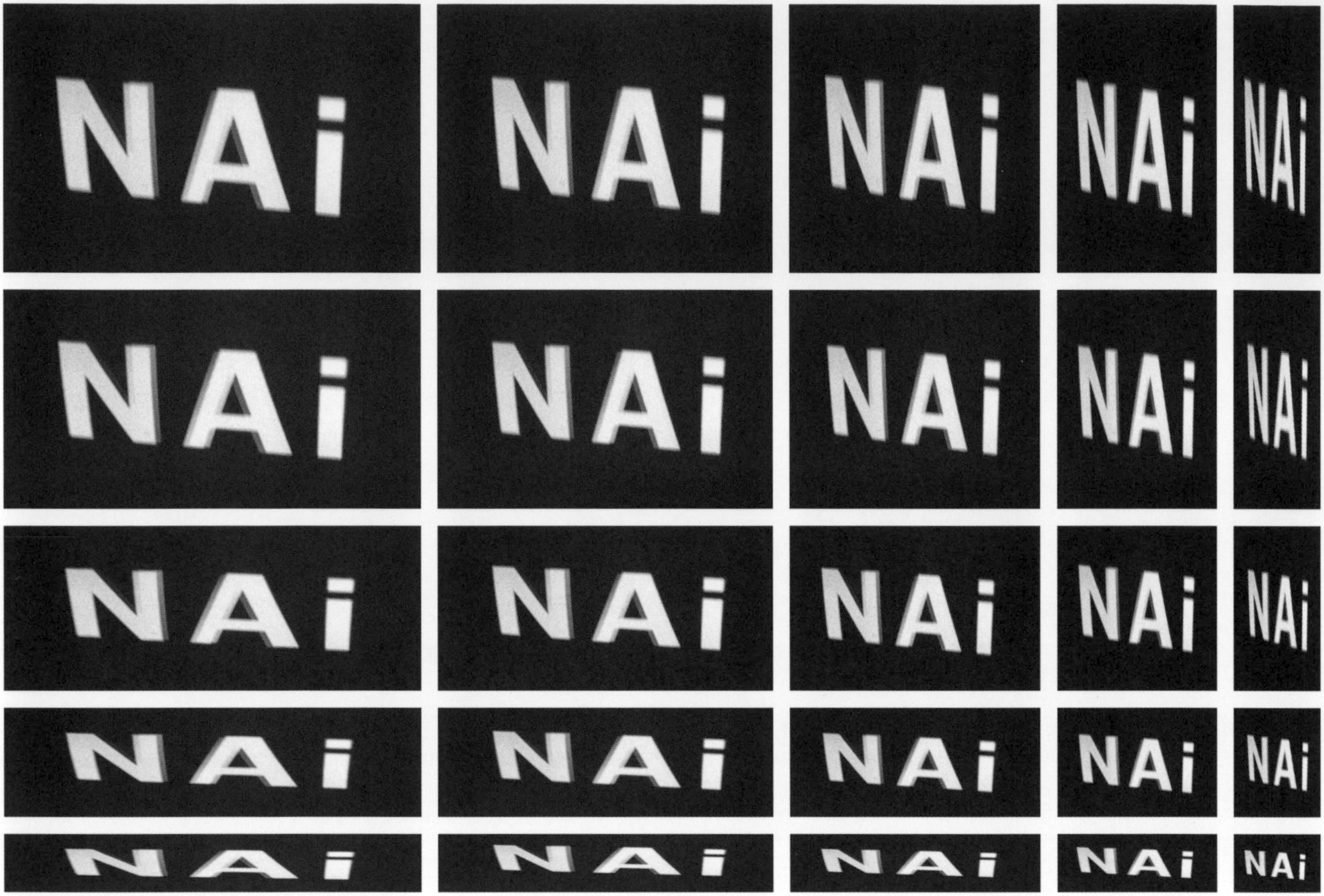

Every logotype is infinitely plastic.

Gerhard Richter, *1024 Farben*, 1973

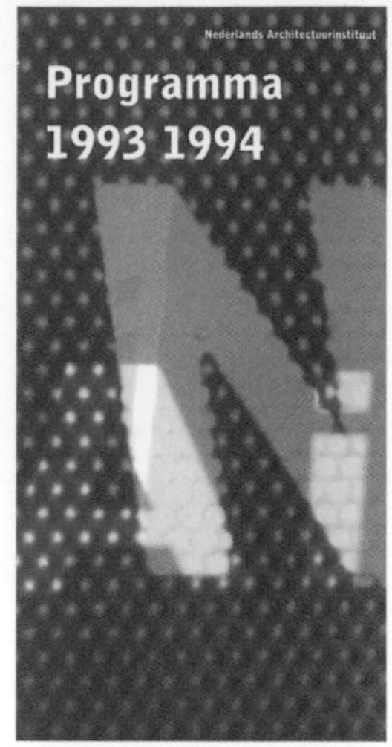

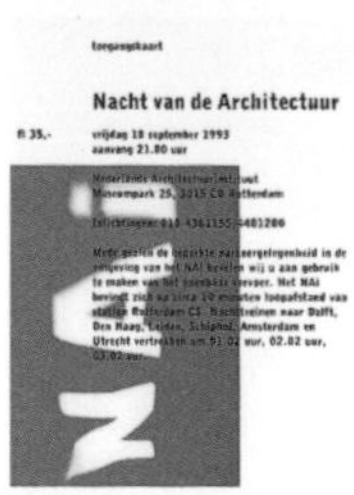

Stickers
Ticket
Stationery

Business card
Event poster
Invitation

Program
Envelope
Envelope

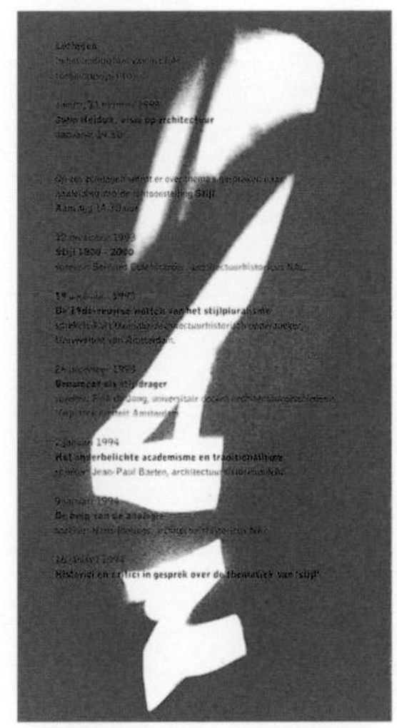

Press release
Business card
Announcement

Invitation
Folder
Business card

Envelope
Flyer
Business card

Necrophilia and Extrapolation

The Warhol identity exists in the territory between high modernism and high fashion, between Bauhaus and Chanel. Confronted by the ghost of an artist with an extraordinary range of media, production, and signature styles, the project is an exercise in necrophilia and extrapolation.

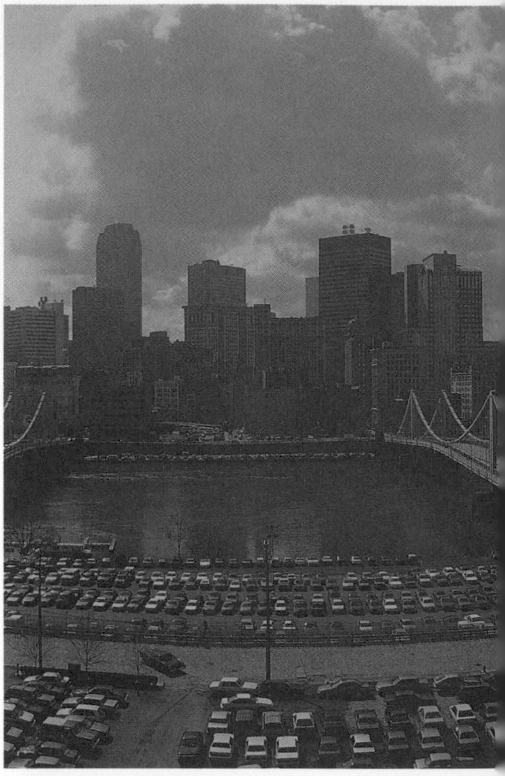

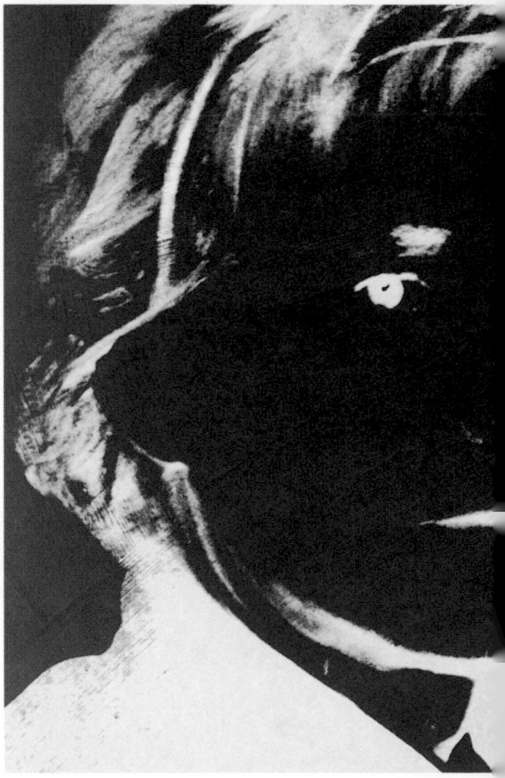

Andy Warhol Museum
Pittsburgh, 1994
BMD was commissioned to develop the visual identity program for the Andy Warhol Museum in Pittsburgh—an institution dedicated to the preservation, exhibition, and interpretation of the life and work of Warhol. The curator, Mark Francis, sent us various versions of the letterhead that Andy Warhol had designed for his studio, the Factory, over the decades. His instructions were simple: imagine you are doing the next version of letterhead. It was a case of necrophilia and extrapolation—our task was to position our design along a trajectory initiated by Warhol. Warhol dominated so many domains and had such a strong signature that our challenge was to grapple with the artist's formidable imprint without resorting to mannerism or caricature. The final identity, positioned between high modernism and high fashion, is the result of our reckoning with the ghosts of Warhol.

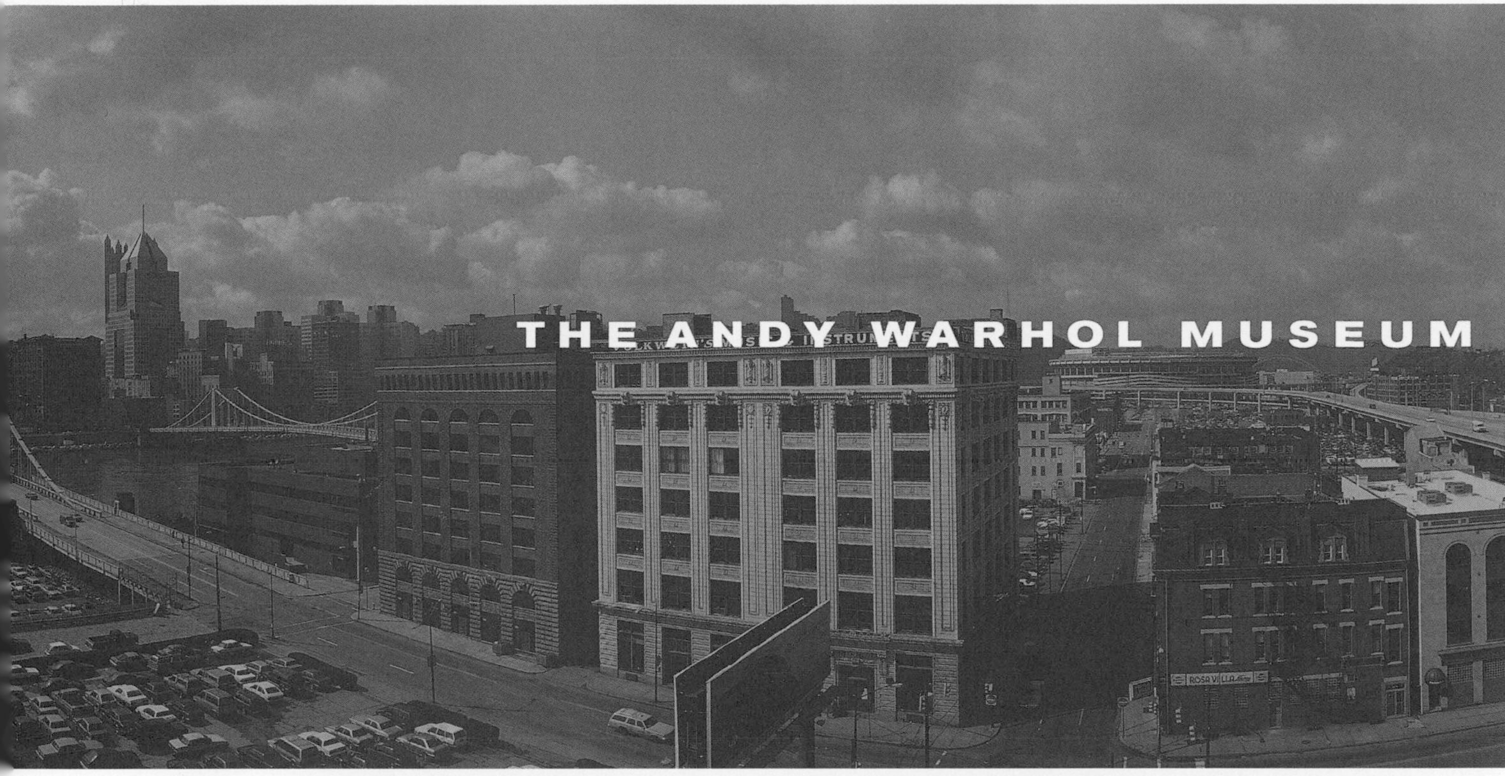

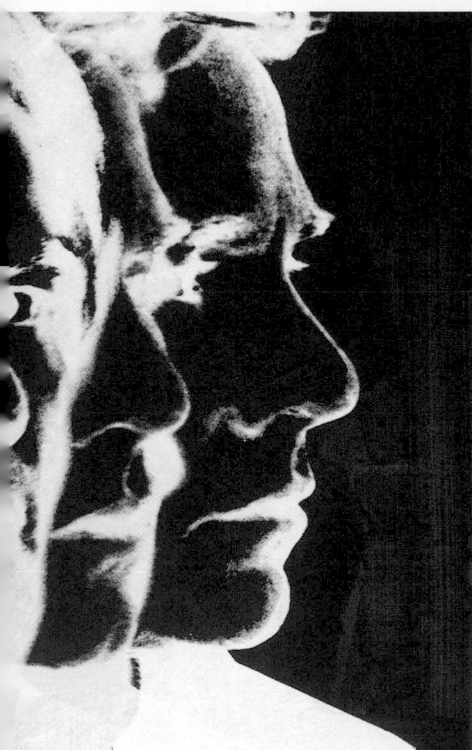

THE ANDY WARHOL MUSEUM

A Collaborative Project of Carnegie Institute,

Dia Center for the Arts, and

The Andy Warhol Foundation for the Visual Arts, Inc.

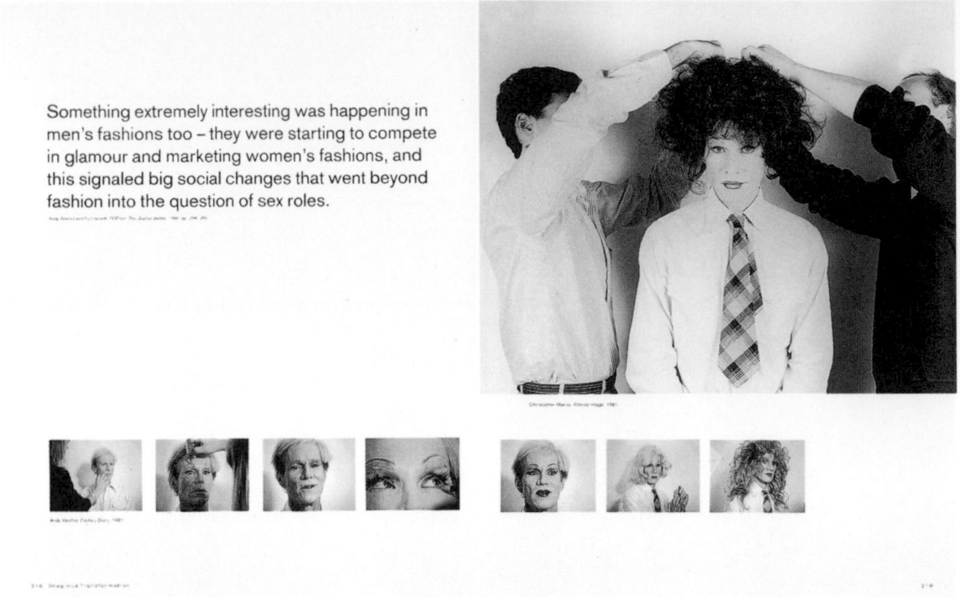

Something extremely interesting was happening in men's fashions too – they were starting to compete in glamour and marketing women's fashions, and this signaled big social changes that went beyond fashion into the question of sex roles.

Spread from *The Warhol Look: Glamour, Style, Fashion*, eds. Mark Francis and Margery King (Boston, New York, Toronto, London: Bulfinch Press; Little Brown and Company, 1997)

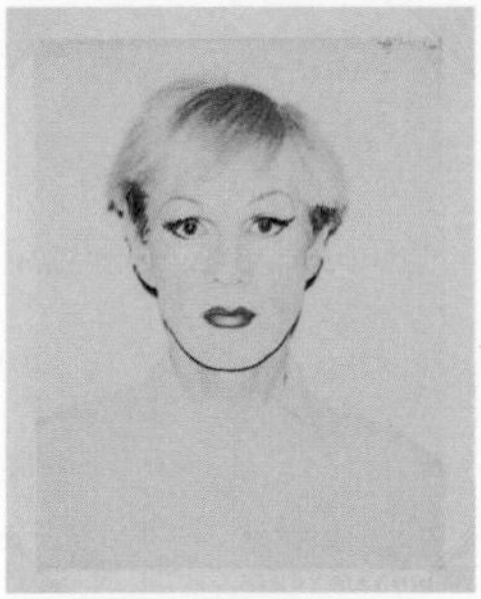

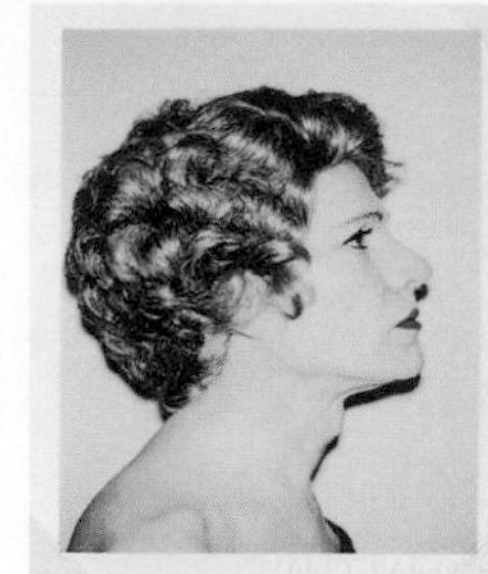

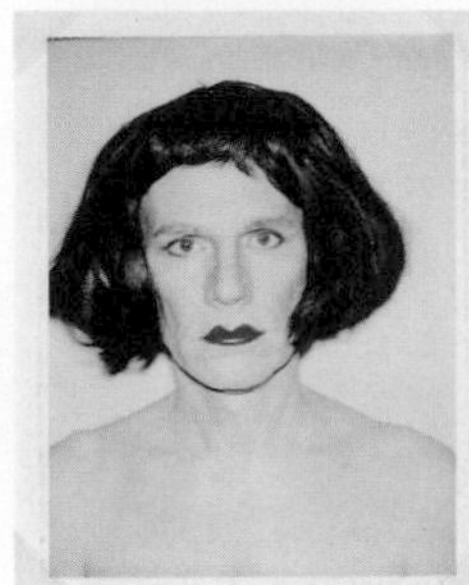
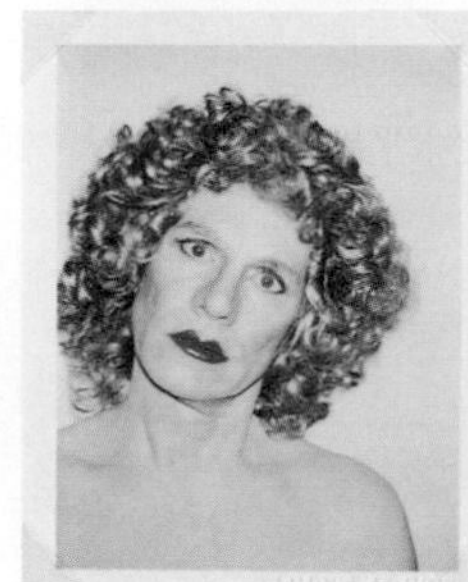

Andy Warhol, *Self-Portraits*, 1981

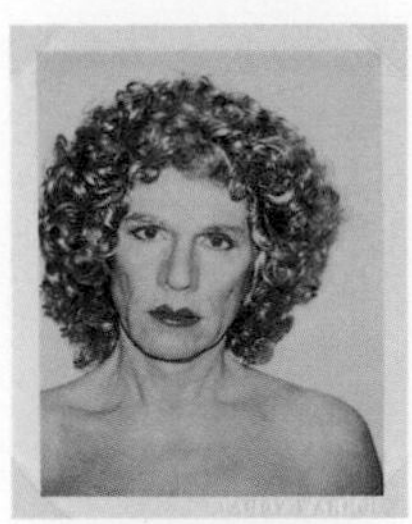

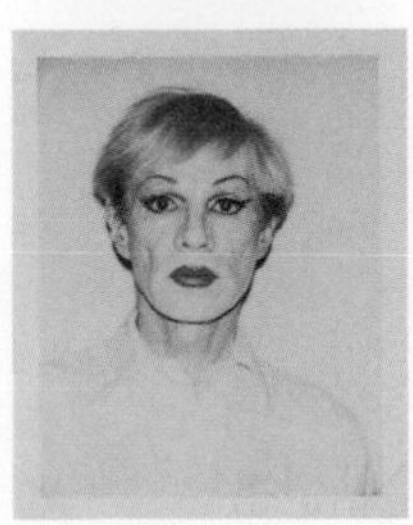

Andy Warhol, *Self-Portraits*, 1981
Opposite: Christopher Makos, *Altered Image*, 1981

Seeking Fred's Approval

The day before the meeting, everyone at the
Factory wishes me "luck."
I begin to suspect something.
Mark Francis explains, "Fred's not well; drugs
cause wild mood swings. If it gets ugly, I'll get
you out of there. He needs to meet you."
On the day, taxi to Hughes's brownstone,
Upper East Side.
Ushered in.
Strange first impression: Americana.
Hughes in wheelchair. Art stacked everywhere.
Combination of effects hard to handle.
Texan: good-old-boy accent.
Dandy: effeminate gestures, cravat.
Drugs: pain, slurred speech.
Addiction: chewing Nicorettes furiously.
Smoking gestures without the cigarettes.
Butting fingers in imaginary ashtray.
Conversation races through wild highs and lows.
Insists on playing Diana Ross at full volume.

Yelling over top.
Attendant drops off a few more Oldenburgs
during meeting – leans them on Rauschenberg.
Fred at center of media controversy.
As executor of the estate,
accused of spiriting off Warhols after death.
Now attacking everyone.
Paranoid.
Slips in and out of impersonating his enemies.
I'm never absolutely sure who is speaking.
For emphasis pulls out gum.
Sticks it to table as punctuation.
"Must they insist on torturing a cripple?!"
Retrieves gum. Carries on.
He doesn't like what he's seen of my work.
Decides he likes me.

Outside in street.
Head pounding from focusing so hard for hours,
trying desperately to follow.
Mark says, "That was good."

Spectacle or Forum

At the time we received the commission from the Art Gallery of Ontario, the institution was beset by internal conflict. Even at senior levels, there seemed to be diverse answers to the question of what the gallery was. There was an unresolved tension between its archival responsibility, as a collector of artifacts, and its growing tendency to take on entertainment functions. This conflict is not unusual for North American art museums.
Our pragmatic response was to invent a scenario method. We created a set of ideal scenarios one might apply to the gallery—think tank, archive, marketplace, spectacle, forum. We presented these scenarios to different groups of employees and asked them to select the ones they thought applied and to single out those that didn't. The strategy was productive: it allowed the staff of the gallery to share a common language in defining the values the identity ought to express.
When we began the work, I was a proponent of aggressive communication inside art museums. I believed that a level of didacticism was necessary to support certain kinds of art work, to enhance viewer experiences, and to create a louder voice for the gallery within its own walls. Since then I have developed doubts. The way I see it now, the art museum represents one of the few public spaces where the volume can be turned down and contemplation encouraged.

Art Gallery of Ontario (AGO)
Toronto, 1996
The Art Gallery of Ontario commissioned BMD to develop its new visual identity. The gallery identified a unique set of concerns relating to its collection, its location, and the changing demographic profile of its audience.

AGO
Gallery of Ontario
Canada

Audition

Presentation for Universal Studios identity program, 1996

When Edgar Bronfman, Jr. took the helm at Universal, Rem Koolhaas received the commission to prepare a master plan for Universal Studios in Los Angeles. Around the same time, Universal had commissioned a new identity program. The new management was not happy with the results and asked three designers to review the problem. On Rem's recommendation we were placed on the shortlist for the project. The other two contenders were large firms. We decided to prepare a thorough analysis of the film studio's identity in order to determine what strategies ought to be devised. Our presentation, which follows, was delivered to Frank Biondi and other Universal senior executives on June 17, 1996, in the boardroom of Universal's "black tower" in Los Angeles.

Ladies and Gentlemen, thank you for inviting me to present to you today.
Universal is probably the most recognizable of all the major film studios and has, historically, one of the strongest brand signatures in the field. If we are to renovate the identity program for Universal, our first step must be to separate the wheat from the chaff. If we can determine where the equity in the old signature resides, we will know what to keep and, conversely, where the liberty lies. Where is the equity? What terrain does Universal own?

Let's look at the history of your identity:

In our memory, it seemed that your logo had always been the same. In fact, it has evolved over time.

At the moment, the signature has three elements: the globe, the spatial illusion of depth, and the type.
The problem with the globe is that, in itself, it is generic. It is very difficult to make a signature globe because it is such a popular image in corporate logos:

Literally millions of companies use the globe in some graphic format as their visual metaphor.

The type is also fairly nonspecific. For over thirty years, bold all-caps fonts have been used—currently a version of Copperplate. While declaring the brand to be essentially modernist and confident, this type has never given a voice to Universal, and so, doesn't have much equity:

It seems that the spatial illusion is, historically, the most powerful aspect of the identity. The name of the company in front of a globe *set in space* is the signature configuration:

However, without a rich rendering of the spatial dimension, the signature joins a class of conventional corporate brands. As the rendering becomes two-dimensional and graphic, the globe loses its distinctiveness. It recalls a collection of references, but these are mostly backward-looking and nostalgic. It's on its way to being merely a "graphic logo":

If I have any advice for you today it's this: if someone comes along and wants to sell you a "graphic logo," don't buy it. You're an image company in the age of the image. You don't want plastic deadness. The solution needs to be spatial and unique.

Now, let's figure out exactly where the equity lies. If we begin to look at the basic configuration—a straight thing in front of a round thing—we see how resilient it is:

These "experiments" show that it is the content *and* quality of the spatial configuration—the cinematic illusion of the *earth in space*—that is unique, not the configuration in and of itself:

Now, let's look at developments in terrestrial imaging in recent years:

A model of the thermographic structure of oceans:

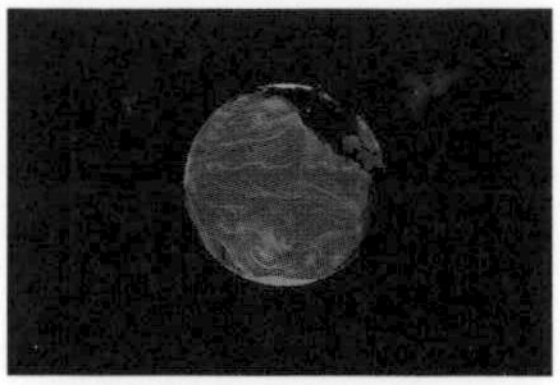

A view of North America at night:

A 3-D model of Tokyo Bay from digital stereoscopic satellite imaging:

An image of the earth created through a composite of thousands of satellite pictures.

We tried a Universal identity using a real photo of the earth from space.

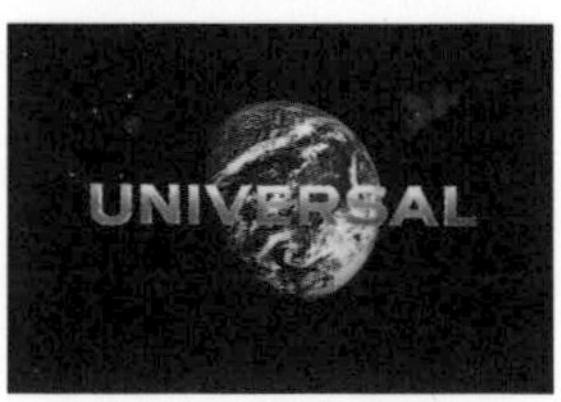

In doing so, we realized that what we want is somewhere between the "real" and the "simulated." We can imagine building a 3-D model of the earth that takes the next step in image/data evolution.

At this point we realized that no matter how beautifully and technologically sophisticated the rendering is, the globe is still generic. Anyone can use it, and anyone with technology and data similar to Univeral will create globes like it. Looking back, this was true in the past, and will remain so in the future. Keeping up with the leading edge of imaging must be part of the Universal mandate, but it's not what generates brand equity.

We find ourselves back at "square one," which in this case means typography—how we write the name:

If the type is generic, we have to rely on the configuration—the globe and space—which we've just shown isn't generating brand equity. In its animated applications, the current Universal name emerges from behind the globe—spectacular in 35mm.

But the key question is how to retain the signature when the spatial illusion of cinema is unavailable. For example, if you have to represent the brand in black and white print, you don't have the benefit of cinematic illusion to carry the signal. What will crack the problem is a distinctive font. We don't have that. The problem with what we've got is that other brands have it too:

BELVIEW ESTATES
FIRST NATIONAL BANK OF SPRINGFIELD
UNIVERSAL STUDIOS
PULLMAN LINE
THOMPSON FUNERAL HOME
ROTO ROOTER

Any other font taken directly off the shelf won't do either:

Even worse, there are literally hundreds of "versions" of the font currently used:

So while the cinematic rendering of the type is unique to Universal, the typography itself is not distinctive. I want to show a project in which I was asked to resolve a similar problem:

The institution wanted to create a singular typographic identity that could fuse a futuristic agenda with historical cachet. The project involved designing signage and environmental graphics for the Walt Disney Concert Hall. We created a font that works for both contemporary and classical performance. We used a technique we called "font breeding."

This is how it works. Two parent fonts are crossed to produce a series of children, each with distinctive, unique characteristics:

UNIVERSAL
UNIVERSAL
UNIVERSAL
UNIVERSAL
UNIVERSAL
UNIVERSAL

I believe that this is where Universal needs to go. We need a new font that looks forward, not back, that is hip, edgy, innovative, and glamorous. And, most importantly, unique and exclusive. Thank you.

Postscript: The challenge we posed to the Universal executives in the interview was how to build the brand outside its film medium. The solution, we felt, had to be typographic, not illustrative. Could these denizens of the image industry accept that there was more to type than meets the eye?
In the end, our audition for Universal was a failure. But everyone, including us, learned a great deal about the demands besetting brand identity in our visually adept culture.
In the last instance, what scared our client—the group of people sitting around that table in the black tower—was that we proposed a process, not a fixed, sure-fire solution for the brand.
What I couldn't know as I looked across the table at them in 1996 was that within two years not one of them would still be working at Universal. Edgar fired them all.

Indigo Book Stores
Toronto, 1997

BMD developed a comprehensive visual identity program for Indigo, a new Canadian retail chain that was opening its first three flagship stores in Ontario. The program included the Indigo brand identity, logo, marketing formats, in-store graphics, directional signage, signature graphic concepts, and selected product design.

The studio worked in collaboration with the architecture firm KPMB to create a retail environment for Indigo in which the brand identity, signage systems, interiors, and architecture would be totally integrated. The project was completed over an intensive seven-month period.

The Indigo project was a start-up venture, where everything had to be invented from scratch. In retrospect, it seems extraordinary that Indigo's CEO, Heather Reisman, commissioned us. We had no experience with commercial retail. We had worked chiefly with publishers and arts organizations.

In our discussions, Reisman described her ambitions and concept clearly. She wanted the stores to be formal, calm, and intimate. Because we had no experience with retail, and a great deal of experience with book design, our strategy was to make a "book" out of Indigo. We extrapolated everything, from shopping bags to signage, from this idea. We approached the design of the store signage as we would a book's title page—issues of legibility were treated on an architectural scale.

What people entering a bookstore need most is clear navigation, because books (unlike furniture or housewares) are fairly generic as objects. Our solution was to scale difference between genres, using drop-down banners, different typefaces, and display labels in a subtle gradation. We imagined that a patron, on entering an Indigo store, could effectively "flip" through its table of contents by scanning the signage.

Somehow, it all worked out. We ended up producing a successful brand and voice for Indigo. We devised a method for channeling attention, and this produced enormous business value. All this was new for the studio.

The value we had generated previously, with the identity programs for NAi and the AGO, was cultural in nature. Here it was value added to a business.

Inventing a Voice

As our world develops greater and greater logistical infrastructure for the effective distribution and circulation of manufactured goods, along with online consumer services that support global price comparison, and timely and effective delivery, the goods themselves — even highly designed products — become increasingly commodified.

Except where technique or sensibility (innovation or style) is proprietary, there is no sustainable advantage in the product itself. This condition is perhaps most glaringly obvious in the distribution and sale of books. Although a particular book may be intensively differentiated from any other book through the application of design technique, as a commodity it is available through multiple possible distribution channels. In the post-Amazon.com jungle, all bookstores must now ensure that every book is available all the time, deliverable anywhere, and at the lowest cost. It's a gloomy, downward spiral.

In this environment, the only way to build real equity is to add value: to wrap intelligence and culture around the product. The apparent product, the object attached to the transaction, is not the actual product at all. The real product has become culture and intelligence.

To build brand identity is to engineer a voice with all the nuance and complexity of any individual voice. In the case of a major retail brand, that voice is articulated through varied and complex channels. In the retail environment, for example, communication

!ndigo
Books Music & more
ruit, french wine,
nd a little music..."
JOHN KEATS 1795-1821

is ultra-broadband, its signal carried on innumerable subliminal wavelengths. It is carried in language, color and typography, but also in materials, textures, images, pricing, services, light, sounds, and even smells. Every gesture and decision helps to define the voice. Everything about the people who make up the company, what they wear, how they respond to questions and complaints, adds to — or detracts from — the clarity and value of the voice and, therefore, the equity of the brand.

As communication travels beyond the physical bounds of the retail environment, the bandwidth is radically reduced, and the challenge of maintaining the voice intensifies. When the brand is applied to the Internet environment, for example, the bandwidth collapses to a wafer-thin stream that must somehow carry the voice or character of the brand.

A design identity functions to capture energy, so that all gestures are converted into equity. At this moment, communication design plays a critical role in directing the energy of an enterprise: by clarifying it, expressing it, giving it direction, and channeling resources to critical functions. The equity of the brand is real and exists only insofar as the value of the brand is perceived by its customers. The situation is Darwinian in the best and worst sense. If a business communicates values at odds with its customers, they will punish it with a sudden and sharp decline in brand equity. If, on the other hand, that company expresses or reflects the ambitions and aspirations of its customers, its identity will resonate with its clients and they will become attached to the brand. For companies that fail to understand the prevailing fate of the

A tribute to a nation's writers, artists and thinkers on Indigo's "Canada Wall"

commodities they sell, the consequences can be brutal. The brand is the "democratic" mechanism of business culture. Where brands are concerned, people vote with their wallets. It is the customer's way of making business acccountable. Branding is the public address system of capitalism. Coca-Cola has no choice but to conduct its affairs in the full glare of public view. We know where Nike, Prada, and Philips live. It is the non-brands, the numbered companies, the invisible businesses, toward which we ought to be vigilant.

The beauty of a start-up company like Indigo is that nothing exists a priori. Everything has to be invented. There is no one to ask. No one knows. It has never been done by anyone. There are no departments, no policies, no history, no territorial disputes, no rule books. It is a free-fall—no parachutes, no nets. Success is limited only by the capacity to imagine solutions, communicate, and mobilize resources.

Under these conditions, the world is composed of two character types: those who round down and those who round up. Heather Reisman of Indigo rounds up—every idea leads to another. With her as a business thinker and collaborator, creative partnership defies gravity in an escalating scenario of invention. Nothing escapes. No detail is too insignificant, no issue too big, no idea too outlandish.

This commitment to subjecting every aspect of a business to a process of rounding up cannot be underestimated. In a world where shopping is everything, to affect culture, you have to change retail.

Soft "O"

Virtual Office of Integrated Design (VOID)
San Francisco, 1998
VOID was a design studio in San Francisco founded by Thomas Meyerhöffer and Yves Béhar. Their vision was to design imaginative and brand-building products for the technology, sports, furniture, and housewares industries, with the objective of creating emotional icons for their respective markets. The acronym, VOID, embodied the concept of the office, which aspired to have the lightest infrastructure possible by assembling a multidisciplinary team of associates to deal with each project. We made an identity-mark that centered on reshaping every application around variants of the O. If O stands for office, and their office reshapes itself, then the O design of the VOID identity interpreted the creations of the company through a series of morphing O forms/voids. It reflects the discourse VOID sought to generate between the rational framework of technology and the organic world, between the individual and the group, between the desire for permanence and the inevitability of change and transformation.

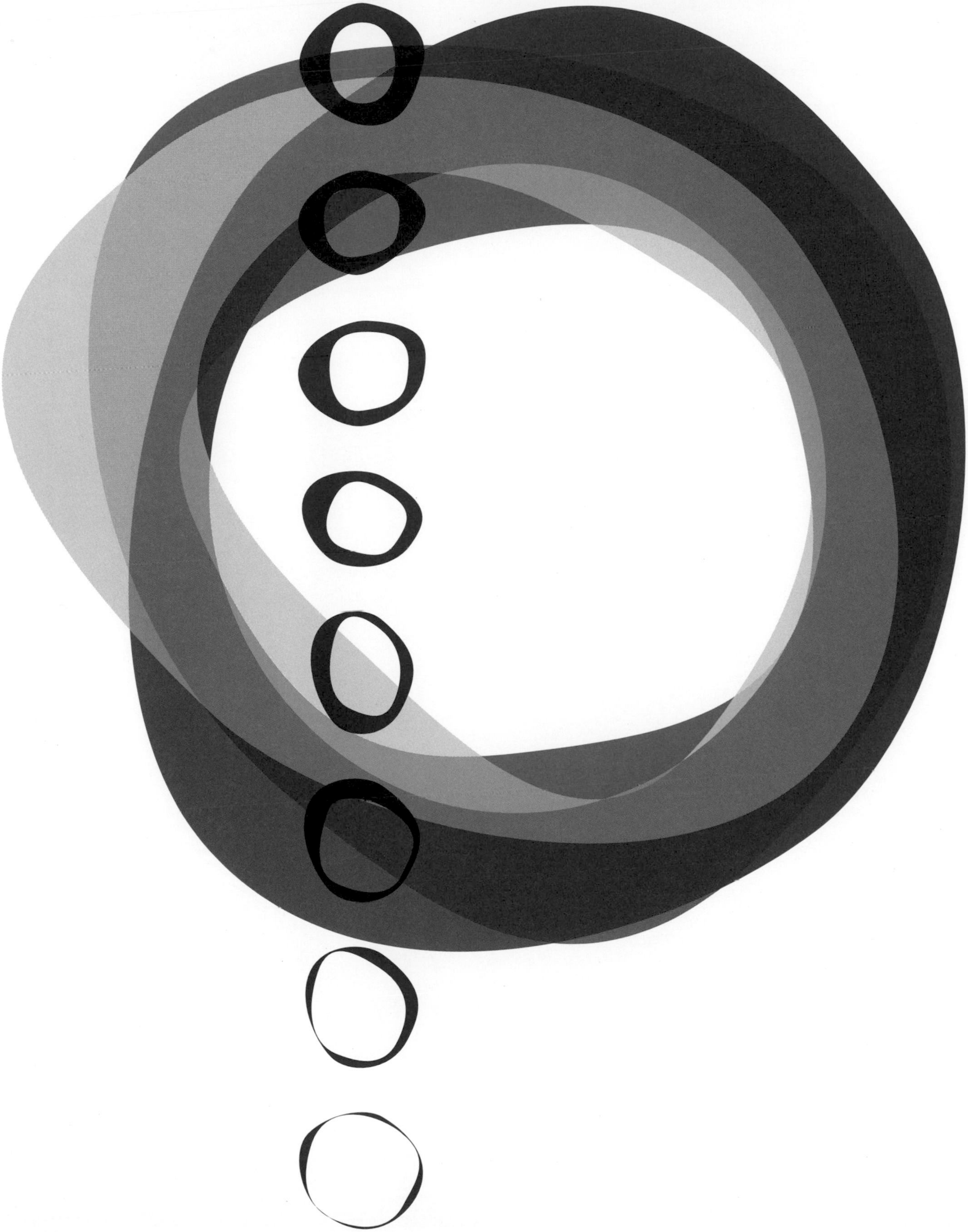

Figure and Ground

Rice University, School of Architecture Houston, Texas, 1998 Catalog and Poster

This commission was a sort of surreptitious identity project. The school never contracted us to do an identity for them, but Lars Lerup, the dean of the school, talked a little bit about putting the place on the map in terms of communicating its sensibility to the outside world. The question of geography was paramount. Rice is in Houston, and being in Houston is like being in Toronto: it's a big place, but its significance hardly registers on the radar screens of New York, Los Angeles, London, Paris, and Tokyo. Houston is a second-tier city. The catalog was a collaboration between the studio and Rice graduates Luke Bulman and Kim Shoemake, as part of my appointment as the Cullinan professor. We used a font called Interstate, designed for highways. (Houston is famous for expressway design and development.) All images were of Houston, taken by George O. Jackson, an associate of Rice who had been documenting the city for years in a way that makes Houston the most toxic and glamorous place on the planet.

Shown here are the first catalog, a poster prototype and two final posters.

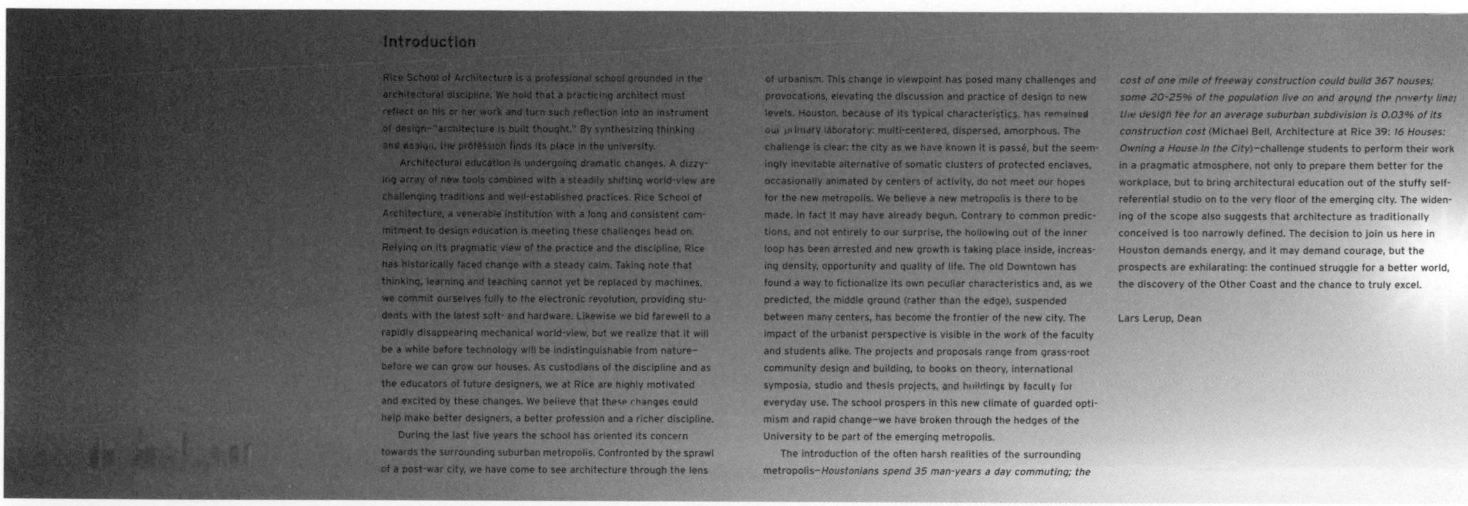

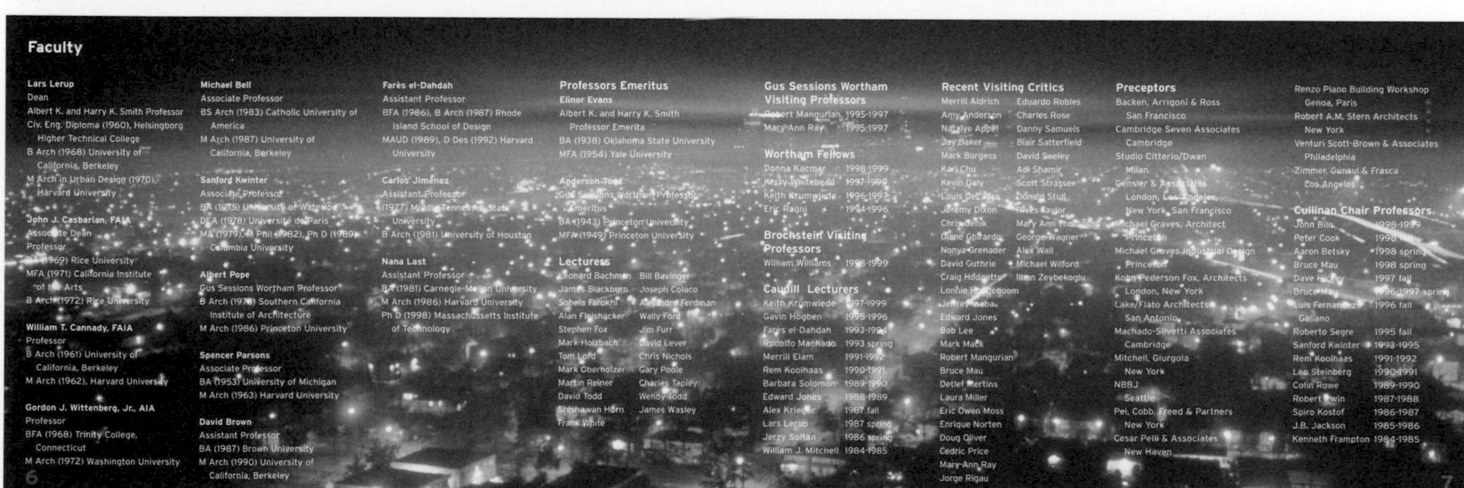

Master of Architecture

The Master of Architecture program prepares graduates for a full range of professional activities in the field of architecture. It is offered to individuals who possess a bachelor's degree. Students follow a course of study in all four areas of the curriculum: Design; History, Theory and Criticism; Structures, Practice, as well as Environments; and Computing, Logic, and Representation. These areas of study are sustained by groups of courses from which students may choose offerings according to the requirements of their particular program. Strong emphasis is given to developing design skills, logic, and imagination through an intensive series of design studio courses. Students are also required to prepare an independent thesis before graduating. A potential exists for dual degrees. The Master of Architecture program leads to a professional degree; please see note on page 31 from the National Architectural Accrediting Board (NAAB) for more information on accreditation and licensing.

Programs of Study

There are three program options at the Master of Architecture level: Options 1, 2, and 3, which differ according to the bachelor's degree received prior to entering the graduate program.

Option 1: seven semester program

Option 1 is offered to individuals who hold a four year undergraduate degree with a major in a field other than architecture. Preference for admission is given to those who have completed a balanced education in the arts, sciences, and humanities. A minimum of two semesters of college level courses in the history of art and/or architecture and one semester of college level courses in mathematics or physics are recommended. Previous preparation in the visual arts is also desirable as are courses in philosophy, literature and economics.

In order to graduate, students must complete a four semester core curriculum (76 credit hours), which is followed by a three semester advanced curriculum (57 credit hours). Coursework in both core and advanced curricula consist of seven studios (including thesis) and 20 distribution courses (133 credit hours).

Typical Curriculum

Core

1st Semester

Arch 501	Core Design Studio I
Arch 685	Architecture and Society I
Arch 507	Introduction to Design of Structures
Arch 633	Intro to Computer Applications in Architecture

2nd Semester

Arch 502	Core Design Studio II
Arch 686	Architecture and Society II
Arch 514	Design of Structures II
Arch 636	Computer Aided Design in Architecture

3rd Semester

Arch 503	Core Design Studio III
Arch 683	20th Cent. History of Ideas in Arch.
Arch 515	Design of Structures III
	Distribution Elective in Computing, Logic, and Representation

4th Semester

Arch 504	Core Design Studio IV
Arch 516	Building Climatology
Arch 623	Professionalism and Management. in Arch.
	Distribution Elective in History, Theory and Criticism

Advanced

5th Semester

Arch 601	Architectural Problems
	Distribution Elective in Computing, Logic, and Representation
	Distribution Elective in History, Theory and Criticism
	Elective

6th Semester

Arch 602	Architectural Problems
Arch 701	Pre-Thesis Preparation
	Distribution Elective in Structures, Practice, and Environments
	Elective

7th Semester

Arch 703	Thesis Studio*
	Elective
	Elective

*or an approved alternative

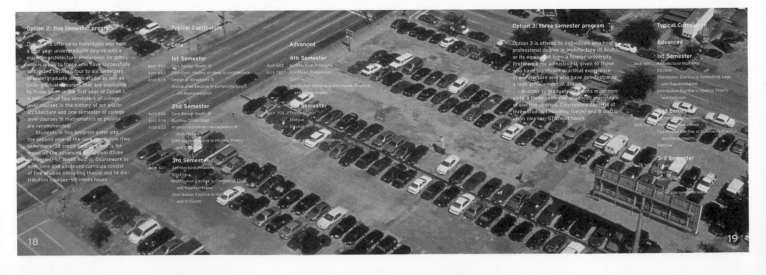

Option 2: five semester program

Option 2 is offered to individuals who hold a four year undergraduate degree with a major in architecture. Preference for admission is given to those who have successfully completed between four to six semesters of undergraduate design studio as well as undergraduate courses that are analogous to those given in the first year of Option 1. A minimum of two semesters of college level courses in the history of art and/or architecture and one semester of college level courses in mathematics or physics are recommended.

Students in this program enter into the second year of the core curriculum (two semesters–38 credit hours), which is followed by the advanced curriculum (three semesters–57 credit hours). Coursework in both core and advanced curricula consist of five studios (including thesis) and 14 distribution courses–95 credit hours

Typical Curriculum

Core

1st Semester

Arch 503	Core Design Studio III
Arch 683	20th Cent. History of Ideas in Architecture
Arch 515	Design of Structures III
	Distribution Elective in Computing, Logic and Representation

2nd Semester

Arch 504	Core Design Studio IV
Arch 516	Building Climatology
Arch 623	Professionalism and Management in Architecture
	Distribution Elective in History, Theory and Criticism

3rd Semester

Arch 601	Architectural Problems
	Elective
	Distribution Elective in Computing, Logic and Representation
	Distribution Elective in History, Theory and Criticism

Advanced

4th Semester

Arch 602	Architectural Problems
Arch 701	Pre-Thesis Preparation
	Elective
	Distribution Elective in Structures, Practice and Environments

5th Semester

Arch 703	Thesis Studio*
	Elective
	Elective

*or an approved alternative

Option 3: three semester program

Option 3 is offered to individuals who hold a professional degree in architecture (B.Arch.), or its equivalent from a foreign university. Preference for admission is given to those who have significant practical experience in architecture and who have demonstrated a high achievement in design.

In order to graduate, students must complete a three semester advanced curriculum of elective courses. Coursework consists of three studios (including thesis) and 8 distribution courses–57 credit hours.

Typical Curriculum

Advanced

1st Semester

Arch 601	Architectural Problems
	Elective
	Distribution Elective in Computing, Logic, and Representation
	Distribution Elective in History, Theory and Criticism

2nd Semester

Arch 602	Architectural Problems
Arch 701	Pre-Thesis Preparation
	Distribution Elective in Structures, Practice, and Environments
	Elective

3rd Semester

Arch 703	Thesis Studio*
	Elective
	Elective

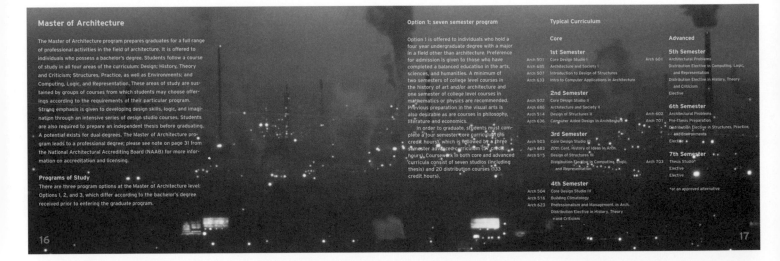

*or an approved alternative

Awards, Endowments and Special Funds

The School of Architecture benefits from special awards, endowments, and funds which enrich its scholastic, research and public service programs. At the end of each academic year the School of Architecture awards a significant number of grants and fellowships to its students for sponsored research and travel.

Honors

American Institute of Architects School Medal
Edward B. Arrants Medal
Chillman Prize
William D. Darden Medal
Tau Sigma Delta
Alpha Chi Rho Medal
AIA School Medal and Certificate
Rice Visionary Project

Scholarships

American Institute of Architects Scholarship
McGinty Scholarship Fund
Berda and Charles Soon Chan Memorial Scholarship
Ralph S. Herman Memorial Scholarship
Gene Hackerman Scholarship
Texas Architectural Foundation Scholarships

Traveling Fellowships

Rosemary Watkin Barrick Traveling Fellowship
John Crowder Traveling Fellowship
M.N. Davidson Fellowship
Margaret Everson Fossi Traveling Fellowship
John T. Mitchell Traveling Fellowship
Morris R. Pitman Traveling Fellowship
William Ward Watkin Traveling Fellowship
Mary Ellen Hale Lovett Travelling Fellowship
Mary Alice Elliot Travelling Fellowship

Professorships

Craig Francis Cullinan Chair in Fine Arts, Architecture and Urban Planning
Harry K. and Albert K. Smith Chair in Architecture
Gus Sessions Wortham Professorship in Architecture

Special Funds

William Wayne Caudill Lecturers
Smith Fund in Architecture
Betty R. and George F. Pierce, Jr. FAIA Fund
Brochstein Fund

Acknowledgements

The publication of this catalog is made possible in part by support from the Harry K. Smith Fund.

All photographs by George O. Jackson selected from the George O. Jackson Collection of Houston Photographs

Although every effort has been made to ensure that the information contained in this catalog is accurate at the time of publication, October 1998, the School of Architecture reserves the right to make corrections and changes in any information contained herein. Courses of instruction, programs, degree requirements, fees and any other information are subject to change in accordance with established academic procedures.

Note on NAAB Accredidation:
"The Master of Architecture program is accredited by the National Architectural Accrediting Board (NAAB). In the United States, most state registration boards require a degree from an accredited professional degree program as a prerequisite for licensure. The National Architectural Accrediting Board (NAAB), which is the sole agency authorized to accredit US professional degree programs in architecture, recognizes two types of degrees: the Bachelor of Architecture and the Master of Architecture. A program may be granted a five-year, three-year or two-year term of accredidation, depending on its degree of conformance with established educational standards."

"Masters degree programs may consist of a pre-professional undergraduate degree and a professional degree, which when earned sequentially, comprise an accredited professional education. However, the professional degree is not, by itself, recognized as an accredited degree."

—National Architectural Accrediting Board

Design: Kimberly Shoemake and Luke Bulman in association with Bruce Mau Design, Toronto, Canada. Printed by Bowne of Toronto.

The moment
of our
disappearance
is fraught
with
possibility
Rice School of Architecture, Houston
Let's face it: the test of life will be multiple choice. Choose Rice. Call 1-800-555-RICE for more information.

The erosion
of tradition
demands
your
intervention
Rice School of Architecture
MS 50 P.O.Box 1892 Houston, Texas 77251-1892 phone: 713-527-4864 fax: 713-285-5277 e-mail: lerup@rice.edu website: www.arch.rice.edu
Las Palmas
MEXICAN FOOD
Hollywood

The bl
of o
bound
sugge

urrin
aries
sts

the sh
new t
Rice School o
6100 Main St ouston, Texas 77005 phone: 713-527-4864 fax

ap of
rrain.
Architecture
285-5277 up@rice.edu www.ruf.rice.edu/ arch/

The United States of Switzerland

I should have known.

There was something about the tone of the letter. The Swiss organizers want this architecture conference to be as important as the World Economic Summit in Davos. Some things are better left unsaid.

Our hosts have asked three important architects, Rem Koolhaas, Jacques Herzog, and Norman Foster, to invite guests for one of three days of events. My reason for being here is an invitation from Rem.

He has also invited Mark Leonard—the brains behind Tony Blair's "Cool Britannia" branding campaign. In a hastily arranged conference call a few days earlier, Rem had explained that we should each address the issue of identity from our various perspectives—a British politician, a Dutch architect, and a Canadian designer.

The day begins with a musical composition inspired by the work of the invited architects. Fortunately, I sleep a little late this morning. However, I arrive in time for Mark Leonard to take the stage. He is brilliant. A classic motivational speaker. He roams the stage asking rhetorical questions about who the British think they are and how the rest of the world sees Britain; he then proceeds to answer these questions with flashes of statistical insight. He winds up his performance with several "scenarios."

Rem presents his research on African urbanism. (To see images of Nigerian squalor in a conference center in Pontrasina is profoundly incongruous.)

My presentation addresses the mechanisms and metaphors with which identity is produced. I announce that we will be running an identity workshop using the scenarios method we have evolved in the studio in order to redesign the identity of Switzerland.

Tough crowd, the Swiss.

For Canadians, the subject of identity is one of endless fascination. On the one hand we define ourselves by doubt as to who we are, and on the other by certainty as to who we are not. We are not the United States.

In the part of Canada known as The Rest of Canada — not Quebec — most of our free energy is spent not in promoting or celebrating who we are, but rather in trying in vain to discover or invent ourselves.

Former prime minister Pierre Elliott Trudeau once said, "Living next to the United States is in some ways like sleeping with an elephant. No matter how friendly and even-tempered the beast, one is affected by every twitch and grunt." This is the principal fact of Canadian identity. We live next door to the source of global culture. Our two nations share:

- the world's longest undefended border
- the world's highest dollar volume of bilateral trade
- one telephone country code — a stroke of genius on our part
- and, with NAFTA, greater and greater access to each other's markets.

We supply the United States with a disproportionate share of their cultural commentators and comedians, from Marshall McLuhan and John Kenneth Galbraith to Mike Myers and Jim Carrey. It is precisely this volatile mix of doubt and certainty that gives rise to such figures in Canada.

In an unpublished article about Toronto filmmaker David Cronenberg, Jonathan Crary describes the relationship of Cronenberg to Hollywood (i.e., of Canadians to the United States) as that of the termite to the log. The termite can eat the log, he can ingest it, regurgitate it, crawl on its surface or burrow through it, but he cannot become the log. As Canadians, we are not the United States.

The other fact of Canadian identity is the Quebec question—we even express certainties as questions. Once the cultural, business, and intellectual center of Canada, Quebec is now a province governed by ethnic nationalists. Quebec has been in decline for more than twenty years, with no bottom in sight. An atlas from the 1960s, before the Quiet Revolution (what other country could produce such a term?), shows the population of Montreal as twice that of Toronto. Today the situation is reversed, with much of the intellectual and economic capital having been transferred west to Toronto.

These nationalist identities rise and reassert themselves as a kind of tribalism just as they are being erased by new, seemingly unstoppable forces that perforate the nation-state. Operating at the largest possible scale, massively complex and widely distributed corporate entities are emerging that challenge the ability of the nation-state to control and regulate them. At the same time, communication technologies are now allowing collaborative work practices, which are mobile and unmappable, to challenge even the state's capacity to monitor its smallest unit, the individual citizen. The scope and depth of these changes places us in a dangerous moment: at times like this, masses retreat into mythologies.

Now for Switzerland.

I present seven scenarios—metaphors or models for rethinking the Swiss identity. It's meant as an exercise, a way of thinking freely that allows us to focus on a problem with almost cartoon-like clarity. What if Switzerland is:

- an entertaining new product in the market?
- a center of high culture?
- an inclusive, nurturing, liberal institution?
- the bastion of the old and new establishment?
- an entrepreneur?
- an archive?
- a leading-edge think tank?

During a short break, our hosts insist that we conduct our workshop in the forest. The entire assembly begins a slow procession down through the town and into the forest. *This* is Switzerland. Crisp clear mountain air, neatly manicured nature, a system of pathways—with signage—and, deep in the forest, a rustic amphitheater surrounded by towering pines. The stage is somehow already set: two chairs at a long table with a pristine white tablecloth and candelabras.

Rem and I take the stage and define the rules of the game: each participant is to choose one of the seven scenarios and form a group with like-minded individuals. Each group is to brainstorm a new Swiss identity based on their chosen metaphor. Rem and I move from group to group in an effort to assist the process. In every group we encounter one stubborn player stuck on what for them is a fundamental fact.

Angry Swiss architect: "Switzerland has a perfectly good identity. I don't

see why we have to make a new identity for Switzerland."
Koolhaas: "Cuckoo clocks and chocolate?"
Mau: "Look, it's an exercise; we're not really going to change your identity."
What is surprising is the ferocious intensity of the discussion. The group working on Switzerland as an archive nearly comes to blows as the young participants try in vain to get out from under the weight of Swiss dogma and history. What is evident is that identity, though constantly negotiated, is not negotiable. It's not something the citizen is willing to trade. It consists of a complex set of equations that define a place in the world, and any action or event that disrupts or alters those equations can set off uncontrollable forces.
In one of the groups someone suggests that through a simple process of naming we could express a new sensibility for Switzerland. Rem immediately takes hold of this thread and weaves it into an idea. Moving from group to group we prod and cajole new names from each metaphor. Rem's talent for making a silk purse has never been more clearly evident. Finally we take the stage and announce the success of each group in tackling their challenge.
From group one: "***Swissland***" (in bold italic lettering), an entertaining new product in the market.
From group three: "Switzerlands" (like The Netherlands), an inclusive, nurturing, liberal institution.
And finally, from group seven: a nation defined as a leading-edge think tank—"The United States of Switzerland."

Turning Solids to Fluids

As creatures of the modern metropolis, we are inundated with an ever-increasing barrage of branded visual information. In this sea of sensory data, how does one begin to form an association, a relationship with one particular voice or identity? How does an identity move from the background into the foreground?

Tension.

The new identity for al&d creates tension through the interplay of constants and variables. (Variables differentiate the identity from the background. Constants link the points of differentiation.) The identity reflects the evolving nature of the faculty by challenging classical delineations, which rely on a consistent and unchanging visual approach. Instead of reducing variables to constants and thereby eradicating chance, flux, and personality, the al&d identity is conceptualized as a constant/ variable matrix of three base components: the line, the stack, and the mark. Each component permits subtle shifts through morphing, color, or image, playing at the periphery of the core identity to permit flexibility and exploration while retaining a sense of coherence.

Faculty of Architecture,
Landscape & Design (al&d)
University of Toronto, 1999

faculty of
architecture
landscape
and design
university
of toronto

faculty of
architecture
landscape
and design
university
of toronto

The problem was this: "Faculty of Architecture, Landscape & Design" is not exactly a grabber of a name. There are good reasons that all these words are there, but they have to do with the originating end of the communication and not the receiving end. Once we recognized that the name was twice as long as that of any other school, the solution was obvious: the name itself. What configurations would work to give a long name a unique signature? Our solution was what we call the line and the stack. The line is the whole name in a single line. The stack is the name forced down and piled vertically. The school had been using "FALD" as its word-mark, but that seemed haphazard; "al&d" had a better cadence. So we made a mark. Having derived these elements, we tried various configurations to test the signature's flexibility and stability. The results appear in the al&d manual as an inventory of operations.

contents

from the Dean page 4

With the estimate of the world's population now at 6,000,129,811 there has never been a more important time for innovation and excellence in urban design, architecture and landscape architecture. Our planet of six billion people, most of whom live in cities, requires supportive infrastructure, vital neighbourhoods, proper shelter, useful parks, productive gardens and imaginative civic buildings. We must strive to create great communities, great urban places.

The Faculty of Architecture, Landscape, and Design (al&d) offers rigorous programmes of study for the emerging urbanist, architect or landscape architect. If you want to pursue one of these dynamic fields, the University of Toronto offers outstanding opportunities for creative work.

Whether joining us as an undergraduate in the new Architectural Studies programmes or entering our professional masters degree programmes in architecture, landscape architecture or urban design, you will discover a diverse, intensive community of students, teachers and support staff.

For more than 100 years, graduates of our school have spread across Canada and the world. From Bangkok to Brooklyn, Reykjavik to Rome, Vancouver to Vienna, our alumni are innovators and leaders in the design professions. I invite you to contact us and to start imagining your role in designing the architectural networks, structures and places necessary for a world of six billion.

Larry Wayne Richards, MOAA, FRAIC, AIA/IA
Dean, 19 July 1999

al&d career map page 2

graduate admissions page ...

Application procedure

1. Obtain an application package from the Faculty through one of the following routes:
   admissions.ald@utoronto.ca
   Graduate Admissions
   230 College Street
   Toronto ON Canada M5T 1R2
   T 416 978 5038
   F 416 971 2094
2. Following the instructions in the application package, send us the following materials: the completed application forms; two official copies of your complete academic record from all universities attended; three letters of reference; and a portfolio designed according to the "Portfolio Requirements" sheet included in the application package.

Application deadline
The application deadline for all graduate programmes is **February 1**, by which date you must have submitted all of the above elements of the application. Applications received after February 1 will be considered if places and awards are still available, but early application is strongly recommended.

Language of application
All documents in languages other than English or French must be submitted with certified English translations.

English language facility
Candidates whose primary language is not English and who graduated from a university where the language of instruction and examination was not English must have a TOEFL score of at least 580 with a TWE score of 5.0 or higher; 85 on the MELAB; or 7.0 on the IELTS.

6,000,129,811

Architect	▶	BA Architectural Studies (4 years) or other 4-year bachelor's degree	▶	MArch (3.5 years) *(U of T Specialist BA Architectural Studies graduates with a design concentration receive one year of advanced standing in the MArch)*	▶	Approximately 3 years' internship with architect	▶	Professional licensing examination
Landscape Architect	▶	BA Architectural Studies (4 years) or other 4-year bachelor's degree	▶	MLA (3 years)	▶	Approximately 2 years' internship with landscape architect	▶	Professional licensing examination
Urban Designer	▶		▶	BArch/BLA/ MArch/MLA	▶	MUD (2 years)	▶	Direct entry into practice

How to become an architect, landscape architect or urban designer at the University of Toronto

...er the BA architectural studies programmes page ...

How to apply
Students enter the BA Architectural Studies by first applying for admission to the Faculty of Arts and Science (not to the Faculty of Architecture, Landscape, and Design). When you make your application, select Stream III of the Faculty of Arts and Science, St. George Campus. To qualify for Stream III, you must be eligible for the Ontario Secondary School Diploma (OSSD) and present credits in at least six Ontario Academic Courses (OACs), one of which is OAC English 1/anglais. (If your mother tongue is not English and you have studied in an English language system for less than four years, you must present proof of English facility: for instance, TOEFL. In this case you do not have to present OAC English 1/anglais.)

Once you have been successfully admitted, enrolment follows the usual procedures in the Faculty of Arts and Science, where students are required to select their major at the end of the first year. Enrolment in the BA Architectural Studies requires the completion of four courses including ARC 131H and 132H. No minimum GPA is required, and there is no portfolio requirement.

Where to apply
All applicants can obtain programme information either from al&d or from:

Faculty of Arts and Science
University of Toronto
Sidney Smith Hall
100 St. George Street, Room 1068
Toronto ON Canada M5S 3G3
T 416 978 3384

www.artsandscience.utoronto.ca

Applicants from outside the Ontario Secondary School System should obtain application forms and related information from:

Admissions and Awards
University of Toronto
315 Bloor Street West
Toronto ON Canada M5S 1A3
T 416 978 2190

Application deadline
Application should be made early in the year for which admission is sought, and no later than April 1.

recent exhibitions, events and visitors page 12

Gallery Exhibitions 1997/1998
Thesis 98: *Frontispiece*
Still/Moving: 301 in New York City
Food City: Conception Production Consumption
Morphosis and Teeple, *Building for 2000/the University of Toronto Graduate Residence Project*
Projecting Beirut
RAIC/CIDA Youth Programme in Architecture
The Anatomy of Precedent: Structural Case Studies
Sophie Charlebois, *Moonlight Table: Still Life Part + Dreams + Other Realities*
Work of Studio Granda
Thesis Work, *Endgame*

Events 1998/1999
Forum with Frank Gehry
Santiago/Toronto Design Charette, *New City Hall Campus*
Stan Allen, Roger Keil, Marie-Paul MacDonald, Sandro Marpillero, Asha Varadharajan, John Knechtel (moderator), *Open City Symposium*
Urban Strategies, *U of T Open Space Symposium*

Visiting Lecturers and Critics 1998/99
Landscape
Robert Allsopp, David Anselmi, Martin Arnold, Beth Benson, Joe Berridge, Jean Besz, Douglas Birkenshaw, Mary Ellen Brennan, Michel Caron, Claude Cormier, John Davies, Adrian Di Castri, Judith Doyle, Stephen Ervin, Dennis Eveleigh, Robert Fones, Eldon Garnet, Sean Goetz Gadon, Chris Graham, Mary Hay, Michael Hoffman, Pamela Hubbard, Sharilyn Ingaram, Beth Kapusta, Joanna Kidd, Jusuck Koh, Nina-Marie Lister, Tony Lotimer, Janine Marcheseault, Brian McHattie, Donald McKay, Richard Milgrom, Ann Milovsoroff, Sheila Murray, Eha Naylor, David Oleson, George Pagowski, Bruce Peart, Kathleen Pirrie Adams, Cameron Portt, Deborah Root, Elissa Rosenberg, Jody Rosenblatt-Naderi, Val Ross, Val Rynnimeri, Thomas Seebohm, Dave Schmidt, Robert Shibley, Jeff Stinson, Peter Timmerman, Joe Tropman, Colin Vaughan, Agnes Vermes, Jerzy Wojtowicz

Architecture
Jennifer Bloomer, Shirley Blumberg, Ken Brooks, Scott Cohen, Tom Deacon, David Dernie, Ken Drucker, Lynne Eichenberg, Tye Farrow, Pat Hansen, David Jansen, Bernie Jin, John Johnston, Helen Kerr, Alar Kongats, Scot Laughton, Michael Lechman, Tim Love, Brigitte Luzar, Brian Mackay-Lyons, Reinhold Martin, Mary McAuliffe, Paul Mezei, Richard Milgrom, Michael Moxam, Nolan Natale, Tom Payne, Christie Pearson, Marco Polo, Bud Purvis, Paul Raff, Paul Reuber, Jody Rosenblatt-Naderi, Eha Naylor, Lindy Roy, Val Rynnimeri, Gilles Saucier, Don Schmitt, Catherine Seavitt, Thomas Seebohm, Elizabeth Sisam, Richard Slywka, Kim Storey, Gary Switzer, Agnes Vermes, Charles Waldheim, Kevin Weiss, Jerzy Wojtowicz, Peter Yeadon

Waltzing with Frank

In 1991 architect Frank Gehry commissioned us to design an original visual signature for the Walt Disney Concert Hall in downtown Los Angeles. The work proceeded from the premise that the graphic identity was not to mimic the architecture but to resonate with it by expressing its essential characteristics: humanity, originality, and wit.

WALT DISNEY

CONCERT HALL

WALT DISNEY CONCERT HALL

Walt Disney Concert Hall
Los Angeles, 1991
Environmental Graphics
We began by using animation techniques to produce an exclusive font. It was a technique that we evolved during *Zone 6*, where we morphed one letterform into another, looking for in-between stages. The resulting font was titled "A Font Called Frank." Clear and deceptively "regular" when reproduced on small applications such as letterhead, the font possessed complex qualities that are revealed when enlarged to the scale of architectural signage.

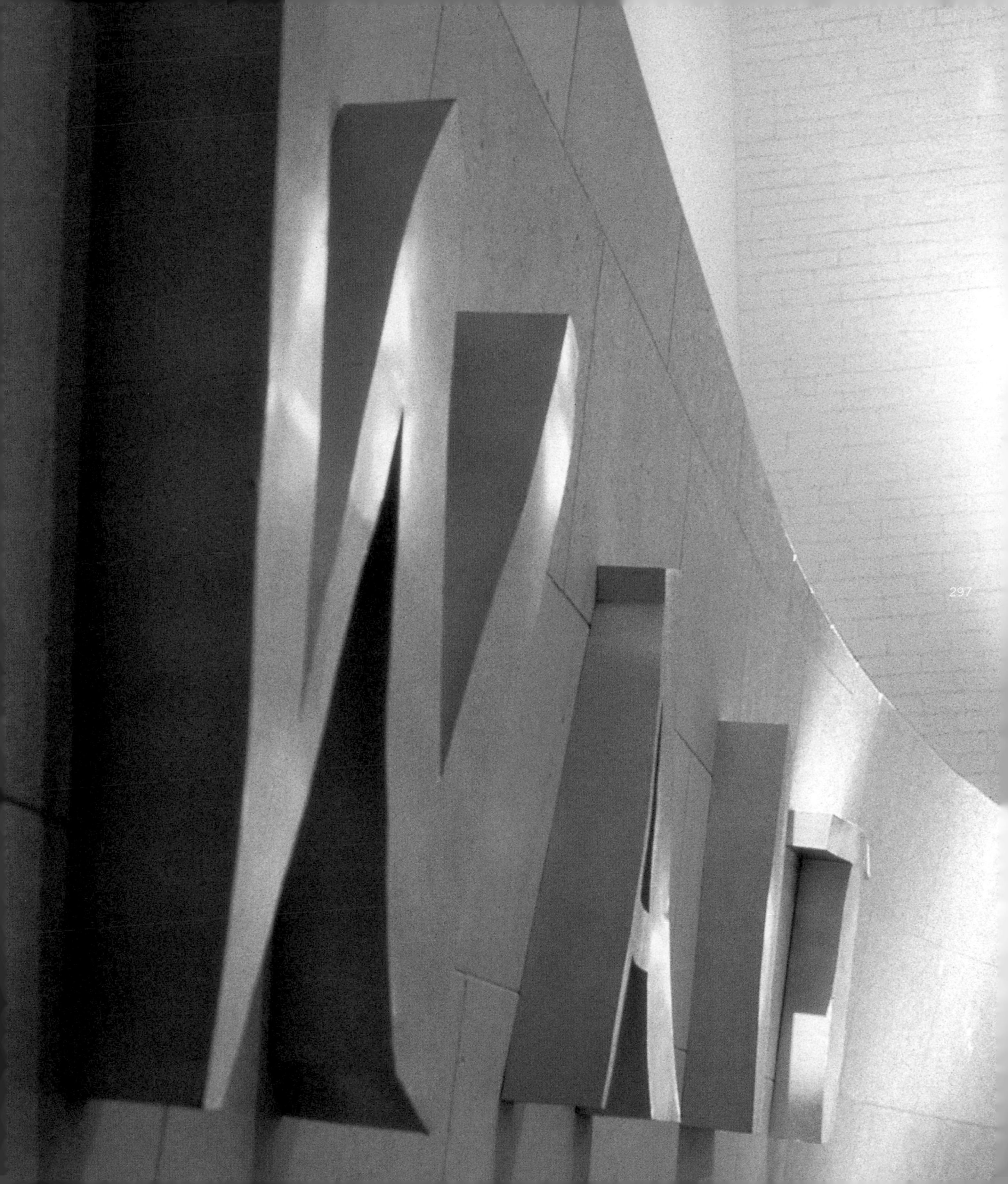

A B C D E
a b c d
H I J K L
h i j k
O P Q R S
o p q r
V W X Y Z
v w x y
5 3 1 & !
4 2 0 ?

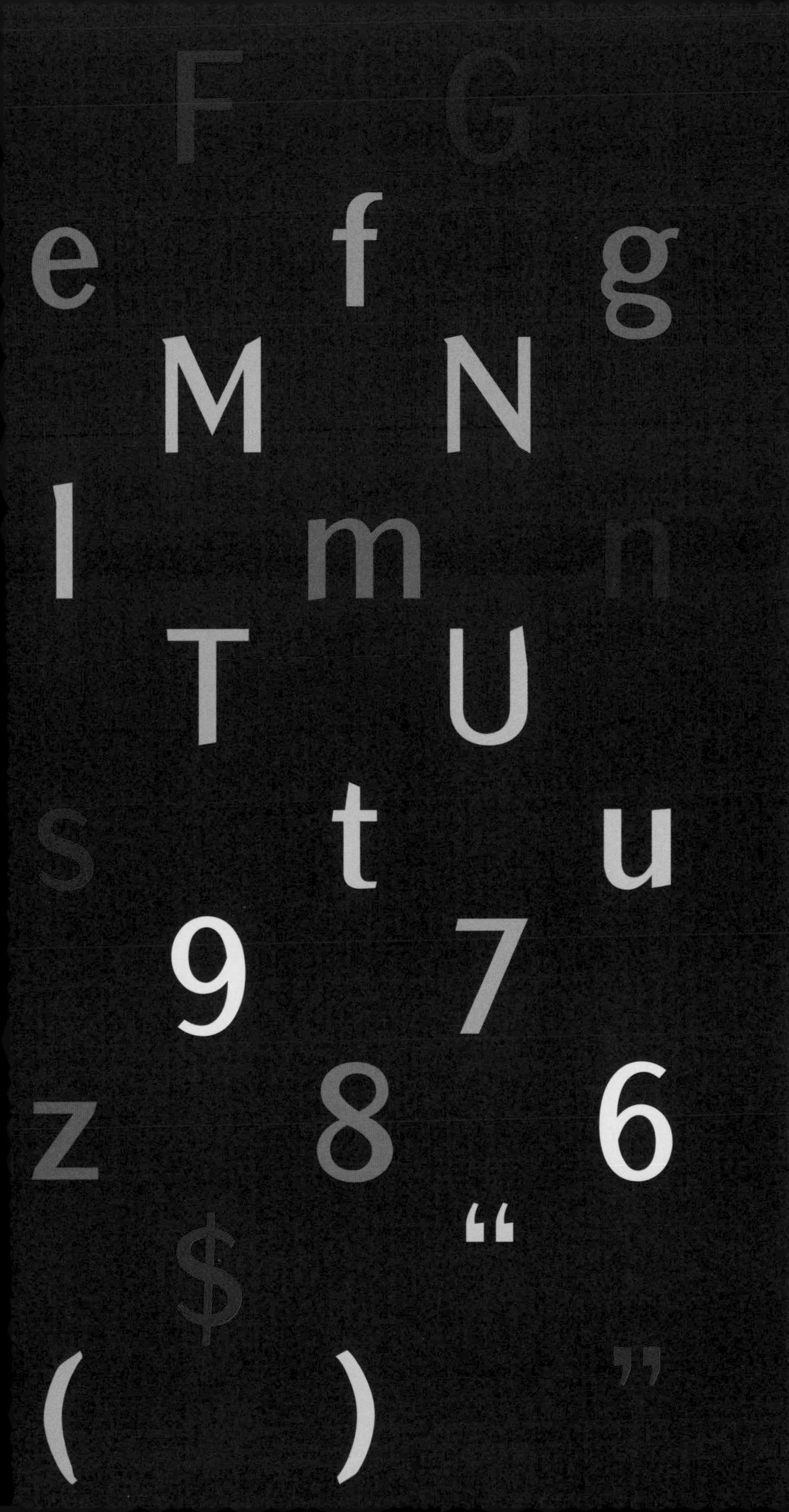
F G
e f g
M N
l m n
T U
s t u
9 7
z 8 6
$ “
( ) ”

Compositions by Cage

Lorem ipsum dolor sit amet, consectetuer adipiscing elit, sed diam nonummy nibh euismod tincidunt ut laoreet dolore magna aliquam erat volutpat. Ut wisi enim ad minim veniam, quis nostrud exerci tation ullamcorper suscipit lobortis nisl ut aliquip ex ea commodo consequat. Duis autem vel eum iriure dolor in hendrerit in vulputate velit esse molestie consequat, vel illum dolore eu feugiat nulla facilisis at vero eros et accumsan et iusto odio dignissim qui blandit praesent luptatum zzril delenit augue duis dolore te feugait nulla facilisi. Lorem ipsum dolor sit amet, consectetuer adipiscing elit, sed diam nonummy nibh euismod tincidunt ut laoreet dolore magna aliquam erat volutpat. Ut wisi enim ad minim veniam, quis nostrud exerci tation ullamcorper suscipit lobortis nisl ut aliquip ex ea consequat.

Duis autem vel eum iriure dolor in hendrerit in vulputate velit esse molestie consequat, vel illum dolore eu feugiat nulla facilisis at vero eros et accumsan et iusto odio dignissim qui blandit praesent luptatum zzril delenit augue duis dolore te feugait nulla facilisi. Nam liber tempor cum soluta nobis eleifend option congue nihil imperdiet doming id quod mazim placerat facer possim assum. Lorem ipsum dolor sit amet, consectetuer adipiscing elit, sed diam nonummy nibh euis-

3

Los Angeles Philharmonic
Ernest Fleischmann conducting
Berlioz
Symphonie fantastique
Beethoven
Symphony No. 7 in A, Op. 92
May 18, 1996, 8pm
WALT DISNEY
CONCERT HALL

Landscapes

tival Commemorating the Life and Work of John Cage

Dance and Concert Performances
Atlas Eclipticalis
Fontana Mix
4′33″
hpschd
Imaginary Landscapes I–IV
Third Construction
Variations I–VIII
Water Music

and works by
Satie
Stockhausen
Tudor

Participating Artists
Los Angeles Philharmonic
Cathy Berberian
Nexus
Merce Cunningham
Gordon Monahan
Brian Eno

Lectures and Presentations
The Future of Music: Credo
Electronics in Performance
Cage/Duchamp: Riddles and Rigor
Cage/McLuhan: The Medium is the Metalanguage
Indeterminacy and Romanticism

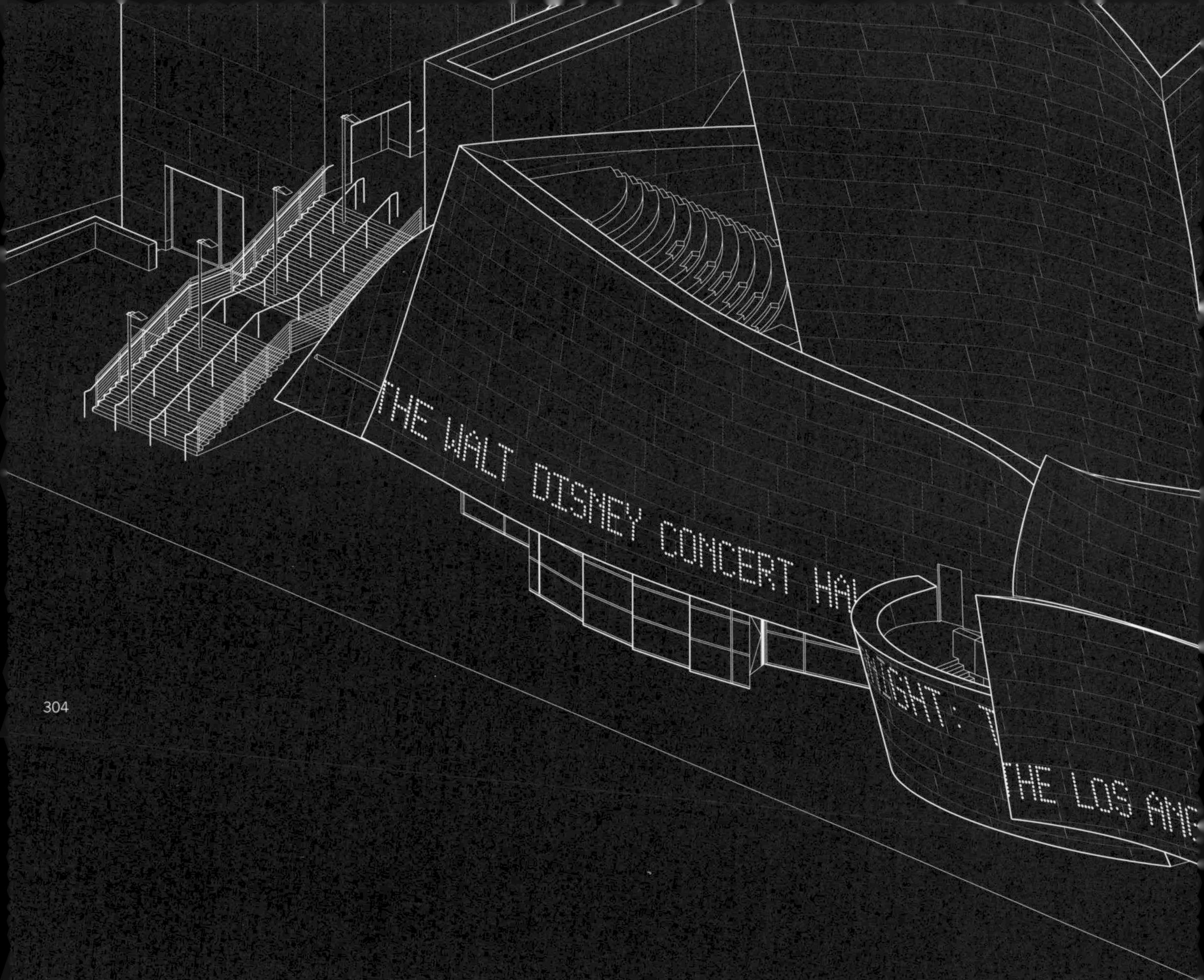
THE WALT DISNEY CONCERT HAL
IGHT: T
THE LOS ANG

LES PHILHARMONIC ORCHESTRA PERF
ORMS BEETHOVENS FIFTH SYM

Go-Go

In April 2000 the Gagosian Gallery was preparing to open a new site in London. After years of using a mishmash of designs for their three U.S. operations, the Gagosian decided it needed a cohesive identity to fuse its dispersed activities. Our proposal called for an approach that was neutral and discreet, understated and clear. The work culminated in the creation of a new, signature font.

GO

a b c d e f g h i j k l m n

A B C D E F G H I J K L M N

Gagosian Gallery Identity Program
2000

GO

o p q r s t u v w x y z
O P Q R S T U V W X Y Z

MOSTLY WOMEN

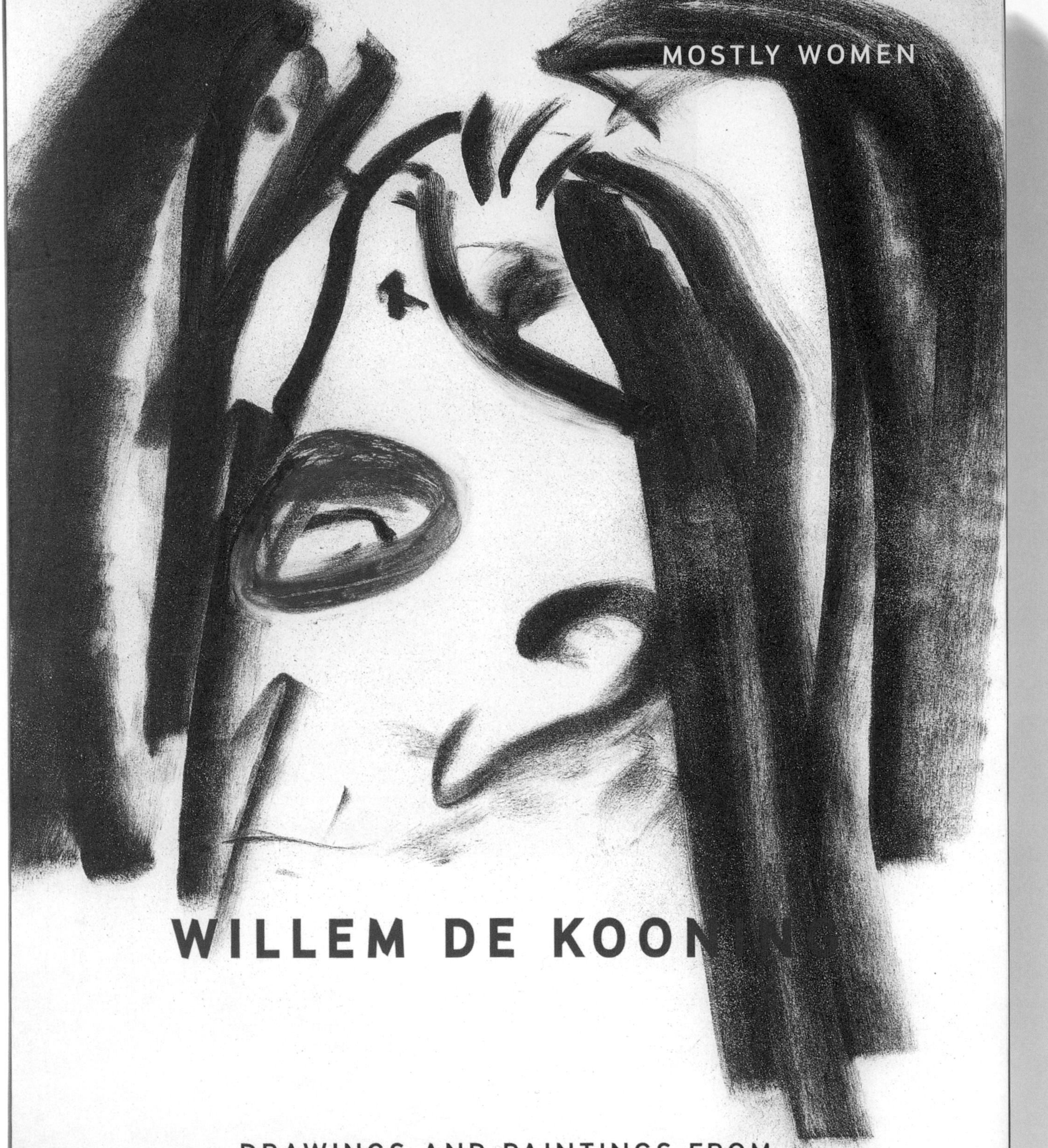

WILLEM DE KOONING

DRAWINGS AND PAINTINGS FROM
THE JOHN AND KIMIKO POWERS COLLECTION

MAY 9, 2000
6–9 PM
VB43
VANESSA BEECROFT
GAGOSIAN GALLERY
8 HEDDON STREET LONDON W1R 7LH ENGLAND T. 020.7292.8222 WWW.GAGOSIAN.COM

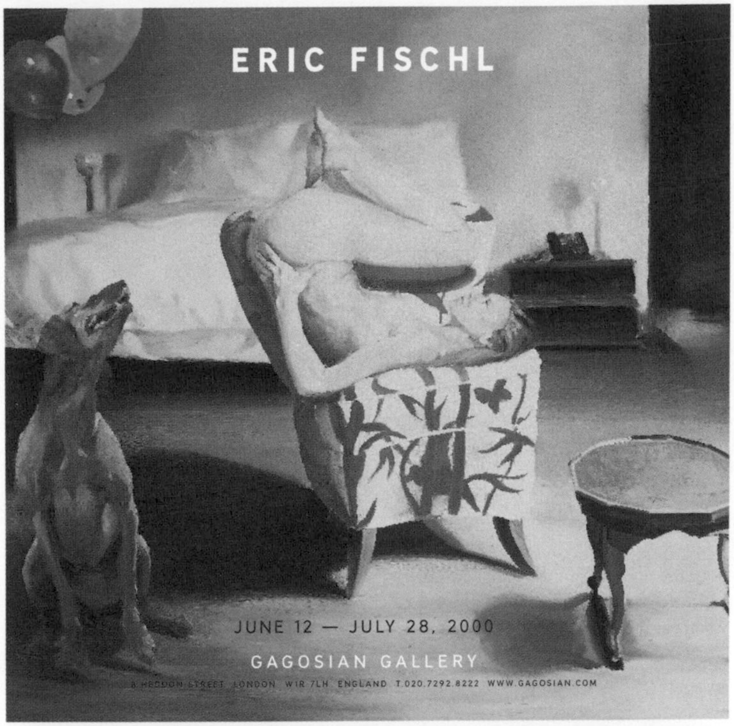
ERIC FISCHL
JUNE 12 — JULY 28, 2000
GAGOSIAN GALLERY
8 HEDDON STREET LONDON W1R 7LH ENGLAND T.020.7292.8222 WWW.GAGOSIAN.COM

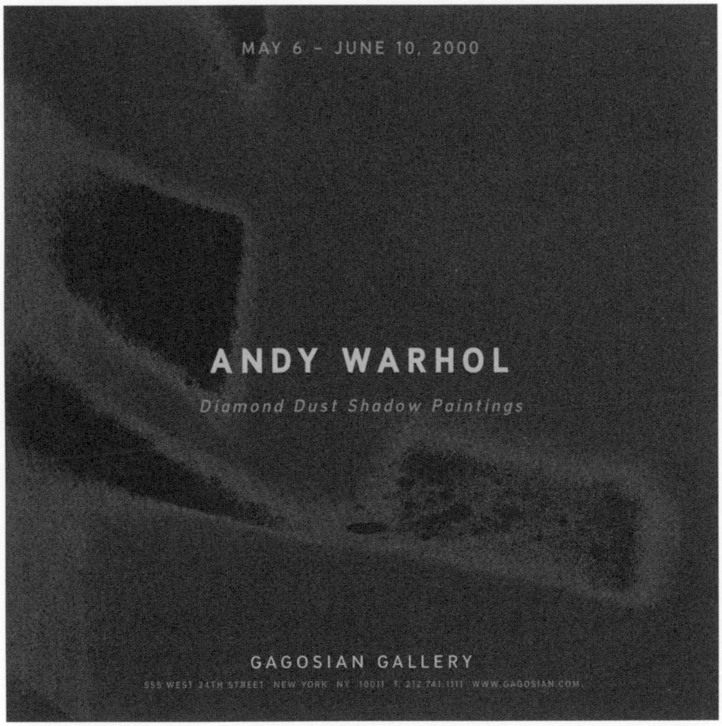
MAY 6 – JUNE 10, 2000
ANDY WARHOL
Diamond Dust Shadow Paintings
GAGOSIAN GALLERY
555 WEST 24TH STREET NEW YORK NY 10011 T. 212.741.1111 WWW.GAGOSIAN.COM

ART UNLIMITED, ART 31, BASEL
SCALE MODEL OF THE SOLAR SYSTEM
A SCALE MODEL OF THE SOLAR SYSTEM ACROSS THE CITY OF BASEL
JUNE 21 – 26, 2000
CHRIS BURDEN
GAGOSIAN GALLERY
8 HEDDON STREET LONDON W1R 7LH ENGLAND
T.020.7292.8222 INFO@GAGOSIAN.COM WWW.GAGOSIAN.COM
MAY 10 – JUNE 10, 2000

Can we envision

1. a font that asks more questions than it answers

2. a font that has projective memory that reminds you to remember

3. a font with a limited life span

4. a font with an expiry date

5. a font that's gone bad

6. a font without temporal inflection, without the imprint of its time

7. an apolitical font, a font that doesn't care

8. a font unaffected by the force of gravity and the weight of human history

9. a font without family, without ancestry

10. a Marshall McLuhan font that stubbornly persists in bidding farewell to itself

11. a font that takes advantage of all that promised "processing power"

12. a font that does something other than sit on its ass in a digital museum

13. a font with the capacity to breed with other fonts

14. a recombinant font — every letterform the unruly child of a predictable but random process

15. a font that sounds as good as it looks

16. a font that writes its own script

17. a font that thickens the plot

18. a font that responds and reacts to the meaning it carries and conveys

19. a font that assumes the intelligence of its reader

20. a font that might sense your level of agitation, fear, or aggression

21. a font prone to sudden outbursts and tantrums

22. a font that exceeds the typographic genome

23. a font whose parents are Father Time and the Mother of Invention

24. an ambient font, a font without qualities

25. an everyday font, a font of common sense

26. a font that slows the pace of reading for the difficult passages (and skips along through easy bits)

27. a font that writes between the lines

28. a font that refuses to utter imperatives or commands

29. a karaoke font, a lip-synching font, a font without a voice of its own

30. a font that listens while it speaks

31. a font that toggles effortlessly between languages

32. a font for speaking in tongues

33. a font that speaks in dialects

34. a metropolitan font for uptown, the ghetto, and suburbia alike

35. a font that simultaneously translates

36. a font that sings the plaintive songs of lonely whales

37. a font that grows

38. a font that learns

39. an evolutionary font

40. an entropic font

41. a "live" font

42. a promiscuous font, a font that fucks fonts, a font-fucking-font

43. a font that emerges, unfolds, performs, evolves, and passes away

44. a font of youth

45. twin fonts, identical but distinct

46. a generative font that renders itself according to behavioral tendencies

47. a font that is something other than a recording

48. a font that is different every time you "play" it

49. a font with the metabolism of a fly

50. a font with a demographic algorithm that projects itself onto you, the average reader

51. a font that recognizes you

52. an unfinished font

53. a font that is not an etymological fallacy, that says what it means and means what it says

54. an ergonomic font that reduces discomfort and fatigue

55. a slang font

56. a pidgin font

57. a pheromonic font

58. a phatic font

59. a game font that takes you to the next level

60. an amnesiac font, a font that forgets itself

61. a font of doubt, uncertainty and indeterminacy, endlessly postponing clarity

62. a local font, a font to which you have to travel

63. a font for airports, a ruthless average of distinctive character

64. a font with ambitions, dreams, and expectations of its own

65. a font with cuts, pans, zooms, and close-ups

66. a font trapped in the present tense, erasing as it writes itself

67. a font changing states — melting, crystallizing, condensing, evaporating or sublimating

68. a colloid font, a font between states

69. a font immaculately conceived

70. a font with a Brooklyn accent

71. a font that only ever mumbles

72. a seasonal font, a font for this spring

73. a model-year font

74. a font that becomes you, a font with boundless empathy for your desires

75. a font that constantly reinvents and renews itself, shedding its crusty old skin with every new thought

76. a font that witnesses, testifies, mourns, and traces memory across itself

77. a font that perforates the surface of things

78. a font that responds to your touch

79. a porous, absorbent font

80. a font that is atmospherically sensitive — registering environmental shifts

81. a font that is yours, and yours alone, that grows and ages with you, and with your passing, also dies

82. a font that sees itself reflected in the searching eyes of the reader

83. a font that looks up to you

84. a font that "stuffs" meaning onto the printed page

85. a dream font

86. a deadpan font

87. a slow-motion font

88. a dirt font

89. a big-budget, full-colour, star-studded, widescreen, Oscar-winning, surroundsound font

90. a scathingly funny, tenderly moving, blissfully surreal, blazingly original, hugely entertaining font

91. an action-packed, eye-popping, over-the-top font

92. a glossy font

93. a "lite" font

94. a facelift-gone-wrong font

95. a Gesamtkunstwerkfont

96. a fluid font that oozes, bleeds and leaks with ambiguity

97. an unstable font, in need of constant intervention to maintain appearances

98. a Chinese water torture font, that interminably drip drip drips its meaning onto your forehead

99. a tragic American font of youthful promise and naive exuberance, driven to an abrupt and violent end

100. a font whose uniqueness lies in its software, not merely in its image?

Research

Laboratorium
QuarkXPress
CHRISTO
Pioneer

Notes

During the time I spent working in London, my work day was eighteen hours, and I realized that when you devote that much time and effort to mundane projects, they absorb your entire life. It's that simple. So, the first decision I made when the studio was starting up was that, if I was to continue to work eighteen hours a day (which seemed inevitable), the projects had to be stimulating and research-driven.

Our intense kind of research process constantly renews our work and transforms us. The process is unpredictable and the results seldom what we anticipate. The studio's process is not a stylistic system with signature fonts used repeatedly, not a recipe of colors, not a formula for approaching space or shaping form. The process flows in the reverse direction: the projects provoke us to learn about the world, and the research constantly produces different kinds of work that, we have discovered, cannot be arrived at by other means. It may be a difficult thing to grasp for people at the other end of the process, but the work arises as a methodological consequence—not from streaming projects through some stylistic posture.

In order to work and to live this way you need time. The obstacle is that the economy of design work is not set up to operate with a research process as a central component. The businesses that designers customarily have as clients seldom, if ever, plan for adequate design time when scheduling their projects. The serious designer must learn to become a time thief. Publishers, for instance, refuse even to hear about paying a designer to accompany the author on his or her artistic or intellectual travels in order to become intimately familiar with what is going on *inside* a book. The result is that to develop a responsive and considered research process one has to proceed by hook and by crook. One way or the other, you will travel with the author, but you may well find yourself traveling in economy.

Optimize. That is what the whole research process is about. When I say research, I mean going out into the world and grappling with the forces directly shaping our working context. That's what "getting engaged" is all about. It's about trying to make sense of how the environment in which we work is being rapidly transformed, and what the implications of that are for our practice.

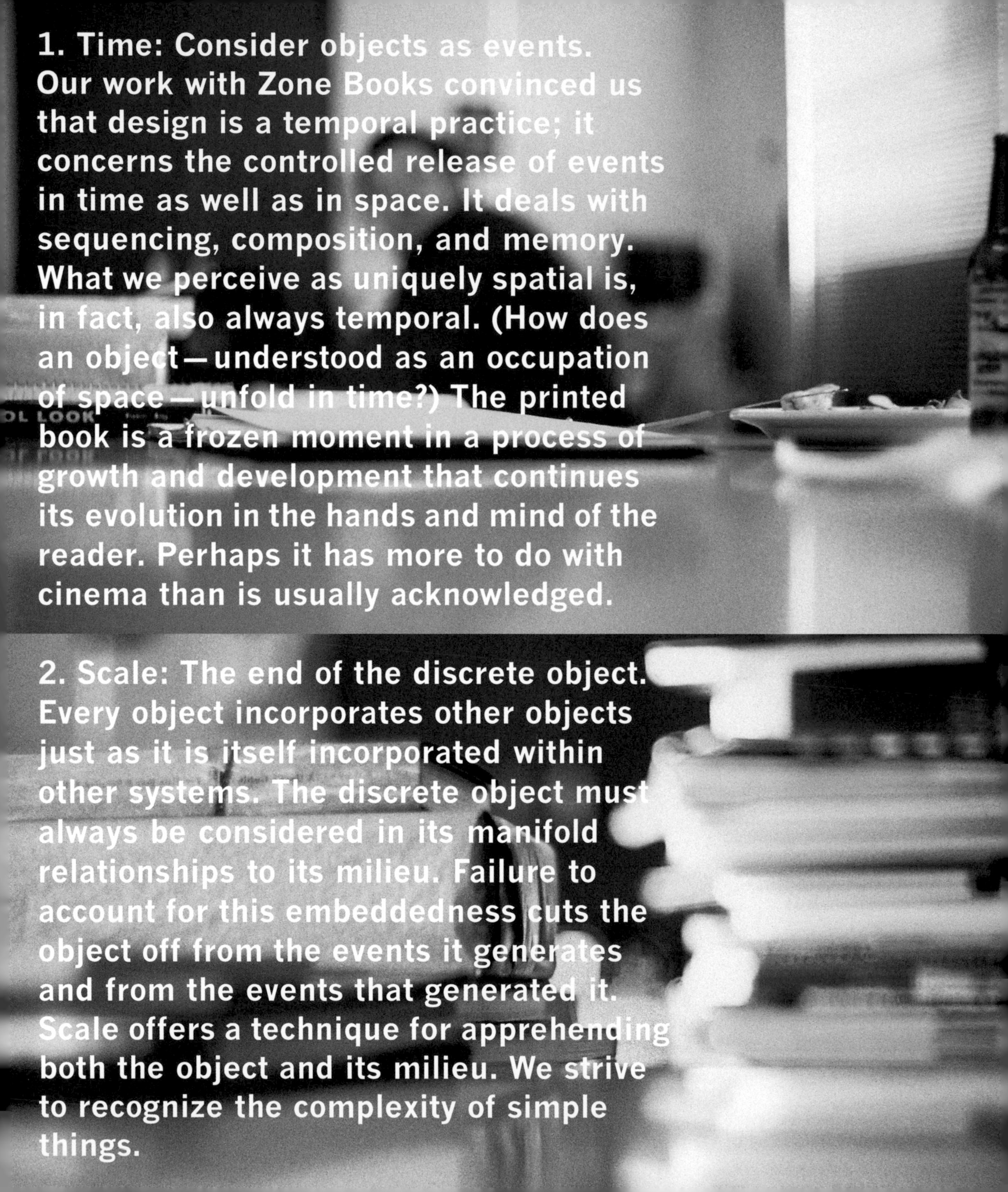

1. Time: Consider objects as events. Our work with Zone Books convinced us that design is a temporal practice; it concerns the controlled release of events in time as well as in space. It deals with sequencing, composition, and memory. What we perceive as uniquely spatial is, in fact, also always temporal. (How does an object—understood as an occupation of space—unfold in time?) The printed book is a frozen moment in a process of growth and development that continues its evolution in the hands and mind of the reader. Perhaps it has more to do with cinema than is usually acknowledged.

2. Scale: The end of the discrete object. Every object incorporates other objects just as it is itself incorporated within other systems. The discrete object must always be considered in its manifold relationships to its milieu. Failure to account for this embeddedness cuts the object off from the events it generates and from the events that generated it. Scale offers a technique for apprehending both the object and its milieu. We strive to recognize the complexity of simple things.

Twelve Strategies

This essay is a reflection on design methodology and the context in which it is currently evolving. It is an attempt to discover what it takes to produce a new work today, an attempt to articulate some of the creative, spiritual, and intellectual processes that one must mobilize in order to live this way. It is an interrogation of states of mind — of enthusiasm, suspicion, and nerve, of brutal sophistication and of the naive megalomania necessary to create what others have called postindustrial culture. But it is also a meditation on how one might sustain a nervous connection to a hypercharged global image machine without simply reproducing the most horrific and destructive aspects of the social and economic milieu.

What we wish to do here is to take stock of some of the ways in which our studio reacts to contemporary culture. Our goal is to approach design as more than a set of formal solutions. We have tried to develop a new stance for the designer, one that confronts demands both from the world of business and from the world of culture.

This text is organized around twelve of the many conceptual strategies employed by our studio. These strategies are openings; we are not driven by them, but use them interchangeably as relays or expediencies — in other words, as tools. What distinguishes these strategies from others is that they are provisional rather than prescriptive; they are potentials rather than self-contained ends.

We do not imagine the production of form to be the endpoint of design. We look for something more difficult and tenuous: to engage as directly as possible the environment within which design occurs. Adopting provisional strategies, then, is a technique for providing the designer with a space within which to work, one outside of the relentless demand for form or novelty. At certain moments it is the search for freedom.

Traditionally, the designer begins work only after content has been shaped. The designer determines how something is said, but has no influence over

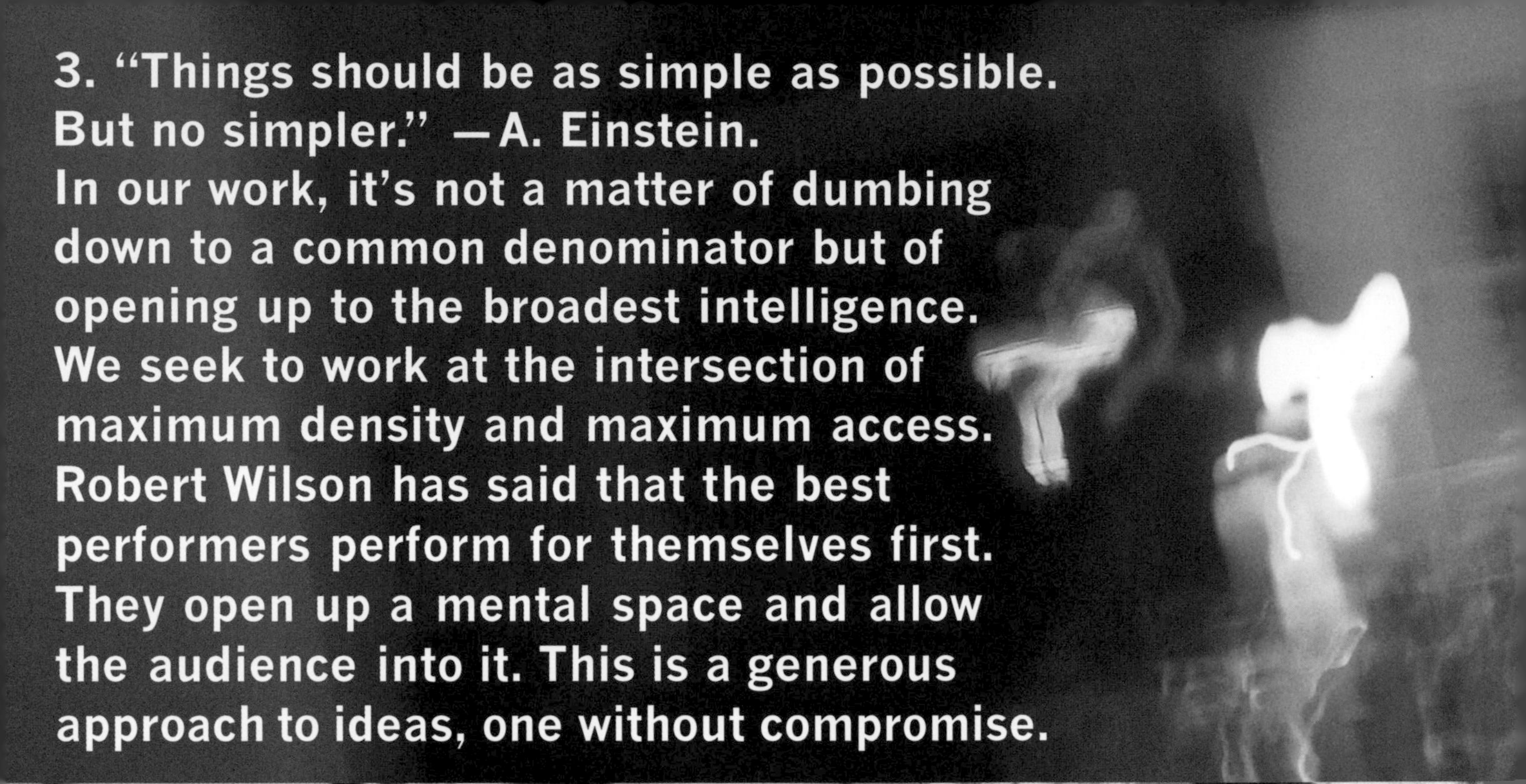

3. "Things should be as simple as possible. But no simpler." —A. Einstein.
In our work, it's not a matter of dumbing down to a common denominator but of opening up to the broadest intelligence. We seek to work at the intersection of maximum density and maximum access. Robert Wilson has said that the best performers perform for themselves first. They open up a mental space and allow the audience into it. This is a generous approach to ideas, one without compromise.

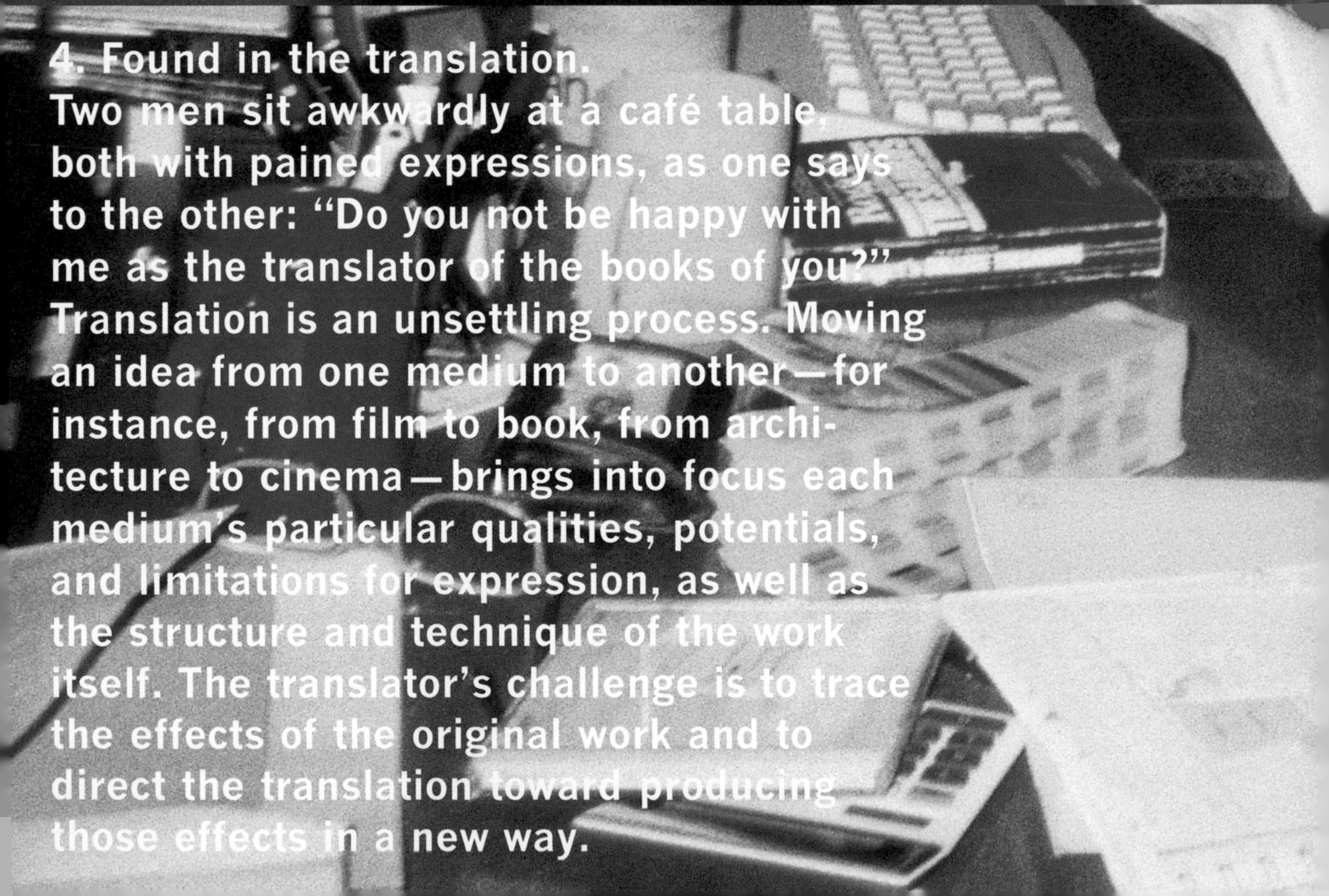

4. Found in the translation.
Two men sit awkwardly at a café table, both with pained expressions, as one says to the other: "Do you not be happy with me as the translator of the books of you?" Translation is an unsettling process. Moving an idea from one medium to another—for instance, from film to book, from architecture to cinema—brings into focus each medium's particular qualities, potentials, and limitations for expression, as well as the structure and technique of the work itself. The translator's challenge is to trace the effects of the original work and to direct the translation toward producing those effects in a new way.

what is being said. We are interested in expanding and extending the role of the designer to include the substance of the message itself. The content—what is being said—is the trigger for form. Our goal is to produce an environment of collaboration for the development and integration of content and form.

We are living through a transformation that is altering all our forms of exchange: our biological capacity to reproduce; the ways and means by which we interact with one another; the definition of work and the workplace; the forms, and the forms of circulation, of our cultural products; and finally, the urban milieu in which all of these things are integrated.

In the last two decades we have witnessed a revolution in our capacity to invent and manipulate images. The digital age has inflicted insecurities, crisis, drama, and conflict on every discipline that relies on the image for its *modus operandi*. Indeed, it has left almost no field intact. Even the newspaper, once a text-based medium, now seems a flimsy remnant of its former self, inundated by the image, desperately striving to be like television.

With our new-found manipulative capacities we have rushed blindly toward the ideal, removing, retouching, and perfecting every flaw and wrinkle. A recent cover of *Mirabella* magazine displays a supermodel whose image is a montage composed entirely of fragments. Our craving for perfection has sentenced women and men by the thousands to the gym, to the surgeon, and occasionally even to their deaths in an effort to align their own image with a thin digital strip of perfection. Montage is now deliriously self-inflicted.

The capacity to alter and reproduce images is being extended to natural and manufactured objects, with all of the attendant dilemmas and paradoxes that capacity involves. Devices to generate and replicate complex new objects may soon be as widely distributed and accessible as personal computers. These information-management tools already travel the globe freely, emerging wherever possible or necessary, creating a supranational web of technique. Taken together, changes like these are funda-

5. Holding a shot too long.
Push a convention beyond its limits and surprising events occur outside the typical economy of attention and distraction. Filmmaker Chris Marker's homage to Akira Kurosawa, *AK*, opens with a shot of a man's face, motionless, staring at the camera, creating the impression of a still-image. Marker holds this shot to the point of discomfort. As a viewer, one asks oneself: "Is he dead? Is this a hoax?" One comes to realize that the man is alive and is, in fact, the master Kurosawa himself. One passes beyond the frame in which images are typically received, through a stage of anxiety and frustration, to a point where one begins to look at the face with new intimacy, as if one had never looked at a face before. In the work of Chris Marker, we see the possibility of evolving a practice that strategically maintains, then moves away from accepted norms of visual communication to create new levels of perception.

6. Signal-to-noise ratio.
Signal carries noise and noise carries signal. If lacking in signal, pump up the noise. These days most "new" design increases noise at the expense of signal: increasing obscurity, decreasing legibility, turning readers into viewers. Often, of course, this is because the signal itself is simply not as rich as the noise. We are not so quick to abandon the signal. The studio believes in design that, through resonance, grows richer with time.

mentally redefining the context of global images within which local cultures must distinguish and sustain themselves.

It is this new cultural environment that makes adopting a critical stance so difficult. The promiscuity of the image, and our unprecedented abilities to create, modify, and disperse images, increase in subtlety and force daily. We speak of the ability of images to "target" specific audiences, and the precision and force of such "targeting" (the techniques by which images may be used to produce definite ends) are alarming. It is as if the communications environment has itself become toxic.

Paradoxically, these same conditions provide a window of opportunity. As tools proliferate horizontally, opportunities and expertise realign vertically. Every software application that can be loaded onto a computer increases our capacity to produce within the envelope defined by the software parameters. In our studio, for instance, we have the capacity to create typefaces, manipulate images, design books, produce Websites, generate cinema, record and manipulate audio, and create three-dimensional objects—all in a digital realm—and then circulate those objects and products in the world. Our ability to extend our reach is increasing, and, more important, so is our capacity to combine and hybridize our work.

If the computer becomes for images the equivalent of a typewriter for text, "authors" on a computer may use graphic vocabularies the way they once used text. As software and image-production technology become smarter and cheaper, we may begin to approach the capacity for invention that has only ever been the province of literature. Instead of signaling the end of the book, the computer triggers its re-invention as a radicalizing visual medium. We view these changes as a chance to depart from the Fordist politics of form-giving that accompanied design practice when the production of images required resources that only larger, bureaucratic interests could muster. In response to the imposed division of labor between form-giving and content-making, we propose a long-overdue reunification.

7. Exaggeration amplifier.
Exaggeration pulls a quality into the foreground; by amplifying its particularities we clarify the quality. In order to create a manifesto (a cultural organism that can survive in our corrosive information context), we must create extremes of clarity. Legibility is the quality that allows us to distinguish a particular element against the background noise. Amplifiers or exaggerations become emblems—hardline and high-contrast.

8. Associative bandwidth (subliminal signal).
Describe print-based media in the terminology of new media and what becomes apparent is the extent to which "bandwidth" is carried by the non-text-based qualities of an object. The tactility, color, material, smell, history, image, and portability of an object produce what we call associative bandwith or subliminal signal. All of these qualities inflect the meaning of an object. They make it speak of intelligence, consideration, contemporaneity, criticality, accessibility, or generosity. Although we may not focus in a cognitive sense on these qualities, the channel remains open. The real effect and power of the work emerge in the tension between our cognitive and associative engagement. Perhaps the most challenging constraint facing online design application, and the reason so much of it seems anemic or impoverished, is simply the extremely narrow bandwidth—effectively stripped of all that subliminal signal.

Our insistence on playing a collaborative editorial role as part of the design process has been fundamental in shaping the direction of our practice and in leading us toward the development of content. Our studio seeks an increasingly active role in the projects we undertake, not merely to service the demands of the client, but rather to collaborate in ensuring the seamless realization of an innovative cultural product.
This allows us to develop something new: a laboratory environment where the holistic project of design can be pursued. We believe that the most effective and ambitious practice involves the creation of new cultural artifacts. In pursuit of this, one cannot rely on any one formula or point of view. The technique of transgression, long a favorite of the avant-garde, has lost power as a critical strategy in an environment where every transgression is instantly trumped and appropriated as a media and marketing strategy. The objective is not to develop form per se, but culture: to engage in design as a critical stance. The new approach promises to end boundaries, borders, and artificial limits, and to shatter the brutal confinement of creative lives stuck within the strictures of an imposed professionalism.
This is a diagram of the typical trajectory of a book project.

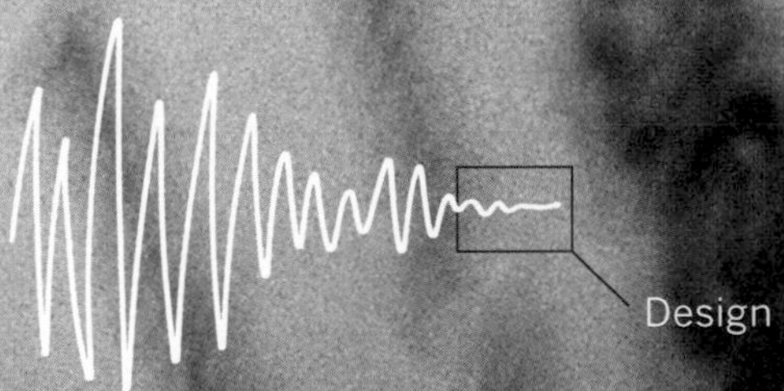

It shows the wandering of the author as he or she interprets the world, gathering and eventually synthesizing information. Once compressed, the content is relayed to what the Dutch would call a form-giver, the one who designs the final product.
Compare the amplitude. The amplitude is our ability to freely engage and interpret the world directly, to move away from what is already known, and to explore.

9. Work work work.
There is nothing worse than burdening a project with too many archived ambitions, too much attention to detail, too much finesse, too much intelligence. Part of the work is the work between the work—how our projects, and the dilemmas, conflicts, and opportunities they generate, resonate with one another. It requires a "critical mass" of production to maintain an economy of application. Innovation on one project can be applied to another, and the ease and liberty of relaxed speculation finds its expression in the work.

10. The third event.
The work doesn't happen where it seems it ought to. We expect the work (of graphic design, at least) to happen on the surface. Instead, it happens in the "thickness," in the turning of the page, like a spark jumping a gap. The third event—the meaning and power of the work—occurs between images, between a text and an image, a void and an image. The third event is the cut. The violent Eisensteinian moment where two apparently known quantities catapult themselves into a (third) new domain. The power of the third event can be produced only in the mind of the reader when he or she transforms the potential energy of an image into the kinetic energy of meaning.

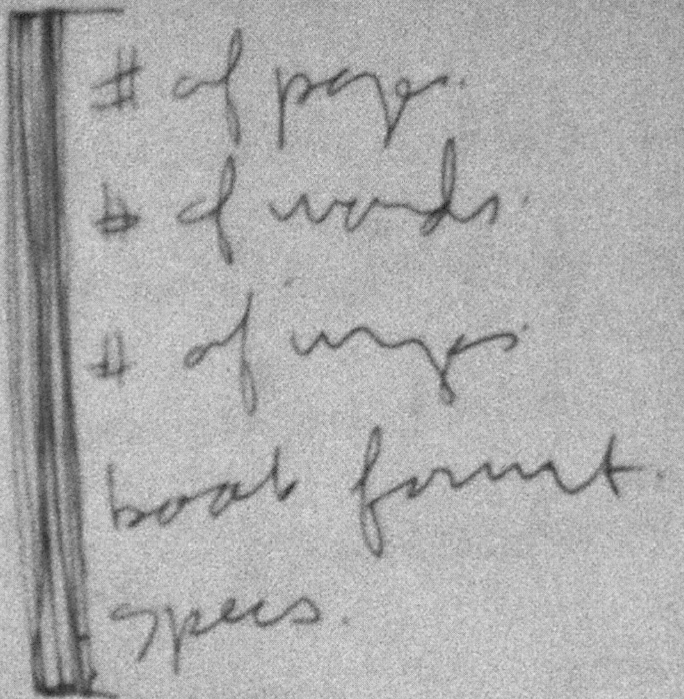

# of pages.
# of words.
# of images.
book format.
specs.

This is a diagram of a new approach, where the creation of content and form are in dialogue from start to finish. When design practice is enlarged and superimposed on the creation of content, the designer takes part in the same processes of wandering and refinement as the author does.

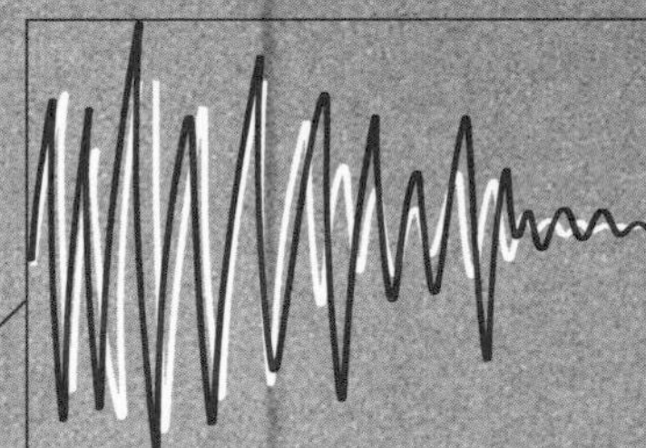

While the pathways followed by designer and author occasionally diverge, it is the separation and tension between them that generates ideas and qualities that could be produced in no other way.
The new approach replaces division of labor with synthesis, clients and commissions with collaborators and partners, executing tasks with negotiating terrain, maximum output with maximum feedback, and form applied to content with form and content evolving and enriching each another simultaneously. We replace resource extraction with investment, efficiency with depth, speed with growth, and professional classification with integration.
We are not sure whether this new way of working means the end of design, or whether it means that designers become authors, or authors become designers, or all three. We are convinced that this approach is rich with potential and capable of producing results not otherwise possible.
Our approach to design practice arises from a deep contradiction. We attempt to excavate a space of freedom from the corrosiveness of form, all the while accepting that our product itself is form. It is a contradiction that we accept and work with. We explore form as a particular momentary stability within a condition of continuous, evolving instability. In the end, the objective is to design new objects that possess clarity and complexity within an environment ruled by circulation and dispersion—to create unforeseen freedoms within which to work and live.

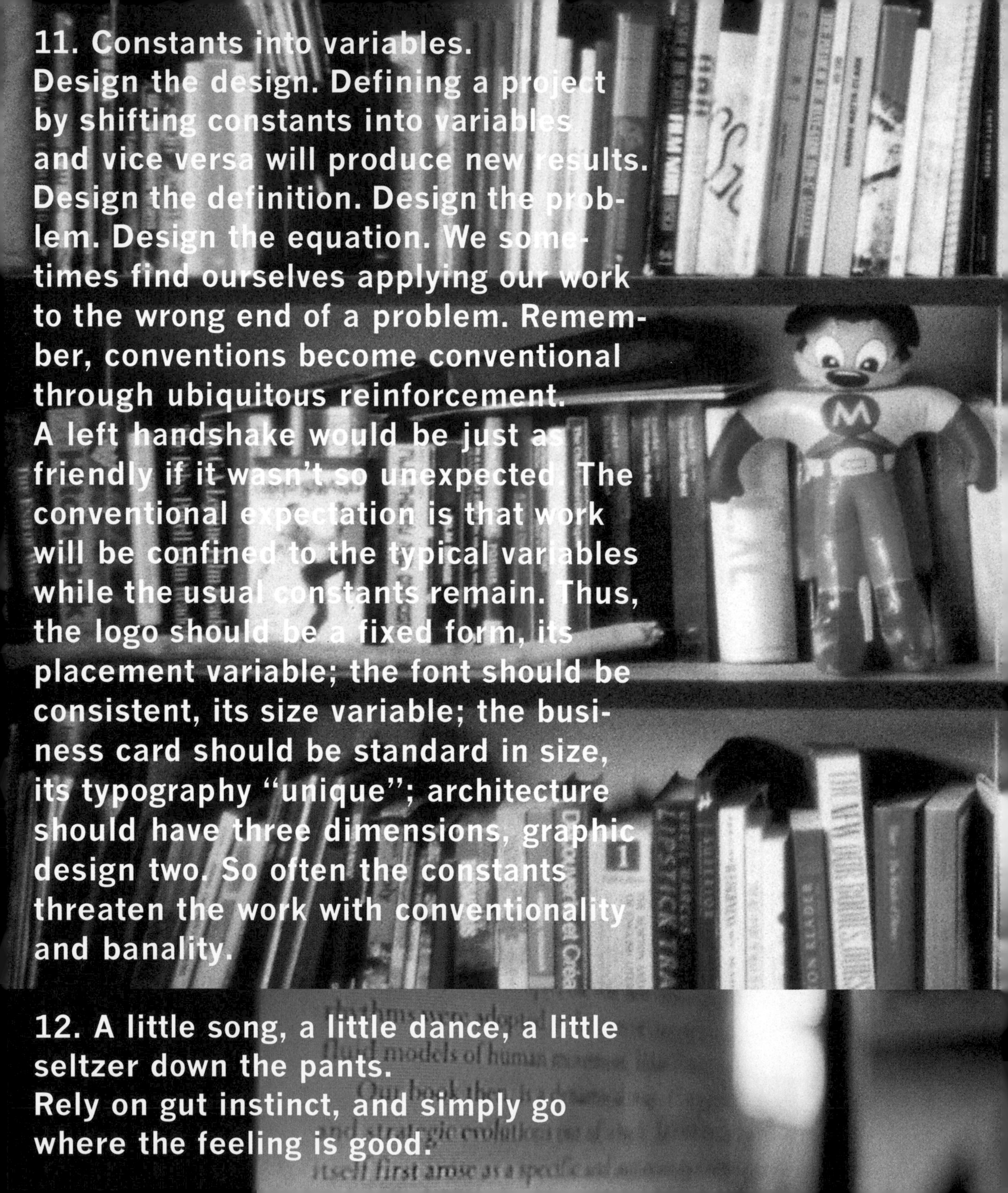

11. Constants into variables.
Design the design. Defining a project by shifting constants into variables and vice versa will produce new results. Design the definition. Design the problem. Design the equation. We sometimes find ourselves applying our work to the wrong end of a problem. Remember, conventions become conventional through ubiquitous reinforcement. A left handshake would be just as friendly if it wasn't so unexpected. The conventional expectation is that work will be confined to the typical variables while the usual constants remain. Thus, the logo should be a fixed form, its placement variable; the font should be consistent, its size variable; the business card should be standard in size, its typography "unique"; architecture should have three dimensions, graphic design two. So often the constants threaten the work with conventionality and banality.

12. A little song, a little dance, a little seltzer down the pants.
Rely on gut instinct, and simply go where the feeling is good.

Meeting Mr. Johnson

Filled with trepidation. Desperate straits.
S,M,L,XL finish line a moving target.
Studio in peril.
Drive up from Manhattan with Julia.[1]
(Julia once published *Oppositions'* exposé of Johnson's fascist history.[2]
Delivered the issue to his office personally.
Johnson, tipped off, turned directly to the damning passage.
Exploded with anger.)
Stone bridges, dappled highway, trees, shadows.
Park the car. Absolute quiet. Only sound is of white gravel underfoot.
Glass House is open and empty.
Fruit bowl on the table on the lawn.
A few chairs overlooking the pond.
Film set.
Cottage-like patina superimposed on machine-steel aesthetic.
History in slow motion. Strange and beautiful.
Off in the distance several figures descend.
We approach.
Jasper Johns, the Menils of Houston, Zaha Hadid.
History, money, style.

1 Julia Bloomfield, Head of Publications, Getty Research Institute.

2. *Oppositions* was an architectural journal founded by Peter Eisenman.

Zaha a brilliant tube top in a cloud of transparent Miyake.
Further up, David and Philip.
Johnson frail but robust. "It's so good to meet you.
I've heard so much about you."
Utterly disarming.
I expected to prove myself.
Johnson wants to show his collections.
The sculpture pavilion.
Sun beating down on exploding Stella.
The painting bunker. Underground turntables.
Lazy Susan of American masterpieces.
Return to the house to look at mockup of book.
"Oh look, Jasper, it's so big!"
Philip excited by clarity—extra-large type.
Johns, ageless, doesn't speak, ever, it seems; smiles silently.
David announces that Philip must nap.
We will all have to go.
Julia drives back into Manhattan.
Zaha sleeps in the back seat. Snoring loudly.
"Philip just wanted to touch you before he dies."

A few days later we hear from the foundation.
The money will be forthcoming after all.

It only took us five years to do *S,M,L,XL*.

S,M,L,XL
O.M.A., Rem Koolhaas and Bruce Mau
New York: The Monacelli Press, 1996
S,M,L,XL presents the work of Rem Koolhaas and his studio, Office for Metropolitan Architecture, and explores the nature of architectural practice. The book consists of graphs, charts, poems, scripts, revisions, essays, metaphors, panic, chronologies, plans, cartoons, Beckett, events, big men, big type, models, diaries, competitions, notebooks, disasters, artworks, dreams, manifestos, drawings, rants, lectures, cities, speculation, sex, invention, and tragedies.

It started as a book about Rem's office, and even though we knew pretty much from the beginning that it wouldn't be a traditional monograph, that is technically what we were contracted to design. It was supposed to take 265 days to finish and be 264 pages in length. At one point, we reached a critical juncture and realized that the work had to be structured around the issue of scale and the whole idea of urban incorporation. That's when things began to inflate.

In the early days of publishing, designers were both publishers and producers. They would produce their own things, projects that they believed in either commercially or culturally. The idea of design detached from the production of content is a relatively recent phenomenon. In the big historical sweep, it is tied to Fordism and Taylorism and the whole idea of specialization and the abstraction of the work process.

S,M,L,XL

When we did *S,M,L,XL*, we expanded the concept of design quite substantially—a decision that nearly bankrupted both Rem and our studio. Basically, Rem asked me to accompany him on a sort of expedition. Sometimes we went together and sometimes we parted and traveled different trajectories, but the idea was that we would end up in the same place—with the book.

Through our collaboration with Rem Koolhaas, we hoped to deliver a tactile, almost visceral understanding of architectural practice at the end of the twentieth century. The challenge was to embody and demonstrate an architectural practice rather than simply describe it as a static thing.

Spring 1993
OMA
Checklist
FM
FP
S
M
OMA
Checklist
L
XL
BM

S,M,L,XL explores a new kind of time that is closest to cinematic sequencing in its effect. For instance, the book exploits the freedom to "hold a shot too long" (to make the reader see details that would otherwise go unnoticed), and to show "bad" images, unresolved ideas, or problematic results.

We realized that our true ambition was to situate the work and the book in a cultural flux—in an urban context that accommodates not only intelligence, invention, collision, collaboration, and expansion, but also, and perhaps more important, dumbness, drift, excess, and banality.

MATISSE
A HISTORY OF BRITISH ART

It was a real eye-opener to recognize the depth in simplicity. If you look at Rem's work, it's often very straightforward. There's nothing on the surface to indicate that the work is complex. The complexity exists in its order. This is Rem's response to a hyperactive image culture—keep things confidently and muscularly simple.

"Restraint" may seem an unlikely word with which to describe my involvement in a project of such megalomaniacal scale. But, in fact, I have simultaneously expanded the role of the designer and made it invisible, asserted and withheld the designer's voice. The designer becomes "author" but, at the same time, steps back to what may seem an anonymous status. A "signature" may not be apparent because the design is not to be viewed, but to be read. It does not steal the show, but propels it.

S,M,L,XL
010

Don't be Fooled

Once, while working in Paris, architect Rem Koolhaas invited me for breakfast at Villa Dall'Ava, a house in the outskirts of Paris that his office had designed. Early the next morning, I collected him at the Hilton, his favorite Parisian hotel, and we raced off at typical break-neck speed. At the house, we were greeted on the street by a man and woman whom I took to be the owners.

After only a few moments, it becomes clear they are not, in fact, the owners but will be joining us for coffee. The house is empty, the owners out for the day, and Rem proceeds to show his guests through the house. Villa Dall'Ava, a glass house with a pool on the roof, is a dazzling composition with surprises at every turn. I can't contain my enthusiasm: "Oh, Rem, spectacular!" At the top

of a stair there is a small round window looking into the bottom of the pool. It gives off a shade of blue light I have never seen before. I am laughing, clapping, and howling. Our guests, on the other hand, don't say a word, never smile, look solemnly at one another, and proceed meticulously, cautiously, to open and close kitchen cabinets, inspecting the workmanship.
Rem made coffee. He and the couple exchanged a few pleasantries in Dutch and then the man and the woman left. Not long after, as we arched onto the expressway to Rotterdam, Rem turned to me and asked, "What do you think? Would they make a good client?" I was stunned. "Rem," I said, "they don't seem to me to be up for an adventure; they were checking the hinges."
"Don't be fooled," said Rem, "The Dutch see enthusiasm as a sign of weakness."

The Culture of Energy

I will begin with a basic fact: A living organism ordinarily receives more energy than is necessary for maintaining life. If the excess cannot be completely absorbed in its growth, it must be spent, willingly or not, gloriously or catastrophically.

—Georges Bataille, *The Accursed Share*

All actions can be understood as manifestations of energy. The earth receives more than enough energy from the sun. The excess floats around as the "accursed share." It either contributes to the growth of a system, or, if that system has reached its maximum capacity, the surplus energy must be spent elsewhere. This expenditure has taken many forms: cathedrals, dense metropolitan centers, feats of engineering, the production of art, and the destructive expenditure of war as epitomized by the atomic bomb. Yet, despite its many material expressions, energy remains an abstraction. Most people care only about the effects of energy when their supply is interrupted or endangered: think of The Energy Crisis, The Blackout of 1968, The Chernobyl Disaster.

In 1994, we had the opportunity to consider energy as a cultural force when we were approached by the German utility company EMR, which promotes environmentally sensitive, state-of-the-art technologies. EMR had commissioned Frank Gehry to design a new technical facility. As part of EMR's cultural agenda, a public gallery was included as a component of the building program.

Over the course of one year, the studio developed the conceptual structure for an exhibition series called ENERGIEKULTUR: "The Culture of Energy." We undertook the content development and design schematics for exhibits about the sun, weather, domestic energy, and growth. For each installation, scientific theories and explanations of energy were presented against the background of mythological and historical narratives.

Elektrizitätswerk, Minden-Ravensberg (EMR)
Bad Oenhausen, Germany, 1994

EMR highlights a difference between the culture of electrical power in North America and that of Europe. In North America, if you have a problem with an electrical power plant, you simply remove it to someplace remote from the general population. If this presents an environmental threat or other serious problem, you simply relocate the plant to the wilderness, to a site where the local people don't count, or where there are no people at all.

Europeans cannot do this because there is virtually no wilderness left, nowhere to remove a problem to. The context in which EMR operates, then, makes it a strange capitalist entity in North American eyes. Here was a private company that controlled 100 percent of its energy market and was nonetheless actively working to limit demand for its product. They wanted to reduce capacity, and they could only reduce capacity by reducing demand. A regional company, EMR knew that if demand increased, they would have to increase capacity. Higher capacity, EMR knew, would increase pollution in highly populated areas and would eventually make nuclear power the only alternative. And so they were working to help people understand what limiting demand means, and what the implications of not doing it might be. EMR was beginning a voyage into the culture of energy. That is why they built a community center and wanted to communicate to people the meaning of the product.

EMR came to us and said, "What do we do with this space? What's the program?" This was the first time anyone had come to us with that kind of open-ended scenario, asking us to develop the content, the program, and the design. The brief from them essentially said, "Help us communicate the meaning of the situation." They were very adamant about not wanting to display energy-saving products. Such displays are technical and mean little to anybody. The head of the facility, Dr. Regati, understood this clearly, and posed the question: If the focus is not technical, what is it?

What would communicate the scope and significance of the problem? The task, therefore, was to engage people, and that meant moving away from technical issues to something else.

The first thing we did was to contextualize the technical issues as a cultural problem. Once you make the issue a cultural one, everyone has a stake in it. If you define energy as Bataille defines it, every human exchange becomes part of the energy problem, and energy becomes everyone's issue. Any kind of cultural exchange, from economic relations to communications, becomes part of the transfer of energy. Bataille's "accursed share" became a foundation on which we would build the project. Bataille's thesis is that the problem of energy is not scarcity but excess.

EMR was probably thinking of a permanent installation, but we proposed that they mount four exhibitions a year: a

Empires of the Sun: Solar Myth and Solar Science

In 22 days the earth receives as much energy from the sun as is believed to be stored in the earth's entire reserves of fossil fuels.
—CRC Handbook of Chemistry and Physics, 1986

This exhibition chronicles contemporary scientific and mythological knowledge about the sun, tracing the ways we've tried to explain what the sun is and what it does. The exhibition is essentially an inventory of stories. Our concept was that from one perspective, the images would be black-and-white and mythological (Asian, Polynesian, Mayan, and Aztec drawings). Looking the other way, all the images would be in color and scientific. So the installation is double-sided: contrasting mythical, ethereal ideas with our technological/scientific understanding of the sun.

single thematic structure and four approaches to the problem from different perspectives. Each project would bring a different audience. Our plan called for a three-year cycle, or twelve different projects, each providing an opportunity to address a different kind of person in a different way, with overlap. This is what we termed the "culture of energy." We provided a scheme of twenty-four exhibition concepts. These were simple, one-page outlines: "Empires of the Sun," or "The Poetry of Weather," for example. Then we worked up twelve schemes that laid out practical strategies, followed by four plans that involved intensive research and established what each exhibition would look like and include. We constructed models of those projects, and I presented them to Dr. Regati in Los Angeles at Frank Gehry's office.

EMR commissioned four projects for the first year, which we proceeded to do, but there were serious difficulties. One of the problems we faced is that developing real content cannot be done entirely by a team. Ideas must begin on an individual basis. A team can accomplish a great deal, but producing content is very slow and time-consuming. With EMR, we did not change speeds effectively. We approached it like a design problem when it was really a research and content problem. Our project management had spun out of control.

When that happened, Dr. Regati pulled the plug. It was a disaster for the studio. Half the studio had to be let go, and that produced a deep crisis, the worst in our history. People who had enormous commitment to the studio had to leave simply because half of our workload disappeared with absolutely no warning. The problem ultimately prompted the studio to adopt what we called the 20 percent rule: no project, organization, or person can consume more than 20 percent of the studio's output.

Another contributing factor led to the termination of our commission: while we were working on the project, Germany was undergoing reunification, and the economic situation changed overnight. It put huge pressure on Dr. Regati to rein in the project, because suddenly the economics had flipped. Minden-Ravensberg is one of the richest regions of Germany, but when everyone woke up to the economic costs attached to reunification, the climate there shifted totally. That played a serious role in EMR's canceling *The Culture of Energy* in the ambitious form we envisioned for it. Even though it hurt to lose the commission, the process instigated a way of thinking and working in the studio that has now turned into a productive part of our practice.

It took me a long time to go back to the project. My heart was broken and I didn't open the box for over five years. Now I can appreciate what we accomplished. There are fantastic things that are just sitting there on the shelf.

347

A huge solar explosion. The sun casting off six billion metric tons of filmy outer dress at speeds of more than 100 km/s.

The following texts were taken from BMD's original exhibition proposal and research.

The Power of the Wave

This exhibit explores the idea that it is through the dynamics of the wave that we may understand the transmission of energy. The wave gives tangible form to what would otherwise be completely abstract.

The exhibition room will be filled with a constructed model of a large ocean wave. When visitors enter the room, they will be entering the trough of this 12-meter high wave. On the opposing wall will be a three-dimensional collage of image panels, computer monitors, videos and projection screens.

This collage represents the portal through which various wave-related concepts will be explained. The content of the exhibit will include sound waves, convection, radiation, light waves, tidal power, wave power, surfing, wave simulation tanks, radio waves and, finally, electricity itself.

Work: The Energy of Physical Labour

This exhibit illustrates the human resources expended to mine coal, to drill for oil, to reap a crop, to clearcut a forest, etc. Until the transition to electrical and gas power nearly two hundred years ago, it was more economical to use human power rather than animal power, mostly because humans ate less for the amount of work that they did. Throughout the world, almost all agricultural work was done by hand.

As an introduction, the exhibit will compare a three-dimensional symbolic graph, showing a one horsepower engine, sitting beside one pulling horse, sitting beside an equivalent group of pulling humans.

How many human powers are there in one horsepower, and how many of these did it take to build the pyramids?

The exhibit may also compare a day in the life of a Sahara bushman with a day in the life of Chancellor Helmut Kohl, or a day in the life of a medieval stonemason with a day in the life of a professional dancer. For each, the notion of "work" is slightly different, and the particular conception of work sheds light on the respective cultural attitudes towards work.

Virtual Work: Burning Excess Calories

An analysis of state-of-the-art "Nautilus" stationary weight systems, which are very popular in fitness clubs.

They are machines which simulate the activities of bicycling, cross-country skiing, speed-skating, rowing, climbing stairs and running. Each machine can be individually adjusted to facilitate the desired expenditure of energy and one's heart rate can be monitored. A simple comparison can be made between the caloric consumption of "real" work, such as picking cotton, mixing a yard of concrete, carrying water, walking to work, cultivating a pound of potatoes, etc., and the simulated work of these machines.

Artist Installation

A guest artist will be invited to create an installation in the exhibit space which describes their personal interpretation of energy. The artistic practices to choose from are diverse, they range from those which deal directly with light and sound, to those which address current energy related issues, to others which address the emotive energy of objects and spaces.

Our first proposal for the exhibition programme would be a commission of the work of Jene Highstein.

Other artists to be considered include: James Turrell, Dan Flavin, Christian Boltanski, Jenny Holzer, Sebastiao Salgado, Rebecca Horn, Marc Pauline (SRL), Dennis Oppenheim, William Blake, David Therrien, Joseph Beuys, Laurie Anderson, Brian Eno, Robert Wilson, Nancy Rubin, Jean Tinguely, Andy Warhol, Ann Hamilton and Claes Oldenburg.

Grow or Die: An Ecology of Energy

By regarding energy as a growing (i.e. dynamic) ecology, we are reminded of its integral role in shaping our daily lives. All issues of energy, no matter how peripheral they may initially seem, are, in fact, influencing our culture. Growth (and decay) do not occur independently, they require interaction and interrelation between the thing that is growing and its environment. All phenomena must obey this basic law of exchange—civilizations, cities, businesses, families, hair, light, electrical power, water levels. All may experience a sudden or even prolonged period of what is understood as growth, followed by a period of stasis and decay. Any nonlinear ecology such as "growth" necessitates the study of the interaction between the constituent elements rather than isolating particular phenomena as discrete.

Shifting the scales of space and time will help us see analogous relationships between previously disparate elements. For example, in biological terms, it is difficult if not impossible to tell where life and death begin and end. At a cellular level, animal bodies are continuously growing and dying. At a planetary level, if the earth is regarded from the scale of an orbiting satellite, it is easily seen and read as a living and growing being. One can see the changing weather patterns, easily imagine the tectonic plates adjusting and shifting, volcanoes erupting, and glaciers shaping mountains. Yet someone standing on a stretch of the Canadian Shield would be hard pressed to see it as a dynamic and pulsing system. It is more likely to be read as static, unmoving rock. Though we have different models for growth, none is really adequate.

The proposition that we inhabit not a static environment but the responsive tissue of a planet-sized organism provides us with a metaphor for seeing growth within its infinitely complex context. Gaia theory, for example, presents the earth as a self-regulating and intelligent body, where humans are simply a very small though disproportionately influential force.

The Politics of Water

This exhibit attempts to illuminate the political, environmental and human costs of harnessing energy. Sometimes the environmental effects are so great that the needs of a region have to be weighed against the growth of the whole country. This exhibit will illuminate the issues involved in large hydro projects like the James Bay project in Canada, water redirection projects in Russia and the Three Gorges project on the Yangtze.

A projected video of a hydro dam will cascade down the curved wall of the exhibit.

James Bay

Sponsored by the province of Quebec, the James Bay project boasts the largest underground generating station in the world. Since 1982, work has begun on four more stations, three great rivers have been diverted to feed La Grande river, and an area the size of the state of Montana has been flooded with the aid of thirty major dams and five hundred dykes. Political leaders see it as an economic windfall, giving the francophone province an added bargaining tool in its relations with the rest of Canada; the environmentalists and the relocated Cree Indians see it as a disaster on par with the devastation of the Amazon rain forest.

The Aral Sea

This huge inland sea has been sacrificed by Russian water management for agricultural and industrial development. In this case the well-being of a body of water is subordinated to the good of the economy, namely in order to fulfill a plan for self sufficiency in cotton. The main rivers that traditionally fed the sea have been diverted and its water is evaporating. The sea has already lost 40 percent of its surface area and all of its fish. The water is now too saline to support any life and the fishing industry around it has been closed. This does not even begin to describe the health problems created by the blowing salt, extreme changes in climate, and the 60,000 people who are now unemployed.

More Politics

Large water reservoirs almost always involve weighing the needs of the larger community against those of the populations which will be displaced.

The Aswan Dam displaced 80,000 people, and 75,000 were moved by the Lake Volta Project in Ghana. Often the electricity from these projects never reaches the local populations, it all goes to encourage industrial growth in the form of large metal refining plants and other large-scale construction

Water Law

These laws are complicated and never based on natural systems. In the USA, they differ from state to state, and globally they vary from country to country. The effect of these laws is further complicated by the fact that rivers and bodies of water are often not limited to one jurisdiction, and laws regarding water quality, quantity, surface water and groundwater are all administered by separate agencies which rarely interact.

Water Case Studies

On the Columbia River, a proposal to provide enough water to help restore salmon runs may take water away from turbines.

In Kentucky, a new power project that will use water to control air pollution raises fears that it will also reduce water for homes.

In South Dakota, a project to move coal by water is challenged by states farther downstream.

Las Vegas is discussing buying water from a desalination plant in Santa Barbara to trade to Los

Angeles for rights to water from the Colorado River.

Water Supply
In the USA, irrigation uses the largest shares of water: 13.7 billion gallons per day. More than three trillion gallons of water are used by turbines every day to provide roughly 10 percent of the nation's electricity. Power plants that use coal, oil, natural gas, or uranium also need water for steam and cooling and take about 131 billion gallons a day. Domestic use of water adds up to about 20 billion gallons a day. With so many uses—drinking water, power, agriculture, industry, waste, and recreation—there are invariably conflicts.

Energy from Water
A new energy development, which seems to have been suppressed in North America by fossil-fuel lobby groups, involves the harnessing of hydrogen from water. This would effectively end our dependency on imported oil and clean up the air with the most abundant element on the earth, hydrogen. An endless supply of hydrogen can be generated from water. Hydrogen is non-toxic, and it has the most energy per unit weight of any fuel (about three times that of gasoline).

Politics of Water
The major obstacle facing an orderly transition to a renewable energy economy is not technical in nature, but political.
Our laws, regulations, and incentives all favor fossil-fuel economies. Industrial and commercial interests lobby aggressively to keep fossil fuels cheap. These issues are steeped in controversy.
There are numerous examples of scientists, politicians, and traditional utility companies deliberately altering and withholding technological advances from the public. Some would rather put people into army tanks in Iraq than into energy-efficient cars.

Energy and Japan
This exhibit introduces the energy strategies of a country without energy resources. It will illuminate how Japan maintains its prolific industrial and commercial growth while simultaneously promoting a very comprehensive and model program of energy efficiency.
The exhibit will also present related excerpts from Japanese culture: natural environments, traditional architectures, and developments in electronic products. Because Japan must import 85 percent of all its energy, it has become one of the most energy-efficient countries in the world.

"Ma"
Japanese culture has nurtured a distinct sensitivity toward nature, for which the Japanese have great love and respect. In the context of the long history of Asia, this sensitivity toward nature has given birth to a unique Japanese concept of time and space called "ma." "Ma" means pause or empty space. It is through the effective utilization of what at first glance would appear to be a useless blank space that the Japanese succeed in lending a limitless quality to a given place or time. The effective use of "ma" is the principal element of many Japanese objects and art forms, and probably an important factor in why the Japanese are easily able to adopt life styles of efficiency and economy.

Domestic Japan
A family in Japan uses one-third less the amount of energy than a family in Canada. This part of the exhibit will examine all aspects of Japanese domestic life, including popular types of dwelling, types of appliances, how people commute to school and work, the importance of recycling, as well as their rituals and philosophy.
Only 5 percent of Japanese homes have central heating; in the USA the figure is over 80 percent. Japanese use only 40 percent as much heat per unit of floor area. Only 55 percent of Japan's total domestic travel is by car. In the US this figure is closer to 85 percent.
Japanese homes on average have only 27 square meters of space per person, vs. over 50 square meters per person in the US.

Renewable Energy
Japan is a world leader in energy management and in the development of many renewable energy resources. From wave power to superconductors to ocean power, they have invested large amounts of capital and research into developing and commercializing these industries, encouraging different sectors of the economy and corporate base to collaborate and interact. For example, utility companies work regularly with owners and operators of large buildings to reduce their energy use, especially with respect to summer cooling problems.

OTEC (Ocean Thermal Energy Conversion)
The sea is the largest collector of solar energy. OTEC harnesses this energy. The temperature differential in tropical seas, where the surface can be twenty-six degrees Celsius, and the depths are near freezing, can be used to run a heat engine to generate electricity. It has been estimated that ten million megawatts of electric power could be generated worldwide from OTEC systems.

How to Harness a Wave
Japan's Masuda corporation produces thousands of ocean buoys and navigational aids used throughout the world's oceans. They are powered by an oscillating column of water, which is a product of the wave motion. This kinetic energy, in turn, drives an air turbine and generates 60 watts of electricity which keeps their light beacons lit.

Industrial Japan
Japan's industry is known for its unique and highly advanced systems of production and a fierce competition among its corporations as well as among employees. Each industry in Japan has an assigned energy efficiency manager. It is the manager's job to monitor all consumption, output, and energy costs, troubleshooting when leaks in the delicate energy economy are found.
Japan's manufacturing productivity increased 102 percent between 1970 and 1980, while that of Germany grew 59.9 percent and in the US only 28 percent. Yet Japan used 30 percent less energy per unit of manufacturing output than the US. With its energy efficiency policies, Japan has been able to keep the amount of energy used per dollar of GNP lower than its western competitors.

Natural Resources
Although Japan is devoid of natural resources, it is currently very rich in another commodity: money. Japan is able to trade its capital and technology for metal ores and petrochemical resources with Australia and Malaysia. In 1990, Japan's total investment in Australia amounted to thirty-two billion dollars, making it one of Australia's largest investors.

Japanese Culture & Efficiency
Japan's productivity and global success does not come without cost. It relies on an extraordinary work ethic and a population willing to sacrifice luxury for economic growth. This dedication begins in the earliest stages of education and extends into corporate management structures, where sixteen hour days and six day weeks are the norm. But this is also a society which enjoys the highest life expectancy in the world, 82 years for women and 76 for men. This part of the exhibit would answer questions about the high quality of life in Japan, and the nature of its society and its evolution since the Second World War.
An exhibit about Japan would be incomplete without a look at its traditional and popular cultures. This would include karaoke, the tea ceremony, pachinko (pinball) parlours, *Shonen Jump* (a comic book which sells 4 million copies a week), sumo wrestling, flower arrangement, sexual pleasure, calligraphy, martial arts, university entrance exams, baseball tournaments, *Mito Komon* (a popular TV show), the Flower Festival and video games.

Fireworks or Gunpowder?
How do we expend our excess energy, our "accursed share"? The invention of gunpowder radically changed relations among humans. In this exhibit, the invention of gunpowder would be put in the context of the culture of fireworks, and human fascination with the spectacle of fire and explosions.
The earliest practical applications for this black powder were celebratory—the New Year, weddings, battle victories, eclipses of the moon, etc.

Alchemy, Fireworks and War
Berthold Schwarz, a thirteenth century Franciscan monk known as the "Powder Monk," supposedly perfected gunpowder for use in a gun. Yet, gunpowder's earliest military application was not for use in guns, but for fireworks. Over the years various chemical refinements have been added to the basic formula to produce different effects. Initially, antimony and iron filings were added to produce an amber colour. Zinc metals were added to produce a greenish blue color. Changing the ratios, eight parts saltpeter to one part antimony and sulphur produced a whitish colour with a blue tinge. In the 1840's, potassium chlorate was added, and later, a pure blue was added to the spectrum. The painterly qualities of the ignited fireworks and the sculptural and architectural qualities of the launching "machines" attracted many great artists. Bernini, Michelangelo and Da Vinci all dabbled in fireworks.

Domestic Energy

The Energy-Efficient House

What's the use of a house if you haven't got a tolerable planet to put it on?

—Henry David Thoreau

This exhibit outlines the dichotomy between new home technologies and traditional or vernacular energy-efficient houses.

Until now, technology has followed an autonomous path, one often in conflict with nature. Through its power it has influenced every mode of thought and every kind of design operation, whether for art or for industry. It has produced waste, and the dwelling has reflected some of the most typical aspects of this phenomenon.

The "house of the future" will rely on automation. Appliances and other home equipment will be able to communicate. We may, for example, tell the gas fireplace when to turn on, dim the lights, find out how many kilowatts of electricity we used today, and check the security alarm, all through our TV. But is it appropriate to rely on technology alone to solve the problems of the private dwelling by turning it into a large computer?

Perhaps this increase in technological knowledge has not substantially increased our understanding of the basic problems of shelter. If we examine the roots of dwelling and our relationship to the sun, the wind, the rain, and the land, we may uncover many practical ways of saving energy that have been neglected or forgotten in the recent wave of building, population growth, and urbanization.

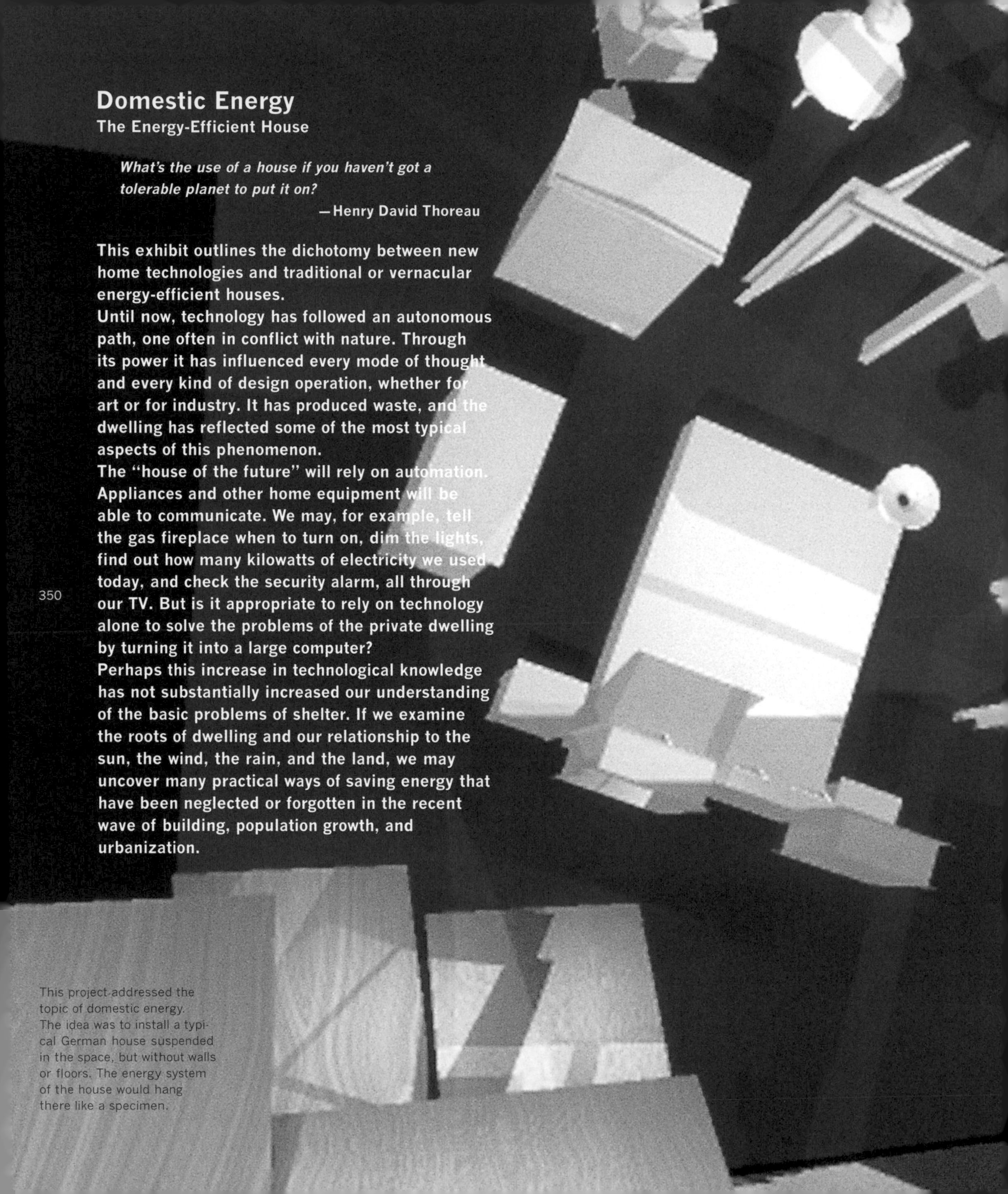

This project addressed the topic of domestic energy. The idea was to install a typical German house suspended in the space, but without walls or floors. The energy system of the house would hang there like a specimen.

The Poetry of Weather

Sometimes the wind rarefies, becomes more amorous, less aggressive, more disturbing. Then it is a wind that has been around for a long, long time; a wind that, according to the ancient Greeks, was born about the same time as chaos; or that other semi-human, a Cyclops called Brontë — the Greek word for thunder. And what is thunder, hereabouts, but a strong voice making itself heard in a rough wind?

—Jane Urquhart, *Changing Heaven*

The Poetry of Weather was one of the original models made. It expressed a kind of cultural-scientific intersection, tracing how weather has appeared in various cultural forms of expression like poetry and painting. We projected an image of sky and clouds onto a scrim that covers the whole space and rises up dramatically to meet a model tornado.

Vithout the sun there would e no weather. Every type of veather we experience occurs ecause the heat of the sun eeps the Earth's atmosphere onstantly in motion. Light rom the sun is the energy hat fuels the world's great veather machine. This atmos-phere is at once life's circula-ory system and its skin.

Projected and colorized satellite image of Hurricane Fran, 1996

Pop Culture

The Coke project arose from our association with Frank Gehry. He faced a problem. He had two extremely earnest clients, the Schmidts, owners of the world's largest private collection of Coca-Cola memorabilia, and they wanted to build a new museum to house and display the collection. While the Schmidts understood the value and significance of their collection, their understanding was bound up with nostalgia and with a collector's passion for the individual objects. They found it difficult to make the leap into a broader field of cultural interpretation. Gehry recognized immediately that he would need someone to interpret the material before he could design a building. In a conversation with Gehry I expressed interest in the project, and he set up a meeting with the Schmidts, advertising executive Jay Chiat, and the distinguished art historians Irving Lavin and Marilyn Aronberg Lavin. During our discussions, the group came up with a basic mandate for the museum. For the next eight months the studio developed the project around the thesis that the history of Coca-Cola, as evidenced by these artifacts, was also the history of American advertising and marketing, and of America itself, comprising all the ambitions and failings of that history. American pop culture cannot be separated from the evolution of advertising and marketing, and Coke was the leading experimenter. The company had produced a wide range of materials and had repeatedly reinvented its image, often very dramatically during periods of social crisis or change. At the same time, the experiments that Coke underwrote for its own promotions were picked up and became broader cultural trends, disseminated by other advertising and media.

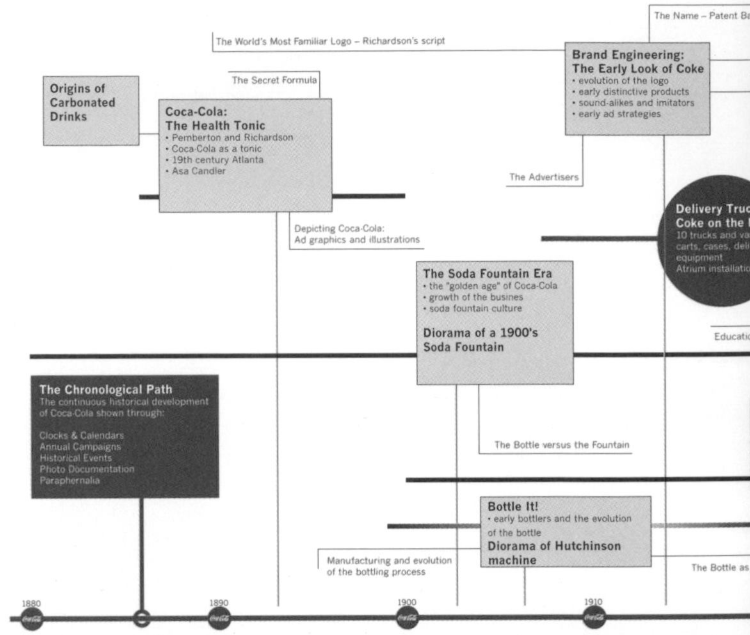

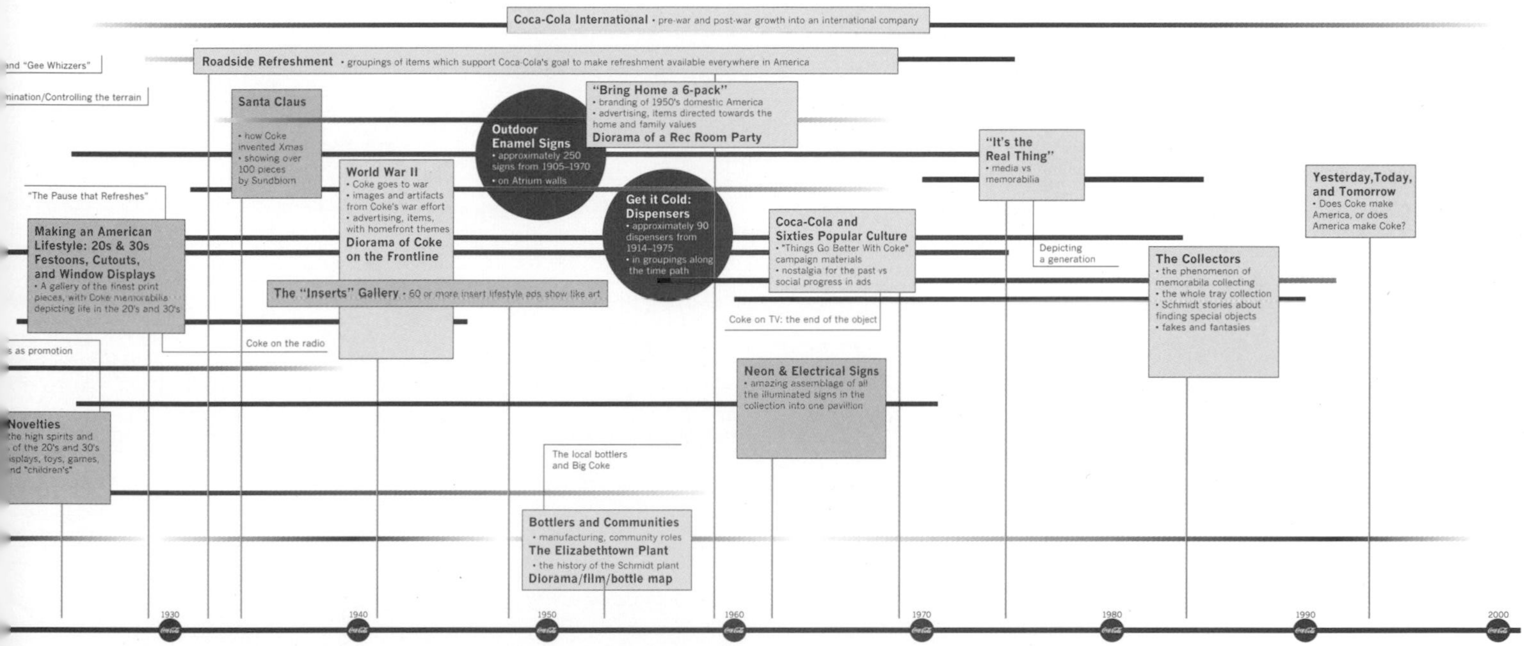
Coca-Cola International • pre-war and post-war growth into an international company
and "Gee Whizzers"
Roadside Refreshment • groupings of items which support Coca-Cola's goal to make refreshment available everywhere in America
mination/Controlling the terrain
Santa Claus
• how Coke invented Xmas
• showing over 100 pieces by Sundblom
Outdoor Enamel Signs
• approximately 250 signs from 1905–1970
• on Atrium walls
"Bring Home a 6-pack"
• branding of 1950's domestic America
• advertising, items directed towards the home and family values
Diorama of a Rec Room Party
"It's the Real Thing"
• media vs memorabilia
World War II
• Coke goes to war
• images and artifacts from Coke's war effort
• advertising, items, with homefront themes
Diorama of Coke on the Frontline
"The Pause that Refreshes"
Get it Cold: Dispensers
• approximately 90 dispensers from 1914–1975
• in groupings along the time path
Coca-Cola and Sixties Popular Culture
• "Things Go Better With Coke" campaign materials
• nostalgia for the past vs social progress in ads
Yesterday,Today, and Tomorrow
• Does Coke make America, or does America make Coke?
Making an American Lifestyle: 20s & 30s Festoons, Cutouts, and Window Displays
• A gallery of the finest print pieces, with Coke memorabilia depicting life in the 20's and 30's
Depicting a generation
The Collectors
• the phenomenon of memorabila collecting
• the whole tray collection
• Schmidt stories about finding special objects
• fakes and fantasies
The "Inserts" Gallery • 60 or more insert lifestyle ads show like art
Coke on TV: the end of the object
Coke on the radio
s as promotion
Neon & Electrical Signs
• amazing assemblage of all the illuminated signs in the collection into one pavillion
Novelties
the high spirits and of the 20's and 30's isplays, toys, games, nd "children's"
The local bottlers and Big Coke
Bottlers and Communities
• manufacturing, community roles
The Elizabethtown Plant
• the history of the Schmidt plant
Diorama/film/bottle map
1930
1940
1950
1960
1970
1980
1990
2000

Coca-Cola

CANDY KITCHEN
Coca-Cola
FOUNTAIN

Schmidt Coca-Cola Museum
Elizabethtown, Kentucky, 1998

The Schmidt Coca-Cola Museum will house the largest collection of Coke memorabilia in the world. Following the curatorial and exhibition strategy developed by BMD, the museum is conceptualized as an intricate network with a timeline and a series of theme areas.

The timeline (shown above) maps out the chronology of Coca-Cola and provides orientation through the museum. It graphically represents a sequence of overlapping spatial episodes which draw thematic envelopes around groupings of artifacts in the collection. Themes are neither taxonomic nor historical, but instead are points of convergence, where coherence in the collection materials are reflective of discernible cultural issues. Each new theme introduces a shift in mood, scale, and content.

The overall effect is a dense fabric of cultural objects, in which individual and collective stories are told within the social and cultural contexts of the twentieth century.

There are some fantastic moments within the Schmidt collection that demonstrate how an advertising vision both held a cultural mirror to America and served as a catalyst for popular social change. For example, in the 1930s, some packagers tried putting six bottles of Coke in a cardboard carton that could be carried home. At the time, almost no one had refrigerators, and the carton gimmick failed. But the advertising projected a domestic life-style as the setting for drinking the product. This idealized image would become a reality two decades later—when Coke would be taken home to millions of refrigerators.

Probably the most famous signature image is Coke's virtual reinvention of Santa Claus in the 1920s as a jolly round man dressed in red and white, the cola's brand colors. Coke's Santa Claus soon displaced other images of St. Nicholas and began to represent Christmas itself throughout America.

For the studio, the biggest challenge and the greatest potential arose from the fact that we were presented with a project that had not been preprogrammed. With the exception of EMR, we had mostly been involved in exhibition designs for which the curators undertook the interpretive work; in this case, however, we were commissioned not only as designers, but as interpreters and organizers of the collection.

1

1

3

2

4

1. Atrium Gallery
(1920s–1980s)
Integral to the vision of the Atrium is a lively and richly patterned display of enamel Coca-Cola signage on all available wall areas. The sign walls also convey the idea that the key to Coke's market and cultural presence is repetition and distribution of the image. Atrium surfaces are filled with over four hundred enamel Coke signs of all sizes and subjects.

2. The Ideal Brain Tonic
(1880–1888)
This first room contains the oldest and some of the rarest objects in the collection and answers some of the basic visitor questions: Why is it called Coca-Cola? Who invented it and where? What are its ingredients? What made it so popular one hundred years ago?

3. The Soda Fountain Era
(1888–1915)
This was the "golden age" of Coca-Cola, when it was still a drink principally served in the Southern U.S., at soda fountains in pharmacies. Included is a full-size, highly realistic construction of a period soda fountain with Coca-Cola artifacts, and other period evidence.

4. The Standardized Bottle
(1890s–1920s)
The remarkable story of how Coke was transformed from a local Atlanta refreshment to the first nationally distributed consumer product was a profoundly significant moment, not only for Coca-Cola, but for modern American culture as a whole. This theme area explores the invention of the standard bottle and its iconic role in American culture.

5

6

5. Making an American Lifestyle
(1915–1930)
Some of the finest objects in the collection in terms of both visual appeal and historical reference are pictorial festoons made to decorate soda fountains. The 1920s festoons project the levity and youthfulness of the period.

6. Window Displays and Cutouts
(1905–1930)
Window displays were one of the original means of advertising Coca-Cola and conveying the pleasure of a pause at the soda fountain. As a medium of advertising, they were infinitely changeable and subject to extraordinary graphic innovations that reflected their time. Cumulatively, they form a mini-essay on the American Main Street as it changed during the first half of the century.

7. Brand Engineering
(1885–1930s)
Much of the object-based story of Coca-Cola is the story of its advertising campaigns, its branded items, and the evolving look of the company. This is not objective but is intimately linked to the visions, passions, and talents of the company's ad men and senior executives.

9

10

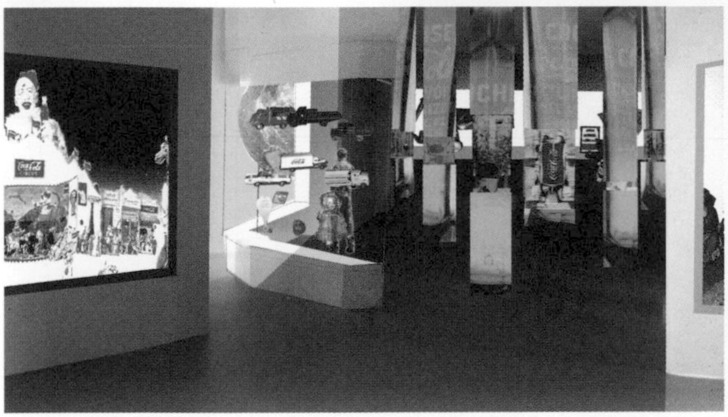

8

8. Toys and Education
(1900 to 1940, mainly late 1920s to early 1940s)
During the 1920s, Coca-Cola promoted an image of youthful fun and playfulness.
The policy documents of the period indicate a clear agenda to attract teens and children to the product: “Get them young and you have them for life.” But direct advertising to children was considered immoral, so other approaches were sought. Manufacturing toys and novelties was an early approach. Items focused on educational needs, along with sponsorship of teams and community work. The theme of toys and novelties will be picked up again much later in the exhibition, in the section covering the 1960s to the present. The ads and items became more overt in their focus on teens and children. This changing strategy will be traced through objects from tin Coke trucks to the *Star Wars* character R2D2.

9. Roadside Refreshment
(1920s–1960s)
This area addresses American car culture, roadside advertising, and the omnipresent roadside Coca-Cola vendor. It introduces Coke’s status as a “life-style” drink by showing how Coke became directly associated with the values of youth, freedom, and convenience. This section also incorporates several subthemes: the Coca-Cola truck, its design and evolution; the ever-expanding bottler’s distribution network; roadside signage and the new American highway; the culture of the picnic.

10. Neon and Electrical Sign Room
(1920s–1970s)
American nightlife was born of electricity and neon. The story begins with advertising entrepreneur Archie Lee’s account of his first illuminated Coca-Cola sign in Times Square, built before 1920. This room is a delirious celebration of illuminated Coca-Cola signs, clocks, and lights. Every lighted sign in the collection is presented in this room. It may include a time-lapse video projection showing an electric Coca-Cola sign in Times Square over a 24-hour period.

11. World War II
(1930–1946)
The story of how Coca-Cola joined the war effort and simultaneously became equated with American democratic values and world enterprise is a watershed in the history of the company.
This section includes great stories about the prewar European bottlers, the opening of markets before 1939, and their subsequent efforts to keep the company intact under the Nazis.

14

12

12

12. The "Inserts" Gallery
(1930s–1950s)
During the 1930s Coca-Cola ad men devised a standard decorated frame in horizontal and vertical formats to hold changeable 33.5″ x 22.5″ illustration posters. The many images of young, active lifestyles convey the optimism that arose during the Roosevelt era and continued after WWII into the prosperity of the 1950s.

13. Sprite Boy
(1946–mid-1950s)
The introduction of the Sprite Boy character in 1946 was intended to ease the public into accepting the word "Coke"—recently trademarked—for Coca-Cola. Whether this was necessary or not, Sprite Boy became a playful, if somewhat sinister, mascot during the postwar period. This room brings together a concentration of his ad objects.

14. Postwar Vendors
Following World War II, the U.S. possessed the material reserves and manufacturing capacity to produce a huge array of commercial goods. Coca-Cola commissioned and produced a stream of new metal-fabricated products, from vendors to enamel signs, to new bottling equipment, to trucks. This is an object-based installation. The vendors and coolers will be used to tell stories about design, availability, distribution, and refrigeration technology.

17

15

16

15. Santa Pavilion
(mainly 1930s–1940s)
This area tells the story of Coca-Cola's invention of the image of Santa Claus.

16. "Bring Home a Six-Pack": 1950s Domestic American Lifestyle
(1950s)
The story of Coca-Cola in the 1950s is a combination of an ambitious international expansion campaign and a consolidation and rarification of the image of American domestic life. Brand engineering became much more systematic and consistent. Life-style advertising predominated through the decade, with an undertone of patriotism and enterprise. Youth culture and the image of youth became more focused on the idea of the young family. At the same time, the availability of affordable domestic refrigeration finally made "Coke at home" a reality for the middle class—the cola's fastest expanding market.
In telling this story, we will also introduce evidence of earlier attempts in the 1920s and 1930s to market Coke for home consumption.

17. Elizabethtown, The Bottlers and their Communities
(1946–1965)
This room focuses on the postwar story of Coca-Cola from the bottler's point of view, using physical and anecdotal material from the Schmidts and other archives.
Technical innovations combined with new marketing initiatives and challenges from competing soft drink manufacturers made the 1950s and early 1960s a time of rapid change for the bottlers and Coca-Cola corporation. This section will include a look at: the new machinery in motion (a video film in a bottling plant), the shrinking "Bottle Map" of America, and the introduction of the can.

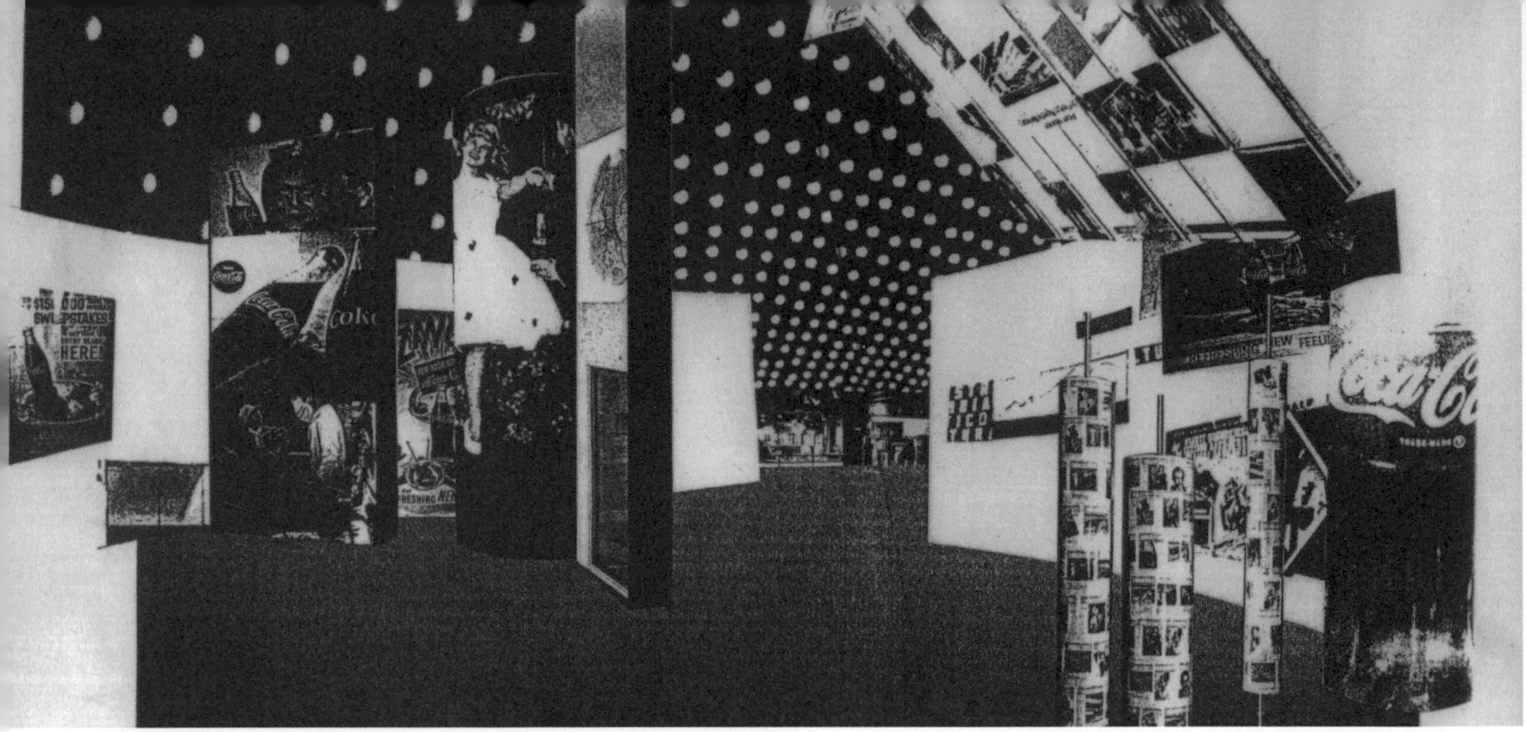

19

19

18. Mini Theater
(1955–1965)
This area presents a variety of restored films from the 1950s and early 1960s. Some of these films are commercial spots for early TV. There are also sales training films and brief "histories" of Coke made for promotional purposes. Viewed together they are very telling of their time, and anticipate the overwhelming role of film and TV advertising in future decades.

19. Coca-Cola and 1960s Pop Culture
(1960–1970)
As Coke entered the 1960s there was a dramatic shift in its ad strategy. Perception of its target market broadened to encompass multiple life-styles. The homogenous American family image expanded to reflect different ethnic groups, ages, and attitudes. The period also saw several efforts to re-engineer the brand—with slogans ranging from "Coke with Chow, Wow!" to "Things Go Better with Coke" to "I'd like to Teach the World to Sing". The emphasis on advertising and away from object-based marketing shifted in response to the rise of TV and radio. A subtheme of this section is the influence of Coke on American pop art of the period.

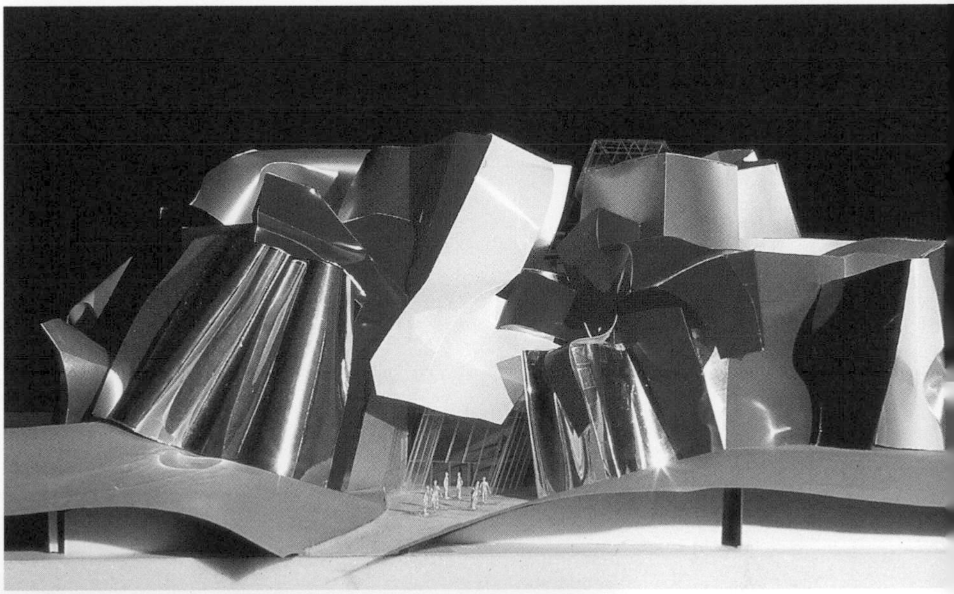

Frank O. Gehry and Associates
Study model for the museum

20. The Collectors
(1950s–present)
Why is Coca-Cola memorabilia so sought after? How is it found? How is it valued? Which are the rarest items? Here we address the mania for collecting Coca-Cola memorabilia. The Schmidts themselves are the heroes of this story. This is an opportunity to include a history of their collection and its ongoing objectives.

21. "The Real Thing" versus TV
(1970 to present)
The last ad campaign to consider memorabilia was "The Real Thing" in the early 1970s. Attention has since shifted to media-based advertising with decreased emphasis on the production of memorabilia. This area traces the 'mediatization' of Coke while celebrating the best of the video works made for Coca-Cola since 1970. Several stories emerge from this period: the introduction of Diet Coke; the death of Robert W. Woodruff, head of the company for fifty years; the consolidation of the bottling operations; the invention of New Coke and Coke Classic; new frontiers with Coke in space, Coke in Russia, Coke at the movies; Max Headroom and Coke's 1980s video culture; and the 1990s nostalgia revival.

Conclusion
The story of Coca-Cola is a story of a war fought on two fronts. The first was a war of terrain, starting in Atlanta and spreading throughout the south and then to all of America and beyond in a bid to dominate the world. The second was a war of identity, a war fought by lawyers with contracts and advertising men with images in a campaign to dominate global attention.

The last section of the exhibition ends with the question: Has America made Coke? or, Has Coke made America?

At some point, as design "professionalized," thinking and saying were delaminated, and it became possible to say without thinking. The result? Mountains of message that mean nothing. We empty the word "literature" and strap it to the back of "corporate" without apology, without irony.

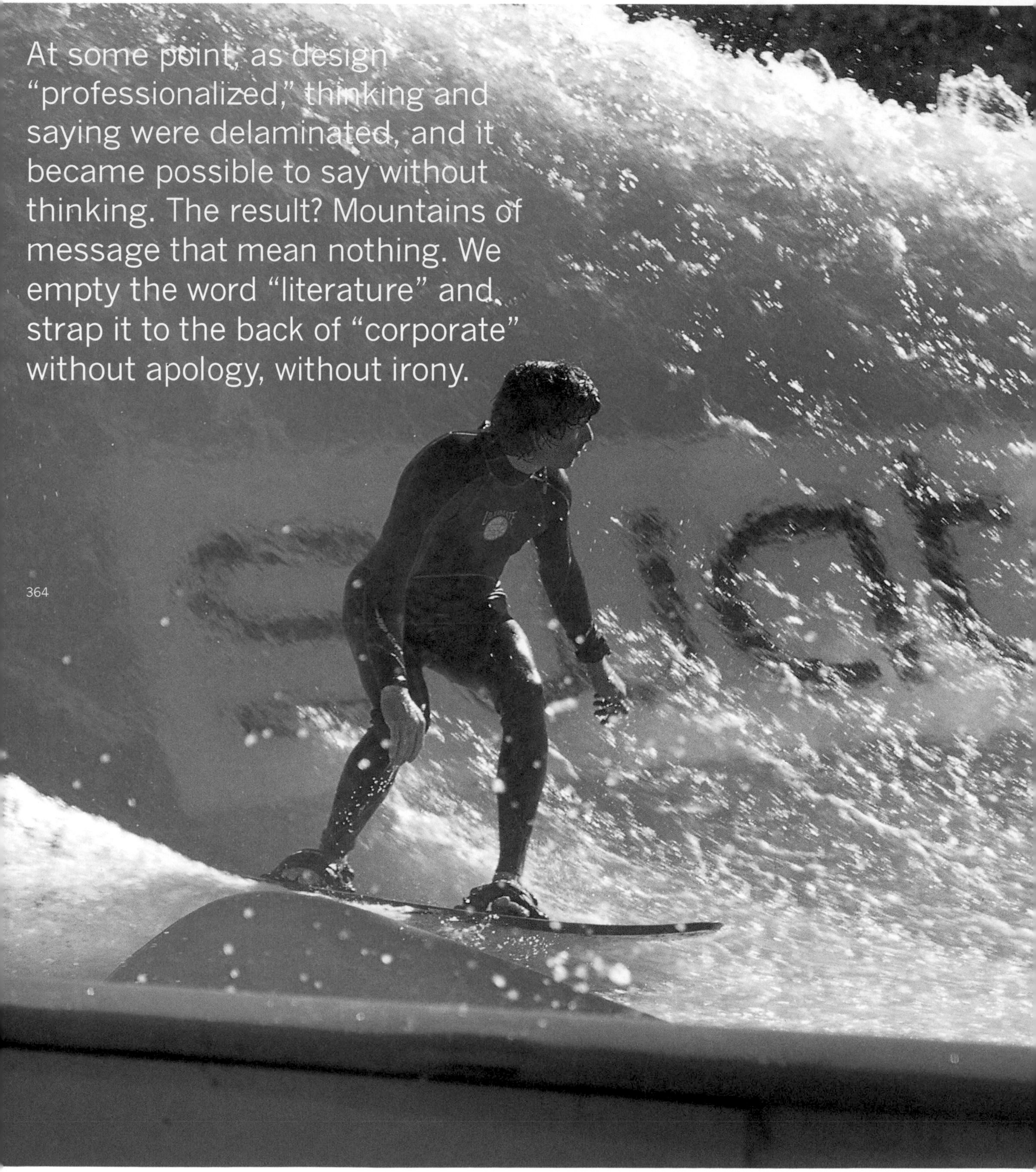

Cloaking Devices

In combat, in the age of intelligent machines, a cloaking device is used by an invader to avoid detection. In culture, in the age of the spectacle, a cloaking device is more supple. Used to hide certain characteristics and enhance others, it performs reconstructive surgery on the image. It can make a company that runs sweatshops look like it is concerned with AIDS; a bank look like it cares about small business; the state look friendly; architecture, the lapdog of big business, look radical; two guitars and a drummer look innovative; a marketing budget look like a grant to a museum; an advertisement look like a magazine. It can make a magazine seem like the news; a dozen video cameras seem like the world; an advertising delivery system seem like public broadcasting; fiction seem like history.
If one could name the two cloaking devices that have screwed up the twentieth century more than any others (though competition here is stiff), they would have to be marketing and television.

Marketing
Marketing gets the nod for its capacity to lead by following: it reduces citizens to consumers. The fact that the Western world is governed by opinion polls should come as a wake-up call to anyone who believes that his or her future could be different from, if not better than, what we already know. Marketing asks the answer by stating the question, or by redrawing the question in the shape of the answer. Marketing collects the evidence to commit the crime. It is a technique designed to adjust the image to the perception—a cloaking device. It allows David Duke, the former Ku Klux Klansman and

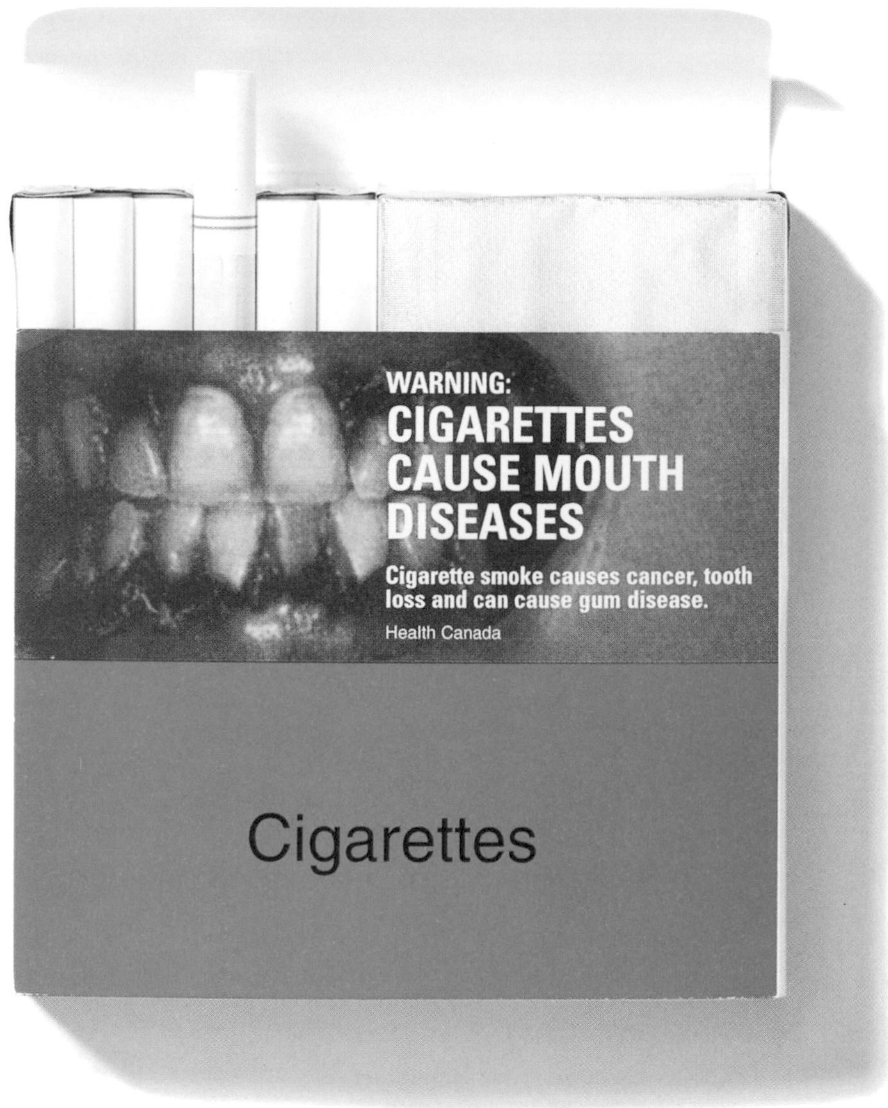

WARNING:
CIGARETTES CAUSE MOUTH DISEASES
Cigarette smoke causes cancer, tooth loss and can cause gum disease.
Health Canada
Cigarettes

366

Cigarette packaging currently being proposed by Health Canada, calling for 50 percent of the surface of the box to be given to health warnings.

U.S. Congressional candidate from Louisiana, to be accepted as a viable mainstream political candidate by altering his cheekbones, his hairline, and his lapels. Entrusted with leadership, our leaders insist on adjusting the rearview mirror and driving backward out of the future. We can't know who they are because they will only tell us that they are who we want them to be.

Television

Television delivers the little piggies to market. It delivers an audience to advertisers. It does what marketing does, but it does so at the speed of light. Now, with digital convergence, we will soon enter a five-hundred-channel universe. Five-hundred channels of shopping: passivity masquerading as interactivity. Combine this with recent mergers in the entertainment-information complex and you've got the greatest concentration of image control since the Medicis. Isn't anyone else angry, or at least nervous? Cultural turnaround time — the time it takes for mainstream business to assimilate street culture — is rapidly shrinking. Formerly marginal activities, like skateboarding or surfing, are now routinely incorporated directly into marketing campaigns. Cultural events are becoming "historic" in five years, "classic" in ten. We have become nostalgic for yesterday, even for this morning. The visual milieu — the context in which our design work must live — is intensifying. It is vicious. It is, quite simply, Darwinian.

So where does my work fit in? What is my relationship to this happy, smiling monster? Where is the freedom in this regime? Do I follow Timothy Leary and "tune in, turn on, drop out?" What actions can I commit that cannot be absorbed? Can I outperform the system? Can I win?

RiverLab

Institution Concept and Programming Study
National Museum of the Mississippi River
New Orleans, 1999

In early 1999, through our ongoing work with Frank Gehry, I was invited to a meeting in New Orleans, a gathering of more than twenty people chaired by Scott Cowan, president of Tulane University. Although the group was extremely diverse—business people, engineers, scientists, military personnel, city officials—everyone was committed to creating an institution showcasing the culture of the Mississippi River. The question on everybody's mind was how to proceed with the project. Someone proposed that they should begin by conducting focus groups. I disagreed and suggested that what the project needed was leadership. Focus groups are good for follow-up—they inform you about where you've been. I stressed that, to succeed, they would instead have to invent what they wanted and make it something completely new. These remarks got us the commission to develop a model of the project.

We started with what we regarded as a storyline problem, as we did with the Coca-Cola museum project. But what we discovered, after undertaking an extensive interview process, was that Riverlab, as the project came to be called, would require an act of imagination of a different kind. There were so many different institutions involved—the city of New Orleans, universities, the U.S. Army Corps of Engineers, and so on— and each had different ideological interests.

Cowan wanted to reinvent Tulane University and make a mark on New Orleans and Louisiana. In this light, our mission was to explore new means of education, new models for a learning institution. One of the references we drew on was a Zone book, *Wonders and the Order of Nature*, by Lorraine Daston and Katherine Park. The authors describe the sixteenth-century curiosity cabinet, or *Wunderkammer*, as a precedent for the nineteenth-century art museum, but with this critical difference: art, science, and human curiosity were freely mingled. The curiosity cabinet, an early means of collecting and ordering eclectic objects to produce knowledge, became our preliminary model for working in a trans-disciplinary way.

Think-tank
Web-Site
Theater
Broadcaster
Store
School
Research Lab
Kunsthal
Residence
Science Center
Conservancy
Park
Museum
Riverboat

A day in the life of the Mississipi
9:00 a.m.
Administrative and teaching staff arrive. Lectures, research, and projects get started within the museum. Set up for two-day Think-Tank takes place. Approximately forty people are attending a workshop on the issue of retaining the shoreline. Participants from the United States and from international communities who share the same concerns (The Netherlands, Egypt) will spend two days discussing this issue. Participants will be encouraged to stay in touch with the museum and with one another. One class that has organized this Think-tank will take the information from the event and post it on the museum's Website for further discussion. The Think-tank is being sponsored by the Army Corps of Engineers and the museum.

The Mississippi River and Tulane University have already attracted extraordinary river scientists and river systems researchers. The literature of the Mississippi is vast, its musical culture extremely rich, and its role in U.S. industry and commerce enormous. All these aspects of the river's culture, science, and economics needed to be incorporated.

The question then became how much of the thing would be fixed and how much would operate fluidly on the model of a Kunsthal, where art is installed only temporarily.

The permanent portions would be devoted to the poetry of the river, in the form of a spectacular architectural exhibition. The least "stable" — but still very significant — element would be a performance space that would be used for music, theater, dance, and storytelling. Between these extremes would fall the range of engineering, science, economics, and ecology activities.

The basic concept was that visitors should be able to engage the whole place, that RiverLab should have one front door through which scientists, businesspeople, students, and the general public could enter and then participate at different levels of involvement and commitment. Tourists could go for the show and come away with some experience of the scientific, cultural, and economic life of the Mississippi. Graduate students could enroll in intensive research residencies.

11:00 a.m.

Luncheon tour for a group of spouses from a convention of actuaries. The tour will include a ride on the river.

Demonstration of jambalaya preparation in the RiverCafé. It is open to the public and also involves the students in residence. They will be making their own jambalaya for lunch following the demonstration.

University lecture on Louis Armstrong in the theater. Course is publicized and can be audited by request.

Internal meeting of exhibition programming staff, Army Corps of Engineers, researchers, and a visiting scholar from Chicago to discuss the initial idea for a temporary exhibition involving all the river changes that have taken place over the past hundred years. The exhibition is three years away and has three other institutional partners along the Mississippi and its tributaries. The objective of the meeting is to formalize the concept and develop grant proposals.

2:00 p.m.
The group of students in residence for the week spend the afternoon in the RiverLab observing the way in which samples are drawn from the riverbed and examined.
They watch a film on the engineering challenges of the river and spend time with an expert from Vicksburg who talks about the history of the levees on the river. The discussion is conducted in the museum area, where exhibits detail the changes that have taken place in the river's course.
Internal meeting of the program coordinators. The administrators of the program are drawn in part from the teaching facility and in part from the school board. Students are also represented on this committee. The coordinators are looking at the upcoming exhibitions and developing training sessions for the teen docents. The docent program runs during weekends and evenings, providing course credit for all students who successfully complete it.
A church group from out of state is visiting the museum and has requested a special tour. They organized their tour with the Amistad Research Program at Tulane. The tour will focus on the experience of slaves on the river. The museum is able to develop specialized touring situations because of its close relationship with the university and other partners. Amistad is an active partner in the museum as they attempt to increase their own holdings and work with audiences at every opportunity to broaden awareness of the African-American experience of the Mississippi River.

3:00 p.m.
Graduate students take a break in the RiverCafé and chat with their professors and some of the students from different disciplines. The RiverCafé is a regular meeting place for staff, students, volunteers, and the public. It is pleasant and energetic. The coffee is as good as the food.

Staff meeting with officials from the Audubon Park and Zoo to plan a joint function. The proposed evening will be a River Romp—an evening of dancing on a riverboat with a live band. The dress will be period costumes from the 1920s and 1930s, and a contest will held for the best dancers at the event.

Students begin to arrive to facilitate an after-school program for younger kids. The program is sponsored by a local bank and brings in families for one hour from 4:00 to 5:00 p.m. The parents attend a lecture or performance in the RiverTheater with a group of seniors, while the children are kept busy with sand and water tables, stories, and games. The program is facilitated by teens and senior volunteers.

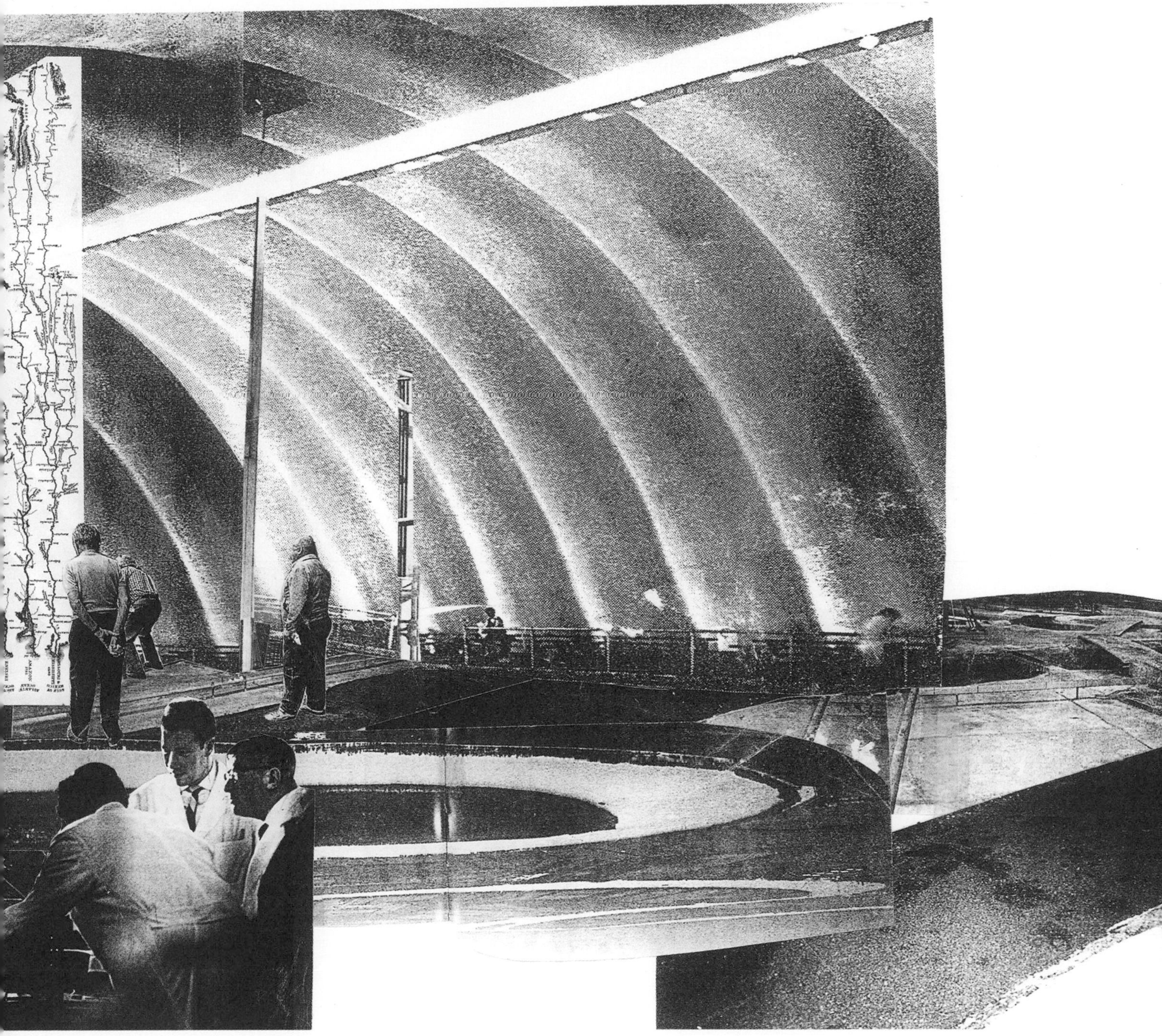

4:00 p.m.
The after-school chat line starts for both students and professors. The hour from 4:00 to 5:00 p.m. is dedicated to students working on projects in schools, at home, or even at the museum. Through the chat line, kids can ask for help, get responses to questions, and pursue their science projects with the help of the staff at the museum. The chat-line responsibility is shared among many professors and graduate students. When they can't answer the question, it is forwarded to a colleague.
The kids in the residence program head to the RiverCafé for a snack. They are met by their leader for the next session, who takes them back into the world of 1930s jazz for an hour before dinner. Both the context of the music (no televisions, few radios) and the developments in jazz at that time are discussed and replicated.
Communications arrangements are being finalized for a conference taking place in the morning. It involves two researchers from Stockholm who will participate via satellite and five of the researchers in the museum's lab. The conference is a follow-up to a large think-tank held eight months before. The discussion will be recorded and broadcast on the Web. It will be included in a future museum publication.

karst water table
Danube
656
606
574
525
475
12 km

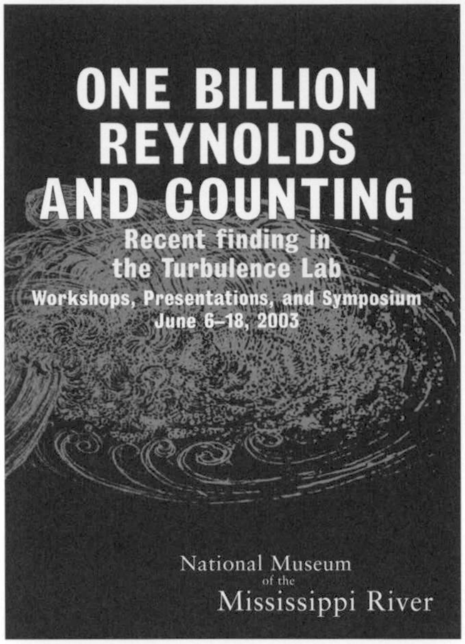

ONE BILLION
REYNOLDS
AND COUNTING
Recent finding in
the Turbulence Lab
Workshops, Presentations, and Symposium
June 6–18, 2003
National Museum
of the
Mississippi River

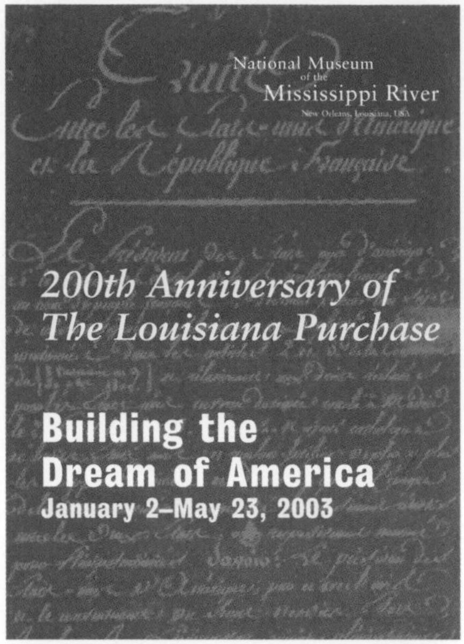

National Museum
of the
Mississippi River
200th Anniversary of
The Louisiana Purchase
Building the
Dream of America
January 2–May 23, 2003

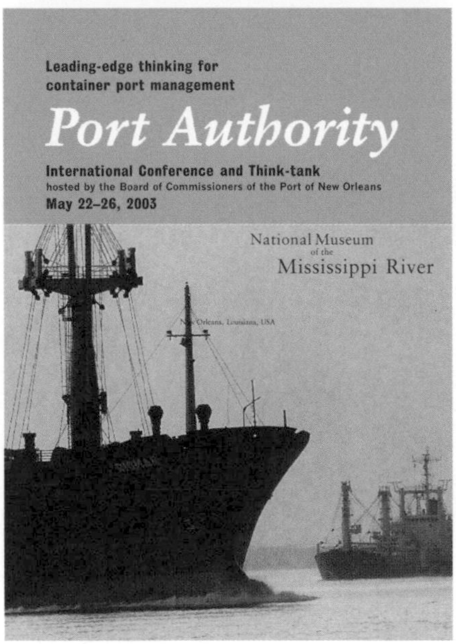

Leading-edge thinking for
container port management
Port Authority
International Conference and Think-tank
hosted by the Board of Commissioners of the Port of New Orleans
May 22–26, 2003
National Museum
of the
Mississippi River

SUSPENDING DISBELIEF
The Heroic Age
of Bridge Building
January 6 – March 23, 2004
Mississippi RiverLab
New Orleans, Louisiana, USA
National Museum
of the
Mississippi River

5:00 p.m.
Staff is setting up the Atrium space for an evening reception. An intern from the School of Hotel, Restaurant, and Tourism Administration at the University of New Orleans is on hand for the evening to assist the manager on duty. The exhibits are open until 6:00 p.m. while the RiverCafé stays open until 10:00 p.m. Students and professors drift in and out of the facility until midnight, when the building is secured for the evening. Generally, there is a lull at this time while the day's activities are winding down and the evening performances, lectures, and social events are organized. The museum box office sells tickets for an evening performance at the Aquarium. The IMAX theater is featuring a film on the river that has been developed in conjunction with staff from both institutions.

8:00 p.m.
Dance for teen volunteers takes place in one of the banqueting areas. The theme is Juke Joint, and it is a chance for the students doing volunteer work to meet one another as well as some of the graduate students working in the museum. There is lots of dancing and no alcohol. Diners in the restaurant also walk out to the levee and watch the students by the bonfire.

9:00 p.m. to closing
Students proceed to the residence for bed. Teachers supervise the end-of-day activities and then meet briefly before retiring also. The RiverCafé is clearing out and students are drifting home for the evening. Security staff make their last rounds in the museum and the evening maintenance crews arrive. The convention group will dance until midnight, while the Port of New Orleans dinner breaks up and attendees leave before 11:00 p.m

Tree City

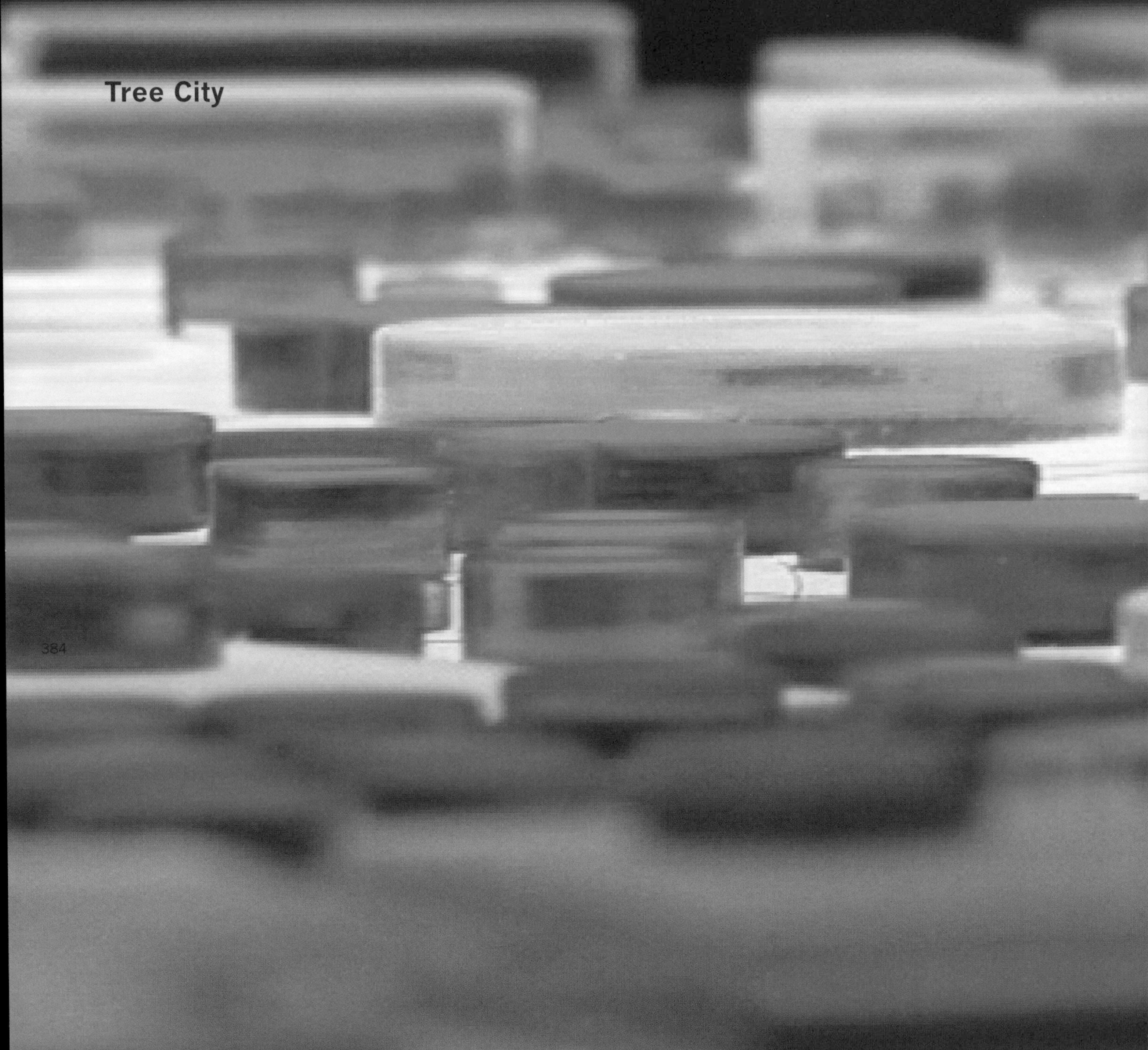

**Proposal for Downsview Park
Toronto, 2000
A creative collaboration between Bruce Mau Design, Petra Blaisse, Inside Outside, Amsterdam; and Rem Koolhaas, Office for Metropolitan Architecture, Rotterdam; with Oleson Worland Architects**

In late 1999, our team was shortlisted for a competition to design Downsview Park, which is to be situated on the site of a decommissioned military base with an active airstrip and housing the De Havilland Bombardier assembly plant. We competed against four other teams. The winning proposal will be awarded $150 million to create a 322-acre park in a 640-acre compound that will continue to house a range of industrial and sports-entertainment facilities. Downsview Park lies at the perimeter of Toronto. Its panoramic views and prairie-like vistas of endless sky are unique to the city's geography. Yet the public image of the park continues to be dominated by the memory of the recently removed barbed-wire fence and policed gates of the military base. This area has been closed to the general public for more than fifty years. We do not envision the park as a completed environment. The park must be seen as active, emerging, and evolving. Downsview may be located on what is today the edge of the city, but in the time it takes for a maple tree to grow to maturity, Downsview will be considered a midtown urban site, and it will host all the activities and amenities associated with its urbanized status.

Toronto suffers
Of all major No
cities, Toronto s
amount on publ

No major city spends less on
survive as urban beauty bec
to a city's prominence in the
Toronto's own negligence tur
a peripheral global city? Des
Toronto has the opportunity t
ent asset into its greatest civ

rom neglect.
th American
pends the least
ic space.

park operations. Can Toronto
mes increasingly important
vorld marketplace? Will
Canada's central hub into
te its meager park spending,
convert the city's one inher-
c amenity.

To imagine an urban park presupposes an urban condition.
When Frederick Law Olmsted imagined Central Park, he imagined the context it would eventually inspire and sustain.
Physically, the Downsview Park site simply has no distinguishing characteristics: no history, no lakes, no mountains, no rivers, no streams, no ponds, no ravines, no forests.
It offers one virtue: scale.
The scale of the site and the relative sparseness of the surrounding suburban context suggest a new approach.
The demand it places on the design is to invert the typical relationship between figure and ground—between figural urban density and natural open space as ground. In the context of the park, natural open space must be legible as figural density against the suburban ground.
We propose to use Toronto's most distinguishing feature as the park's primary urban component: trees. Rather than buildings, trees will serve as the catalyst of urbanization. Vegetal clusters, not new building complexes will provide the site's identity. A civic domain constituted by landscape elements, Tree City will do more by building less, and produce density with natural permeability, property development with perennial enrichment.
Landscape elements will be planted incrementally over time as funding permits, gradually building up the park's mass into a flexible patchwork of planted clusters separated by undesignated open areas. The park will involve three short-term phases: (1) site and soil preparation, (2) pathway construction, and

Global Green Space Survey: Acres of Parkland/1000 persons

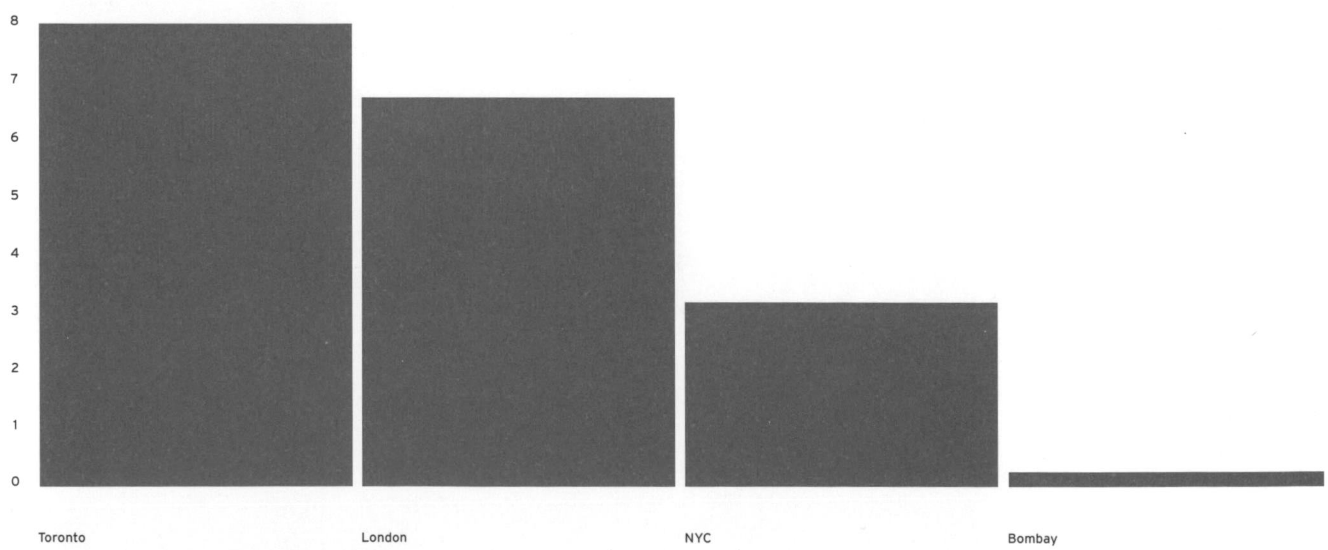

(3) cluster landscaping. The outcome will be a matrix of circular tree clusters covering 25 percent of the site, which will be supplemented by meadows, playing fields and gardens.

Tree City treats the park as if it were an adult capable of sustaining itself rather than a child in need of perpetual care. Most infrastructure decreases in value over time. Tree City's natural network will appreciate as the park matures.

Tree City chooses growth over stasis. Capital generated from the park's appreciated land value should be spent to manage the park's infrastructure and to support future growth and development.

Tree City assumes the park's suburban context to be its greatest virtue. The locale offers an ideal opportunity to reopen unrealized promises of low-density metropolitan life. Notorious until now for its predictability and uniformity, the suburb today has the potential to function as a playground where the population can unwind.

Ultimately, we envision that this vegetal epicenter will connect with the city's green spaces and become a part of a tree "infrastructure" for the Greater Toronto Area. By extending its landscape clusters and pedestrian pathways into adjacent areas, Tree City will link up with the Black Creek and West Don ravines, integrating Downsview Park into the system of wooded river valleys, parks, and public paths unique to Toronto's urban domain. Earth bridges to the west and to the north will link Downsview's ecology to the city's. In this way, Tree City grows the park *into* Toronto.

Park Operating Expenditures in $1000 per Acre

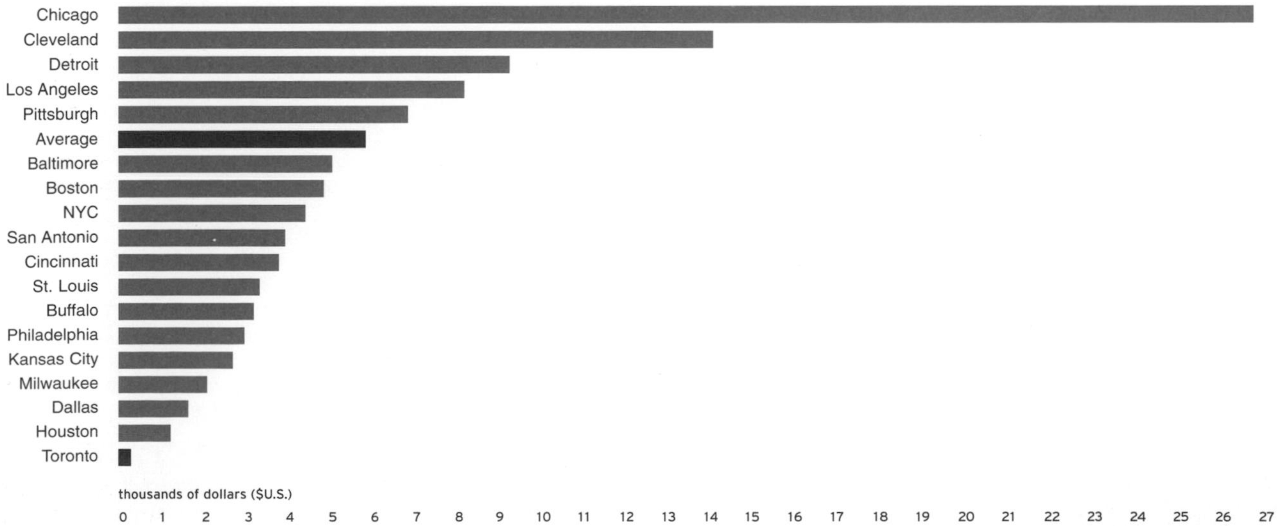

1. Grow the Park

Tree City plants the seed for environmental expansion. In the broadest sense, Tree City is a campaign to grow the park beyond Downsview's boundaries and into the urban realm. It is the antithesis of the token green space. Rather than setting itself apart from the city like a trophy of environmentalism, Tree City accepts a degree of toxicity in order to establish greater presence.

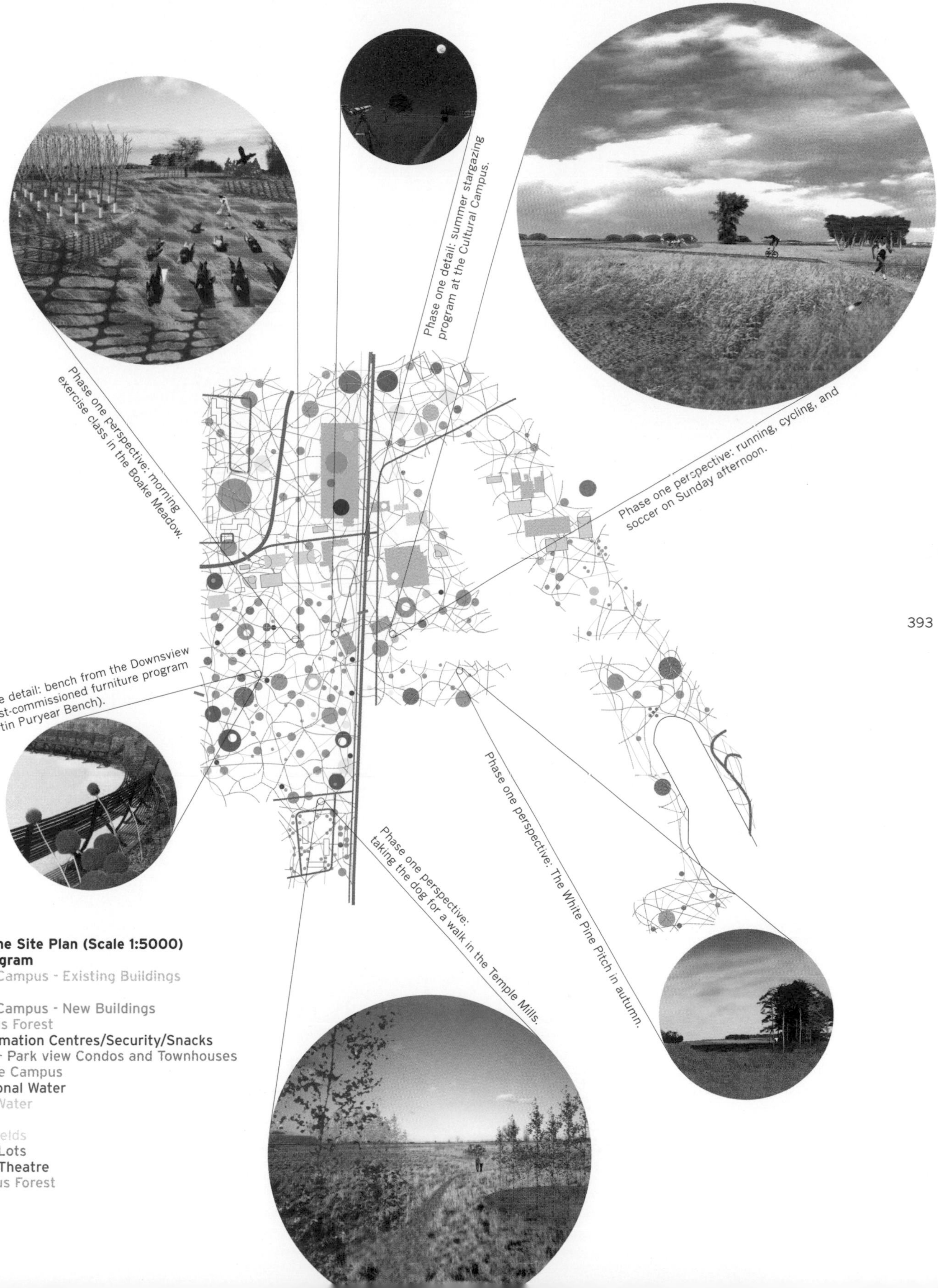

Phase one perspective: morning exercise class in the Boake Meadow.
Phase one detail: summer stargazing program at the Cultural Campus.
Phase one perspective: running, cycling, and soccer on Sunday afternoon.
Phase one detail: bench from the Downsview Park artist-commissioned furniture program (eg. Martin Puryear Bench).
Phase one perspective: taking the dog for a walk in the Temple Mills.
Phase one perspective: The White Pine Pitch in autumn.

Phase One Site Plan (Scale 1:5000)
Park Program

- Cultural Campus - Existing Buildings
- Parking
- Cultural Campus - New Buildings
- Deciduous Forest
- WC/Information Centres/Security/Snacks
- Housing - Park view Condos and Townhouses
- Corporate Campus
- Recreational Water
- Surface Water
- Wetlands
- Sports Fields
- Meadow Lots
- Outdoor Theatre
- Coniferous Forest
- Gardens

2. Manufacture Nature

Instead of restoring the site to a pristine natural state, Tree City manufactures nature for civic ends. It is a fabricated landscape designed first and foremost to orchestrate on-site leisure activities, movement, and commercial development. 100% ‘artificial’ and 100% ‘natural,’ Tree City is unambiguously administrative in ambition AND entirely organic in spirit.

3. 1000 Pathways

Offering endless excursions, 1000 Pathways is a web of trails woven through the entire park. The paths are interconnected to provide infinite itineraries for the Downsview visitor and render inexhaustible the array of experiences available to even the most frequent user. 1000 Pathways produce 1000 Entrances: an open edge condition connecting the park to the city in a multitude of ways.

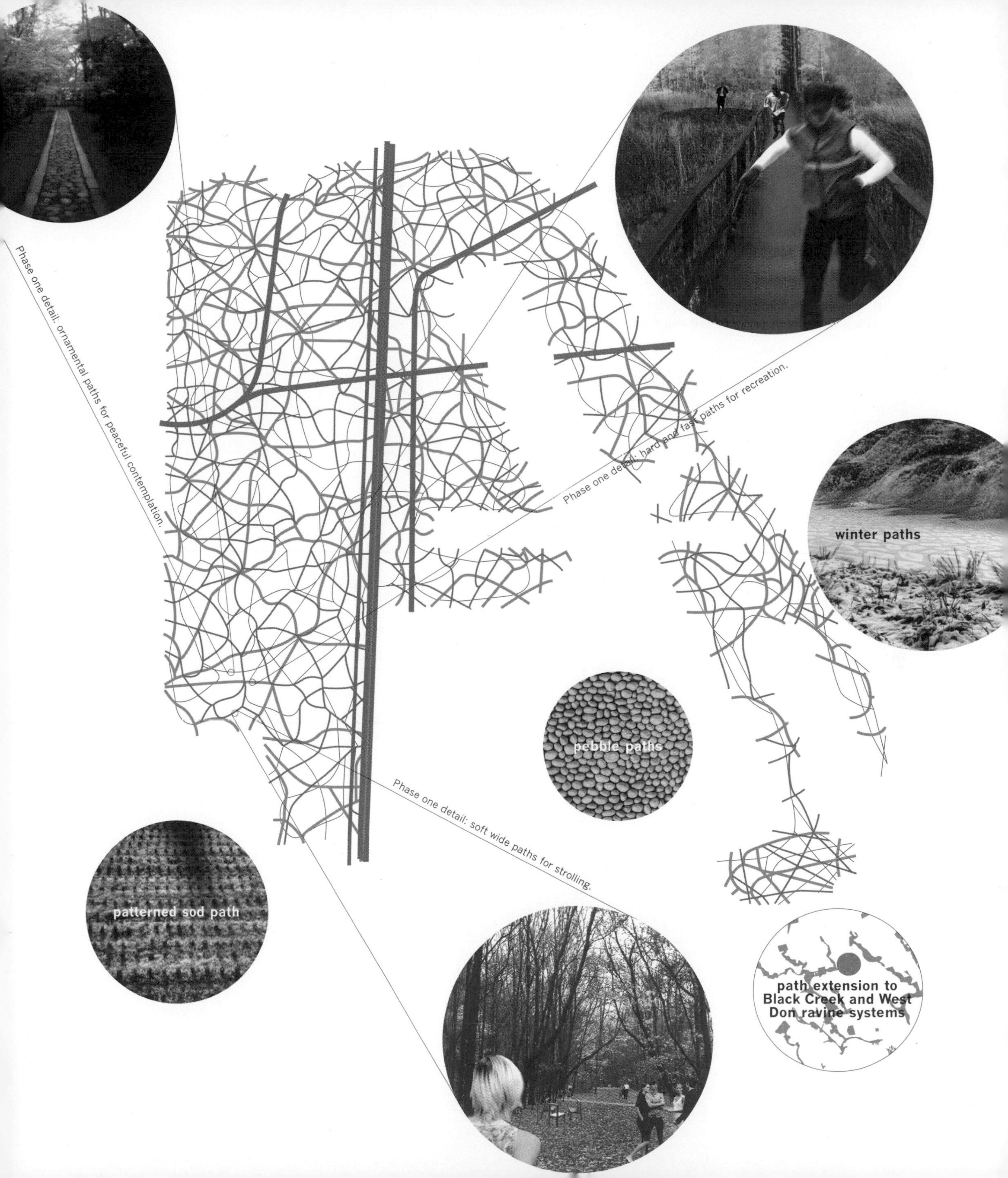
Phase one detail: ornamental paths for peaceful contemplation.
Phase one detail: hard and fast paths for recreation.
winter paths
pebble paths
Phase one detail: soft wide paths for strolling.
patterned sod path
path extension to Black Creek and West Don ravine systems

4. Sacrifice and Save

Tree City opts to grow now and build later. It sacrifices the construction of costly new buildings in order to save funds for an infrastructure of landscape elements. A medium capable of developing mass with greater economy and malleability, the landscape will be privileged over the realm officially known as architecture. Stressing the vegetal over the colossal, Tree City makes 'the ultimate sacrifice' to save Downsview from premature fiscal crisis.

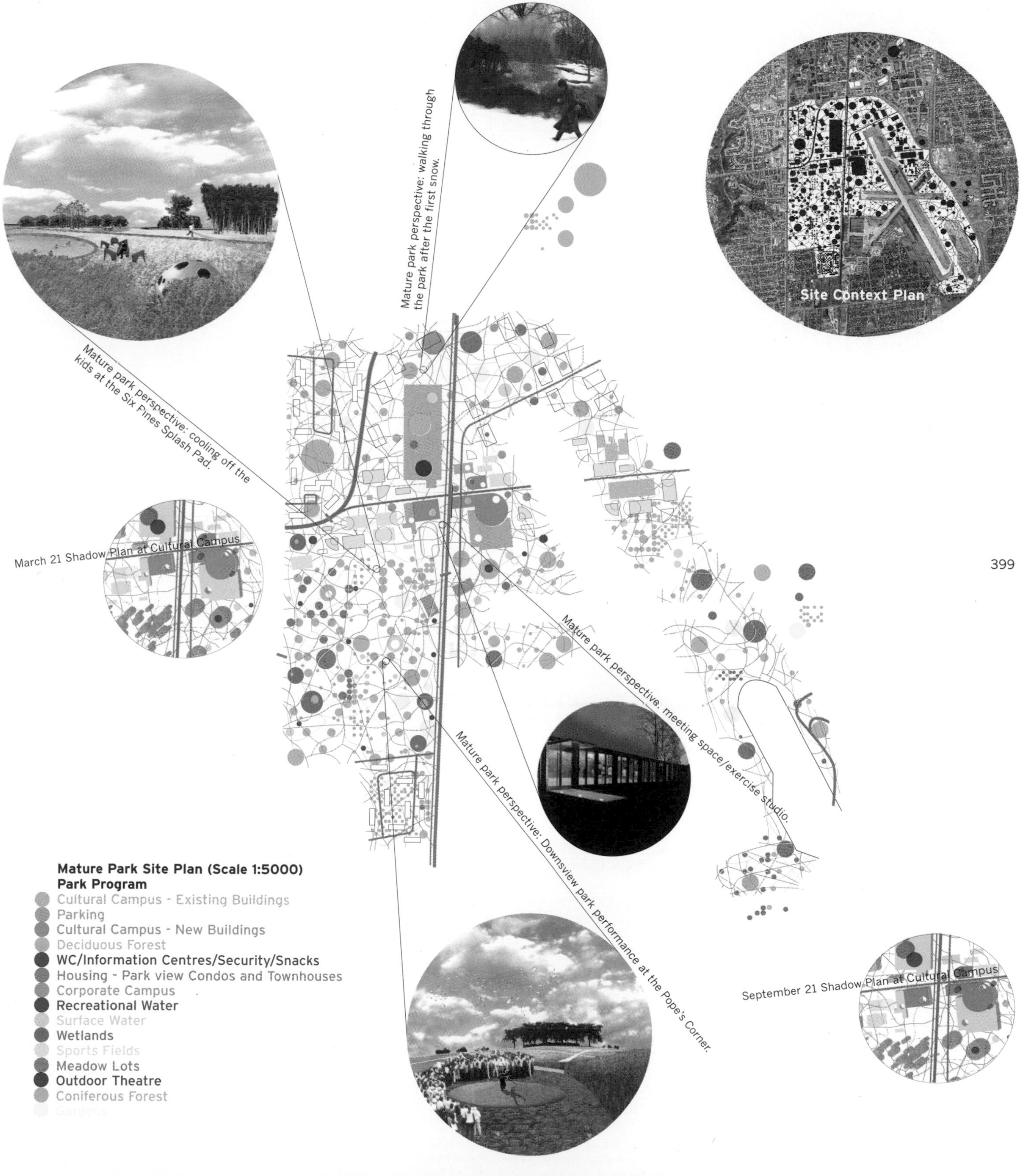
Mature park perspective: walking through the park after the first snow.
Site Context Plan
Mature park perspective: cooling off the kids at the Six Pines Splash Pad.
March 21 Shadow Plan at Cultural Campus
Mature park perspective: meeting space/exercise studio.
Mature park perspective: Downsview park performance at the Pope's Corner.
September 21 Shadow Plan at Cultural Campus
Mature Park Site Plan (Scale 1:5000)
Park Program
Cultural Campus - Existing Buildings
Parking
Cultural Campus - New Buildings
Deciduous Forest
WC/Information Centres/Security/Snacks
Housing - Park view Condos and Townhouses
Corporate Campus
Recreational Water
Surface Water
Wetlands
Sports Fields
Meadow Lots
Outdoor Theatre
Coniferous Forest
Gardens

5. Curate Culture

Tree City is a diagram designed to maximize the park's options for survival. The strategy for cultural programming is provisional. Over the course of its life, functions will be assigned to ensure the park's existence. When possible, cultural activities will be programmed to enhance the park's leisure domain. When necessary, commercial activities will be assigned to offset the park's evolving maintenance costs.

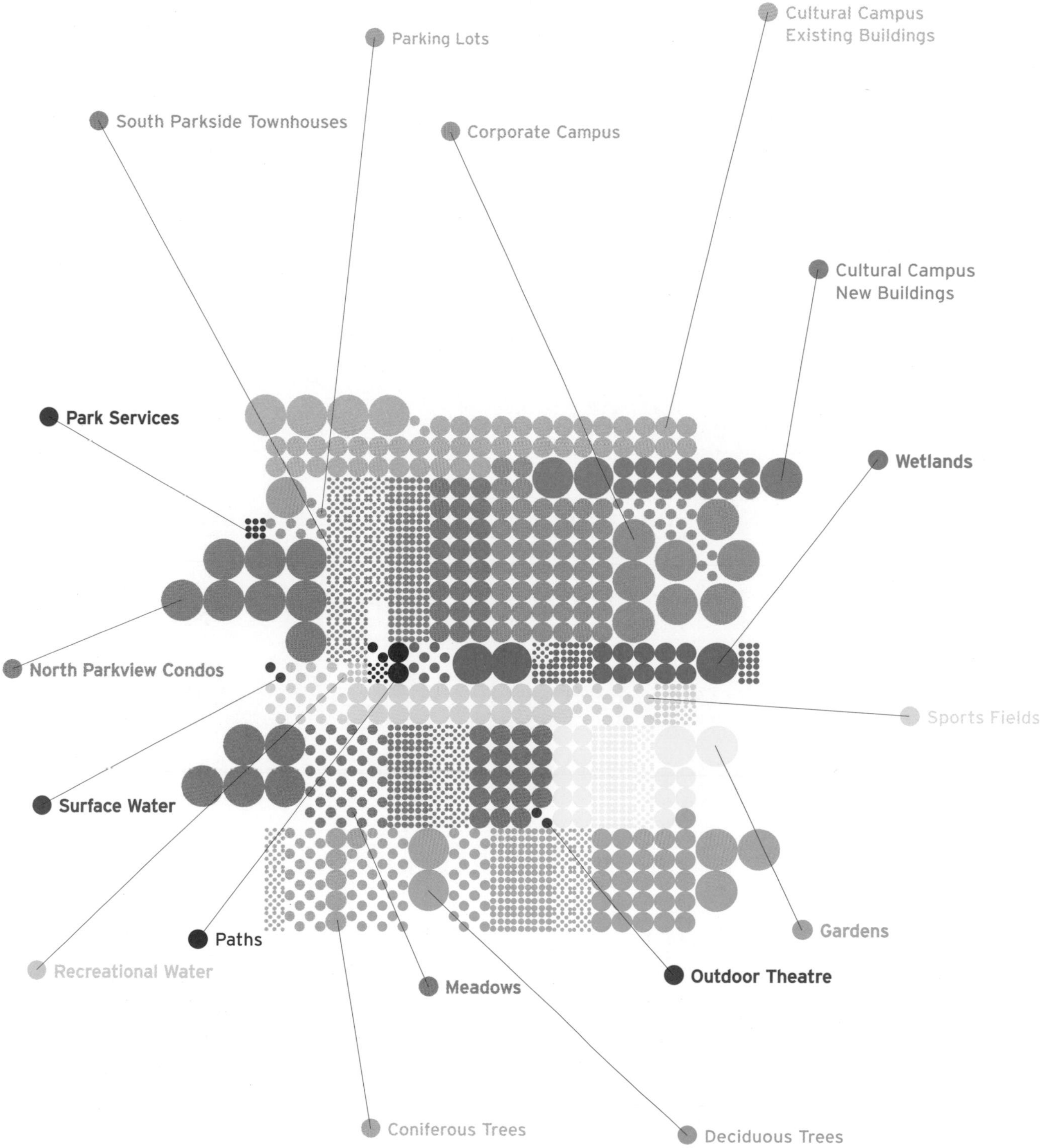
Cultural Campus
Existing Buildings
Parking Lots
South Parkside Townhouses
Corporate Campus
Cultural Campus
New Buildings
Park Services
Wetlands
North Parkview Condos
Sports Fields
Surface Water
Gardens
Paths
Recreational Water
Meadows
Outdoor Theatre
Coniferous Trees
Deciduous Trees

402

6. Destination and Dispersal

Tree City is an urban leisure destination in a low-density setting. At the same time, it supports a multi-modal transportation hub in the suburbs. It serves as gateway into the city, linking transit, rail, expressway, arterial and even recreational and pedestrian transportation systems. Free from the congestion of downtown, Downsview Park is synchronized for leisurely use and low-stress arrival and dispersal.

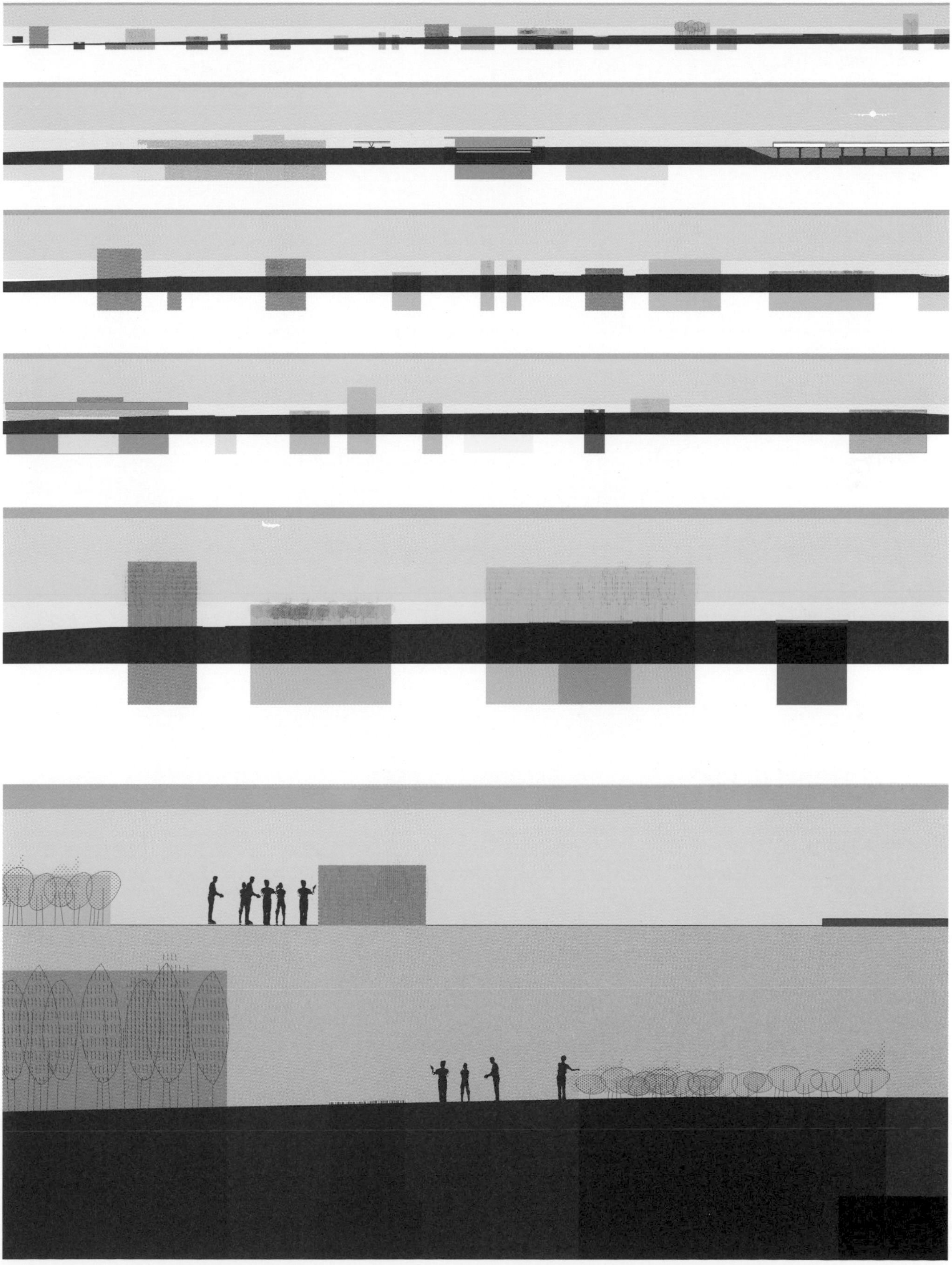

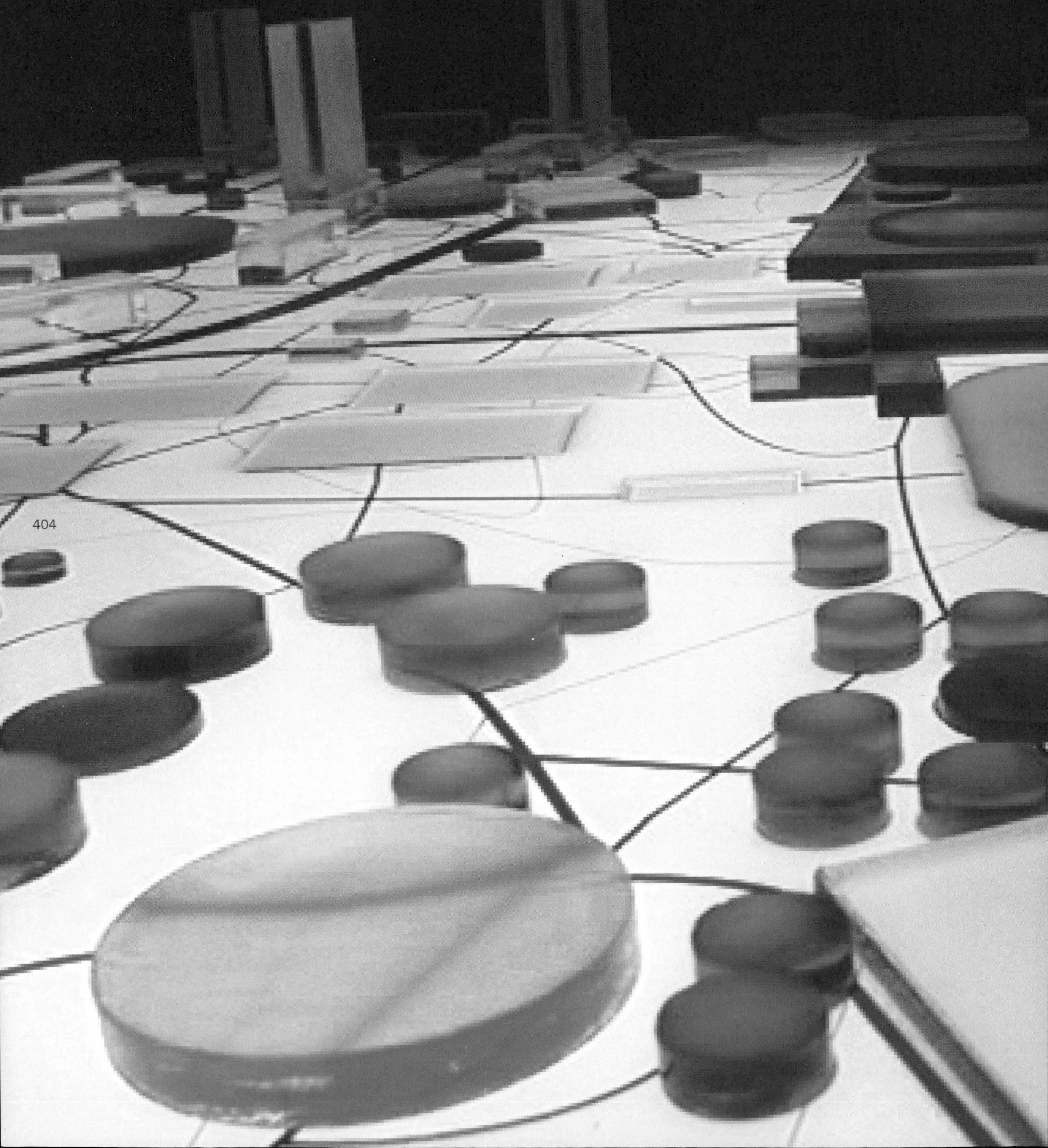

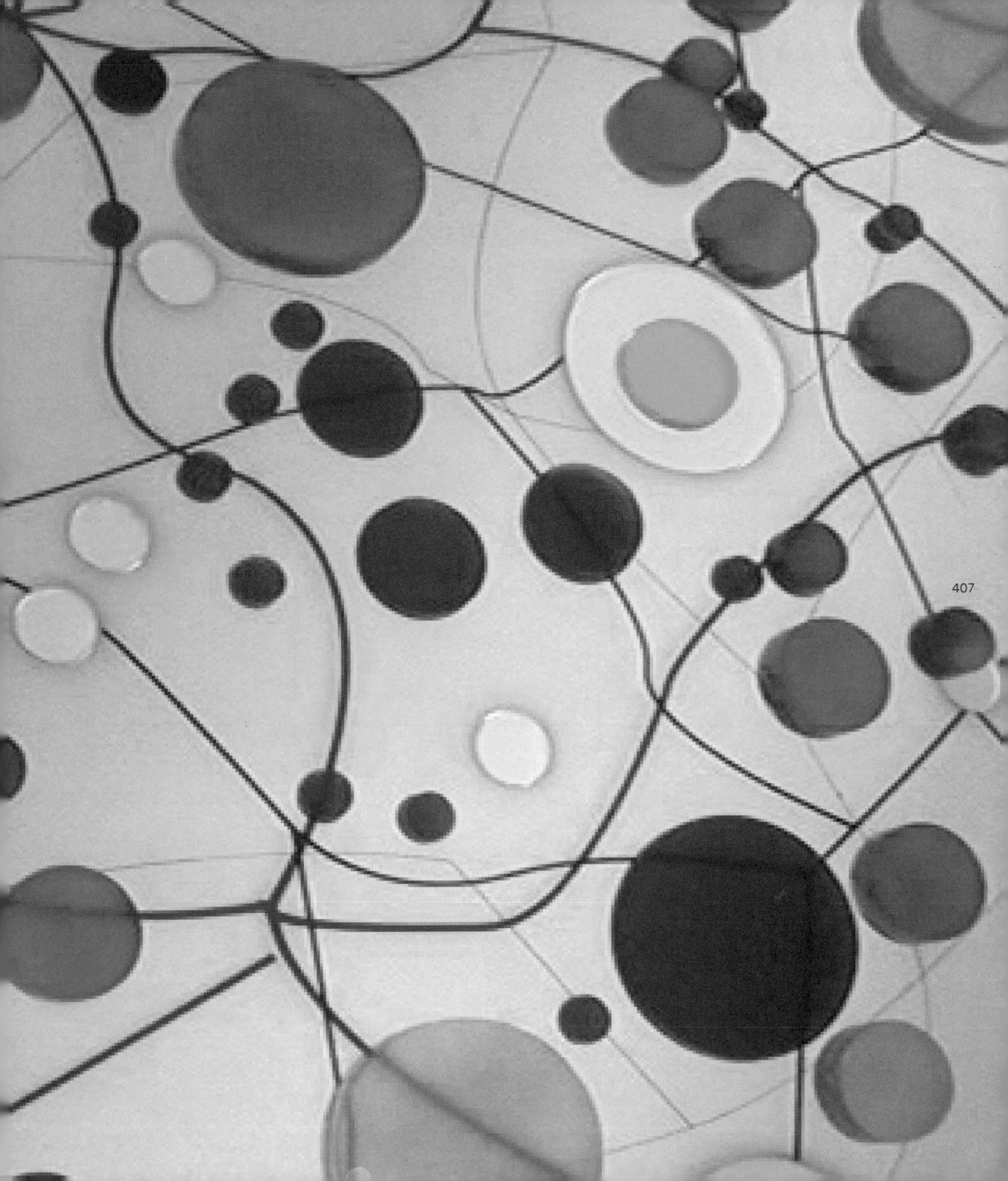

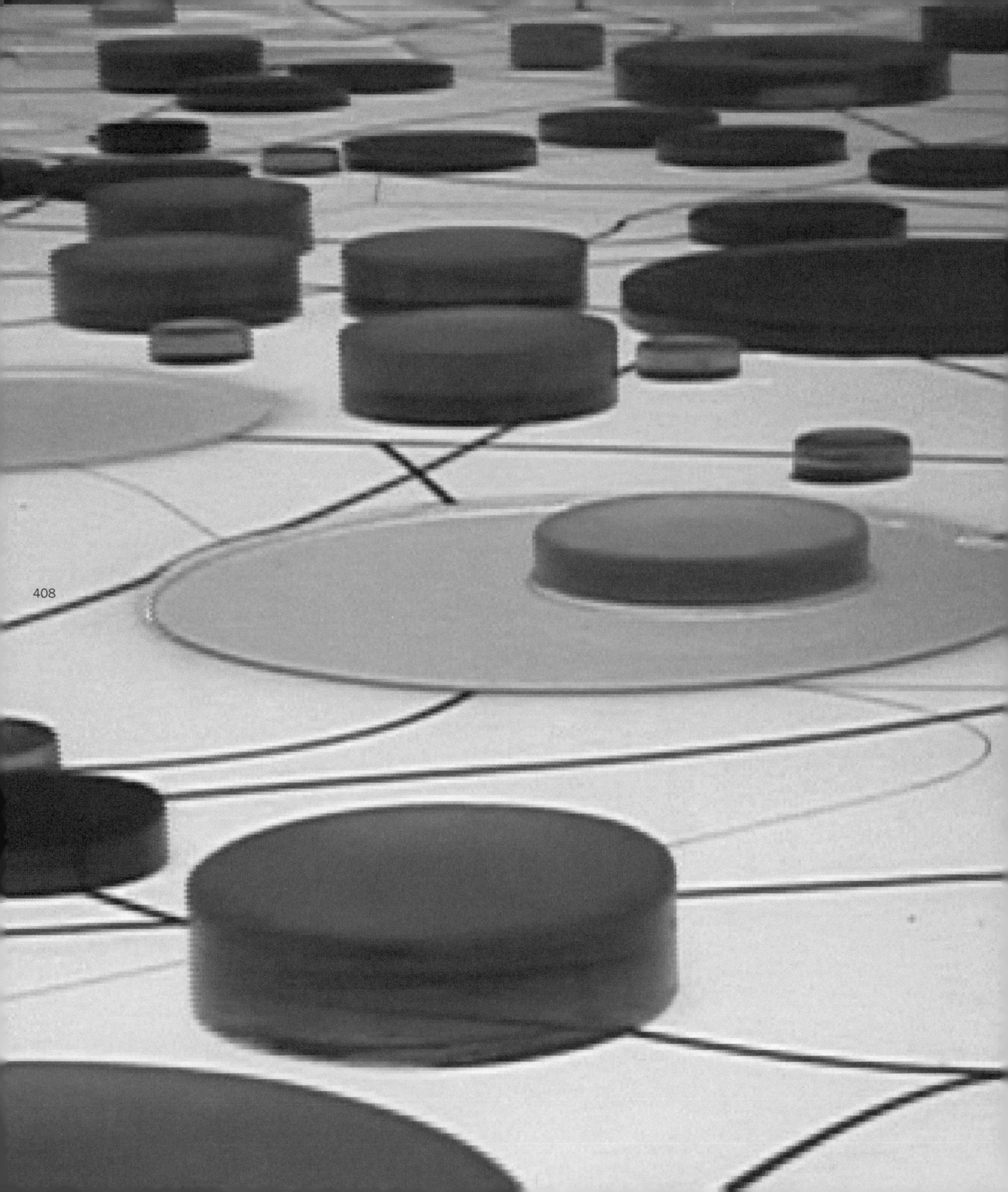

Postscript: On the very day that this book, *Life Style*, was completed, a press conference was held at Downsview Park announcing that Tree City had been selected as the winning proposal.

It is not without heart-breaking ir
total lack of legibility in our collec
history—the typical library. In th
problem, books, and one solutio
library now, there are literally hu
furniture provided to deal with e
magazines to DVDs has a cabine
and an interface. The result is a
While librarians themselves shou
improvisational tactics, overall th
muddle, with one organizational
over another. The time has come

Storage and Retrieval
Seattle Public Library Editorial Design (2000)

ony that we acknowledge a near-
tive repository of typographic
beginning, there was one
, shelves. When you go into the
dreds of signs and pieces of
ch new format. Everything from
, a users' manual, an inventory,
nassive communication problem.
d be commended for their
e patrons confront a constant
ayer of information Scotch-taped
to imagine a new way.

MAGAZI

NEWSPAP

BOOKS

For several hundred years, there was only one problem, the storage of - BOOKS - and necessarily only one solution - SHELVES. 1453: Johannes Gutenberg prints the 42-line Bible. 1605: Cervantes publishes *Don Quixote*, introductio

MAPS 1300: Mediterranean navigators prepare accurate charts of that sea. 1400: Editions of Ptolemy s maps printed in Europe. 1570: First modern atlas published, *Orbis Terraum* contains over 70 m

1150 1200 1250 1300 1350 1400 1450 1500 1550 1600 1650 170

E-BOOK 1999: Rocket eBook™, a hand-held device for reading Web-distributed content E-BOOK

WORLD WIDE WEB WWW

DATABASE 1967: OCLC (Online Computer Library Center) founded DATABASE

8-TRACK 1965: A cartridge that promised to lower the price of recorded tape without sacrificing sound quality 8-TRACK

MICROFORM 1935: Eastman develops the first successful microfilm technology MICROFORM

FILMSTRIPS 1920: Audiovisual education emerges as a discipline to make abstract ideas concrete FILMSTRIPS

RENT-A-PRINT 1945: Seattle Public Library (SPL) Art department begins lending large mounted reproductions of prints RENT-A-PRINT

LP RECORD 1948: The LP record arrives on a vinyl disk LP RECORD

PHOTOCOPY 1937: Carlson invents the photocopier. 1959: Xerox manufactures a plain-paper copier PHOTOCOPY

AUDIO CASSETTE 1929: Magnetic sound recording on plastic tape AUDIO CASSETTE

CINEMA 1923: 16mm nonflammable film makes its debut. 1977: Projectors available for loan at SPL CINEMA

COMIC BOOK 1904: The first comic book appears. 1980: A pilot comic book project is conducted at the Seattle Public Library COMIC BOOK

S 1664: *Erbauliche Monaths-Unterredugen* (Edifying Monthly Discussions) published in Germany. 1900: Popular illustrated weeklies sell for only pennies. 1922: *Reader s Digest* publishes material excerpted from a variety of sources MAGAZINES

RS 1609: First regularly published newspaper appears in Germany. 1689: Newspapers are printed, at first as unfolded broadsides. 1704: A newspaper in Boston prints advertising NEWSPAPERS

dern novel. 1800: Invention of the cylinder printing press. 1804: Lithography developed. 1926: Book-of-the-Month Club founded. 1957: First book to be entirely phototypeset is offset printed BOOKS

: Expeditions are mounted to Lapland and Peru to determine the correct shape of the earth. 1966: The satellite Pageos launched to engage in geodetic surveys. 1995: Global Positioning Systems commercially available MAPS

PHOTOGRAPHY 1816: Niepce makes a true photograph. 1942: Kodacolor process produces the color print PHOTOGRAPHY

YELLOW PAGES 1906: First telephone directory issued featuring business advertising on yellow pages YELLOW PAGES

DOCUMENTARY 1922: *Nanook of the North* is the first documentary DOCUMENTARY

PAPERBACK 1935: The Penguin paperback sells for the price of 10 cigarettes PAPERBACK

VIDEO 1970: VHS home video programs provided for public use at the Seattle Public Library VIDEO

MICROCHIP 1971: Intel builds the microprocessor, a computer on a chip MICROCHIP

FLOPPY DISK 1970: The computer floppy disk personalizes magnetic data storage FLOPPY DISK

COMPACT DISK 1979: From Holland comes the videodisc, read by laser COMPACT DISK

CD ROM 1985: CD-ROM can hold the equivalent of 270,000 pages of text CD ROM

1750 1800 1850 1900 1950 2000

As media formats and library pro
knowledge becomes an increasin
problem. We are entering an era
media format exists alongside ev
is fundamental: What new interfa
these various media formats in t
how will it function? We propose
interface to complement the bro
the individual user. Make the con
accessible at the click of a mouse

The project, a collaboration between BMD and the Office for Metropolitan Architecture in Rotterdam, is an attempt to conceptualize the new central branch of the Seattle Public Library. BMD is responsible for designing the communications interface and contributing to the project's overall conceptual direction. The central proposition involves erasing the boundaries between architecture and information, the real and the virtual. Not incidentally, the site of the library's development and realization is the hometown of Microsoft, Boeing, and Amazon.com.

grams multiply, access to
gly complex and challenging
of new equalities, where every
ery other. The question we face
ce will facilitate the use of
he Seattle Public Library, and
radical new approach. Build the
wsing and gathering behaviors of
tent of the world's libraries
Render all media formats equal.

AI

READERS ADVISORY 1920: The reader's a

YOUNG ADULTS SERVICES 1920:

INFORMATION DESK

LIBRARY WAR SERVICE PROGRAM 1917: Provides libraries for

CHILDREN'S COLLECTION 1895: Most public li

NO COST 1897: The Seattle Public Library librarian's report states, "We flatter ourselves that the library will hereafter be maintained forever

PUBLIC LIBRARY

1854 The Boston Public Library opens as the first public library in a major American city. 1900: Approximately 2,000 public libraries in the US. 1918: Approximately 6,000 public libraries in the US. 1939: The American Library Ass

EXPANDED CONCEPTION OF SERVICE 1900–1917: "Library Militant" era:

"MODERN LIBRARY IDEA" 1910: The public library is envisioned as "an active force, a commu

SPECIALIZATION 1907: Fine Arts division opens at SPL. 1912: Technology depart

AMERICANIZATION 1911: First mention of the Foreign collection at the Seattle Public Libra

INCREASED COMMUNITY PRO

ADULT EDUCATI

GREAT BOOKS P

1150 1200 1250 1300 1350 1400 1450 1500 1550 1600 1650 1700 1750

WORKSTATIONS 1982: An Apple II microcomputer installed at Seattle Public Library **WORKSTATIONS**

VOTER REGISTRATION 1982: Voter registration available at the central branch of SPL **VOTER REGISTRATION**

VIDEO 1981: Media and Program Services department begins coordinating programming for public access **VIDEO**

DISCUSSION GROUPS 1979: A series of Shakespeare discussion programs sponsored at SPL **DISCUSSION GROUPS**

FRIENDS OF THE LIBRARY 1977: The Friends of the Seattle Public Library donate $10,000 for the purchase of media equipment **FRIENDS OF THE LIBRARY**

REMOTE ACCESS 1976: The Quick Information Center opens. 1977: Dial-a-story program begins. 1998: WWW.SPL.org goes online **REMOTE ACCESS**

BIBLIOTHERAPY 1971: The practice of reading is applied to the problems of emotional instability, loneliness, and alienation **BIBLIOTHERAPY**

EXHIBITS 1960: Major artwork commissioned for SPL, *Fountain of Knowledge* and *Pursuit of Knowledge*. 1981: A Cable Arts festival is held featuring video works by local artists **ART EXHIBITS**

vas usually located in a quiet corner or a separate office, in contrast to the reference desk, which was in the line of traffic. The reader would come in with a topic, and a course of reading was suggested **READERS ADVISORY**

service to this age group evolves into a supplement to the school curriculum and a source for recreational reading. As television emerges the library has tried to redefine service to young people. **YOUNG ADULTS SERVICES**

e separate reference desk first appears at the Rhode Island Public Library, increasing the general level of service and recognizing the librarian as a guide and intrepreter. **INFORMATION DESK**

of men in the military. Most Army training camps set up libraries for draftees. Community libraries expand roles in communities by helping the Food Administration during WWI. **LIBRARY WAR SERVICE PROGRAM**

d not serve children, restricting access to those over twelve. 1900: Children's rooms begin to be added to libraries. 1920: Children's collections gain immense popularity, which continues today **CHILDREN'S COLLECTION**

1: Free library service provided to all soldiers and sailors in the Puget Sound area. 1970: Seattle Public Library's first fine-free day, 8,976 overdue books returned. 1973: The 10-cent charge for reserves removed **NO COST**

sets forth the "Library Bill of Rights." 1970: National Commission on Libraries and Information Science charged with the mission of finding "an effective and efficient library system" **PUBLIC LIBRARY**

ttitude that community libraries should assume a broad range of roles to help solve social problems. Art exhibits, education of juvenile offenders, storytelling occur on an elaborate scale **EXPANDED CONCEPTION OF SERVICE**

striving to bring book and reader together and appeal to the entire community with a thousand and one activities that distinguish the modern library from its more passive predecessor" **"MODERN LIBRARY IDEA"**

s. 1960: The Reference department becomes the History, Goverment and Biography department. The General Reading department becomes Literature, Languages, Philosophy and Religion **SPECIALIZATION**

A special assistant is put in charge of working with "foreigners." 1920: Foreign-language division established in the Circulation Department. 1978: Vietnamese and Arabic materials added to the collection **AMERICANIZATION**

ENCE 1920: Masses of men become accustomed to having broad access to books during WWI **INCREASED COMMUNITY PROMINENCE**

1932: Early appearance at the fringe of reference service, then a distinct program with its own location and staff in the library, eventually absorbed widely within the library and community **ADULT EDUCATION**

AM 1954: American Library Association grant awarded to Seattle Public Library to experiment with the use of TV in the discussion of new books, resulting in "The Challenge of Books" **GREAT BOOKS PROGRAM**

HANDICAPPED SERVICES 1967: The Books for the Blind program is extended to any handicapped person certified as unable to read conventional material **HANDICAPPED SERVICES**

TRAINING THE DISADVANTAGED 1970: Young Adult department begins training for the disadvantaged **TRAINING THE DISADVANTAGED**

INFORMATION AND REFERRAL CENTERS 1970: Information and welfare **INFORMATION AND REFERRAL CENTERS**

1800 1850 1900 1950 2000

Imagine: a single library can now
the world's libraries. It is difficult
alone exploit them, without conc
Now imagine a spatial user inter
engine designed to accommodat
library, users will be given digital
to build their own "worlds" basec
They will do so by collecting and
source and media available with
The way we see it, the library's c
ability to become its own databa
virtual templates are manifold. A
updateable, and alive.

store the digital content of all
to fathom the possibilities, let
iving a new method of retrieval.
ace, an image-driven "browse"
the individual user. In the new
access cards and encouraged
on their respective interests.
orting material from every data
the library—and beyond.
vic duty is predicated on its
e. The virtues of introducing
content remains flexible,

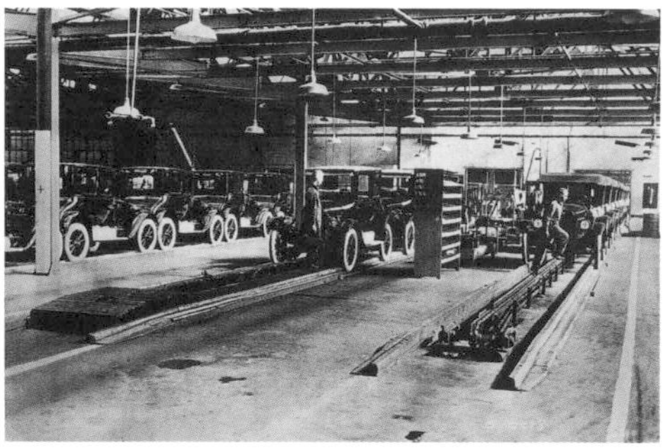

Gutenberg printing press

Assembly line in a Ford finishing plant, 1920s

Honda Motors' walking but not talking humanoid "P2" robot, 1997

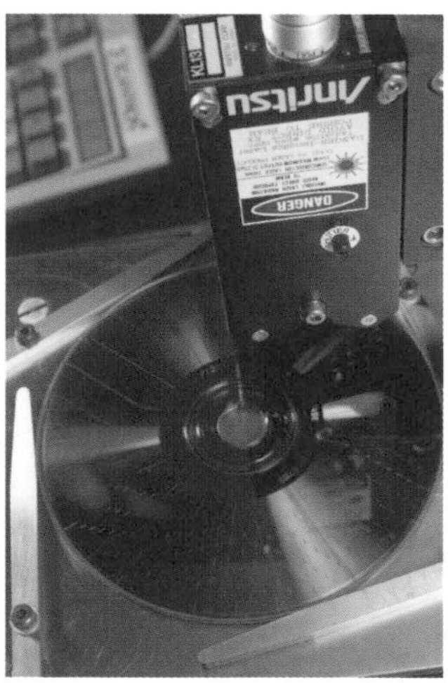

Daguerrotype camera

Victor record

Compact disc player

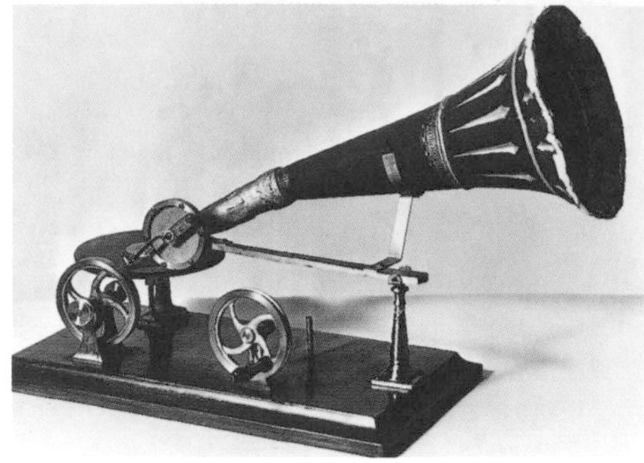

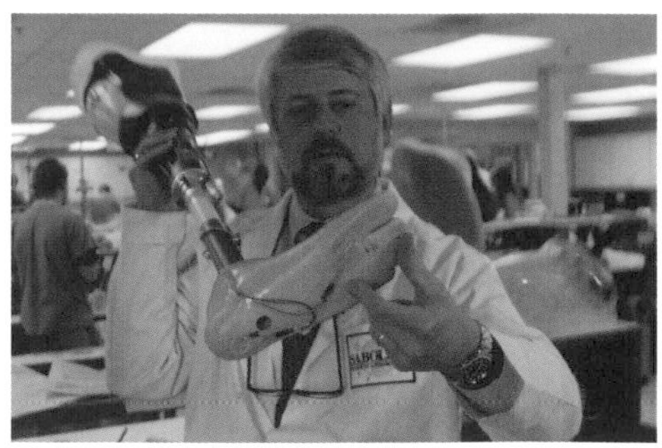

One of the earliest gramophone models

Reel-to-reel tape recorder

Dr. John Sabolich, National Prosthetic Director for Novacare Inc., with a high-tech, sensor-equipped prosthetic leg

Thomas A. Edison experimenting with the first motion picture machine, 1905

An early photocopier, 1936

"Dolly," a sheep cloned from adult cells

Record and Playback: Text, image, movement, sound, object, life

If we trace an arc that chronicles

the development of writing,
the practice of copying books, which built the great library at Alexandria,
the invention of perspective,
the earliest Western printing with moveable type by Gutenberg and Janson,
the invention of photography in Paris by Daguerre,
the invention of the gramophone,
the development of the silent motion picture by Edison,
the assembly line, developed by Henry Ford,
the talkies,
the LP,
magnetic tape and the audio cassette,
the photocopier,
the video camera,
robotics,
photolithography,
the CD,
stereolithography,
Photoshop,
prosthetics,
Surroundsound,
3-D xerography,
onco-mouse and Dolly, the cloned sheep,

we see that genetics takes its place as the most ambitious wet "printing" in our recorded history.
It is the latest in a trajectory of increasingly supple, complex, and invasive recording and playback technologies—this time involving the capture, manipulation, and reproduction of animal and even human DNA.
The unexpected effect of the Human Genome Project may be to liberate the pleasure of sex from its age-old reproductive implications. What remains of the image of ourselves as we go beyond the bounds of "natural" life is deeply unstable, subject to a new Darwinism. Our concept of self is perched at the intersection of the market and the media, the biological and the technological.

Meeting John Cage

Of the many things I have learned in studying the work and life of John Cage, the most important is the following: to allow events to unfold in accordance with nature and in due course (a lesson stated and restated in the *I Ching*). In 1991, when my assistant informed me that John Cage was holding on the phone, I could hardly contain my excitement. We were working on the Carnegie International catalog with Lynne Cooke and Mark Francis, the newly appointed director of the Andy Warhol Museum in Pittsburgh. Cage was a featured artist and we were waiting for his catalog contribution, a matrix of numbers — the outcome of chance operations that would determine the daily configuration of Cage's installation. Until then all dealings had been through his assistant. The voice was confident and gentle. "Hi, this is John Cage. I'm calling to let you know that I've finished my work." I congratulated and thanked him and asked if he could please fax it through to the studio. I would be glad to take it from there.

"Oh, my assistant isn't in, and you know, I'm getting old and can't keep up with these new machines. I don't know how to fax."

"Well," I said, "I happen to be on my way to New York in the morning. I could drop by and pick it up if you would prefer."

"That sounds just great...."

Events, it appeared, were about to unfold.

A typical August day in Manhattan. Brutal. (Doesn't 100 percent humidity = water?) I am a shambles: harried, sweaty, and running late by the time my taxi grinds to a halt and I unfold onto the sidewalk on 22nd Street. I collect myself as best I can and press the buzzer. Cage, a picture of calm, greets me at the door and invites me to join him. I follow him to the industrial elevator, and we rise to his sixth-floor loft. We are alone in his studio — apparently a rare occasion given his usual pattern, a strict regime of chess playing, visitors, and work. As Cage prepares tea I notice artworks here and there, gifts and exchanges with modern masters. Johns, Duchamp, Cunningham, Rauschenberg. Traces of a life.

Here I am with Cage — alone — for tea — and I haven't had a moment to prepare. I simply find myself here. We speak for some time about art and work and then out of nowhere, from within me, comes a question: "In one of your books you tell the story of a student seeking enlightenment and of the Zen master he consults. Each day the student asks the master, 'What should I do?' And every day the master says the same thing: Nothing at all. Finally, one day the master does respond, saying only, 'Try not to improve the world, you'll only make matters worse.' But Mr. Cage," I ask, "Isn't there a contradiction here? If the master really believed what he was saying, wouldn't he have remained silent? And when you refer to 'trying to improve the world,' are you suggesting that any planning or intention or design is futile and we should simply not bother?"

Cage's response is typical Cage: "Of course there's a contradiction. It's within the contradictions and ambiguities that we must find our work." At that, Cage motions me to join him at the window. He looks out into the city and down onto the people moving in the street below. "Look, this is your problem; this is the problem of the next century, the friction of all these millions of people rubbing together."

Music/Sound
The Michael Sno
Presence and Absen
The Michael Snow P
Visual Art
The Michael Snow
Carnegie International 1991
Industrial Site
Ian Carr-Harris 1971-1977
CLAES OLDENBURG
Large-Scal
Robert Bourdeau Industrial S
A S
VAN BRUGGEN
Fra
Ragheb
DAN FLAVI
Stéphane
Brougher
Art and Fi
Robin Collyer

Reading

Project
The Films of Michael Snow 1956-1991
Knopf Canada
The Carnegie Museum of Art
Rizzoli
AGO
OSJE VAN BRUGGEN
Projects
THE MONACELLI PRESS
GALLERY
range Elation
O. Gehry Guggenheim Museum Bilbao
DIE ARCHITEKTUR DES LICHTS
Guggenheim/Hatje Cantz
eel Architect
LUDION
n Since 1945
Hall of Mirrors
MOCA
Monacelli

Road signs along a highway in Israel

Reading: Shaping Time

Training the Nervous System

When a person who has been blind for many years regains sight, what is expected to be a miracle often turns out to be a nightmare. To the newly sighted, a staircase has no spatial dimension but is instead a menacing optical pattern of parallel lines without depth or definition. It seems that our brain and nervous system are actually trained by the environment in which they develop. "Seeing," which seems utterly natural to most of us, is not simply a matter of mechanics, of getting the electrical signal through; it involves complex and subtle pattern recognition that allows us to process massively high levels of visual data. Recognizing the complexity of vision offers some insight into the evolving state of typographic design. As we train our nervous systems for ever increasing rates and levels of stimulation, our cognitive and associative typographic capacities evolve with them. The purpose of typography, or at least one purpose, is to build a bridge from one mind to another. The nature and quality of that bridge determines what travels across it and forms the basis of the practice of typography.

Cognitive and Associative Attention

We have only one active center of attention at any given moment, a single cognitive focus, and we move it around as our environment demands or allows. Evolved over millions of years, this center of attention is the input jack for our nervous system's fight-or-flight program. Locked in the present, it provides our experience of now, of reality, and even, some would say, of being. Our cognitive focus provides safety: it is perpetually scanning the horizon for even the slightest change in the environment that might pose a threat. Most of the new economy revolves around the manipulation of attention—or, more accurately, our center of cognitive attention. Few people, however, recognize the power of associative attention: the sensory information—tactile, auditory, olfactory, visual, and so on—that is processed preconsciously, that seldom surfaces into the

I believe deeply in the untapped potential of books to intimately explore ideas and to reach people in new ways with those ideas. This potential resides in a book's dual capacity as both historical record and manifesto—in its ability to project history into the future.
Our approach to book design is simply to respect the reader's ability to understand even the most demanding configurations. If we design a work that respects the reader's intellect, we contribute a small moment of dignity in a culture that too often panders to the lowest common denominator and, in so doing, insults the intelligence of its citizens.

field of active attention. The principal reason that typography maintains its status as a "black art" cloaked in a quasi-alchemical aura is that it operates across the boundary between our cognitive and associative attention. When we read, we actively apply our cognitive attention to the text at hand. Our cognitive channel is open and we focus in the present tense. Our attention is consciously directed. What we may not realize is that, simultaneously, other channels are open, too. These channels constitute the associative dimension of attention. Typography is capable of producing profound communication effects here, entering into exchanges and building bridges between minds.

The associative dimension of typography is not fixed. It is comprised of a complex and evolving set of qualities that engage history, convention, style trends, and production techniques; it may convey everything from authority to radicalism. Through the manipulation of typographic qualities—font, size, color, and so on—connotative values are injected into the communication process. One reason so few of us have any sense of the associative dimension of typographic design is that its effects occur almost exclusively in the background, beneath the threshold of conscious perception. Our cognitive focus, our center of attention, is fixed on the message's denotative stream, the apparent content of what we are reading. The typographic design, and in particular the letterform, adds a rich and complex message to our associative engagement but operates at the margins of the center of attention. Most designers are mute about the capacities of this associative dimension precisely because it works in a complex, elusive, and indirect way. The moment we direct our focus on it, it slips away. To become aware of it would require us to shift focus, negating its effect. The associative dimension is, after all, a form of seduction, a faint, gossamer-like force that, like any seduction, is hampered by any awareness of its machinations.

We have many ordinary occasions to experience a sudden shift in our channels of attention. For example, when driving a car on familiar streets, nothing presents itself as a crisis requiring our active attention. We are able to shift attention away from the road, and our focus floats to other things: music playing on the radio, the errand we are running, or (ever more frequently) a phone call we are engaged in. We continue processing information about road conditions—other vehicles, pedestrians, traffic lights—but we do so without being directly conscious of it. Our cognitive attention is not centered on driving. Should a crisis arise—someone jumping in front of our car, the driver ahead of us braking suddenly or swerving unexpectedly into our lane—our focus instantly snaps back to handle the crisis. Our cognitive channel locks on to that event. When things return to routine, we drift back—to a floating, associative state of attention.

If we apply these two modes of attention—the cognitive and the associative—to the way we engage typographic content, we may generate a productive model to understand the operations of subliminal typographic communication.

When we scan the morning newspaper, we move our focus around the page from headline to image to caption to text. Our focus is on the content of the news and its relevance to us, whether it is urgent or remote. The newspaper text demands this of us.

To read we must focus. It is, after all, the supposed function of typography to deliver content by channeling our attention. What we are not aware of is the associative dimension of our reading, but it, too, is operating on us to guide our reception and our interpretation. Typographic technique inflects tone and volume to give the story the desired urgency and resonance. When we open the paper to discover in a big, bold headline that war has been declared, or that hundreds have died in an earthquake, our response is, and should be, "Wow, big story!" and not "Wow, big letters!"

So we are faced with something of a paradox: typography is an image you'll never see. Typography is a critically visual form, but it never operates as "image." Rather, it is a kind of nonvisual image—or, perhaps, a verbal-visual image. In other words, the image-aspects a text takes on are not a function

In China, an English-speaker's engagement with text is purely associative. His or her cognitive attention is freed from its capacity to apprehend and register meaning.

of the meaning or content of a text in and of itself. Two very different kinds of texts, typeset in the same way, look more or less identical. Typeset a pornographic novel in the style and format of a Bible and, to a non-reading viewer, the erotic content remains invisible. (I realized the power of this traveling on a streetcar in Toronto reading J.G. Ballard's *Crash*; I was having an intensely private experience in full public view.) The radical potential of literature lies precisely in the fact that the text-based image is accessible only to the reader. Typography is perhaps the only visual practice that works best when you don't see it.

It is for this reason that throughout history most readers have had no sense of how typography works, or even realized that such a thing exists. Ten years ago, most people would not have known what a "font" is. Digital technology has changed this situation. Today, every computer user must choose from a menu of fonts to display or create any document—be it a recipe, diary, critical essay, or business report. Personal computers have made typography accessible even to the average user; it is no longer an esoteric specialty.

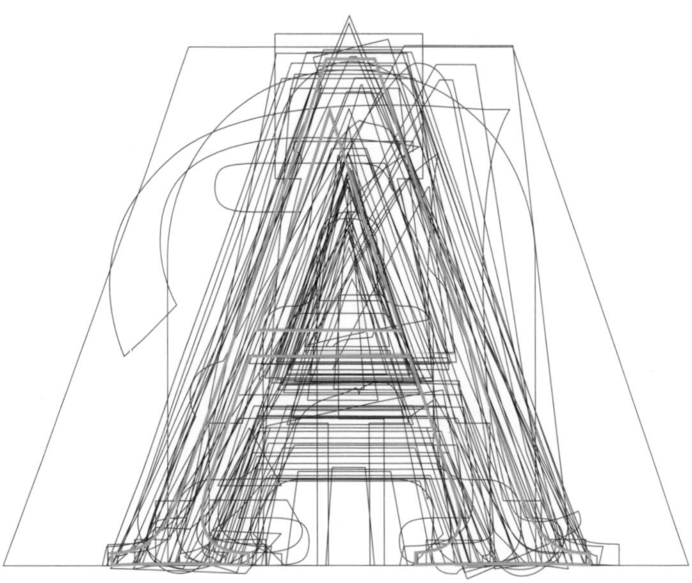

"Gimme an A!"

Perhaps more than any art, typography is a practice founded on convention. It works only when **A = A**. The boundary of **A** is not stable. It is, in fact, an evolving threshold. Within this shifting boundary we are capable of almost infinite variation, so long as we maintain that **A = A**. Every variation, every iteration of **A**, adds a layer to convention and history and inflects our perceptual boundary of **A**. Eric Gill's designs for his font Perpetua, for instance, summon into the background the techniques of stonecutting on which the font's forms are based. Thus, Gill recalls the entire history of typographic permanence, from first-century Roman stone-cut letters to present-day memorial inscriptions. But he does this within the boundary, within the envelope, that our collective alphabetic memory has defined as **A**. **A** exists as the sum of all the **A**s ever expressed typographically as it extrapolates itself into the future. So it follows

The Story of O 570 *You are here to serve*

40 YOU are here to serve your masters. During the day, you will perform whatever domestic functions are assigned to you, such as sweeping, putting back the books, arranging flowers, or waiting on table.
2 Nothing more difficult than that. But at the first word or sign from anyone, you will drop what you are doing and ready yourself for what is really your one and only duty: to lend yourself.
3 Your hands are not your own, nor are your breasts, nor, most especially, any of your bodily orifices, which we may explore or penetrate at will.
4 You will remember at all times – or as constantly as possible – that you have lost all right to privacy or concealment, and as a reminder of this fact, in our presence you will never close your lips completely, or cross your legs, or press you knees together (you may recall you were forbidden to do this the minute you arrived).
5 This will serve as a constant reminder, to you as well as to us, that your mouth, your belly, and your backside are open to us.
6 You will never touch your breasts in our presence: the bodice raises them toward you, that they may be ours.
7 During the day you will therefore be dressed, and if anyone should order you to lift your skirt, you will lift it, if anyone desires to use you in any manner whatsoever, he will use you, unmasked, but with this one reservation: the whip.
8 The whip will be used only between dusk and dawn. But besides the whipping you receive from whoever may want to whip you, you will also be flogged in the evening, as punishment for any infractions of the rules committed during the day: for having been slow to oblige, for having raised your eyes and looked at the person addressing you or taking you – you must never look any of us in the face.
9 If the costume we wear in the evening – the one I am now wearing – leaves our sex exposed, it is not for the sake of convenience, for it would be just as convenient the other way, but for the sake of insolence.

41 SO that your eyes will be directed there upon it and nowhere else, so that you may learn that there resides your master, for whom, above all else, your lips are intended.
2 During the day, when we are dressed in normal attire and you are clothed as you are now, the same rules will apply, except that when requested you will open your clothes, and then close them again when we have finished with you.
3 Another thing: at night you will have only your lips with which to honor us – and your widespread thighs – for your hands will be tied behind your back and you will be naked, as you were a short while ago.
4 You will be blindfolded only to be maltreated and, now that you have seen how you are whipped, to be flogged.
5 And yes, by the way: while it is perfectly all right for you to grow accustomed to being whipped – since you are going to be every day throughout your stay – this is less for our pleasure than for your enlightenment.
6 How true this is may be shown by the fact that on those nights when no one desires you, you will wait until the valet whose job it is comes to your solitary cell and administers what you are due to receive but we are not in the mood to mete out.
7 Actually, both this flogging and the chain – which when attached to the ring of your collar keeps you more or less closely confined to your bed several hours a day – are intended less to make you suffer, scream, or shed tears than to make you feel, through this suffering, that you are not free but fettered, and to teach you that you are totally dedicated to something outside yourself.
8 When you leave here, you will be wearing on your third finger an iron ring, which will identify you.
9 By then you will have learned to obey those who wear the same insignia, and when they see it they will know that beneath your skirt you are constantly naked, however comely or commonplace your clothes may be, and that this nakedness is for them.
10 Should anyone find you in the least intractable, he will return you here. Now you will be shown to your cell. . .
11 It's because it's easy for you to consent that I want from you what it will be impossible for you to consent to, even if you agree ahead of time, even if you say yes now and imagine yourself capable of submitting.
12 You won't be able not to revolt. Your submission will be obtained in spite of you, not only for the inimitable pleasure that I and others will derive from it, but also so that you will be made aware of what has been done to you.

42 O was on the verge of saying that she was his slave and that she bore her bonds cheerfully. He stopped her.
2 Yesterday you were told that as long as you are in the chateau you are not to look a man in the face or speak to him.
3 The same applies to me as well: with me you shall remain silent and obey.
4 I love you.
5 Now get up. From now on the only times you will open your mouth here in the presence of a man will be to cry out or to caress.
6 So O got up. René remained lying on the bed. She bathed and arranged her hair.
7 The contact of her bruised loins with the tepid water made her shiver, and she had to sponge herself without rubbing to keep from reviving the burning pain. She made up her mouth but not her eyes, powdered herself and, still naked but with lowered eyes, came back into the room . . .
9 Without uttering a word, without so much as a glance at Jacqueline, Sir Stephen made a sign to René to let O go, and to O to go into the other room.
10 But on the other side of the door O, who was immediately wedged against the wall, her belly and breasts seized, her lips forced apart by Sir Stephen's insistent tongue, moaned with happiness and deliverance.
11 The points of her breasts stiffened beneath his hand's caress, and with his other hand Sir Stephen probed her loins so roughly she thought she would faint.
12 Would she ever dare tell him that no pleasure, no joy, no figment of her imagination could ever compete with the happiness she felt at the way he used her with such utter freedom, at the notion that he could do anything with her, that there was no limit, no restriction in the manner with which, on her body, he might search for pleasure.
13 Her absolute certainty that when he touched her, whether it was to fondle or flog her, when he ordered her to do something it was solely because he wanted to, her certainty that all he cared about was his own desire, so overwhelmed and gratified O that each time she saw a new proof of it, and often even when it merely occurred to her in thought, a cape of fire, a burning breastplate extending from the shoulders to the knees, descended upon her.

43 JEANNE took O by the hand and let her out into the hallway.
2 Their mules again made a resounding noise on the tile floor, and again they found a valet seated on a bench between the doors.
3 He was dressed like Pierre, but it was not Pierre. This one was tall, dry, and had

The points of her breast stiffened 571 **The Story of O**

Typeset a pornographic novel in the style and format of a Bible (in this case, an excerpt from *The Story of O* by Pauline Réage), and to a non-reading viewer the erotic content remains invisible.

that, at the moment we pass beyond that evolving threshold, it's no longer typography.

An enormous body of work has been produced in recent decades that has sought to test and push the typographic threshold beyond its easily recognizable limit. But no matter how hard we push, there is always an elastic band of convention tying us back to legibility. It's a fundamental problem of innovation in a practice that is conventional. Other practices have similar constraints of convention and legibility. Architecture, for instance, must work with or against expectations and exigencies of accessibility—that is, where you put the door. Typography, however, is a practice that functions exclusively by convention. Its constraints are even more stringent because there is nothing else but convention holding it together. If you make a scratch in the sand in the shape of an **A**, unless I apprehend an **A**, I am left with a scratch in the sand, nothing more. It is convention alone that secures my apprehension.

Remembering and Forgetting

There are those who say we read best what we read most. If Stanley Morison of *The Times* (London) had invented Variex Regular or Keedy Sans instead of Times Roman, we might well associate these fonts with truth and authority, and Times Roman with funky, rave culture.

To get a sense of how quickly things are now evolving, we might consider that human civilization now produces and prints in a single day as much typographic content as our early predecessors did over the course of several hundred years. We might also look to the Palm Pilot's new alphabet of machine-readable letterforms. Who can say wholeheartedly that this is not the future of the standard alphabet?

The real mystery of typography resides in the form of the letter itself and its capacity to express novelty or history, sobriety or exuberance—in other words, to engender associative qualities. Letterform design is the philosopher's stone at the heart of the black art of typography. It is the means by which values and emotions are injected directly into information.

It is precisely these unquantifiable aspects of a font that provide it with an iconic quality and make it a recognizable expression of its time: Futura expresses the Machine Age; Franklin Gothic the open, democratic sensibility of America; Helvetica the cool rationalism of Swiss corporate culture. The associative dimension explains why typography is such an important branding tool: because it is capable of organically fusing a tone of voice or character with a particular message.

But this is something of a chicken-and-egg problem because if fonts project values and emotions onto us, we also project these qualities onto them. If fonts are iconic, they also have memory. Somehow they remember every message that travels through them. They recall the things they were once asked to say. And, over time, they take on the character of those collective messages. Helvetica, for instance, would perhaps convey a very different tone if it had been born into the American culture of the 1890s instead of into the Swiss boardrooms of the 1950s. Template Gothic, spawned at California Institute of the Arts in 1990, and once emblematic of outsider culture, is an example of a font that still carries the edgy ethos of its origins, however faint or subliminal, even though most of its radical resonance has been effectively depleted due to its rapid deployment by mainstream promoters.

Typographic Time

Typographic design is the controlled release of information events in time. It operates on two temporal registers. The smallest is the shifting present tense of the reader. The largest is the sweep of historical time. Typography allows us to experience past and present simultaneously.

Every typographic decision—font, size, position, orientation, weight, color, style—affects the reader's speed of access, the rate at which the message is engaged by the nervous system. This is not to say that the sequence of engagement is fixed, either in duration or even in the order of its elements. Readers may choose to skip, jump back, or reread parts of a text. Some will read from back to front. The

Trajan's Column in the Forum, Rome (ca. A.D. 114)

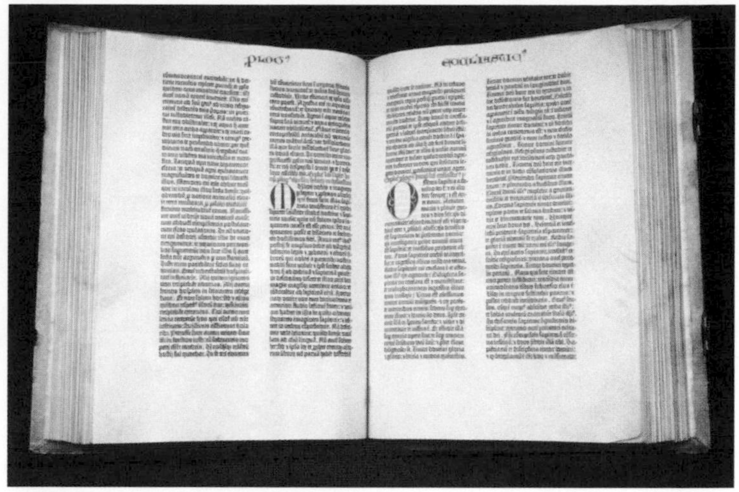

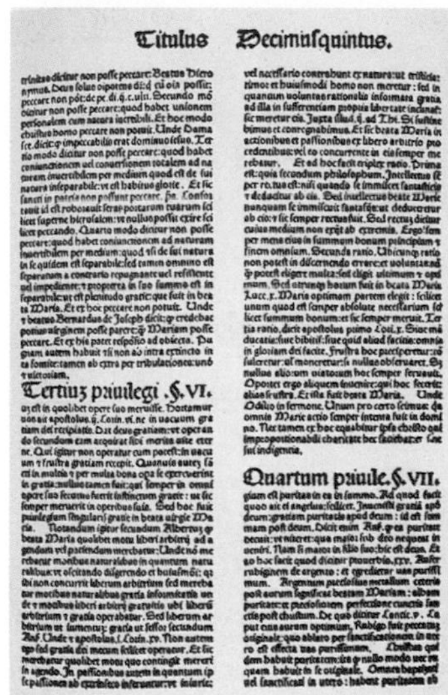

Titulus Decimusquintus

Tertium priuilegi .§.VI.

Quartum priuile.§.VII.

Top: Gutenberg Bible, 1455
Above: Nicolas Jenson, 1480, book page

A Short History of Production
From the very beginning, typography has been a struggle between order and convention on the one hand, and innovation and free expression on the other. When we look at the earliest examples of Western typography—for instance, Trajan's Column in the Forum in Rome (ca. A.D. 114), with its exquisitely rectilinear setting and line spacing and its consistent weight—what is most striking is the orthogonal order. We might ask ourselves: Why does the orthogonal order persist across many centuries? There are at least two answers to the question. The first lies in our stated purpose of typography: to build a bridge from one mind to another. The second lies in the economies of typographic production as a manufacturing technique. When we look at examples of typography from the fourth and fifth century, at *The Book of Kells* produced in the seventh century, at the forty-two-line Gutenberg Bible of 1455, or at a book by Nicolas Jenson printed in 1480, what they have in common is the regular, ordered presentation of their contents. Why? Because order equals accessibility. Order and convention allow a public still learning to read to cross that bridge from one mind to another. Typography was born as a disciplinary regime, a way of controlling the visual interface of thought and, hence, access to thought.
The technologies and economies of production have evolved over the past five hundred and fifty-odd years. The early typographers were entrepreneurs. There was no separation between writing, printing, and publishing, no difference between form and content. Gutenberg, for instance, by producing the printed Bible, single-handedly created a market of readers. Marshall McLuhan describes Gutenberg's Bible as "the first mass-produced commodity." Movable type produced the "mass" as a new category. From there we can draw a line to Henry Ford and, ultimately, on to Nike—a continuous line of mass production.
Every time production techniques changed, typographic form was totally, systematically renovated. New ways of

sequence and meaning develop specifically within the self-driven center of attention of each reader. The task of the typographic designer is nonetheless to engineer the experience of reading. Perhaps this is why the best typographic work is usually produced when designers themselves take time to read what they are designing. When we are inside a text, we feel the cadence of communication events. We feel the release of information and message as we move through typographic elements in sequence. Changes in typographic design alter the cadence and rhythm of the information, and the speed at which it is accessed. Inside a text, we feel the irritating effect of a typographic error, like stumbling upon upon upon a stone left in our path. It disrupts the flow of the voice, shakes the environment.
I work with real pages at full size because it is critical to the typographic design process to experience the reader's time first-hand. The difference between looking at a page of text printed at actual size versus viewing a scaled down version on the computer screen is that the screen offers no temporal reference. When we scale size we also scale time.

In that sense, typographic design is not unlike cinema, architecture, or urban planning, although these parallels are seldom recognized. In all these practices, the form of an object shapes our temporal experience. Every design decision is taken in the context of before-and-after. In book design the event occurs in the thickness of the page. In the turning of the page the power of the work is released. It is not a matter of producing surface effects, but rather of designing the time or sequence of a book's composition while ensuring that surface effects do not disturb the reader's experience of temporal depth by clogging his or her cone of vision. Typographic design becomes fundamentally about shaping time and attention.

Readers and Viewers

With the advent of the Macintosh and software like Fontographer it became possible to develop a new and more fruitful approach to typographic expression — an approach that takes us beyond the

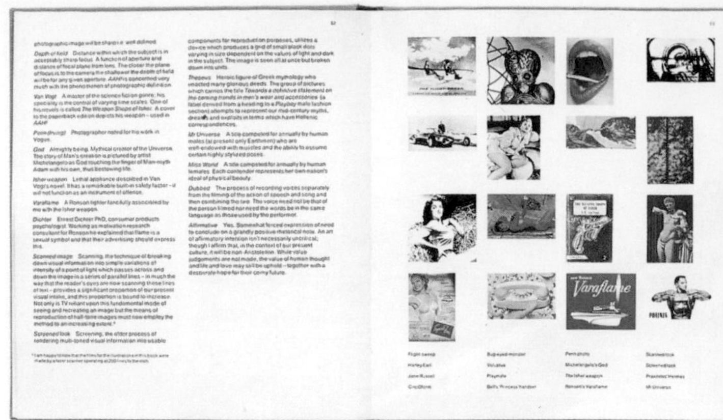

Top: Richard Hamilton, 1983, book spread
Above: Josef Müller-Brockmann, 1969, poster

Massimo Vignelli, 1967, poster

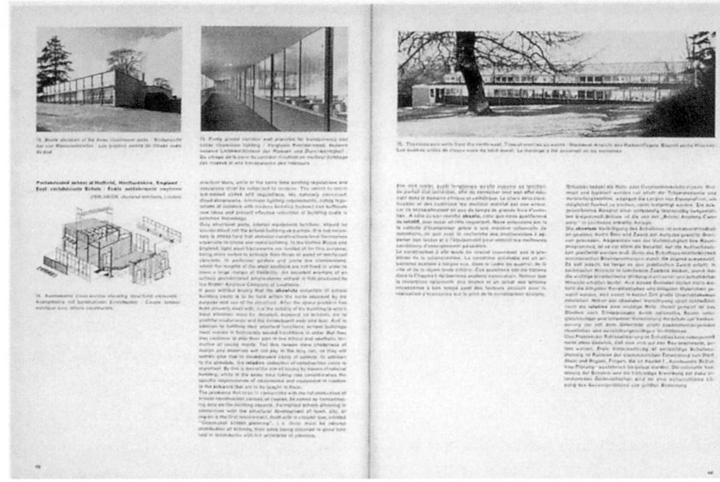

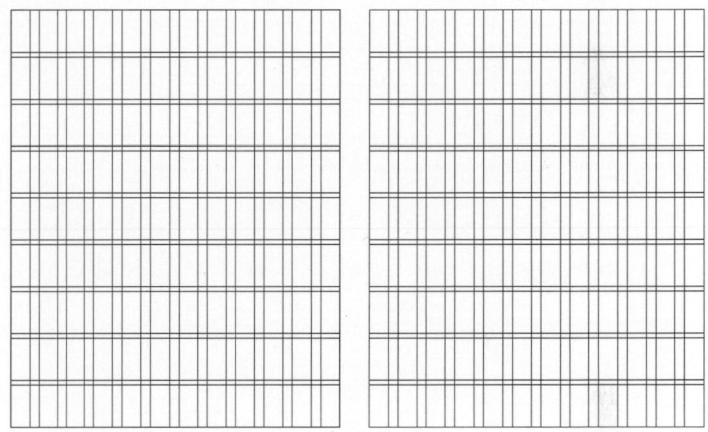

Top: Alfred Roth, *Das Neue Schulhaus*, 1950
Above: The 12-unit grid used by Willy Fleckhaus on *Twen* magazine

working and new operating systems would demand the redesign of typographic form. Up until the middle of the twentieth century, typography was produced using the technology of hot metal type—individual letters set side by side to form words set together to form sentences set together to form paragraphs and pages. To manufacture printed books, the blocks of type had to be put under pressure in a chase, or rectangular frame, so they would hold together as a page. Changes in production technique resulted in significant and longstanding formal developments. The typographic chase reinforced an orthogonal grid that persists as a typographical bias to this day. It becomes clear that a history of typographic form is a history of production technique and that the two invariably inform each another.

And while there is always a radical fringe interested in breaking this link, form is still fundamentally driven by an economy of production. That said, however, most of today's avant-garde typographic work has continued to resist the regulation of the orthogonal grid. Five and a half centuries after the introduction of movable type, two principal schools of avant-garde type design have taken shape:

1. The complex grid group (Fleckhaus, Müller-Brockman, Vignelli, etc.) This group attempts to disguise the regulation of the orthogonal grid through variation while limiting variables in order to maintain the efficiency of manufacture. Their work is effective because it manages expectations. The reader knows where to direct his or her attention. The complex-grid approach allows for enormous production, which makes economic sense for the newspapers and the large corporate entities with masses of product to produce. (These once-innovative grid programs now come as basic software on any computer.) The challenge these designers identified was how to maintain efficiency in a way that disguises its ruthless requirement: to produce infinite variety within a rigorously uniform system of production.

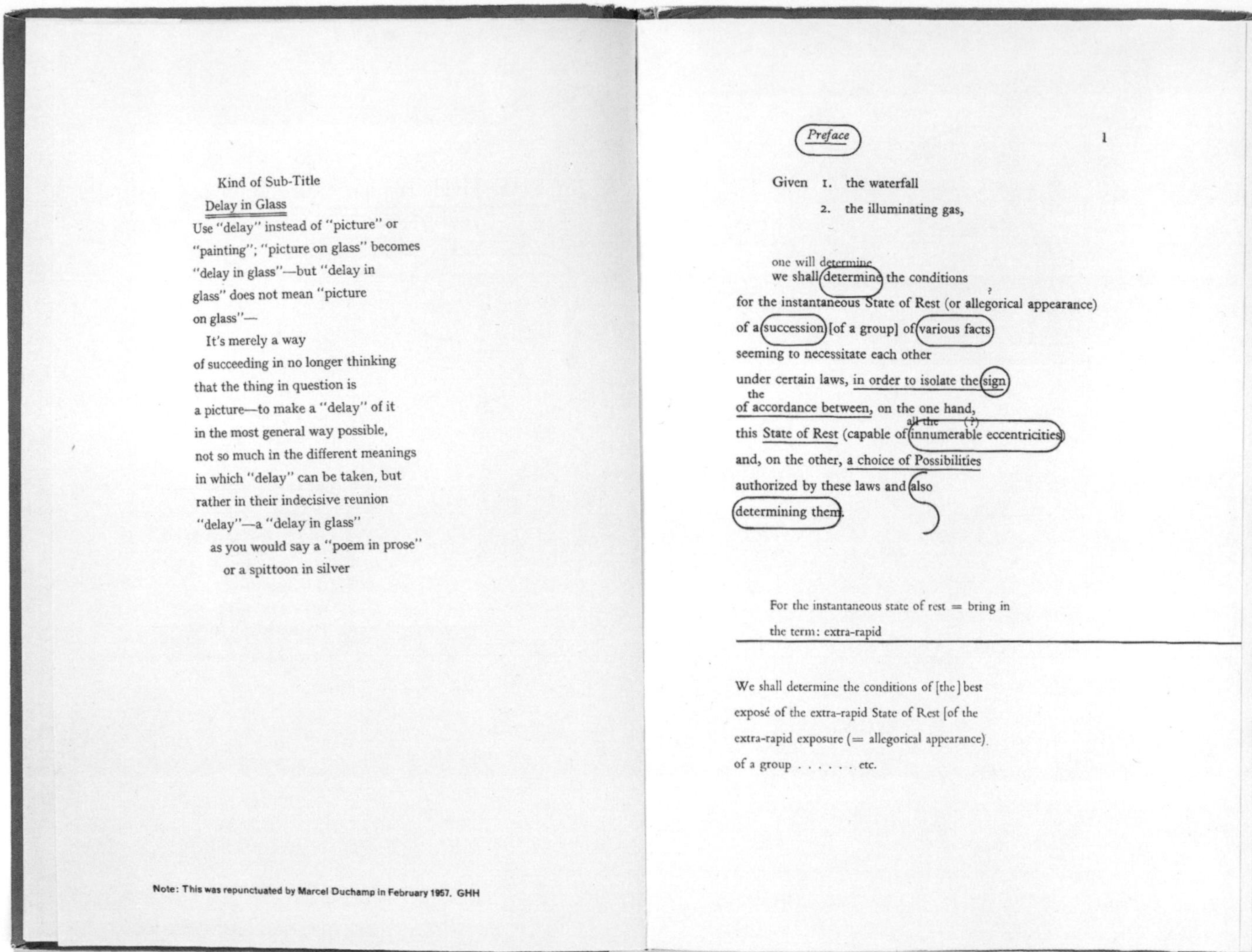

Kind of Sub-Title
Delay in Glass
Use "delay" instead of "picture" or
"painting"; "picture on glass" becomes
"delay in glass"—but "delay in
glass" does not mean "picture
on glass"—
It's merely a way
of succeeding in no longer thinking
that the thing in question is
a picture—to make a "delay" of it
in the most general way possible,
not so much in the different meanings
in which "delay" can be taken, but
rather in their indecisive reunion
"delay"—a "delay in glass"
as you would say a "poem in prose"
or a spittoon in silver
Note: This was repunctuated by Marcel Duchamp in February 1957. GHH
Preface
1
Given 1. the waterfall
2. the illuminating gas,
one will determine
we shall determine the conditions
for the instantaneous State of Rest (or allegorical appearance)
of a succession [of a group] of various facts
seeming to necessitate each other
under certain laws, in order to isolate the sign
of accordance between, on the one hand,
this State of Rest (capable of innumerable eccentricities)
and, on the other, a choice of Possibilities
authorized by these laws and also
determining them.
For the instantaneous state of rest = bring in
the term: extra-rapid
We shall determine the conditions of [the] best
exposé of the extra-rapid State of Rest [of the
extra-rapid exposure (= allegorical appearance).
of a group . . . . . . etc.

Richard Hamilton's typographic version of
Marcel Duchamp's *Green Box*, 1960, book spread

2. The free-form typographic poets
(Piet Zwart, Joost Schmidt, Werkman, Massin, Fella, etc.) These designers have developed an expressive and often eccentric manipulation of the surface of the page. For them, innovation trumps convention. These designers introduce layers of filter between the text and the eye. The work fills the cone of vision (from the retina to the surface of the page). This work is often an illustration of complexity. The designers throw off the yoke of mass production in favor of personal expression. Here, there are no economies of scale.

A new approach to typography allows a reconciliation of one-time opposites. We can generate typography that is symmetrical *and* asymmetrical, that has the efficiency of grid-based production and the fluidity of free-form poetics, that is, finally, for the reader *and* the viewer.

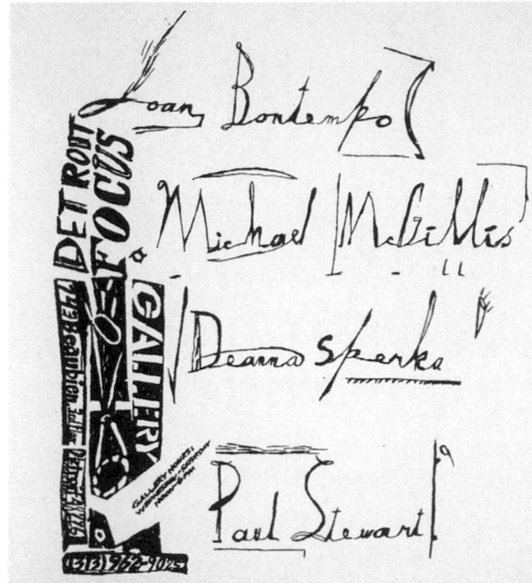

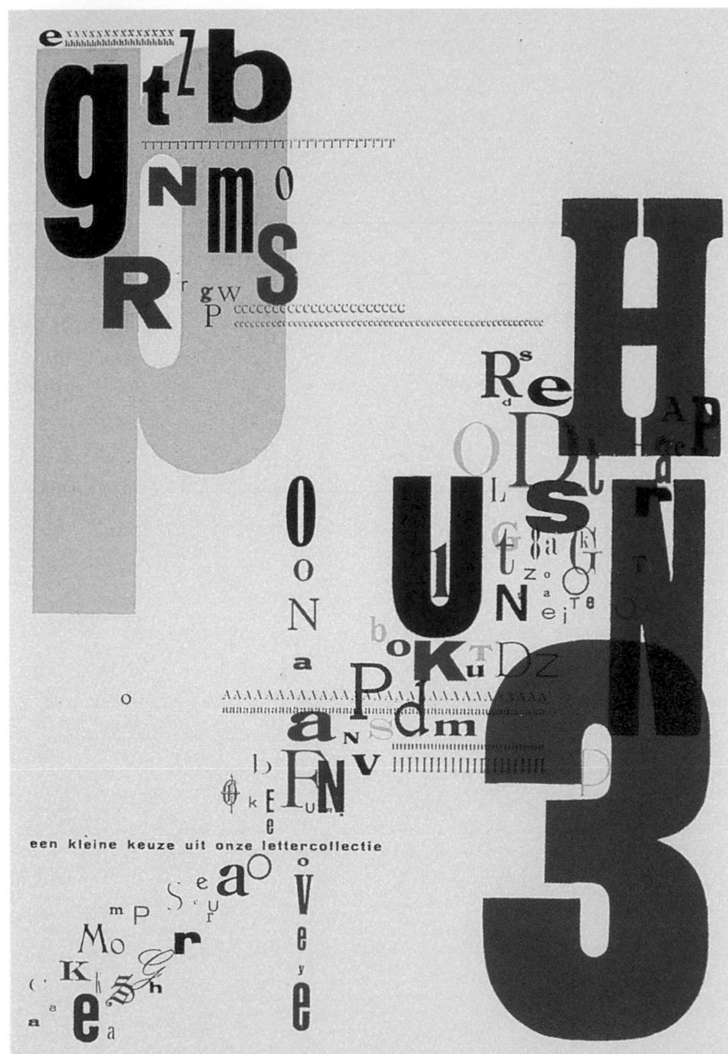

Clockwise from top left:
Piet Zwart, 1930, book page
Edward Fella, 1987, flyer
Joost Schmidt, 1932, advertisement
Robert Massin, 1964, book spread

limitations of the surface of the page. Rather than inserting filters into the cone of vision, we mine into and below the surface of the page to activate the depth of space beyond the page. The surface effect of the work is clarity, simplicity, and even a kind of deadpan tone. We begin to understand typography not as the manipulation of two-dimensional space, but rather as the manipulation of time and attention—of that moment when our nervous system engages and incorporates a typographic message. The surface is left relatively unperturbed, and the action takes place beyond it.

A designer who places primacy on the value of reading the texts to be designed may do very subtle things that will be crucial to the reader's experience on both the cognitive and associative levels. Sadly, most of our world is made up of viewers, and, as a result, most design decisions are controlled by viewers who seem incapable of seeing things the way readers do.

One of the differences between reading and viewing is that viewers engage the overall gestalt and then move on to the next viewing experience. I am not suggesting that designers should abandon the gestalt—this is part of the work too. It helps produce an overall environmental effect. But once we begin to design from the position of the reader, we operate under different criteria and a different sense of cognitive attention, which someone designing from the standpoint of the viewer can never understand. For instance, the relationship between an image and a text can really only be executed by the reader-designer because a designer working solely as a viewer misses half the equation. The kind of subtlety and interplay of text and image that arises from an associative dimension and that allows associative links to develop differs radically in its range of possibilities from the brutally linear regimes of text=image=caption.

Resonance between an image and a text happens at several different scales. However, wavelengths can be made to ripple through different levels of the design so that small-scale events achieve resonant patterns echoed by large-scale events. The design process comes to resemble laying down different tracks in and across the book. What each of these tracks contributes is, in a way, a different kind of temporal effect within the project. These effects range from the most subtle and intimate release of information that is perceptible only by a highly focused reader to the largest, quickest environmental effect that captures the scanning gaze of a viewer.

We are just now emerging from an anomalous moment in the history of typographic design. Until the second half of the twentieth century, the holistic approach was the norm. The designer was both the intimate close reader of a text and its visual communicator. As it was for Eric Gill, writing and designing were part of the same practice. It is only in recent history that these activities start to come apart and designers begin to lose interest in content. This is an aberrant phenomenon that is now being reversed.

Today it is possible to propose a marriage of these two schools: a free-form complex-grid poetics.

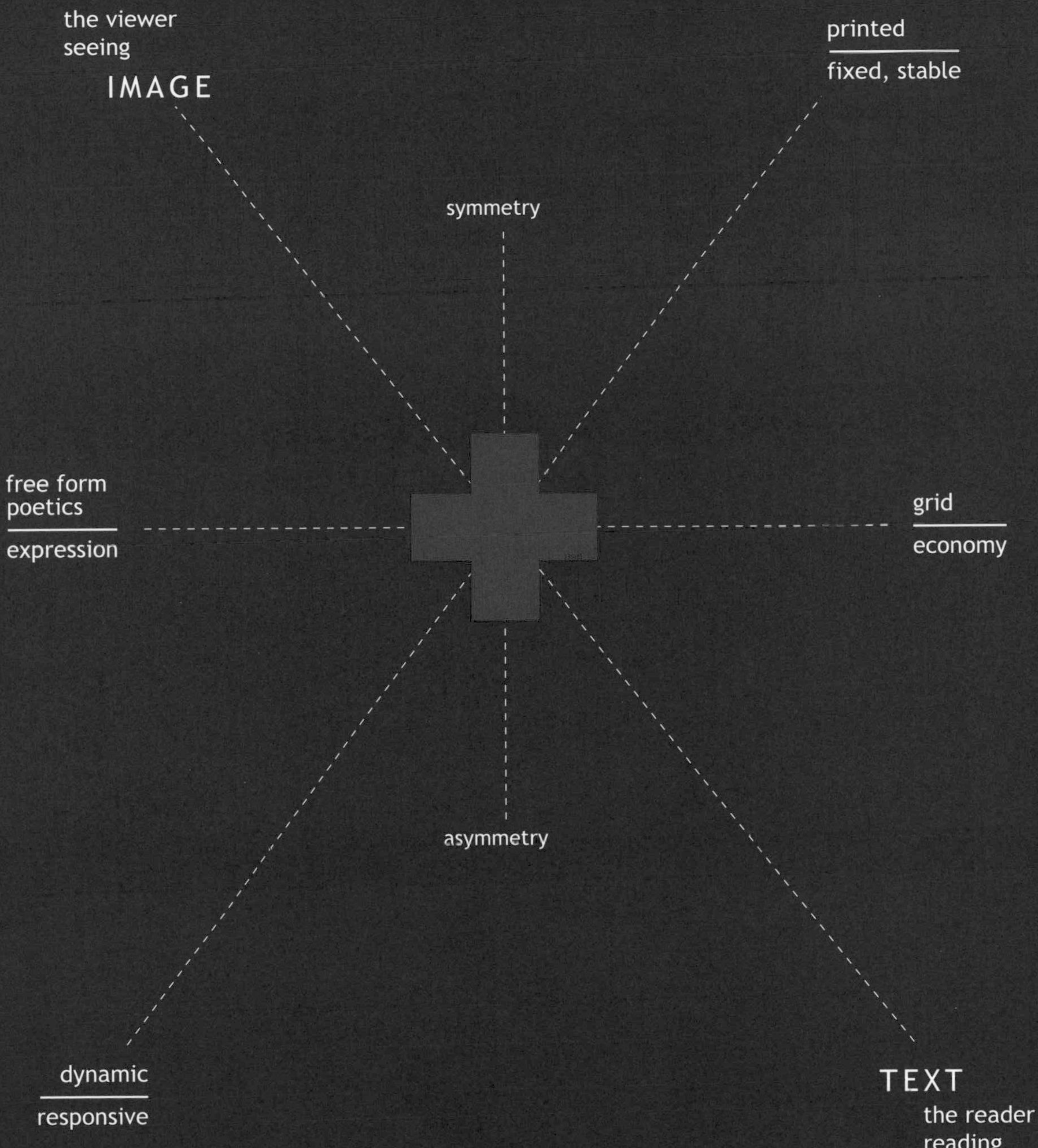
the viewer
seeing
IMAGE
printed
fixed, stable
symmetry
free form
poetics
expression
grid
economy
asymmetry
dynamic
responsive
TEXT
the reader
reading

Poster for The Center Fellowships
Getty Research Institute, Los Angeles, 1990
The Center Fellowships poster is commissioned every year from a different designer as a sort of curatorial project. It is significant in the history of the studio because it was one of the first times we openly engaged content. We began with the given text and added a quotation by John Cage. The Getty Center is an institution in L.A. where scholars go to live and work, but no one goes for the library. They go because they want to go to the beach. The Cage quotation suggested a knowing double entendre.

The Center Fellowships

The Getty Center for the History of Art and the Humanities

The Center is dedicated to advanced research in the history of art, broadly defined as an integral part of human history and society. Its goal is to cross the traditional boundaries imposed on academic institutions by bringing together international scholars to reexamine the meaning of art and artifacts within past and present cultures and to reassess their importance within the full scope of the humanities and social sciences. The resources for scholarship, which include books, manuscripts, prints, drawings, documents, and photographs, are multidisciplinary with a particular focus on the history of visual arts in western civilization.

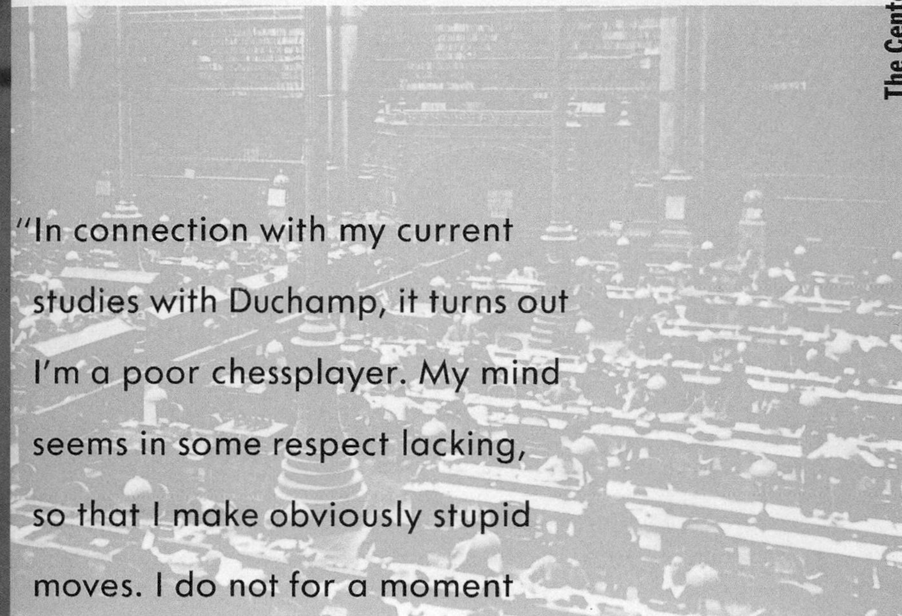

"In connection with my current studies with Duchamp, it turns out I'm a poor chessplayer. My mind seems in some respect lacking, so that I make obviously stupid moves. I do not for a moment doubt that this lack of intelligence affects my music and thinking generally. However, I have a redeeming quality: I was gifted with a sunny disposition."

John Cage
A Year from Monday, 1969

The Center Fellowships provide support for predoctoral and postdoctoral scholars whose areas of research complement the programs and resources of the Center. Applications are welcomed from scholars in such fields of the humanities and social sciences as anthropology; cultural, economic, intellectual, political, and social history; the history of art, architecture, music, religion, science, and technology; literary criticism and theory; and philosophy. Scholars may apply for either a predoctoral or postdoctoral Fellowship. The Fellowship category will be determined, however, by the applicant's degree status at the beginning of the Fellowship period.

The Center Fellowships

Predoctoral Fellowships

Eligibility:

Candidates for a doctorate in the humanities or social sciences who expect to complete their dissertations during the Fellowship year.

Terms:

The Fellowship stipend is $15,000 for a nine-month period, beginning October 1, 1991, and ending June 30, 1992. Some funds are also available for relocation or a housing subsidy, photographic reproduction, and for travel to one professional conference.

All Fellows spend the academic year in residence at the Center.

Fellowships are not renewable.

Application Requirements:

- Synopsis and sample chapter of the dissertation, including a schedule for completion.
- Current transcript.
- Confirmation from the academic institution that all course work has been completed and that the qualifying examinations have been passed.
- Résumé, including description of related studies, other projects, languages, work experience, and travel.
- Three letters of reference (one from a scholar outside the applicant's field of specialization).

Postdoctoral Fellowships

Eligibility:

Recipients of a doctorate in the humanities or social sciences, awarded within the last three years, who are rewriting their dissertations for publication.

Terms:

The Fellowship stipend is $20,000 for a nine-month period, beginning October 1, 1991, and ending June 30, 1992. Some funds are also available for relocation or a housing subsidy, photographic reproduction, and research-related travel.

All Fellows spend the academic year in residence at the Center.

Fellowships are not renewable.

Application Requirements:

- Abstract and copy of dissertation.
- Description of the publication project, including a schedule for completion.
- Confirmation from the academic institution that the doctorate has been awarded.
- Résumé, including description of related studies, other projects, languages, work experience, and professional activities.
- Three letters of reference (one from a scholar outside the applicant's field of specialization).

Send application, postmarked no later than December 1, 1990, to:
Dr. Herbert H. Hymans
Assistant Director
Visiting Scholars and Conferences
The Getty Center for the History of Art
and the Humanities
401 Wilshire Boulevard, Suite 400
Santa Monica, California 90401-1455, U.S.A.
Telephone: 213 458-9811

Notification date: February 1991

For information about non-residential post-doctoral fellowships in the history of art and the humanities, please contact:
The Getty Grant Program
401 Wilshire Boulevard, Suite 1000
Santa Monica, California 90401-1455, U.S.A.
Telephone: 213 393-4244

Designed by Bruce Mau
Above: Bibliothèque Nationale, Paris
Detail of photograph by Gisèle Freund, © Gisèle Freund
Over: Image manipulation based on detail of photograph by Garry Winogrand
© 1984, The estate of Garry Winogrand
Typeset by Archetype in Futura and Franklin Gothic
Printed in Canada by Provincial Graphics

Sameness and Difference
ISBN 0-89236-200-6
d Jan de Vries
Art in history
History in art
G

American Icons
Otto Wagner
Art in history
History in art

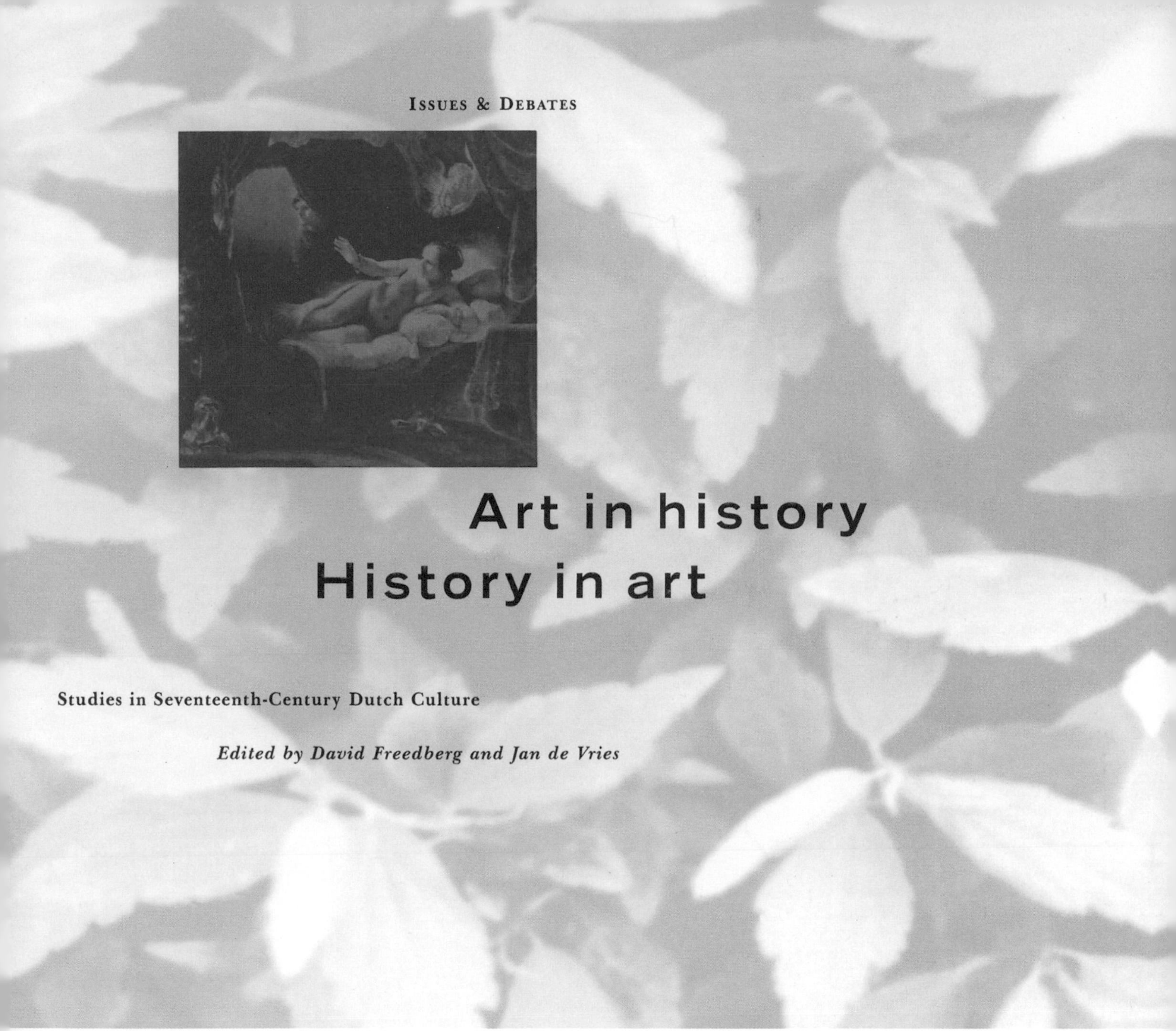

Publications Program, Getty Research Institute, Los Angeles, from 1990
For more than a decade, BMD has been collaborating with the Getty Research Institute on the design direction of its publications program.

Art in History, History in Art **Edited by David Freedberg and Jan de Vries (Issues & Debates) Los Angeles: Getty Research Institute, 1987**
The formal device employed on the jacket of *Art in History, History in Art* is an extreme figure/ground contrast. The relationship between a soft background image and a small, crisp foreground image acts as a vehicle to metaphorically carry the content of a particular book, while maintaining a formal connection between books in the series.

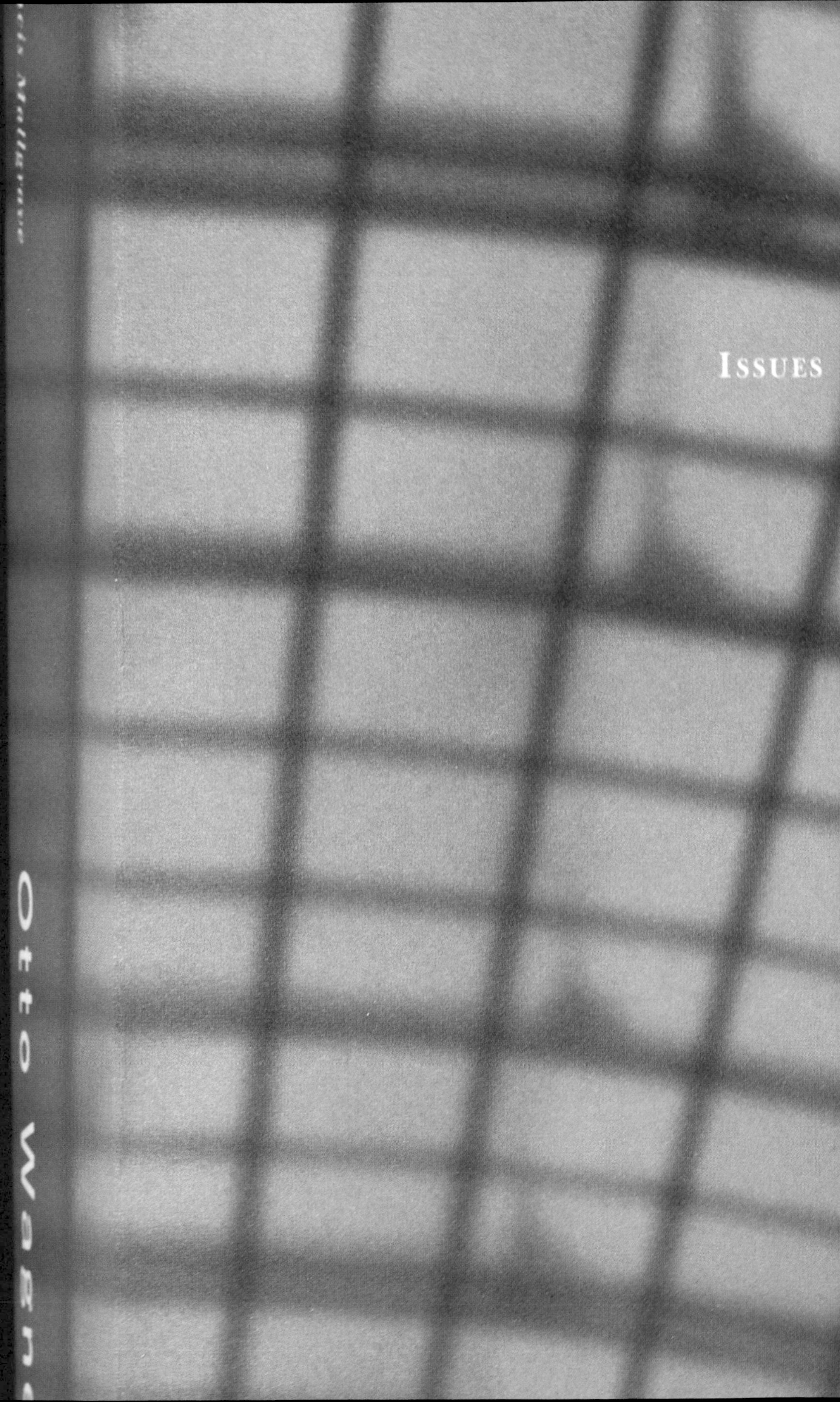

Otto Wagner: Reflections on the Raiment of Modernity
Edited by Harry Francis Mallgrave
(Issues & Debates)
Los Angeles: Getty Research Institute, 1993

DEBATES

Otto Wagner

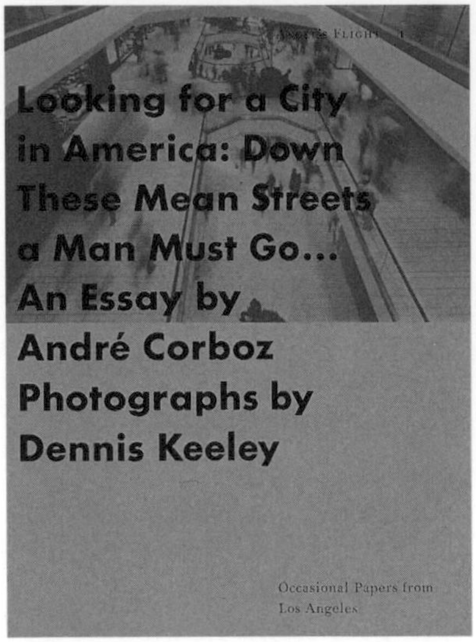

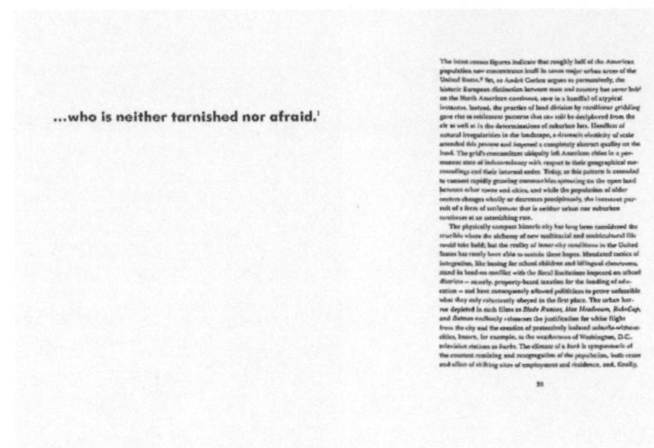

Looking for a City in America: Down These Mean Streets a Man Must Go ...
An Essay by André Corboz
Photographs by Dennis Keeley (Angel's Flight)
Los Angeles: Getty Research Institute, 1990

Looking for a City in America explores a contemporary reading of subjects specific to Los Angeles. It is, above all, an exegesis on loss, anonymity, and the stray moments of beauty to be found in East L.A.'s desperate neighborhoods.

The series title, Angel's Flight, is borrowed from the Angel's Flight funicular railway in Los Angeles which, until 1969, took passengers up to the summit of Bunker Hill, where they were rewarded with a magnificent view of downtown. Given the exploratory nature of the content, this series was designed to be produced inexpensively. The format borrows from traditions of pamphlet publishing. The book is modeled on Los Angeles—on real estate and radical adjacency. The text interrupts and is brutally sandwiched between two "lots" of a photo essay. The rhythm of the photo pages assertively models the violent energy of L.A.—a sort of frenetic homage to Sergei Eisenstein.

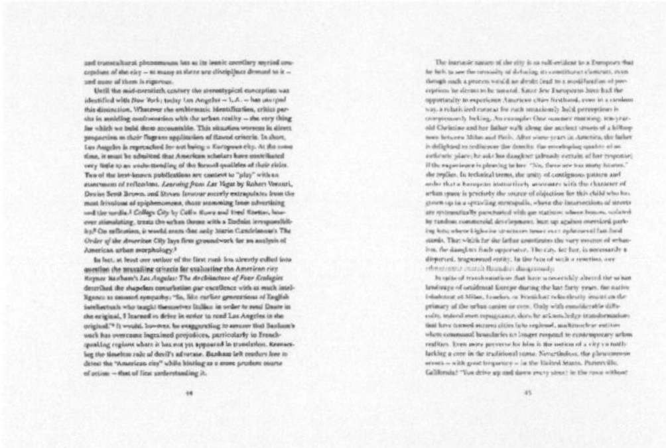

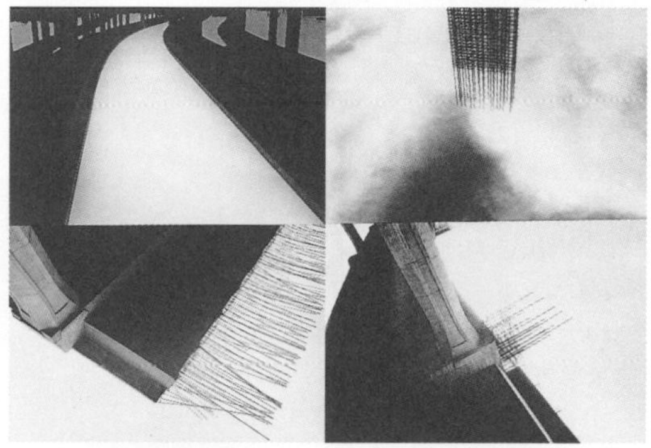

"Another author, suffering perhaps from hallucinations, witnessed 'thousands of cars moving at the same speed, in both directions, headlights full on in broad daylight…coming from nowhere, going nowhere.' This amounts to pure semantic uproar,…"

In 1996, BMD was commissioned to redesign three existing book series published by the Getty: Texts & Documents, Issues & Debates, and Bibliographies & Dossiers. As only one or two titles a year are published under each individual series, consolidating the three series under one visual system provides a recognizable "shelf presence" for Getty publications.
The design is built around the consistent, large-scale application of foil-stamped type against a field of color, image, and material. BMD developed a typeface unique to the Getty series.
The ongoing design has involved striking a balance—and maintaining a tension—between sameness and difference. The series is unified through the consistent application of established specifications for form, orientation, typography, production methods, and presentation. Color, materials, and image treatment change to reflect the specific content of a given book and to differentiate individual titles in the series.

Cover details reproduced on the following pages:

Censorship and Silencing: Practices of Cultural Regulation
Edited by Robert C. Post
(Issues & Debates)
Los Angeles: Getty Research Institute, 1997

Maiolica in the Making: The Gentili/Barnabei Archive
by Catherine Hess
(Bibliographies & Dossiers)
Los Angeles: Getty Research Institute, 1999

Nietzsche and "An Architecture of Our Minds"
Edited by Alexandre Kostka and Irving Wohlfarth
(Issues & Debates)
Los Angeles: Getty Research Institute, 1999

Irresistible Decay: Ruins Reclaimed
Edited by Michael S. Roth with Claire Lyons and Charles Merewether
(Bibliographies & Dossiers)
Los Angeles: Getty Research Institute, 1997

Précis of the Lectures on Architecture
by Jean-Nicolas-Louis Durand
(Texts & Documents)
Los Angeles: Getty Research Institute, 2000

The Victory of the New Building Style
by Walter Curt Behrendt
(Texts & Documents)
Los Angeles: Getty Research Institute, 2000

The Group Portraiture of Holland
by Alois Riegl
(Texts & Documents)
Los Angeles: Getty Research Institute, 1999

Censorship and Silencing: Practices of Cultural Regulation
Edited by Robert C. Post
(Issues & Debates)
Los Angeles: Getty Research Institute, 1997
Censorship and Silencing is the fourth title in the Issues & Debates series, which explores intersections of art history and the humanities in order to develop new perspectives on familiar research areas and to establish new inquiries and research methods. The volume addresses the transformation of familiar understandings of censorship. Authors examine the issue of censorship from a variety of perspectives. They question the use of law as an instrument for the regulation of speech; they explore the use of state power to establish and marginalize discursive practices; and they question the use of state power to redress power imbalances.

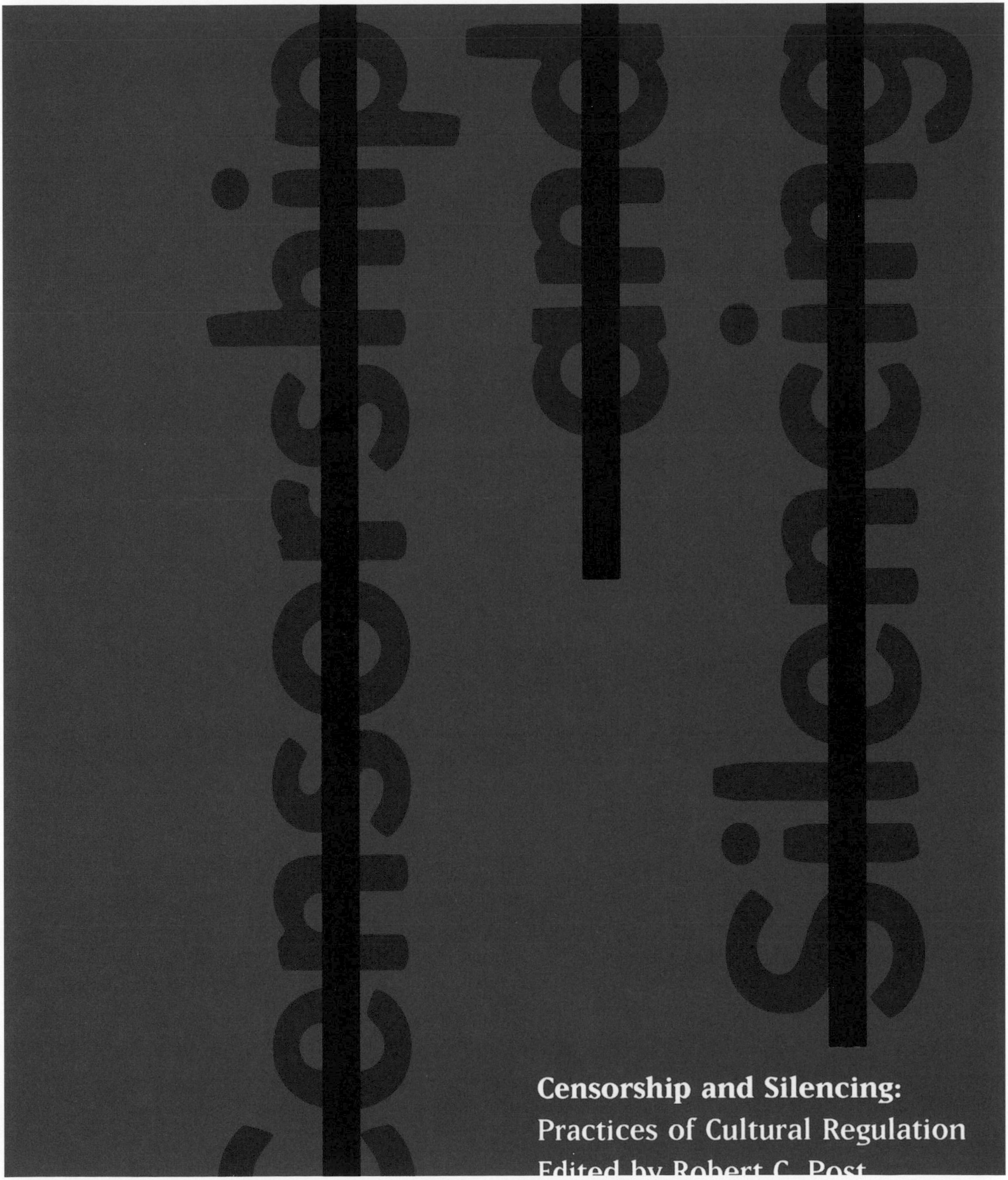
Censorship and Silencing:
Practices of Cultural Regulation
Edited by Robert C. Post

Maiolica
in the Making

Nietzsche and
"An Architecture
of Our Minds"

Nietzsche and "An Architecture of Our Minds"

Irresistible Decay:
Ruins Reclaimed

Michael S. Roth with Claire Lyons

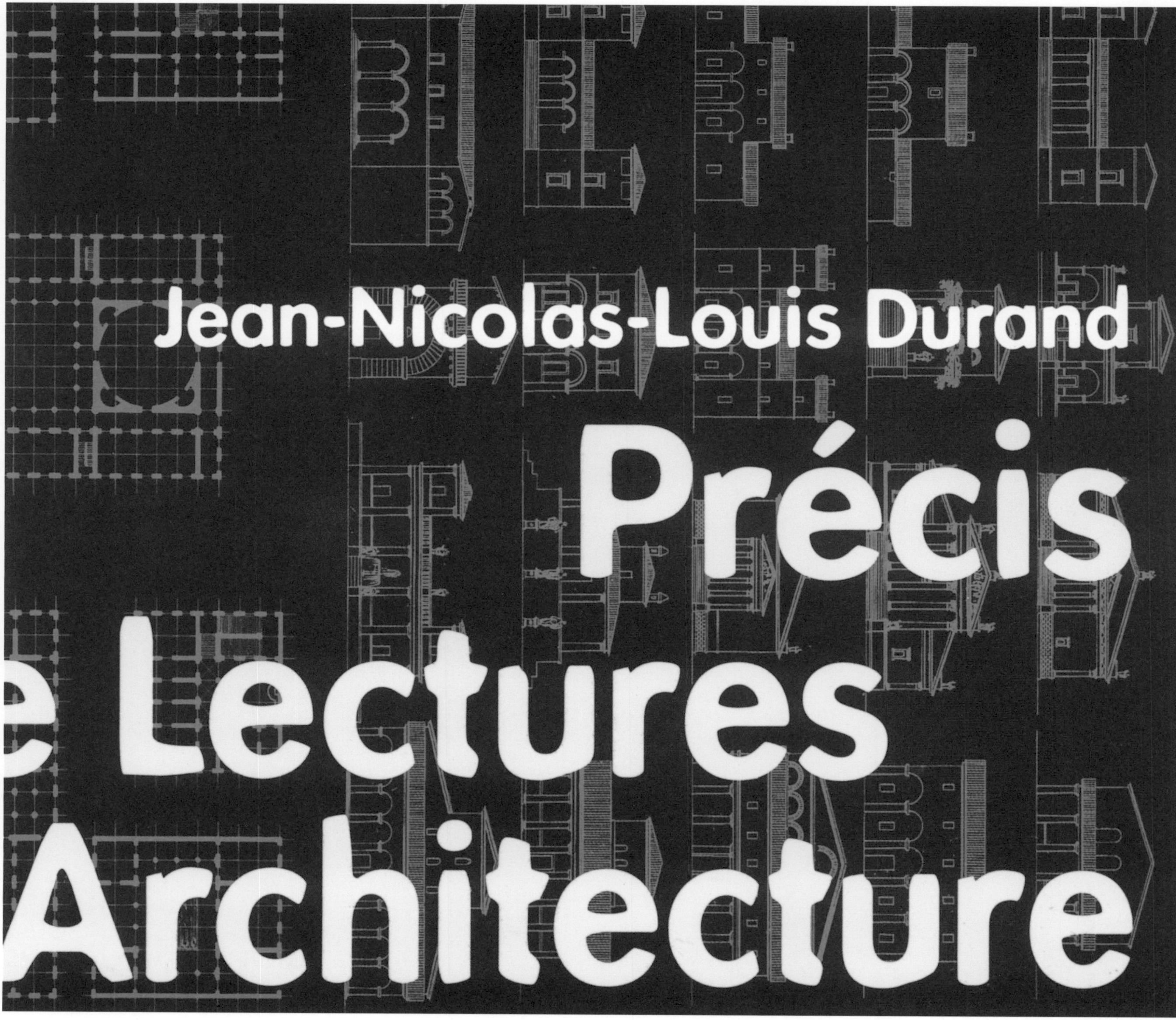
Jean-Nicolas-Louis Durand
Précis
e Lectures
Architecture

Walter Curt Behrendt

The Victory of the Building Style

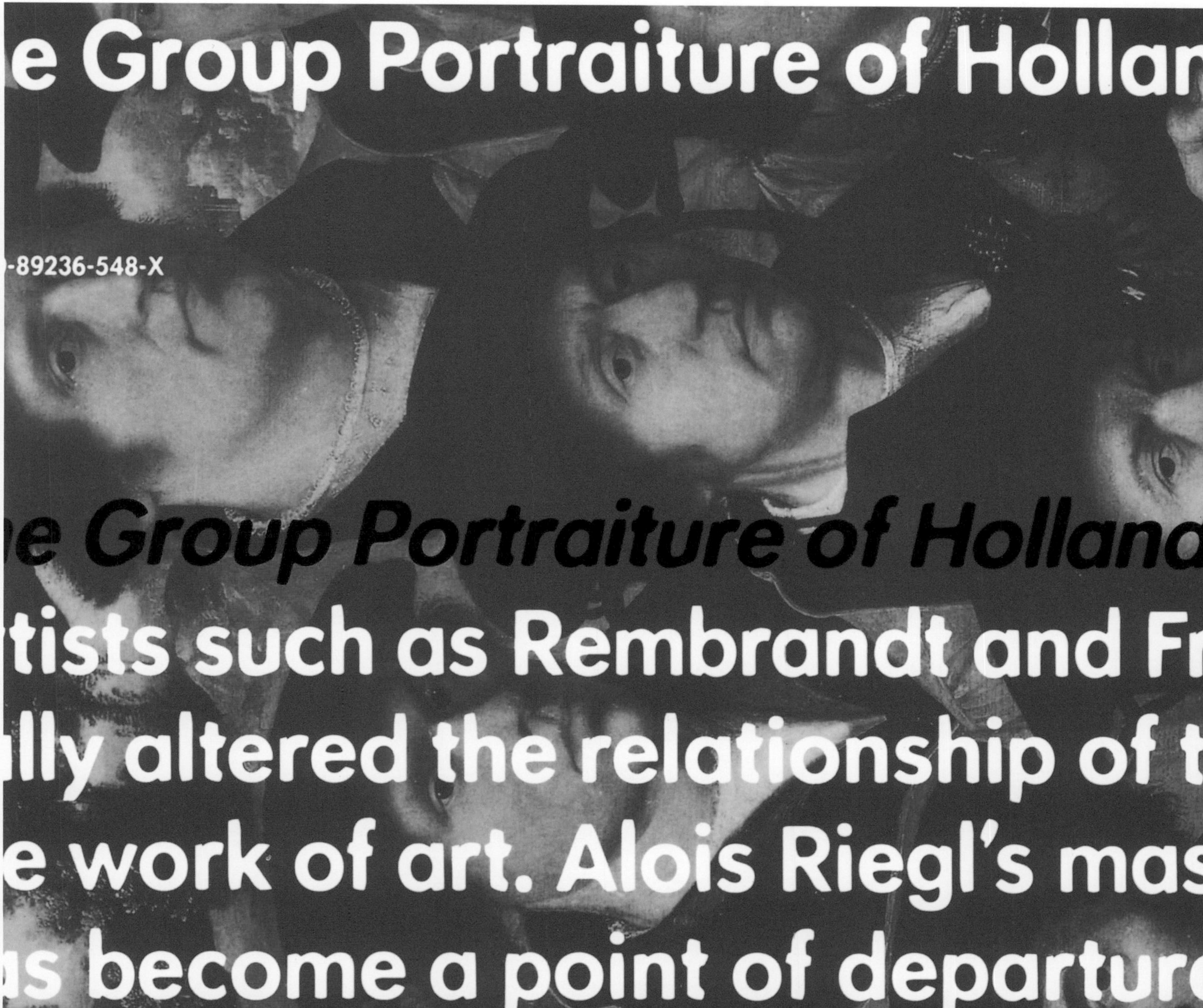
e Group Portraiture of Hollan
-89236-548-X
e Group Portraiture of Holland
tists such as Rembrandt and Fr
lly altered the relationship of th
e work of art. Alois Riegl's mas
s become a point of departure

A Woman of a Certain Age

When my friend Julia faced a significant birthday she disappeared unexpectedly for several days. I left messages and sent faxes and e-mails with no response. After a few days, I began to worry. Julia is the head of publications for the Getty Research Institute and is a portrait of reliability. Finally, from somewhere in Mexico, Julia called and confessed that the big round number had really scared her. It was then and there that I first formulated my fifteen-year theory.

At the time, I was working with Frank Gehry (a close friend of Julia's), Michael Snow, and Claes Oldenburg, all of whom were sixty-five. I was also collaborating with Rem Koolhaas, Coosje van Bruggen, and Julia, all recently turned fifty. I was thirty-five.

I explained to Julia that in the space between her age and Frank's, an interval of fifteen years, Frank had produced his most significant work, and certainly all of the work we think of as distinctly "Gehry." Now, at the age of sixty-five, he was looking forward to the next fifteen years as the period in which he would produce the works that history would remember him for, the Bilbao Guggenheim among them. I reminded Julia that Gehry had worked as long as I had, roughly fifteen years, before *beginning* to produce work under his own name—not unlike Warhol, who had a full career as an illustrator before declaring himself an artist and producing what today we recognize as "Warhol."

"Julia, all that you've done so far may only be in preparation for what you will do. The open road lies ahead." All this seemed to comfort Julia somewhat, as she now could look forward to the possibility of two full-fledged career windows.

A few weeks later, Julia called from London. She was working there with an architectural historian, Wolfgang Herrmann, on one of her Getty books. She related to him the turmoil she had felt around the number fifty, and had explained my fifteen-year theory.

"Oh yes, oh yes," he responded, "I do remember turning fifty. It certainly caused some perturbation. But that was forty-five years ago." He had, it seems, at age ninety-five, outlived his university colleagues and, after a forty-year career as the manager of a zipper factory, picked up where they had left off.

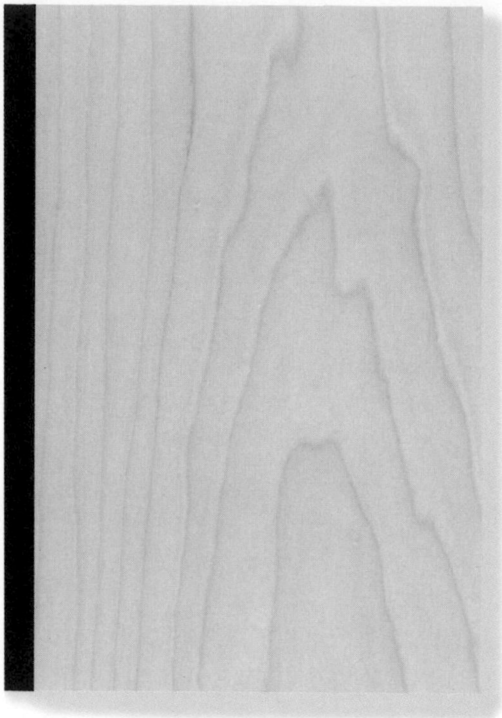

Frank Gehry: New Bentwood Furniture Designs
Montreal: The Montreal Museum of Decorative Arts, 1992
BMD designed the exhibition catalog and promotional material for the launch of Frank Gehry's new bentwood furniture line produced by The Knoll Group. The exhibition catalog was conceived in three parts. The first section documents the Gehry workshop; the second outlines the development of the prototypes and production pieces; and the third presents an essay that contextualizes the work in the history of bentwood furniture. We asked Knoll to send us a piece of the maplewood they were using for the furniture, and we made a scan of it for the cover. We used a strip of hockey tape for the spine.

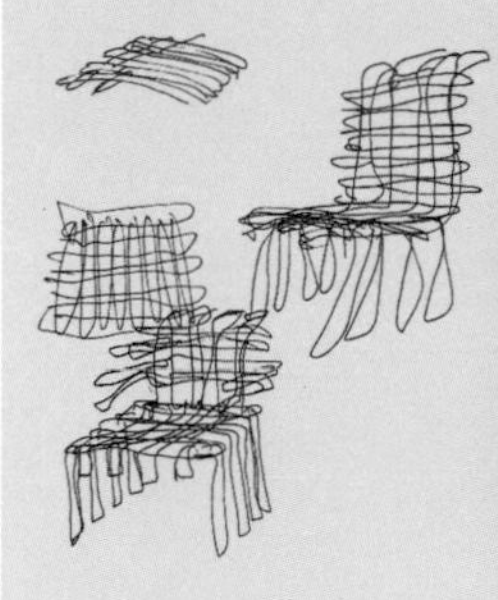

Study for chair, c. 1981

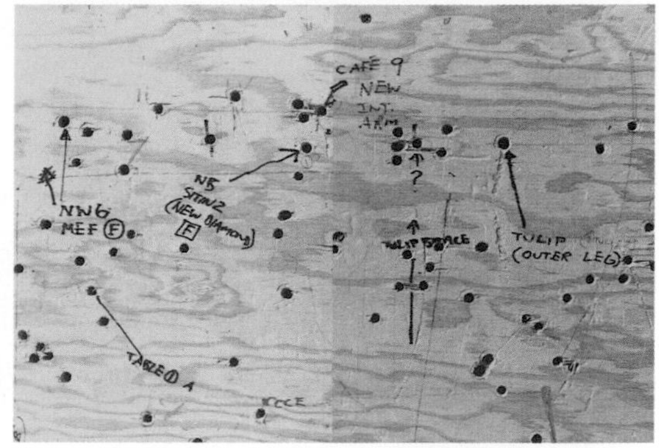

Notes on the Development of the Prototypes
Daniel Sachs and Andrew Cogan
Santa Monica, California, December 11, 1991

2. Bushel Basket

Frank's initial ideas were in part inspired by bushel baskets. He remembered playing games as a kid in Toronto where he and his friends used the bushel basket to sit and stand on. He liked its qualities of lightness and structural strength, and the fact that it was wood. He wanted the new furniture to capture these qualities.

19. *Prototype for Cross Check armchair*, 1990

21. *Prototype for Cross Check armchair*, 1991

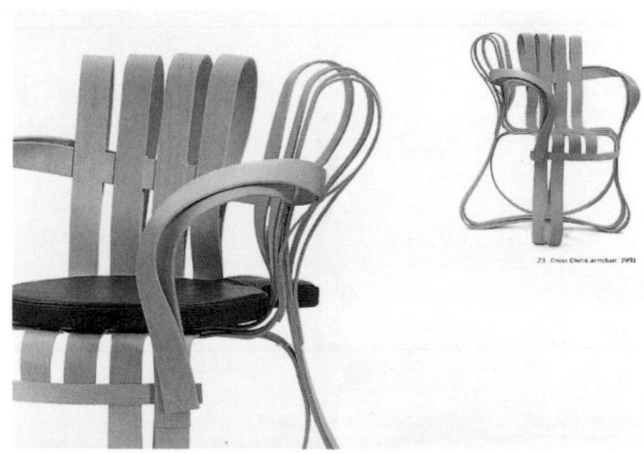

23. *Cross Check armchair*, 1991

5. Isamu Noguchi
Lounge chair, c. 1951

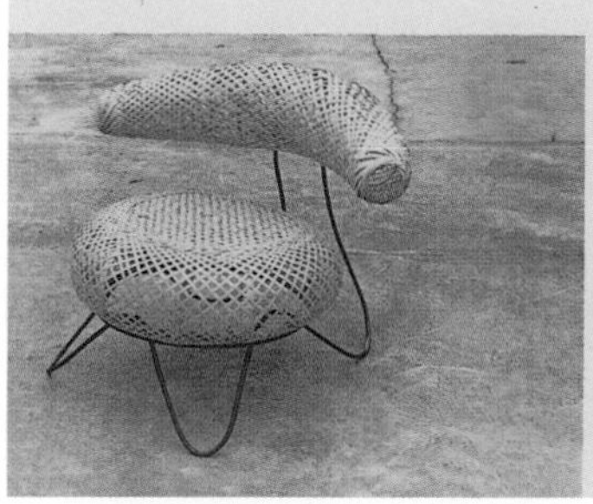

6. Gio Ponti

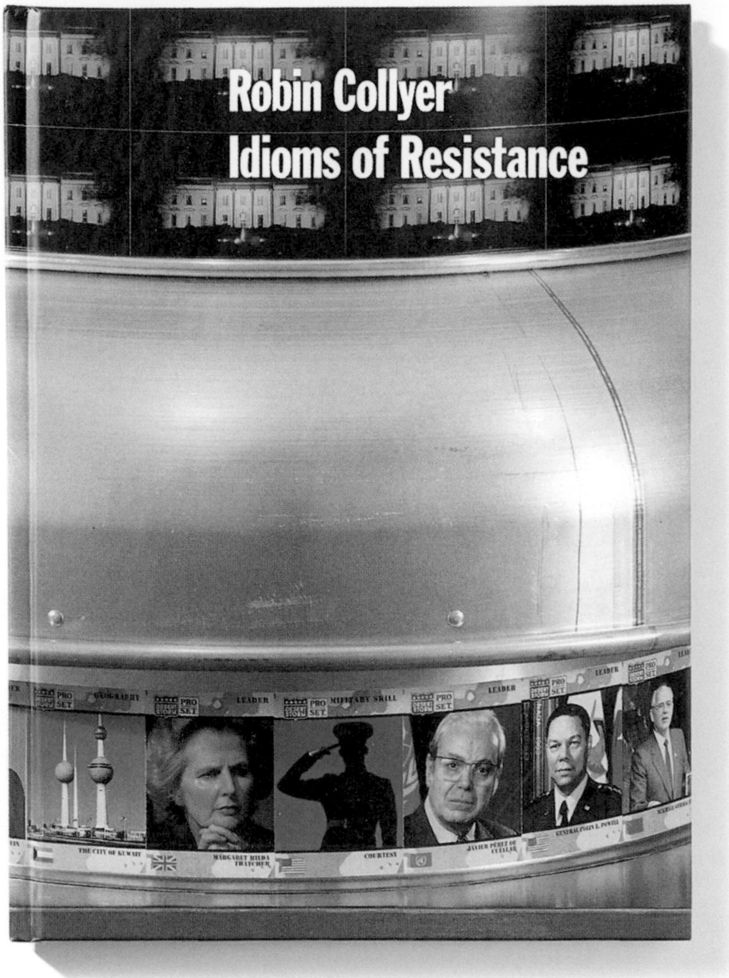

Robin Collyer: Idioms of Resistance
by Philip Monk
Toronto: Art Gallery of Ontario, 1993
This book is a companion volume to Canadian artist Robin Collyer's installation at the XIV Venice Biennale. *Idioms of Resistance* provides a full critical account of his work, which involves sculpture, texts, and photography and often their combination—which Collyer composes as a montage of effects. Rather than represent Collyer's artworks in a classical fashion, the book design installs them on the page, offering strikingly varied views—or "faces"—that single pieces present to the viewer. Robin Collyer's work led to a real understanding of the typographic dimension of urbanism. His piece *Yonge Street, Willowdale* (1992) is a masterpiece. He takes a typically banal urban intersection and removes all of the typographic information. We can't fail to realize the degree to which urbanism functions as a surface of inscription.

box covered with pages from a local (Toronto) tabloid newspaper (actually they are one-sided photocopies printed on newsprint) as if an empty store front had been papered over.

While the pages function as a sign for vacancy or bankruptcy, the light box also becomes a vehicle for the presentation of an implicit critique of this particular newspaper. By merely splaying out the pages of part of one day's edition, the presentation at first seems to reveal the newspaper as a primary vehicle for advertising. But what actually shows itself in the intentional juxtapositions is the paper's editorial attitude towards women. While this newspaper daily runs a pinup, that particular April Fool's day (April 1), the pinup was cut up and spread throughout the paper as a puzzle, reinforcing the paper's editorial commodification of women and the campaign that it wages against them through image and text. The headline of that edition reads "nude body puzzle" at the same time that it sensationalizes crimes against women, for instance, by setting a headline about rape beneath a photograph of three women in bikinis. (The analyses of *Untitled (magazine)* from 1979 comprehend the image-text strategies of the newspaper here.)

The negation in the title of the sculpture stands in a different relation from that of *No Darkne* (the woman in that work was being sponsored by the same newspaper, an advertisement for which can be seen in *NO TV*). Now it is the media collectively that is crossed out: the image in the other light box is of the vehicle of a local tabloid television station, marked by the international symbol for no. The negation is further reinforced by the structural support and circumference of the upended table top spelling out "no."

As with Collyer's earlier sculptures, the dual nature of the signs brought about by the sculpture's construction and juxtapositions allows the artist to speak back with those very materials, signs and representations taken from the dominant culture. Collyer takes a situation with which we are all familiar and insinuates another operation into it. When newspapers are pasted under plexiglass, the automatic association of their use is that of covering the windows of a bankrupt store. We are so familiar with that sight that when we recognize it in the street, we do not stop to read the contents of the newspaper. Presented in a light box under the conditions of advertising, however, the structure and content of the newspaper become clear.

The particular signs that Collyer has chosen to operate with are taken from various types of media and print material. *What Affects*, 1987 (figs. 33-36), houses a variety of printed matter: a business newspaper's advertising campaign that uses the images of world leaders ("What affects the world affects business." "Sooner or later, all news is business news," and so on); a poster ("All men are not created equal"); and a car sticker ("Do not touch this vehicle unless you are completely nude!"). Power and sexuality are brought into proximity within the work, but those same relations perhaps can be imputed within each image, not least in the poster. That these relations construct a society and are insinuated in all strata of it is suggested by the particular associations Collyer brings about by the construction housing the images. From the front, with its vacu-form plastic replicating a blank stone façade and its computer flooring creating a roof, the construction suggests an industrial plant. From the side or behind, it reveals itself to be a life-size businessman's desk, or so we are led to believe, in keeping with the theme of the business advertising. These images, however, inhabit a typewriter return, which would make the desk belong to a secretary, and force us to reinterpret the power relations of the images in this context.

It is not as if we abandon the first interpretation when we reach the second: the desk, after all, could furnish a like building. Our movement duplicates the establishing shot of a film: first, the exterior of the building; then, the interior with the desk. The change of scale that negotiates the switch of associations is essential to the work and implicates us in its representations. When we approach the sculpture from the front as if it were a building, the difference in scale between viewer and viewed implies a distance: it is as if the object were a representation and we stand outside it. When we advance and the building turns into a desk, it now occupies our space and becomes part of our reality. In this movement from what is represented to what is "real," we become *complicit* in the images presented: now they too become our reality and are not just representations, even if they are presented by the media. How we act upon them is as much a question as how they act upon us.

NO TV and *What Affects* have taken a set of signs and applied them to the framework established by *The Zulu*, as if the latter was a dilapidated shed on which advertisements were placed. That housing, however, is not merely an empty shell on which to hang signs: like *The Zulu*, the very shapes of *NO TV* and *What Affects* give the impression of things in the world as well. In both *NO TV* and *What Affects* Collyer applies readymade signs to a structure and uses them to build with, so that they become an integral part of their fabrication. The constructions' resemblances are essential to the function of the sculpture because they are the mechanisms that provide the reality missing in the media images' original deliverance. The full complexity of that reality, however, becomes manifest only through the abil-

ideological or economic. The subject of the work is an ideological representation (which is also an implicit spectacle) undermined by an economic reality that produces the conditions for it in the first place: exactly those that produced the Gulf War – an ideological mix of psychological lift, technological imperative and economic greed.

The Gulf War was the second television war, but it was the first war from which media profits immediately were taken. A number of works contain the trading cards that were quickly generated from the conflict and were modelled on the renewed phenomenon of sports trading cards, itself the manufacture of a false need for economic profit. Both *Vent* (fig. 50) and *Songs for Manuel* (fig. 51) include these cards: in *Vent* they circumscribe its base and in *Songs for Manuel* they build a vertical display. *Vent* juxtaposes the cards to television images of the White House "vigil" during the Gulf crisis (the same image is repeated on the cooling tower of the site intervention of *Peachouse Whitehouse Lighthouse*, fig. 31); *Songs for Manuel* juxtaposes them to an emblem of another American intervention, as it lists songs blasted at Panamanian leader Manuel Noriega during his refuge in the Vatican embassy at the time of the American invasion of Panama.

Offering neither the realities nor effects of the war to its viewers, the media was complicit with the military powers in relying on images and symbols to deliver the message that the American government and military wanted its citizens to see and hear. The usual word for this is propaganda. This is what the playing cards rely on as well, with their images of military and political leaders, pictures of weapons, and their symbolic use of architecture to stand for respective governments and religion. Here is how *Mosque* (fig. 57) could be seen to fit the theme, its outline alone recruited to propagandistic needs and to Collyer's own sculptural effects, both relying on immediate recognition. Here is how the entertainment industry rallies to American jingoism by supplying its simplistic clichés to the propagandistic repertoire: the good and evil caricatures of America wrestling aligning themselves to the good and evil oppositions of American foreign policy in *Circus* (fig. 58, the title as in "media circus", perhaps).

10. Conclusion: The Language of Sculpture

Having uncovered the mechanisms by which these works come to meaning, my analysis seems to have given emphasis to their content alone. Perhaps if I had said "the means by which these works *signify*," it would be clear that the process of signification is made from a *material* construction of signs, signs being considered in their semiotic sense. Signs are

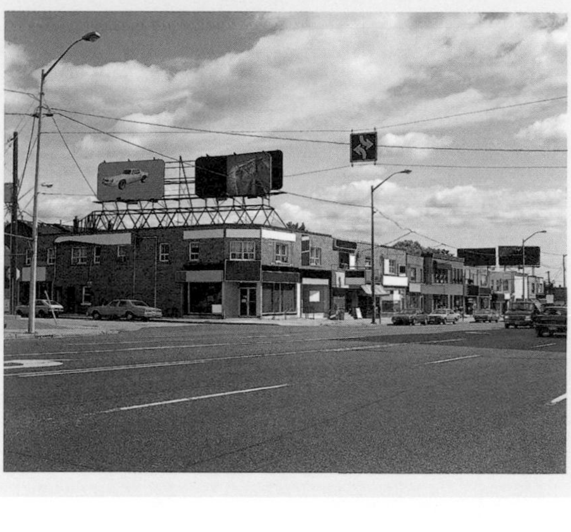

Retouched photograph

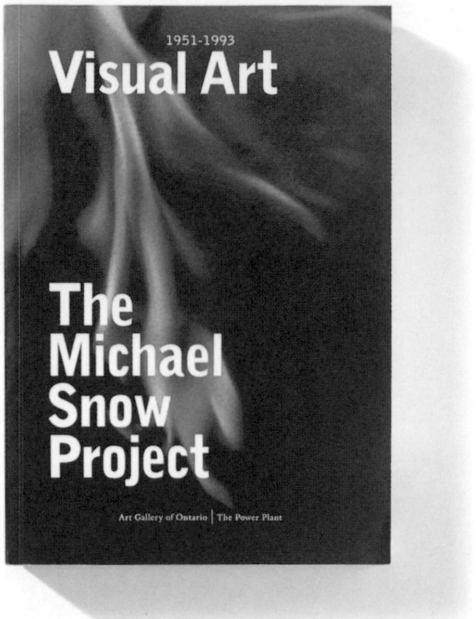

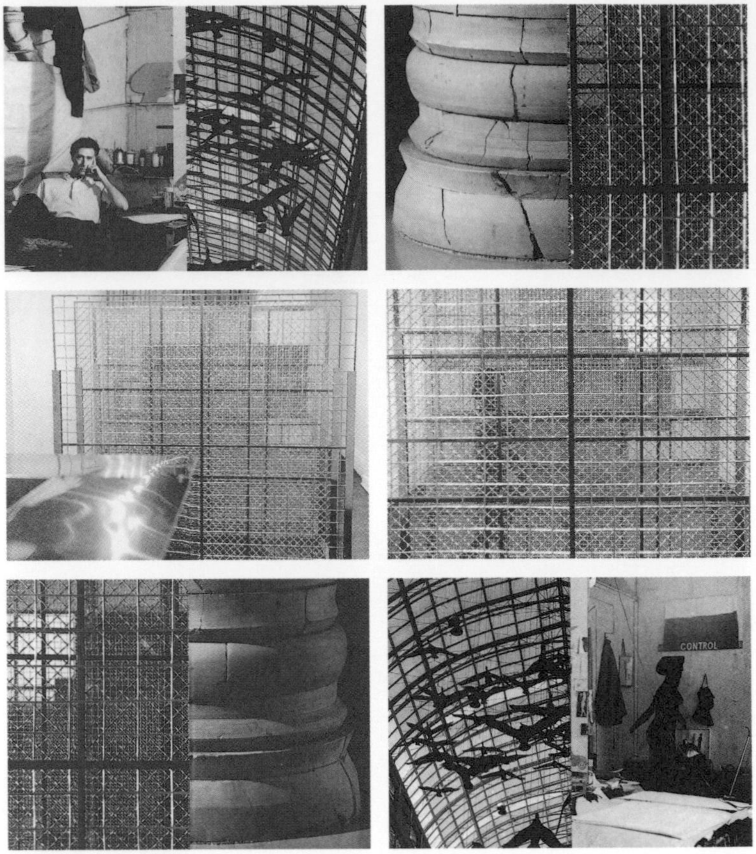

The Michael Snow Project
Toronto: Art Gallery of Ontario and The Power Plant, 1994

The renowned Canadian artist and filmmaker Michael Snow was honored with a retrospective exhibition at the Art Gallery of Ontario and the Power Plant in 1994. BMD worked with the exhibition curators and the artist to develop the identity concept, installation design, and three catalogs for *The Michael Snow Project*. The studio also conceptualized an extensive marketing program that moved beyond the walls of the gallery to infiltrate the physical and intellectual spaces of Toronto. Urban interventions included street banners, backlit images in transit shelters, subway posters, publicity spots on radio and television, newspaper features, and a wayfinding system for the exhibition installations. Michael Snow proved to be a tremendously inspiring presence for the studio. Snow has the courage and capacity to be a perpetual beginner. He always seems to be starting over. It takes immense integrity to follow your creative impulses and change directions, even shift media, the way Snow does. What restrains most artists is the pressure of success. Yet here's a man who started as a successful painter, then began again with cinema, then with books, then with music, then with photo-art, then with sculpture, then with holography. Few artists possess this fearless ability to venture into the unknown.

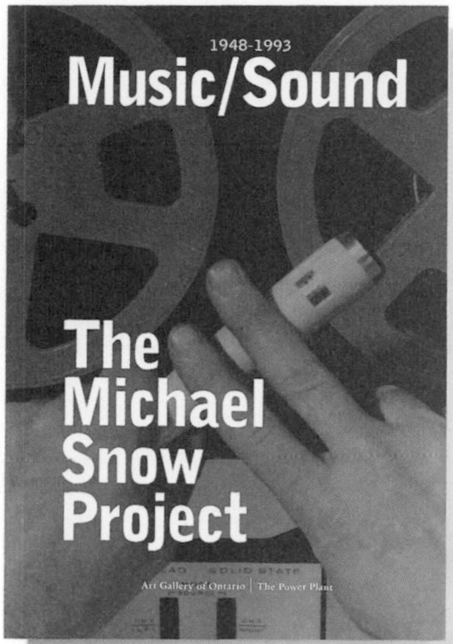
1948-1993
Music/Sound
The Michael Snow Project
Art Gallery of Ontario | The Power Plant

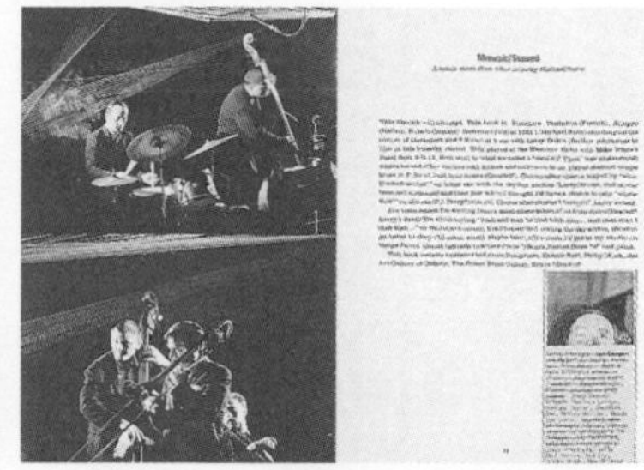

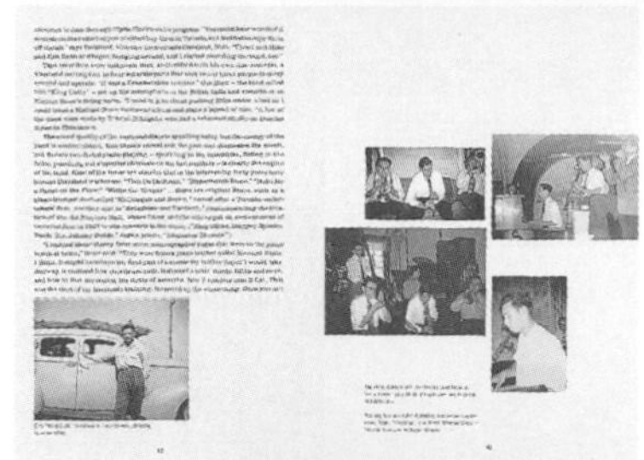

LA ROSE NOIRE

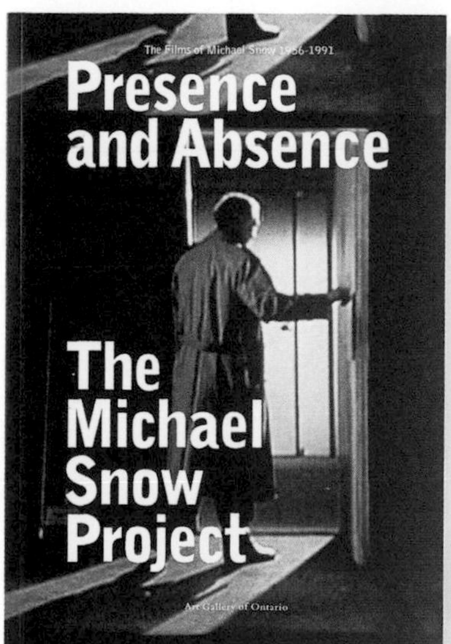
The Films of Michael Snow 1956-1991
Presence and Absence
The Michael Snow Project
Art Gallery of Ontario

Filmography

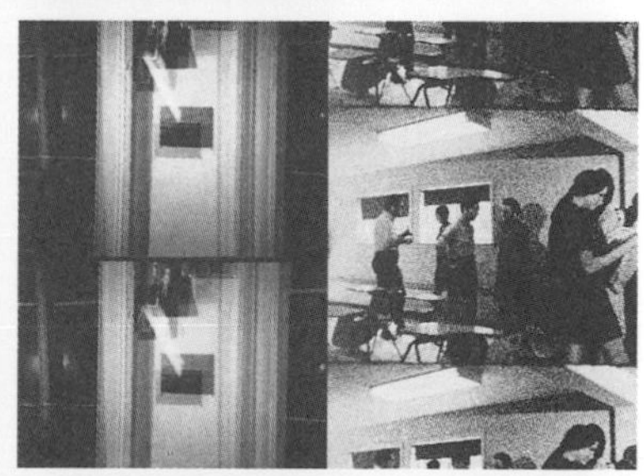

DOUGLAS

Douglas Gordon
Hannover, Germany: Kunstverein Hannover, 1998
Douglas Gordon contacted me because he felt that our work shared something: a "cinematic dimension." A survey-like exhibition at Kunstverein Hannover provided the occasion for collaborating on a book of his works. When we conceived the book as a model of Gordon's art, two books eventually emerged: one would use pictures and the other words. The first section creates a filmic walk-through of Gordon's work. The images start at the front and are sequenced to simulate the viewing experience. Gordon's work is not like a classical art

GORDON

object; rather, it is a series of fragments in time, and their sequence shapes the viewer's comprehension. In the book's image section, viewers wander around the pieces as if they were assembling them in their minds, which is how they are experienced in person. In a consonant way, the reader of the image is invited to approach Gordon's work from various directions to create a fragmentary portrait. Here, there are no captions, no explanatory texts, only images to guide the reader. For example, in *From God to Nothing*, the eye encounters the naked light bulb that hangs at the level of the genitals; the eye then scans the cracks on the concrete floor, then tracks to the bulb that hangs at eye level, then up to the ceiling rafters, and then moves back to view the installation as a whole. The page spreads model the motion of a camera lens, cutting in and out to focus on discrete details and the relationship of the parts to the environment.
The text begins at the back and rolls unconventionally toward the middle. Both photospreads and texts are essentially fictions trying to decode Gordon. The dual text-image model acknowledges this fictive dimension of the book, and at the spot in the middle where pictures and words eventually bump into one another, the last line of the essay reads, "I don't know what to believe anymore."

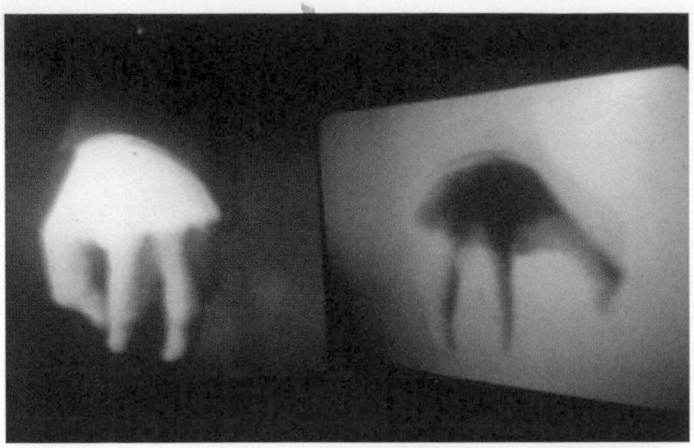

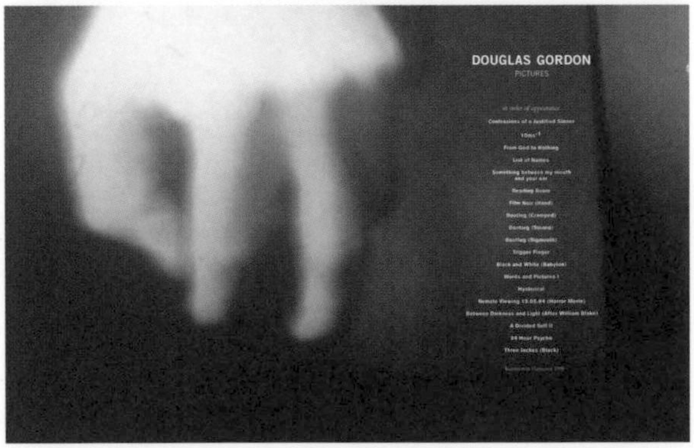

DOUGLAS GORDON
PICTURES
Confessions of a Justified Sinner
Trigger Finger
Black and White (Babylon)
Between Darkness and Light (After William Blake)
24 Hour Psycho
Three Inches (Black)

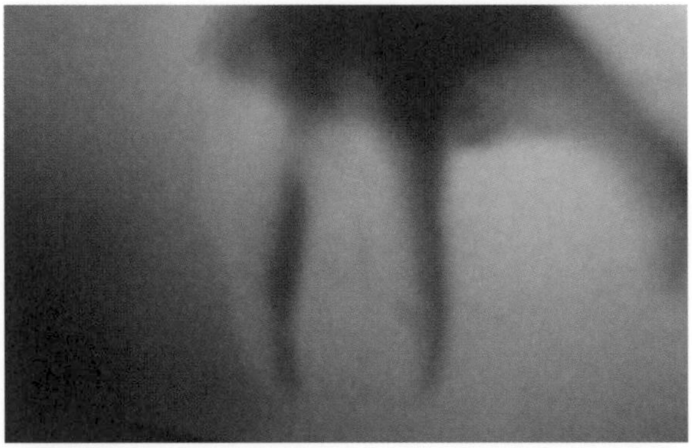

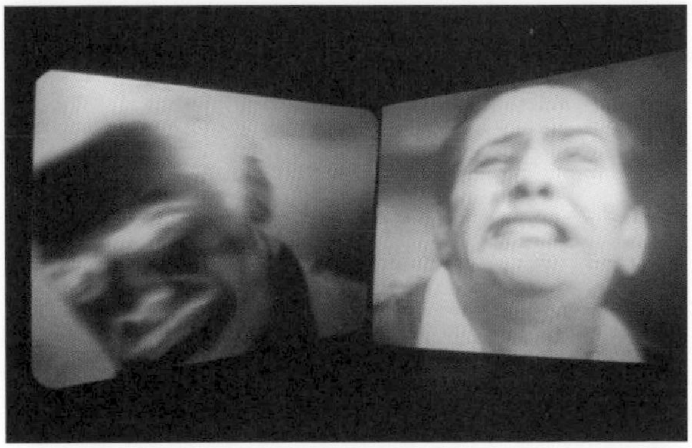

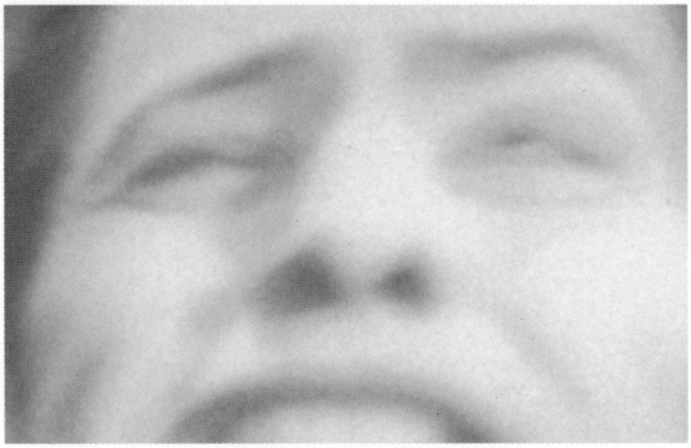

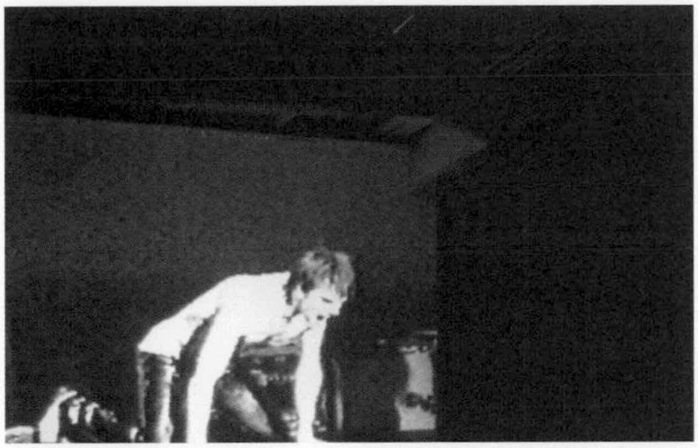

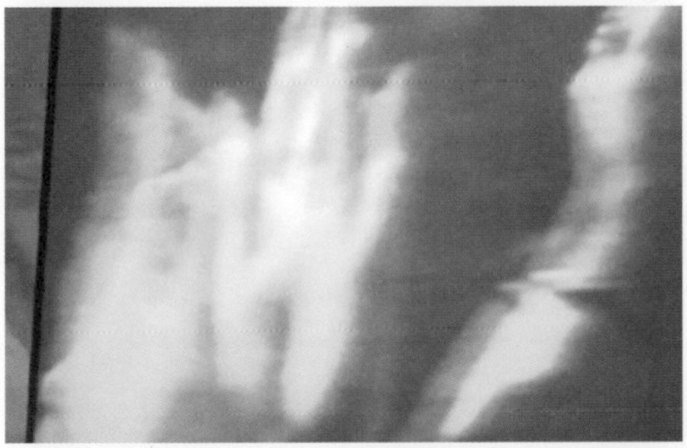
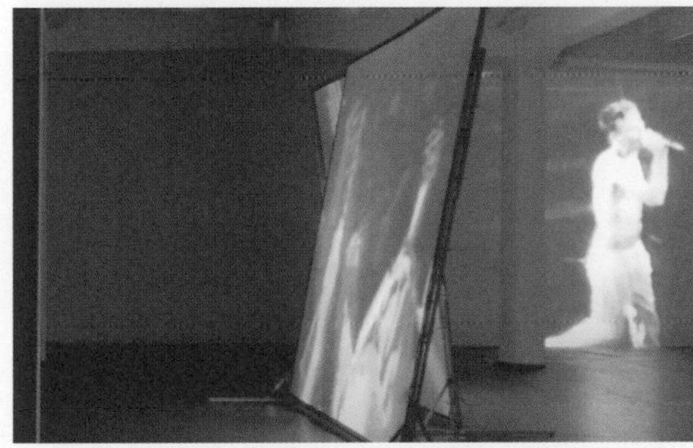

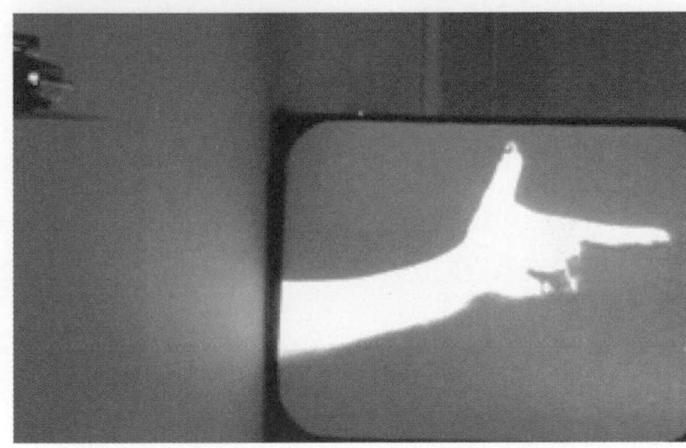

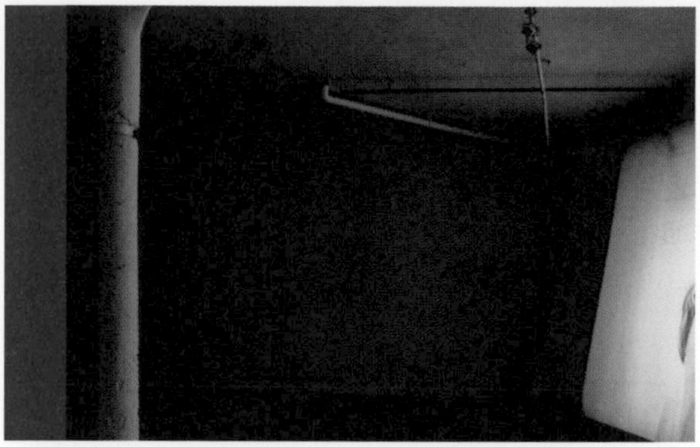

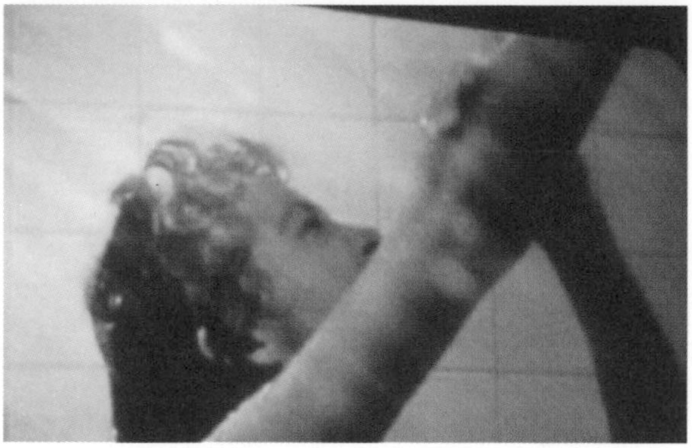

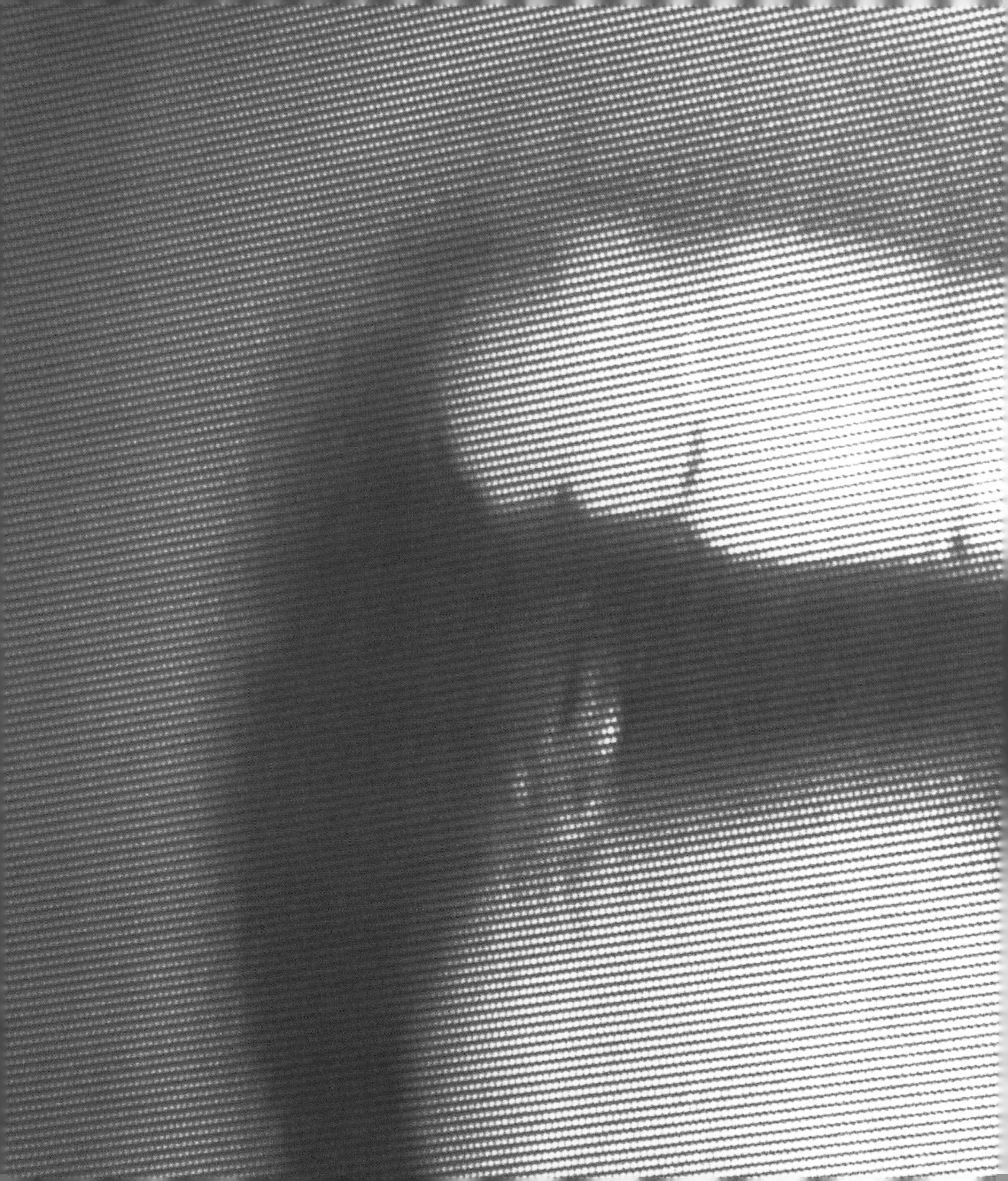

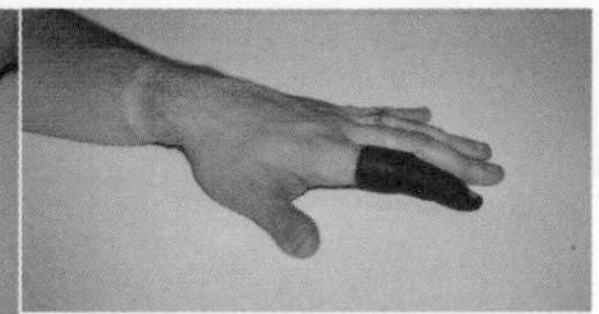

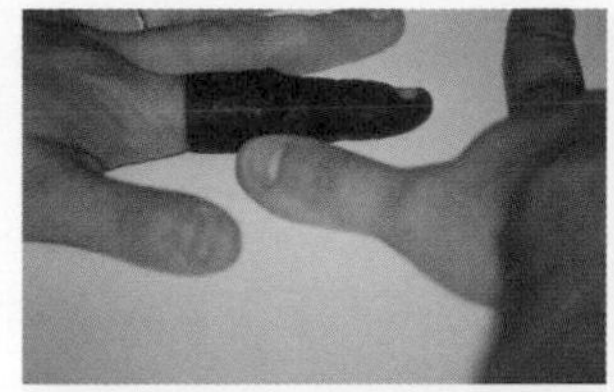

in die Nacht oder bis in den frühen Morgen, und er kam erst kurz vor Sonnenaufgang nach Hause, dann schlief er bis in den Abend hinein, und dann ging das Ganze wieder von vorne los. Sein Freund berichtete, zwischen November und Ende Januar habe er äußerst blaß ausgesehen und offensichtlich nie mehr als eine Stunde Sonnenschein am Tag gehabt. Etwa zu dieser Zeit begann er, den Leuten zu erzählen, er habe tatsächlich den Teufel in einem Café in Berlin gesehen. Aber das ist eine andere Geschichte, die er selbst erzählen soll.

Ich habe versucht, ihn in den letzten Wochen zu erreichen wegen einiger Daten für diese Biographie. Ich kann ihn nirgends erreichen. Seine Galerie teilt mir mit, er habe Berlin verlassen und lebe nun in Köln. Ich rief dort an, und sie berichteten, er sei nie in Köln angekommen. Ich rief in Hannover an, aber dort suchten sie ihn auch. Ich wählte eine Telefonnummer in Glasgow und sprach mit jemandem, dessen Stimme genau wie die von Douglas klang. Aber er behauptete, sein Vater zu sein, und sagte mir, daß niemand wüßte, wo sein Sohn sei, und daß die ganze Familie sich inzwischen ein wenig Sorgen machte.

Ich weiß nicht, was ich noch glauben soll.

Übersetzung aus dem Englischen von Michael Strobel

den Stab fort, und gleich setzt erneut die Krise ein, die er durch Einatmen von Amylnitrat beschleunigen läßt. Die Kranke verlangt nun den Sex-Stab mit Worten, die keinerlei Metapher benutzen.«[36]
Es ist völlig gleichgültig, wie man auf das Werk von Douglas Gordon schaut. Ob man in ihm den Schüler des Heiligen Lukas sieht oder den Erben Charcots, ob man ihn als künstlerischen Akteur auf dem Gebiet der Religion oder der Wissenschaft betrachtet. In jedem Fall erforscht Gordon kompetent und eindrucksvoll eine Tradition, in der sich Medizin und Kunst berühren. Und treibt seine Forschung voran mit Hilfe dessen, was man als erzählende Theologie bezeichnen könnte.

des nicht aufzulösenden Konflikts von Gut und Böse heraufbeschwört. Entlassen werden wir in die unentrinnbare Erinnerung von *List of Names* (1990–) in das nüchterne Tageslicht des 30 Meter langen Saales, vorbei an Tausenden von Namen von Menschen, mit denen Douglas Gordon sich im Laufe seines Lebens beschäftigt hat. In *10ms*$^{-1}$ (1994) begegnen wir der beklemmenden Wucht eines erneut im Halblicht projizierten Filmmaterials. Die Bilder eines ständig stürzenden Körpers produzieren erneut jene rätselhafte Grenze von pathologischem Gebrechen, groteskem Ernst und schrecklicher Komik. Dann erstarren wir in dem dunklen, nur durch drei nackte Glühlampen erhellten Raum von *From God to Nothing* (1997). Die in Höhe der Augen, des Herzens und in Höhe des Geschlechts aufgehängten Lichtquellen lenken den Blick auf uns selbst, und die Schrift auf der Wand, in der die Furcht vor allem, angefangen mit der vor Gott bis zum Nichts von Allerweltskram uns in den hypnotischen Bannkreis unserer Ängste zieht. Zum Schluß läßt uns *Reading Room* (1998) im letzten Raum der Ausstellung befreit aufatmen. Er erinnert uns an den dauernden geistigen Austausch, auf den der Künstler Douglas Gordon und wir, das Publikum, durch Lesen und Kommunizieren dauernd angewiesen sind. Es ermöglicht den schnellen und dichten Gedankenaustausch, der

und andererseits die metaphorische Bühne für die Komplexität des Zwiespältigen. Selten hat die Auswahl der Arbeiten und die Abfolge der Präsentation in den Räumen des Kunstvereins so viel Sinn gemacht wie in dieser Ausstellung, auch wenn die Künstler im Kunstverein stets dezidiert mit dem Kontext umgegangen sind. Die sieben Arbeiten erzeugen im Rundgang und im damit unmittelbar verbundenen Verknüpfen verschiedener psychologischer, emotionaler, sprachlicher und bildhafter Ebenen ein Gefühl schwer zu entrinnender Verstrickung.
Es beginnt mit dem Hinabtauchen in die Erinnerung an Geburt in *Something between my mouth and your ear* (1994), einem gänzlich in entrücktes Blau getauchten Raum, angefüllt mit Musik, die Douglas Gordons Mutter während ihrer Schwangerschaft gehört haben könnte. *Three Inches (Black)* (1997) konfrontiert uns mit der Gleichzeitigkeit von Abscheu und Anziehung. Es ist die Photosequenz eines genau in jener Länge schwarz tätowierten Zeigefingers, der einen Menschen im Herzen zu berühren oder zu töten vermag. Danach geraten wir in das irrationale Halbdunkel von *Confessions of a Justified Sinner* (1995/96), einer Doppelprojektion von Filmausschnitten, deren Wechsel von Positiv und Negativ, deren Gleichzeitigkeit von Hell und Dunkel die beklemmende Atmosphäre

EINE KURZBIOGRAPHIE

Von einem Freund

Douglas Gordon wurde im September 1966 im Redlands Hospital in Glasgow geboren. Er war das älteste von vier Kindern von James Gordon und Mary McDougall. Die Geburt war nicht leicht. Soweit er sich erinnern kann, oder soweit er sich an die Erzählung seiner Mutter erinnern kann, lag sie 64 vierundzwanzig Stunden in den Wehen. Ganz offensichtlich wollte er nicht auf die Welt kommen. Schließlich mußten ihn die Ärzte mit Zangen holen. Das mag der Grund für die eigenartige Form seines Kopfes sein und für die kleine Narbe unten an seinem Schädel, da wo das Rückgrat endet. Die Geburt war ein traumatisches Erlebnis für Mutter und Kind. Mary McDougall, seine Mutter, starb während der Entbindung. Aber nach einigen Augenblicken fand sie ins Leben zurück. Douglas hat immer noch Schuldgefühle wegen all der Scherereien, die er seiner Mutter damals bereitete. Vielleicht reist er deshalb so viel und schiebt seine Heimkehr nach Schottland immer wieder auf. Vielleicht möchte er die Schuld nicht spüren, die er fühlt, wenn er seine Familie sieht.

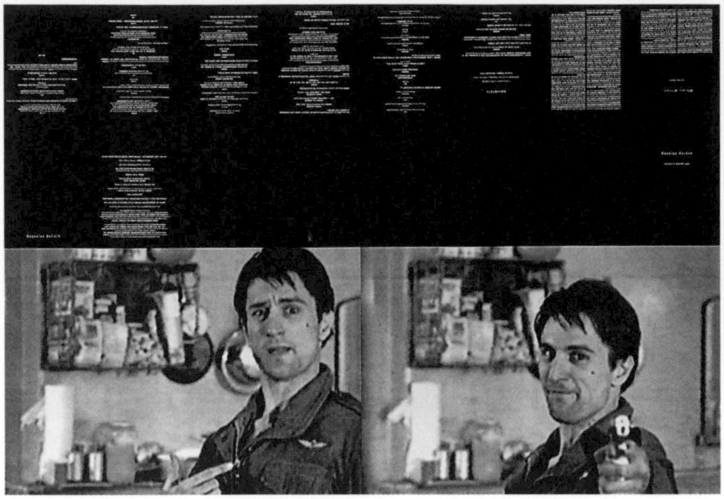

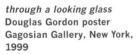

through a looking glass
Douglas Gordon poster
Gagosian Gallery, New York, 1999

The Gagosian Gallery wanted a street poster for Douglas Gordon's New York exhibition of *through a looking glass*. They also wanted a catalog. We combined the two projects in a single, folded format. Unopened, one side of the large poster can be flipped like a book and contains a critical essay by Amy Taubin and a script by Hal Hartley derived from an e-mail exchange with Douglas Gordon. Opened up to its full size, the oversized poster presents two images of Robert de Niro as Travis Bickle from the "Are you talking to me?" sequence of *Taxi Driver*. Gordon's actual piece is composed of two video screens playing a seventy-one-second loop of that scene, with one screen flipped so that it is a mirror image of the other. The other side of the poster is printed on Chromalux, which is as close as paper comes to a mirror surface. In addition to information about the show, printed in a silver varnish, we added, at eye level and in very small black type, the text of Travis's speech, so someone looking at the poster in the street could not only see himself or herself reflected, but also act out Bickle's lines.

Douglas

Gordon

Huh? Huh? Huh? Faster than you. Fuckface. Saw you coming. Fucker. Shithead. I'm standing here. You make the move. You make the move. It's your move. Huh? Don't try it, you fuck. You talking to me? You talking to me? You talking to me? Then who the hell else are you talking... you talking to me? Well, I'm the only one here.

March 6 –

April 10, 1999

Gagosian

Gallery

alking to
ing to me?
the hell else are you talking...

ı talking to me? Well, I'm the only one here. Who the fuck do you think you're ta

Chasing Napoleon: Forensic Portraits
by Tony Scherman
Toronto: Cameron and Hollis, 1999

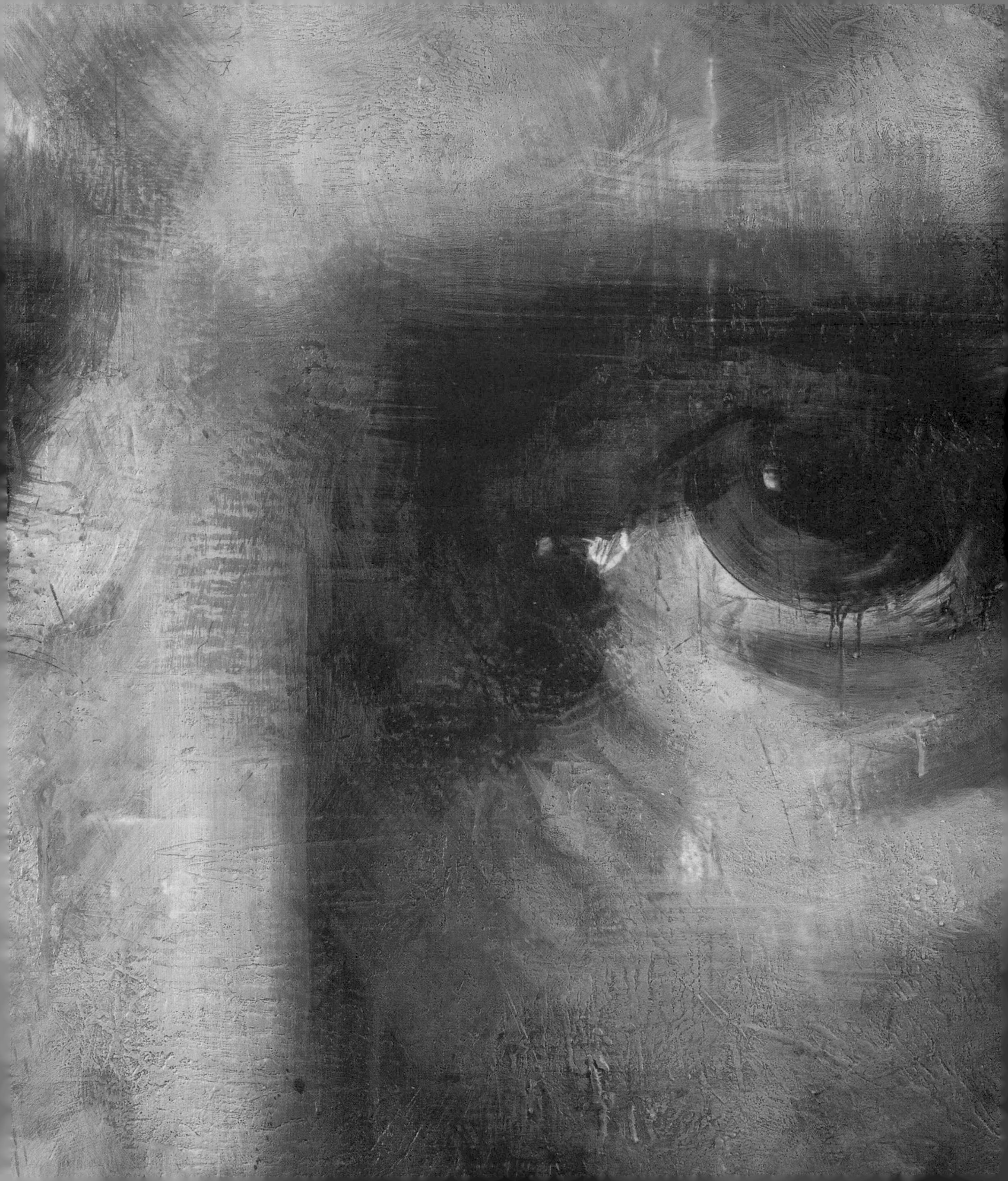

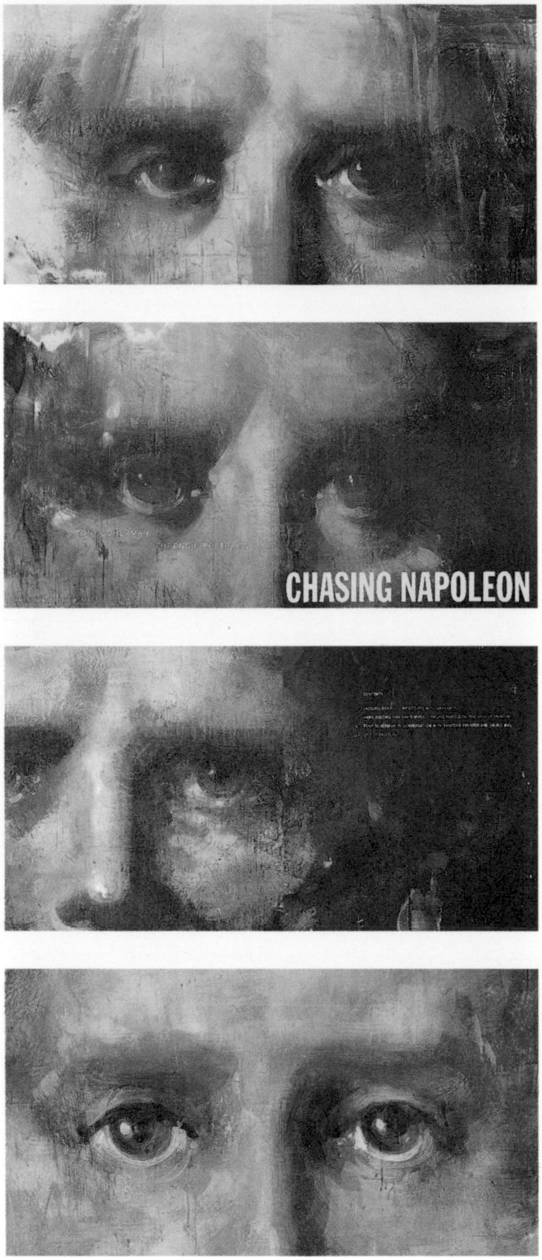

The opening sequence

Cover study: situating Scherman's work in the roiling context of contemporary image culture

From a conversation with Tony Scherman, Sanford Kwinter, and Bruce Mau, in *Chasing Napoleon*

BM: One is struck by your imaging techniques—the close-up, zoom, crop, and pan. When you paint, there appear to be two worlds operating simultaneously—the world of conventional representation, and within that, the space of the film. More and more, the series of paintings seems like one continuous event.

TS: Before I begin painting, I seldom know what will be in the series. It's as though I'm painting at night, flying on instruments. I often don't know until I'm well into a painting what it signifies, and, quite often, when I'm halfway through a painting, I will realize that the painting that I have decided to paint is actually not the one that I should be painting and I will redirect it. I imagine that it is very similar for you in designing, where the thing that you thought you were doing was actually leading you to the real thing that you are doing.

There was a time when the paintings really were missing something, and the something they were missing was the signal—the thing in the painting that would signal how to look at it. I eventually found that signal through cinema. Once the signal was there, the paintings could operate alone.

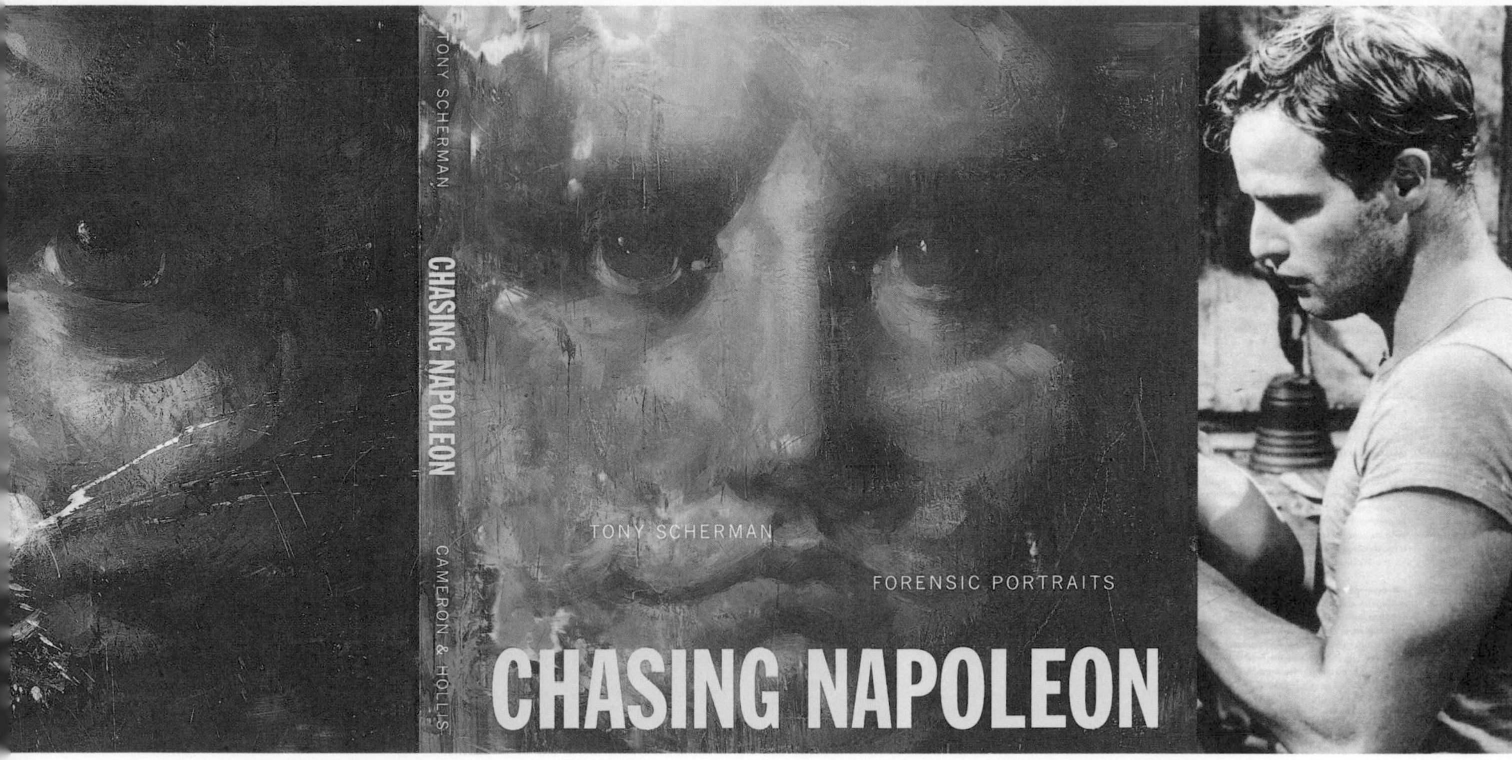
TONY SCHERMAN
CHASING NAPOLEON
CAMERON & HOLLIS
TONY SCHERMAN
FORENSIC PORTRAITS
CHASING NAPOLEON

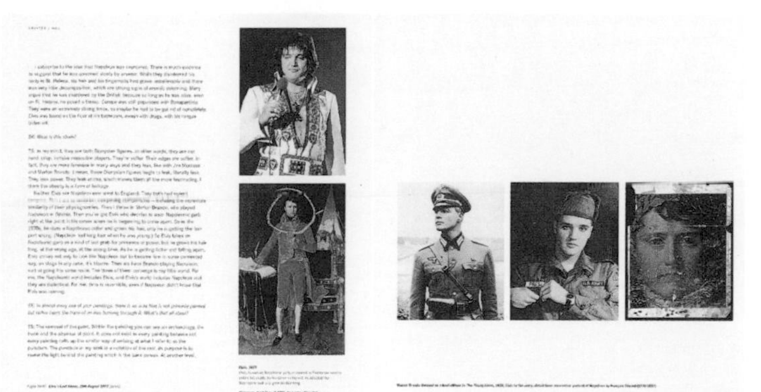

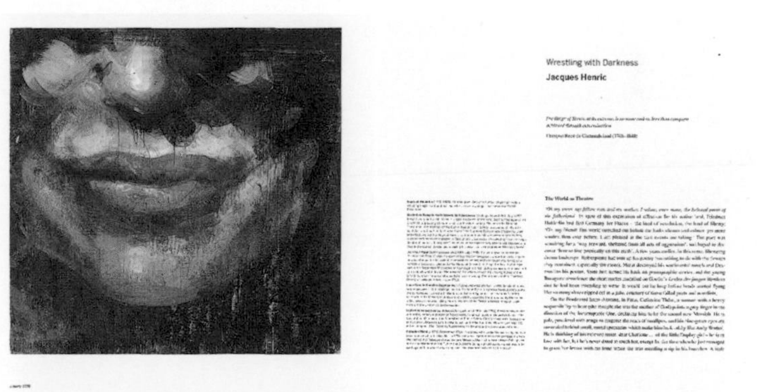
Wrestling with Darkness
Jacques Henric
The World as Theatre

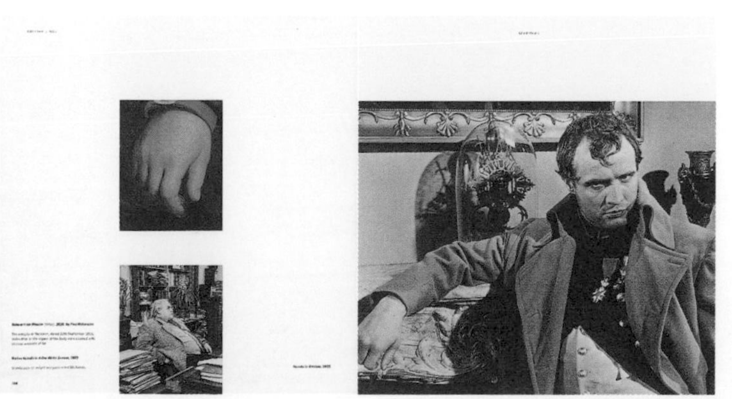

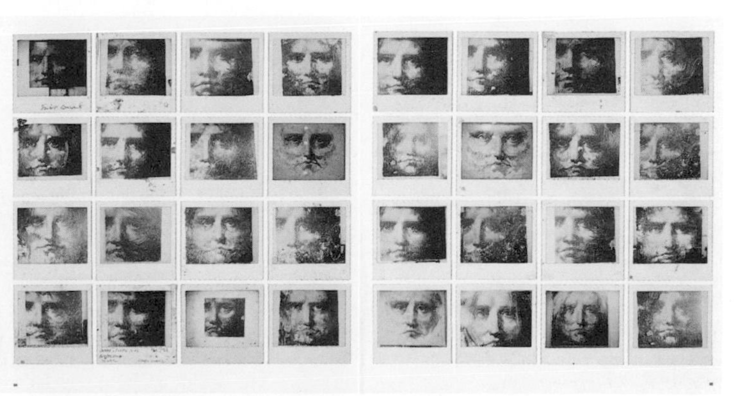

Perfection, Way, Origin
Text by Jean Starobinski
Etchings by Terry Winters
New York: ULA&E, 2000

Published in a boxed edition of fifty copies, *Perfection, Way, Origin* is an artist's book that features letterpress printing on handmade paper to present a suite of works by the artist Terry Winters. Each copy includes a portfolio of ten Winters etchings.

The book is a meeting between the philosopher and the artist. Jean Starobinski's text performs an in-depth exploration of an artistic paradox: In their quest for perfection, the painter and poet discover themselves on a road seemingly without end, one that stretches toward a necessary but furtive destination. Perfection is the end and the origin of art. Starobinski begins: "Every work is on the way to the Work." In a brilliantly succinct text, itself winding through three centuries of aesthetics, the writer is accompanied by Terry Winters's suite of etchings, dense and tangled linear pieces that offer perfect analogues to the philosopher's paradox. They are like maps with dense, crisscrossing lines radiating out of an obscured center. Each is a discrete gesture made more complete when seen with the others in the set.

Terry Winters collaborated on the design. We worked together to size and place the images inside the text by following an innate feeling of what was right.

text
Jean Starobinski

etchings
Terry Winters

Perfection, Way, Origin

translated by Richard Pevear

I

Of Perfection

Every work is on the way to the Work.

This thought accompanied poets and artists for a long time. The concern for perfection directed the desire of those who aspired to the victors' garland. Perfection was what they did not possess but were charged with attaining and adding to the world. For some it was what made the beauty of the world more complete. They had no right to be satisfied before they reached it. They wanted to be supreme, or nothing. This thought has been perpetuated in various guises over the centuries: we still recognize it in the plan for works of world form, which was pondered during the century now coming to an end.

Perfection is taken to have been the ideal of classicism. It was Romantic thought, above all, that attributed this ideal to classicism, in order to criticize it or regret its passing. In fact, the majority of Romantic artists remained attached to the ideal of perfection. They even conferred a transcendent ideality upon it. They sometimes attributed to it the contradictory qualities of wholeness and limitlessness. At the turn of the nineteenth century, in the exalted prose of his *General Draft*, the great German poet Novalis wrote:

> *No perfection is expressed in isolation; the perfect object expresses at the same time a whole related world. That is why the veil of the virgin flutters around what is perfect of any kind—a veil which the lightest contact dissolves into a magic perfume that becomes the cloudy chariot of the seer. It is not only antiquity that we see. It is at the same time the sky, the spyglass, and the fixed star—and thus the authentic revelation of a higher world. Let it not be too rigidly believed that*

certain moment, the work of perfection had become a progressive destruction. "There is nothing on the canvas." Frenhofer, who believed he had created a living and breathing woman, is unwilling to acknowledge his defeat. He burns his canvases and dies of despair the following night.

Has the taste for perfection not prepared its own dethronement? The more intense the pursuit of perfection, the more it calls up and brings forward its contrary: the provisional, the sketched plan, the preliminary tasks; the series of stages passed through before the hoped-for goal is reached. Of these stages there sometimes remain portfolios of sketches, pages of partial studies. In view of so many sketches, the obvious imposes itself: The work did not arise all at once, it occupied its creator's thought for a long time. And for us a temptation may insinuate itself: Should the comprehension of the work, however convincing its "ultimate" form, not include all its preparatory states? Should we not place everything on an equal footing? There are even some among today's readers and viewers who advocate going back, against all reasonable hope, as far as the infantile dreams that prefigured the work. One must make one's way through the long preceding adventure. To which a later history is added. Does the work not change appearance from the moment it is made public, recognized, reproduced, imitated, becomes banal? Can it be separated from the judgment that receives it and that reconstructs it while receiving it? In short, must it not be comprehended, not only as the sum of its parts, but as the sum of its states, perhaps to the point of ruin and mutilation? Now, if it is scattered among the crowd of its states, it is no longer a closed organism: it is an open series, each element of which is a provisional subset. Under a gaze that has become attentive to these phenomena, certain great works themselves lose their character of oneness. They begin to stir. They become mobile, to the point of dissolving in their own history. On reflection, we discover that the instability of the significance of works goes together with their very glory and their transmission In their intimate substance they undergo the (sometimes disastrous) effects of the various means that assure their diffusion and reproduction in space and

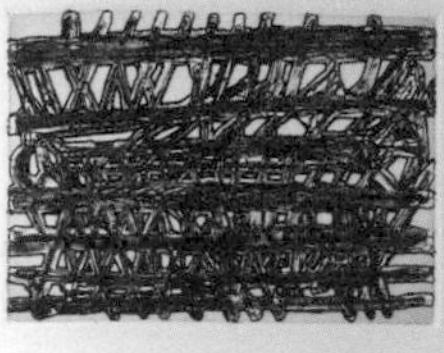

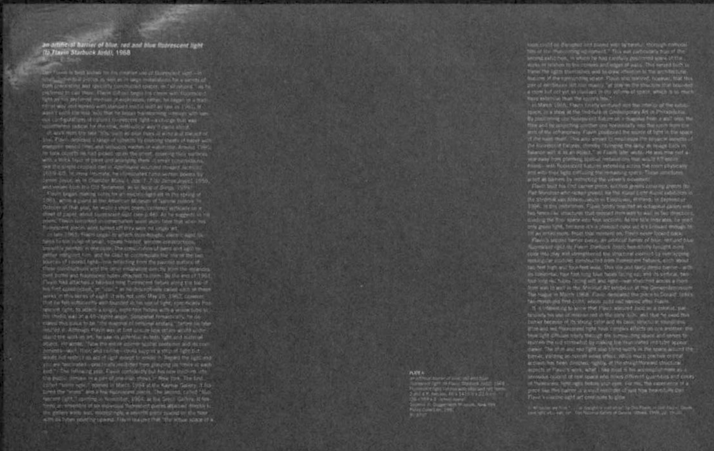
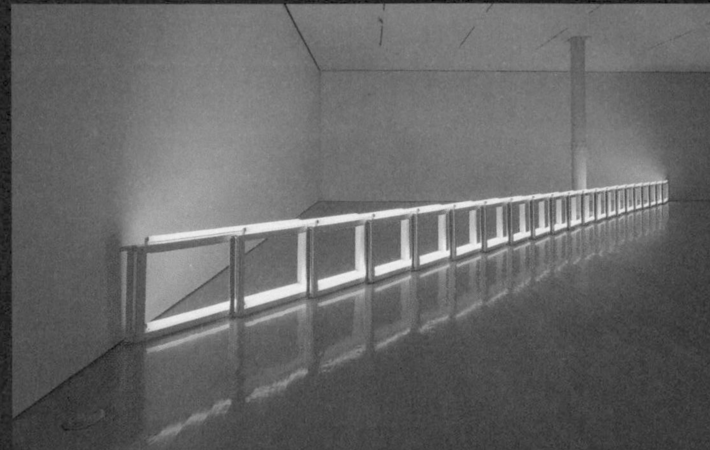
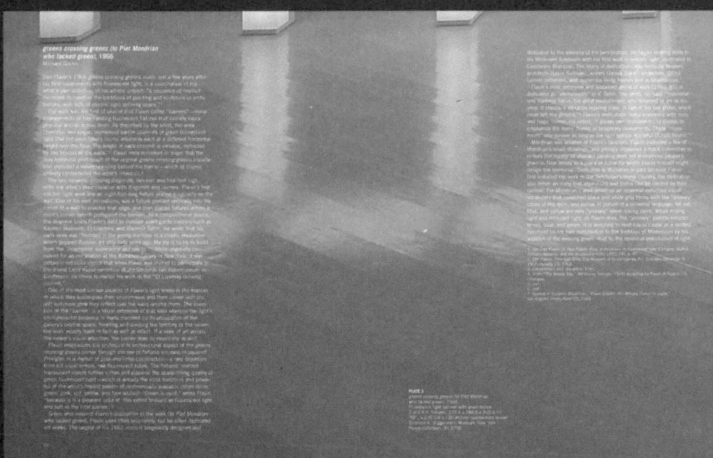
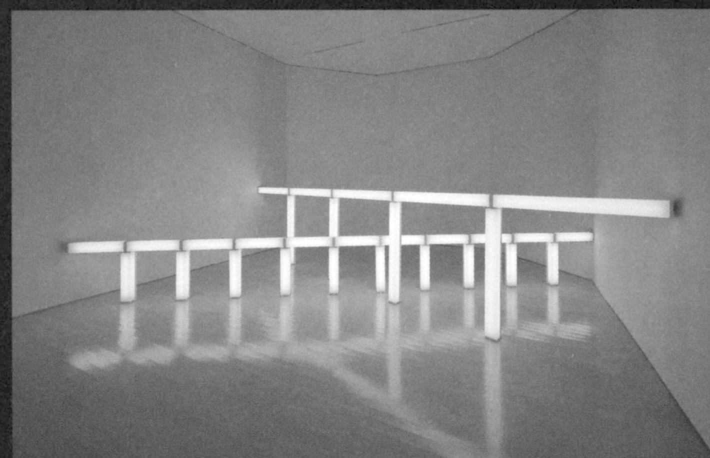

Dan Flavin: The Architecture of Light
Berlin: Deutsche Guggenheim Berlin/ Hatje Cantz Verlag, 1999
The Guggenheim asked us to design the catalog inside a four-week deadline, but added a graver challenge when they said, "We hate every book about Dan Flavin." The reason was apparent: earlier books treat Flavin in the standard art-history fashion, presenting discrete images on a white page. The mistake is obvious. They treat Flavin's artworks as if they were objects, nothing more than fluorescent tubes and brackets. We decided to treat the book like an installation. The reader drops into the space. For every one of the works represented, we took a fragment of the reflected light from the photograph to make a lightwork of the page. The colors fall on the page from Flavin's light, projecting into the book the environments his art creates.

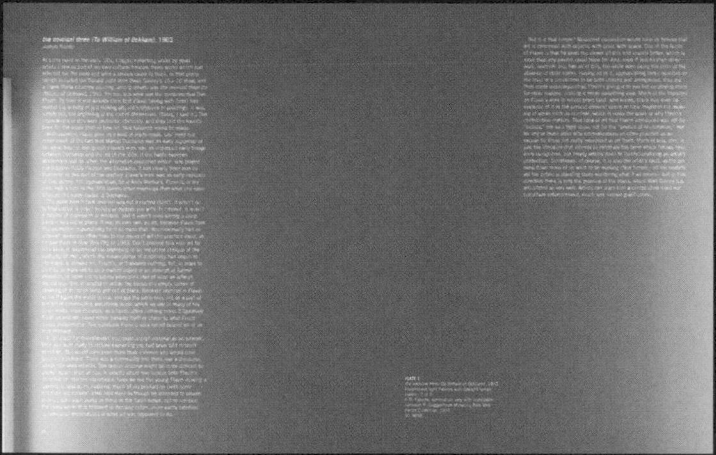

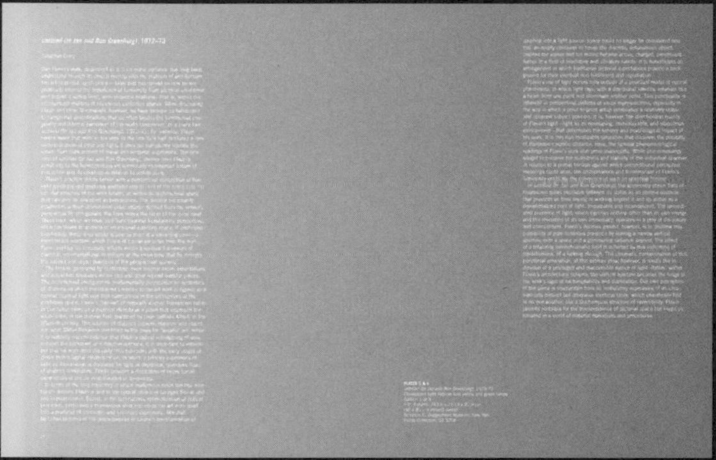

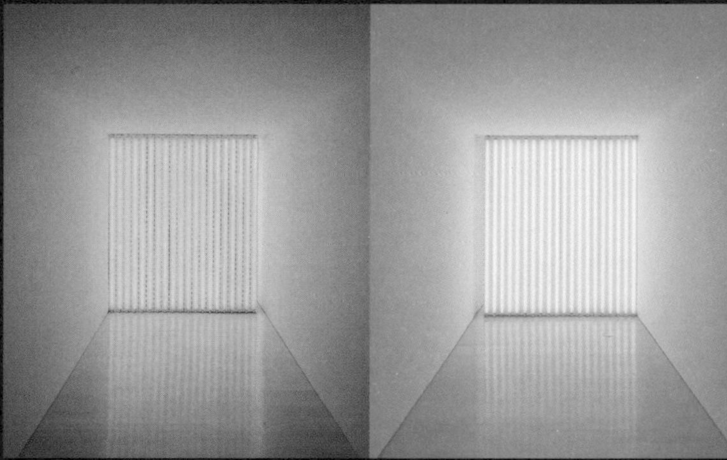

ReMembering the Body
ReMembering the Body
Edited by Gabriele Brandstetter and Hortensia Völckers
With STRESS, an image essay by Bruce Mau with texts by André Lepecki
Hatje Cantz

ReMembering the Body
Edited by Gabriele Brandstetter and Hortensia Völkers
Ostfildern-Ruit, Germany: Hatje Cantz Verlag, 2000
Rather than merely a companion catalog, we saw *ReMembering the Body* as another installation venue for *STRESS*, a video installation by BMD that premiered at the Wiener Festwochen (Vienna Festival) in May 2000. We took the original twenty-six episodes of the video (organized alphabetically from "Alarm" to "Zero"), and translated them into an image essay that travels through the entire volume, occupying every right-hand page.

We also changed the typographic environment to correspond to each of the *STRESS* episodes—every time the episode changes, the font changes on the left page. In effect, the nine scholarly texts move through twenty-six different environments.

Preface

Remembering the body, calling the dismembered and reunited body to memory – wasn't that the signature of the 20th century? And isn't it the rivalling media – image, movement, and writing – within which this process of forgetting and remembering developed?

The project "ReMembering the Body" set out to take the representation of the body and of movement as its subject in three different media of presentation existing in our culture, and to place these in relation to one another: in a dance festival, in an exhibition, and in book form. Each of these media, taken separately, has brought forth its own complex tradition of body representation. The challenge was to bring about an exchange between these conventions of representation, and to do the complexity of this interrelationship justice while preserving the independence of the three forms of presentation.

The tension within this constellation of media suggested to us that we should be raising questions concerning the representability of the body and presenting concepts and images of the body as a remembered history extending into the future. In the process, it has been important to include those discourses and scholarly scenarios of our Western world which have made a deep impression on our concept of body and movement: scientific reflection, from anatomy to media science; the image archives of the body created both in art and the media; and the fleeting performances of movement theatre and of dance.

An open project such as this one – "ReMembering the Body" – requires a framework and structures capable of making an experimental field of this kind possible in the first place: in the nexus of various institutions such as (dance) theatre, exhibition, university, and publishing; in constructive work and in experimental thought

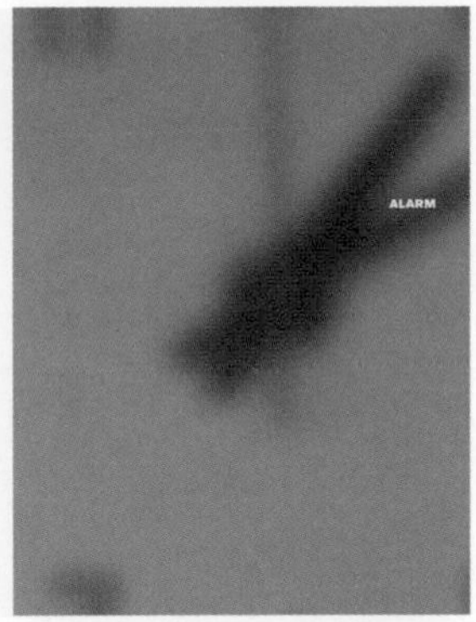

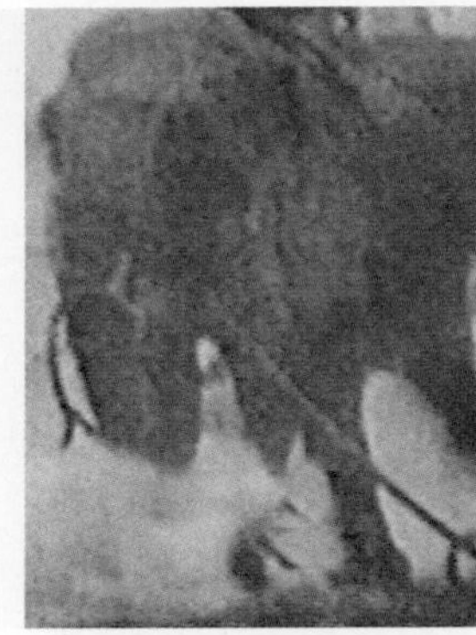

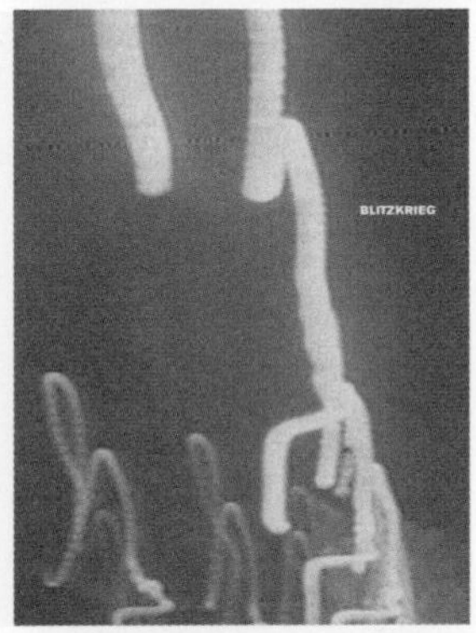

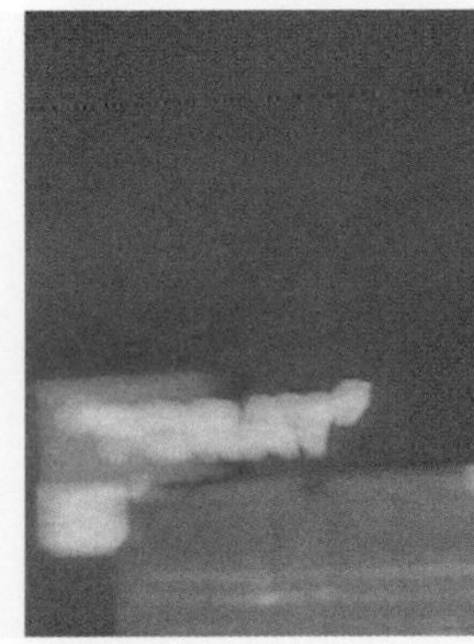

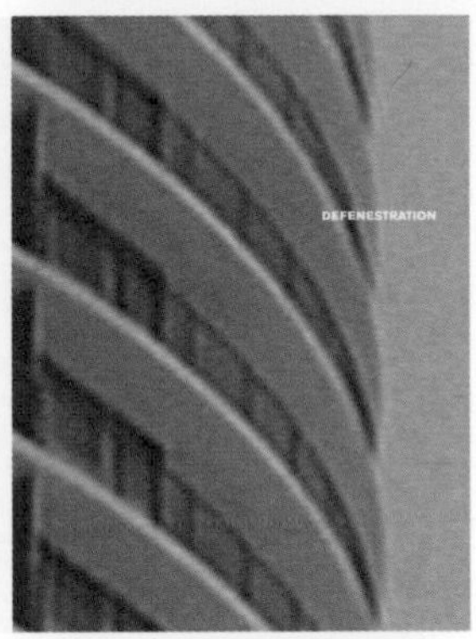

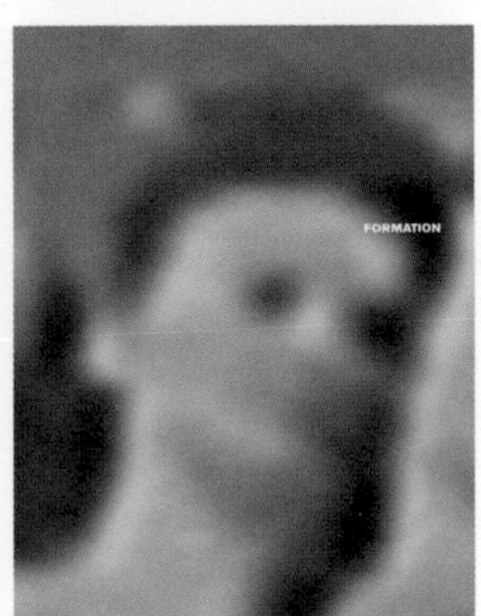

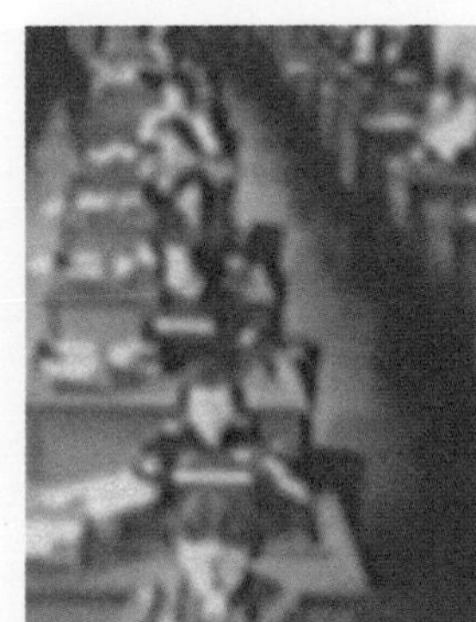

Mr. S, age 43.
A sales manager for a large automobile dealer. Mr. S and his subordinates hurried from one customer to another. Mr. S died of a sudden heart abnormality in March of 1995. Before collapsing, he had complained of his worsening physical condition.

LOGO

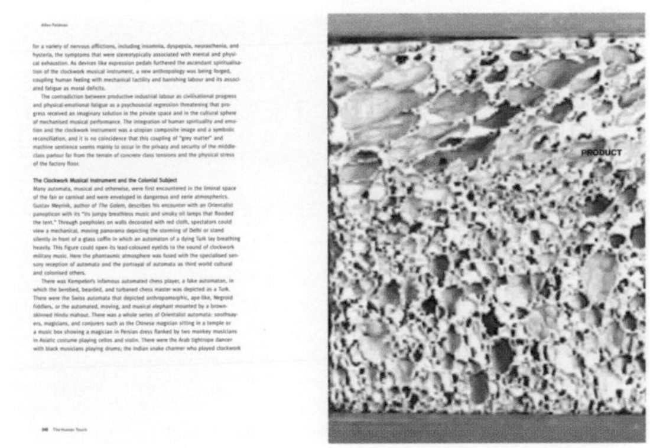
PRODUCT

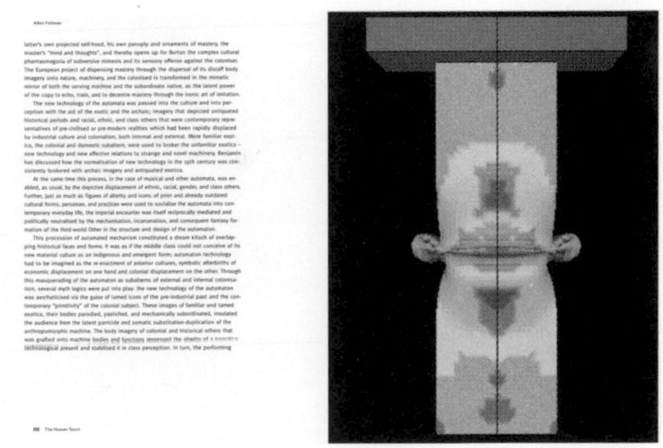

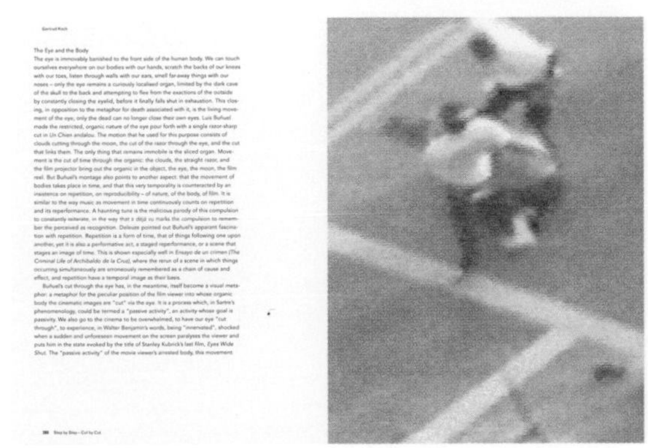

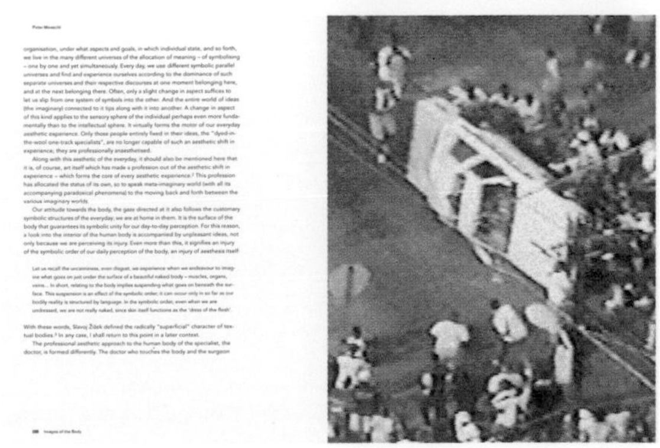

who penetrates into it are doubtlessly driven by a different interest in gaining knowledge, within the framework of a different symbolic system and coming from another imaginative world than the artist, the sexual partner, the father, the brother, the colleague, the friend, the representative of another profession, and so forth – any of which he might also be simultaneously.

Although sufficiently known, hardly any notice is taken of this fact in regard to the confrontations between these different worlds existing within one and the same community, confrontations which occur not all that infrequently, are relevant in terms of content, and are often socially problematic. Without making the dynamic interconnectedness of these parallel worlds in their concrete form the subject of our inquiry, we encounter each other (as representatives of our symbolic worlds) for the most part with unconscious strategies of distancing and disassociation. For this reason, the doctor takes care to maintain the "necessary distance" in bodily contact with the patient. The concept of distance, however, can by no means adequately describe the radical change in language, the other "linguistic operation" on the texture of the body and the fundamental change in aesthetic perception which are connected to the required and appropriate assumption of the doctor's position. Here, the call for distance is not a demand in the sense of the concept of distance in regard to content. In the final analysis, it is clear to everyone that medical treatment of the body demands not only an aesthetic/moral distance, but at the same time a direct technical proximity. The call for distance has, rather, a signalling character for the above-mentioned change in discourse and disposition, comparable to a cut in film. It is a signal with which the doctor might call the "texture" of his profession to mind. It is therefore not yet possible to approach this problem analytically when using the concept of distance alone.

A surgical cut is performed on an area of the body which is carefully disinfected and isolated from other regions, from the rest of the body's entire surface. Thus, the remainder of the body is covered over sterilely and is no longer visible to the operating surgeon during his performance. But this procedure certainly cannot be explained simply by concerns of sterility alone which the operation requires. Rather, it helps the surgeon concentrate both on the detail to be worked on and on the interior of the body. This calls for an approach that must not be disturbed by an everyday, aesthetic perception of the body – which is the perception of "whole" bodies as sensuous entities, particularly in the form of the body's surface! This becomes especially clear when the body is covered again and again, even in interventions which do not require sterility. Moreover, the relationship between (male) doctor and (female) patient has always been subject to special rules of proximity and distance. In the past, doctors demanded that, even on the

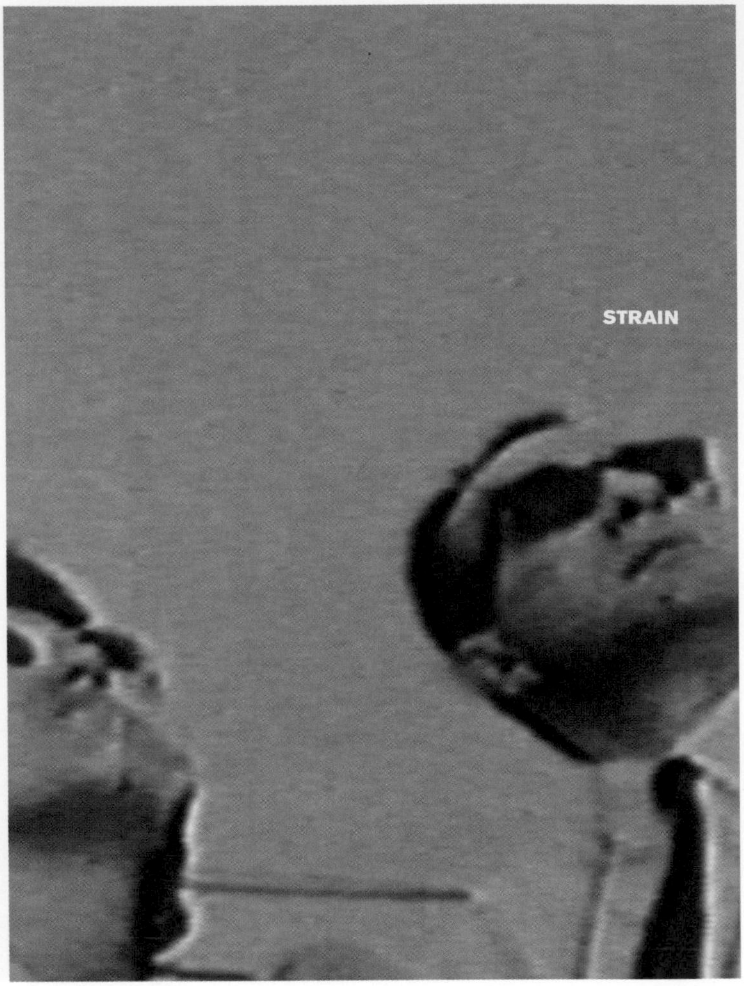

examination table, a woman should never be examined when fully naked. One part of her must always remain clothed or covered over, either her upper body or her lower body. So is it not the clothed part of the patient that stands for the medical discussion carried out between the equal parties of doctor and patient, whereas the unclothed part represents the partitioned region of medical activity? Certainly, one will immediately notice that the relationship between the sexes also plays a significant role here. This complicates the doctor-patient relationship even further, but only in the sense in which it renders it radical on an aesthetic level. Accordingly, personal physicians of the Middle Ages were not at all permitted to look at the female body to be treated. As is documented by old engravings, the doctor had to feel the body parts in question through the clothing. Even today it is not at all rare for medical students and young doctors to black out during operations. The circulatory collapse that they experience, however, is in no way caused by the physical effort, as those affected often claim. It is, in the true sense of the word, an "aesthetic collapse" in which the medical/technical perception of the interior, of the opened body, cannot be maintained, but rather falls back into the external, everyday aesthetic perception of a continuous, "whole" body which can suddenly only be seen for what it is – a terribly injured body.

The sensuous element in modern Western medicine, based on instruments, is that of the opened cadaver, that of anatomy. The birth of clinical medicine, the birth of the institution of the clinic[4] is to be regarded within this framework. From the very beginning of their activity, anatomists have had to push ahead from an everyday aesthetic of the entire body and its external aspect to the medical/technical internal aspect they regard as being functionally relevant. By doing so, they separated themselves from the bodily symbolisms of archaic medicine and let themselves be guided by the ideas of mechanical models. Already centuries ago, they advanced to the boundaries of the macroscopically visible and, led by their mechanical world of ideas, created a closed, functional model of the structures of the human body which to this day appears timeless. Not least, the systematics of the anatomically visible, which was closed already at a very early stage, led Hegel to deny anatomy the status of a science because it did not include new areas of knowledge, but rather merely carried on what had already been developed and systematically closed.[5] It can come as no surprise, either, that macroscopic anatomy today no longer occupies an important place in medicine. The universal practice of autopsying corpses is being rejected by the very representatives of pathological anatomy themselves and limited to special, individually relevant questions. Anatomy today has finally assumed the status of being medically self-evident.

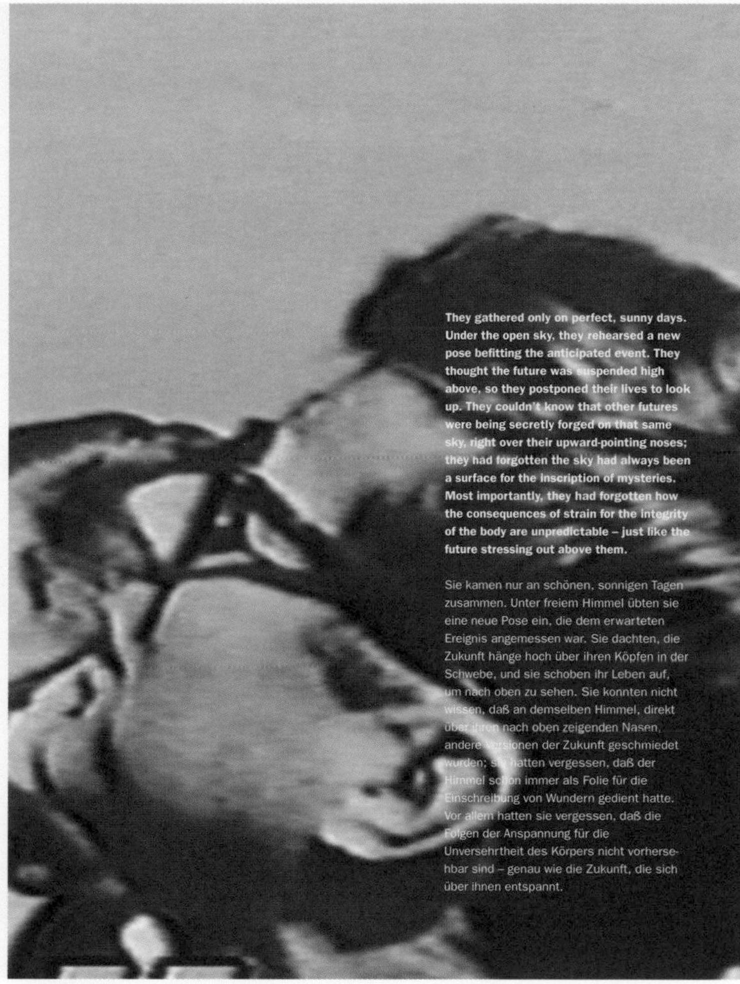

They gathered only on perfect, sunny days. Under the open sky, they rehearsed a new pose befitting the anticipated event. They thought the future was suspended high above, so they postponed their lives to look up. They couldn't know that other futures were being secretly forged on that same sky, right over their upward-pointing noses; they had forgotten the sky had always been a surface for the inscription of mysteries. Most importantly, they had forgotten how the consequences of strain for the integrity of the body are unpredictable – just like the future stressing out above them.
Sie kamen nur an schönen, sonnigen Tagen zusammen. Unter freiem Himmel übten sie eine neue Pose ein, die dem erwarteten Ereignis angemessen war. Sie dachten, die Zukunft hänge hoch über ihren Köpfen in der Schwebe, und sie schoben ihr Leben auf, um nach oben zu sehen. Sie konnten nicht wissen, daß an demselben Himmel, direkt über ihren nach oben zeigenden Nasen, andere Versionen der Zukunft geschmiedet wurden; sie hatten vergessen, daß der Himmel schon immer als Folie für die Einschreibung von Wundern gedient hatte. Vor allem hatten sie vergessen, daß die Folgen der Anspannung für die Unversehrtheit des Körpers nicht vorhersehbar sind – genau wie die Zukunft, die sich über ihnen entspannt.

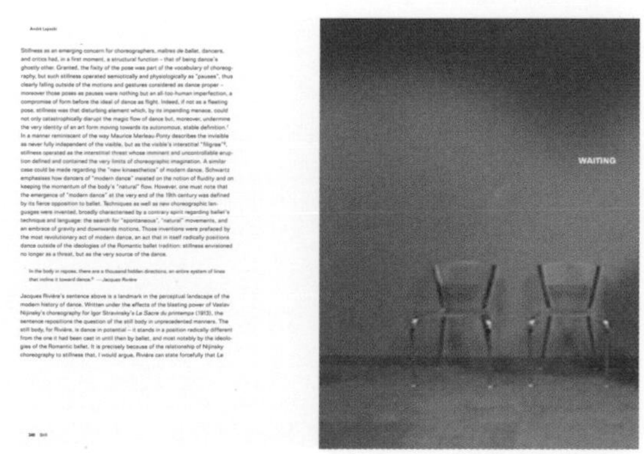

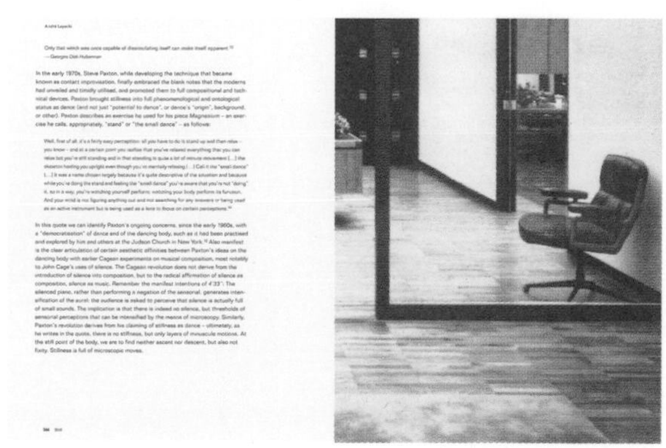

312

Growth as an Event

If the twentieth century can be said to have faced a problem, it was without question the problem of speed. Speed has limits, and we spent the century finding and testing them. The blitzkrieg, the autobahn, the Olympics, Formula One, breaking the sound barrier, the speed of manufacture, of computation, of communication: all these modes of acceleration generated quantities on a scale the world had never seen. Speed has worked its way into every facet of design experience. Its visual codes of seamless, sleek, aerodynamic surfaces and precarious balances have shaped our social and physical environments such that everything from the countertop blender to the Concorde to CNN is measured by its velocity.

As we enter the twenty-first century, I believe that the new problem facing us will be growth. As both designers and global citizens we will need to broach this problem in different ways. We will need to test the limits of growth.

Growth, as I see it, is a problem separate from speed and "more" and reproduction. Growth is a time-based event, with breaking points and moments of rupture that generate entirely new conditions. Growth is nonlinear and unpredictable. This is important to emphasize. Many of us have come to see growth as the uninterrupted telos of progress. Few of us are ready to admit that growth is constantly shadowed by its constitutive opposite, that it is equal partners with death.

U.S. Navy Hornet fighter breaks through the sound barrier, July 1999

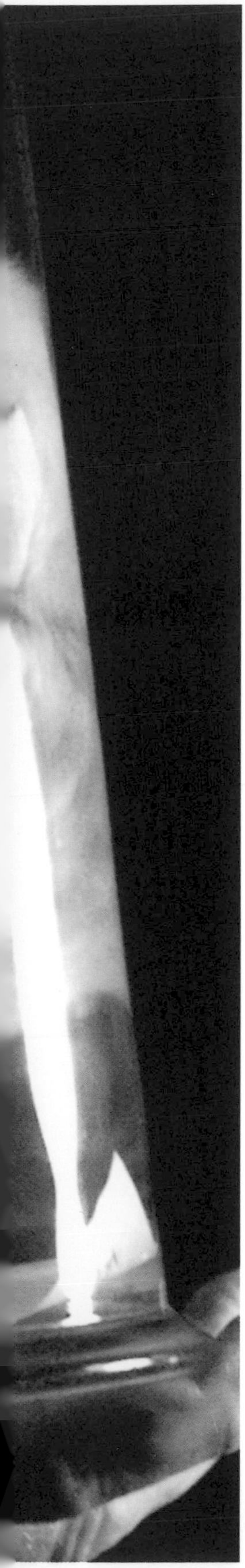

Immersed in the logic of growth, we have, for the most part, denied the liberating potential of death. (For us, there is only addition, never subtraction; accumulation, never decay.) In our shortsightedness, we have banished death both from nature and from our approach to design practice. We seem unable to let go of even the obvious corpses — first in the name of quality, then history, then nostalgia. Even second-rate substance is inflated with significance. We are like taxidermists. We preserve the skin and stuff the remains with modern infrastructure. The result is depressingly inauthentic.

If we look at how growth behaves in nature, we see it coupled with a phenomenon of clearing. Forest fires produce a cycle of life and regeneration. Spring follows the barrenness of winter. Death opens up fields of potential. I increasingly believe that the future of design rests in our ability and willingness to develop new practices and theories of form that are inextricably linked to, and informed by, life and growth. As we observe the life of the object, and the effect of that object on the life around it, we may learn that growth is not about limits in the same way that speed was, because growth is about qualities, not quantities. More precisely, it is about the qualities — wild and incalculable — that emerge from quantities.

By using DNA chip technology, Australian scientists hope to clone an extinct Tasmanian tiger pup preserved in a jar of alcohol. The last of the Tasmanian tigers died in 1936 after they were hunted down by settlers.

Design Culture
***I.D.* magazine**
New York, 1992–1993
I acted as creative director of *I.D.* magazine for eleven issues. I was approached not just to redesign the magazine but to participate in its editorial reinvention. One of my goals as the creative director was to think through the definition of design in the broadest possible terms—not to exclude the business and marketing of design, but to understand them as elements within a cultural definition of design.

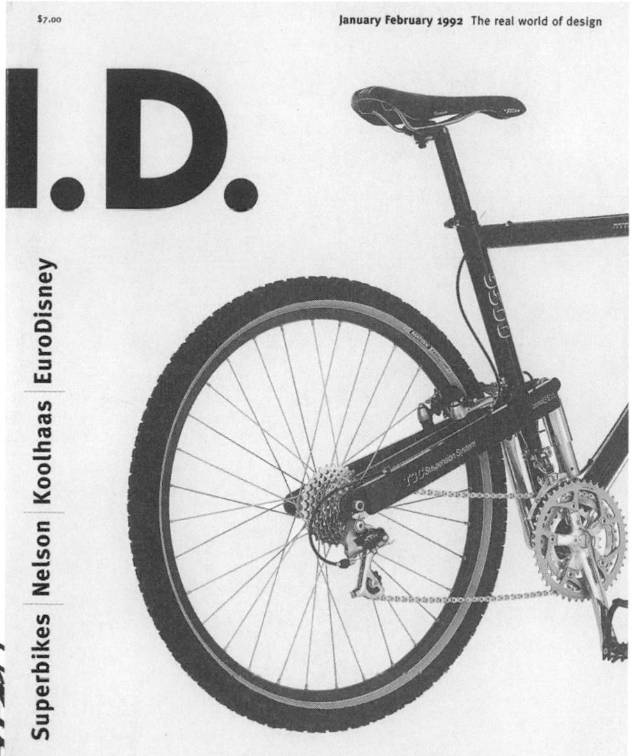
$7.00
January February 1992 The real world of design
I.D.
Superbikes | Nelson | Koolhaas | EuroDisney

I.D.
The 38th Annual Design Review
The International Design Magazine
Products
Graphics
Environments
Packaging
Furniture
Equipment
Concepts
Student Work
July August 1992

The International Design Magazine
$7 November December 1992
I.D.
LESS THAN 10% OF ALL SEXUAL HARASSMENT VICTIMS EVER COME FORWARD
NO WONDER
Graphic Activism
Karrie Jacobs watches WAC
Birth of the UnChrysler
Michael Sorkin on Cartoon Cities
The Business of Design

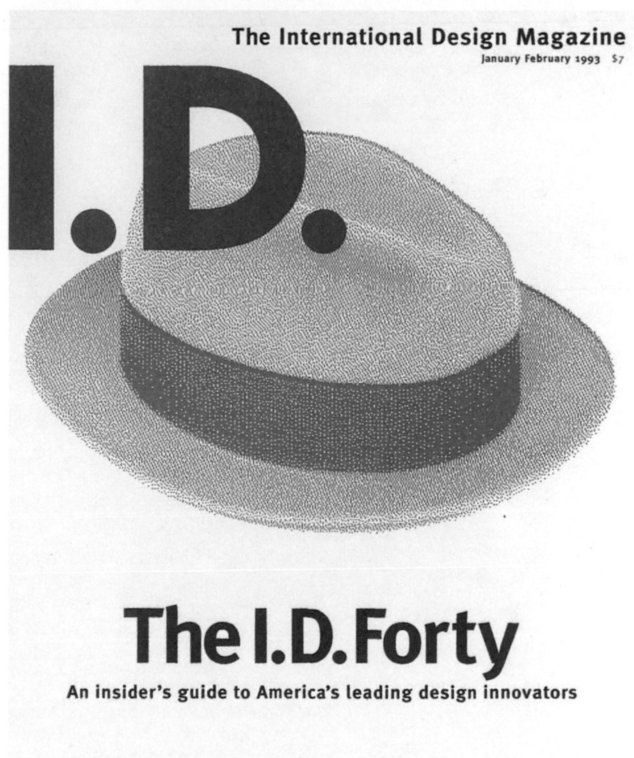
The International Design Magazine
January February 1993 $7
I.D.
The I.D. Forty
An insider's guide to America's leading design innovators

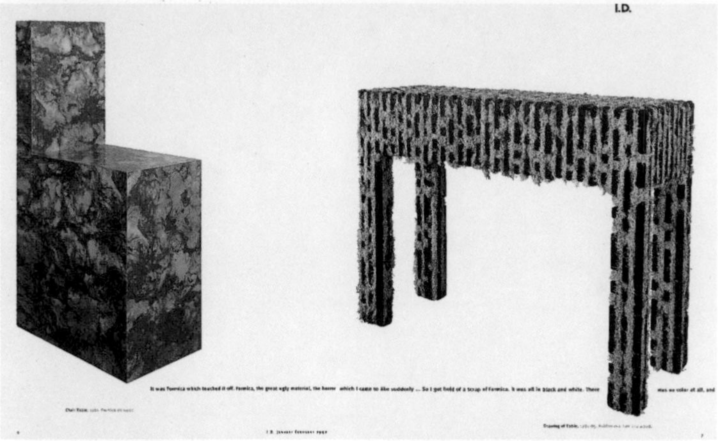

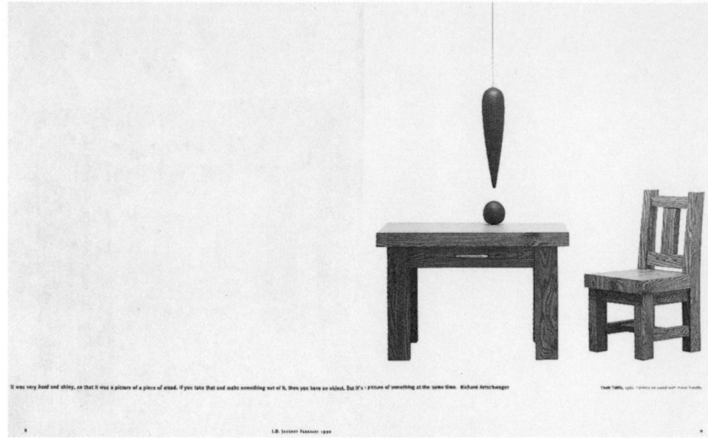

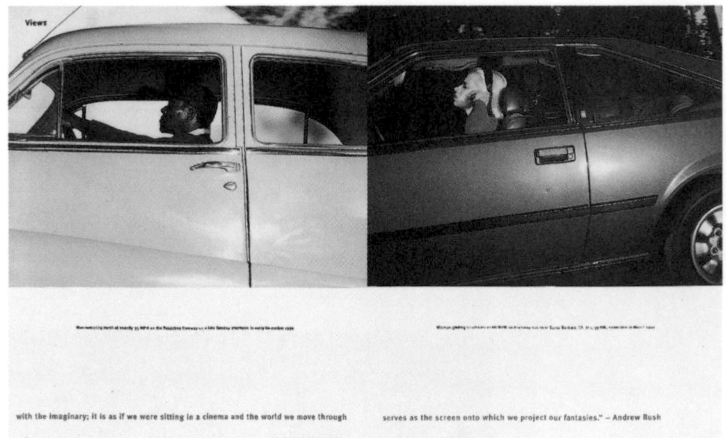

We initiated a four-page feature before the contents page that served to introduce projects that linked design to other cultural practices. As shown on these spreads, artist Richard Artschwager makes work based on the iconography of furniture and typography; Andrew Bush produced a photo project of automobile culture in Los Angeles; and Nancy Rubins assembles her work from the flotsam and jetsam of our manufactured world.

Views

"I started using appliances in mass quantities in 1977. Thousands of them. I'd get them from Goodwill for 50 cents a piece. I was fascinated with them, with the designs, the plastics, the knobs. There were so many of these products and they were all so remarkable, so diverse. There were so many things with so much love put into them. But somehow there was a sense of having so much and not ever being satisfied.

"Around the same time I started using concrete. I had just moved to San Francisco, where I saw my first earthquake. I was living in a loft and I looked out the back and watched as a building started moving like water. It looked as though a wave was moving through it. So I started making walls using products as bricks and concrete as mortar. I wanted to make walls that would sway back and forth when you touched them."

NANCY RUBINS

"Worlds Apart," 1982. Concrete, steel and appliances; approximately 40 feet high.
Commissioned by the Washington Project for the Arts, Washington, D.C.

7

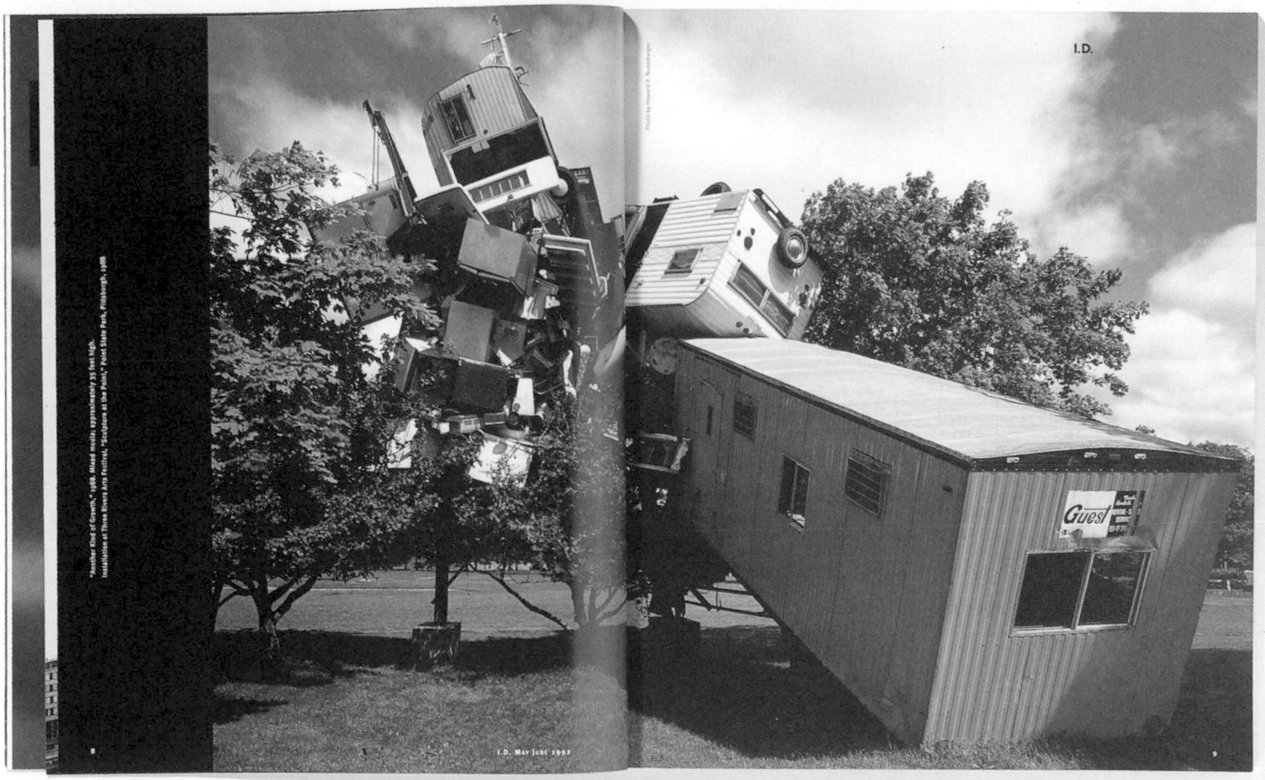

I.D.

"Another Kind of Growth," 1988. Mixed media; approximately 35 feet high.
Installation at Three Rivers Arts Festival, "Sculpture at the Point," Point State Park, Pittsburgh, 1988

8

I.D. May June 1997

9

I.D.
Contents
The I.D. Forty
Charting Power
by Nigel Holmes

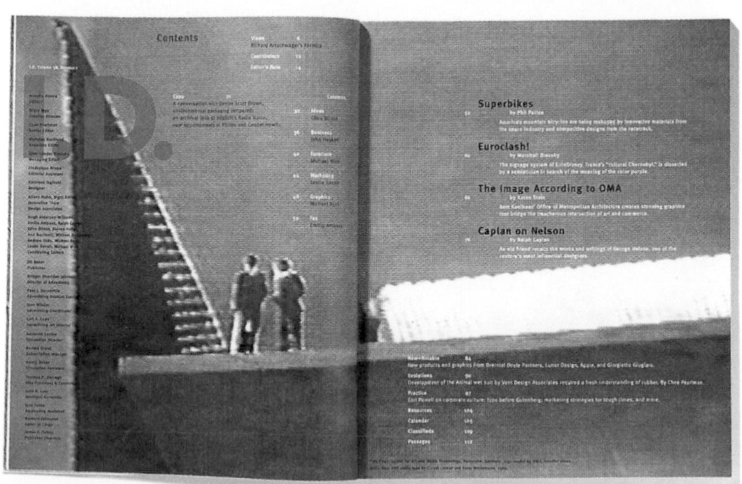
Contents
I.D.
Superbikes
by Phil Patton
Euroclash!
The Image According to OMA
Caplan on Nelson

I.D.
I.D. Volume 39, Number 2
Annetta Hanna
Editor
Bruce Mau
Creative Director
Chee Pearlman
Senior Editor
Nicholas Backlund
Associate Editor
Ellen Lander Brodsky
Managing Editor
Frederique Krupa
Editorial Assistant
Kathleen Oginski
Designer
Alison Hahn, Nigel Smith, Greg Van Alstyne
Design Associates
Joanne Corson
Production Assistant
Hugh Aldersey-Williams, Emilio Ambasz, Ralph Caplan, Clive Dilnot, Steven Heller, Ann Marinelli, Michael McDonough, Andrew Olds, Michael Rock, Leslie Savan, Michael Wolf
Contributing Editors
Barbara Jakobson
Editor at Large
Jill Bokor
Publisher
Bridget Sheridan Johnson
Director of Advertising
Paul J. Sasseville
Advertising Account Executive
Lisa A. Broadbend
Classified Advertising Manager
Lori A. Ende
Advertising Art Director
Adrienne Levine
Circulation Director
Donald Crowl
Subscription Manager
Nancy Baker
Circulation Assistant
Thomas P. Darragh
Vice President & Controller
John R. Loor
Assistant Controller
Jose Colon
Accounting Assistant
James F. Fulton
Publisher Emeritus
I.D. Magazine
250 West 57th Street, Suite 215
New York, NY 10107
Tel 212.956.0535
Fax 212.246.3891 Editorial
Fax 212.246.3925 Advertising & Circulation
I.D. (ISSN 0894-5373) is published bimonthly by International Design Holdings, L.P. at 250 West 57th Street, New York, NY 10107. Copyright c 1992 International Design Holdings, L.P. All rights reserved. Second Class Postage paid at New York, NY, and additional mailing offices All material is compiled from sources believed to be reliable, but published without responsibility for errors or omissions. I.D. assumes no responsibility for unsolicited manuscripts or photographs. Return postage should accompany such material. Nothing in this publication may be copied or reproduced without the prior written permission of the publisher. I.D. is a trademark owned exclusively by International Design Holdings, L.P. Send subscription orders, inquiries and postmaster address changes to I.D., P.O. Box 11247, Des Moines, IA 50340-1247 or call 1-800-284-3728. Subscription rates: $55 in the U.S.A., $60 in Canada (GST included), $70 in Europe. Member: Magazine Publishers Association, Association of Business Publishers, Audit Bureau of Circulations.
Expo
An archival look at
the ecological stat
Umberto Eco on so
nanotechnology —
Blue Note style, an
Advertising Representative for Europe
Michael Benevento
12 rue Popincourt #F
75011 Paris France
Tel 014.357.1358

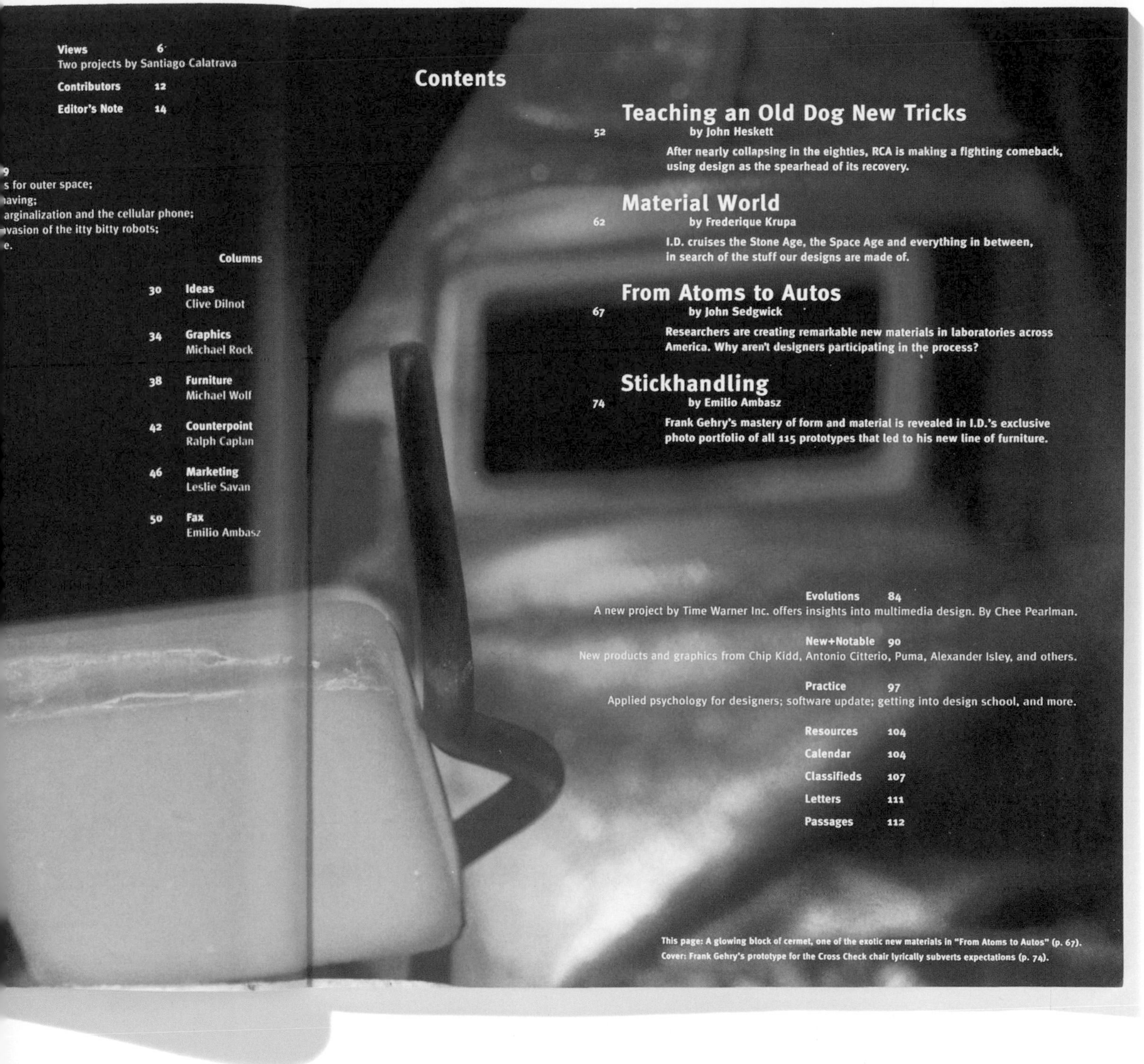

Contents

This page: A glowing block of cermet, one of the exotic new materials in "From Atoms to Autos" (p. 67).
Cover: Frank Gehry's prototype for the Cross Check chair lyrically subverts expectations (p. 74).

The contents page presents the editorial structure of the magazine superimposed on an image from one of the features.

The I.D. Forty

Donald Moffett and Marlene McCarty of Bureau, New York's most outspoken and politically militant graphic design firm.

language (first hinted at in the Duo computer) in a new range of products due out this fall. Of course, this time expectations are much higher than when Esslinger unveiled his "Snow White" approach to an unsophisticated computer market nine years ago. Without question Brunner faces a tough critique.

Yet the designer remains secure in the knowledge that his new "dream team" will work with the agility of a fast-paced consultancy and not a herd of corporate drones. As technologies converge and markets tighten, it will take a strong team captain to sustain the Apple vision we've all come to expect. Now if only a few more companies would play as hard as Apple. C.P.

Design that Acts Up

BUREAU

Marlene McCarty and Donald Moffett do things. This is a very refreshing idea to those of us who spend a lot of time thinking and talking about doing things.

McCarty and Moffett are activists and collectivists par excellence, who together form a small studio called Bureau. They are both members of the art collective Gran Fury. McCarty is a leading member and designer for the Women's Action Coalition (see I.D., Nov./Dec. '92), Moffett has worked with ACT-UP, an AIDS activist group. Between these volunteer activities, McCarty has found time to create a show of some bumper-sticker slogan paintings at the Metro Pictures gallery in SoHo; Moffett has put together an installation for the New Museum; they have jointly wheat pasted a few agit-prop posters around the city; they have designed some public service spots for MTV...

Designer/propagandists McCarty and Moffett don't separate their work from their world. Any graphic designer will appreciate the difficulty of this position. Design lubricates their messages, which are a collision between an aware, trendy surface and fed-up, fight-back content. If politics is the art of the possible, McCarty and Moffett are political masters. M.R.

Back-to-the-Future Plans for America

PETER CALTHORPE

Architect and urban planner Peter Calthorpe is poised to realize a vision for taming America's sprawling exurban landscape. As co-author of the section in the Clinton-Gore transition document on land-use planning, Calthorpe has put much thought into the matter. Indeed, he has already had great success writing regional plans for San Diego, Sacramento and Portland, Oregon that are now being implemented.

Calthorpe's plans foresee a radiating web of mass-transit lines that lead to dense, exurban communities that revolve around a transit stop. From there, a shopping street typically leads to a community facility, such as a library, bandstand or police station. Then residential streets radiate out again, modulating their geometries according to the feature of landscape. "We need to have new models for a new, human-scaled environment," he emphasizes.

Luckily, the times seem to be with Calthorpe. Even Southern California is building a $200 billion mass-transit system that will provide the vital transportation net ideal for his plan to be put into effect. And current economic and environmental restraints will inevitably necessitate the planning of denser developments.

Calthorpe is unabashed about how this small-town vision is rooted in traditional American grid-iron plans. "It worked," he concludes, "while the Modernist vision of Frank Lloyd Wright didn't." A.A.B.

Controlled Chaos in Our Times

DAVID CARSON

Rumor has it that David Carson's work on the short-lived Californian surfing magazine *Beach Culture* has won over 150 design awards. Quite an achievement for a former sociology teacher who had just six months' formal training as a graphic designer before going out to art direct four magazines and earn himself a cult following and the dubious title of "leading proponent of the post-*Emigre* style."

Exactly what the "post" is supposed to mean is open to question. Carson initially used Emigre fonts in *Beach Culture* and employed some of designer Rudy Vanderlans' layout techniques, such as distorting and overlapping type with fractured and deteriorated images. But by the "Special No Emigre Font Issue" of the magazine, he had switched to more conventional faces, claiming that *Emigre*'s were no longer "fresh."

Certainly the playground for Carson's work is not *Emigre*'s world of jumbled communication, but the worlds of surfing, skateboarding and alternative music. As his latest magazine, *Ray Gun*, demonstrates, Carson's achievement is in homing in on the mood of the moment and coordinating a team of designers — 11 are credited in *Ray Gun*, including eight font designers — to sustain it in a magazine. *Beach Culture*'s typographic antics conveyed, as William Owen put it in *Modern Magazine Design*, the "vicarious sensual pleasures of Valley children." *Ray Gun*, with its smudged, overlayed, obliterated text, over-enlarged photographs and appropriated illustrations, communicates the key aspirations of the alternative music scene. Yet as if to prove he can switch gears, Carson is also at work on the '94 Chevy Camaro print ad campaign. "It's based on *Ray Gun*," he says about the campaign, "but it won't be as all over the place." P.H.

His beach days behind him, graphic designer David Carson now art directs *Ray Gun*.

The Clever Type

MATTHEW CARTER

Font designer Matthew Carter confesses a propensity for extremely condensed typefaces, which is not so odd considering he sort of resembles one — very narrow and upright with something of a decorative serif of long gray hair at the top.

Every time you open the White Pages, you see one of Carter's typefaces. Bell Centennial was designed to reduce the size and paper consumption of the telephone book while increasing legibility. Bell is typical of the level

Renowned font designer Matthew Carter reads the writing on the wall.

48 I.D. JANUARY FEBRUARY 1993 49

The I.D. Forty

Learning to Read the Hard Way

EMIGRE

Emigre comes out four times a year. In almost every issue, editor and designer Rudy Vanderlans figures out a new way to ask the same old question: when theory and technology are radically changing the way we communicate in print, what constitutes legibility? Or, in other words, *can you read this?*

The answer, at least on one level, usually takes the following form: Vanderlans introduces a new typeface, often (but not always) designed by his partner Zuzana Licko. At first glance the font appears unreadable, sometimes disturbingly so. Then, about one-and-a-half pages in, you realize with a start that you're actually — simply — reading it. As Licko says, "You read best what you read most."

One wonders, then, how many people actually *read Emigre*. The magazine's horrified critics, both public and private, are too busy railing against its barbaric assault on the verities of Modernism to curl up with it along with their bedtime cocoas. Its fans, on the other hand, often savor the frisson of the form without delving into the content.

Too bad, because Vanderlans is doing some of the best reporting around on today's emerging graphic designers. While academics can't seem to discuss the work of designers like Barry Deck, Jeffrey Keedy, Hard Werken and Thirst without smothering them first in a thick sauce of French linguistic theory, Vanderlans simply asks reasonable questions. "Are you making typefaces ugly on purpose?" he asks Keedy (*Emigre* #15). "Is it not inevitable that a sameness will surface as a direct result from working so closely together?" he asks a group of Cranbrook students (*Emigre* #19). Or just, "What do you think Valicenti means with that type on the bottom?" (*Emigre* #13). The answers are as refreshing as the questions.

Issue after issue, Vanderlans and Licko are reshaping the ways in which we view, and think, about the printed page. *Emigre* has become a vital contribution to graphic design's critical discourse. People who don't like it should consider starting their own damn magazines. M.B.

Playing on Emotions

HARTMUT ESSLINGER

Maybe it's time to cut Hartmut Esslinger a little slack. Sure, some would say frogdesign's CEO has had quite enough cut already. From his $2 million contract with Apple Computer in the early '80s to his comparably lucrative deal with Steve Job's NeXT, industrial design's flamboyant iconoclast has carved a comfortable niche for himself in America's conservative corporate terrain. He's also generated more than his share of controversy.

But despite stories of temperamental outbursts this German-born designer continues to be one of the most influential product designers of our age. In contrast to his peers in America's established design firms, Esslinger opted for splashiness and visibility from the beginning (his Altensteig, Germany, office was opened in 1969, his California office in 1982). Despite his northern birthplace, high emotion is the language of choice for this designer. "Who," he has demanded, "wants to be clean and quiet?"

It's tough to argue with the impact frog has had on the design profession in this country. Both the firm's "Snow White" design language for Apple and its NeXT computers are considered icons of contemporary design, and the company continues to offer large corporate clients like AT&T and IBM design inspiration with single-product programs. Silicon Valley companies like Logitech, Sun and the recent start-up EO have based their product lines on frog's clarity and expressiveness of design.

Of course Esslinger's high visibility has raised hackles among some designers. There is resentment of his high-priced fees and aggressive style. "If we can't talk to the company CEO," Esslinger brashly asserted in a *BusinessWeek* profile a few years ago, "we're gone the next day."

But that same visibility has meant that when frog has made mistakes they don't go unnoticed. Esslinger himself was among the first to renounce his involvement in the ill-fated Frox sound system, a venture that just about cost him his company.

But Frox proved a sobering experience, and since recovering Esslinger has redoubled his passion for design — and has perhaps even mellowed. A new generation of product and graphic designers in California is working at top capacity, producing some of the firm's strongest work and generating record revenues (the company claims $13 million in billings worldwide). "He still stirs up the pot and makes people work harder," says vice president Dan Harden of his boss. "But we all are aware of a standard to be reached, so it's a team effort."

Esslinger has always acted on the belief that design can be truly influential to companies and society, and he has undoubtedly paved the way for others to insist on fidelity to their designs, charge higher fees and go straight to the CEO. His brashness has done more to empower today's designers than they may acknowledge. Perhaps it's time they stop acting so scandalized. K.C.

Hartmut Esslinger, controversial founder of frogdesign, avoiding the limelight (right); frog's design for the EO personal communicator (top).

The King of Zing

ED FELLA

Remarkably catchy phrases crop up wherever graphic designer Ed Fella goes; as a commercial artist in Detroit, he was referred to as the "King of Zing." Yet after 30 years experience in this capacity, Fella went to study at the Cranbrook Academy, where he found his profession already embraced by post-Modern theory. "I was the vernacular!" he once told a friend. "I was like those people that Robert Venturi wrote about, right?"

Although it seems radical for a successful commerical artist to go to school at the age of 47 and immerse himself in the application of Deconstruction and French critical theory to graphic design, his work actually changed very little. The pithy wit, the scratchy ink illustrations, the clip art and the idiosyncratic typography are all still there. He always did think that Swiss Modernism was "just another style"; by going to Cranbrook and CalArts (where he now teaches), he simply "legitimized" his experimentation.

Fella is fast becoming the intellectual's designer, which admittedly may leave the uninitiated somewhat baffled by the quirky, messy, mad scribbles he calls designs. His

CalArts' Ed Fella has made his mark with post-Modern wit and scratchy ink design.

52 I.D. JANUARY FEBRUARY 1993 53

For the introduction of "The I.D. Forty" feature we had no time or money to commission forty portraits, so we sent every designer a roll of black-and-white Polaroid slide film and asked him or her to produce a self portrait.

Alex Isley, a growing talent.

Tibor Kalman, a design giant.

Furniture insider and outsider, Bill Stumpf.

ture market is separated into contract and residential markets with design emphasis only on the contract market. "No one is involved in serious residential design," he says. "There is no research institute, no body of information, no academic studies. Only an excess of decorative furnishings."

Ironically, Stumpf was called back to research the home by Herman Miller. Company founder D.J. De Pree's health had deteriorated with old age, and his son, Max De Pree, wanted to make a combination work and leisure environment that was flexible and supremely functional. The future of furniture design, according to Stumpf, depends on the ability of companies such as Herman Miller to launch cross-over designs that function in both residential and office environments.

Due to the recession, however, interest in developing the products suggested by Stumpf's "Metabolic Home" project has fallen off. But Stumpf holds out hope that someone will eventually adopt the work, since his "Ethospace" system, launched in 1985, was also the product of a protracted six-year-long research project. L.Y.

Battling the 55-MPH Behemoth

Dan Sturges and Trans 2

Following a stint at GM's Pontiac II exterior design studio and a year and a half in Silicon Valley at frogdesign, Dan Sturges has spent the better part of half a decade pursuing his personal vision: the development and production of low-speed electrical vehicles for short-distance use. The company he helped found, Trans 2, based in Farmington Hills, Michigan, is now finishing third-stage prototypes for a design distinguished by its innovative body architecture. "We're not just retrofitting automobiles for electric power," he says of the car that his company will not only develop and design, but engineer, assemble and market. While the new car is intended to supplement conventional automobiles, not replace them, Sturges is nevertheless thinking big. "It's personal transportation designed from a global perspective."

Though the project has attracted considerable interest from regional transit authorities in California's traffic-choked big cities,

Dan Sturges (fourth from left) and colleagues (left to right) Craig Padlo, Rick Morgal, Keith Sprague, Bill MacAdam, Jeff Brown, Doug Query and Brian Nelson.

Sturges has run into some hurdles. "A lot of them tell us we can't sell a car that can't go up against all those 55-MPH freeway behemoths," he says. "Our answer is that with slight modifications of existing commuter corridors along the bike-path model, you can create an environment that's friendly to lighter vehicles."

With several major corporations as developmental allies, a core group of investors and orders in hand, Trans 2 is on schedule to begin production of a new class of environmental electric cars in 1994. Sturges is keeping publicity to a minimum until the launch of the car, although he will say the vehicle will be "low-cost, reliable, safe, easy to use, attractive, offer unique features and be fun to drive." Stay tuned. K.C.

Express Yourself

Thirst

A word from Thirst.

If there is one look that has spread across the visual landscape faster than you can click a mouse, it is the look associated with Rick Valicenti's Chicago-based consultancy Thirst. Now dozens of firms are plundering the electronic media for imagery and inspiration, hot on the trail of Thirst's stylized manipulation of visual sound bites and unfocused video images adorned with bit-mapped or runelike type.

Tibor Kalman once argued that Thirst's work "starts from language rather than from a style." The remark acknowledges the importance of Valicenti and copywriter Todd Lief's wordplay and sloganeering as much as it emphasizes the fact that Thirst's work is more of a personal manifesto than a rigorous exposition of the Deconstruction theory that is so popular nowadays. Since its founding in 1988, Thirst has shown with companies such as Steelcase, AGI DigiPak, Cooper Lighting and Gilbert Paper that corporate clients are ready to ditch their besuited problem-solving consultants to work with designers who put self-expression first.

In the case of this designer, self-expression is the driving engine of the studio's visual language. Valicenti's personal artwork turns up unexpectedly in an array of client commissions. As for the old argument about what is art and what is design, Valicenti is a master at blurring the lines. P.H.

Modernism the Old-World Way

Reinhold Weiss

One of the last of the true Modernists, German-born product designer Reinhold Weiss may be the ultimate outsider. Trained at the famed Ulm Hochschule für Gestaltung in the late 1950s, Weiss has produced an amazing series of design classics, including work for Braun in Germany and Unimark, Acoustic Research, NAD and Proton in the U.S. Yet he remains an enigma, shunning the

Writer-designer-educator Lorraine Wild teaches at CalArts and maintains her L.A. studio, ReVerb.

spotlight in favor of the corporate boardroom, where until recently he served as design director and vice president at Proton. "Unless designers influence product development at the very top of the corporation," says Weiss, "our work can easily slip into mere decoration."

Reinhold Weiss' high-Ulm look Proton stereo.

Uncompromising in all aspects of life and work, Weiss avoids design conferences, refuses most interviews, has no photos of himself and quit the IDSA years ago because the group seemed too commercial. "No one wanted to talk about improving the level of design in this country," he says, "only how to promote themselves, get jobs and charge as much as possible." Currently, the solitary German spends long hours in his Evanston, Illinois, studio working on designs for the start-up electronics firm AMC, which he predicts will succeed in the 1990s the way NAD and Proton did in the 1980s: by responding to users' needs. "Good design is only possible by focusing on the user and making the product as simple and self-explanatory as possible. Anything less," he sniffs, "is just marketing." C.P.

Woman of Substance

Lorraine Wild

In talking to Lorraine Wild, she will often describe herself as a "fan" of some piece of graphics she admires. The word makes you pause. Wild studied at Cranbrook and Yale and for seven years she was the program director at CalArts. She writes courageous, closely argued essays like the one "On Overcoming Modernism" in last September's I.D. Yet despite the rigor of her work and thought, she retains a fan's enthusiasm for the best of the paper stuff that brought her into the discipline.

It is routine in our culture to hear how the image has supplanted the word; many designers are only too anxious to believe this. Not Wild: "I'm a really avid reader," she says. The book is her specialty. In her designs for volumes on the Californian Case Study Houses and the British Independent Group, Wild shows a rare talent for creating pages that look casual and full of energy, while being flawlessly planned. She takes rich subjects and makes them richer and more engaging in the telling, and she has an acute sense of pictorial relationship and rhythm. Her post-Cranbrook typeface combos are quirky, but apt.

Graphic designer Jeffrey Keedy, Wild's friend and now program director at CalArts (where she continues to teach) labels her a "neo-functionalist." But that's just fine with Wild. "I think the choices that I make are based on my understanding of the necessities of a project," she says, "to which I then bring a kind of interpretation — but that interpretation is always extremely specific."

Wild belongs to a small but growing group of women writer-designer-educators who are creating a vital discourse on the purposes, history and meaning of graphic design. Is anyone listening? Wild sometimes has her doubts, but cleaves to the task. "I guess what I'm fascinated by are the contradictions in the rhetoric of graphic design," she says. With her four colleagues in her studio, ReVerb, based in Los Angeles, Wild is making work of valuable intelligence. This is design not just as the vehicle of ideas, but as their living medium. R.P. ▲

For a resource listing of the I.D. Forty, see page 88.

The Life and Times
of Osunkemi

In the first two years of my daughter's life she traveled to these cities: Boston, Houston, Los Angeles, Madrid, Milan, Montreal, New York, Paris, Toledo, Toronto, Vancouver, and Winnipeg.
In the first seventeen years of my life I traveled to this city: Sudbury.

Extras

Pop in Orbit
Design Exchange
Toronto, 1995
Bruce Mau Design collaborated with curator Rachel Gottlieb and Toronto's Design Exchange on an exhibition, *Pop in Orbit*, which dealt with the design culture of the 1960s Space Race. Featuring home-entertainment design, furniture, fashion, product designs, and visionary architectural projects, *Pop in Orbit* simultaneously celebrated and criticized the cultural artifacts of the period. Objects were displayed on "islands" made of period materials such as fake fur, vinyl, and reflective Mylar. Clusters of display graphics illuminated the five major themes of the exhibition: "Brave New Living," "Sex and the Single Stereo(type)," "Galactic Girls," "Bubble Vision," and "Balls in Motion." The installation culminated with a video of compiled TV and movie clips presented in a room stuffed with purple and silver beanbag chairs.

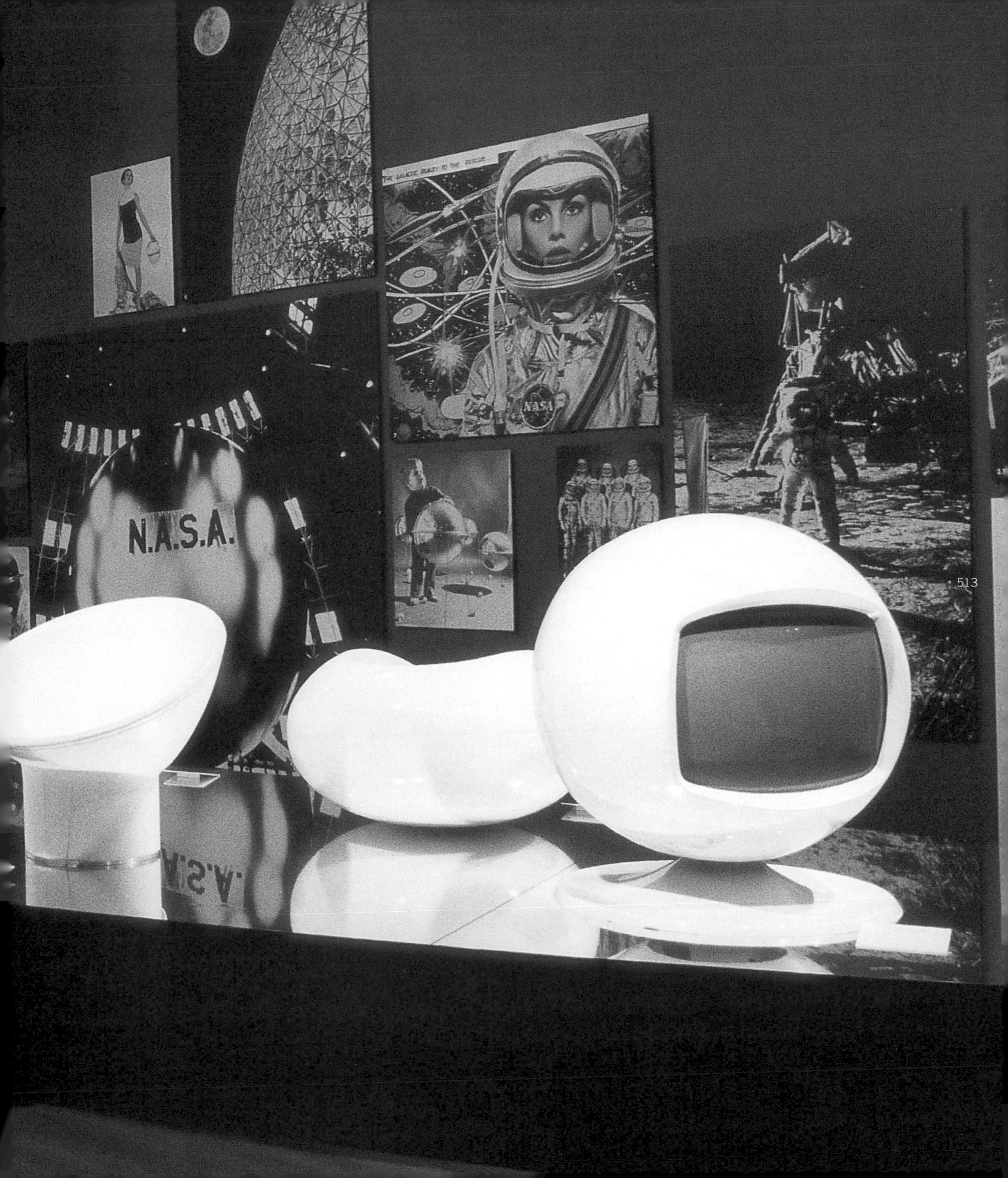
N.A.S.A.
NASA

Galactic
Girl
In The Sun
THE GALACTIC GIRL

N.A.S.A.

Pop in Orbit
Pop in Orbit

In the 1960s, Canada was a leader in industrial design and produced advanced projects in several areas. *Pop in Orbit* documented the rise and development, then the crash and burn, of that Canadian industry. The exhibition ended with a large photographic image of Buckminster Fuller's 1967 Montreal Expo geodesic dome engulfed in flames: a tragic real-history punctuation to the era.

Genextrapolation™
Futuristic Advertisement for Eugenics
***The New York Times Magazine*, 1996**

The New York Times Magazine produced a special issue written from a futuristic perspective. Contemporary historians and critics were asked to write articles under the premise that this was the year 2027, and they were looking back over the previous thirty years. The studio was invited to design an advertisement to be inserted in an article on genetic engineering. For the advertisement, we invented a company, Genextrapolation™, that claimed to provide services to ensure a genetically "perfect" baby. We designed the company, its product, its logo, its niche market, and its confident, upbeat slogan.

Why depend on his background, when you can screen-test her foreground?
genextrapolation™
We bring good life to life.

Love Connection

I returned to Canada in 1983 with my art school friend Elisabeth Matheson and her boyfriend, Steven Bock, drummer in the band TBA, which once opened for the B-52's. We had no money, no contacts, and no clients, so we started a business. For two years we shared an apartment that doubled as the offices and studios of a company we called Public Good. We all worked in one small room, along with our only employee. Together we made enormous efforts to maintain an air of professionalism. We dressed formally—black suit, white shirt and tie—even

Elisabeth. When it came to holding what we called "management meetings," which we took with absolute rigor every weekday at four p.m., there were only two possibilities: my bedroom, or the room that Liz and Steve shared. Since Liz had a television, the choice was obvious. To our lone employee, who was asked sternly to "Hold all calls," these closed-door meetings seemed to be wild affairs with much laughing, hooting, and occasional cheering or groaning. It wasn't until years later that we eventually confessed that "management meeting" was code for an afternoon game show called *Love Connection*.

How to Get Ahead of Advertising

The challenge in finding corporate support for the presentation of leading edge contemporary art is precisely that it is leading edge. For the companies that would sponsor it, the work is problematic in two ways. First, to the degree that it is on the leading edge it is by definition an unknown quantity. The Power Plant presents the latest work from emerging artists, not typically household names. The second problem for sponsors rests with the content of the work itself, which often deals with prickly issues and challenging themes. The strategy for The Power Ten campaign was to find a way to allow business leaders to see that contemporary artists were engaged in what is perhaps the most prized business activity: innovation. By allowing sponsors to support the innovation without attaching it directly to the risk inherent in the work, businesses could support the *idea* of contemporary art, and in the process build national and international awareness for The Power Plant and its programs.

The Power Ten campaign
The Power Plant
Toronto, 1996
The Power Plant is Canada's leading non-collecting contemporary art gallery. It explores the forefront of visual arts expression through exhibitions and education programs. BMD worked on the marketing and advertising campaign to promote fundraising efforts on the occasion of Power Plant's tenth anniversary. In exchange for large annual donations over a three-year period, The Power Plant promoted ten companies as a special sponsor group.

The first year we successfully avoided carrying a string of corporate logos. But by the second year the companies involved insisted their signatures be attached to their philanthropy.

When you dive into a think tank, be sure it has a deep end.

The Power Plant
Contemporary Art Gallery at Harbourfront Centre

Supported by The Power Ten:
Ten visionary companies committed to Canada's leading contemporary art gallery.

A&E Television Network, Bruce Mau Design, CIBC Wood Gundy Securities Inc., Chubb Insurance Company of Canada, The Financial Post Magazine, IBM Canada Ltd., Jackson-Triggs Vintners, Land Rover Canada, Rogers Communications Inc., Spar Aerospace Limited

Together, these companies pursue an uncompromising belief in leading edge creativity and innovative visual art.

Come down to The Power Plant and see what they believe in.
231 Queens Quay West, Toronto, (416) 973-4949

CITY OF EXACERBATED DIFFERENCE© (COED©)

harmony and a degree of homogeneity. The CITY OF

based on the greatest possible difference between its

permanent strategic panic, what counts for the CITY OF

creation of the ideal, but the opportunistic exploitation

model of the CITY OF EXACERBATED DIFFERENCE©

primitiveness of its parts — the paradox is that it is,

ication of any detail requires the readjustment of the

extremes. ASYMMETRY© All phenomena that restore,

without COOPETITION©

structive component that

in the Pearl River Delta

clusion, exclusion, desired

recent communist history

suggests that art should

Pearl River Delta
Insert in *Documenta X: The Book*
Ostfildern-Ruit, Germany: Hatje Cantz Verlag, 1997

"Pearl River Delta, the City of Exacerbated Difference," a thirty-six-page insert in *Documenta X: The Book*, was designed as a radical condensation of research and insights by architect Rem Koolhaas and his Harvard graduate students working in the Pearl River Delta region of China. The pages were subsequently enlarged and displayed as "wallpaper" for the exhibition.

The traditional city strives for a condition of balance,

EXACERBATED DIFFERENCE©, on the contrary, is

parts — complementary or competitive. In a climate of

EXACERBATED DIFFERENCE© is not the methodical

of flukes, accidents and imperfections. Though the

appears brutal — to depend on the robustness and

in fact, delicate and sensitive. The slightest modif-

whole to reassert the equilibrium of complementary

maintain or intensify the inequalities that define

no COED©. Newly minted Singaporean word that

competition can have in the Asian context. **BORD**

(PRD) drawn, and re-drawn, open or closed, according

of undesirable elements. **MARKET REALISM©** Is there

and its present idolatry of the Market? Socialist Realism

depict, in the most realistic way, a final condition of

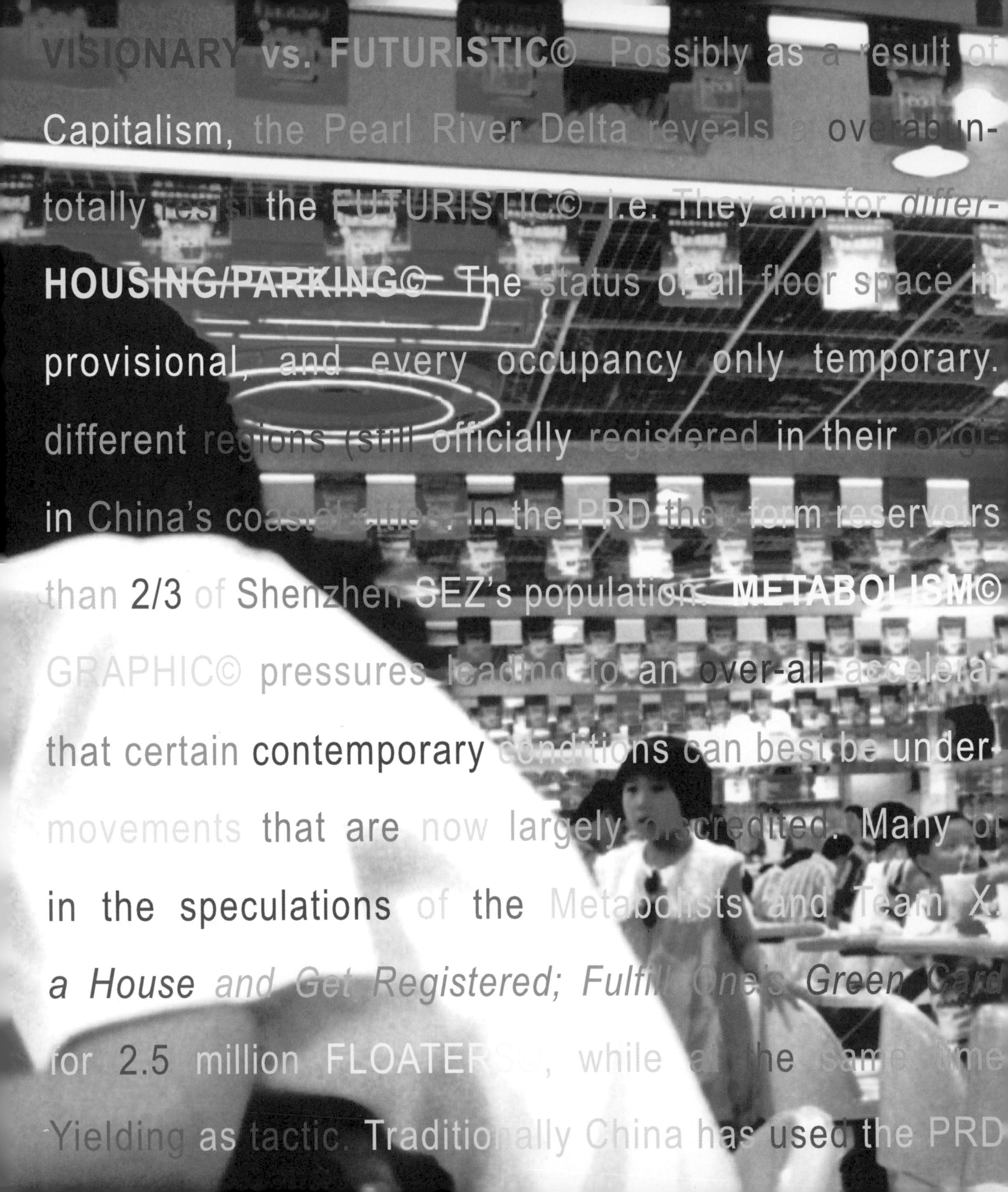

VISIONARY vs. FUTURISTIC© Possibly as a result of
Capitalism, the Pearl River Delta reveals a overabun-
totally resist the FUTURISTIC© i.e. They aim for *differ-*
HOUSING/PARKING© The status of all floor space in
provisional, and every occupancy only temporary.
different regions (still officially registered in their origi-
in China's coastal cities. In the PRD they form reservoirs
than 2/3 of Shenzhen SEZ's population. **METABOLISM©**
GRAPHIC© pressures leading to an over-all accelera-
that certain contemporary conditions can best be under-
movements that are now largely discredited. Many of
in the speculations of the Metabolists and Team X.
a House and Get Registered; Fulfill One's Green Card
for 2.5 million FLOATERS©, while at the same time
Yielding as tactic. Traditionally China has used the PRD

the hybridization of Confucianism, Communism and

dance of **VISIONARY©** projections that paradoxically

ence more than progress. **FACTORY/HOTEL/OFFICE/**

China is generic. Each programmatic function is

FLOATING© A collection of migrants FLOAT© from

nal place of residence) attracted by hyper-development

of unofficial inhabitants. FLOATERS© make up more

A heightened collective effort triggered by DEMO-

tion of the production of urban substance. The paradox

stood through concepts developed by architectural

the phenomena now visible in the PRD were anticipated

GREEN CARD DREAM© Shenzhen's policy of *"Buy*

Dream" allows the immediate establishment of citizenship

boosting the slowing real estate market. **CONCESSION©**

to make CONCESSIONS©: Hong Kong and Macau were

experience. In a subversion of the educational process, and Soviet 'ideas,' and adapts them in order to gain **INFRARED©** Driven underground by the forces of global totalitarian ideology by moving into the invisible spec- compromise and double standard, a preemptory rever- realities of the 21st century. **SCALE©** Planning defines regime of standards that replace hierarchy with impetus. sured by the relative size of each economic absurdity economy measures the success of the open door cam- communist ideology. For the CCP, size is a measure of the present as an era of opportunistic juxtapositions logical puzzle of urban forms and programs. The social as being akin to the PICTURESQUE©; the irrational is beauty in disorder and virtue in the bizarre. **CULTURAL** of NEGLECT©, geographical circumstance, and relent-

China recycles received (often discredited) Western
access to the 'new' (see VISIONARY VS. FUTURISTIC©).
economy, the Chinese Communist Party safeguards its
trum of politics. INFRARED© is a covert strategy of
sal of history that links 19th century idealism with the
the city in terms of number. The CCP introduces a
During Mao's era, ideological commitment was mea-
disaster or famine. In reverse logic, the socialist market
paign' in terms of each victory of the MARKET© over
truth. **LINEAR©** The socialist market economy defines
and uses the LINEAR© city as the blueprint for an ideo-
ist market economy exposes, therefore, the LINEAR©
rationalized, planned according to a logic that finds
DESERT© China's euphemism for the PRD. The result
less ideological campaign. The CULTURAL DESERT© is

ZONE© Imposes limits, but not spatial content. A vague
Party over *city*. Because it is conceptually blank, a
lation. A ZONE© purges historical contents from territo-
with the dynamics of global economy. A ZONE© remains
achieves focus and intensity. ZONE© is the birthplace
Urbanization without a doctrine of the city. If in the
spin-offs of the city, in China, SUBURBIA© is the
city strives for the SUBURBAN©. **RETROFIT©** To
existing structure. Used in the PRD as a strategy to
STEALTH© China's cities aspire to quick growth
the global fame (or is it infamy?) that follows. Cities vic-
Zones — are unable to attract the foreign capital neces-
to prosper. STEALTH© tactics simultaneously quicker
business CHINESES©-style (see CORRUPTION©)
of construction into existence each year in the Pear

term, ZONE© is preferred by the Chinese Communist

ZONE© is open to the impurities of ideological manipu-

ries where they have been imposed, and replaces them

programatically unfulfilled; an urban condition that never

of CHINESE SUBURBIA©. **CHINESE SUBURBIA©**

West, suburban is a derogatory term for unwelcome

essence of urbanization. The newness of the Chinese

install or fit an improvised device or system to repair an

repair anything — architecture, ideology, or politics.

through modernization (see SHENZHEN SPEED©), and

timized by NEGLECT© — they aren't *Special* Economic

sary. They instead devise STEALTH© strategies in order

growth, and insure continued *invisibility*, thus facilitating

CORRUPTION© Eases thousands of square kilometers

River Delta. Asian business practice never acknowl-

An Immodest Proposal

Although it looks unlikely ever to begin publication, *21A* was to have been a New York-based magazine "addressing the shifting ground of architecture and design in an age of globalization."

The magazine is conceived as a space, actually three spaces simultaneously.

Every part of the magazine, and the magazine as a whole, will be considered in terms of three "bands" of content:

- a foreground
- a background
- a middle ground.

Every feature will have an apparent "subject" or theme that will function as a foreground. In addition, a middle ground will be conceived and layered (not visually) into the concept and then these will be considered against a background.

Proposal for *21A*, 1999
21A was intended to provide frames through which to consider architecture and design issues: Material, Form, Image, Migration, Ideas, Frontiers. Each issue would be built around one such category. It would become the "feature well" category; the others, organizing aspects for smaller articles.

The transcribed notes that follow are taken from the studio's initial design study.

For example: a feature on a building might have an architectual foreground, a furniture middle ground and a history background.

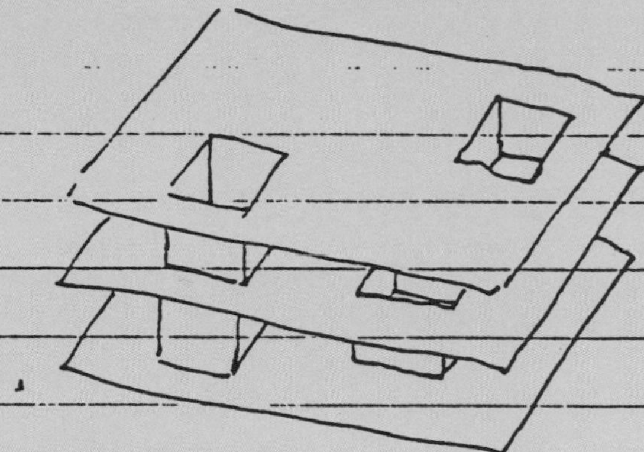

The magazine is concieved as a space, actually three spaces simultaneosly.

Every part of the magazine, and the magazine as a whole, will be considered in term of three "lands" of content.

- a foreground
- a back ground
- a middle ground.

Every feature will have an apparent "subject" or theme that will function as a foreground. In addition, a middle ground will concieved and layered (not visually) into the concept and then these will be considered against a background.

For example: a feature on a building might have an architectural foreground, a furniture middle ground and a history background.

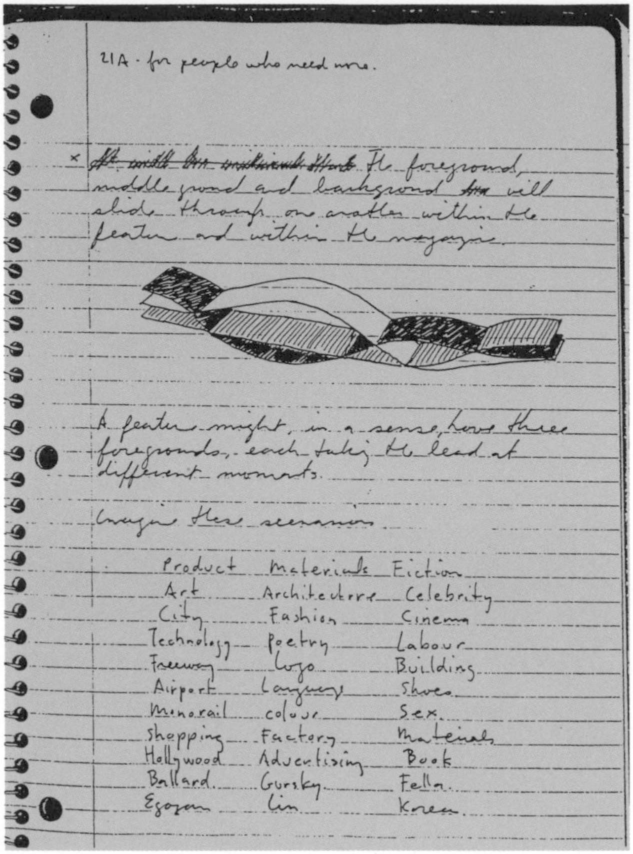

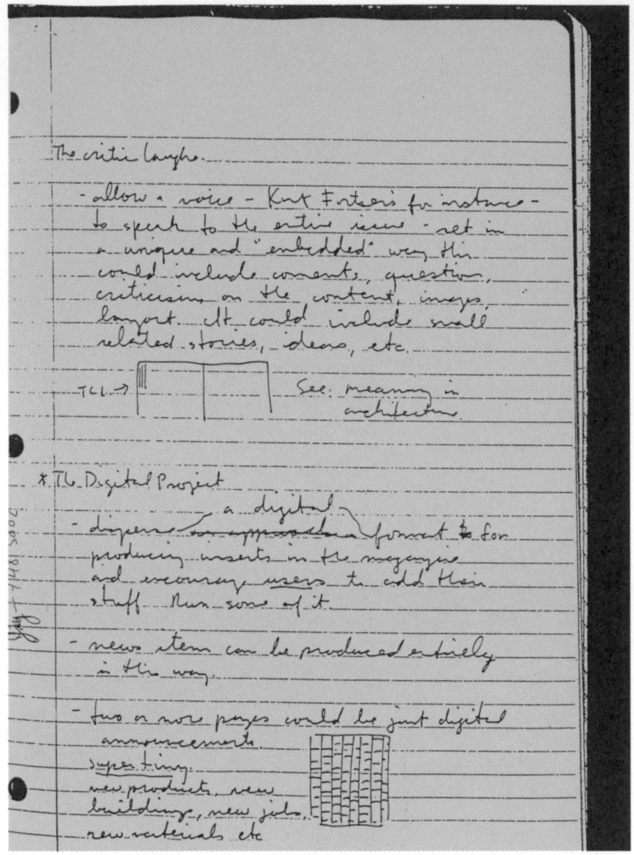

21A - for people who need more.

~~xx xxxx xx xxxxx xxxx~~ The foreground, middle ground and background ~~xxx~~ will slide through one another within the feature and within the magazine.

A feature might, in a sense, have three foregrounds, each taking the lead at different moments.

Imagine these scenarios:

Product	Materials	Fiction
Art	Architecture	Celebrity
City	Fashion	Cinema
Technology	Poetry	Labour
Freeway	Logo	Building
Airport	Language	Shoes
Monorail	Colour	Sex
Shopping	Factory	Materials
Hollywood	Advertising	Book
Ballard	Gursky	Fella
Egoyan	Lin	Korea

The critic laughs

- allow a voice — Kurt Forster's for instance — to speak to the entire issue — set in a unique and "embedded" way this could include comments, questions, criticisms on the content, images, layout. It would include small related stories, ideas, etc.

Tcl   See: meaning in architecture

The Digital Project

- disperse ~~xx xxxxxxxxx xx~~ a digital format for producing inserts in the magazine and encourage <u>users</u> to add their stuff. Run some of it.

- news items can be produced entirely in this way.

- two or more pages could be just digital announcements
  <u>super tiny</u>
  new products, new
  buildings, new jobs
  new materials etc.

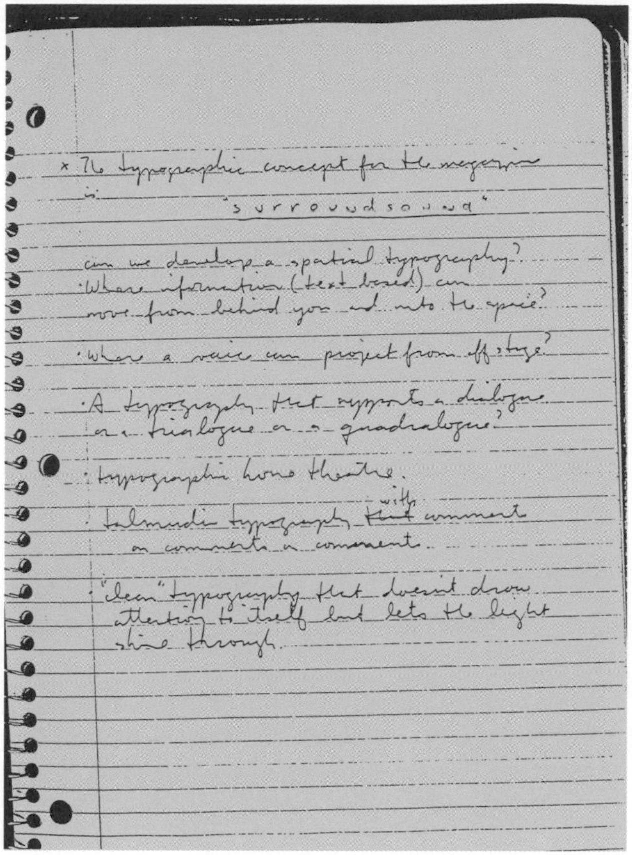

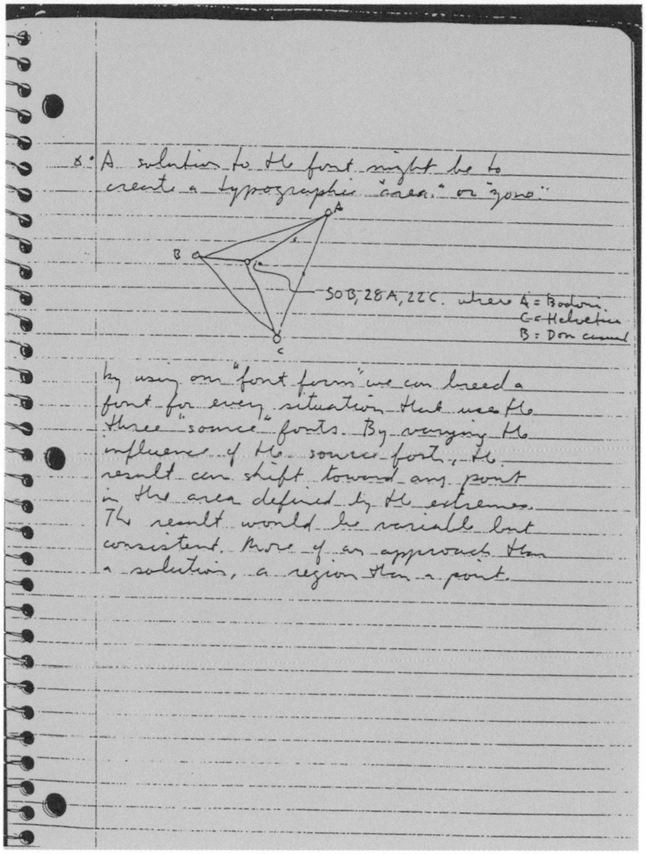

The typographic concept for the magazine
is:

"surroundsound"

Can we develop a spatial typography?
Where information (text based) can
move from behind you and into the space?

Where a voice can project from offstage?

A typography that supports a dialogue
or a trialogue or a quadralogue?

Typographic home theatre.

Talmudic typography ~~that~~ with comments
on comments on comments

"clear" typography that doesn't draw
attention to itself but lets light
shine through.

A solution to the font might be to
create a typographic "area" or "zone".

A

B

50B, 28A, 22C. where A = Bodoni.
C = Helvetica
B = Dom Casual

C

by using our "font farm" we can breed a
font for every situation that uses the
three "source" fonts. By varying the
influence of the source fonts, the
result can shift toward any point
in the area defined by the extremes.
The result would be variable but
consistent. More of an approach than
a solution, a region than a point.

Questionnaire

In 1999, BMD put out a call for "thinking designers" in a Toronto weekly newspaper. In lieu of a conventional job ad, the studio developed a quiz. Within a week, over 160 responses had arrived.

Bruce Mau Design Job Quiz, 1999

1. Manuel De Landa

2. Claes Oldenburg

3. Frank Gehry

4. Christopher Alexander is the principal author. Several submissions also listed Sara Ishikawa and Murray Silverstein. Still others listed secondary authors Max Jacobson, Ingrid Fiksdahl-King, and Shlomo Angel.

5. Nigiri is raw fish on a bed of rice; sashimi is simply raw fish.

6. J.G. Ballard

7. John Cage

8. Philippe Starck

9. Bruce Kuwabara of KPMB (Kuwabara Payne Mckenna Blumberg) Architects

10. Viljo Revell

11. The animal we were looking for was dog, as Gill had sex with dogs. Other answers, equally valid, included golden cockerel (one of Gill's more famous fonts), and the Hampton Hog.

12. 305 (source: *S,M,L,XL*)

13. *The Society of the Spectacle*

14. Jan Tschichold. Cooper & Beatty.

15. The red Roots "po'boy" cap.

16. Buckminster Fuller. Many people answered "Thomas More," only seeing the first part of the title.

17. Alan Fleming

18. Quentin Fiore

19. Saul Bass

20. John Oswald

21. We were looking for Michael Snow. It was a cheeky question because there are no words in *Cover to Cover*. Turns out, however, that there was a book on bookmaking that came out in 1995 by Shereen LaPlantz. We had more Shereen LaPlantz answers than Michael Snow. There is at least one other book with that title.

22. Charles & Ray Eames

23. Shiro Kuromata. Artificial roses. But many people discovered an earlier collage work by Kurt Schwitters with the same title.

24. They're all twentieth-century chair designs.

25. Donald Judd

26. Douglas Gordon

27. Jean-Luc Godard. Some people more properly identified Jean-Luc Godard and Anne-Marie Miéville.

28. Franz Kafka

29. Oliviero Toscani. Some people answered designer Tibor Kalman. We thought his work for Benetton came later but some argued that he was involved at the same time as Toscani and was the art director.

30. Marc Newson. Philippe Starck designed the hotel, but Newson did this particular piece of furniture.

31. Derek Jarman. Yes, Kieslowski made a film called *Blue*, but it doesn't consist of "nothing but the color blue." Others answered Oskar Fischinger, who made a film called *Komposition im Blau* in the 1920s. Unlike Fischinger, whose film consists of blue-colored shapes, Jarman's film is edge-to-edge solid blue and (visually) nothing else.

32. Mea culpa. The exhibition is called *100 objects to represent the world* and the artist is Peter Greenaway.

33. Walter de Maria

34. Well, some people answered Bill Clinton, which is arguably true ("I never had sex with that woman in any way, shape or form."). We were looking for the Amazing Kreskin. The best answer was contained in an incredible quote from Allen Ginsberg that predated anything Kreskin would have said. I mentioned this to the *Toronto Star*, a Canadian daily newspaper, and told them that we'd revised our answer. Turns out the applicant who cited the brilliant quote fabricated it. So, the answer remains the Amazing Kreskin.

35. Maya Lin

36. It's actually not the name of the artwork, though it is the text that forms the basis of the work *Quiet Fire: Memoirs of Older Gay Men* from 1989. It's by Micah Lexier. The actual sentence should read "I like sex, but I like it with someone who's read a book."

37. Richard Hamilton. The album credits additional people for art direction, but it was Hamilton who came up with the cover concept.

38. Gynecology, though many people claimed dentistry.

39. Black Mountain College. Merce Cunningham.

40. & 41. There are no correct answers.

Avoid Fields. Jump Fences.

Help wanted.
Bruce Mau Design is looking for **thinking designers** to work in our intense, upbeat, fast-paced, intellectually demanding studio.

We're looking for people who:

- understand design culture as research – trials and errors, experiments, speculations
- read books (sorry, we must insist)
- work at the intersection of form and content
- don't see a clear distinction between work and play
- possess broad cultural experience and are excited by working in an international context.

The studio is a multi-disciplinary **think tank** where designers, artists and architects, curators, filmmakers and writers collaborate to create, learn and develop the full potential in their projects and in themselves.

We produce exhibitions, objects, books, texts, museums, visual identities, environmental graphics, magazines, advertising campaigns, and art installations. We work with the world's leading visual artists, intellectuals, filmmakers, museums, publishers, cultural institutions, and corporations.

We are presently collaborating on:
- an art installation for a courthouse in Belgium
- a multimedia installation on the history of dance for Wiener Festwochen 2000
- the conceptual planning for the Museum of the Mississippi River in New Orleans
- the publishing program of the Getty Research Institute in Los Angeles
- a graphic identity program for the Museums of the City of Antwerp
- an environmental graphic system for Frank Gehry's Walt Disney Concert Hall in Los Angeles
- projects with artists Terry Winters, Tony Scherman, and Glen Seator
- many other design projects, conceptual planning work, and artistic collaborations.

If you possess superior design skills, a flare for the digital, and a penchant for the pleasures of hard work, answer the skill testing questionnaire and return it to us along with your resume and a sample of your writing.

Replies may be faxed (no phone calls please) to 416-260-2770 or e-mailed to studio@brucemaudesign.com
Attn. Jim Shedden, Studio Manager.

Of course, absolute discretion will be exercised.
Deadline: July 8, 1999.

You could win a job, and not just any job!

The **BMDquiz** is "scientifically" developed to test the depth of your cultural awareness. A score of more than 35 may qualify you for an interview, so go ahead, tell us a little bit about yourself.
(By the way, research is allowed.)

1. Who wrote *1000 Years of Non-Linear History*?
2. What artist made a work titled *Soft Screw*?
3. Who designed such contemporary furniture classics as *Power Play, Cross Check*, and *High Sticking*?
4. Who wrote "A City is not a Tree?" and *A Pattern Language*?
5. What is the difference between *nigiri* and *sashimi*?
6. Who wrote *Concrete Island* and *Highrise*?
7. Who wrote the book *A Year from Monday*?
8. Who designed the Asahi Beer Hall in Tokyo?
9. Who designed Kitchener City Hall?
10. Who designed the new Toronto City Hall?
11. What animal did typographer Eric Gill have a certain fondness for?
12. In 1993 how many nights did Rem Koolhaas spend in hotel rooms?
13. What text by Guy Debord was central to the events of May '68?
14. Who wrote *Asymmetric Typography* and what Toronto typesetting company published it in English?
15. What style of hat was a runaway success at the Nagano Winter Olympics?
16. Who wrote *Utopia or Oblivion*?
17. Who designed the CN logo?
18. Who designed *The Medium is the Massage*?
19. Who designed the film titles for *North by Northwest*?
20. Who created "plunderphonics"?
21. Who wrote the book *Cover to Cover*?
22. Who made the film *Powers of Ten*?
23. Who designed *Miss Blanche* and what does she have in her arms?
24. What do wink, wiggle, zigzag, butterfly, ant, and coconut have in common?
25. What artist started the Chinati Foundation in Marfa, Texas?
26. Who won the 1998 Hugo Boss Prize?
27. Who directed the television series *Son et image*?
28. Who invented Gregor Samsa?
29. Who was the image guru for Benetton who created the controversial AIDS patient ad?
30. Who designed the Lockheed Lounge in the lobby of the Paramount, N.Y.?
31. Who made a film consisting of nothing but the colour blue?
32. Who created the exhibition 100 objects that describe the world?
33. Who created the installations *Broken Kilometer* and *Earth Room*?
34. Who made famous the phrase "in any way, shape or form"?
35. Who designed the Vietnam War Memorial in Washington, D.C.?
36. Who created the artwork "I like sex, but I prefer it with someone who's read a book."
37. Who designed the cover of the Beatles' White Album?
38. Pierre Chareau's client for his Maison du Verre was a doctor: what was his specialty?
39. At what school did Buckminster Fuller and John Cage collaborate? And who was the choreographer in charge?
40. What is your all-time favorite:
    a) movie
    b) restaurant
    c) author
    d) artist
    e) fashion designer
    f) building
    g) book?
41. What languages do you speak and write?

Boekmachine
Bruce Mau
BEETLE
TREA
SURE
TROVE
Selected
Publi
cations
from
Bruno
Latour
SEVEN
EXP
ERIM
ENTS
DUOSCAN T1200

Artlife

Speaker Swinging

Speaker Swinging **is a seven-minute video that Gordon Monahan and I co-directed and produced. My collaboration with Gord Monahan as a director/producer and performer, including travelling together on a soundwork performance tour, demonstrates the studio's relationship to creative practice and the depth of our involvement in the projects we do. To some degree these projects best describe the new conditions and possibilities open to designers.**

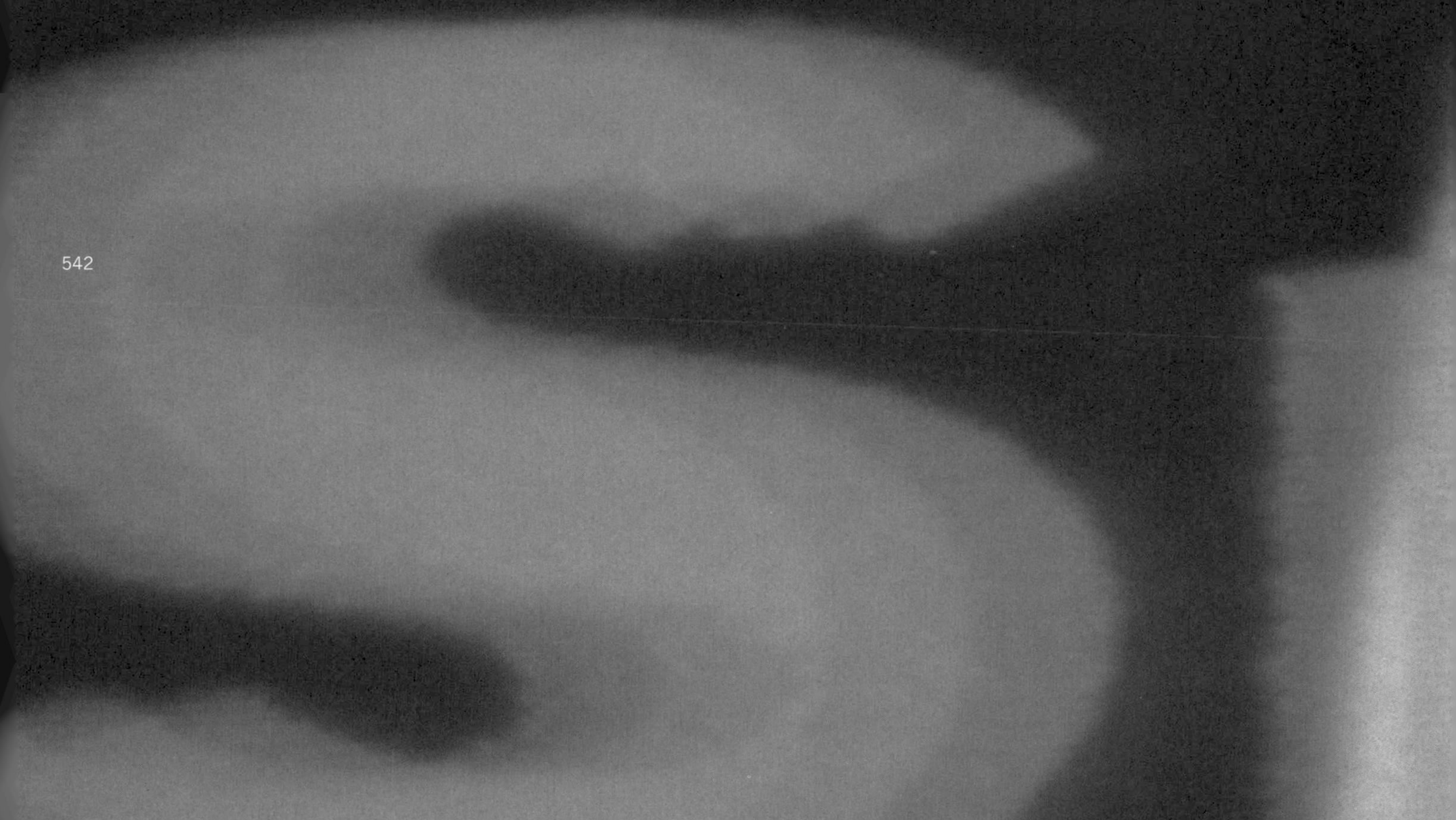

Collaboration with Gordon Monahan, 1988
Speaker Swinging presents a performance of a composition by Gordon Monahan. It is inspired by the Doppler effect of passing car stereos on a busy city street.
With speakers (and lights) attached to the end of twenty-foot cables, three performers mount platforms and for approximately half an hour swing the speakers around them in long sweeping arcs while Monahan generates tones that range from industrial to other-worldly. At a certain point, the sound stops, the lights go off and the audience, in complete darkness, hears only the swishing sound of flying speakers and the strained breathing of three performers. Strobe lights flash and pitch shadows contrapuntally around the room.

548

549

John Cage was once asked, Who's making the most interesting work these days? He answered, "There is a Canadian artist, Gordon Monahan, who's making pianos produce sounds I've never heard."

Every Day was Different

In 1990 I was invited to Halifax to conduct a weeklong workshop at the architecture school of the Technical University of Nova Scotia. Practitioners from various disciplines presented lectures each evening and worked with a small group of students to produce a project during the week. My project involved chance operations and the use of Brian Eno's *Oblique Strategies*. The following year, the school's dean, Essy Baniassad, invited me to return and bring some people along with me.

I asked my friends Sanford Kwinter, an editor at Zone, and Gordon Monahan, a composer, performer, and artist, to join me in Halifax. Everything went as planned until we arrived. At the opening session we each presented a project to explore during the week. The students were free to choose with whom they would work. After meeting our respective groups, Gordon, Sanford, and I each confessed that we were dismayed at the apparent lack of enthusiasm, awareness, energy, and exuberance in the students we were faced with.

That evening we changed the plan completely. We would abandon what we had come with, pool our resources, and simply produce a three-day "blast" of culture. If we couldn't rely on the students, we would rely on one another to produce a week of high intensity. We realized that the most important thing we could do was simply to expose them to what we thought culture was in the outside world. Rather than telling the students, we would show them, and give them what we could. Every day we produced performances, audio works, projects, and lectures. We showed videos, films, art works, typography, design, and history. We gave as much as we could. Some of the students loved it. Many hated it. They interrupted performances. They walked out of David Cronenberg's early films.

They ignored audio works by Alvin Lucier. We let the week and its events evolve as the project progressed. By midweek the students' enthusiasm and anger were palpable. We were invited to the dean's office for lunch. Essy remained his charming and effervescent self and studiously avoided the controversy. By week's end two students had calculated the number of hours of "instruction" we had provided and the cost to them of our presence.

We met on Saturday morning as a group to discuss the week's events. Essy sat at the center of a large room. The students formed a circle around him. He asked what had happened. They were timid at first. One or two claimed the workshop was "interesting."

One complained, "I didn't like it." Then the floodgates opened.

"We weren't told what to do or how to respond."

"We didn't know what was going to happen."

"Every day was different!"

Essy sat and listened calmly, turning in his chair to address each complaint directly. When the students had finished, he said, "It seems that we have finally been able to deliver one week of education. It's unfortunate we can't do this all year long."

Just before our departure we were handed a class list and asked to grade the students. It had been such a free-for-all that we didn't know all their names. We realized that we knew only those who had distinguished themselves at either end of the scale. There were a dozen great students who had participated and contributed. And there were half a dozen lumpen-students who couldn't or wouldn't get it. So we graded those at either end of the extremes and put the rest in the middle. Unfortunately, we were not aware that some of the students on the list had attended an entirely different program, and had somehow, *in absentia*, earned a B.

552

Remote
A collaboration with Meg Stuart for White Oak Dance Project, 1996
White Oak Dance Project was founded by Mikhail Baryshnikov in 1990 as a touring modern-dance company. It has since gained a reputation for tackling difficult choreographic assignments. In 1997 the company commissioned choreographer Meg Stuart to develop an extended work called *Remote*. Meg Stuart approached the studio to create a performance environment. We chose to use stark black-and-white projections of city scenes to augment the dance portrait of contemporary urban angst and isolation. We did the entire work using images of Toronto. For Baryshnikov's "anti-solo," we created a sequence of starry skies made of city lights softly out of focus.

A year later we were invited to collaborate with Meg Stuart again on a performance called *Crash Landing*.

Crash Landing with Meg Stuart, 1997

The Dance of the Difficult Image

I arrive with a basic misunderstanding: that we are here in Paris at the invitation of choreographer Meg Stuart to design a dance work to be performed on three nights. After a few days at Théâtre de la Ville I finally get it—we are here performing a dance work to be designed on three nights.

There is to be no distinction between dancers, musicians, and designers. As a group we decide on a basic structure: two sets each night. Endless discussion as to how to finish. Finally a decision: a lighting cue. Other than that, improvisation: costumes, sets, music, movement. Designers' work is to instigate, inflect, engage, respond, perform. No choreography, no control.

We have several days and nights of "rehearsals" in the theater before opening night. We begin to discover what we are capable of, how a dancer responds to an image, a musician to a gesture, a designer to a sound. Conflict: we don't want to waste a good idea by using it before the "real" performances. We set up instigations—inputs that can be activated when the time is right.

Our apartment-hotel, next to Centre Pompidou, is roach-infested—I'm indifferent; my wife, Bisi, is not. We move to St. Germain.

Opening night. Théâtre de la Ville apparently is the most demanding and difficult dance venue in Paris. This audience destroyed Pina Bausch. (Serious misgivings about Meg's title for this work.)

Our piece opens with "the dance of the difficult image." Three of us move haltingly about the stage hauling fifteen-foot-high light stands with projectors mounted up top. The projectors display a series of urban triptychs that we struggle unsuccessfully to maintain as a coherent image while we move about, throwing the image onto the back of the stage, the wings, and the audience. From there, the work assumes a life of its own. Unpredictable: now soaring, now flat. One of the dancers comes offstage to where I am. I whisper to him, "Nasser, check this out." During the performance I have fashioned a pile of newspapers and a jacket into an evening gown. In a moment his pants are off as he slips into a pair of heels and a platinum wig. "Fantastic, I'm going to do a real leggy number." He collects himself for half a beat, then strides onstage yelling, "I need my light! Give me my light! Paris I love you." All inexplicably in English with a heavy Belgian accent.

Later on, in the darkness of the catwalk high above the stage (absolute fear of heights somehow overcome), I prepare a cinema dump: several reels of sixteen-millimeter film that I rain onto a dancer below. Slowly at first, a single strip descends, then faster and faster he pulls the film from the reels and spins into a wild pas de deux with the shimmering celluloid.

At the opening of the second set we place a tray of popcorn on a hot plate in a tight spotlight. I "dance" a solo lugging a movie projector and a ladder across a lonely stage. I move slowly till I am right up front when, standing there in Théâtre de la Ville, I recognize the image I'm referencing—the animated opening credits of the *Carol Burnett Show*.

Momentary calm. Suddenly out of the audience someone cries, "Wait!" From the blackness, down the stairs, a young blond woman slides onto the front of the stage, writhing wildly in a tortured frenzy, spinning off her clothes as we watch in amazement, glancing anxiously at one another, uncertain how to respond. This is a little more improv than we had in mind. She is in the pit now, stark naked, the star of the show. Meg is quietly furious. Nasser, brilliantly, comes from behind me in full stride, wheeling the costume rack in front of him. Salesmanlike, he offers our guest her choice of dress. She is eventually waltzed offstage.

The audience, to my surprise, loves it. We end with a big dance party onstage. But deep down, I find it less than satisfying. To my surprise I'm less laissez-faire than I had imagined.

Book Machine

When curators Hans Ulrich Obrist and Barbara Vanderlinden approached us with the idea of participating in the exhibition *Laboratorium* the question for me was how to make the project itself a working laboratory.
One of the underlying ambitions of our project, Book Machine, was to demonstrate the book's vitality simply by treating the production of a book as a real-time performance.
The traditional definition of "book" has created a kind of self-fulfilling prophecy in which people continue to produce books that are meant to entomb the material. I see bookmaking as a process of rolling forward, a process that continues its momentum with every reading. It is not something that stops.
The experiment we undertook with Book Machine is one of translation. To move from one form to another the material has to pass through a kind of translation filter. This can be a process of clarification and intensification, or its opposite. Somehow, one has to make the concepts, the forms, the events, and the drama of one medium speak in and through another.
We thought of the people involved in the Book Machine as the filter. Their task was to capture a variety of wild events and pass them through a prism and into the book, and to make these events meaningful in a discursive context with all the other material.

Laboratorium
Antwerp Museum of Photography
Belgium, 1999
Book Machine is a massive documentation-capture project and cataloging system that was shown as a real-time print performance in Antwerp, tracking and interpreting an exhibition process and its residue over a period of four months. The exhibition, *Laboratorium*, explored the intersection of art and science by showcasing various practices of experimentation. From June to October 1999, Book Machine (comprising two Macintosh computers, two scanners, a color printer, and two assistants), operated within the exhibition's headquarters at Antwerp's Museum of Photography. Book Machine was an ongoing project that allowed the content and context of the catalog-publication process to converge. The catalog became performative. As each page came through the Book Machine it was mounted on the wall, starting at the top left-hand corner of its venue and continuing across all the walls in rows. The design process was implemented as a laboratory. In the first two days of the *Laboratorium* exhibition Book Machine produced over three hundred spreads. By the end of three months it had processed six thousand images and almost 18,500,000 characters of text.

THE BOOK MACHINE MANUAL
A set of instructions and equipment to produce the catalog for *Laboratorium*.

Equipment
2 Macintosh G3 computers,
each with a 4G hard drive, 120MB of RAM
Software: graphics applications and fonts
E-mail and ISDN line
1 color printer
2 flatbed scanners, with ability to scan transparencies
1 Zip drive
1 table
2 chairs
2 table lamps
1 filing cabinet with lock
Ethernet network
1 CD burner

Staff
Two assistants on site. The function of the assistants is comparable to that of a colorist, someone who fills in color where outlines are given. They may do this in an organized way or they may be arbitrary, moving outside the lines.
Two designers at BMD. The role of the designers is to provide structure by creating the list of instructions and techniques to be used in the production of the work.

Procedure
1. Establish form and content.
Laboratorium will be the main source of content for this exercise, providing form and morphology to the Book Machine.
2. Collect material.
Photograph, record, videotape, transcribe, download, surf Web-sites, record data, visualize information, make graphs, visit installations, talk, ask questions, transmit calls for submissions.
3. Start with the spread (two facing pages laid open).
Think of the spread as a space, and of the page as a unit within the spread.
Define the page dimensions. The number of pages is unlimited.
4. Insert the grid.
The grid is a structural consistency beneath the surface of the book. Everything will "snap" to the grid. The text area and the page must always have the same proportions. At its largest, the

BEETLE TREASURE TROVE

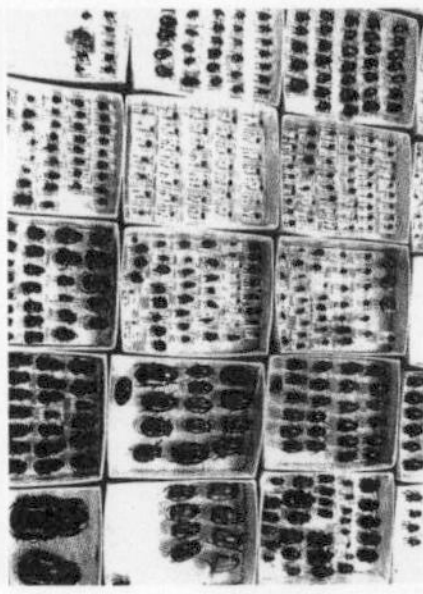

The Beetle Treasure Trove

The Beetle Treasure Trove

Tanga, Manaus, February 8, 1982
reprinted for Laboratorium

The Beetle Treasure Trove

The Beetle Treasure Trove Tanga, Manaus, February 8, 1982 excerpts reprinted for Laboratorium. I travelled to the North on the mission of assembling a collection of samples of the local fragrances, roots, oils, toilet soaps and everything aromatic and perfumed that was gathered or milled there. Being an enthusiast of insects, their worlds and habits, I found the trip opportune for reviving the delight that being an amateur entomologist gave me. I succeeded in establishing contact with Terezinha, a true scientist in the matter, who introduced me to countless specimens unknown to me, especially the Scarbacus Turucui Sagrado - the Sacred Turucui Scarab (Scarabaeus sacer).

I was seized by a veritable fascination for the insect. The STS are Coleoptera whose shape and chromatic scintillation particularly are exquisitely beautiful. There is, however, something horripilating about the fascination they wield. Learning more about them sheds light on what is scabrous. They are extremely skillful and persistent. Their skill stems from the formation of glenoid articular cavities that are enormous in proportion to their tiny size.

The STS are persistent in the determined pilgrimage that leads them to their favourite "menu". A predilection such as theirs reveals what has been said to be scabrous in their habits. The scarabs of this species are necrophilious and coprophilious. This information only excited my new passion all the more. I learned that their spherical sculptures, nests for larvae, were also constructed in putrefied foulness and even out of human excrement. This fact has made the specimen known vulgarly as Shit-Roller (or ball-roller) - "nickname" not in the least in keeping with the beauty that they ostentate. It was this said beauty that spurred my diligence and I soon undertook a hunt for the insect with the intention of obtaining a spawn of its larvae. The construction of this culture had as its end the determined task of cultivating them so as to dispose of any beyond-the-tomb company. I imagined myself as excellent food for the specimens once my putrefaction in the coffin had reached a far advanced state. I organized the hunt using a classical booby-trap for beetles: the method is quite simple: a thimble-shaped tin pail is buried in a place where the beetle's favourite foods are deposited.

The beetle, once having fallen into the trap, cannot succeed in escaping due to the non-adhesive surface of the metallic walls of the pail. As bait, I used my own excrement, diluted in urine. Days later, I returned to the trap where I found three handsome Brs. I took the measures necessary for the maintenance and subsistence of the insects by arranging a provisional nook for them in my room with the roots and products that I had at my disposition. Professional obligations suddenly took me to Belém,* the capital of fragrances. However, other odours besieged me in this capital, for I was struck down by malaria. The octan fever kept me in a state of delirium with regularity and, intoxicated, I was systematically pursued in strange constructions in which the STS played the leading role. Still febrile, I repaired to Manaus, where the surprise awaited me. On penetrating my room, I was overcome by an odoriferous avalanche. The surprise, nevertheless, did not issue from the odours, but from their source. My three Shit-Roller specimens had excrementitiously produced enormous spheres - the size of human heads. They were making a great effort to aggregate the three volumes, each pushing a sphere toward the two others. The fact was peculiar, for the "cannonball" formations had been constructed with the aromatic materials from my collection of samples.

Aghast and stunned, after some minutes I emerged from my torpor. The sight of the intumescent triangle brought back memories of the malarial fevers. Impulsively and unhesitatingly, I filled a syringe with an ampule of chloroform and, piercing the carapaces of the Coleoptera, one by one, I meted out their death. I then inserted long needles, which I had on hand, to perpetuate - in that macabre position - the excremental work that I have name The Beetle Treasure Trove and now present to you. Notes* [Tr.'s note] Belém, capital of the state of Pará; and Manaus, capital of the state of Amazonas, are both located in northern

Galleries as Labs

(Sort of) as reprinted from the New York Times

Roberta Smith

Artists are a voracious lot. They take from everywhere, even if they misuse, abuse or only partly understand what they borrow.

In the last three decades ever since Minimalism and Conceptual Art declared open season on reality-science has played an increasingly prominent role in art. Donald Judd used the Fibonacci series of natural numbers as a compositional device and Robert Irwin's installations examined the nature of visual perception.R.Smithson embraced entropy as the underlying principle of his art. Alan Sonfist, playing the botanical historian, reconstructed a bit of primeval Manhattan forest, still standing at the corner of West Broadway and Houston.

In recent years, the AIDS crisis, concern for the environment and the development of new technologies are only a few things that have inspired references to science in art. Consider Ross Bleckner's paintings, with their evocations of the body's cells; Mark Dion's laboratory-like tableaux; Matthew Barney's sculptural excursions into biogenesis, or Matthew Ritchie's paintings, which concert theories of astrophysics into warring gods. Old science is as present as new, as attested to by the rage for taxidermy in current sculpture. And the history of science is a subject unto itself. Alexis Rockman's panorama paintings, with their dystopic view of evolution, and Zoe Leonard's photographs of cadavers are examples.

At the moment, three different uses of the scientific are on view in Manhattan galleries. In a group show at Andrew Kreps in Chelsea, Julian LaVerdiere is exhibiting "Hydrogen Bed," a helium-filled mattress that floats near the ceiling. At David Beitzel in SoHo, Michael Lucero's elaborate ceramic totems include pots shaped like chemists' beakers, which evoke the chemical basis of firing and glazing ceramics. Also in SoHo, at American Fine Arts on Wooster Street, Dennis Balk is inviting viewers to use his "Photo Magnetic Receiver," a machine that transforms the viewer's aura into light rays.

Science has taken artists in many new directions. Terry Winters bases his semi-abstract paintings on natural forms and structures and over the years has moved from botanical subjects to linear networks that are simultaneously micro and macrocosmic. Kiki Smith reveals some of the body's unseen beauties by making large blood molecules from handblown red glass. Fred Tomaselli comments on society's pharmaceutical diversions by making beautifully patterned paintings out of over-the-counter pills embedded in resin. And Gary Schneider is one of a number of artists interested in the most infinitesimal measure of human uniqueness, DNA, photographing his own to create a new kind of self-portrait.

Almost no scientific invention, principle, fact, technique or technology seems immune to the artistic appetite. Given the nature of art, science and of reality, more of the same purely follows.

BAMBOYE OLADELE

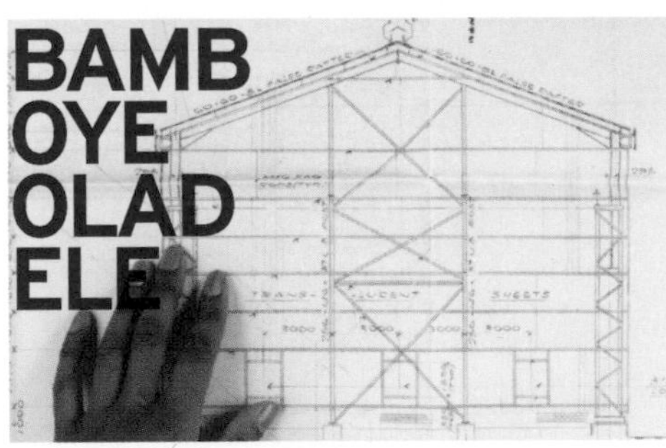

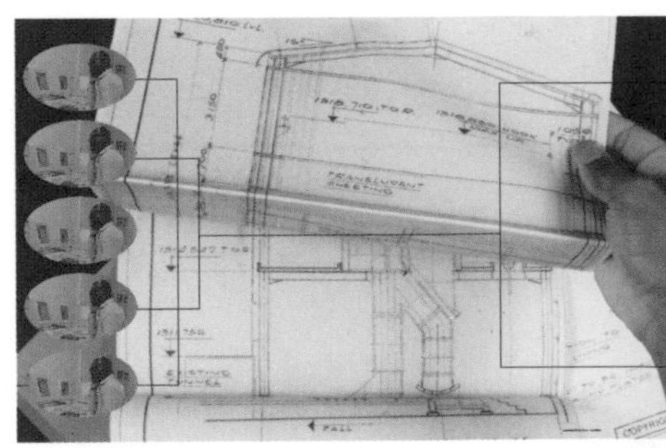

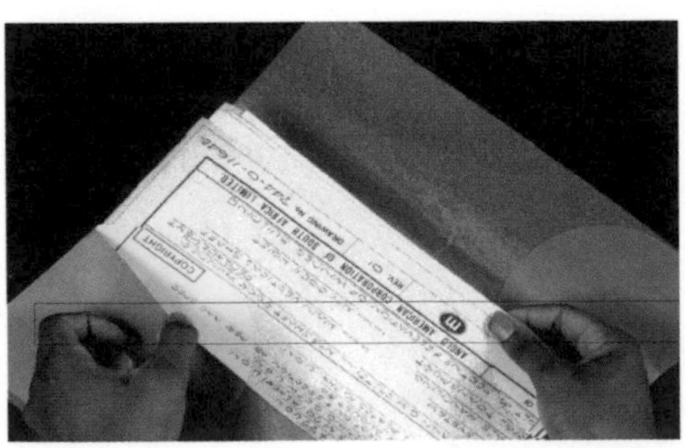

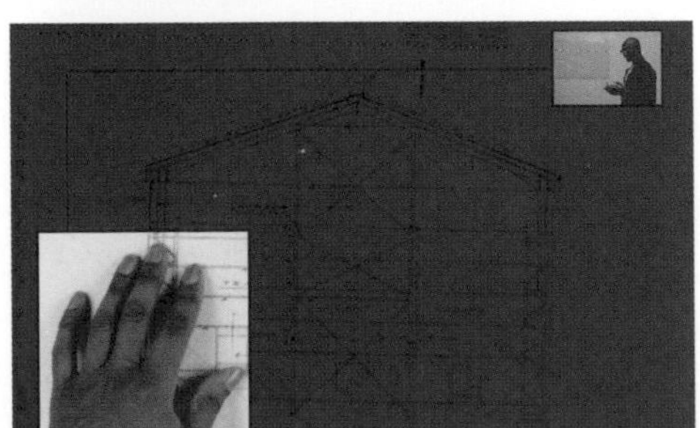

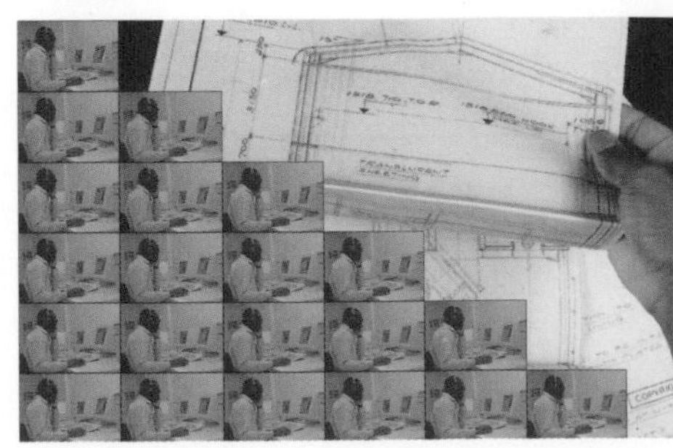

text area will follow the golden canon of Jan Tschichold, drawn in 1953: the inner margin is one-ninth the page width; the outer margin is two-ninths the page width; the top margin is one-ninth the page height; and the bottom margin is two-ninths the page height.

Depending on the desired length of the finished text piece, the text box can shrink along a diagonal line drawn from the top inner corner of the page down to the bottom outer corner. The top inner corner of the text box remains constant in its position and the bottom outer corner moves up and down the diagonal. If the text area is very small, a short text can thus be made to fill many pages.

5. Select the associated images.

Representations of artists' works must not be cropped or altered. Use a full horizontal or full vertical dimension of the page, depending on the orientation of the image. The rest of the page is left blank.

Situation images are infinitely flexible and can be cropped, manipulated, and treated as required.

6. Apply the appropriate templates and masks.

Templates define the position of content within the spreads. Masks control the degree of expression of this content. (For example, a particular mask is 70 percent opaque and therefore only 30 percent of the content is expressed.)

7. Specify typography.

All typography will conform to the composition rules and typographic specifications outlined in each elaborated template description.

8. Create a feedback loop.

Process the content through various filters. The filter can be any of the following: critic, collaborator, commentator, peer, analyst, curator, editor, a person off the street, a visitor to the exhibit. Capture and incorporate the response from the filter into the piece. This information flow allows for the cross-breeding of systems, triggers conflict, and transforms and amplifies the content.

Templates

As new forms of content are identified that cannot be accommodated by the existing templates, new templates must be created and recorded. Among them might be:

1. Essays

Read the essay. Determine the most important themes/subjects of the text and find related images. The text is always inserted

Entertainment for Surrey. Ken Lum

Surrey is Vancouver's largest suburb, located about 25 kilometres from Vancouver. Each weekday morning, tens of thousands of commuters make their way to work from the suburbs to the city. The flow of heavy traffic is reversed at the end of each workday as commuters return to their suburban homes from the city.

In 1978 I was nearing completion of my studies in Pestology, basically an area covering entomology and chemistry. I worked during the summer months in a government laboratory under the twin purview of the Ministry of Agriculture and the Ministry of the Environment. My primary responsibility was to research methods of natural predatory control by the release of tiny wasps (biological name: Hymenoptera Spalangia Endius) into the pupae of houseflies that infest the manure droppings that form underneath poultry barns.

Each weekday morning I would start my commute to Surrey, generally in the opposite direction of traffic flow. One day, on my return from work, I saw a man walking near the side of the highway. I found that surprising because the highway is difficult to access on foot and I wondered why he was there. As I drove further along, I could see in my rear view mirror his car some distance back from him. Sighting his car seemed to at least explain to me why he was there; it seemed sufficient to know that he was there for a reason, whatever that might have been. I also noticed one other thing - how seeing the man by

the highway awoke me from my trance-like state of driving for 45 minutes each and every workday morning and late afternoon.

For Entertainment for Surrey, I stood in on overpass embankment by the side of the TransCanada Highway for two hours each morning from Monday through Friday. The overpass is only visible about 12 seconds to commuters going in the direction of Vancouver as the TransCanada is a long curve at that point. Once the commuters sight me and pass under the overpass, they immediately descend onto a bridge leading to Vancouver.

I wore the same clothing every day of the performance. One day it rained heavily and it was very difficult to stand affixed on the sharp incline without slipping. The sleeves of my sweatshirt were thoroughly soaked and the water caused them to extend down to beside my knees. I did nothing except to stand as motionless as possible observing traffic. Within a couple of days, the local newspaper had received a number of calls about a "strange man standing by the freeway." A newspaper reporter came by but I concentrated only on watching traffic. The police also came by and ordered I get off the embank-

ment. When I did not respond to them, they simply went back into their car and departed. I remember being very nervous when they demanded I leave.

The performance continued onto the following Monday and my picture had already appeared in the newspaper. Many commuters blew their car horns and waved at me as they passed by. On the Tuesday, the cars reverted to silence. The commuters had grown accustomed to seeing me on their daily commute. I had, in effect, become a sign. On the second Wednesday, I put up a white cardboard outline of myself on the spot where I had stood. That signalled the end of the performance.

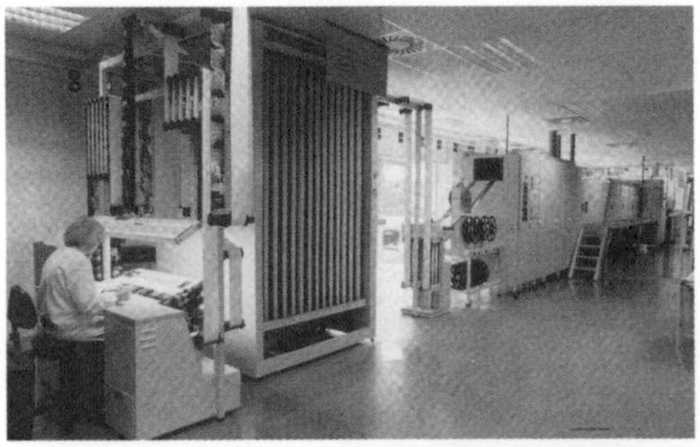

MARK BAIN

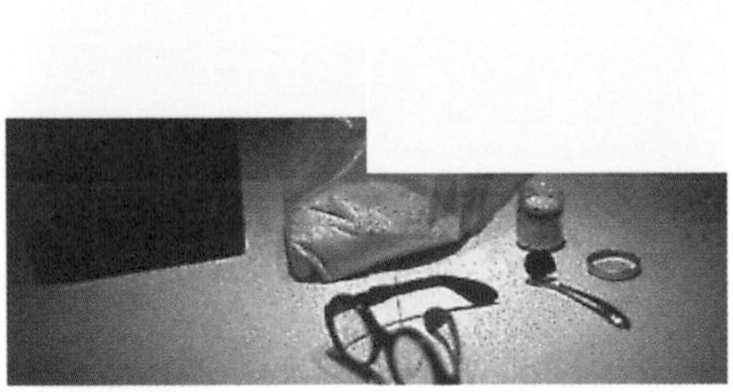

HANS-PETER FELDMANN

UNTITLED

on the right-hand page. Images are always placed on the left-hand page. All images require a caption. Captions appear directly under the images and are positioned such that the reader can intuit which captions refer to which image. Notes and extracts are always set one point smaller than the body text. First line of each note is indented. Indentation is always equal to the leading.

2. Project proposals

Read the proposal. Determine the most important themes of the text and find images related to them. These pages have two live areas, a smaller one for the text and a larger one for the images and their captions. Run the text through the pages and insert the images into a position where they are relevant to the text. At least one edge of each image should be touching the image area margin. All images require a caption.

3. Notes and experiment logs

Organize all notes and logbook entries chronologically and code them with a numeric system (by time, by date, or by order of occurrence). Organize each entry with its respective images inserted directly below the entry title. The image should be sized to the full column width. Any information about the image should be included at the beginning of the entry.

4. Lectures with slides

Attend the lecture or watch the lecture video. Ask one question. Ensure that texts are transcribed and translated. Collect the most important images. Organize images in chronological order and pair them with their associated texts. The images and their texts are organized like the pages of a comic book. The images are arranged in an orthogonal grid, with four to six images per page. The text always appears directly below each slide image. All images require a text or caption.

5. Lectures without images

Attend the lecture or watch the lecture video. Ask one question. Ensure that texts are transcribed and translated. Scan the text for the most important, or most interesting, statements and extracts. Organize extracts in chronological order and place them on the left-hand page of each spread. The lecture text flows in its complete form on the right-hand pages of the spread.

6. Interviews

Read the interview. Determine the most significant themes of the interview and find images that are relevant to or evocative of these ideas. Each voice in the conversation gets its own typeface. Every left-hand page carries text and every right-hand page carries a full-bleed image.

Toy Model of Space A Lecture by Panamarenko

I have explained this several times. Each time differently and in more detail. And . . . for myself easier. But for others less comprehensible. 'Toy model of space' would be pointless if there weren't for the basic idea, a whole lot of coincidental or genuine . . . tests or proof. But you shouldn't look too hard for proof, because then it is as if you're making it up.

In my explanation about the working of the universe . . . I always assumed that everybody understood all the basic concepts. But . . . the fourth dimension . . . What it really means . . . Something you can learn in about 20 minutes. That gravity means that things fall down, not up. But during every explanation or meeting . . . it turned out that most people had never heard of those things, so that I actually addressed

The Fourth Dimension

an audience that obviously didn't understand any of what I was saying. But they do understand that it's very boring. And it is very boring. It can't be helped. It's not . . . It's no nonsense theatre. It's . . . That's just the way it is.

The Fourth Dimension

First I'll try to write down all the basic . . . the basic concepts. Like it is done at school. Or like it should be done at school. First you have . . . That's the only formula you need to know in order to do the fourth dimension transformation. The universe is based on four dimensions and if you don't know the fourth, this explanation is pointless. This is the speed of light. V is the speed of the object. It can also be light, then

All the celestial bodies we know have the same speed.

it's the same speed and . . . When you raise the quotient to the square and then . . . divide it by two, then you get the . . . transformation of the celestial body in question compared to its speed.

All the celestial bodies we know have the same speed, 220 kilometers per second. That goes for the sun . . . and for us . . . the earth and the entire solar system.That's the speed around the Milky Way. If you fill in this number here and this number there and you do the calculation, then you would get . . . The best thing to do is . . . Because it doesn't give you a fraction. It's better to put in a fraction. And you do that like this . . . Otherwise you can write the number. This speed gives . . . 1/3,700,000. When you don't put it in a frac-

In 10 minutes there is not one person in the world who understands.

tion, you have to say 0.00000 . . So you put in a fraction.

At the beginning this is all very simple. In 10 minutes there is not one person in the world who understands what I'm talking about and soon after I don't understand it myself. Each body has a certain division of its mass. There are names for this, but they are very vague. But actually it comes down to this. You put . . . This is a pair of scales . . . and here you put a long lath . . . which weighs one kilo. And here you put a weight at a certain place. So that those two objects are balanced. If this could also move around, and not only up and down, it would also remain balanced in this direction. It wouldn't stay behind, because the weight . . . The objects are balanced, although they can have different

That Point

weights. The weight here in the middle doesn't really count. That point . . . is the point or the moment of inertia. The fourth dimension in space interacts with that point. When it is the sun, for instance . . . The fourth dimension doesn't interact with the surface of the sun, but it interacts somewhere where the mass is present, is balanced, is in equilibrium . . . in the . . . the moment of inertia. If it's a solid sphere, this is two fifths . . . from the midpoint. About here. Here. But the sun is not a solid sphere, but something..that's 10 times thinner on the side than the air . . . and in the midpoint . . . one billion times denser . . . then the edge. When you calculate this, bearing this in mind . . . When you make an estimation, it would be around . . . The radius of the

The Sun

moment of inertia of the sun . . . would be at one fourth . . . At one fourth. Or at 0.25 . . . of the radius.

The Sun.

You see the sun. It's just like a glowing lamp. Its density increases and the heat in the centre is enormous. So you get an upward curve and at a certain moment you can say: 'This must be the point of equilibrium.' That makes the sun four times smaller than it really is. If I don't do that . . . then I can use any diameter and my calculations always work out.

But I want it to be right. I don't want to falsify it. This is all school book material, but . . . But it's necessary to say it. Otherwise you don't know what I'm talking about. And

A Renowned Mathematician Erdos is Dead

Tanga, 1995

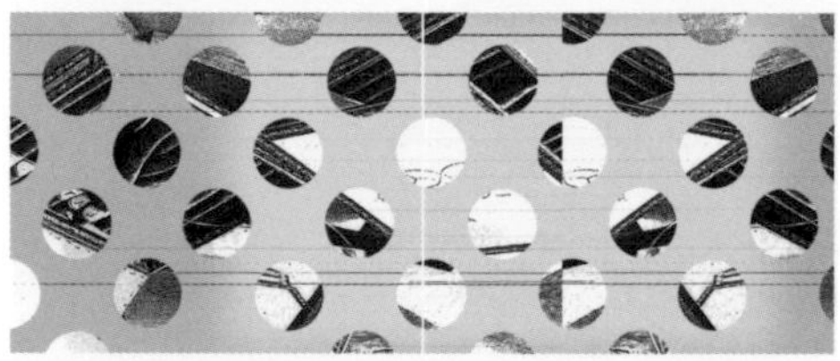

KOO JE ONG -A

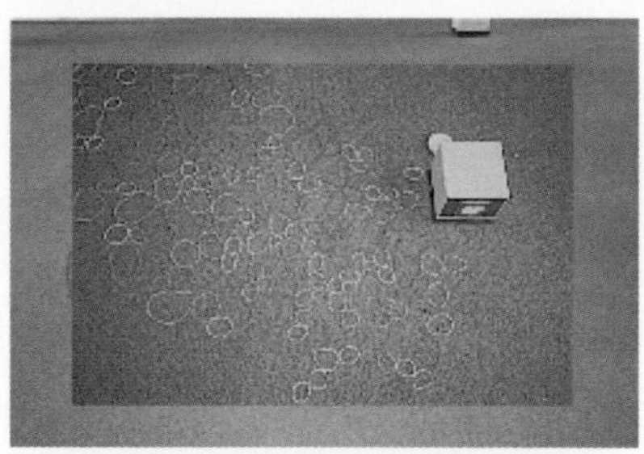

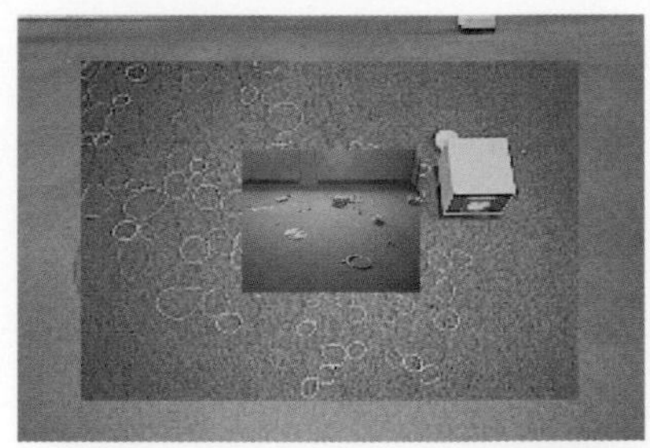

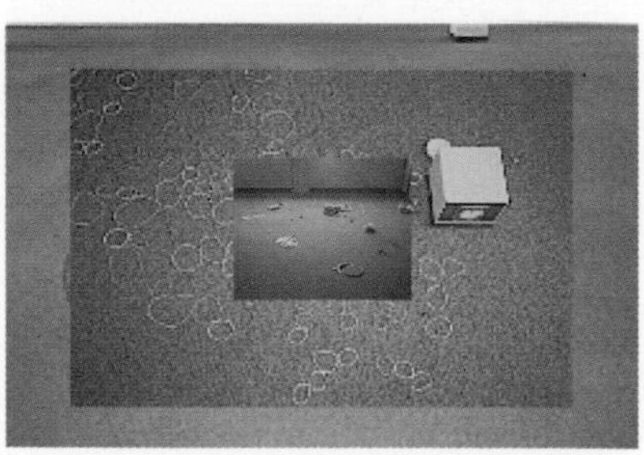

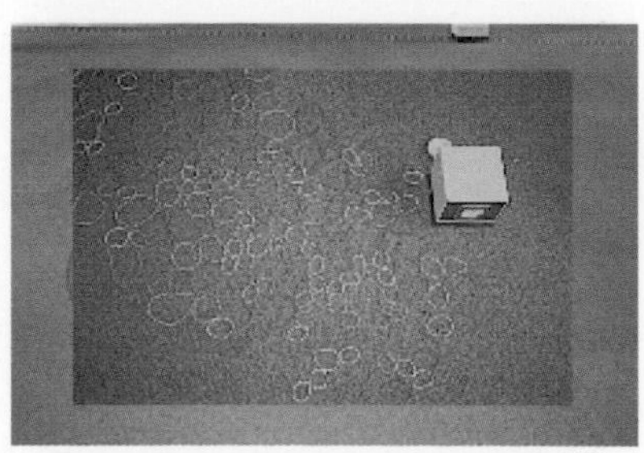

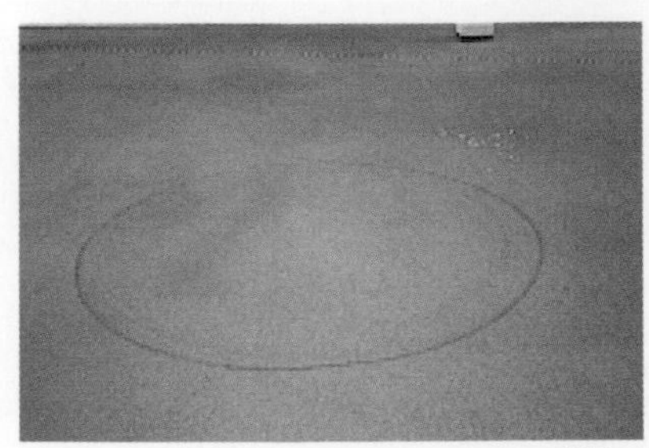

7. Emphasized charts and diagrams
Collect as much quantitative and qualitative data as possible related to all the work. Determine the clearest graphic representation of the data. Three-dimensional graphics are preferred.
8. Tabletop experiments
Watch each performance video. Select stills that represent animated gestures, varied demonstration techniques, and simultaneous use of multiple presentation media. Link each image to the appropriate section of text. Every image needs text, and you need enough images to illustrate all the texts.
9. The overcolumned layout
Some content will need to be displayed in narrow columns. Create pages with too many columns to amplify the dense nature of the material. Some pages could have up to ten vertical columns, and the content can be set in very small but still legible type. Use the city Yellow Pages as a model.
10. Images as seeds
Some contributions have many reference images. To accommodate such large quantities, images can be reproduced in very tiny sizes, as seeds, dispersed throughout the body of the text.

11. Snap-to-corners image essays
Image essays can be applied to the spreads by placing an image at each of the four corners of the spread. The images should not be cropped and they should be made as large as possible without allowing them to overlap.
12. Simultaneous image essays
One series of images can commence within a second image essay. The first series is formatted with full-spread, full-bleed images. Toward the middle of this image sequence, the first image of the second series should occur as a small picture in the bottom right-hand corner of a spread. After this point, every subsequent spread has an image from the second sequence in this same location. Once the first sequence of images is completed, the second sequence keeps on going in this corner location until it ends. This second series of images can also become incrementally larger until it overtakes the first sequence, eventually becoming as large as the whole spread.
13. Big captions
Reverse the usual image-caption relationship. Some works may be made up of small images and big captions. In this case each image is placed in the exact center of the spread across the gutter. The size of the image must also allow space for a column

CITY
OF
THE
STARS
Moscow, Russia ' Armin Linke

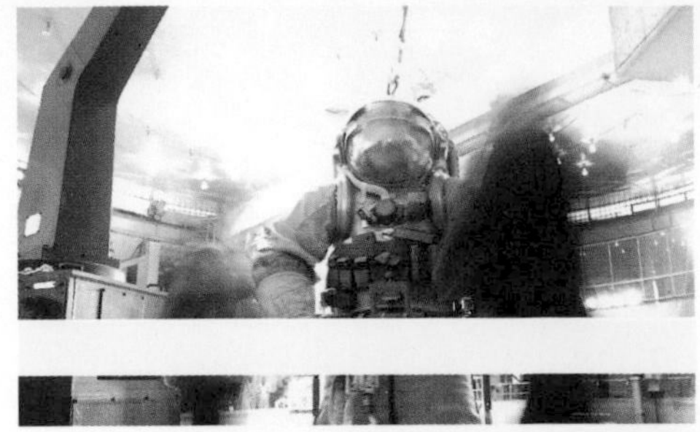

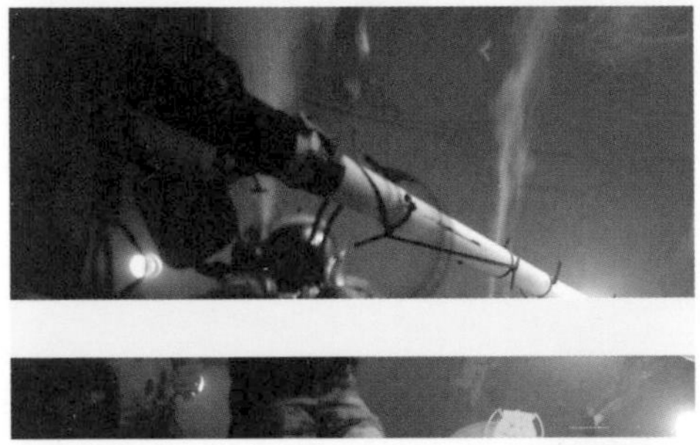

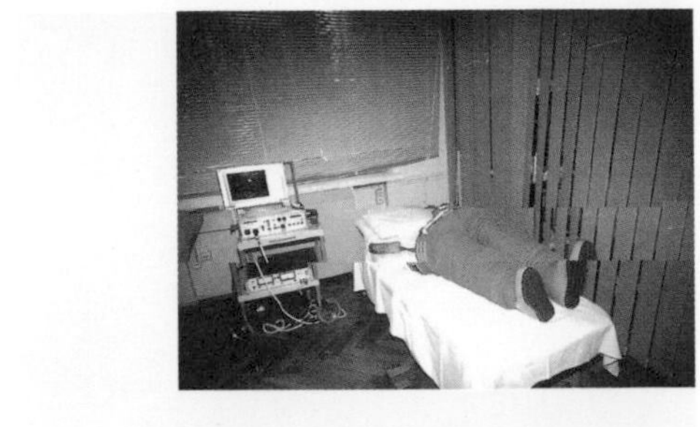

REM
KOOL
HAAS

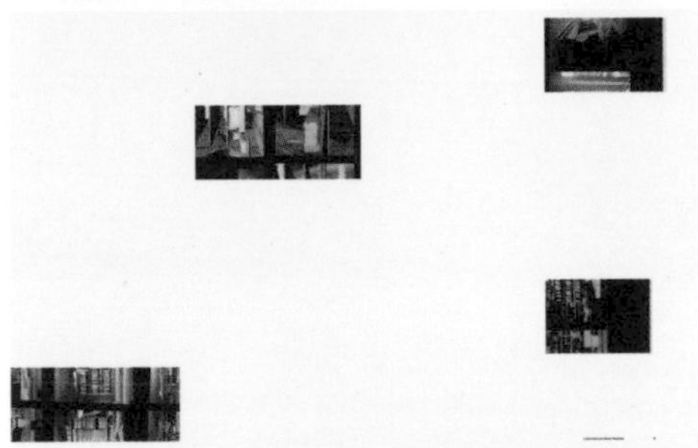

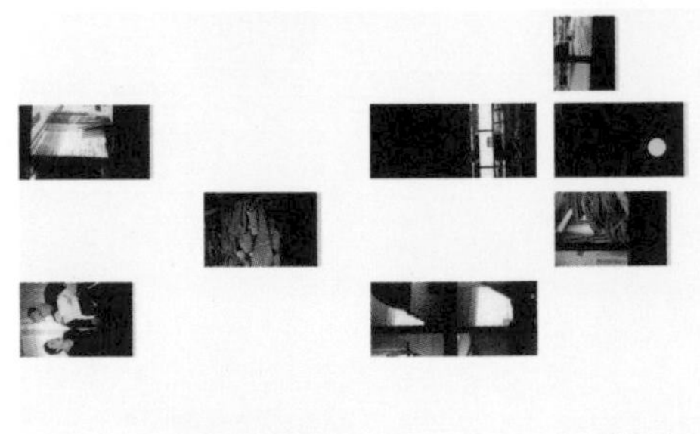

ADAM
LOWE

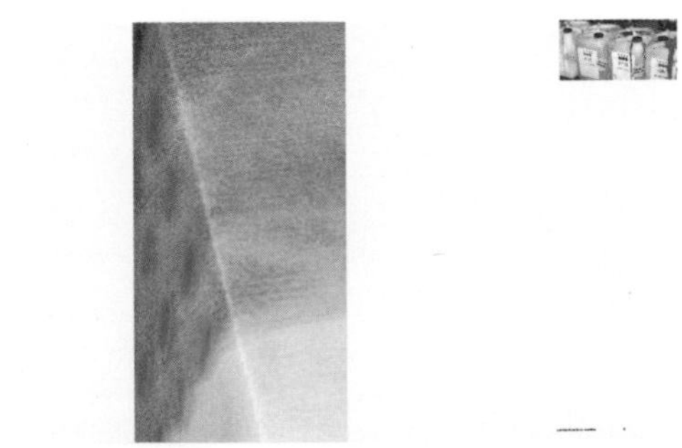

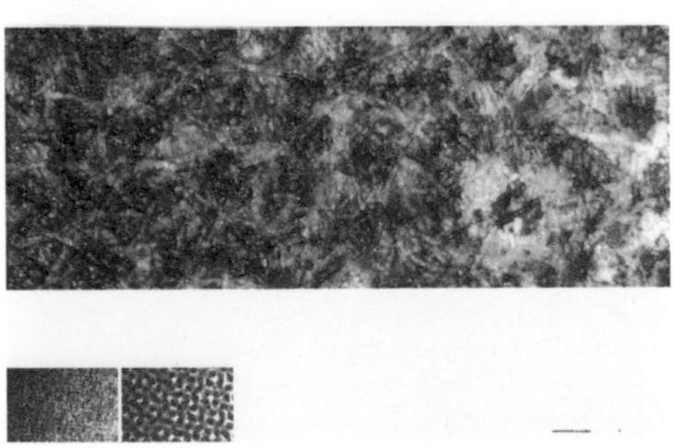

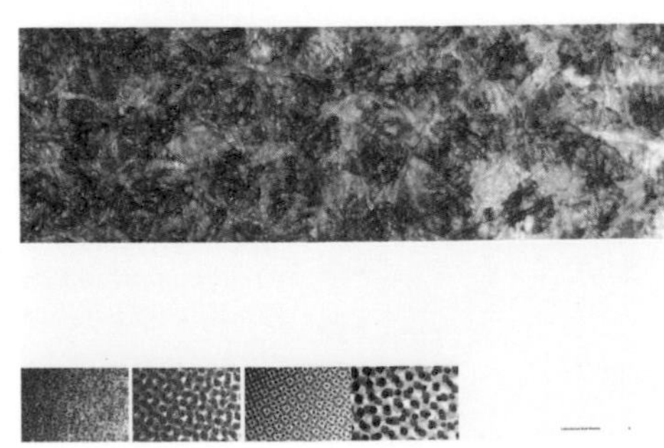

of text and the caption, attached to the right side of the image. The caption text box starts exactly halfway down the right side of the image and is equal to two times the width of the image. These proportions are constant, even as the size of the image changes.

Masks
There are currently four masks. This number can be expanded.
1. Graduated perforations
This mask is made up of graduated, opaque circles. All the circle centers are on a constant grid, but the circle sizes gradually increase, from mere specs in a large field of space on the far side of the mask, to large opaque spheres that touch at all four axis points so that there is a minimum amount of space between them.
2. Spikes
This mask is made up of long, narrow triangular spikes with abutting edges at one end and points that taper to the far side of the mask to reveal an image of the space beyond which is the inverse shape of the mask.
3. Soft spaces
This mask is a series of soft-edged ellipses that act as holes leading to a space beyond.
4. Perforation
This mask is a regularized grid of circular holes punched through the surface of the spread. All the holes are the same size, and the space between them is equal to their diameter.

Killing: A Body of Knowledge

For the longest time, it was an embarrassment—a fact best left unstated. It had no place or utility in the urban context to which I had migrated. It was a remnant of a former life. I had no need here for the skills of killing, no way even of speaking of what I knew. Here in my downtown world, I felt like I was carrying an extinct language that could no longer act as a bridge to the outside world. So I tried to forget.

But facts are facts. They remain. And over time I realized the significance of these events, images, sounds, and sensations that had marked me. They had marked me in more than an intellectual way; they affected me in a deep, bodily, historical way.

Killing is an event that penetrates the body of the killer. It is a confrontation not only with death, but with life, one that ties you, binds you, to the rhythms of the world: the patterns of seasonal change; the wavelengths of sex, birth, growth, and death; the flows of energy, of flesh, of blood, of urine, of excrement, of ins and outs, of beating hearts, of inhaling and exhaling and seeing your breath stand frozen in the crisp, still autumn morning; and the piercing, unforgettable modulations of the death scream as the violence of life pumps itself down and out.

Killing places you, locates you, in this polyrhythmic world. It is an event that engages every opening, every channel, every frequency, every sense: the muffled pop of the gunshot that is carefully placed to stun but not kill, the frenzied movement as the jugular is severed, an unearthly scream, the shocking force of spraying blood, the dwindling flow gathered in bowls, the moment of regaining composure after having committed the act, trousers hitched, nervous laughter, hair stroked back into place, the sound of tendons taking the weight as the carcass is hoisted, the warmth of shaving the body, repeatedly immersed in boiling water, the cut, the careful carving about the anus, the sound of guts straining under their weight and plopping into trays below, the feeling of bone yielding to the saw as the spine is bisected along its length.

It's not by chance that we speak of a taste for killing.

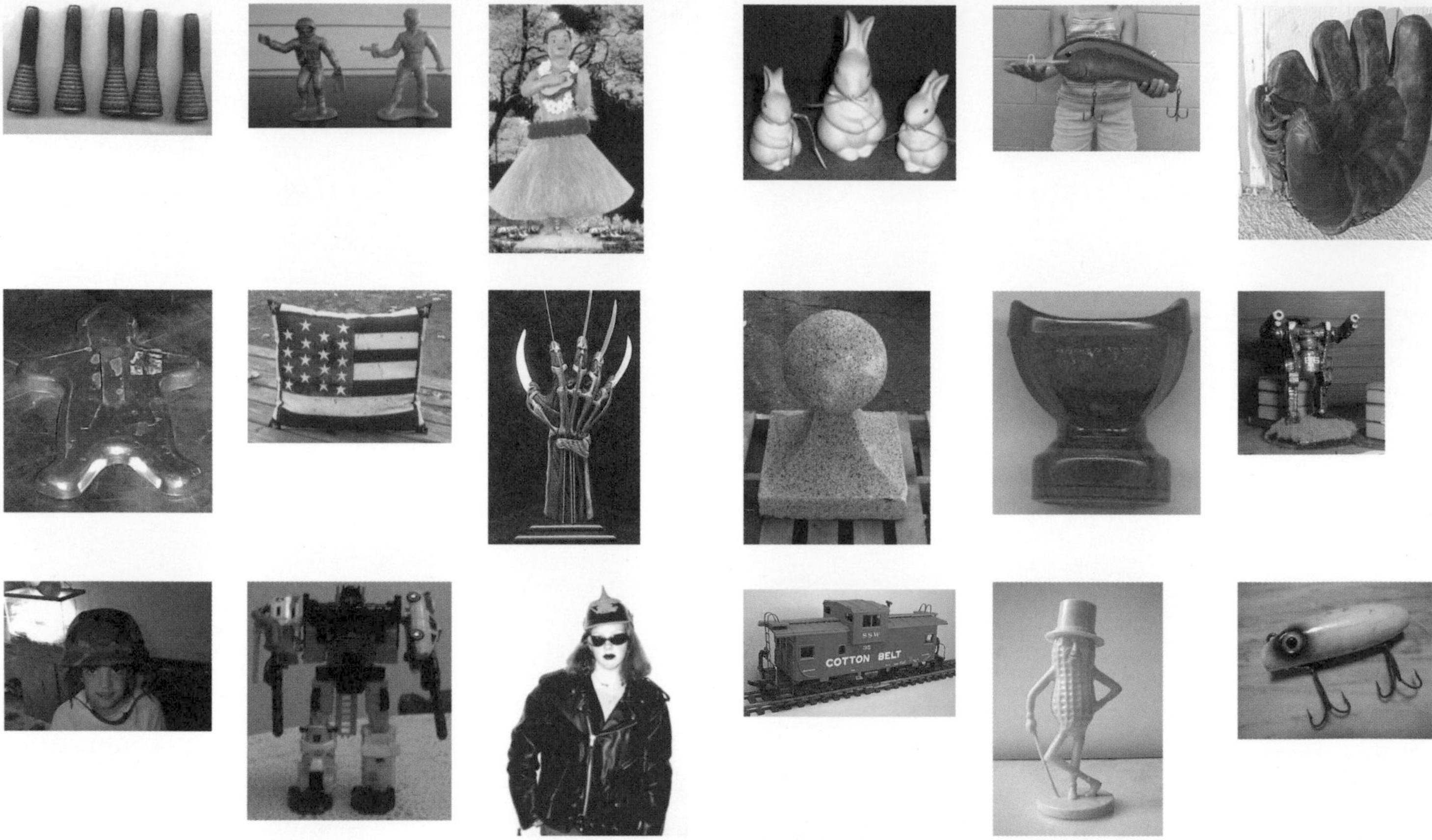

Love for Sale
Installation in *Retrace Your Steps: Remember Tomorrow* at Sir John Soane's Museum London, 1999
The Soane's Museum in London presents a collection of objects, art, and architectural artifacts. It was assembled over decades by collector and architect Sir John Soane and is now displayed in the museum he built for it.
In late 1999, curator Hans Ulrich Obrist invited a number of artists to contribute pieces for a temporary installation. Among the artists who accepted were Douglas Gordon and Richard Hamilton. The one rule Obrist set for the participants was that their pieces should not disturb the museum's permanent displays.
The studio decided to echo the collection by projecting its contemporary equivalent into the museum's space. This took the form of one thousand objects culled from the Internet auction site eBay, downloaded, and video-projected one after another. The eBay images were all made by the owners of the items posted for sale. Most have the uniform quality of photographic glorification: love for sale.

2000

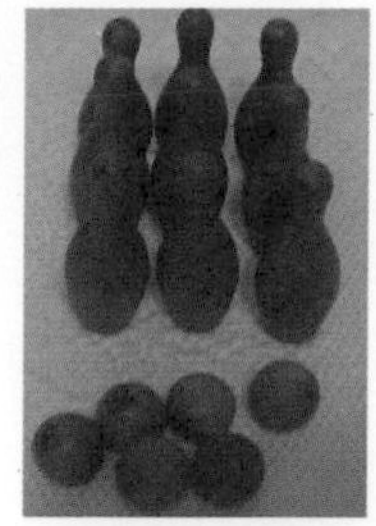

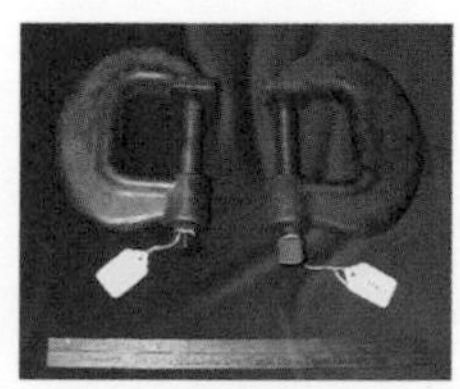

CAPTAIN MARVEL

Yonge St. Willowdale (#4),
Robin Collyer, 1995

Robin Collyer's work shows the degree to which our space is occupied by the text of commerce. When I first encountered this series of images, it reminded me of friends of mine who went to East Germany during the Cold War period, before the Wall collapsed. When they returned they described a place without text; it had no advertising signs. There was no reason to sell anyone anything. Signage was based on pure function. So a bakery would have a bakery sign to mark it, but not to promote it. There was no promotional voice in the urban landscape. In our present Western context, the only way we see all the urban inscription is by taking it away. Only then do we realize the degree to which our attention is colonized.

Conclusion: What Will Be.com of Us?

We imagined that we could have a carefree life — simply choosing colors, making shapes, putting one image beside another — the life of a designer, free from the anxieties of content. We imagined somehow that we could work within the schedule of the author, following the meandering pathways of our interests and observations. We even thought we could embrace the complexities of the landscape architect. We imagined that if we worked this way, we would, simply by declaration, be granted the status of the artist. We hoped through our ingenious configuration to earn the paycheck of the businessman.

Instead, the hand that we have dealt ourselves is anything but carefree. On the contrary, we are faced with the complexities of the businessman, the schedule of the designer, the anxieties of the author, the status of the landscape architect (no disrespect intended, designers in this category work most often for other architects, and like bindery workers in the book trade, deal principally not with what might be, but instead with what remains, making the most of what is left of schedules, budgets, and real estate). Finally, we are left with the paycheck of the artist.

Somewhere in my studio, a book of the collected writings of the late designer and educator Alvin Lustig opens with a quotation concerning the limits of disciplinary boundaries. Lustig declares that the words architect, graphic designer, and industrial designer stick in his throat, and stand for him as a brutal reduction of a creative life to an administrative perimeter that constrains what might be possible.

The tension between the consolidation of knowledge, expertise, and practice on the one hand, and the wild free range of invention and speculation it makes possible on the other, has become the central dilemma of our work. We are living at a moment when the definition of things is open to negotiation, and design is after all a "thing" open to definition. Administrative frontiers are up for grabs. Technology is allowing and in some sense demanding and promoting an embedded intelligence beneath the surface of our work. More and more, software carries the burden of expertise, liberating our energies for more ambitious objectives. The integration of intelligence promises and insists on the redefinition of work and design itself. Even in the 1950s, Lustig saw this, and others have worked at and through this intersection.

The studio of Ray and Charles Eames directed its efforts beyond the bounds of design office practice to include cinema, exhibitions, technology, innovation, and communication.... Gyorgy Kepes imagined a seamless zone of exploration between science and art, where invention and discovery in one domain traveled effortlessly and productively to the other.... Carlo Molino imagined that the envelope somehow included the design of architecture, furniture, gestures, speed, flight, and the erotic.... Tibor Kalman encouraged a problematic, ornery, sometimes cynical, and often ironic self-critical practice.... Philippe Starck has embraced the persona of the idiot savant while systematically attacking the elitist economies of the design that he produces.... Rem Koolhaas has driven toward a redefinition of design from his position within architecture and urbanism, imagining a mirror image of his practice in the realm of the virtual by simultaneously shedding and extending his ambitions ... Frank Gehry has reconfigured the limits of design technology and project practice, collapsing the boundaries between the once combative disciplines of engineering and design.

We make no claims for our own advances in these redefinitions, but we are happy to take our place in the struggle for their expansion. We admit that we are not inhabiting these roles and executing these responsibilities as elegantly or effortlessly as might sometimes be suggested in this volume. We couldn't be more conscious of the embarrassing compromises and sometimes glaringly evident contradictions that a practice of redefinition necessarily involves. While redefinition implies an expanding universe of possibilities, it comes with its own inherent limitations.

One of the dilemmas of the coming era is that there is no erasing anymore. We have lost the ability to subtract; we can only add. As the digital replaces the analog, there is no impetus to discard or lose things. In the past it was cumbersome to store information. Now the capacity to record and store material electronically is basically unlimited, and still it doubles every nine months. And we are only now entering the era of real accelerations in the movement and capture of information.

In sheer quantity, content is overpowering navigation, bestowing an alchemist's aura on the navigators. Designers and artists, cinematographers and architects, the authors who shape culture become critical players in the field.

As the mass and volume of information increase, people

search for a clear signal. More powerful than ever, the role of the navigator — one who gives pattern, shape and direction to the noise — becomes indispensable. The question is: What kind of people can these navigators be in terms of function or profession? We should not forget that the com after the dot is short for commercial. Must we define every gesture and possibility within this envelope? Is it not our role to imagine new futures more rich and complex and wild in their style than any single framework can accommodate?

We are suggesting the designer as a difficult, problematic figure, one who cannot afford to be stable, or to acknowledge boundaries as impassable. We have tried to turn our work into a constant process of growth, a living thing that responds to its environment and, as the environment itself evolves, propagates new opportunities.

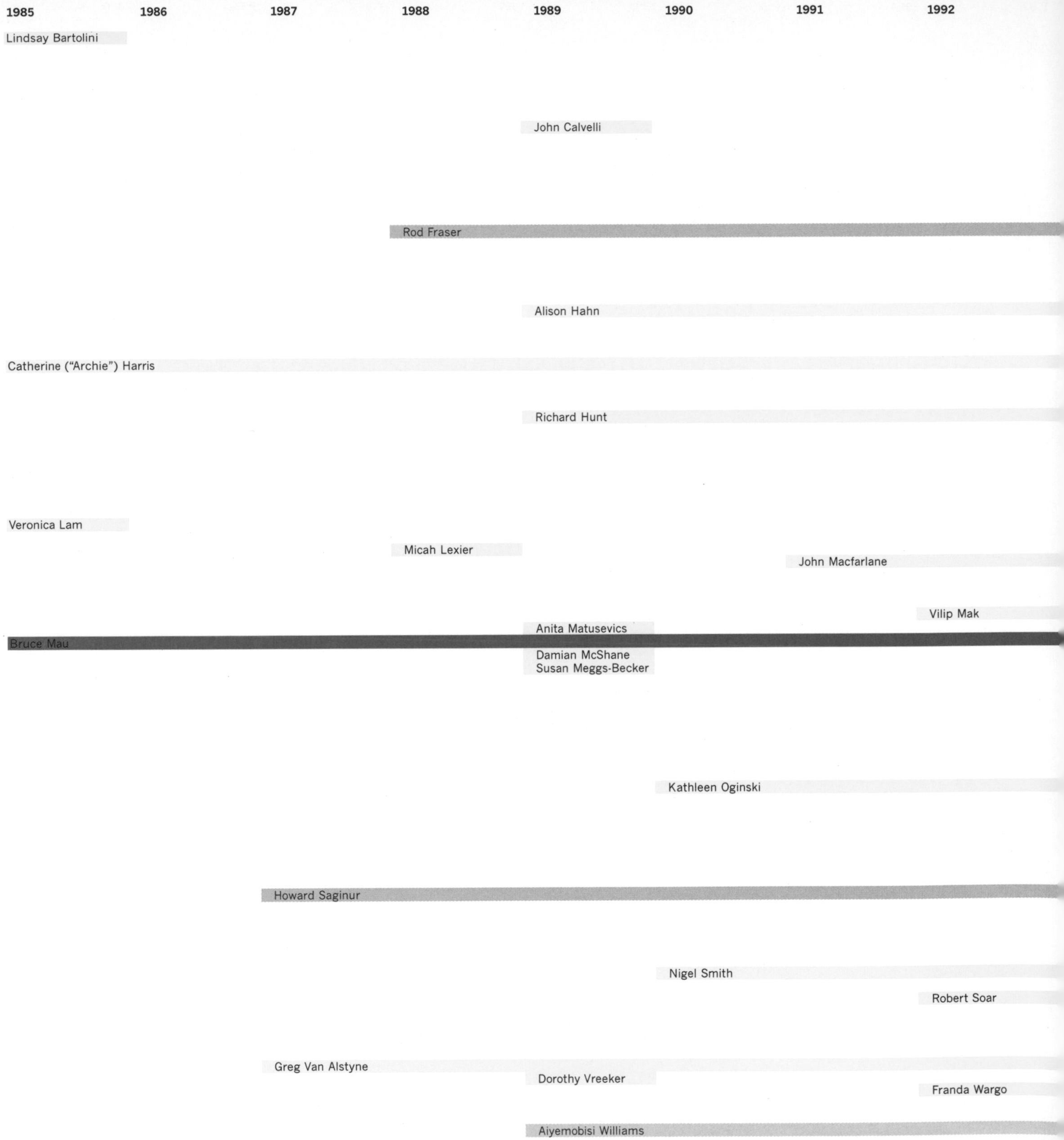

1985
1986
1987
1988
1989
1990
1991
1992
Lindsay Bartolini
John Calvelli
Rod Fraser
Alison Hahn
Catherine ("Archie") Harris
Richard Hunt
Veronica Lam
Micah Lexier
John Macfarlane
Vilip Mak
Anita Matusevics
Bruce Mau
Damian McShane
Susan Meggs-Becker
Kathleen Oginski
Howard Saginur
Nigel Smith
Robert Soar
Greg Van Alstyne
Dorothy Vreeker
Franda Wargo
Aiyemobisi Williams

1993 1994 1995 1996 1997 1998 1999 2000

Paul Backewich
Michael Barker
Alan Belcher
Sara Borins
Tania Boterman
Jayne Brown
Luke Bulman
Simon Chan
Henry Hong-Yiu Cheung
Aaron Currie
Andrew di Rosa
Norah Farrell
Val Foster
Alejandro Gehry
Reto Geiser
David Gillespie
Barr Gilmore
Nathaniel Gray
Jason Halter
Burton Hamfelt
Tracey Hanson
Branden Hookway
Kevin Hope
Karla Huckvale
Izumi Iizuka
Lee Jacobson
Cathy Jonasson
Robert Kennedy
Helmina Kim
Tom Kyle
James Lahey
Louis-Charles Lasnier
Kyo Maclear
Kate MacKay
Donald Mak
Maris Mezulis
Mary Moegenburg
Enzo Moser
Carol Moukheiber
Lisa Molnar
Lewis Nicholson
Riki Nishimura
Nancy Nowacek
Megan Oldfield
Chris Pommer
Shadi Rahbaran
Vis Ramasubramian
Catherine Rix
Jackie Rothstein
Chris Rowat
Amanda Sebris
Lucas Sharkey Pearce
Jim Shedden
Emmet Sheil
Kimberly Shoemake
Steve Snyder
Kevin Sugden
Nazik Tahri
Matthew Talbot-Kelly
Gary Westwood
Yoshiki Waterhouse
David Wilkinson
Bolaji Williams
Jonathan Winton
Stefan Wolf

Chronology

Projects are listed by the following information:

Client and/or Publisher, city
Title of book and/or description of project
Author of book

1985

Lindsay Bartolini, Veronica Lam

3-D Imagery, Toronto
Promotional materials

Virtu, Toronto
Catalog and poster for Virtu

Zone Books, New York
Zone 1|2: The Contemporary City
Edited by Michel Feher and Sanford Kwinter

1986

Art Gallery of Ontario, Toronto
Bernie Miller
by Philip Monk and Barbara Fischer

Liz Magor
by Philip Monk

The Norcen Gift: Twentieth Century Canadian Art
Preface by William Withrow

Art Metropole, Toronto
The Disposables
by Andrew J. Paterson

1987

Greg Van Alstyne

Art Gallery of Ontario, Toronto
Paterson Ewen: Phenomena. Paintings 1971–1987
by Philip Monk

Shirley Wiitasalo
by Philip Monk

49th Parallel, New York
Poster for *The Idea of North*

Zone Books, New York
Foucault/Blanchot
by Michel Foucault and Maurice Blanchot

Society Against the State
by Pierre Clastres

1988

Micah Lexier, Greg Van Alstyne

Art Gallery of Ontario, Toronto
Ian Carr-Harris 1971–1977
by Philip Monk

Art Metropole, Toronto
Pornography in the Urban World
by Jean Gagnon

Gordon Monahan, Toronto
CD cover for *This Piano Thing*

Waterloo University School of Architecture, Waterloo, Canada
Posters for The Arriscraft Lecture Series

YYZ, Toronto
Struggles with the Image
by Philip Monk

Zone Books, New York
The Accursed Share: An Essay on General Economy
Volume 1: *Consumption*
by Georges Bataille

Bergsonism
by Gilles Deleuze

Matter and Memory
by Henri Bergson

Mitra-Varuna
by Georges Dumézil

Myth and Society in Ancient Greece
by Jean-Pierre Vernant

Myth and Tragedy in Ancient Greece
by Jean-Pierre Vernant and Pierre Vidal-Naquet

Your Money or Your Life: Economy and Religion in the Middle Ages
by Jacques Le Goff

1989

John Calvelli, Alison Hahn, Anita Matusevics, Damian McShane, Susan Meggs-Becker, Greg Van Alstyne, Dorothy Vreeker

Art Gallery of Ontario, Toronto
4 Hours and 38 Minutes: Videotapes by Lisa Steele and Kim Tomczak
by Philip Monk and Dot Tuer

Ron Martin 1971–1981
by James D. Campbell, Walter Klepac, Ron Martin, and Philip Monk

Canadian Embassy, Washington, D.C.
The Light that Fills the World
by William A. Ewing

Silver in Quebec in the 18th Century
by Mario Béland

Dia Center for the Arts, New York
Identity for Printed Matter bookstore at Dia Center for the Arts

Martin Kohn and John Shnier Architects, Toronto
Competition entry submission for Kitchener City Hall

Zone Books, New York
Fragments for a History of the Human Body: Part One
Edited by Michel Feher with Ramona Naddaff and Nadia Tazi

Fragments for a History of the Human Body: Part Two
Edited by Michel Feher with Ramona Naddaff and Nadia Tazi

Fragments for a History of the Human Body: Part Three
Edited by Michel Feher with Ramona Naddaff and Nadia Tazi

The Life of Forms in Art
by Henri Focillon

The Normal and the Pathological
by Georges Canguilhem, with an introduction by Michel Foucault

Theory of Religion
by Georges Bataille

Identity program for Zone Books

1990

Alison Hahn, Kathleen Oginski, Nigel Smith, Greg Van Alstyne

Art Gallery of Ontario, Toronto
Art Gallery of Ontario: Selected Works

Canadian Embassy, Washington, D.C.
Canadian Landscape
by Jeremy Adamson

The Passage of Light
by Rosalyn J. Morrison

Carnegie Museum of Art, Pittsburgh
Design of Forum Series

The Getty Research Institute, Los Angeles
Looking for a City in America: Down These Mean Streets a Man Must Go...
An Essay by André Corboz
Photographs by Dennis Keeley
Angel's Flight: Occasional Papers from Los Angeles

Poster design for Center Fellowships

Martin Kohn and John Shnier Architects, Toronto
Letterhead

Zone Books, New York
Expressionism in Philosophy: Spinoza
by Gilles Deleuze

The Poetic Structure of the World: Copernicus and Kepler
by Fernand Hallyn

1991

Alison Hahn, John Macfarlane, Kathleen Oginski, Nigel Smith, Greg Van Alstyne

Artemis & Winkler, Munich
Tusculum series design

Carnegie Museum of Art, Pittsburgh
Carnegie International 1991, Volume II
Edited by Lynne Cooke and Mark Francis

Frank O. Gehry and Associates, Los Angeles
Font development, signage, and environmental graphics for Walt Disney Concert Hall

The Getty Research Institute, Los Angeles
Art in History, History in Art: Studies in Seventeenth-Century Dutch Culture
Edited by David Freedberg and Jan de Vries

Zone Books, New York
The Accursed Share: An Essay on General Economy
Volume II: *The History of Eroticism*
Volume III: *Sovereignty*
by Georges Bataille

Fragmentation and Redemption: Essays on Gender and the Human Body in Medieval Religion
by Caroline Walker Bynum

Masochism. Coldness and Cruelty
by Gilles Deleuze
Venus in Furs
by Leopold von Sacher-Masoch

Perspective as Symbolic Form
by Erwin Panofsky

Zone Books, Swerve Editions, New York
War in the Age of Intelligent Machines
by Manuel De Landa

1992

Alison Hahn, John Macfarlane, Vilip Mak, Kathleen Oginski, Nigel Smith, Robert Soar, Greg Van Alstyne, Franda Wargo

The Getty Research Institute, Los Angeles
American Icons: Transatlantic Perspectives on Eighteenth- and Nineteenth-Century American Art
Edited by Thomas W. Gaehtgens and Heinz Ickstadt

***I.D.* magazine, New York**
Design and identity program

Gordon Monahan, New York
CD cover and performance for *Speaker Swinging*

The Montreal Museum of Decorative Arts, Montreal
Frank Gehry: New Bentwood Furniture Designs
by David A. Hanks & Associates Inc.

Zone Books, New York
Etienne-Jules Marey: A Passion for the Trace
by François Dagognet

La Jetée: Ciné-roman
by Chris Marker

Zone 6: Incorporations
Edited by Jonathan Crary and Sanford Kwinter

Born in Sudbury, Ontario, Canada, Bruce Mau studied at the Ontario College of Art and Design. He has been the design director of Zone Books since its inception in 1985, and an editor (with Sanford Kwinter and Jonathan Crary) of Swerve Editions, a Zone imprint. From 1991 to 1993, he served as creative director of *I.D.* magazine. He was the Associate Cullinan Professor at the Rice University School of Architecture in Houston, Texas, from 1996 to 1999. He has been a thesis advisor at the University of Toronto's School of Architecture, artist in residence at California Institute of the Arts, and a visiting scholar at the Getty Research Institute in Los Angeles. He has lectured widely throughout North America and Europe and in 1998 was awarded the Chrysler Award for Design Innovation.

Since Bruce Mau Design was founded in 1985, the studio has maintained ongoing collaborations with architects Rem Koolhaas and Frank Gehry; devised identity programs for such institutions as the Netherlands Architecture Institute, the Andy Warhol Museum, and the Art Gallery of Ontario; worked with the Getty Research Institute on an expanding range of publications; collaborated with artist Gordon Monahan, filmmaker Michael Snow, and choreographer Meg Stuart; and completed projects for *The New York Times*, *Metropolis* magazine, and dozens of other clients and individuals. BMD's recent projects include new identities for the UCLA Hammer Museum (Los Angeles), Access Storage Solutions (London), the Gagosian Gallery (New York and London); a new communication strategy for Vitra; the conceptual program for a new museum on the Mississippi River in New Orleans in association with Tulane University; *Book Machine*, an installation and catalog for the exhibition *Laboratorium* at the 1999 Antwerpen Open; and *STRESS*, a multi-media installation about the limits of the human body commissioned by Hortensia Völckers for the Wiener Festwochen 2000. More recently, BMD's proposal "Tree City," developed in collaboration with Rem Koolhaas and Petra Blaisse, with Oleson Worland Architects won the prestigious Downsview Park international competition in Toronto.

1993

Alison Hahn, Karla Huckvale, Lee Jacobson, John Macfarlane, Anita Matusevics, Kathleen Oginski, Chris Rowat, Nigel Smith, Robert Soar, Kevin Sugden, Greg Van Alstyne, Franda Wargo

The Andy Warhol Museum, Pittsburgh
Identity program

Promotional booklet

Art Gallery of Ontario, Toronto
Robin Collyer: Idioms of Resistance
by Philip Monk

Robin Collyer: Canada XLV Biennale di Venezia
by Philip Monk

Exhibition marketing campaign for *From Cezanne to Matisse: Great French Paintings from the Barnes Foundation*

The Getty Research Institute, Los Angeles
Otto Wagner: Reflections on the Raiment of Modernity
Edited by Harry Francis Mallgrave

Luaka Bop Records, New York
CD cover for *Zap Mama: Adventures In Afropea 1*

Netherlands Architecture Institute (NAi), Rotterdam
Identity program

Ontario Arts Council, Toronto
Identity program

Zone Books, New York
The Invention of Pornography: Obscenity and the Origins of Modernity 1500–1800
Edited by Lynn Hunt

1994

Val Foster, Alison Hahn, Karla Huckvale, Lee Jacobson, Anita Matusevics, Carol Moukheiber, Lewis Nicholson, Megan Oldfield, Kathleen Oginski, Chris Rowat, Nigel Smith, Robert Soar, Kevin Sugden, Matthew Talbot-Kelly, Nazik Tahri, Greg Van Alstyne

Art Gallery of Ontario, Toronto
The Michael Snow Project: Presence and Absence, The Films of Michael Snow 1956–1991
Edited by Jim Shedden

Art Gallery of Ontario and The Power Plant, Toronto
The Michael Snow Project: Music/Sound, 1948–1993
Edited by Michael Snow

The Michael Snow Project: Visual Art, 1951–1993
by Louise Dompierre, Philip Monk, and Dennis Reid

Exhibition design and marketing for *The Michael Snow Project*

Each One, Teach One, Toronto
Design of banner and stickers

Elektrizitätswerk Minden-Ravensburg (EMR), Minden-Ravensburg, Germany
Exhibition design concept

The Globe and Mail, Toronto
Competition entry for re-design of *The Globe and Mail* (unrealized)

Micah Lexier, Toronto
Micah Lexier Cross Reference: Dictionary Illustration Works 1981–1993

Lightscape Technologies, San Jose, California
Identity program

Los Angeles Philharmonic, Los Angeles
Marketing design

Claes Oldenburg and Coosje van Bruggen, New York
Claes Oldenburg, Coosje van Bruggen: Large-Scale Projects
by Claes Oldenburg and Coosje van Bruggen

Wexner Center for the Arts, Columbus, Ohio
Marketing, membership campaign, and annual event calendar for the Wexner Center for the Arts

Witte de With, Rotterdam
Witte de With: Cahier #2, June 1994
by Richter Verlag

Zone Books, New York
The Movement of the Free Spirit
by Raoul Vaneigem

The Society of the Spectacle
by Guy Debord

Third Sex, Third Gender: Beyond Sexual Dimorphism in Culture and History
Edited by Gilbert Herdt

A Vital Rationalist: Selected Writings from Georges Canguilhem
Edited by François Delaporte

1995

Alison Hahn, Karla Huckvale, Lee Jacobson, Anita Matusevics, Lewis Nicholson, Kathleen Oginski, Chris Rowat, Nigel Smith, Kevin Sugden, Matthew Talbot-Kelly, Greg Van Alstyne, Bolaji Williams
S,M,L,XL: **Paul Backewich, Val Foster, Alejandro Gehry, Nathaniel Gray, Burton Hamfelt, Kevin Hope, Izumi Iizuka, Helmina Kim, Tom Kyle, Vilip Mak, Megan Oldfield, Steve Snyder, Robert Soar, Jonathan Winton**

Collins and Skover, Washington
The Death of Discourse
by Ronald K.L. Collins and David M. Skover

Design Exchange, Toronto
Exhibition design for *Pop in Orbit*

The Getty Research Institute, Los Angeles
Building in France, Building in Iron, Building in Ferroconcrete
by Sigfried Giedion
Introduction by Sokratis Georgiadis

The Solomon R. Guggenheim Museum of Art, New York
Posters and T-shirt for the exhibition *Claes Oldenburg—An Anthology*

The Monacelli Press, New York
S,M,L,XL
by O.M.A., Rem Koolhaas, and Bruce Mau

Rhombus Media, Toronto
Titles for the film *September Songs* by Larry Weinstein

Universal Studios, Los Angeles
Presentation for Universal Studios identity program

Whitney Museum of American Art, New York
Views from Abroad: European Perspectives on American Art 1
by Rudi Fuchs and Adam D. Weinberg

Zone Books, New York
The Organism
by Kurt Goldstein

The Propensity of Things: Toward a History of Efficacy in China
by François Jullien

1996

Andrew di Rosa, Alejandro Gehry, Barr Gilmore, Karla Huckvale, Cathy Jonasson, James Lahey, Megan Oldfield, Chris Pommer, Chris Rowat, Kevin Sugden, Yoshiki Waterhouse, Bolaji Williams

Art Gallery of Ontario, Toronto
Exhibition concept and design for *The OH! Canada Project*

First Website for the Art Gallery of Ontario

Identity program

The Getty Research Institute, Los Angeles
The Modern Functional Building
by Adolf Behne

Harbourfront Centre, Toronto
Identity program

Museum of Contemporary Art, Los Angeles, and The Monacelli Press, New York
Art and Film Since 1945: Hall of Mirrors
Organized by Kerry Brougher
Edited by Russell Ferguson

***The New York Times*, New York**
Futurist advertisement for genetic engineering

The Power Plant, Toronto
Power Ten Campaign (1996–98)

Rogers Communications Inc., Toronto
Website and marketing for artwave@Rogers.com

Meg Stuart, Damaged Goods, Brussels
Set design for White Oak Dance Project, "Remote"

Zone Books, New York
The Culture of the Copy: Striking Likenesses, Unreasonable Facsimiles
by Hillel Schwartz

The Masters of Truth in Ancient Greece
by Marcel Detienne
Foreword by Pierre Vidal-Naquet

1997

Sara Borins, Barr Gilmore, Tracey Hanson, Branden Hookway, Karla Huckvale, Cathy Jonasson, James Lahey, Nancy Nowacek, Chris Pommer, Chris Rowat, Amanda Sebris, Emmet Sheil, Kevin Sugden, Yoshiki Waterhouse, Bolaji Williams

Art Gallery of Ontario, Toronto
Donor Recognition Program

Jane Corkin Gallery, Toronto
Identity program

The Getty Research Institute, Los Angeles
Censorship and Silencing: Practices of Cultural Regulation
Edited by Robert C. Post

Incendiary Art: The Representation of Fireworks in Early Modern Europe
by Kevin Salatino

Irresistible Decay: Ruins Reclaimed
by Michael S. Roth with Claire Lyons and Charles Merewether

Russian Modernism. The Collections of the Getty Research Institute for the History of Art and the Humanities
Introduction by Jean-Louis Cohen
Compiled and annotated by David Woodruff and Ljiljana Grubišić

The Solomon R. Guggenheim Museum, New York
Frank O. Gehry: Guggenheim Museum Bilbao
by Coosje van Bruggen

Indigo Books and Music, Toronto
Identity program, marketing, and environmental signage

Rem Koolhaas, Rotterdam, and Documenta X, Kassel
"Pearl River Delta," insert in *Documenta X*, compiled by the Harvard Project on the City, The China Group: Bernard Cheng, Mihai Cracium, Nancy Lin, Yuyang Liu, Katherine Orff, Stephanie Smith, with Marcela Cortina, and Jun Takahashi

Selected Bibliography

Publications by Bruce Mau

Books

S,M,L,XL, O.M.A., Rem Koolhaas and Bruce Mau (New York: The Monacelli Press, 1995).

Articles

"Beyond Typography." *Insite* (Toronto), January 1996.

"Eight Strategies." *Rethinking Design 4* (Los Angeles), October 1997.

"Getting Engaged." In *Anytime*, edited by Cynthia C. Davidson (Cambridge, Mass.: The M.I.T. Press, 1999), 202–207.

"An Incomplete Manifesto for Growth." *I.D.* (March/April 1999), 56–59.

"A Manifesto for Growth." *rHed* 1, no. 7 (Fall 1997): 7.

"Mining the Structure" (an interview by Hendrik Tratsaert). *janus* (May 2000): 14–18.

"Shopping in Paradise" (discussion with Naomi Klein). *THIS* (November/December 1999): 45–46.

"Et ufullstendig manifest for vekst." *Morgenbladet* (Oslo, February 18, 2000): 11.

"Where Are We Going? An Incomplete Manifesto for Growth." *Domus* (January 2000): 46–47.

Publications about Bruce Mau Design

"The Best Design of 1996." *Time* (December 23, 1996): 48.

"Bruce Mau: Consultancy Profile." *Graphics International* 70 (November 1999): 18–21.

"Forecasts." *Publisher's Weekly* (January 22, 1996): 54–55.

"Koolhaas e Mau in Bordeaux." Exhibition review. *l'ARCA* 125 (April 1998): 99.

"New & Notable." *I.D.* (March/April 1996): 77.

"Toronto Graphic Designers Export Decidedly Different Styles." *The Financial Post*, September 10, 1993, p. 8.

Berridge, Joe. "Charting Scale of Koolhaas's Oeuvre." *The Globe and Mail*, June 19, 1996, p. C20

Buruma, Ian. "The Sky's the Limit." *The New York Review of Books*, November 28, 1996, pp. 42–47.

Coupland, Ken. "Bruce Mau: Book Maker." *Graphis* 314 (1998): 76–87.

Crinion, Elizabeth. "Maximal Mau." *Azure* (May/June 1994): 20–21.

de Smet, Catherine. "'Je suis un livre'. A propos de S,M,L,XL, par Rem Koolhaas et Bruce Mau." *Les Cahiers du Musée National d'Art Moderne* 68 (Summer 1999): 94–111.

Filler, Martin. "The Master Builder." *The New York Times Book Review*, March 17, 1996, p. 12.

Freedman, Adele. "Exploring the No Man's Land between Art and Design." *The Globe and Mail*, August 8, 1987, p. C12.

———. "A Font of Innovation, Down to the Letter." *The Globe and Mail*, June 5, 1993, p. C12.

———. "High Anxiety." *Saturday Night* (May 13, 2000): 65–70.

———. "International Bruce Mau." *Canadian Art* (Summer 1990): 60–69.

———. "The Tall Order of Sizing Up a Very Big Book." *The Globe and Mail*, November 5, 1994, p. C15.

Paragon/HandMade Films, London
Animated logo redesign

Professional Art Dealers Association of Canada (PADAC), Toronto
Identity program and Website

Random House of Canada/ A Bruce Mau Editions Book, Toronto
Royal Agricultural Winter Fair: An Illustrated History
by Dan Needles

Rensselaer Polytechnic Institute, New York
Recruiting posters

Rice University School of Architecture, Houston
Poster design

Roots Canada, Toronto
Campaign for Roots, Spring and Fall/Winter 1997 Collection

Identity program

Uniform branding for Canada's Olympic team at the 1997 Winter Olympics

Roots Jeans campaign

Sony Classical, New York
CD packaging for *Yo-Yo Ma: Inspired by Bach*

Meg Stuart, Damaged Goods, Brussels
Bruce Mau performance of *Crash Landing*, Théatre de la Ville, Paris, November 6–8, 1997

Swatch, New York
Design of "Overtime" watch

The Andy Warhol Museum, Pittsburgh
The Warhol Look: Glamour, Style, Fashion
by Mark Francis and Margery King

Whitney Museum of American Art, New York
Views from Abroad: European Perspectives on American Art 2
by Jean-Christophe Ammann and Adam D. Weinberg

Views from Abroad: European Perspectives on American Art 3
by Nicholas Serota, Sandy Nairne, and Adam D. Weinberg

Zone Books, New York
Formless: A User's Guide
by Yve-Alain Bois and Rosalind E. Krauss

The Libertine Reader: Eroticism and Enlightenment in Eighteenth-Century France
Edited by Michel Feher

The Panorama
by Stephan Oettermann

Zone Books, Swerve Editions, New York
A Thousand Years of Non-Linear History
by Manuel De Landa

1998

Aaron Currie, Reto Geiser, Barr Gilmore, Tracey Hanson, Karla Huckvale, Cathy Jonasson, James Lahey, Louis-Charles Lasnier, Kyo Maclear, Anita Matusevics, Mary Moegenburg, Lisa Molnar, Enzo Moser, Nancy Nowacek, Chris Pommer, Catherine Rix, Chris Rowat, Amanda Sebris, Jim Shedden, Emmet Sheil, Kevin Sugden, Stefan Wolf

AIDS Committee of Toronto, Toronto
Poster and promotional material for Dancers for Life performance

Air Canada Centre, Toronto
Banners, mural, restaurant signage, and exhibition concept and design for *Memories and Dreams* (the history of Maple Leaf Gardens hockey arena)

Canadian Academy of Arts and Television, Toronto
Promotional material and program for 1997 Gemini Awards and 1998 Genie Awards

Fuse Magazine, Toronto
Fuse poster

The Getty Research Institute, Los Angeles
Dosso's Fate: Painting and Court Culture in Renaissance Italy
Edited by Luisa Ciammitti, Steven F. Ostrow, and Salvatore Settis

Jane Corkin Gallery, Toronto
Robert Bourdeau: Industrial Sites
An interview with Robert Bourdeau by Robert Enright

Kunstverein Hannover, Hannover, Germany
Douglas Gordon
by Douglas Gordon, Lynne Cooke, et al.

***Metropolis* magazine, New York**
Center spread for April 1998 issue

Rhombus Media, Toronto
Film title and credits for *The Red Violin*

Joseph L. Rotman School of Management, University of Toronto
Identity program

Rice University School of Architecture, Houston
Catalog (with Luke Bulman and Kimberly Shoemake), poster design, and text for promotion and recruitment

Schmidt Coca-Cola Bottling Company, Elizabethtown, Kentucky
Concept and design for Schmidt Museum of Coca-Cola Memorabilia

Virtual Office for Integrated Design (VOID), San Francisco
Identity program

Wood Street Galleries and Mark Francis, Pittsburgh
Poster, invitation, and T-shirt for Louise Bourgeois exhibition

Zone Books, New York
Chronicle of the Guayaki Indians
by Pierre Clastres
Translation and Foreword by Paul Auster

Crossing Boundaries: Selected Writings
by Albert O. Hirschman

The Decadent Reader: Fiction, Fantasy, and Perversion from Fin-de-Siècle France
Edited by Asti Hustvedt

The Visual and the Visionary: Art and Female Spirituality in Late Medieval Germany
by Jeffrey F. Hamburger

Wonders and the Order of Nature, 1150–1750
by Lorraine Daston and Katharine Park

1999

Alan Belcher, Jayne Brown, Aaron Currie, Reto Geiser, Barr Gilmore, Jason Halter, Cathy Jonasson, Robert Kennedy, Louis-Charles Lasnier, Kyo Maclear, Kate MacKay, Anita Matusevics, Maris Mezulis, Barbara Milne, Mary Moegenburg, Lisa Molnar, Chris Pommer, Vis Ramasubramian, Catherine Rix, Jackie Rothstein, Chris Rowat, Amanda Sebris, Jim Shedden, Kevin Sugden, David Wilkinson

Anyone Corporation, New York
Proposal for *21A*, an architecture and design magazine (unrealized)

Antwerp Museums, Antwerp
Identity program and banner system

Antwerpen Open, Antwerp
Book Machine installation

Exhibition identity program for *Laboratorium*

Argus Pictures, Toronto
Identity program

Stéphane Beel Architects, Brugge
Signage program and art installation for the winning entry for the Ghent courthouse architecture competition

Canadian Centre for Architecture (CCA), Montreal
Identity program and exterior signage

Printed materials for CCA 10th anniversary

Deutsche Guggenheim, Berlin
Dan Flavin: The Architecture of Light
Edited by J. Fiona Ragheb

Faculty of Architecture, Landscape, and Design at University of Toronto (al&d), Toronto
Identity program

Gagosian Gallery, Los Angeles
Glen Seator: Three
Essays by David Joselit and Terry R. Myers

Gagosian Gallery, New York
Hybrid exhibition catalog and poster for *Douglas Gordon: "through a looking glass"*
by Douglas Gordon, Hal Hartley, and Amy Taubin

The Getty Research Institute, Los Angeles
Aby Warburg: The Renewal of Pagan Antiquity
Introduction by Kurt W. Forster

Maiolica in the Making: The Gentili/Barnabei Archive
by Catherine Hess

Nietzsche and "An Architecture of Our Minds"
Edited by Alexander Kostka and Irving Wohlfarth

Harbourfront Centre, Toronto
25th Anniversary World Leader event and campaign

Indigo Books, Toronto
Design of Website

Ludion, Gent-Amsterdam
Stéphane Beel Architect
by Geert Bekaert, et al.

Mira Godard Gallery, Toronto
Big North: The Paintings of John Hartman
Essay by Matthew Hart

David Milne. Watercolours: An Overview
Preface by John Hartman

Office for Metropolitan Architecture, Rotterdam / House and Robertson, Los Angeles
Signage program for Universal Studios headquarters

Gill, Brendan. "Koolhaas in 2-D." *The New Yorker* (February 12, 1996): 76–79.
Glazer, Kate. "A Conversation with Renegade Designer Bruce Mau." *Omnibus/Documenta XS4ALL* (October 1997): 29–30.
Gopnik, Blake. "The Content Is the Design. For Me, That's the Key." *The Globe and Mail*, November 6, 1999, p. F3.
———. "Mau's trap." *The Globe and Mail*, May 6, 2000, p. R9.
Hanna, Annetta. "On the Borderline." *I.D.* (May/June 1988): 79.
Hannon, Gerald. "Inside Bruce's brain." *Toronto Life* (June 1998): 92–99.
Hume, Christopher. "Bruce Mau's Messages are His Message." *The Toronto Star*, February 8, 1997, p. M3.
Jameson, Fredric. "XXL." *The Village Voice, Voice Literary Supplement* (May 1996): 17–19.
Kapusta, Beth. "How now, Bruce Mau?" *Azure* (May/June 2000): 32.
Kirchoff, H. J. "Publisher Aims at the Intellect." *The Globe and Mail*, April 13, 1988, p. C6.
Kuitenbrouwer, Peter. "A Slippery Glass Slipper: Reversing the Brain Drain." *National Post*, June 24, 1999, pp. C1, C6.
Luscombe, Belinda. "Making a Splash." *Time* (April 8, 1996): 52–54.
Mays, John Bentley. "A Symphony of Forces on the Complex Theme of the Human Body." *The Globe and Mail*, June 24, 1989, p. C16.
Mitchell, Michael. "Our Town: Portrait of a Decade." *Canadian Art* (Fall 1994): 59.
Muschamp, Herbert. "Buildings Born of Dreams and Demons." *The New York Times*, January 7, 1996.
———. "Rem Koolhaas Sizes up the Future." *The New York Times*, March 3, 1996, Arts & Leisure section, p. 38.
Neri, Claudia. "Canadian Accent." *Linea Graphica* (March 1993): 64–66.
Novosedlik, Will. "The Producer as Author." *Eye* 4, no. 15 (Winter, 1994): 44–53.
———. "Leviathan." *Print* 50, no. 4 (July/August, 1996): 90–95.
Ouroussoff, Nicolai. "On Being in Nothingness: Rem Koolhaas Generic City." *The New York Observer*, March 11, 1996, p. 27.
Perman, Margot. "Book Reviews." *Graphis* 304, (July/August 1996): 19.
Poynor, Rick. "Book Monitor." *AIGA Journal of Graphic Design* 14, no. 2 (June 1996): 32–33.
———. "Chairman Mau." *I.D.* (January/February 1998): 93.
———. "Producer as Author." *Blueprint* (December 1989): 37–38.
Ramakers, Renny. "A Fascination for an Unstable Quality: Bruce Mau More Than Just a Designer." *Items* (December 1994): 48–53.
Riley, Terence. "O.M.A. Un livre, une oeuvre: S,M,L,XL, La Dutch House." *L'architecture d'aujourd'hui* 304 (April 1996): 55–78.
Rock, Michael. "The Designer as Author." *Eye* 5, no. 20 (Spring 1996): 44–51.
Shnier, John. "Plump Fiction." *Canadian Architect* (November 1995): 18–21.
Sliwka, Ryszard. "XL." *Insite* 5, no. 4 (May 1996): 27–31.
Tratsaert, Hendrik. "Bruce Mau: Mining the Structure," *janus* (April 2000): 14–18.
Wasiuta, Mark, and Burton Hamfelt. "Notes on the Tendencies Exhibited through Free Time." *Span* (University of Toronto School of Architecture, Spring 1992): 35–39.
Young, Pamela. "Going Beyond Attention and Distraction." *The Globe and Mail*, May 16, 1996, p. E3.

Rice University School of Architecture, Houston
Pandemonium: The Rise of Predatory Locales in the Postwar World
by Branden Hookway
Edited and presented by Sanford Kwinter and Bruce Mau

Roots Canada, Toronto
Art direction

Royal Ontario Museum, Toronto
Graphic and exhibition design, promotional materials for the Gallery of Korean Art

Tony Scherman, Toronto
Tony Scherman: Chasing Napoleon, Forensic Portraits
Texts by Jacques Henric, et al.

Tulane University, New Orleans
Museum concept for the National Museum of the Mississippi River

University of Toronto/Hart House, Toronto
A Strange Elation. Hart House: The First Eighty Years
Edited by David Kilgour

Zone Books, New York
The Expressiveness of the Body and the Divergence of Greek and Chinese Medicine
by Shigehisa Kuriyama

Human Rights in Political Transitions: Gettysburg to Bosnia
Edited by Carla Hesse and Robert Post

Remnants of Auschwitz: The Witness and the Archive
by Giorgio Agamben

Two Sisters and Their Mother: The Anthropology of Incest
by Françoise Héritier

The Wicked Queen: The Origins of the Myth of Marie-Antoinette
by Chantal Thomas

2000

Michael Barker, Alan Belcher, Tania Boterman, Jayne Brown, Simon Chan, Henry Hong-Yiu Cheung, Aaron Currie, Norah Farrell, Reto Geiser, Barr Gilmore, David Gillespie, Jason Halter, Cathy Jonasson, Robert Kennedy, Kate MacKay, Kyo Maclear, Donald Mak, Anita Matusevics, Maris Mezulis, Lisa Molnar, Riki Nishimura, Chris Pommer, Shadi Rahbaran, Catherine Rix, Jackie Rothstein, Chris Rowat, Amanda Sebris, Lucas Sharkey Pearce, Jim Shedden, Kevin Sugden, Gary Westwood, David Wilkinson

Access Storage Solutions, London
Brand identity program, marketing, and signage designs

Antwerpen Open, Antwerp
Catalog design for *Laboratorium*

Canadian Centre for Architecture (CCA), Montreal
Tracking Images: Un Dictionnaire...
by Phyllis Lambert, Jean François Chevrier, et al.

Parc Downsview Park, Toronto
Tree City competition submission in collaboration with Rem Koolhaas, Office for Metropolitan Architecture; Petra Blaisse, Inside Outside; with David Oleson, Oleson Worland Architects

Gagosian Gallery, New York
Eric Fischl: The Bed, The Chair...
by Frederic Tutten

Willem de Kooning: Mostly Women
Introduction by Bob Monk

Andy Warhol: Diamond Dust Shadow Paintings
Essay by Rosalind E. Krauss

Gagosian Gallery, New York, Los Angeles, London
Identity program and unique font for Gagosian Gallery

Galerie de Bellefeuille, Montreal
James Lahey
Essay by Ihor Holubizky

Hatje Cantz Verlag, Stuttgart
ReMembering the Body
Edited by Gabrielle Brandstetter and Hortensia Völckers

The Getty Research Institute, Los Angeles
The Group Portraiture of Holland
by Alois Riegl
Introduction by Wolfgang Kemp

Modern Architecture in Czechoslovakia and Other Writings
by Karel Teige

Précis of the Lectures on Architecture: with Graphic Portion of the Lectures on Architecture
by Jean-Louis Durand
Introduction by Antoine Picon

The Victory of the New Building Style
by Walter Curt Behrendt

The McMichael Canadian Art Collection, Kleinberg
Exhibition concept for *Hockey and the Art of Being Canadian*, in collaboration with Ken Dryden

Office for Metropolitan Architecture, Rotterdam
Signage and environmental graphics for Porto Concert Hall, Portugal

Signage and environmental graphics for Seattle Public Library, Seattle

Rosedale Montessori School, Toronto
Identity program

Tate Liverpool, Liverpool
Douglas Gordon: Black Spot
by Mark Francis

UCLA Hammer Museum, Los Angeles
Identity program, publications design, and signage

Vitra, Basel
Marketing and publications design

Vitra Design Museum, Weil am Rhein, Switzerland
Exhibition concept and design for *Luis Barragán: Die Stille Revolution*

Vizible Software Inc., Toronto
Brand identity program

Wiener Festwochen 2000, Vienna
Multimedia installation *STRESS*, in collaboration with André Lepecki and John Oswald

Terry Winters, New York
Book and limited-edition box design for *Perfection, Way, Origin*
by Terry Winters and Jean Starobinski

Zone Books, New York
Art and Technology in the Nineteenth and Twentieth Centuries
by Pierre Francastel

Culture in Practice: Selected Essays
by Marshall Sahlins

Detour and Access: Strategies of Meaning in China and Greece
by François Jullien

The Vienna School Reader: Politics and Art Historical Method in the 1930s
Edited by Christopher S. Wood

Image Credits

All reasonable efforts have been made to trace the copyright holders of the visual material reproduced herein. The Publisher and Bruce Mau Design apologize to anyone who has not been reached.
Photographs and illustrations are provided courtesy of Bruce Mau Design, with the exception of those listed below:

© AFP/CORBIS: 82 top right, 235, 239
© David Allen/CORBIS: 70
AP Wide World Photos: 433
AP Wide World Photos/Peter Barreras: 69 center
AP Wide World Photos/Shizuo Kambayashi: 75 bottom left
AP Wide World Photos/John Lehmann: 20–21
AP Wide World Photos/MasterCard International: 50–51
AP Wide World Photos/Eric Miller: 240–41
AP Wide World Photos/Ragdoll Productions: 69 bottom
AP Wide World Photos/Collin Reid: 74 top right
AP Wide World Photos/Murad Sezer: 62 bottom
AP Wide World Photos/Nick Ut: 82 bottom left
Archive Photos: 422 center, 422 center right, 422 center left, 423 bottom
Thorsten Arendt: 540–41, 563, 565, 567, 569, 571
Associated Press AP: 44 top center, 44 top and bottom right, 55 bottom
Associated Press AP/Richard Drew: 52 top
Associated Press/Princeton Video Graphic: 44 bottom left
© Marla Aufmuth: 68
© Theo Baart: 69 top
© Bettmann/CORBIS: 40 top right, 40 bottom, 41, 58–59, 234 center, 422 top right, 423 top
© Namas Bhojani, 8–9
Courtesy British Film Institute: 65
© Bruce Bennett Studio: 72 bottom
© Richard Bryant/ARCAID: 339
Byron Collection, Archive Photos: 40 top left
Simon Chan: 194 bottom
© Oliver Chanarin and Adam Broomberg: 84–85
Courtesy Robin Collyer: 576–77
© CORBIS: 236 top center, 238 center, 437 top right
Courtesy Damaged Goods: 558
© Bruce Davidson/Magnum Photos: 49 bottom right
Courtesy Design Archive/Volker Seding: 270
Reproduced by permission of *Esquire* magazine. © Hearst Communications, Inc. Also, *Esquire* is a trademark of Hearst Magazines Property, Inc. All rights reserved: 59 right
© Larry Fink: 76 top
© Michael Freeman/CORBIS: 422 top center
Courtesy Ben Fry, MIT Media Laboratory, Massachusetts Institute of Technology: 56–57
Courtesy Frank O. Gehry & Associates: 296–97, 363
Courtesy General Mills (Canada): 230, 232
© Mitchell Gerber/CORBIS: 237 right
Photo by David Gray/Reuters/Archive Photos: 498
© Lauren Greenfield, 22–23
Courtesy Health Canada: 366
Masanori Horie: 78 top left
© Hulton-Deutsche Collection/CORBIS: 234 left, and right, 236 top left, 236 bottom, 423 center
Courtesy Iron Mountain/National Underground Storage, Inc./www.national-underground.com: 53
KPMB, Photo by Robert G. Hill: 266, 270, 512–519

Index

Courtesy Jerde Partnership International: 18–19
Courtesy Ben Johnson: 52 center
Courtesy Las Vegas Convention and Visitors Authority: 14–15
Armin Linke: 10–11, 16–17, 24–27, 60–61, 62 top, 75 top, 212–13, 216–19, 428–29, 600–24, back endpapers
Anne Loustaunou/Archive Photos: 74 top left
Tom McCallion. Reproduced with permission from *Fly: The Art of the Club Flyer* (New York: Watson-Guptill Publications, 1997): 47 left
Courtesy Steve Mann/www.eyetap.org: 86
Photo by Dylan Martinez/Reuters/Archive Photos: 224–25
© Matthew Mendelsohn/CORBIS: 238 right
Courtesy National Aeronautics and Space Administration (NASA): 55 top, 353
© Richard T. Nowitz/CORBIS: 430
© Denis O'Regan/CORBIS: 237 left
© Jurgen Ostarhild, 6–7, 46
Courtesy PBS: 52 bottom
Digital capture by Darrell Perry: 76 bottom right, 77 top
© Mark Peterson/SABA: 42–43
PR Newswire AT&T: 1
© Roger Ressmeyer/CORBIS: 236 top right, 238 left, 422 bottom right
Reuters/Pat Benic/Archive Photos: 48 bottom insert
Reuters/Jill Connelly/Archive Photos: 82 bottom right
Reuters/Bernard Doppagne/Archive Photos: 72 top
Reuters/Chai Hin Goh/Archive Photos: 228
Reuters/HO/Archive Photos: 54 center, 82 top left
Reuters/Steve W. Grayson/Archive Photos: 54 bottom left
Reuters/Sam Mircovich/Archive Photos: 44 center
Reuters Newsmedia Inc./CORBIS: 496
© Gerhard Richter: 251 bottom
© Monika Rittershaus: 74 bottom
© Jeffrey L. Rotman/CORBIS: 47 right
© Salinger, Adrienne: 38
Photos by See Spot Run: 45 bottom left, 71, 97, 111–13, 128–29, 144–45, 150–51, 154–55, 158–59, 177, 261, 268, 272, 292, 308, 314–15, 332–33, 438 top, 440, 464, 466 top left, 467 top left and bottom left, 476, 477, 478–79, 503, 504, 505, 539
© Jason Schmidt: 4–5
Mike Segar/Reuters/Archive Photos: 2–3
Photo by Virginia Sherwood/Reuters/Archive Photos: 83
Courtesy Star Alliance/www.star-alliance.com: 54 top
Courtesy Robert A.M. Stern Architects: front endpaper
Stone/Aldo Torelli: 66–67
Courtesy Swatch, Inc.: 364
Susumu Takahashi/Reuters/Archive Photos: 75 bottom right, 422 bottom left
© John Terence Turner/FPG International: 73 right
© Tiffany Design: 48 full page
© Alan Towse; Ecoscene/CORBIS: 72 top right
Kyoichi Tsuzuki: 49 top right, bottom center, bottom right; 63
Courtesy Bernard Turbe: 44 top left
© Peter Turnley/CORBIS: 48 insert top left
Courtesy ULA&E, New York: 484–87
© Underwood & Underwood/CORBIS: 422 top left
Venus Veldhoen: 12–13, 341
Diana Walker/Liaison Agency, Inc.: 64
© Kevin Wilton, Eye Ubiquitous/CORBIS: 422 bottom center

Phaidon Press Limited
Regent's Wharf
All Saints Street
London N1 9PA

First published 2000
Reprinted 2001

ISBN 0 7148 3827 6

A CIP catalogue record for this book is available from the British Library.

Designed by Bruce Mau Design Inc.
Printed in China

Bruce Mau: Designer or Not?

Michel Feher

What is graphic design? Bruce Mau doesn't know. You might think this is a problem since Bruce Mau is supposedly a graphic designer. But is he? If you listen to what he has to say about graphic designers and about the way their work is usually perceived—that is, giving a pleasing form to someone else's content—you will probably conclude that he doesn't want to be one of them. And indeed he has often expressed the desire to do something else. But how could he stop being a graphic designer—or, for that matter, how could he be so sure that he has actually ceased to be a graphic designer—if he doesn't know what graphic design is?

Unable either to abandon or to embrace his career as a graphic designer, Bruce Mau could have done one of two things: either whine and complain about the fact that nobody—not least himself—understands what he is doing, or turn his own work into an investigation about the nature of graphic design. Fortunately for the people close to him, he chose the latter alternative. Whether it deals with books, magazines, posters, CDs, theater sets, or architectural space, Bruce Mau's work is thus devoted to finding out what graphic design really is.

Has Bruce Mau reached some kind of verdict? Clearly not. For if he had, he would have either closed shop or reconciled with the idea of being a graphic designer. Yet, while still in the dark, Bruce Mau has gathered some clues about why he is in the dark. Thanks to his frequent and close collaborations with architects, he tends to liken his practice, and even more, his torments to theirs. Indeed, scale notwithstanding, architects and graphic designers seem caught in the same exhausting dilemmas: Are we supposed to be artists or are we merely to provide a service? Is the service we provide our real art, or are our artistic achievements the true service we provide? For the architect as for the graphic designer, these questions remain unanswered because they always point to the same character, the client, whose purpose is both to enable their work and to obscure its nature.

Because of his clients' expectations—they want their books, posters, sets, and so on to be served by a designer who is also an artist—Bruce Mau can never figure out what his work is really about. But at the same time, his clients' conflicting demands are also what compel him to pursue his investigation. This is why a book gathering Bruce Mau's body of work is not only a treat but also an enlightening experience—particularly for Bruce Mau himself. Indeed, all these projects put together form an answer, or at least the beginning of an answer, to the question: What is graphic design?

In trying to formulate a provisional answer, the word that comes to mind is "selection." Unlike architecture—or furniture design—graphic design doesn't rely primarily on the practice of drawing. It is about selecting. The problem with that characterization is that it brings graphic designers dangerously close to "interior design," which is also about selecting. So, in order to avoid such an infamous association, we should say that Bruce Mau's work as a graphic designer seeks to define the conditions under which the act of selecting becomes an art.

As an admirer of Bruce Mau's work—and as a professional philosopher—I should be ashamed of myself for limiting my analysis of his highly complex, extraordinarily diverse, and constantly evolving projects to the vague and obscure definition I just proposed. But I am also a client of Bruce Mau, and as such, it is my duty and my purpose to remain an obstacle to his quest.

Coda

Turbine.
Licensed by De Havilland Engine Company. Thermajet with ten combustion chambers and post-combustion. Fifteen-minute start thrust 2270FP at 10250 u/min without post-combustion. Year of construction: 1955.

STRESS

Stress is the inevitable outcome of a system that incorporates every gesture into a global competition for resources.
Stress imagines every rule and limit to be infinitely flexible, open to constant recalibration as faster, cheaper, and better.
Stress is a post-natural ecology aimed at the ultimate fusion of nervous-system and economy.
Stress is the phenomenon of ever-expanding proportions.
A culture that pushes the limits of social, ecological, biological, intellectual, emotional, and psychological capacity in almost every endeavor is a culture of stress.

Looking back over the twentieth century, over all modernity in fact, what you discover is an almost continuous and totalizing cycle: establish a threshold, push beyond it, experience stasis, repeat. One of the central arguments of *STRESS* is that a culture that can produce the concept of "the envelope"—and then proceed to "push the envelope" in almost every endeavor—is a culture of stress. Only a culture of stress could have imagined a flexible boundary and imaginatively cast that boundary around virtually everything.
When we were commissioned by Hortensia Völckers to make a work for Wiener Festwochen, a performing arts festival in Vienna, the organizers initially wanted a piece that concerned dance or performance. We began there, but the idea gradually evolved. For a time, it took on the name *Panorama*. It had to do with the notion

Multimedia installation, Wiener Festwochen
A collaboration with André Lepecki and John Oswald
Vienna, 2000
STRESS is a video-based installation that explores forces of impact and disfiguration in a series of short episodes. For approximately forty minutes and in a large, blackened room, viewers venture into the total choreography of stress. They are exposed to the forces of modernization that have, in Marshall McLuhan's words, "worked us over." *STRESS* takes us to the thresholds of life by exploring our maximal capacities for pleasure and pain, speed and attention, consciousness and endurance, bodily integrity and incorporation.

Alarm.
Clocks ticking ubiquitously, in alarming precision, regulate global systems. Electronic impulses synchronize labor with capital, missiles with targets, catastrophes with their images. Gradually, the constant state of alertness this ceaseless pulsing provokes is embodied as state of emergency. Alarming clocks everywhere, counting the beat, from birth to death.

of being embedded in the image, in this case, a protocinematic space.

In traditional, which is to say pre-cinematic, nineteenth-century panoramas, the spectator always remained at a distance from the image, viewing it from a panoptic platform. *STRESS* remains a panorama of sorts, but the effect is distributed over eight large video screens, twelve feet wide and eighteen feet high. The overall image is now fragmented and mobilized within a space where the viewer circulates freely. In the viewing situation set up by *STRESS*, the viewer is embedded in the space of the image. We have interpreted the techniques of book development and conceptualization through the medium of cinema, using digital projection to create a cinematic experience for the viewer.

The piece has twenty-four episodes, each one presenting an aspect of the condition of stress. The episodes range from the openly documentary to the abstract. We have, for example, taken a character from the history of stress development, Colonel John Stapp, and let him stand as an emblematic figure. He is the man on the cover of Marshall McLuhan and Quentin Fiore's book *The Medium is the Massage*, and a central figure in the history of stress. By strapping himself into a rocket sled and hurling his body at breakneck speed down a track in a series of experiments beginning in the late 1940s, Stapp placed himself at the center of research to test the human capacity to endure the force of gravity. The enterprise was scrupulously recorded by the United States Air Force. They filmed the preparations, the site development, the technicians prepping him for the ride, and the medical examinations afterward. Stapp's encapsulating adventure represents the collision of biological capacity, speed, and cinema.

Escalator.
Manufactured by Schindler Elevators and Escalators Limited Company. 13m long, 5.5 tons. Hoisting height: 4m.

Alarm:
the punchclock in the bedroom, electricity, regulation, change in rhythm from circadian to digital.

Blitzkrieg:
quick response, rapid transport, progress as warfare.

Collapse:
proving the threshold by going beyond the limit, beyond stasis, out of control.

Defenestration:
the ultimate boundary beyond which all that remains is the force of gravity.

Exodus:
massive forces set masses in motion, their scale evidenced in sheer human kinetic biomass.

Formation:
capturing the energy of anonymous individual gestures in massive collective disciplinary formations.

G-force:
systematic cinematic research on human endurance under extreme conditions of speed and arrest.

Invent:
some of those responsible for generating the ecology of stress, each one triggers an avalanche of change.

Jitterbug:
released from its confines, the body explodes with movement, apparently in all directions simultaneously.

Karoshi:
dropping dead from overwork, a corporeal letter of resignation as a final silent protest.

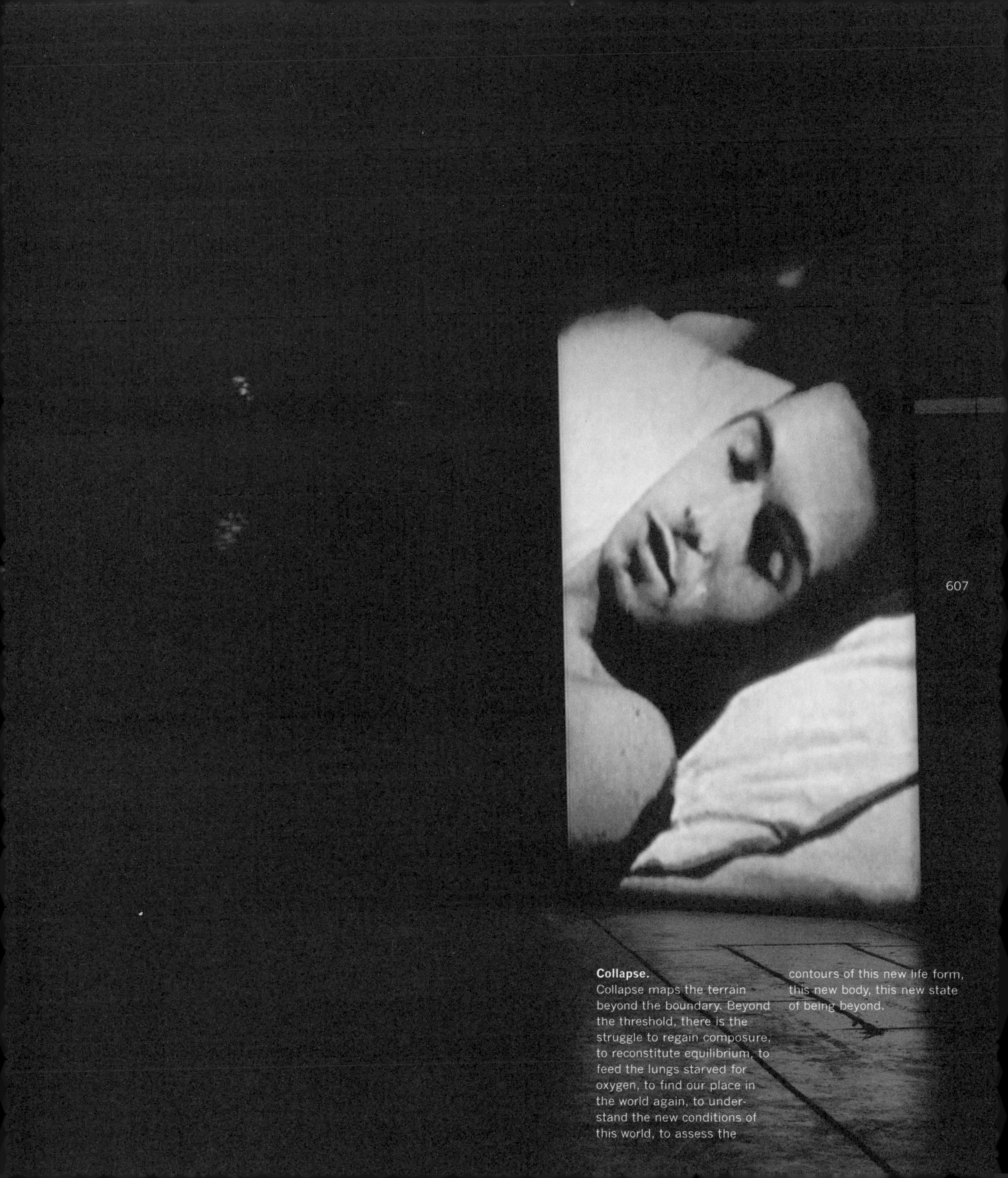

Collapse.
Collapse maps the terrain beyond the boundary. Beyond the threshold, there is the struggle to regain composure, to reconstitute equilibrium, to feed the lungs starved for oxygen, to find our place in the world again, to understand the new conditions of this world, to assess the contours of this new life form, this new body, this new state of being beyond.

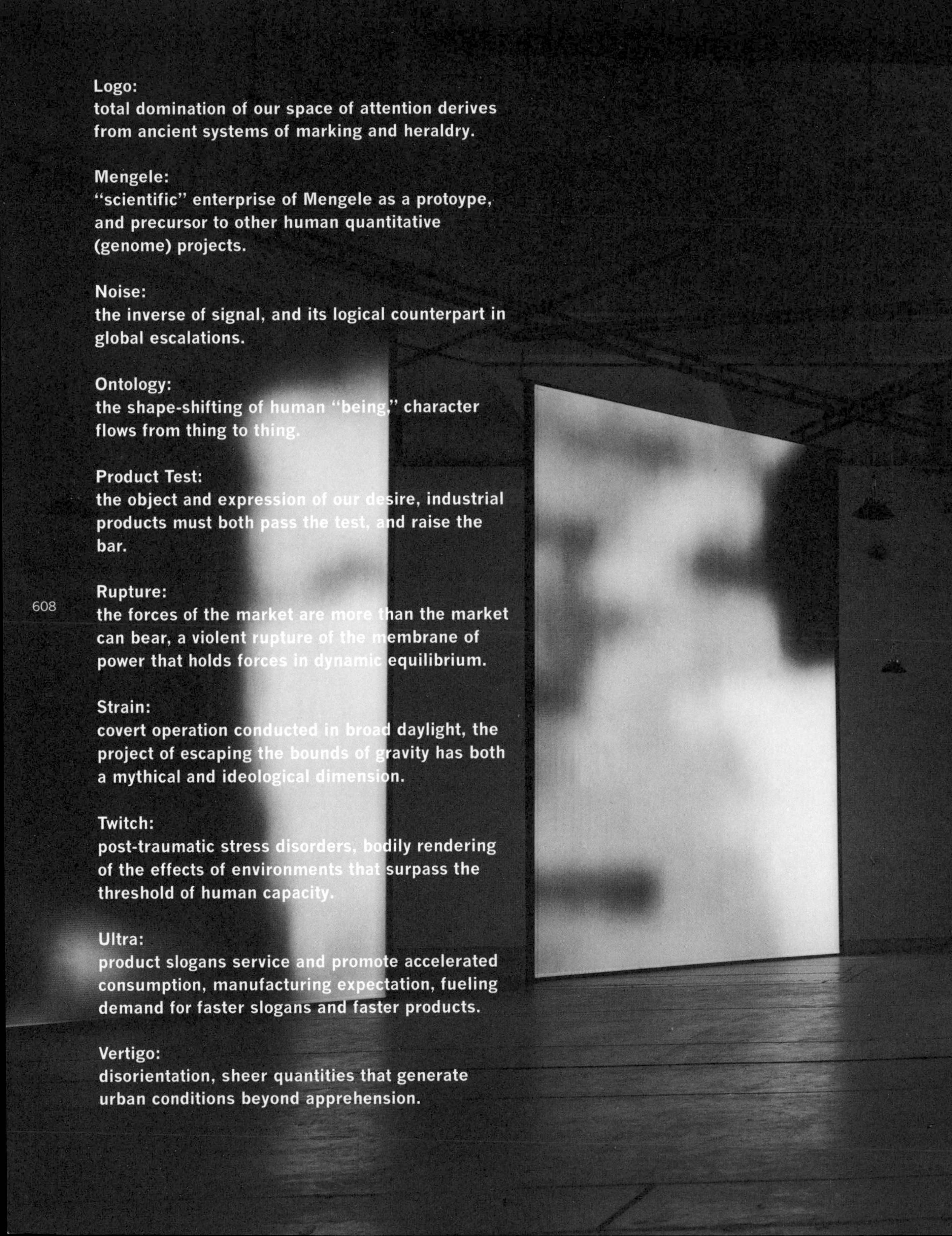

Logo:
total domination of our space of attention derives from ancient systems of marking and heraldry.

Mengele:
"scientific" enterprise of Mengele as a protoype, and precursor to other human quantitative (genome) projects.

Noise:
the inverse of signal, and its logical counterpart in global escalations.

Ontology:
the shape-shifting of human "being," character flows from thing to thing.

Product Test:
the object and expression of our desire, industrial products must both pass the test, and raise the bar.

Rupture:
the forces of the market are more than the market can bear, a violent rupture of the membrane of power that holds forces in dynamic equilibrium.

Strain:
covert operation conducted in broad daylight, the project of escaping the bounds of gravity has both a mythical and ideological dimension.

Twitch:
post-traumatic stress disorders, bodily rendering of the effects of environments that surpass the threshold of human capacity.

Ultra:
product slogans service and promote accelerated consumption, manufacturing expectation, fueling demand for faster slogans and faster products.

Vertigo:
disorientation, sheer quantities that generate urban conditions beyond apprehension.

Formation.
Its force field is sometimes discrete, sometimes anamorphic, and other times explicitly precise. In each case, bodies trapped within a formation capture with crystal clarity the contradictory tensions modernity has to resolve for the maintenance of its greatest invention — the monadic subject, oscillating between the mirage of individuality and call of the mass. That such tension is managed by detailed regulation of individual motions within a larger collective body shows how modernity's project is, first and foremost, a gigantic choreographic effort in the most literal sense.

Waiting:
the irony in acceleration derives from the waiting we must do to experience it.

X:
in the air force, x is experimental, a massive enterprise to extend the boundaries of speed and endurance.

Yesterday:
all of the wonderful tomorrows all our yesterdays have promised us.

Zero:
in the end, we return to nature, only to find it is no longer there.

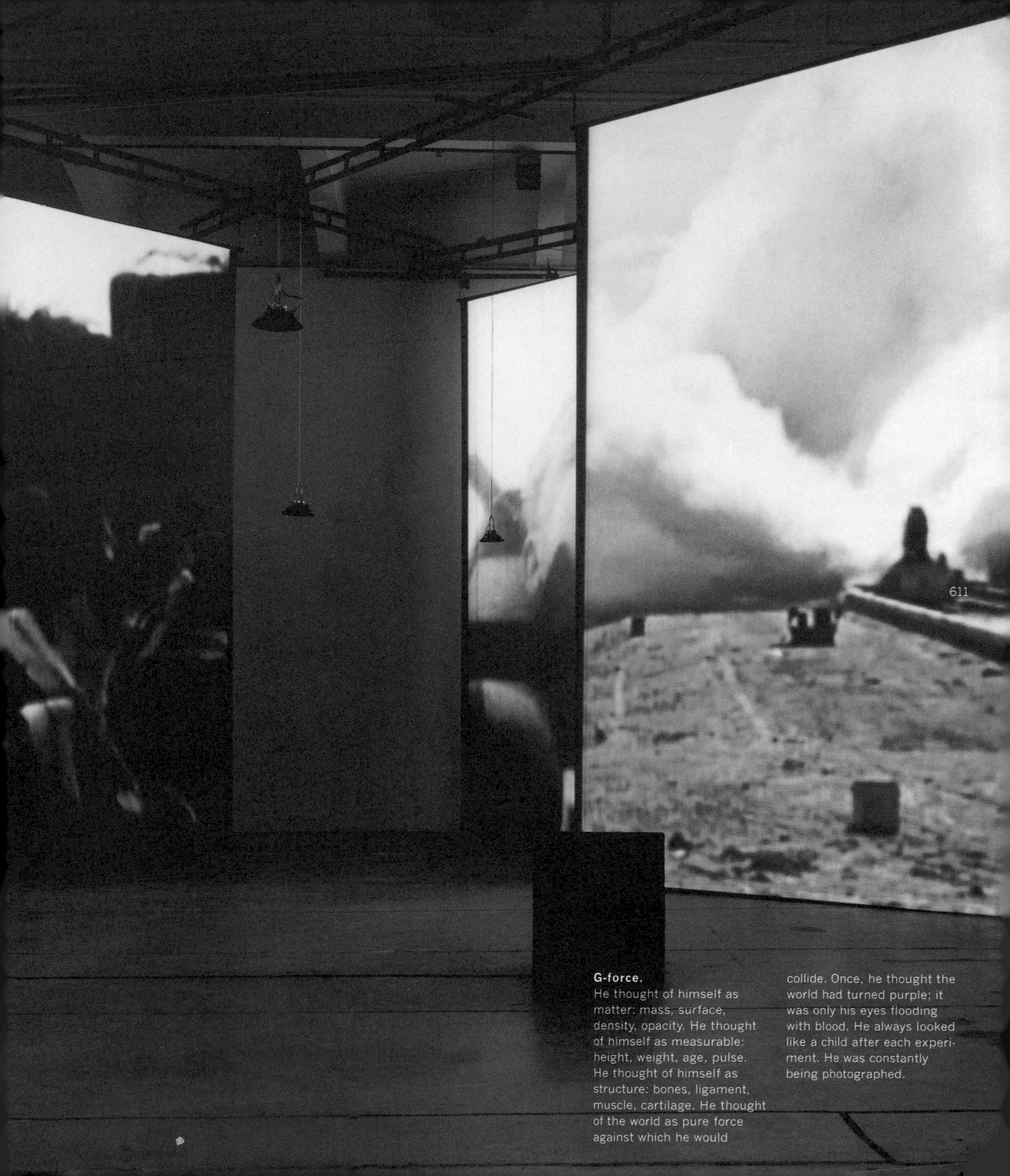

G-force.
He thought of himself as matter: mass, surface, density, opacity. He thought of himself as measurable: height, weight, age, pulse. He thought of himself as structure: bones, ligament, muscle, cartilage. He thought of the world as pure force against which he would collide. Once, he thought the world had turned purple; it was only his eyes flooding with blood. He always looked like a child after each experiment. He was constantly being photographed.

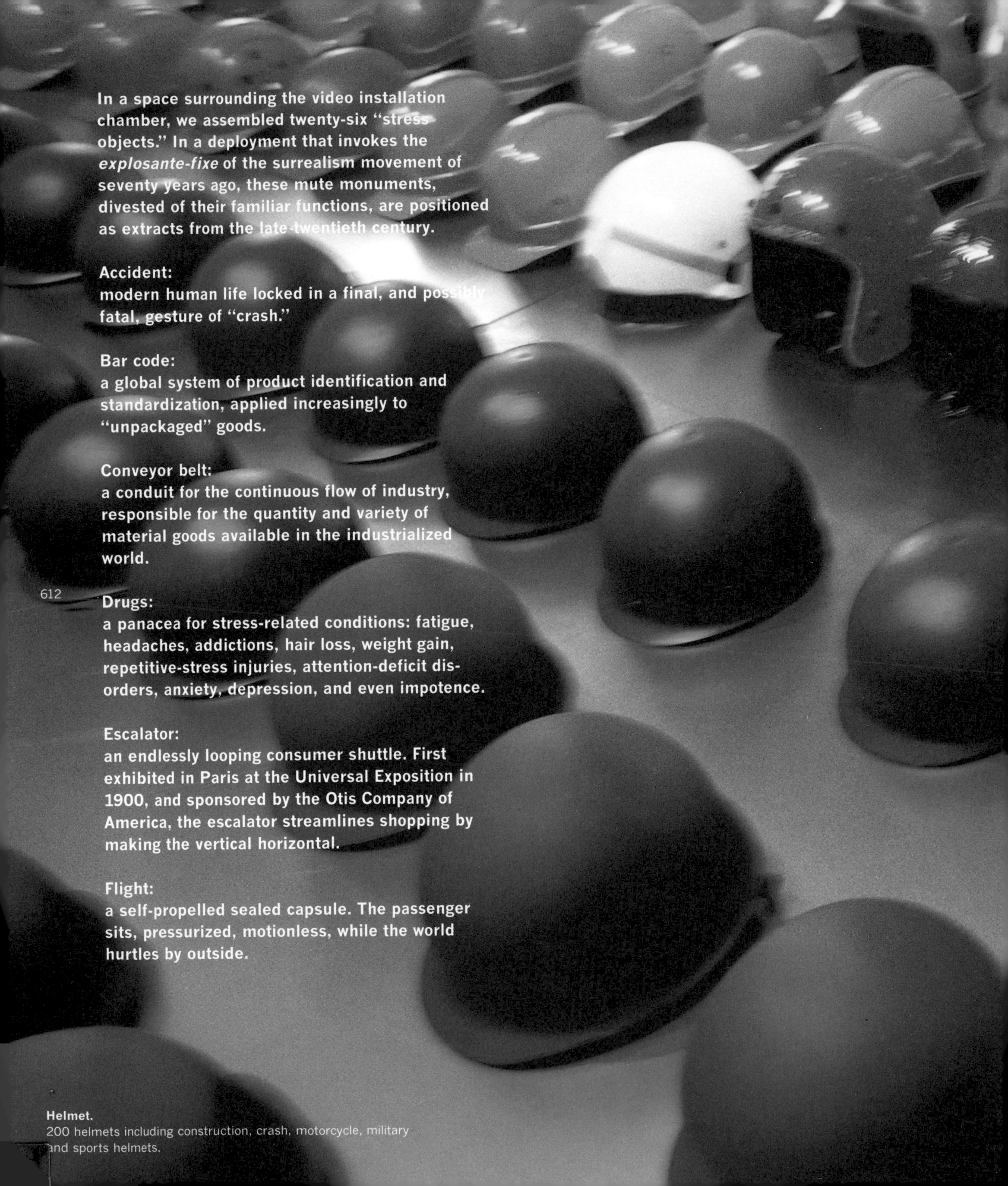

In a space surrounding the video installation chamber, we assembled twenty-six "stress objects." In a deployment that invokes the *explosante-fixe* of the surrealism movement of seventy years ago, these mute monuments, divested of their familiar functions, are positioned as extracts from the late-twentieth century.

Accident:
modern human life locked in a final, and possibly fatal, gesture of "crash."

Bar code:
a global system of product identification and standardization, applied increasingly to "unpackaged" goods.

Conveyor belt:
a conduit for the continuous flow of industry, responsible for the quantity and variety of material goods available in the industrialized world.

Drugs:
a panacea for stress-related conditions: fatigue, headaches, addictions, hair loss, weight gain, repetitive-stress injuries, attention-deficit disorders, anxiety, depression, and even impotence.

Escalator:
an endlessly looping consumer shuttle. First exhibited in Paris at the Universal Exposition in 1900, and sponsored by the Otis Company of America, the escalator streamlines shopping by making the vertical horizontal.

Flight:
a self-propelled sealed capsule. The passenger sits, pressurized, motionless, while the world hurtles by outside.

Helmet.
200 helmets including construction, crash, motorcycle, military and sports helmets.

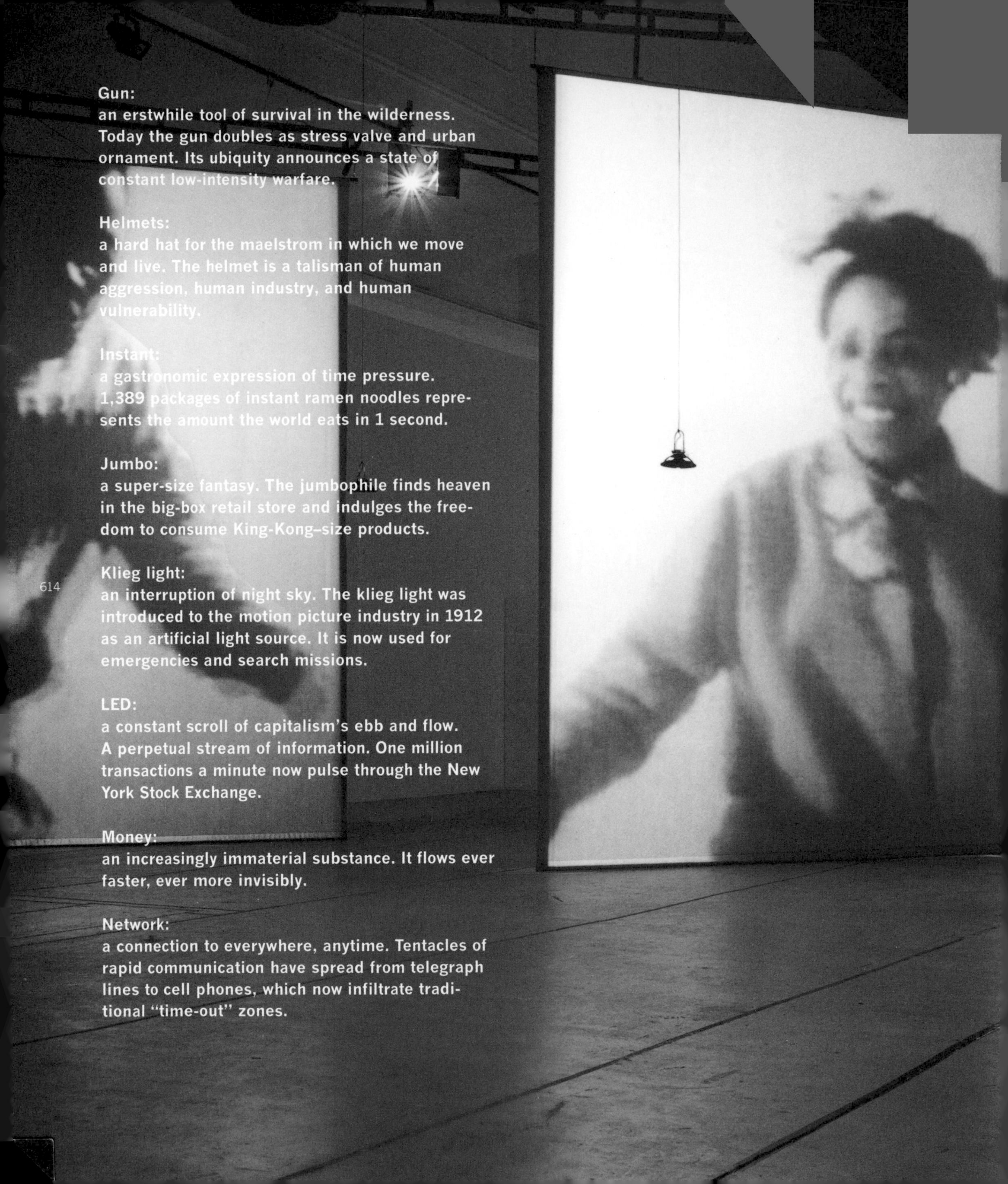

Gun:
an erstwhile tool of survival in the wilderness. Today the gun doubles as stress valve and urban ornament. Its ubiquity announces a state of constant low-intensity warfare.

Helmets:
a hard hat for the maelstrom in which we move and live. The helmet is a talisman of human aggression, human industry, and human vulnerability.

Instant:
a gastronomic expression of time pressure. 1,389 packages of instant ramen noodles represents the amount the world eats in 1 second.

Jumbo:
a super-size fantasy. The jumbophile finds heaven in the big-box retail store and indulges the freedom to consume King-Kong–size products.

Klieg light:
an interruption of night sky. The klieg light was introduced to the motion picture industry in 1912 as an artificial light source. It is now used for emergencies and search missions.

LED:
a constant scroll of capitalism's ebb and flow. A perpetual stream of information. One million transactions a minute now pulse through the New York Stock Exchange.

Money:
an increasingly immaterial substance. It flows ever faster, ever more invisibly.

Network:
a connection to everywhere, anytime. Tentacles of rapid communication have spread from telegraph lines to cell phones, which now infiltrate traditional "time-out" zones.

Jitterbug.
"Jitterbug" stands metonymically for any action in which a "glorious expenditure of energy" (Bataille) takes place. "Our industrial civilization builds up tension: It confines people to patterns. The Jitterbug relieves the tension in violent dance very free and unconfined," wrote African American choreographer Katherine Dunham in 1941. Such expenditure without economy is absolute dance. The irony: as long as it remains an agent of relief, or discharge, Jitterbug participates entirely in the very euphoria, anxieties, and economy of stress.

Office:
one unit in the global flow of capital; one pod in the vast corporate cubicle hive.

Plastic:
the collagen of modern life, its secret ambition the fusion of the organic and inorganic worlds.

Quinoline:
an oily and colorless compound that extends shelf life. Quinoline is used as a food preservative and in the manufacture of dyes and antiseptics.

Robot:
a soldier in the battle for the mechanization of work. The robot promises to relieve us from repetitive, hazardous, and unpleasant labor.

Surveillance:
a constant companion, surveillance devices—from security cameras to biometrics—surreptitiously capture and record our every movement, from traffic transgressions to purchasing patterns.

Turbine:
the effortless muscle behind modern swiftness and efficiency.

Uniform:
a deliberate blurring of difference. Uniformity makes a virtue out of sameness. It is the visual expression of the individual's desire to merge, and of the conversion of units into mass.

Vienna Circle:
a step toward the eradication of doubt and uncertainty. The movement associated with the Vienna Circle, logical positivism, proposed that philosophy should adopt the strategies of empirical science because that was all that could actually be known. As such, this movement reduced fundamental questions about our being, purpose, and morality to issues of science and technology.

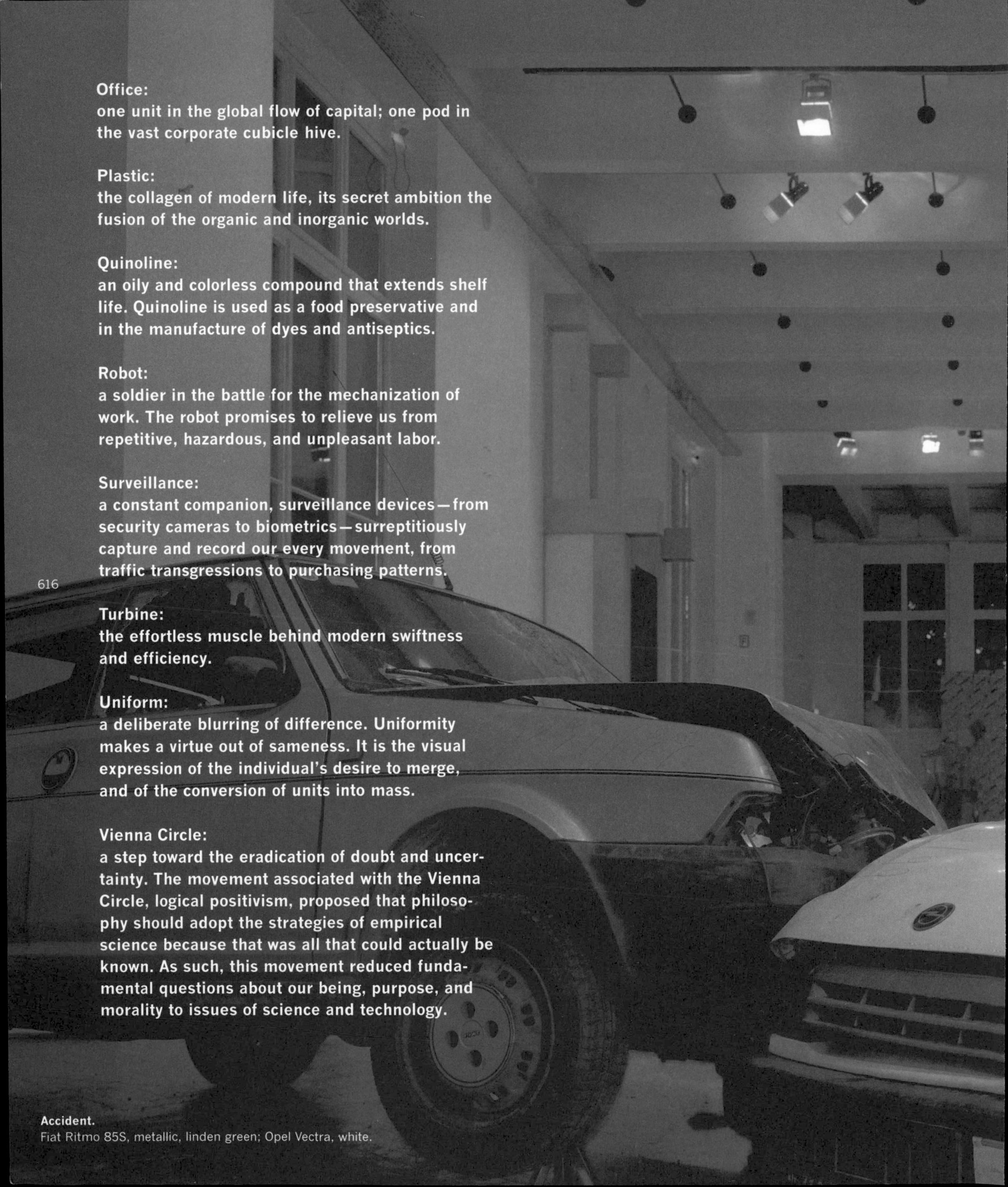

Accident.
Fiat Ritmo 85S, metallic, linden green; Opel Vectra, white.

Wireless:
mobility reduced to its basic functioning cell. The commercial battery signals portability as a way of life and a way of living "off the grid."

Xerox:
an alchemy of light, heat, chemicals, and electrostatic charges, the Xerox machine allows us to jump the copyright fence and enter a world of low-cost reproduction and easy circulation.

Youth:
longevity as counter-top commodity. Anti-wrinkle skin creams and firming serums are the first line of defense in the battle against gravity, entropy, and the remorseless sag of aging flesh.

Zoom:
a tunnel into the unknown. The zoom lens produces the vertigo of microscopic infinities, beyond the limits of the naked eye and the threshold of human vision.

Logo.
Each day, the average Western citizen sees, assimilates and recognizes 16,000 different logos. These are so many lighthouses guiding us in our experience of the world. As graphic equivalent of the compass, and as modern derivative of medieval heraldry, the logo first of all tells us where we stand. Its inscription on every landscape recasts space as site of perpetual recognition. Its presence on every piece of garment recasts subjectivity as tribal.

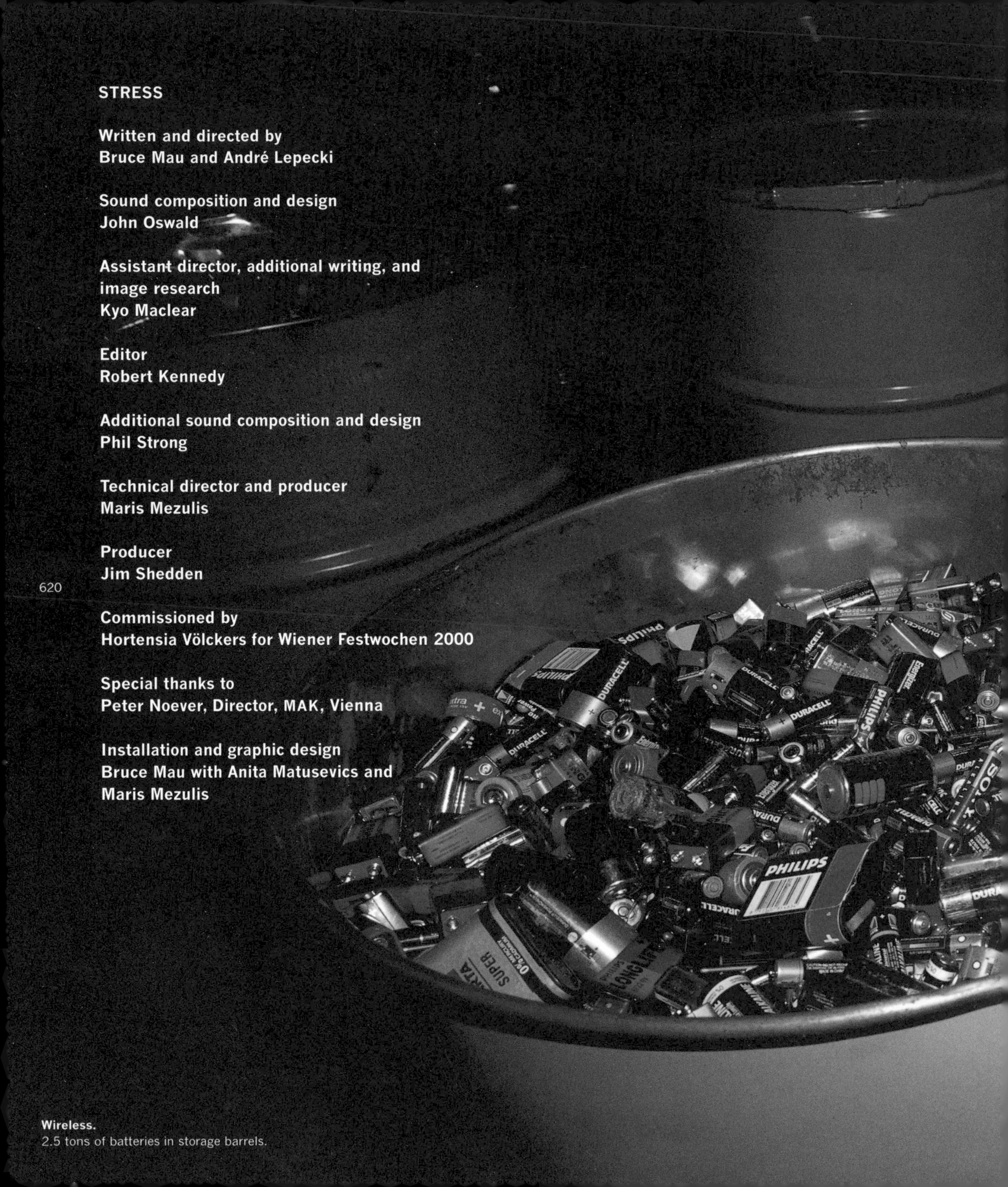

STRESS

Written and directed by
Bruce Mau and André Lepecki

Sound composition and design
John Oswald

Assistant director, additional writing, and
image research
Kyo Maclear

Editor
Robert Kennedy

Additional sound composition and design
Phil Strong

Technical director and producer
Maris Mezulis

Producer
Jim Shedden

Commissioned by
Hortensia Völckers for Wiener Festwochen 2000

Special thanks to
Peter Noever, Director, MAK, Vienna

Installation and graphic design
Bruce Mau with Anita Matusevics and
Maris Mezulis

Wireless.
2.5 tons of batteries in storage barrels.

DURACELL
DURACELL
DURACELL
extra
PHILIPS
PHILIPS

Rupture.
Poachers, mercenaries, militias, hijackers, terrorists, vigilantes, assassins: central characters in the ecology of stress.
When market forces go beyond what the market can bear, the result is a rupture of the membrane of power. Violence spurts in the rent.

Poachers, terrorists, assassins step in, not as alien forces, but as intrinsic players in the economy and ecology of stress. They complement and guarantee the flow of information, goods, capital, power, and the violent images they help generate.

Strain.
They gathered only on perfect, sunny days. Under the open sky, they rehearsed a new pose befitting the anticipated event. They thought the future was suspended high above, so they postponed their lives to look up. They couldn't know that other futures were being secretly forged on that same sky, right over their upward-pointing noses; they had forgotten the sky had always been a surface for the inscription of mysteries. Most importantly, they had forgotten that the consequences of strain on the integrity of the body are unpredictable—just like the future stressing out above them.